OUR
RISING EMPIRE
1763-1803

ARTHUR BURR DARLING

ARCHON BOOKS

We demand independence only for the thirteen States of America which are united among themselves, without including any other English possessions which have not taken part in their insurrection. We do not desire by a great deal that the rising new republic remain exclusive mistress of this whole immense continent.

VERGENNES *to* MONTMORIN, *October 30, 1778.*

Poor as we are, yet as I know we shall be rich, I would rather agree with them to buy at a great price the whole of their right on the Mississippi than sell a drop of its waters. A neighbor might as well ask me to sell my street door.

FRANKLIN *to* JAY, *October 2, 1780.*

However our present interests may restrain us within our own limits, it is impossible not to look forward to distant times, when our rapid multiplication will expand itself beyond those limits, & cover the whole northern, if not the southern continent, with a people speaking the same language, governed in similar forms, & by similar laws; nor can we contemplate with satisfaction either blot or mixture on that surface.

JEFFERSON *to* MONROE, *November 24, 1801.*

This accession of territory strengthens for ever the power of the United States; and I have just given to England a maritime rival, that will sooner or later humble her pride.

NAPOLEON *according to* MARBOIS, *May, 1803.*

CONTENTS

And let me conjure you in the name of our common country, as you value your own sacred honor, as you respect the rights of humanity, and as you regard the military and national character of America, to express your utmost horror and detestation of the man, who wishes, under any specious pretences, to overturn the liberties of our country, and who wickedly attempts to open the flood gates of civil discord, and deluge our rising empire in blood.

Washington to His Officers, March, 1783.

OUR RISING EMPIRE

I

ALLIANCE OR INDEPENDENCE

The Mid-Continent

GEORGE WASHINGTON, the Lees of Virginia, Phineas Lyman of Connecticut petitioned their King for grants upon the Mississippi and its tributaries. The great river flowed southward across the continent to the Gulf of Mexico beyond the Spanish Floridas. Near its sources, the Great Lakes poured their waters to the northeast through the French Valley of the St. Lawrence behind Nova Scotia. Along the Atlantic Coast between the Floridas and Nova Scotia lay the old colonies of England, firmly established now and reaching up to the Appalachian Mountains. Forward-looking men cared not at all that Spaniards on the one hand and Frenchmen on the other laid claim to the rich lands beyond. They were planning new colonies for England. Benjamin Franklin anticipated a population of a hundred million in centuries to come, devoted to agriculture and always dependent upon the mother country for manufactured goods. He believed that the colonies would never be dangerous to her, because she would keep pace with her growing daughters. In the Government, Lord Shelburne too caught the idea of English expansion into the continent of America. But those who lived in the region had a different conception of its future. Indian war parties raked the English frontier with fire and tomahawk as France deserted her Indian allies and surrendered Quebec to England. White men have called this Pontiac's "conspiracy" against the English King. It was a desperate effort of red men to keep the American pioneers from their ancestral lands.[1]

If Frenchmen did not foresee the consequences of these events in America, they did appreciate all too well what had happened to France. Seven years of war had ruined her empire there and in India. Her military and naval power was sapped. Her colonial system was shattered. Such insular possessions as she had left were at the mercy of the English fleet. And most humiliating, that Euro-

1. Alvord, I, 90–101, 184 ff., citing Parkman. Franklin (Smyth ed.), IV, 55. Carter, 103–144. Alden, 1–20.

pean prestige was gone which Frenchmen since Louis XIV had considered theirs by right. It is not surprising, under these circumstances, that French statesmen thought of separating the American colonies from England even before leaders in the colonies considered it for themselves. French overtures reached the Continental Congress before they had decided to frame the Declaration of Independence in 1776. Secret aid from France helped to stop the English army of penetration at Saratoga in 1777. The alliance following that triumph over Burgoyne brought French troops, money, ships, and munitions to increase greatly the forces and the morale which overpowered Cornwallis at Yorktown in 1781. The interest of France had given the United States its opportunity to negotiate for both independence and expansion.

French Agents in America

THE French foreign minister, Choiseul, had moved toward the objective of separating the colonies from the mother country shortly after the fall of Quebec. He renewed the Family Compact with Spain in 1761 and turned Louisiana over to her. France began as quietly as possible to repair her naval forces for another attempt upon English supremacy of the seas. French agents came to spy out the land and to foster sedition in America.[2]

Pontleroy, veteran naval officer, visited New England, New York, Pennsylvania, and Maryland in 1764. He reported upon their resources in grain and timber, their shipbuilding, their seamanship, the rapid increase of their population, and the attitude of their non-English stock. He learned the distances between important settlements, the soundings of ports and rivers, and he drafted military plans for taking Boston, New York, and Philadelphia. The Americans were restive, he said, because they were no longer afraid of French power beyond their western frontiers; and they were irritated by Parliament's new Sugar Act, for the King's ships were now stopping the trade with the French and Spanish West Indies which had been bringing specie into America.

The middle colonies knew their strength, wrote Pontleroy; they were too affluent to persevere in obedience; they hoped to control the fisheries and the fur trade, to throw off Parliament's restrictions upon their navigation, and sooner or later to invade the sugar islands on their own account. Britain, therefore, he declared, should anticipate a revolution. But he had to report that there was also some desire among the Americans to have another war with France in order

2. Corwin, *French Policy and the American Alliance of 1778*, 34–40. This special study is essential to this and succeeding chapters on the period.

that they might seize the French Islands—San Domingo for its markets and Miquelon off Newfoundland for its fisheries. In that case, they might not be so eager for a revolution.[3]

Another French agent, whose name is uncertain, reported on the defenses of Norfolk, Philadelphia, and New York in 1765. They could be attacked, he said, with ease. He wrote while in Virginia that the inhabitants of the county of the "Noble Patriot Mr. henery" were asserting publicly that they would stand by him to the last drop of their blood if the least injury were offered to him, and "Some of them muter betwixt their teeth, let the worst Come to the worst we'l Call the french to our sucour: and if they were in Canada the British parlem't would as soon be Dd, as to offer to do what they do now." And he reported later upon his experiences at the tavern in Annapolis, Maryland: "Where we had nothing but feasting and Drinking, after the Kings health, the virginia assembly, and then Damnation to the Stamp act and a great Deal to that purpose in fine we scarce used to Go to bed sober."[4]

The Baron de Kalb, subsequently one of Washington's generals, toured the colonies for Choiseul in 1767. He wrote that disturbances were increasing from day to day in spite of the repeal of the Stamp Act. For Parliament had reached the same objective in a "circuitous way" without obtaining the consent of the colonies. The Townshend duties on glass, paper, and tea angered the Americans. They contended, he said, that their specie was being drained to England, although he himself believed that it was disappearing from circulation because of private hoarding in the colonies rather than because of the exactions of Parliament. He heard them complain also that they were compelled to support troops which had been sent to oppress rather than to protect them. And yet Kalb believed, notwithstanding their seditious utterances, that the colonials still loved England. It was a quarrel, said he, within a family: "The remoteness of this population from their centre of government makes them free and enterprising; but at bottom they are but little inclined to shake off the English supremacy with the aid of foreign powers. Such an alliance would appear to them to be fraught with danger to their liberties."

So, Kalb could not honestly report what Choiseul had sent him to find, and the foreign minister gave vent to his disappointment with this rebuke: "You returned too soon from America, and your labors are therefore of no use to me. You need not send me any more reports about that country." Into the discard also went Kalb's

---

3. Witt (3d ed.), 407–417. Van Tyne, 446–449.
4. AHR, XXVI, 747.

shrewd opinions that the colonies would some day free themselves
from Britain with no other nation's help. In time, he said, as their
population increased by birth and by immigration from every quarter of Europe, they would threaten and indeed annex the possessions of other European powers on the North American continent.

This was a startling prophecy of things to come. But its meaning
then was too far beyond the range of Choiseul's wishful thinking.
As he saw it, there had to be another war with Britain for the good
of France, and when this war came, the American colonies would
be made to serve her cause. Until she was ready, he would keep up
friendly appearances with Britain, even though he resented the welcome which the Corsican Paoli received in London.[5]

Changing Opinions of American Leaders

THE first response from the American leaders was just as Kalb had
predicted to Choiseul. James Otis hailed the conquest of Canada
although denouncing simultaneously Britain's use of writs of assistance to check trading with her enemy. He had declared to a mass
meeting in Boston that the true interests of the mother country
and the colonies were mutual: "What God in his Providence has
united," said he, "let no man dare attempt to pull asunder." But
then, whether sane one moment and insane the next, James Otis
was always a British imperialist. He did not go with his partner in
agitation, Samuel Adams, beyond demanding local autonomy. James
Otis did not plot independence.[6]

Even Samuel Adams at the time of the rioting over the Stamp
Act in 1765 publicly resented the statement in a London paper that
the American colonies were seeking to be free: "There is at present
no appearance of such disposition as this Writer wd insinuate, much
less a Struggle for Independence; & I dare say there never will be
unless Great Britain shall exert her power to destroy their Libertys.
This we hope will never be done."[7]

But this was the very thing which Samuel Adams soon felt was
being done, as he watched the administration of the Townshend
Acts in Boston and, be it said, found his own influence expanding
in the town and in the colonial assembly. By the spring of 1773, as
he fought the reaction in favor of England following the Boston
Massacre of 1770 and sensed the great value of support by malcontents in other colonies, Samuel Adams was corresponding with Rich-

5. Kapp (1870 ed.), 53–73 at 55, 286–292 at 287. Phillips, 18 n. 29. Perkins, 31.
6. Channing, III, 82, quoting the Boston *Post Boy and Advertiser,* March 21, 1763.
Miller, 89–91. Tudor, 360–362.
7. Adams (Cushing ed.), I, 38, Adams to G–W–, November 13, 1765.

ard Henry Lee of Virginia as if independence were a matter of course. "The Friends of American Independence and Freedom," he wrote, were at fault in not opening "every Channel of Communication," for the colonies were all embarked "in the same bottom"; the liberties of all were alike invaded "by the same haughty Power"; their common rights were subject to "Oppression and Tyranny." Public instructions for Benjamin Franklin, agent of Massachusetts in London, which Adams drafted on March 28, 1774, do not have the same ring of sincerity. They declared that the people of this country wished for "nothing more than a permanent Union" with the mother country "upon the condition of equal liberty."[8]

Benjamin Franklin, writing to his Loyalist son from London on August 28, 1767, had remarked that the French minister was extremely curious to inform himself upon the affairs of America: "I fancy that intriguing nation," he said, "would like very well to meddle on occasion, and blow up the coals between Britain and her colonies; but I hope we shall give them no opportunity." And as late as April 6, 1773, although Parliament was even then discussing the legislation which led straight to the Boston Tea Party, Franklin expected the mother country and colonies to be reconciled by another war with France. He discredited the talk in London that England would make an alliance with France and Spain against Prussia. He wrote to the conservative American, Galloway, that a war with Spain and France would be more to the advantage of American liberty, for: "Every step would then be taken to conciliate our Friendship, our Grievances would be redress'd, and our Claims allow'd." And this would happen, thought Franklin, because the colonies would be of the greatest assistance to Britain against the "House of Bourbon" among its American possessions where it was "most vulnerable."[9]

Responding to the statement of Lord Dartmouth that Parliament could not let pass unnoticed the declaration of the Massachusetts Assembly "asserting its Independency," Franklin remarked on May 5, 1773, that it would be "better and more prudent" to take no notice. "It is *Words* only," said he. "Acts of Parliament are still submitted to there." Parliament would do well "to turn a deaf Ear." Violent measures against the colony would not change the opinion of the people. "Force," he declared, "could do no good."[10]

But such counsels of moderation did not prevail. The King in-

8. *Ibid.*, III, 25, April 10, 1773. Bancroft (1859 ed.), VI, 508–509.
9. Franklin (Smyth ed.), V, 45–48, VI, 33–34.
. *Ibid.*, VI, 48–52, to T. Cushing, May 6, 1773.

sisted upon keeping the tax on tea as a matter of principle, and Parliament gave what amounted to a virtual monopoly of the colonial trade in tea to the East India Company. And so Franklin published in the *Gentleman's Magazine* of September, 1773, his satirical, "Rules by which a great empire may be reduced to a small one." Among them was this: "If you see *rival nations* rejoicing at the prospect of your disunion with your provinces, and endeavouring to promote it; if they translate, publish, and applaud all the complaints of your discontented colonists, at the same time privately stimulating you to severer measures, let not that *alarm* or offend you. Why should it, since you all mean *the same thing?*"[11]

By 1774, Benjamin Franklin had further changed his mind. He was now fostering good relations with the French embassy in London and with merchants on the continent. There is even the hint of overtures to certain parties in case the American colonies might have need for materials of war. But he rejected any dealing with the officials of France and he worked to the very end of his stay in England with Chatham, Howe, and other friends of America searching for some way to reconciliation.[12]

Franklin's hope was that mother country and colonies might have separate parliaments under the Crown. But his personal foe, Wedderburn, and Lord Sandwich and others enraged by colonial behavior cut the issue cleanly as the "dependence or independence of America." In their opinion, Massachusetts had to be punished severely for its Tea Party, and the protests of the Continental Congress spurned.[13]

So Parliament passed the famous "intolerable acts." They closed the port of Boston; altered the charter of Massachusetts; increased the power of military commanders to quarter troops among the people; provided for certain trials of civil and military officers in some other colony or in England if necessary to insure fair decisions; revised the government of Quebec for the gratification of its Catholic inhabitants, and restored the southern and western boundaries of the province at the Ohio and Mississippi rivers as they had once been in the possession of France.[14]

Parliament then obeyed the whip of Lord North's ministry and enacted his plan of conciliation, offering to withhold taxation ex-

11. *Ibid.*, VI, 127–137.

12. Faÿ, *Franklin*, 376. Van Tyne, 461. For Franklin's own account, see Smyth ed., VI, 318–399.

13. Bancroft (1859 ed.), VI, 510.

14. France had put most of the Illinois country under the jurisdiction of Louisiana in 1717. Carter, 6, 11.

cept for purposes of regulating commerce if the several colonies would contribute their "proportion to the common defence." But then, as if distrusting its own sincerity, and before there could be any colonial response to this offer, Parliament proceeded to pass a restraining act, punishing not simply Massachusetts but all New England further by confining its trade to Great Britain, Ireland, and the British West Indies and closing the Northern fisheries to its people. And Lord North himself was no exception. Having heard that the First Continental Congress had adopted an association to prevent trade with the mother country until the "intolerable acts" should be repealed, he declared that "it was but just that we should not suffer them to trade with any other nation."[15]

And so, Benjamin Franklin was on his way home at the end of March, 1775, to find himself immediately upon arrival elected to the Second Continental Congress and, before the year closed, a member of its committee of secret correspondence with "our friends in Great Britain, Ireland, and other parts of the world."[16]

As Governor Trumbull of Connecticut had so accurately foretold in 1767, "if methods tending to violence should be taken to maintain the dependence of the Colonies, it would hasten a separation."[17] Franklin, writing in July, 1775, to his friend Strahan in London, put it: "You are a member of Parliament, and one of that majority which has doomed my country to destruction. You have begun to burn our towns, and murder our people. Look upon your hands; they are stained with the blood of your relations! You and I were long friends; you are now my enemy, and I am, Yours, B. Franklin." Fixing the blame entirely upon Parliament was not just. It was too obviously done even to be considered clever. Perhaps that is one reason why Franklin did not send the letter. But he was recording the change that was coming over American emotions. They were swiftly generating patriotism.[18]

The American Plan of 1776

THE desire for independence grew apace after the bloodshed of Lexington and Concord as one British action followed another through the year 1775 into 1776, intensifying anger with the government of George III. The King scorned the petition of the Second Continental Congress, and declared that this was rebellion in America, "manifestly" for the purpose of establishing an "independent

15. Howard, 304–305.
16. *Journ. Cont. Cong.*, III, 392.
17. Bancroft (1859 ed.), VI, 83–84, to Wm. S. Johnson, June 23, 1767.
18. Franklin (Smyth ed.), VI, 407.

empire." Parliament forbade all trade with the colonies. Colonial
seamen were to be impressed into the Royal Navy and compelled
to fight their relatives. Governor Dunmore of Virginia offered
freedom to all slaves who took arms against the rebels. And Norfolk burned when he could not maintain his authority ashore. The
British fired Charlestown during the Battle of Bunker Hill—from
the colonial point of view, for no good military reason. Falmouth,
Maine, was raided and burned. And finally, the King sent mer-
cenaries to suppress as insurrection what his American subjects
wished to believe was civil war. There is no measuring the destructive effect upon American loyalty to Britain of these simple German soldiers who have come down to us in patriotic legend as the
dreadful Hessians.[19]

Forces were at work, too, within the colonial spirit turning the
demand from redress of grievances to independence. There was victory at Bunker Hill, even though the American troops were forced
to withdraw from the field. There was conquest in the invasion of
Canada, although the expedition failed to take Quebec. The thrill
of self-government, once experienced in the crisis, was not to be
relinquished willingly. Provincial congresses usurped and kept the
powers of the royal governors. And there was a lure in Crown and
Loyalist property. Mere rioters should not steal it. But those who
had governing powers, even though arrogated to themselves, could
condemn such property for a public purpose. The status as belligerents among the nations of the world held advantages far superior to the status of rebels, if they but dared to assert their independence and insist upon its recognition abroad. And then came
Thomas Paine's pamphlet, *Common Sense*, demonstrating the un-
answerable logic of events. No matter what they said or thought
about loving King George and hating his wicked ministry, the fact
was that they were fighting for independence.

Common Sense also admonished the patriots that they should
"form no partial connection" with any part of Europe. "It is the
true interest of America," wrote Paine, "to steer clear of European
connections." He was aiming the argument at Britain. But it was
as applicable to France, Spain, and others in 1776. Connection with
any one of them would involve the American States in the "wars
and quarrels" of Europe which he wished henceforth to avoid.

This idea is especially interesting as a forerunner of Washington's Farewell Address in 1796, Jefferson's Inaugural in 1801, and
the Monroe Doctrine of 1823. But Thomas Paine knew in 1776 that
these youthful states were by no means ready for so much inde-

19. Channing, III, 188, citing *Parl. Hist.*, XVIII, 696.

pendence from Europe. They would have to get help in Europe if they were to gain freedom from Britain. If they were to break what he called the "alliance" with Britain, they would have to risk an alliance with France. This would have to precede isolation from European affairs. The difficult task would be to make such an agreement that, once separate from Britain, they would have no obligations to France which they would not then care to meet.[20]

Leaders in Congress realized no less than Paine that the rebellious colonies must have aid from Europe and that they themselves must act as if they were independent states before they could get it. The plan which John Adams had advocated early in the summer of 1775 rapidly gained supporters as the forces within the colonial spirit, the sting of British actions, and increasing bloodshed drove the conviction deep: "We ought immediately to dissolve all Ministerial Tyrannies, and Custom houses, set up Governments of our own, like that of Connecticutt in all the Colonies, confederate together like an indissoluble Band, for mutual defence, and open our Ports to all Nations immediately." By the spring of 1776, the slower patriots, Dickinson, Rutledge, Jay, and others who would try still to shun France and find reconciliation with England, gave way to the Adamses, Franklin, the Lees, who would tell the mother country that they were free, and seek arrangements with France, Spain, and any other powers of Europe which would recognize them.[21]

Americans turned to the ancient enemies of Englishmen. The "Gallic Peril" in North America lost its fearfulness. France took on the quality of benevolence. The committee of secret correspondence appointed Silas Deane on March 2, 1776, to go to Paris. His instructions were twofold. He was to secure "articles for the Indian trade" and "other supplies" for the colonies. And with Vergennes' "permission," he was also to discover "on what principal conditions" France would enter into a "treaty or alliance with them, for commerce or defense, or both," if they should be "forced to form themselves into an independent State."[22]

But the Adamses, Franklin, the Lees had no intention of waiting to be forced. Congress adopted on May 10 their resolution that the "respective assemblies and conventions of the United Colonies" should establish governments of their own. And on June 7, Richard Henry Lee moved, with John Adams seconding the motion, that "these United Colonies are, and of right ought to be, free and independent States"; that "it is expedient forthwith to take the most

20. Paine (Conway ed.), I, 88–89. See below, pp. 19–22, 148–151.
21. Warren–Adams Letters, I, 75. For Adams' recollections, see *Works,* II, 407 ff.
22. Burnett, I, 376.

effectual measures for forming foreign Alliances"; and that "a plan of confederation be prepared and transmitted to the respective Colonies for their consideration and approbation."[23]

Edward Rutledge wrote to John Jay that he would move to postpone the question. "A Man must have the Impudence of a New Englander," said Rutledge of South Carolina, "to propose in our present disjointed state any Treaty (honorable to us) to a Nation now at peace." But that impudence sprang from knowledge of the French interest in what was happening, as well as from anger with the mother country. It was the insolence of vision. It would not be stopped by provincial rivalries or sectional fears of the "present disjointed state."

Congress appointed the committees necessary to Lee's resolutions on June 11 and 12, and came on July 1 to the decision whether the colonies should declare themselves free from Britain. There were changes in the draft which had been made by Thomas Jefferson. But the resistance of Dickinson, Rutledge, and their associates collapsed. Congress adopted the resolution on the next day, and on Thursday, July 4, 1776, formally agreed to the Declaration of Independence.[24]

The Articles of Confederation prepared by John Dickinson were debated for months and were not submitted to the States until November, 1777. But the "plan of treaties" reported in the handwriting of John Adams on July 18, 1776, was considered in its final form on September 17 as the agreement to be proposed to France. Congress drew the instructions for the commissioners to France on the twenty-fourth and two days later named Franklin, Deane, and Jefferson. Jefferson declined because of his wife's health and Congress on October 22 appointed in his place Arthur Lee who was already abroad. Franklin left immediately for France, where he arrived in December and received an informal audience with the French foreign minister on the twenty-eighth.[25]

The price set in advance by those rebels in America for reducing the power of Britain and restoring French supremacy in Europe was very evident in the "sketch of the proposed treaty" which their commissioners left with the French minister after their first interview. Materials of war and financial aid were on their minds. But they had "principal conditions" of their own about which they were determined to treat. Seriously "disjointed" though they might

23. *Journ. Cont. Cong.,* IV, 342, V, 425.

24. Burnett, I, 477. *Journ. Cont. Cong.,* V, 431, 433, 507, 510.

25. *Ibid.,* V, 546, IX, 935; V. 576, 768. Jefferson (Ford ed.), II, 91–92. Franklin (ᶜ ᵛ ed.), VI, 477. Corwin, 95.

be at home in regard to other matters, they were united in expecting of Europe two things. They would have the exclusive right of
conquest in North America. They would have freedom for their
commerce on the seas when they were neutrals. And it was obvious
that they intended to be so just as soon as possible after they had
won this war for independence.[26]

The American "plan" of 1776 stipulated that the King of France
should "never invade, nor under any pretence attempt to possess
himself" of any parts of the continent "which now are, or lately
were under the Jurisdiction of or Subject to the King or Crown of
Great Britain, whenever they shall be united or confederated with
the said United States." Second, France was to agree that "free Ships
shall also give a Freedom to Goods"; that is to say, when neutral,
American ships were to have the right to carry the goods of France's
enemies, excepting contraband. But contraband was to be confined to arms, ammunition, and armor. It was not to include ships'
stores of any kind, nor shipbuilding materials, nor anything else
which was not specified in the treaty as contraband.[27]

These rebels in America, furthermore, were reluctant to commit
themselves to Europe in return for these things. Although Franklin, Deane, and Lee may not have told the French minister as much
in their first interview, if ever, Congress had amended the draft of
their instructions on September 24 so as to withhold from them the
power to go beyond making a treaty of amity and commerce. The
original draft had permitted the commissioners to agree to "wage
the war in union with France" and not to make peace with Britain
until France had regained possessions in the West Indies which she
had lost in 1763, if this were necessary to get France into war with
Britain. But this clause had been struck out. And then Congress
had drawn additional instructions before Franklin left for France.
The commissioners were to take great care when negotiating with
other European governments. They were to make no treaty inconsistent with the treaty which they might obtain with France. But
neither were they to make with another power any agreement
obliging the United States to become "a party in any war" which
might happen in consequence of their treaty with France.[28]

Principles for the guidance of America's future were in clear
view before that future was at all assured. But these principles were
not to be established, nor that assurance won, until after the United
States had entered into alliance with France, become involved

26. *Ibid.*, VII, 9.
27. *Journ. Cont. Cong.*, V, 770, 775. September 17, 1776.
28. *Ibid.*, V, 817, VI, 884. October 16, 1776.

in dangerous commitments and guarantees, and experienced grave threats to their isolation from the "wars and quarrels" of Europe. The French foreign minister, too, had his price to set in advance.

"Secret Aid"

THE effect of bloodshed in America had been as immediate upon France. The revolution which Pontleroy had foretold was happening. Choiseul's hopes were real. The opportunity to humble Britain had arrived. And Vergennes, successor to Choiseul in the French foreign office and heir to his plans, was as determined to make the most of it. But Vergennes, though he might be "a mere clerk with his feet under the table," as Carlyle has written, and lacking the brilliance of Choiseul, was far too experienced a diplomatist to be hasty. A certain Bonvouloir offered himself, it is said, to undertake a mission in the summer of 1775 to the American Congress at Philadelphia. His offer was accepted. But Vergennes ordered Garnier, French representative in London, to say that the French Government knew nothing of it and to protest that the King's "delicacy and sense of justice would prevent such an act."[29]

Even so, instructions reached Bonvouloir which had come from Vergennes. He was to avoid giving the impression that he had been authorized, for it might prove desirable to repudiate him entirely, if Britain threatened to act at once because of his mission, or if the American Congress should fail to show strength and purpose. Bonvouloir nevertheless was to have it well understood in Philadelphia that France was interested in the fortunes of Congress. He was to discover the conditions in America and report back immediately to the French Government. And above all, he was to make the Americans believe that France had no intention of taking advantage of their situation to restore her own power in Canada.[30]

Vergennes knew at the start the vital importance of such a disclaimer. Canada was "the jealous point for them." "It is necessary," said he, "to make them understand that we dream of it not at all." For they would not care to help him reëstablish French supremacy in Europe only to face French troops again in their own back country. They might not keep up their struggle with the mother country. They certainly would not leave the side of Britain and swing over to France, even if they did finish the job and gain independence from King and Parliament.[31]

Word from Bonvouloir reached Paris on February 27, 1776. He

29. Corwin, 56. Van Tyne, 469 n.
30. Doniol, I, 129.
31. *Ibid.*, I, 152–156. Vergennes to Guines, August 7, 1775.

had talked with Franklin and the committee of secret correspondence. They wanted the aid of France but they also wished to know
what the price for it was going to be. Bonvouloir's favorable report
on conditions in America, written December 28, 1775, did not
come, however, until late in the following spring, too late to do
more than support the decision which had been made. By that time
Silas Deane had arrived in Paris; Vergennes already had a good idea
as to what the Americans expected; and the King had adopted his
plan to aid them secretly and to exploit the Spanish quarrel with
Portugal, Britain's ally.

This had been done over the weighty objections of the minister
of finance. Turgot had opposed on account of the risks involved,
the poor condition of the French Treasury, and the very great
probability that the American colonies would break from their
mother country of their own accord regardless of what France
might do. But so much wisdom could not prevail with the King.
Turgot was soon out of office.[32]

To aid the American rebels would be an extremely delicate operation, as it would invite war with Britain. But, argued Vergennes,
so would failure to help them. For Britain would attack the French
colonies, he said, as soon as she had reconquered her own; and if
she were defeated, she would then form a coalition with the new
American States to do the same thing. Mere conjectures, these, and
flimsy reasons for risking a war with Britain, but they were the
means by which the foreign minister persuaded his King. It was
not long before Deane was getting supplies, many from the arsenals
of France, and shipping them to America through the fictitious
"Hortalez et Cie." of the famous playwright, Beaumarchais. There
is evidence, also, of negotiations with Spain for sending supplies to
the American rebels through Louisiana. Vergennes was not averse
to having a war with Britain. He wished to choose the time, the area
of combat, and to control France's associates.[33]

Portuguese aggression in the La Plata Valley of South America
was even more fragile material, and Vergennes was reluctant at first
to use it, although the Spanish ambassador, Aranda, was eager. If
Spain were to absorb Portugal, Spain herself might endanger French
supremacy in Europe. Even if Spain should not grow arrogant with
success, the attack on Portugal would bring Britain ashore to the
aid of her ally, and that would upset the equilibrium which Vergennes was striving to maintain among the interests of Prussia,
Russia, Austria, and other European states. He was afraid of war

32. *Ibid.,* I, 265, 280–283, 287–292.
33. Lyon, 57.

in Europe. But at length he was willing to take that chance, too, if in so doing he could break the power of Britain. For after all, as he argued in the King's council on July 7, 1776, not Spain nor any other continental power, but Britain was "the sole enemy" whom France "could and ought to fear."[34]

The considerations entering into this decision had been assembled by Garnier on May 15, 1776. He wrote to Vergennes that if Spain were to invade Portugal, Britain certainly would come to the aid of her ally. But a general war would result, he reasoned, and it would ruin Britain. France therefore ought to help the American colonies even if Spain did attack Portugal. Britain would have to give in to her colonies because she would become so involved in Europe. And the logical outcome would be that having thus lost her greatest colonial resources Britain would be unable to dispute French supremacy on the continent of Europe.[35]

So Garnier's reasoning wove about the central theme of revenge and restoration of French prestige. But we should note that it did not meet the equally logical arguments of Turgot. What if the general war should ruin France as well as Britain? What if France obtained the independence of the American States for them and then should not be able to hold them closely in friendship and coöperation against Britain? Would the gain from the policy of Garnier and Vergennes be complete?

It was precarious, but Vergennes was determined to try. When he learned toward the end of August, 1776, that the United States had declared themselves independent, he urged upon the King that the advantages of war with Britain outweighed the "inconveniences." Those Americans who had made the "enormous conquests" so humiliating to France in the last war were now on the side of France. It was they, he asserted, and not the British, who had broken French power in North America. Their connection with France, he declared, could not fail to last. And evidently the King agreed, for Vergennes got his scheme off to Spain promptly with Aranda's assistance. It purported to show that Spain had the same interests, motives, and reasons as France. She had her own quarrel with Britain behind Portugal, her own griefs over British interpretations of contraband and "encroachments."[36]

There might have been war with Britain then and there in the fall of 1776, if Spain had acted at once upon Vergennes' proposals. For he defied the British complaint that Deane had been allowed to

34. Doniol, I, 527–528. Council at Marly, July 7, 1776.
35. Corwin, 83. Stevens, No. 868, Garnier to Vergennes, May 15, 1776.
36. Corwin, 84–85. Doniol, I, 567–577 at 570 and 574, 585.

enter France. The King, said he, was master in his own house. Louis XVI did not have to account to anyone for the strangers whom he chose to admit into his dominions.[37]

But the authorities in Madrid were not so eager as Aranda. They agreed that a war with Britain would be "just." But they were not ready to start it. If Britain were weak then, she would be more so after two or three months of added losses in her "civil war." It is apparent, besides, that the advisers of the Spanish King did not relish having the Americans for allies. If they had made those "enormous conquests" before, they might try again—next time to the "humiliation" of Spain.[38]

Consequently, when the Spanish acceptance of Vergennes' proposals finally did reach Paris, it came at the same time as discouraging news from America. Washington had been defeated on Long Island. The British had taken New York City. And Vergennes was in quite a different mood. Lafayettes, Steubens, Broglies—romanticists, soldiers, egotists—might join or think of joining the American patriots, and they would have Vergennes' good wishes. But as for him, responsible to the King for the management of foreign affairs, secret aid would remain yet a while the "better part of valor." They would wait and see if the American armies had better luck. They would debate further the Spanish plan of conquest in Portugal. And in the meantime, they would try to take the edge from their defiance by sharing with the British ambassador, Stormont, that "joy which the satisfactory news had given him regarding the success of British arms in Connecticut and New York."[39]

The Alliance

THEN Benjamin Franklin arrived at Paris in December, 1776, with the American "plan of treaties." His fame as a scientist, philosopher, and man of the world, the quaintness of his manners, were charming to the French élite. His audacity was captivating. He expected eight ships of the line completely manned, thirty thousand stand of muskets and bayonets, ammunition and artillery sent under convoy to America. But Vergennes was keenly aware that Franklin and his fellow commissioners did not offer an alliance in return. They spoke of American rights of conquest and neutrality on the seas, not of commitments and guarantees in war and peace. Here was little prospect of American States torn from Britain and held to the side of France to assure her supremacy in European

37. *Ibid.*, I, 583.
38. *Ibid.*, I, 603–613 at 612, Grimaldi to Aranda, October 8, 1776.
39. Corwin, 85. Doniol, II, 107 n. 2. October 21, 1776.

affairs. Vergennes could congratulate himself that he had made his defiance of Britain in September no stronger. He demurred.

Sensing this situation, Franklin, Deane, and Lee pledged themselves to one another on February 2, 1777, to do what Congress had included and then had withdrawn from their instructions. They would undertake an alliance with France, if necessary, to get her into the war. But as it happened a letter written on December 30, 1776, was already on its way from the committee of secret correspondence reinstructing them to make "such tenders to France and Spain." And it appears to have arrived in time to save them from having to act on their own responsibility. Aroused further by the news that Burgoyne was preparing to invade the United States from Canada, they made specific proposals to both France and Spain.[40]

Deane wrote to Vergennes on March 18. They had just received new advices, he said, from Congress. If France would come into the war, the United States would offer to make common conquest of Nova Scotia, Newfoundland, Canada, St. Jean, the Floridas, the Bermudas, Bahama, and other islands. One half of the fisheries of Newfoundland and all the sugar islands would go to France. The United States would have the other conquests. They would furnish the supplies for the attack upon Britain's sugar islands. They would agree to restrict the commerce of France and the United States exclusively to the shipping of both nations. They would bind themselves to make no peace except by mutual consent. And Spain would be assured the conquest of Portugal if she came into the alliance.

Deane, however, included a scarcely veiled threat at the end. If France did not enter the war, the United States at least would ask her to get the European troops (those Hessians) out of America. And they would seek her advice whether they ought, perhaps, to offer peace to Britain on condition that Britain recognized their independence. It was a diplomatic way of warning France that if she did not enter the war, the American States might come to terms with their mother country without independence. Deane, Franklin, and Lee knew what Vergennes did not want.[41]

Franklin made similar proposals to the Spanish ambassador, Aranda, on April 7. But he added the stipulation that the United States would help in capturing Pensacola if their own inhabitants were allowed to use its harbor and freely navigate on the Mississippi

40. Corwin, 97. Wharton, II, 240, 260.
41. Doniol, II, 319–322.

River. American ambitions in that quarter were fully assertive.[42]

Again the Spanish ambassador "took fire." It was the foreign minister of France who still consulted caution. Vergennes met Deane's overture obliquely by making another retort to Britain. He answered her complaint that American merchantmen were getting protection in French ports by declaring that France as a neutral would grant the same privileges to American vessels as to those of any other power on friendly terms with her, whether or not at war with Britain. It was France's right, he asserted, under the old Treaty of Utrecht. But this was strong language. Neutrals did not then have the right to distinguish between insurrection and civil war in another state, of their own volition and without giving offense to that state. This right has grown into international law since the war of 1861–65 between the North and the South in the United States. Vergennes was almost declaring then that he was willing, if not quite ready, to fight.[43]

But he was not quite ready. The Americans had indeed offered to meet his price. They would enter an alliance in war and peacemaking. Under those circumstances, Deane's threat to deal alone with Britain was not very disturbing. Nor was his suggestion that Spain conquer Portugal as distressing as one might think, for Spain herself was changing the character of that problem. But Spain was balking more than ever against France's lead. And that was disturbing. It would be well if France could hold things in suspense until her own navy reached full strength and further news came from the battlefields of America.[44]

However exuberant Aranda might be in Paris, the authorities in Madrid felt differently. They were settling their controversy with Portugal. The lure of Jamaica, the Floridas, and especially Gibraltar was great. But they were averse to fighting Britain for the direct purpose of giving independence to those American States who claimed territorial rights in the Mississippi Valley, whose pioneers were spreading along the Ohio, Cumberland, and Tennessee rivers toward Louisiana, whose leading representative in Paris demanded the use of Pensacola and free navigation of the Mississippi. They would give secret aid to the rebels. That would injure Britain. But they would not recognize the American cause. Grimaldi stubbornly turned Arthur Lee back at the French border from his mission to Madrid.[45]

42. Wharton, II, 304.
43. Doniol, II, 334. March 21, 1777.
44. *Ibid.*, II, 325.
45. Corwin, 98–104. Doniol, II, 432. Wharton, II, 280–283. Yela, I, 161–180.

So Vergennes had the choice either of persuading the Spaniards to endanger their interests in America for the sake of Gibraltar, or of convincing himself and the King that France could go ahead without them. He was not yet sure of the latter. He chose to hold on to the American offer while he negotiated further with the Spaniards. His plan of financial aid and guarantees to the American States might be made to free them from Britain but keep them in practical dependence upon France and Spain jointly. Then came the news. Burgoyne had surrendered on October 17, 1777, at Saratoga![46]

Now American armies were winning battles. France's secret aid had been successful. And Vergennes had the United States committed to war and peace in common with her. The opportunity was too great for misgivings in case Spain did not join. Nor was this the time to worry whether American aggressiveness in the Mississippi Valley and aspirations on the seas would threaten later the interest of France as well as Britain and Spain. The moment had come for France to rise again to "grandeur"—upon·the ruins of the British Empire. Once more Vergennes moved the King with fear. If he did not attack Britain, the United States would join with her to despoil his West Indian possessions! He had to make this alliance with them if he would get them out of Britain's control. He should go on without Spain. The King agreed. Vergennes came quickly to terms with Franklin on February 6, 1778.[47]

The common object in this "defensive alliance," it said, was "to maintain effectually the liberty, Sovereignty, and independence absolute and unlimited of the said united States, as well in Matters of Gouvernement as of commerce." And each party was bound not to conclude either truce or peace with Britain, without the formal consent of the other, until that object had been "formally or tacitly assured by the Treaty or Treaties that shall terminate the War."[48]

Our first reaction to these statements may be that they meant triumph for Franklin, the Adamses, the Lees over Dickinson, Rutledge, and others who were reluctant to break with the mother country. And so they did. But they suited Vergennes' purposes equally well. Those words "or tacitly" were significant. They left as much discretion to France as to the United States in regard to the peacemaking and the subsequent status of the United States.

46. Doniol, II, 502, 564, 570, 575–578.
47. Corwin, 114–120.
48. Miller, *Treaties,* II, 37–40.

It might be "tacitly assured" that the United States were nominally independent but actually under the guardianship of France and Spain in the society of nations.

France undertook to renounce forever "the possession of the Islands of Bermudas as well as of any part of the continent of North america which before the treaty of Paris in 1763, or in virtue of that Treaty, were acknowledged to belong to the Crown of Great Britain, or to the United States. . . ." France agreed to guarantee not only the independence of the United States after the treaty of peace which should close the war but also any conquests which the United States might make during the war of British territory in the "Northern Parts of America, or the Islands of Bermudas." France, too, was to be free to acquire the British islands in or near the Gulf of Mexico. And the United States undertook to guarantee at the end of the war such conquests by France together with her existing possessions.

Again the primary purpose of Vergennes was revealed. The United States would be at liberty to enlarge their territory, if they could, and France would even guarantee within limits after the peace what they had acquired during the war. But France would make sure first of her major objective. It was separation of the American colonies from Britain. And then she, too, would have such conquests as she might have obtained in her particular sphere of interest. Besides, many things could happen before the war came to an end and the necessity should arise of guaranteeing the independence of the United States and the conquests which they had made. Not the least of these was that Spain might have entered the war and made conquests of British territory east of the Mississippi for herself. France's renunciation in favor of the United States did not restrict Spain.

An "act separate and secret" was adopted on the same day to supplement the general statement in the Treaty of Alliance that other parties might make common cause against Britain in redress of their grievances. The American commissioners agreed, "in consequence of the intimate union" subsisting between the King of France and the King of Spain, that the latter might participate in both the alliance and the commercial treaty of France and the United States. This had the appearance of opening the alliance to Spain upon terms of equal obligation as well as privilege. But it also said that if the King of Spain took exception to any of the stipulations therein, he might propose other conditions "analogous to the principal aim of the alliance and conformable to the Rules of equality, reciprocity & friendship." It was more than probable that the King of Spain would take serious exception to the provisions in the alliance for conquest by the United States.[49]

What if that clause designating the "Northern Parts of America" did lie open to interpretation so that Spain might appropriate the Floridas on the south as spoils of war? What if France had been careful to stipulate that she would guarantee to the United States only "the whole as their Possessions shall be fixed and assured to the said States at the moment of the cessation of their present War with England"? Vergennes would answer those questions only when he got to them. Conditions then, he obviously hoped, would be different. France might be supreme again in Europe. As for Franklin, Deane, and Lee, they were attempting to solve no problems now that were not actually confronting them. Conditions later would be very different, indeed, for the United States. They expected to be free and independent in America. As for the King of Spain, he knew that conditions would certainly be different; but would they be better? His own point of view was not likely to change. But would he look out upon French supremacy in Europe, and American independence on the other side of the Atlantic, with as much pleasure and self-esteem? Would he be so sure of his position at home and his possessions abroad? These were very ominous questions to be answered to his satisfaction before he undertook any renunciations or guarantees in an alliance with France and the United States.

The commercial treaty which Vergennes accepted with the alliance contained all that the American Congress had conceived with regard to neutral rights on the seas. It proclaimed the principle that *free ships make free goods*. It stipulated the right to carry enemy goods excepting contraband. And it defined contraband so as to exclude from its meaning naval stores and shipbuilding materials and anything else not expressly stated in the treaty itself as contraband. It gave the right to trade with enemy ports except those "at that time beseiged, blocked up or invested."[50]

Vergennes was too much of a realist to think, because he wished it so, that Britain's power on the sea would necessarily decline with the separation of the American States from her empire and the reëstablishment of French supremacy on the continent of Europe. But the neutral rights of the new power in America might serve France in the future against the mistress of the seas, if they could be joined with the neutral rights of other states in Europe.

49. *Ibid.*, II, 45.
50. *Ibid.*, II, 21, 22–23.

Other provisions in this commercial treaty with the United States, however, would help France immediately. It was agreed that the ships of war and privateers of either party should enter and depart from the ports of the other at pleasure with prizes taken from an enemy. But no enemy could bring his prizes into the ports of either, except under stress of weather, and then only under the commitment that he would be forced to leave as soon as possible. Both parties agreed that their subjects or citizens who took service as privateers against either should be treated as pirates. And it was stipulated that foreign privateers in enmity with either party would not be allowed to fit their ships in the ports of the other party, nor to sell what they had taken, nor to exchange their ships and merchandise or any other lading in any way whatsoever, nor even to purchase victuals except those necessary to take them on to the next port of their own "Prince or State."[51]

The Prospect of 1778

THUS France dropped the mask of neutrality long since transparent, entered into an alliance with the rebels in America, took up the cause of neutrals on the seas for her own advantage, and prepared to throw her armies and fleets once more upon the only foe whom she "could and ought to fear." The quarrel between Britain and her American colonies, which had begun over colonial trade, self-government, westward expansion, and grown into a war for independence, was now to become a world struggle involving practically every nation of Europe arrayed against British power either as a belligerent or as an armed neutral. And, even though the League of Armed Neutrality of 1780 never reached solidarity against British violations of neutral trade with France, Spain, and the United States, the parts which Russia, Denmark, Sweden, and Holland played did affect the outcome of the war. The pressure of the League upon British opinion had value for Americans in quest of their independence and Western territory that cannot be measured by tons of shipping and dollars in merchandise.[52]

The prospect seemed good for both France and the United States in February, 1778. To Frenchmen, their "tradition de grandeur" gave promise of reality again. And to Americans, the alliance with France pledged independence "absolute and unlimited." These words appeared definite and sweeping enough. But were they? Or did they mean simply independence from the government of King and Parliament in London? Were they going to mean release also

51. *Ibid.,* II, 16–17, 19–20.
52. Fauchille (Scott ed.), *The Armed Neutralities of 1780 and 1800,* 579–586.

from the "wars and quarrels" of Europe as Thomas Paine wished?
Were they going to assure freedom from French and Spanish interference with America's neutral commerce? Did they guarantee, with
no reservations, the right of the United States to conquer North
America at the expense of Britain?

There were Spaniards in high position who thought decidedly
not, and intended to see that these things did not happen. There
were Frenchmen also, if not those in authority at the moment, who
would soon rise to power and strive to make sure that they did not
happen, but that France regained an empire in North America.

Vergennes himself, within two months after accepting the
treaties, was giving significant instructions to Gérard who had
signed with Franklin and was to go as minister to the Congress in
Philadelphia. One point was very important to the King, wrote
Vergennes, and it would exact all of Gérard's "dexterity." It was
the reservations to be made in favor of Spain. So far she had no part
in the treaties, but she would want Jamaica, the Floridas, and a share
in the fisheries of Newfoundland. Jamaica was already, he said, at
the disposal of the King, and the fisheries would be to a great degree. But the Americans were planning to conquer the Floridas.
Gérard was to make it his business to stop them. And he should discourage any attempt to take Nova Scotia and Canada. For the principal aim of the King, declared Vergennes, was the independence of
North America and "its permanent union with France." The King
therefore considered it "useful" to leave Canada in the hands of the
British. If the Americans were kept "vigilant" and "uneasy," they
would be made to feel the complete "need" which they had of the
King's friendship and alliance. Gérard might help them plan an attack upon Canada, if that were necessary to please them, but he was
to make no agreement that France should participate in the campaign.[53]

French Aims—"A Very Hard Law"

WHAT was the motive behind all this jockeying to get France into
the American war, to make the United States independent of Britain, and yet to keep them from taking Canada and the Floridas?
One conjecture since has been that France entered the war so that
she could be in position afterwards to exploit the trade of the
United States. But this explanation was effectively dismissed at the
time by Vergennes himself. He could evade and obscure with the
best when it served his ends. He was frank and direct if there was
no point to being otherwise. He declared on June 20, 1778, in the

53. Doniol, III, 153–157. March 29, 1778.

midst of trying to involve Spain, that her ministers would be mistaken if they thought France was making her decision to get new trade. This motive, said he, was only "very slightly accessory." American commerce, "subjected to the monopoly of the mother country," was without doubt "a great object of interest" to Britain. But "open in the future to the eagerness of all nations," he declared, "it will be perhaps for France only a trifling matter." He was theorizing still as a good mercantilist that colonial trade had little value unless it were monopolized. But his policy was in fact one of *"statecraft* rather than of *economics."* And he foresaw with remarkable accuracy what was going to happen when the United States did become independent. Britain lost her colonies but kept the greatest part of their trade.[54]

Another conjecture as to the French motive cannot be set aside so readily. It relies upon the hope of many Frenchmen that they might regain Canada from Britain and take back Louisiana from Spain. It presumes that the statesmen of France had these ultimate purposes in their minds as they made the alliance with the American States.

Historians who venture with caution to build upon circumstantial evidence reject this explanation because they have discovered no documents confirming it. They note that France expressly renounced all claim in the Treaty of 1778 with the United States to that part of North America which was British after 1763; and they do not give corresponding weight to the fact that France's renunciation carefully excepted the Spanish territory west of the Mississippi and the island of New Orleans, so recently her own possessions. To them, this reservation was made only for the benefit of Spain under the Family Compact, and not to safeguard French interests of future time against American encroachment. They do not consider that hope was kept alive of restoring the empire of France in America. They pass by the extreme dissatisfaction with Spanish rule of the French in Louisiana, the presence of French settlers and traders in the Illinois country near St. Louis, and the French population of old Quebec. And they minimize popular sentiment in France and private memorials to the French ministry for that end. They do not take seriously the proposal of the French naval commander, D'Estaing, on March 19, 1769, that Louisiana should be made into a free state under the protection of both France and Spain, for the benefit of French commerce in the Mississippi Valley.[55]

54. Corwin, 15. Doniol, III, 140, Vergennes to Montmorin, June 20, 1778. See below, p. 149.
55. Phillips, 14–17 n. 26. Villiers du Terrage, chaps. x–xiii.

France's statesmen may indeed have been honest in renouncing claim to British North America, but they had the very best of reasons for doing so. Revolutionary feeling would not have spread so fast in America if they had not. Nor would Spain have been impressed so much by their offer of Jamaica and the Floridas, nor even by the promise of Gibraltar. Nonetheless, it may be true that they did abandon thought of restoring the empire of France so long as the struggle continued for American independence. That was their primary objective. But it is as true that they did not take long thereafter to revive the hope at the expense of both Spain and the United States—once Britain had acknowledged in the Peace of 1783 that the United States were independent.[56]

A third explanation came straight from the foreign office. France would have to enter the war, it was said, to protect her possessions in the West Indies. If she did not, and the Americans won or grew tired of fighting, they would join with the British to invade the French colonies. And if Britain won, those colonies would be in still greater danger. France, therefore, had to take the side of the American rebels, help them to victory, and bind them to guarantee her colonies. Apparently, Vergennes and his agent, Beaumarchais, prevailed upon the King with these solemn assertions. But we should not be affected by them to the extent of believing that they displayed the French motive. Governments have been prone in every age to justify aims of aggression or revenge with arguments of self-defense.[57]

The American historian, Bancroft, enthusiast for democracy and a practicing Democratic politician, ascribed the participation of France to the movement for liberty then fascinating many of her élite. And the French historian Faÿ, improvising upon this theme, has endeavored to show that there was a moral affinity between French liberal thought and American discontent, in which French ideas had the greater generative force. He has maintained that Thomas Jefferson was guided when writing his famous Declaration, though unconsciously perhaps, by Rousseau and Voltaire more than by John Locke. But were this true, it would not explain the revolutionary spirit of America. The Declaration of Independence was not so much the cause as the product of American discontent.[58]

Such a view does not take properly into account the effects upon loyalty to Britain of colonial evasion of the mercantile system through a century before Thomas Jefferson took up his pen. It does

56. See below, pp. 117–122.
57. Corwin, 121 ff., 155 n. Loménie, II, 99–106.
58. Bancroft (1892 ed.), V, 256. Faÿ, *Revolutionary Spirit*, 81.

not consider that by habitual indulgence in an illegal practice, Americans came finally to think of it as their right. This view does not comprehend the popular reaction in America as Britain attempted to revise and to enforce her navigation laws when the Peace of 1763 had greatly complicated her problems of empire. It disregards years of friction between royal governors and colonial assemblies over the conflicting interests of creditors and debtors, and other disputes of practical importance and bitter political significance. It overlooks the rancor, indigenous in America as elsewhere, of humbler and poorer people toward richer and more fashionable neighbors who seemed to hold office not because they were talented but because they had favor with the governor. And it ignores altogether the temper of frontiersmen in America who had never heard of Rousseau and Voltaire, nor pondered the metaphysics of the *contrat social* if they had.

But quite apart from these obstacles to the theory that France came to the aid of the American Revolutionaries primarily because her own liberal ideas were their generative force, such an explanation of the French motive is blocked by evidence in the archives of France, given by the man more responsible than any other for getting France into the war, her foreign minister, the Count de Vergennes. M. Faÿ has written that no impartial mind can help being struck by the fact that there was no question of acquiring territory or of ruining England in the letters of Beaumarchais and the reports of Vergennes. The word *ruin* may have to be construed relatively. But the statements of Vergennes are to be examined with more care. He wrote on June 20, 1778, to Montmorin, French ambassador in Madrid, in regard to the motive of France:

> What ought to have persuaded her and in reality has persuaded her to join with America, is the great enfeeblement of England, brought about by the removal of a third of her empire. I shall not repeat here, sir, what has been said on twenty other occasions of the resources, vast and of every kind which she may draw therefrom to affront at her pleasure the domains of the two Crowns in America, and, in consequence, the point of security which they acquire by this separation. . . .

And he instructed Montmorin to tell the Spanish minister, Floridablanca, that France was determined to accomplish it.[59]

The enthusiasm of the *salon* nourished the policy of France, but that policy originated from cool reasoning in the ministry of foreign affairs. The aim was to attack Britain where she was most assailable

59. *Ibid.*, 61. Corwin, 23–24. Doniol, III, 140, Vergennes to Montmorin, June 20, 1778.

and when the most damage could be done to her vital interests. And this was to restore the French monarchy to that European prestige which it had enjoyed under Louis XIV. The aim was not to favor those liberals in America beyond the exact commitments in the treaties of 1778. If further proof is necessary, it is at hand. For Vergennes was writing again to Montmorin in Madrid before the year 1778 was out: "We do not desire by a great deal that the rising new republic remain exclusive mistress of this whole immense continent. Self-sufficient before long for her own needs, the other nations would be likely to reckon with her, because she, able to do without everything, would very certainly make a very hard law for them."[60]

60. *Ibid.*, III, 561–562, Vergennes to Montmorin, October 30, 1778.

II

THE SPANISH ENCUMBRANCE

Floridablanca's Thoughts

THE American contract with France was in jeopardy from the beginning. Floridablanca, dour successor to Grimaldi as prime minister of Spain, cared even less for those liberals across the Atlantic. Their republican principles were a menace to the Spanish Empire. Their diplomatists talked of their right by nature to the outlets through Spanish territory. Their armed bands were coming nearer to Spain's possessions as the war progressed. No matter what Montmorin declared at Madrid or Gérard accomplished in Philadelphia, American ambitions would collide with Spanish interests. And the King of France was bound by the Family Compact to respect those interests. The peace of mind of Spain's colonial governors, the ease and self-esteem of her King were not to be disregarded as Vergennes had disregarded them in making his agreements with Franklin.

To soothe the King, but more to halt American independence, Floridablanca tried first to mediate between Britain and France. But the British Government would not respond as he wished. His sincerity was at least questionable. And it was France that had taken the aggressive. A disavowal by her of the American Alliance was in order before mediation, and possibly reparations also for damages to Britain. Besides, Englishmen were not yet ready to concede that they could not subdue their own rebels without taking the governments of Europe into consultation. And so the Spanish minister had to find another way of holding the American States in check.[1]

Floridablanca's second thoughts reached Congress eventually through Vergennes and Gérard. These were to the effect that there should be a truce with Britain. The King of France would keep all his pledges to the United States, but they should look to Spain and France for protection of their independence. This proposal Vergennes communicated to Franklin "under the seal of secrecy" and without the knowledge of his fellow commissioners. It would be a "premature confidence," wrote Vergennes on December 25, 1778,

1. Corwin, 180–182.

to Gérard, to let Congress know about it just then. But the French minister in Philadelphia was to prepare the way, and get it before Congress in time.[2]

Vergennes informed Montmorin in Spain that Franklin would accept this "imperfect recognition." Franklin seemed to agree that the question whether independence was a right or a fact was not important if the United States got the "sweets of peace, or of a truce"; it might be good, as a matter of fact, to have an interval of peace in which they could put their own house in order. This undoubtedly was welcome news in Madrid. But if the members of Congress heard of Franklin's opinion at all, and it is very unlikely that they did from him, they did not have the same faith in the intentions of Spain and France that Vergennes attributed to Franklin. Or else, they were not yet as susceptible to French and Spanish influences in Philadelphia as they were to become.[3]

Congress passed by the hints from Gérard that there should be a truce under the guardianship, and we need hardly add the dictation, of the Bourbon monarchies. It voted instead on August 14, 1779, that the negotiations for peace with Britain should be based upon acknowledgment in advance by the mother country that the United States were "Sovereign, free and Independent." And on September 27 Congress elected John Adams minister plenipotentiary to Great Britain. He had just returned from France where he had taken the place of Silas Deane.[4]

Congress instructed Adams to obtain treaties of both peace and commerce with Britain. This certainly was not looking to Spain and France as special guardians. John Adams went back to Europe immediately, to behave in France and in Holland as if he were the minister of a sovereign State—much to the annoyance of Vergennes. Even Adams' modified instructions of October 18, 1780, had little in them really to please the foreign minister of France. Although Adams was then advised that he might accept a truce for a long period, he was ordered to place it firmly upon French recognition before the world that the United States had the "character of an independent and sovereign people." And the condition for such a truce was that Britain would remove her land and naval armaments from their territory. Congress was determined still to have freedom

2. Doniol, III, 56–80, 613–615, Vergennes to Gérard, December 25, 1778.
3. *Ibid.*, III, 595, 599, Vergennes to Montmorin, December 4, 24, 1778.
4. *Journ. Cont. Cong.*, XIV, 956; XV, 1113. Adams, *Works*, VII, 121. The quarrel between Lee and Deane which led to Deane's recall, and Deane's defection from the American cause are not pertinent to this story. For a sympathetic treatment, see Clark, *Silas Deane*.

from all foreign powers in fact, whether or not they acknowledged it in a truce or a formal treaty of peace. It was not yet to be "tacitly assured."[5]

The King of Spain, however, had decided in the meantime to take advantage of the international situation as it was and to make war on his own account. Something might fall into his hands if Britain were severely shaken. The secret agreement with France at Aranjuez, April 12, 1779, stipulated that Spain should get Gibraltar. France in return was to have control of the fortifications at Dunkirk, or some equivalent. Spain would receive the island of Minorca in the Mediterranean. If France obtained Newfoundland, Spain was to have fishing rights there. Around the Gulf of Mexico, Britain was to be driven from the Bay of Honduras, the Campeche Coast, the river and fort of Mobile, Pensacola, and the shores of Florida along the Bahama Channel. But Spain carefully reserved the right to deal with the United States for herself alone. In short, Spain refused to join with France in recognizing their independence. As Montmorin reported to Vergennes in August, the King of Spain looked upon the Americans as rebels. He did not intend to recognize them until the general peace at the close of the war—that is, until he might be compelled to do so.[6]

La Luzerne's Purse

THE American States stood to lose rather than profit from Spain's entrance into the war. Britain now would have to face another enemy and defend Gibraltar, but France could not throw her greatest strength against British positions in America. She would have to include Gibraltar, Minorca, and Jamaica in her naval objectives as well as the Atlantic Coast. More dangerous for the United States, Spain's desire to retake the Floridas and conquer British territory from the Mississippi toward the Appalachians soon caused activities in Philadelphia which threatened to divide Congress and corrupt some of its members.

The French historian, Doniol, has recorded an episode decidedly in point. It appears that Gérard and his successor, La Luzerne, under instructions from Vergennes, tried again and again to correct that wayward decision of Congress which had made John Adams sole negotiator for peace and commerce with Britain in 1779. By June 15, 1781, La Luzerne had persuaded Congress to submerge Adams in a commission of five and further to revise their instructions.

5. *Journ. Cont. Cong.*, XVIII, 949. October 18, 1780.
6. Doniol, III, 753 n.; 803–810, for the Treaty of Aranjuez.

Henceforth the American peacemakers were to maintain "the most candid and confidential communications" with the French ministers, and "undertake nothing in the negotiations for peace or truce without their knowledge and concurrence."[7]

La Luzerne explained in his despatch of May 13 some of the means which he had employed: ". . . he had just 'opened his purse,' in other words taken into his pay General Sullivan, newly become a member of Congress. The old and queer commander of the army of Rhode Island was then on the point of being purchased by Clinton. In any case, La Luzerne persuaded him. He designated other deputies to whom a situation like that which was obtained for him would yield great service." According to Doniol, subsequent reports from La Luzerne and his subordinate, Marbois, assigned to General Sullivan a good share in other decisions by Congress, notably the selection of Robert Livingston as secretary of foreign affairs. There is a glimpse here of the rivalry in New York between the Livingstons and the Clintons.

At the end of his report on June 11, four days after the final action of Congress, La Luzerne wrote:

> I attribute the promptness with which Congress yielded to my representations to two principal causes; the first is the absence of Mr. Samuel Adams. . . . The second is the rupture of the coalition of New England States and the destruction of the system which it had proposed for prolonging the war. It is to General Sullivan alone that I am obligated for it; this delegate has displayed in the whole of this affair as much patriotism as attachment to the alliance, and I believe I can consider that the efforts to re-establish this coalition will be useless for so long a time as he shall remain in Congress. I think that it will be just as profitable for the alliance to nourish his attachment to us, even after he shall have returned to the State of New Hampshire where he enjoys much influence.

We do not have to accept La Luzerne's assertions about General Sullivan as the truth to realize the danger to American independence and hopes of empire in such activities at Philadelphia.[8]

While the American Revolution continued, the statesmen of France may have had no thought, as they professed, of restoring a French empire in America. Bonvouloir had been sent to give that promise, and the Treaty of 1778 made his statement official. But neither had Vergennes any intention of losing the support of Spain in Europe at this juncture by thwarting her aims in America. On the contrary, he saw as good reason to foster those desires in the

7. *Journ. Cont. Cong.,* XX, 651. Wharton, IV, 503–505.
8. Doniol, IV, 608 n.

Floridas as to let Britain stay in Canada; both would keep the Americans uneasy and dependent upon their alliance with France. Before he had done with the question, he conceded that Spain had a right to invade other British possessions east of the Mississippi.

This concession not only lay in the path of American aspirations; it came very near to breaking the pledges of renunciation and guarantee which France had given to the United States. Vergennes was quite within his legal rights when making the subsequent Treaty of Aranjuez with Spain. But if he would save France from compromising those prior agreements, he would have to persuade the United States to accept a newer interpretation of their contract with France. It would have to mean that Spain was entitled to compete with them for the British possessions east of the Mississippi, not only the Floridas which had once belonged to Spain but also the Ohio, Cumberland, and Tennessee valleys which never had. Gérard received instructions amounting practically to just that. And he went farther in collusion with the Spanish agent, Miralles, to obtain the result.

Which ally of France was to receive her support at the peace conference if both Spain and the United States should happen to have made such conquests? Among those Americans who had or were gaining experience in the diplomacy of Europe, it was a question to create doubts of their success, particularly as they knew that Britain's statesmen would turn every misunderstanding among her enemies to her own advantage in the negotiations for peace.[9]

Jay's Experiences at Home

THE immediate experiences in Philadelphia of John Jay, still a young man in his thirties, and his actions later at Madrid and Paris, had a great deal to do with preventing such disaster to the independence and inland empire which Washington, Franklin, and many another American by this time had clearly perceived.

Jay had been slow to take up the idea of independence, but once it was declared, he threw himself into the patriot cause, utterly scorning what his brother did. (Sir James Jay, after profiting from the cause, withdrew to England in circumstances ruinous to his honor.) John Jay was not so sure, however, that there was wisdom in making an alliance with France to accompany the Declaration of Independence. As he wrote to Gouverneur Morris, April 29, 1778, when news of the agreement reached him: "What the French treaty may be, I know not. If Britain would acknowledge our independence, and enter into a liberal alliance with us, I should prefer a

9. Corwin, 304–309, for the "tangle" of French commitments. Also see below, p. 73 f.

connexion with her to a league with any power on earth." Now at
the end of the same year, when he had become the presiding officer
of Congress, he sat long after dinner, pipe in mouth, listening to his
host, the French minister. The Spaniard, Miralles, also was present.[10]

The purport of Gérard's conversation for two hours was that the
welfare of the American States demanded a permanent line of separation between the possessions of Spain and theirs, and he reported
to Vergennes that his reasoning had won approval. The president of
Congress seemed to be impressed. But Jay knew what Gérard was
about. He remarked that Spain was as interested as America in the
arrangements. And Gérard, sensing that no specific proposal as to
where the line should be drawn was forthcoming at that time from
Jay, turned the conversation to a discussion of the same idea, but
in general terms—whether too extensive boundaries would be dangerous to the United States. It is evident that Gérard knew quite
well there were territorial rivalries between the sections within the
American confederation. So did Jay. He agreed with Gérard merely
that the bounds should be those of the colonies at the outbreak of
the Revolution.[11]

How far to the west were those limits? If we accept over the objections of the American patriots the view that the King's Proclamation of 1763 and the Quebec Act of 1774 had determined the
western frontiers of the seaboard colonies, we assume that John Jay
was assenting on that occasion to an interpretation which would
have held the American States back from the Mississippi River. If
we defer to the patriots, however, and give more weight to the
French alliance and its stipulation that the States were free to reduce
the British power remaining in the "Northern Parts of America,"
we conclude that Jay thought of the boundaries of the United
States as enclosing the territory from the Appalachians to the Mississippi. So far as we can ascertain from Gérard's report to Vergennes
at the time, the president of Congress did not say.

That John Jay was not including the Floridas in his thoughts,
however, does appear certain. For Gérard had been taking great
pains to follow Vergennes' instructions and to tell his American
listeners that France would not continue the war in order to help
the United States succeed to the rights or claims of Britain on the
continent which were still open to acquisition by Spain. This could
mean nothing less than the Floridas, as they had been Spanish possessions as recently as 1763.

What the president of Congress thought at the time about the

10. Monaghan, 215. Jay, II, 23. For Miralles, see Yela, I, 385–399, II, 274–275.
11. Circourt, III, 260–263. December 22, 1778. Doniol, IV, 35–36.

navigation of the Mississippi, the minister of France did not even try to discover. He reported to Vergennes that he had carefully abstained from discussing the exclusive acquisition of the course of the Mississippi. That object, said he, had indeed to be handled "secretly and with dexterity." But Gérard felt encouraged to believe that he was getting on with his mission, for in closing his report of January 28, 1779, he declared that Jay was sincerely attached to the alliance with France, hostile to Britain, and enthusiastic in the conviction that the triumvirate of France, Spain, and America could defy all the world.[12]

Writing some months later, after he had arrived in Spain, Jay himself recorded his views at the time of Gérard's activity in Philadelphia as these:

> I was early convinced that provided we could obtain independence and a speedy peace, we could not justify protracting the war, and hazarding the event of it, for the sake of conquering the Floridas, to which we had no title, or retaining the navigation of the Mississippi, which we should not want this age, and of which we might probably acquire a partial use with the consent of Spain. It was therefore my opinion that we should quit all claim to the Floridas, and grant Spain the navigation of her river below our territories, on her giving us a convenient free port on it, under regulations to be specified in a treaty, provided they would acknowledge our independence, defend it with their arms, and grant us either a proper sum of money, or an annual subsidy for a certain number of years.[13]

Concede that in large part this was the result of afterthought, when the chance of making the triple alliance of France, Spain, and the United States was growing remote and personal disappointment was increasing. It is a case, nevertheless, where a man's recollection is to be taken for his opinion. Jay had not been thinking that the western borders of the American States lay in the Appalachian Mountains at the line of the King's Proclamation of 1763, as he had listened to Gérard's argument. His idea, as Gérard had reported then to Vergennes, was an alliance with Spain in war against Britain for the purpose of obtaining American independence. And we should observe that he spoke now, not of admitting that Spain had a legal right to close the Mississippi River within her own territory, but of granting her control of the river below American territory on condition that the United States should have a convenient free port under regulations specified in a treaty.

12. Circourt, III, 264–266. January 28, 1779. Doniol, IV, 69–70.
13. Jay, I, 95–101.

Jay's Mission to Madrid

JOHN JAY went to Spain as John Adams returned to negotiate for peace and commerce with Britain. In spite of Gérard's efforts among the members of Congress, Jay was instructed on September 28, 1779, always to insist upon free navigation of the Mississippi into and from the sea for the inhabitants of the United States. He was to obtain some port below the thirty-first degree of latitude, free for all their vessels and goods. He was to seek a loan of $5,000,000. He was to secure treaties of alliance and commerce similar to those with France. And before negotiating the loan, he was to ask for a subsidy in return for guaranteeing the Floridas to Spain.[14]

It seems unmistakable, from these expectations, that the American Congress knew nothing, officially at least, of the Treaty of Aranjuez in which Spain had been so noncommittal and yet so clearly hostile to the United States. Jay too must have been uninformed. But Gérard's curiosity about his instructions did not escape his notice on their voyage to Europe together. And he had plenty of time before arriving in Cadiz to think over the episodes which had involved Gérard with the Spanish agent, Miralles, at Philadelphia. In any case, the instructions which he gave to his secretary, Carmichael, who preceded him to Madrid, show that he was searching for the realities behind appearances. Carmichael was to discover how far the influence of France entered into the counsels of Spain. And when speaking of American affairs, he was to do justice to Virginia and the Western country near the Mississippi.

John Jay's mind was already questioning the chances of success at Madrid. Was he to get the recognition of American independence, money, acknowledgment of the right of the United States to use the Mississippi, undisputed title to the intervening territory, the alliance? Would he even be officially received?[15]

Floridablanca's first letter, although personally cordial, informed him that he was not "to assume a formal character." All was at once clear to John Jay. He reported immediately to Congress. This letter told them, he said, that the independence of the United States would be acknowledged only if they acceded to certain terms of a treaty. Gérard had tried often to persuade him that the negotiations would be ruined if Congress maintained its resolutions. But he had replied that Congress had taken the ground with too much deliberation to quit it: "And indeed, as affairs are now circumstanced, it would, in my opinion," he said, "be better for America to have no

14. *Journ. Cont. Cong.*, XV, 1113, 1118–1120. Wharton, III, 353. Yela, I, 415–458.
15. Pellew, 129. Wharton, III, 472. January 27, 1780.

treaty with Spain than to purchase one on such servile terms. There was a time when it might have been proper to have given that country something for their making common cause with us, but that day is now past. Spain is at war with Britain." Many things induced him, he concluded, to suspect that France was determined to manage between Spain and the United States so as to make them both her debtors.[16]

John Jay had discovered the realities in March, 1780, before he reached Madrid. France was as committed to Spain as to the United States. Spain had gone to war without making an alliance with the United States, and had done so purposely. She was likely to pursue her own ends without undertaking any commitments to the United States, unless they made concessions in regard to the Western country, particularly the closure of the Mississippi to American traffic. So it was to prove.

In his preliminary conference with Jay on May 11, 1780, Floridablanca broached the question of the Mississippi as the obstacle to a treaty. The King, he declared, would never relinquish his position, but perhaps "some middle way might be hit on which would pave the way to get over this difficulty." Jay replied that "many of the States were bounded by that river and were highly interested in its navigation." But "they were equally inclined to enter into any amicable regulations," he observed, "which might prevent any inconveniences with respect to contraband or other objects which might excite the uneasiness of Spain." In other words, the United States wished to allay the fears of Spain that the river might be used against her in war, but they would expect both recognition of their right to the Mississippi and its use for commercial purposes.[17]

Cumberland in Madrid—Straight Talk

THE appearances of the moment were that there was some basis for agreement. But the arrival on June 18 of the British agent, Cumberland, changed them. And after him came the news in July that General Lincoln had surrendered to the British at Charleston, South Carolina.

Cumberland had little chance of making peace with Spain. His instructions had been explicit that he should return to England at once if the Spaniards asked him to cede Gibraltar. As this playwright described the scene years later, he found Floridablanca "in the hands of D'Estaing, and more than half persuaded that the

16. *Ibid.*, III, 515–516, February 24, 1780; 529–530, March 3, 1780.
17. *Ibid.*, III, 724. May 26, 1780.

cooperation of France would put him in possession of Gibraltar, that coveted fortress, which I would not suffer him even to name, and for which Spain would almost have laid the map of her islands, the keys of her treasury at my feet." Yet, upon finding this out, he did not return at once to England. Nor did his Government thereupon recall him immediately. In fact, his superiors had ordered the ship which put him ashore at Lisbon to return so promptly that it looks as though, from the start, they had neither expected him to succeed nor wished him to return immediately if he did not. He was hardly given time to make the journey from Lisbon to Madrid and back.[18]

This affair may have been just another of Lord George Germain's blunders during the American Revolution. For Cumberland had great difficulty later in getting reimbursement for his expenses. But there are other facts that are not to be overlooked. Germain himself knew beforehand, and so did Cumberland, that the exuberant Irish priest, Hussey, who seems to have been the instigator of the mission and who accompanied Cumberland as his confidential secretary, was a Spanish agent. Germain and Cumberland, in fact, were party to the scheme whereby Hussey had been provided with papers, ostensibly secret documents, regarding the Navy and the defenses of Gibraltar, which he had sent on to Floridablanca. Cumberland may have given this circumstance less and less thought later as he warmed to Hussey's real charm and the attentions of the Spanish Court. Cumberland's letters home seemed guileless. But were they? Did he not suspect that Hussey might be—as he was—making copies for Floridablanca? Was Cumberland, too, deceiving nobody? Had he forgotten completely that his secretary was a Spanish spy?[19]

It is most improbable that the British foreign office forgot, whether or no the exhilaration of moving in high diplomatic circles dulled Cumberland's memory. It was worth while to keep him in Madrid regardless. His presence there was useful, though not in the way it was supposed to appear. He settled no issues with Spain. But his mission did follow up the irresponsible (and subsequently repudiated) activities in Lisbon of the naval officer, Johnstone, whose suggestions had lured Floridablanca into showing his hand to the British Government. The Spanish minister had virtually confessed that he would let France down and compromise the Family Compact if he could get for Spain what she wanted from Britain. This was Gibraltar, but Minorca and West Florida also if possible. Cumberland's stay in Madrid, therefore, put the French foreign minister,

18. Bemis, *Hussey-Cumberland*, 49. Cumberland, II, 12, 46.
19. Bemis, *Hussey-Cumberland*, 14–15, 71, 83.

Vergennes, upon an extremely anxious seat. It accelerated his nego-
tiations roundabout through Russia and Austria for a truce with
Britain. And, especially, it helped to check whatever inclination
Floridablanca might have had to find a real "middle way" with the
American envoy. John Jay did not upset British plans for peace with
Spain so much as Richard Cumberland, with the aid of the ambidex-
trous Hussey, worried the French Government and stalled Ameri-
can hopes in the Mississippi Valley.[20]

John Jay did not know but he sensed that Floridablanca's "middle
way" for the United States was not to the Mississippi. It was, in
fact, to be a "middle road" back to some kind of "feudal dependence" upon the mother country that would release France from her
alliance with them. This was to be justified by the casuistry that
Britain had never declared war upon France. It therefore was not
yet a defensive war; the alliance had not yet gone into effect; France
was not yet bound to win American independence "absolute and
unlimited." This was a road for Spain, too, that might take her into
Gibraltar by separate agreement with Britain, apart from but co-
incident with the treaty of peace.[21]

Since everybody seemed to have reason to suspect that everybody
else was double or triple dealing in this whole affair, we can hardly
believe that anybody fooled anybody else, except perhaps Floridablanca. It does look as though he tricked himself. If there was humor
in it for anyone, it was reserved for the British ministers in London.
But they may have shared a bit with the French, for Cumberland
eventually found his way back to England through France with
passports supplied by Montmorin, French ambassador at Madrid.[22]

The misfortune of the American troops in Charleston appears to
us now as only a discouraging episode in the successful course of
events to Yorktown. It was not so then. Jay reported to Congress
that the effect of the news from Charleston was "as visible the next
day as that of a hard night's frost on young leaves." Floridablanca
made the choice of a successor to Miralles in Philadelphia an excuse
for delay. He declined to see Jay in the morning, pleading illness,
but did see the French ambassador and rode out as usual in the
afternoon. And he neglected to answer Jay's letters. Such trivialities
were annoying enough. But when the French ambassador undertook
to advise Jay that he ought not to be affected by this inattention,
that he should always have in view the importance of Spain, and
remember that the United States "were as yet only rising States, not

20. *Ibid.,* 40–43, 64, 75–76.
21. *Ibid.,* 42–43, 92–95 n. 9.
22. *Ibid.,* 64–98.

firmly established or generally acknowledged," John Jay perceived
that he had come to a crisis.

It was time for straight talk both to the French ambassador and
to the Spanish minister, for it was apparent that Montmorin was as
often intermediary for Floridablanca as representative of America's
ally:

> I answered [said Jay in his report to Congress, November 6, 1780] that
> the object of my coming to Spain was to make *propositions,* not *sup-
> plications,* and that I should forbear troubling the minister with further
> letters till he should be more disposed to attend to them. That I con-
> sidered America as being, and to continue, independent in *fact,* and
> that her becoming so in *name* was of no further importance than as it
> concerned the common cause, in the success of which all the parties
> were interested; and that I did not imagine Congress would agree to
> purchase from Spain the acknowledgement of an undeniable fact at the
> price she demanded for it.

He would await patiently, he said, the fate of the bills which Congress had drawn upon him in anticipation of establishing credits
upon the loan from Spain. Then he would write Floridablanca another letter on the subject of the treaty. If it brought no results, he
would consider his mission at an end and plan to return to America.
For he was "inclined to think it the interest of America to rest content with the treaty with France, and by avoiding alliances with
other nations, remain free from the influence of their disputes and
politics." Thomas Paine would have been pleased.[23]

Jay's outburst annoyed Montmorin. He asked if Jay were satisfied with the conduct of France. Jay replied that he was, so far as it
had come to his knowledge. He was satisfied, he said, with Montmorin's treatment of him personally, but he was still in ignorance
as to what if any progress had been made in the mediation with
Spain which Vergennes had promised. Montmorin demurred that
he could negotiate between Floridablanca and Jay only in cases
where they could not agree upon matters for their treaty.

This was expert hedging. It is significant that at this point in
their conversation Jay heard no defense based upon the Treaty of
Aranjuez. Evidently he was not supposed to know that France had
been obliged to accept Spain's reservation practically refusing to
join the alliance. That he did not know is almost certain, for he
came very near to accusing the French ambassador of delaying action which was within his power.

Jay may have done Montmorin some injustice, but he was prop-

23. Wharton, IV, 131.

erly concentrating his diplomacy upon the needs of his own country: "How far the tone of this conversation may be judged to have
been prudent I know not," he reported to Congress. "It was not
assumed, however, but after previous and mature deliberation. I
reflected that we had lost Charleston, that reports ran hard against
us, and therefore that this was no time to clothe one's self with
humility." He was fighting as grimly for American independence
on the European front as Washington in America.[24]

Franklin's "Street Door"

YIELDING to Montmorin's earnestness, however, Jay did make another attempt to get in touch with Floridablanca. But the representatives of the minister, Gardoqui and Del Campo, who came to him
tried to persuade Jay that he should give up the navigation of the
Mississippi in return for the loan which he was seeking. And they
insinuated that some of the American States were on the point of
submitting to Britain. The insult was almost too much, for Cumberland was still in Madrid and messengers were passing back and forth
to London through Portugal.

Then on September 13 Gardoqui reappeared with a verbal message from Floridablanca. Exigencies of state, said he, would prevent
the payment of any more bills. Jay retorted sharply. It seemed extraordinary to him that the minister should take three months to
consider a loan which was not in his power to make. And he wrote
directly to Floridablanca to inquire what aids, if any, the United
States might expect from Spain. This ultimatum brought a reply
from Gardoqui on the fifteenth that Spain would supply $150,000,
but criticism also that the United States were proposing no equivalent, and further insinuation that they had some understanding
with Britain.

Jay accepted the money, but resented the insinuation. He asked
Congress to stop the drafts upon him for the time being; it was
obvious that Spain would not supply money in any adequate quantity. And with Montmorin's consent, he submitted the problem of
his unpaid bills directly to Vergennes.

The rising temper of the American envoy must have had some
effect upon Floridablanca, for at last on September 23 came the
long-delayed conference between them with regard to a treaty. But
Floridablanca reached the vital question only after many remarks
about the bills of exchange and further insinuations that the States
were seeking peace with Britain on their own. Miralles, he stated,

24. *Ibid.*, IV, 132.

had informed him that Congress would surrender its claim to the navigation of the Mississippi. And he declared "with some degree of warmth" that unless Spain could exclude all nations from the Gulf of Mexico, "they might as well admit all." As for himself, he considered it "the principal object to be obtained by the war"; it was "far more important than the acquisition of Gibraltar," and if they did not get it, "it was a matter of indifference to him whether the English possessed Mobile or not." Apparently, the negotiations through Hussey and Cumberland so far had been as complete a failure as Floridablanca should have expected from the beginning.[25]

Jay did not reply to this declaration about the Mississippi, for very good reasons. He had established his own position on behalf of the United States. He would yield it no more willingly than Floridablanca now would consider a "middle way." Their conference closed with nothing further accomplished.

Before long, however, Jay had the satisfaction of a letter from Franklin in Paris, dated October 2, 1780. It read: "Poor as we are, yet as I know we shall be rich, I would rather agree with them to buy at a great price the whole of their right on the Mississippi than sell a drop of its waters. A neighbor might as well ask me to sell my street door." Congress further instructed him on October 4, in response to his report of May 26 that Spain would not yield on the Mississippi River. He was to stick to his original instructions. He was by no stipulation to relinquish the right to the free navigation of the river. He was in fact to ask in addition for the use of the waters running through West Florida, in case the Spaniards acquired the territory from Britain.[26]

John Jay repressed his anxiety and grief over Mrs. Jay's illness and the death of their child at Madrid. He rose above the intrigues and quarrels of his secretaries. He struggled on with the bills which Congress drew upon his account. He endured the prying of Spanish officials into his mail. But he grew more outspoken with the French embassy as he gathered intimations that France had pledged herself to Spain at the expense of the American States and as he learned what La Luzerne was doing in Philadelphia.[27]

Then came the news that Congress had revised its instructions on February 15, 1781, upon the motion of Virginia "to promote the general object of the Union" and to hasten "an alliance between his Catholic Majesty and these States." Jay was to recede from demanding free navigation of that part of the Mississippi which lay below

25. *Ibid.*, IV, 145–146.
26. *Ibid.*, IV, 75. *Journ. Cont. Cong.*, XVIII, 900–902.
27. Pellew, 135. Monaghan, 153–160. Wharton, IV, 129, 137.

the thirty-first degree latitude, and from asking free ports there. He was to do this, however, only if Spain unalterably insisted upon it, and he was still to exert every possible effort to obtain those concessions. But what could have been more baffling? To make his situation worse, he did not hear of these additional instructions until May 18, 1781, until after the Spanish minister had heard and sounded him through the French ambassador about them.[28]

Jay stood his ground. He would follow his instructions as a whole concerning an alliance, recognition of independence, and a loan. He would not be guided merely by this revised portion about the Mississippi River. When, therefore, Floridablanca in the midst of evasive generalities on May 23 let fall the telltale remark that all these matters, navigation of the Mississippi, exclusive use of the Gulf of Mexico, the treaty of union and commerce, might well wait until the general treaty at the end of the war, Jay refused to concede that Spain had any right to close the Mississippi to American shipping and goods unless she agreed to a treaty of alliance and recognized the independence of the United States before the treaty of peace was made.

That settled it. Jay did not submit his final statement of the terms which he would accept until September 22. And he lingered at Madrid into the spring of 1782. But his mission to Spain had come to its end.[29]

Nor did Floridablanca make any effort to negotiate upon Jay's proposals. He even permitted a number of American bills to go to protest. He did attempt to soften personal feelings by inviting Jay at last to dinner. There was a hint, also, through the French embassy that if Jay were personally in need of funds he might obtain them. But John Jay would neither dine with the Spanish minister nor accept personal aid, even though hard pressed. He would not dine with the minister as a private citizen so long as recognition was denied to his Government. He would compromise neither his own independence nor that of his country.[30]

Vergennes' Plan for Mediation—"Jealous of Us"

SUCH personal thoughts, however, did not distract Jay's mind from other matters so entirely as has often been presumed. He welcomed the release which Franklin's summons to Paris gave him from the humiliations at Madrid. But more revealing was his quick agree-

28. *Journ. Cont. Cong.*, XIX, 151–153. The motion and the draft of the instructions were in the handwriting of James Madison.
29. Wharton, IV, 745–746, 760–761.
30. *Ibid.*, V, 356, 376, Jay to Montmorin, April 27, 1782.

ment with Franklin's wish that they might obtain at once the paltry
$170,000 or so which they had borrowed from Spain, pay that im-
pecunious creditor, and have done with her. Montmorin had admitted during the preceding winter that Spain wanted to "modify"
American independence and "keep herself in a situation to mediate"
between Britain and the United States in the general peacemaking.
"I suspect," declared Jay, "that there has been an interesting conversation" between the Courts of Spain and France.[31]

Jay had already protested the instructions of June 15, 1781, from
Congress to its peace commissioners. He had said in September, when
arranging his last proposals to Floridablanca, that such orders to
undertake nothing in the negotiations for peace or a truce without
the knowledge and concurrence of the French ministers breathed "a
degree of complacency not quite republican"; but more to the
point, that they put it out of the power of the commissioners "to
improve those chances and opportunities which in the course of
human affairs, happen more or less frequently unto all men." Jay's
mind had been focused then upon the problems of the Mississippi in
relation to Spain. But now, as he reported on April 28, 1782, to
Robert Livingston, secretary for Congress, John Jay was thinking
these things over in conjunction with the British surrender at Yorktown in October, 1781, and news since then that Parliament had
advised the King to stop all offensive operations against the United
States. Jay questioned now whether it could be wise to instruct the
American commissioners "to speak only as the French ministers
shall give them utterance." Marbois in Philadelphia, he said, was
gleaning "every scrap of news." His letters were "very minute."
They detailed "names and characters."[32]

Had John Jay known as much about the correspondence of Vergennes with Montmorin, and Vergennes' negotiations during the
past two years with Austria and Russia, he would not have sent his
protest to Secretary Livingston in a rhetorical question nor offered
his opinion of France as a mere suspicion. While La Luzerne "opened
his purse" in Philadelphia, Vergennes was formulating a plan for
peace that would have held the United States short of the commitments of France in the Treaty of Alliance.

The scheme, as it had been put on paper in February, 1781, by
Vergennes' secretary, Rayneval, was that Austria and Russia should
mediate to end the war. Britain would agree to evacuate New York
and grant independence to the United States by a treaty or a truce

31. *Ibid.*, V, 296, 370, 368, Jay to Livingston, April 28, 1782. For Franklin and Jay
on Spain, see *ibid.*, V, 369–370.
32. Monaghan, 173–175. Wharton, IV, 716–718; V, 373.

of twenty years or more. But, if it were necessary in order to get France out of a struggle which was taxing her severely, the mediators might agree that Britain should keep South Carolina and Georgia. And the King of France would engage that Congress should accept the truce, provided he had secret assurance from Britain that she would not keep New York too. Is it strange that Vergennes told John Adams on the eighteenth of July following that there were certain "preliminaries" concerning the United States which were to be settled before Adams could appear at the Austrian Court and allow himself "the smallest ministerial act in the face of the two mediators"?[33]

Vergennes, however, had some scruple about this scheme. For Rayneval had set down the statement that the King himself could not propose to Congress that the truce should be joined with the *status quo*. Certainly he could not, if he were to honor the intent of the Treaty of Alliance. But the way around that was easy. The mediators, acting upon their own responsibility, might link the truce with the *status quo*. And if they got their negotiations with Britain to the point of agreement upon such a basis, the King of France might then accept what he had not been at liberty to initiate. Then he could revive his conscience by offering a new convention to the Americans in which he would undertake to defend them against British attack at the expiration of the truce. In line with this complicated thinking, Vergennes had instructed La Luzerne on March 9 to advise Congress that the King might accept the mediation of Russia and Austria "conditionally," for both himself and the United States. What John Adams thought on the subject was simple and point-blank. He told Vergennes in July that not thirteen States but the United States of America would be represented in any congress at Vienna, and as "a free, sovereign, and independent State, of right and in fact." "There is upon earth," said he, "no judge of a sovereign State but the nation that composes it."[34]

Vergennes had directed Rayneval to close his memorandum of February, 1781 with this statement: "It is from necessity and not from choice that the King makes war upon Great Britain." Possibly the French "tradition de grandeur" had been fully rationalized by this time as a European necessity, in the mind of Vergennes at least, though peace would seem to have been much more requisite for France. But we need probe here no farther into the mystery of Vergennes' mental processes to appreciate what his scheme would have

33. Bemis, *Hussey-Cumberland*, 106–120, 185–192. Adams, *Works*, VII, 443.

34. Bemis, *Diplomacy of the American Revolution*, 185. Doniol, IV, 556. Adams, *Works*, VII, 437–438.

meant for America if it had been put into effect before Yorktown. It not only would have broken the confederation of the States on the Atlantic Seaboard. It would have destroyed their claims, through the colonial charters of South Carolina and Georgia, upon the Indian country westward to the Mississippi. Spain would surely have preferred Britons to American pioneers as neighbors above the Floridas. The "rising new republic" would have found it very hard indeed to become "mistress of this whole immense continent."[35]

If John Jay had no inkling of this plan while he was still at Madrid in April, 1782, he was fully aware as he considered the news from Yorktown that time now was playing into his hand. "Time is more friendly to young than to old nations," he said, "and the day will come when our strength will ensure our rights." The United States should no longer try to make a treaty with Spain, for Spain would require concessions which later they would not have to yield. John Jay, too, had the vision of American empire. And he went up to the peacemaking at Paris certain that both Spain and France intended to frustrate it. "Both courts," said he, "are watching and jealous of us." Was he so very mistaken? By September Rayneval was arguing openly with him that Spain ought to have the Indian country beyond Georgia, that Britain should keep the territory above the Ohio, that the American States were asking too much. But Vergennes' secretary succeeded in proving to John Jay only that the American commissioners for peace must deal separately and secretly with the British.[36]

35. See above, pp. 22, 25.
36. Wharton, V, 373.

III

INDEPENDENCE AND EMPIRE:
FRANKLIN'S PART

Overtures to Franklin and Adams

A SEPARATE PEACE with the mother country was beyond the preliminary stages when John Jay arrived in Paris. Conditions after Yorktown had been too wearing for the English people. Loyalists could not hold the reconquered areas as the King's armies moved on to other disaffected colonies. It had become increasingly difficult to supply those armies across the Atlantic as rebel bands kept them from foraging the countryside. The participation of France, then Spain, and finally Holland had forced Britain to the defensive in spite of her great strength upon the sea. Attacked by a European alliance, opposed by a league of armed neutrals, and sinking deeper into debt, Englishmen realized that they must have peace with their rebellious colonies whether or not it broke the Empire. But the surrender of Cornwallis at Yorktown in October, 1781, ironically so much the result of Spain's delay in using the French West Indian fleet for her own purposes, changed the course of events in Europe far less to the injury of Great Britain than of France and Spain.[1]

Lord North endeavored to carry on, but he could get new loans only at high rates of interest. He was relieved in the spring of 1782 to drop the authority which he had retained long since merely because the King insisted. Rockingham, heading a coalition, was summoned to take over the Government. The rivalry in this ministry between Shelburne and Fox complicated matters, but it was to hinder no more than it assured negotiations with the United States. Nor was the King's reluctance to acknowledge their independence to stand in the way. For these Rockingham Whigs had been responsible for repealing the Stamp Act in 1766, and some of them had defended the colonial cause in Parliament, and even championed American independence. Their agents now were soon in touch with Benjamin Franklin and John Adams.[2]

1. Corwin, 312–313.
2. Bemis, *Diplomacy of the American Revolution*, 190–194. This work is especially valuable for this and the following chapter.

Franklin had rebuffed his friend Hartley's suggestion of a separate treaty in January. There was, said Franklin then, not a man in America, except a few Tories, who "would not spurn at the thought of deserting a noble and generous friend for the sake of a truce with an unjust and cruel enemy." But Hartley's ideas had not been confined to leaving France in the lurch. They implied something else. He had failed to make any stipulation regarding American independence. And Franklin could not have overlooked this fact. Until Britain's statesmen dropped their reluctance to discuss the point, there was little chance of their getting this American diplomatist, at least, to speak of France in any terms but devotion and praise.

Benjamin Franklin, however, was keeping watch upon the changing temper of Parliament. By March he had observed enough to encourage him to approach Shelburne directly. Perhaps, he said, they might have a "*general peace.*" Accordingly Oswald, a Scottish merchant with American interests and connections, arrived in Paris with a letter from Shelburne remarking that he was more interested in the "means of promoting the happiness of mankind" than in the "best concerted plans for spreading misery and devastation." Oswald, he said, was "fully apprized" of his mind. No panegyric is needed here upon the exalted philosophy concerning freedom of trade and other benefits to humanity which Shelburne shared with Franklin, and Franklin with Shelburne, by correspondence between London and Paris. Shelburne was announcing that he was ready for what Franklin had to offer and that Oswald was his man. Benjamin Franklin understood. His retort to Hartley had not missed its mark.[3]

John Adams, too, found himself waited upon at Amsterdam. The Englishman, Vaughan, brought word that Henry Laurens, just released from the Tower, was at Haarlem and wished to see him. Adams honored the request of the former president of Congress, though he could not talk with Laurens as a fellow commissioner of peace, for Laurens was still on parole. But he could listen. And he heard that Lord Shelburne and others among the new ministers were "anxious to know whether there was any authority to treat of a separate peace, and whether there could be an accomodation upon any terms short of independence."[4]

Franklin and Adams immediately compared notes. They found that both of them were for peace, but with independence and empire. Britain, they agreed, should expect to give up Nova Scotia and

3. Hale, *Franklin in France*, II, 47. Franklin (Smyth ed.), 358, 381–382, 405, 420. Wharton, V, 112, 303, 535–536, Shelburne to Franklin, April 6, 1782.
4. *Ibid.,* V, 543–544.

Canada. Neither was yet willing to sacrifice the French alliance or even to conclude a separate peace with Britain. But Franklin was a shade more ready at this moment than Adams to respond to Shelburne. Franklin replied to Adams on April 21, 1782: "I like your idea of seeing no more messengers that are not plenipotentiaries; but I cannot refuse seeing again Mr. Oswald, as the minister here considered the letter to me from Lord Shelburne as a kind of authentication given that messenger, and expects his return with some explicit propositions. I shall keep you advised of whatever passes." Franklin was building upon the recent Act of Parliament which provided that Americans held captive were not to be tried as traitors to the King but were to be treated as prisoners of war. This was, said he, "a kind of tacit acknowledgement of our independency."[5]

As a matter of fact, Franklin had already made proposals to Oswald upon that assumption. He had suggested that Britain should voluntarily turn Canada over to the United States and make reparations for the houses and villages which her troops and Indian allies had burned. She should do this, he said, if she wanted more than "a mere peace," if she wished "reconciliation." The United States then would assure her free trade with Canada. Vacant lands there might be sold to pay the reparations, and also to indemnify the Loyalists for their confiscated estates.[6]

Whether he explained these proposals to Vergennes also, Franklin did not record. But Oswald told Thomas Grenville that Franklin had asked that Shelburne keep them secret from France. It may be, therefore, that Vergennes did not know their nature and would have interfered if he had. Franklin's distinction between "a mere peace" and "reconciliation" might have disturbed him. Certainly he would not want reconciliation if it left the American States in any connection with Britain to the disadvantage of France. But the proposal that Britain cede Canada could have surprised Vergennes not at all. Franklin was only expressing what had been an American aim since his mission to Quebec for the Continental Congress in 1776, what Vergennes himself had known well before this and taken steps to counteract if he could. He had carefully enveloped this aim in the Alliance of 1778. The French guarantee of American territory had been so guarded that it was not to come into effect until peace had been made at the end of the war. As for reparations and indemnifying the Loyalists, Vergennes might have been informed, and amused, if Franklin had told him. But, all things considered, it is doubtful that Vergennes much cared whether he did or did not,

5. *Ibid.*, V, 544–545.
6. *Ibid.*, V, 541, Franklin's "notes for conversation."

if indeed he did not, know the exact nature of Franklin's first proposals to Oswald.[7]

The greater point is that Vergennes had no objection to separate negotiations. In fact, he preferred them. He advised La Luzerne on April 9 that they would be agreeable. Only, said he, the allies would have to come out of the war together and sign their treaties at the same time. No quicker way perhaps could be had to make Britain acknowledge that the United States were independent of her and that their alliance with France was superior. Necessarily, one treaty should not be without the other.[8]

It was never part of French policy to block the American States from gaining self-government. Vergennes had considered some status for them short of it because of Spain's counteractivities and his fears that France might have in self-preservation to stop fighting. But that was before Cornwallis' surrender. After Yorktown, autonomy for the United States, at least, was not one of Vergennes' worries, though he may have wondered whether they could maintain sufficient union among themselves to preserve it.[9]

What Vergennes was now decidedly anxious about was the extent of the territorial domain which these new States might get from Britain. He had a very good idea from the instructions of Congress to their peace commissioners what they were likely to ask. It might be just as well for France if she were free in her own negotiations to throw her weight against the ambitions of the American people. She had commitments to Spain besides those to the United States. They might appreciate their need of the French alliance more if they had to stand "vigilant" and "uneasy" upon their own responsibility.[10]

Vergennes already had evidence that these new States might desert the lead of France in world affairs if they got an imperial domain as well as freedom from their mother country. He could be sure perhaps of Franklin among these commissioners of peace. Franklin was in fact placing high value upon the French alliance, and continued to do so to the end of the negotiations. But how about this John Adams? Vergennes had already felt compelled to admonish him that he should lay the foundations of peace before he talked of commercial agreements with Britain apart from France. He had reminded Adams with some asperity that Franklin, not

7. *Ibid.*, V, 537–538. Adams, *Works*, I, 375. Russell, Fox, I, 363, 376–380. Grenville to Fox, June 4, 16, 1782.

8. Corwin, 329 n. Doniol, V, 78–79.

9. See above, pp. 18–19, 27–29.

10. See above, pp. 22, 25–26, 29.

Adams, was the American minister to France. He had advised La Luzerne to discredit Adams with the Congress in Philadelphia. And what of this John Jay, now coming from Madrid to Paris? Would he be as enthusiastic as Gérard had once reported? Would he still think that they should have a triumvirate of France, Spain, and the United States and defy the world? Vergennes had doubts. His secretary, Rayneval, was soon to deal with Shelburne in London accordingly.[11]

Franklin's proposals had been put in the form of unofficial "notes for conversation" which he allowed Oswald to take over to Shelburne. But Franklin reacted quickly against himself. He regretted that he had offered to compensate the Loyalists. He was ashamed of his "weakness" in letting the paper get out of his hands. And so, although he wrote dutifully to Adams about his suggestions on April 20, he did not enclose a copy of them and he did not tell Adams that he had let fall the hint about the Tories.[12]

Possibly here is one reason why John Adams wrote in his diary in the following October, after he had finally arrived at Paris to take his part in the negotiations: "Franklin's cunning will be to divide us; to this end he will provoke, he will insinuate, he will intrigue, he will manoeuvre." But Adams had declared years before this that Franklin should not be left alone in Paris even with a competent secretary, for he was "so indolent, that Business will be neglected"; and, although he had "as determined a soul as any Man," his constant policy was "never to say Yes or No decidedly but when he cannot avoid it. . . ." And, notwithstanding the fact that the American commissioners made the separate treaty without division, John Adams still had it on his mind to say about Benjamin Franklin—"I can have no Dependence on his Word. I never know when he speaks the Truth, and when not." But perhaps this is less revealing of Benjamin Franklin than of John Adams, for he went on to say:

> It would be Folly to deny, that he has had a great Genius, and that he had written several things in Philosophy and in Politicks, profoundly. But his Philosophy and his Politicks have been infinitely exaggerated, by the studied Arts of Empiricism, until his Reputation has become one of the grossest Impostures, that has ever been practised upon Mankind since the Days of Mahomet.[13]

11. Corwin, 273–278, 294–296. Wharton, IV, 3–6, 16–17. Doniol, IV, 551 n., 589. Vergennes to La Luzerne, April 19, 1781. See above, p. 28 f., 43, and below, pp. 81–83.
12. Wharton, V. 542.
13. Adams, *Works*, III, 300. October 27, 1782. Warren–Adams Letters, II, 74, 209–210. See below, pp. 89–91.

Oswald's Perception

WHEN Oswald returned to London, the British cabinet agreed on April 23 to treat for a "general peace" as Franklin suggested, and in Paris as Vergennes desired. But they declared that "the principal points in contemplation" should be the independence of the United States "on condition that England be put into the same situation that she was left in by the peace of 1763." Such were the words as Franklin remembered them from Oswald's report to him.[14]

They were not so enigmatic as they were elusive. They could mean a qualified independence for the United States, with France in some way held responsible to Britain—as those previous French and Spanish schemes for a long truce had implied. They could also mean retention by Britain of those dominions on the north and west of the United States which American arms had not freed from British control.[15]

Franklin chose not to think so. He asserted that they meant the return of the West Indian islands which had been taken by France, and these of course the United States had no authority to return. On his part, Vergennes rejected the idea that France would be in any way responsible now for the kind of American independence. He remonstrated to Fox's new representative in Paris, Grenville, that the United States did not ask independence of Britain. "There is Mr. Franklin," said Vergennes, "he will answer you as to that point." And Franklin complied with: "To be sure we do not consider ourselves as under any necessity of bargaining for a thing that is our own, which we have bought at the expense of much blood and treasure, and which we are in possession of."[16]

In the meantime, Rodney had ended all conjecture about the West Indies by defeating the French fleet under De Grasse on April 12. Whatever France had seized there was again within British reach regardless of opinions or dispositions at Paris.

What then did the words of the British cabinet mean? Their import was clear to Shelburne, if not yet to Fox and the rest of the ministers. Britain would break the alliance between France and the United States, and retain Canada besides. But, if it had to be done in order to separate the United States from their ally, Britain would turn Canada over to the United States along with their independence. Shelburne let no one except Lord Ashburton see Franklin's "notes for conversation." He sent the paper back with Oswald. He

14. Wharton, V, 548.
15. See above, pp. 18–19, 27–29, 41–44.
16. Wharton, V, 550, 552.

ordered Oswald to show a copy of the cabinet's decision to Franklin, though not to leave it with him. And he gave Oswald definite instructions in regard to Franklin's proposals.[17]

Oswald was "to insist in the strongest manner, that if America was to be independent, she must be so of the whole world, and not attempt any connection, secret, tacit, or ostensible with France." He was to declare that Britain, if the negotiation failed, would retain all her rights in America as they were before. He was not to conceal from Franklin that Shelburne did not wish to see the United States completely independent. Shelburne hoped they might remain in a federal union with Britain; but he would support American independence if that had to be. Oswald was to say that Britain expected much from Rodney in the West Indies. He was to demur strongly to Franklin's ideas about Canada. Britain would make no reparation for the property which had been destroyed by her troops and Indian allies. And a more friendly way than the cession of Canada, it was to be hoped, could be found for preventing future wars. It was out of the question to use the Canadian lands for indemnifying the Loyalists, after those lands had come into the possession of the United States. Shelburne would not listen, he said, to acknowledging the independence of the United States unless they took care of the Loyalists. He would never give up the Loyalists. He would expect compensation also for New York, Charleston, and Savannah, still occupied by British forces. He would keep Penobscot. In short, he would not let Canada go as yet on anything like Franklin's terms. Besides, Oswald was to make "early and strict conditions" to secure all debts whatever that were due to British subjects.[18]

According to Franklin, however, Oswald spoke only in general terms about "reconciliation" when he came to talk again in the first days of May. As for the subject of Franklin's "notes," he had reason to believe, said Oswald, that the matter might be settled to the satisfaction of the United States "towards the end of the treaty," though he himself wished that it might not be mentioned at the beginning. Shelburne, he remarked, had not imagined that reparation would be expected, and he wondered whether Franklin knew if it were to be demanded. Then Oswald announced that Fox's representative, Grenville, was on his way to take up the negotiations with France.[19]

Oswald went with Franklin to tell Vergennes also of Grenville's mission. But he said nothing else of importance there. And when he had returned to Franklin's quarters, he merely repeated what he had

17. Fitzmaurice, II, 124, 126–128.
18. *Ibid.*, II, 127–128.
19. For Grenville's experiences in Paris see his letters to Fox. Russell, *Fox*, I, 347–383.

said before in regard to Canada. The matter would be settled to American satisfaction, he thought, toward the end of the negotiations. Then, having remarked that Spain would offer "the greatest obstructions," he wandered off upon the subject of Russia. She was England's friend. Lately she had made great discoveries "on the back of North America." She could establish posts there. She might easily "transport an army from Kamchatka to the coast of Mexico and conquer all those countries."

Whether Franklin took this reference to Russia as an indirect threat to the territorial ambitions of the United States, he did not say. It is difficult to believe that he did not comprehend. But he merely recorded in his journal: "This appeared a little visionary at present, but I did not dispute it."

Franklin had been able to learn so little about Shelburne's "sentiments" from Oswald that he wondered why the Scot had been sent to him again. And he supposed that Grenville "might be better furnished." Vergennes, too, thought it "odd" that Oswald had come back with nothing more explicit. Was it, as often surmised, that Oswald was maladroit in imparting to Franklin the sense of his instructions from Shelburne?[20]

Quite a different view is tenable. Oswald was "fully apprized" indeed of Shelburne's thoughts. He knew that Shelburne did not want to concede independence to the United States unless they were separated completely from France. And he knew that Shelburne would yield Canada only if necessary to separate them from France. But he found upon returning to Paris that Franklin was working as closely with Vergennes as ever. Oswald was not maladroit. He was shrewd. He knew that his job was to come between Vergennes and Franklin. His instructions, if fully imparted to Franklin, would have served just the opposite purpose.

Evidence supporting this view is in the reception which Vergennes and Franklin gave to Grenville's hint that France had brought about America's independence. Franklin declared that it was already established, and Vergennes "grew a little warm" as he continued the argument. The breach had been made, independence had been declared, he asserted, long before the United States had received the least encouragement from France. He defied the world to give the smallest proof to the contrary. "There sits Mr. Franklin, who knows the fact," said he, "and can contradict me if I do not speak the truth."

Benjamin Franklin did not choose to contradict Vergennes, not even to himself in his private journal. But it cannot be that he had

20. Wharton, V, 547–550.

so readily forgotten the mission of Bonvouloir to America in 1775 nor the experiences of Silas Deane in France during the spring of 1776.[21]

Franklin, as he said, may have been "a little surprised at the suddenness" of Oswald's resolution after a conference with Grenville to return at once to London. We should not be. There was quickness but no uncertainty in the action. It was apparent that Shelburne would have to loosen his instructions about Canada, if he expected Oswald to get between Vergennes and Franklin. The United States were going to keep their independence and the French alliance too, if Shelburne did not take care.[22]

The Way Open

FRANKLIN had information from London by May 26 revealing in large part the "sentiments" of Shelburne which Oswald might have purveyed, if he had been maladroit. Hartley sent over "preliminaries" for Franklin to consider. He had left a copy, he said, with Lord Shelburne. These propositions were that the British troops should be withdrawn from the "Thirteen Provinces" and a truce made to last for ten or twenty years. Then there should be a negotiation between Britain and the "allies of America." If it should not "produce peace," the war should continue between Britain and those "allies," and America should "act and be treated as a neutral nation." Whenever peace did come, the truce between Britain and "America" should then be converted into a "perpetual peace"; the independence of "America" should be admitted and guaranteed by Britain; and a commercial treaty settled between them. In short, the plan was to hold the American States dependent if possible, independent if unavoidable, but always in the British system. When Franklin acknowledged these suggestions from Hartley, however, it was September, and conditions were far different.[23]

Grenville came to Franklin on the same day in May. His courier, he said, had returned from London, and he now had full powers to treat for peace *"with France and her allies."* Mr. Oswald had arrived in London, so Grenville said, about an hour before the courier came away. Franklin then gave Grenville the copy of the Franco-American Alliance which he had requested, and Grenville lent Franklin the London *Gazette* containing an account of Rodney's victory in the West Indies. This would make no difference, said

21. *Ibid.*, V, 552. See above, pp. 12–13.
22. *Ibid.*, V, 555.
23. *Ibid.*, V, 562–563. Franklin (Smyth ed.), VIII, 596. September 17, 1782. See below, pp. 78–81.

Grenville, in the British plan to treat for peace. But Franklin had doubts; and within two days he learned something from Vergennes to increase them. For Grenville's power, as submitted to the French Court, was to deal only with France.

Vergennes assured Franklin that he would tell Grenville plainly that France would not treat with Britain for the United States:

> They want to treat with us for you, but this the King will not agree to. He thinks it not consistent with the dignity of your state. You will treat for yourselves, and every one of the powers at war with England will make its own treaty. All that is necessary for our common security is that the treaties go hand in hand and are signed all on the same day.

France, that is to say, would not compromise the very thing for which she had entered the war—disruption of the British Empire. She would not stop short now of making the American States independent of the King and Parliament in London.[24]

What Vergennes did not assert was that the King wished the American States to treat with Britain entirely by themselves for the purpose of winning both acknowledgment of their independence and a continental domain. Nor did he intend to say any such thing. That would jeopardize the interests of both Spain and France in North America. France had other plans, already formulated, which she would complete before she undertook to guarantee American territory at the end of the war. France, too, after the several treaties of peace had been signed, wished to hold the United States—apart from Britain and within the French system.[25]

Franklin learned more about Grenville's instructions from Grenville himself on June 1. He readily admitted that his written "power" was to deal only with France. But he dismissed that fact as resulting from the careless use of an old official form. His instructions, he said, were adequate. It might be premature, but he would not hesitate to tell Franklin confidentially that he now had authority *"to acknowledge the independence of America previous to the commencement of the treaty."*

It was clear in the light of Hartley's propositions and Grenville's statements. The purpose of the British Government was to separate the American States from France. This was the aim of both Shelburne and Fox. Shelburne was more reluctant to admit that the United States were independent; but both of them wished to convince Franklin that the United States should not stand by France and Spain. For, as Grenville asked Franklin, "If Spain and Holland,

24. Wharton, V, 563–564.
25. See above, pp. 25–26, 41–44.

and even if France should insist on unreasonable terms of advantage to themselves, after you have obtained all you want, and are satisfied, can it be right that America should be dragged on in a war for their interest only?"[26]

Then came Oswald again on June 3 to tell Franklin something of his recent conversations in London with Rockingham, Shelburne, and Fox. Oswald had given them his opinion, in consequence of his previous talk with Franklin, that Canada should be ceded to the United States. Rockingham and Shelburne had spoken "reservedly," said Oswald, but they had not seemed "adverse" to the idea. It was Fox who "appeared to be startled at the proposition." But Oswald was "not without hopes that it would be agreed to." Evidently Fox had not seen Franklin's "notes for conversation" nor Shelburne's instructions to Oswald in reply. It is equally apparent, however, that Franklin was not to think this fact would make any trouble for him within the British Government, if he wished to proceed with the negotiations.[27]

There were further hints to Franklin. Oswald brought a "paper of memorandums" written by Shelburne. He was ready to correspond "more particularly." The "enabling act" was passing through Parliament. Commissioners would be named, "or any character given to Mr. Oswald, which Dr. Franklin and he may judge conducive to a final settlement of things between Great Britain and America." That settlement, as Franklin himself "very properly" had said, required to be treated "in a very different manner from the peace between Great Britain and France." They had always been "at enmity with each other."

Shelburne, however, had caught up Franklin's remark about the Loyalists. He insisted that the several States should be influenced to agree to "fair restoration or compensation for whatever confiscations have taken place." This was the announcement of a British prerequisite. But it was also a suggestion of a loophole for the American commissioners of peace.[28]

The way was open now for Franklin. But although suggesting separate negotiations, he still was not eager for separate negotiations which should lead to a separate peace. He would cling to Oswald as the negotiator with whom he would deal in preference to Grenville, not really because Oswald had "an air of great simplicity and hon-

---

26. Wharton, V, 566–567. See also Sparks Mss., XL, 9, Oswald to Shelburne, June 9, 1782.

27. Wharton, V, 572. Grenville reported from Paris to Fox regarding Franklin's "notes" on June 4. Russell, *Fox*, I, 363.

28. Wharton, V, 571.

esty." He was Shelburne's man. He offered the better approach to empire beyond mere independence. Franklin needed time for argument to get out of the hole in which he had put himself with his remark about compensating the Tories. He was irked by Grenville's impetuous assumption, and release to the British press, that the French alliance would not keep the United States from separate negotiations. He was fearful of the effect in England of Rodney's victory. Most disturbing of all, he was not certain that, even if the United States did get entirely satisfactory terms of peace with Britain, they could go along without the French alliance. He might agree, as Vergennes wished, to separate negotiations, but he was not so sure that he wanted a separate treaty of peace. It could result in another war.[29]

Franklin went on June 11 to talk over this possibility with Vergennes and his secretary, Rayneval. What were the British about? Vergennes believed that they were sincere in their desire for peace; but he consented to discuss their attempts to disunite France and the American States, and the prudence, consequently, of "holding together and treating in concert." "It was possible," remarked Franklin, "that after making peace with all they might pick out one of us to make war with separately." It might be well for the powers at war with Britain, therefore, to have another treaty engaging themselves to renew the general war if Britain should turn upon any one of them. This should be done, he thought, before the forthcoming treaties of peace were signed.

Vergennes "seemed to approve of" the suggestion; but nothing was eventually to come from it. Franklin had been persuaded that separate negotiations would do no harm. By the time that discouragement at Gibraltar warranted new agreements among Britain's enemies, the American commissioners had gone so far along the road of separate negotiations to a separate peace, and so advantageously, that Franklin himself was no longer so anxious in case the United States might have to stand alone. He was content by that time with the guarantees of 1778.[30]

Grenville reappeared on June 15 to tell Franklin he had notified Vergennes that he had full power also to deal with the American commissioners and declare "the independence of America" before the negotiations. He hoped, therefore, that "all difficulties were now removed" and that they might proceed "in the good work." Franklin, however, had not yet abandoned the mood of his recent conversation with Vergennes. He asked about the enabling act of Par-

29. *Ibid.*, V, 570, 574–575. Sparks Mss., XL, 8–11, 13–14.
30. Wharton, V, 577. See below, pp. 84–87.

liament. Grenville had to admit that it had been delayed in the House of Lords, though merely, he said, because of other business; they could get on with the "reconciliation." Still Franklin would not respond. Grenville found him "as silent as ever."[31]

It did look at this moment as though the British, having failed to separate Franklin from Vergennes, might be trying to reach the same objective in another way. They talked of American independence, but they might refuse to concede it in the end despite the promises of Hartley, Oswald, and Grenville. After all, these men were merely agents who could be repudiated at pleasure. Possibly Britain would make more of Rodney's victory than Grenville had asserted, to subdue France and to destroy her protectorate over the new States in America. Rayneval told Franklin on the twenty-eighth that the French were informed that Carleton had orders to propose terms of reunion with the mother country similar to those which were being made for Ireland. British emissaries, he said, were to go among the people and get them to put pressure upon Congress.[32]

These were thoughts which Franklin could not ignore. Besides, John Jay was on the way from Madrid. And the part which Spain had played and was still likely to play in the negotiations was not to be overlooked. The fate of Gibraltar involved all parties that summer as the French and Spanish forces tightened the siege. It was in fact to have more influence upon the eventual terms of the peace than Franklin could have foreseen as he rebuffed Grenville and waited for Jay at the end of June, 1782.[33]

Jay in Paris—Franklin's "Hints"

JOHN JAY arrived in Paris on the twenty-third of June. His experiences with both Floridablanca and Montmorin intensified his dislike of the instructions which Congress had given largely, as a matter of fact, at the direction of Vergennes through La Luzerne. Jay came to Paris already of half a mind to disregard them. He had seen just enough of French solicitude for Spanish welfare in Madrid. He would not follow the lead of the French ministers if he saw them do anything which looked as though it might subordinate American interests. And he was fully minded to reverse the situation with Spain, if the negotiations were to continue in Paris. He would call upon the Spanish ambassador politely, but the Spaniard would now have to say what Spain would like to have.[34]

31. *Ibid.*, V, 579–580. Russell, *Fox*, I, 380, Grenville to Fox, June 16, 1782.
32. *Ibid.*, V, 584.
33. See below, pp. 84–87.
34. Wharton, VI, 21. Jay's report to Livingston, November 17, 1782.

This Aranda proceeded at once to do, cautiously behind the guard of the French foreign ministry. Rayneval assured Franklin and Jay that he had authority to tell them that they would be well received. They did call on the twenty-ninth, and they were well received indeed, the Spaniard going so far as personally to open the folding doors before them when they departed. It was, wrote Franklin, "a high compliment" in Paris. But during their conversation Aranda had said nothing of his instructions, merely rambling on about the "nature of things"; "Thus, says he, if there is a certain thing which would be convenient to each of us, but more convenient to one than to the other, it should be given to the one to whom it would be most convenient, and compensation made by giving another thing to the other for the same reason." Unraveled, did this mean that navigation on the Mississippi River was one of those matters of convenience?

Benjamin Franklin had made a direct statement in the spring of 1777 about the navigation of the Mississippi, and had fired Aranda with enthusiasm for it. But he did not try that device now. Conditions had changed. Spain had lost her chance. The argument that the United States would make an alliance with Spain was good still to worry Britain a little. It was no longer part, however, of Franklin's policy. He agreed with Jay. Time was playing the hand of the young nation. Franklin translated Aranda's verbiage simply. The Spanish ambassador had in view "something relating to boundaries or territories, because, he added, we will sit down together with maps in our hands, and, by that means, shall see our way more clearly."[35]

Franklin and Jay did not come away trying to see Spain's intentions "more clearly" that day. No further progress was then made, as Jay was seriously ill with influenza until August. There was as yet no indication that Aranda had authority to deal on equal terms with Jay. Spain had not yet recognized the independence of the United States. Franklin and Jay did not much care. Jay wrote later to Montmorin that he suspected the Spanish Court was "at last, in earnest." But that was a question which "facts and not words" would have to determine. It really did not matter much.[36]

And yet, both Franklin and Jay were rather despondent at this moment. They had written on June 25 to Robert Livingston, secretary to Congress, that since Rodney's victory Britain would prolong the negotiations. Franklin was afraid that another campaign

35. Ibid., V, 585.
36. Ibid., V, 523. This letter was begun on June 26, but the part referring to the visit with Aranda was not written until after Jay's recovery from illness in July.

might pass before they agreed. Something might even happen to break off negotiations. They had better be "prepared for the worst." And on the twenty-eighth, he wrote again:

> It looks as if, since their late success in the West Indies, they a little repented of the advances they had made in their declarations respecting the acknowledgement of our independence; and we have pretty good information that some of the ministers still flatter the king with the hope of recovering his sovereignty over us on the same terms as are now making with Ireland.

He feared that private agents would influence Congress to accept Carleton's scheme of reunion. He felt helpless. He could only exhort. Americans would draw upon themselves the contempt of Europe, he pled, if they accepted the King again, and they would never find another friend to help them. But then came the shrewdest comment: "The firm, united resolution of France, Spain, and Holland, joined with ours, not to treat of a particular but a general peace, notwithstanding the separate tempting offers to each, will in the end give us the command of that peace."

Franklin was depressed; he was afraid to leave the protection of France, but he was sensitive to the future. The prospect was bright before the American States, if they could weather immediate uncertainties at London, Paris, and Philadelphia. The "system" which had been "attended with so much success" did promise "to make America soon both great and happy"—if only America could gain her particular ends while all were making the "general peace."[37]

The British Government changed at this juncture as Rockingham died. Fox resigned, and Shelburne took charge. While he was reorganizing the ministry on June 30, he informed Oswald that he was adopting Franklin's "Idea of the method to come to a general Pacification by treating separately with each party." The way was open again for Franklin's natural opportunism.[38]

It does not matter who originated the idea. Possibly it was more Vergennes' than either Shelburne's or Franklin's. It does not matter who accepted it or whether he did so eagerly or reluctantly. Notwithstanding Franklin's misgivings of what would come after the peace when the United States stood alone, the idea was excellent for both Britain and the United States. Both gravely needed a "general Pacification." Each wanted to guard its own particular interests. And here was their opportunity. Oswald opened negotiations on

37. *Ibid.*, V, 511, 516, 526. For Carleton's efforts in America, see Bemis, *Diplomacy of the American Revolution*, 201–202.
38. Sparks Mss., XL, 11–13. Shelburne to Oswald, June 30, 1782.

July 6 with Franklin upon this basis. If Franklin played now with any finesse at all, he would indeed have "the command of that peace."[39]

There were not many things, ventured Oswald, to be settled with the United States after their independence had been granted, and that was already "in a manner acknowledged." He hoped that there were none. But if Franklin thought there were others, he might give some "hint of them." He was to do so only "as a Friend," of course; but then it was the universal opinion in England that he was a "Friend of England." Oswald went on to say that, although he expected no information inconsistent with particular engagements, he "could not help thinking that the Commissioners of the Colonies, had it much in their Power to give dispatch to the general Treaty, and to end it on just and reasonable terms, even notwithstanding their particular Treaty with France." In other words, here is your chance, Dr. Franklin, to show how much more sensitive you are to the welfare of the United States than to their relations with France. And on the side, you may be able to do England a favor in the process.

"Upon this the Doctor said they had no Treaty with France but what was published." Oswald replied that he was glad, for he saw nothing there "against a separate peace" excepting the "Great Article of Independence," and for him that was no longer in question. Then he remarked that he had been happy to hear Laurens say soon after his release from the Tower that the treaty with France would end when the States obtained their independence. But Oswald did not "think it proper to quote" to Franklin at this point "what Mr. Grenville said the Doctor himself had told him on the 11th or 12th of May last, to the same purpose." Instead, he kept the conversation upon France by declaring that whatever she "might desire beyond the separation of the thirteen Colonies would be more than she had just reason to expect. . . ."

The Doctor got his cue. It was not to confirm Laurens' opinion or to restate what he himself had said to Grenville in May. It was to say that there were some "hints" which Oswald might take to England on his next trip. He would not like it known that he had suggested them; but if Oswald would come to him on Wednesday the tenth he would show him "a minute of some things which he thought might be deserving of notice upon the occasion." Meanwhile Oswald should ponder the resolutions of the Maryland Assembly greeting the arrival of General Carleton in America to make peace. Their purpose was that there should be no "separate Peace,

39. See above, pp. 47–48. Sparks Mss., XL, 15. Oswald to Shelburne, July 8, 1782.

or Peace of any kind with England, until their Independence is acknowledged." And Oswald should remember that there "would be no Solid Peace" so long as Canada remained "an English Colony." Oswald made sure to report that to Shelburne immediately.[40]

Franklin gave Oswald eight points to consider on the tenth, but this time he would not let the memorandum out of his hands. The first four, he said, were *"necessary* for them to insist on." They were: Independence, "full and complete in every sense," had to be granted to the "13 States" and all troops withdrawn from them. Settlement had to be made of the boundaries between *"Their* Colonies" and the "Loyal Colonies." The bounds of Canada had to be held at least to what they were before the Quebec Act of 1774, and should be contracted farther "on an Ancient footing." And fourth, the Americans had to be assured "a Freedom of Fishing on the Banks of Newfoundland and elsewhere as well for fish as Whales." Franklin did not mention the right of drying fish ashore in Newfoundland, and so Oswald discreetly did not remind him of it.

The second four points, said Franklin, were "not absolutely demanded," but they were "such as it would be *advisable* for England to Offer for the Sake of Reconciliation and her future Interest." They were: Reparations to the amount of five or six hundred thousand pounds for towns burned and destroyed; acknowledgment in an Act of Parliament, or otherwise, that Britain had been in error; reciprocal rights for ships and trade between the American States and Britain and Ireland; and fourth, surrender of "every part of Canada."

Shelburne might find these terms rather sweeping, but Franklin felt that a voluntary offer of reparation on the part of England would "diffuse a universal Calm and Conciliation over the whole Country." He expressed himself, said Oswald, "in a friendly way towards England." He was "not without hopes" that "if we should settle on this occasion in the way he wished, England would not only have a beneficial Intercourse with the Colonies, but at last it might end in a Federal Union between them. In the meantime we ought to take care not to force them into the hands of other People." This was an amusingly oblique reference to the French alliance, a curious way of intimating that Shelburne had a chance to lure the Americans from association with the French in the future.[41]

Franklin's idea of "federal union," however, was not that which Shelburne was hoping to establish. For Franklin expressly notified him and his colleagues not to entertain any expectation that George

40. *Ibid.,* XL, 16, 18, 32–33.
41. *Ibid.,* XL, 19–23, Oswald to Shelburne, July 10, 1782.

III could have "some sort of sovereignty" over the American States such as "His Majesty had of Ireland." If they thought he could, they would find themselves "much disappointed," for the Americans "would yield to nothing of that sort." What then was in Franklin's mind? His ideas were predicated upon his first point—American independence "in every sense." After that was certain, then possibly he thought that Britain and the United States might enter into some kind of a customs union of both shipping and goods, perhaps one of concerted international policy.

This is conjecture insofar as it suggests that Franklin had in mind at that time any specific moves in the field of international affairs which the United States would make with Britain in the future. What is not conjecture is the revelation Franklin had thus given to Oswald of his changing attitude toward that alliance which he had signed with Gérard in 1778.

Franklin showed Oswald the "State of the Aids they had received from France." This was to impress upon him, as it were, that those debts constituted "the only foundation of the Ties France had over them, excepting Gratitude, which the Doctor owned in so many words." But while Oswald thought as much, he was also "entirely persuaded" that Franklin was not taking "the least step," not even "in such as his late communication with me, but what has been settled between him and the Count de Vergennes. . . ." If then Franklin was now favoring an *entente cordiale* with Britain, or "federal union" as he expressed it, which in the future might put a severe check upon American relations with France, he was doing so only upon the assumption that the mutually specific undertakings of France and the United States in the past should continue to stand.[42]

Oswald, nevertheless, was encouraged by this conversation with Franklin, and rightly, to report to Shelburne that they could "put an end to the American Quarrel in a short time." When that was done, he said, negotiations with the other powers would go on more smoothly. He believed that the Americans should be handled differently from the French, for the Americans were showing a "desire to treat, and to end with us on a separate footing from the other Powers." They displayed "a greater appearance of feeling for the future interests and Connections of Great Britain" than he had expected. They would not take subordination to Britain, but neither would they be subservient to France. Their commissioners were free agents. The French retained, he thought, only the power of ap-

42. *Ibid.*, XL, 27–28, Oswald to Shelburne, July 11. See also Franklin to Vergennes, July 24, 1782, in Smyth ed., VIII, 570.

proval at the time of ratification. He hoped that the Americans would not be "any way stiff" as to Franklin's "advisable" points or would drop them altogether. The "necessary" should offer hardly any "obstacle." "And I really believe," wrote Oswald, "the Doctor sincerely wishes for a speedy settlement, and that after the loss of Dependance, we may lose no more; but on the contrary that a cordial Reconciliation may take place over all that Country."[43]

Franklin indeed had come far from his timid position of the month before when he sought out Vergennes and Rayneval to propose a new treaty for protecting the United States in case they were set apart for punishment by Britain after the general peace. He was now laying the actual groundwork for the separate treaty of peace between Britain and the United States. There were still to be many anxious moments with both Britain, Spain, and France. John Jay was still to learn the limits to the oscillation of British opinion between "acknowledgement" of American independence and a "federal union" with the United States. But Benjamin Franklin was already beyond those uncertainties and on to details of the final settlement. Oswald heard him say at this time that it would be impossible for the commissioners to make any provision in the treaty for compensating the Loyalists. They would have to leave those victims of the war to the mercy of the several States. And the "back Lands in Canada" would have to be ceded to the United States without any stipulation for "the Loyal Sufferers." It was the rough draft of the final agreements on those matters.[44]

Oswald's Fear of America—Jay's Misgivings

Two things, however, were still bothering Oswald. He saw that Franklin was disturbed by the report which he had from England that Shelburne was not "so well disposed to end so quickly and agreeably with the Colonies." And Oswald himself felt that "the chance of a total or partial Recovery" in this "American Business" was "desperate." He heartily wished "we were done with these people, and as quickly as possible, since we have much to fear from them, in case of their taking the Pet, and throwing themselves into more close connections with this Court and our other Enemies." The Scottish merchant with American connections did not wish to pay out independence so slowly nor to wait for events at Gibraltar. He was even more worried on the next day, July 12, when he received a note from Franklin, as he reported at once to Shelburne, putting "a sort of stoppage upon the Preliminaries of Settlement."

43. *Ibid.*, XL, 22, 25, 26, 29.
44. See below, pp. 91–93.

Franklin wrote that he had heard that Shelburne's opposition to Fox's "decided *plan of unequivocally acknowledging American Independency* was one cause of that Gentleman's resignation." And further, that "Mr. Grenville thinks Mr. Fox's Resignation will be fatal to the present negotiation." Perhaps, said Franklin, this opinion was groundless; but until he had assurance straight from Lord Shelburne that the independence of the United States was acknowledged before they began negotiating the treaty, he would not go on with "Propositions and discussions." Nor could he enter into particulars without Mr. Jay. He might have added that he had just answered by courier an old letter from Vaughan speaking of a "proposed dependent State of America." He had told Vaughan that it was "impracticable and impossible," and he had expressed doubt of Shelburne's intentions. But it was not necessary to tell this to Oswald. It would reach Shelburne through Vaughan before Oswald could relay it to London. Franklin's finesse was approaching "command" of the peace.[45]

Alarmed and provoked, Oswald remonstrated to Shelburne that it was the first time he had heard of the "reserve intended in the Grant of independence." He had always supposed, he said, that the grant was meant to be "absolute and unconditional." He had never used the latter term, but only because he had thought such qualification unnecessary. How could anybody have been "so wicked as to throw this stumbling Block in the way"? It obstructed not only peace with the "Colonies" but the "general treaty." It disturbed the peace at home. It threw blame upon the new ministry and Shelburne himself.[46]

There was indeed more to Shelburne's "reserve intended" than rumor started by his political opponents. But he realized too well the strength of Oswald's arguments and Franklin's position in Paris to blur his reply. The American alliance with France was still in existence. Shelburne responded in a way that could hardly have been more gratifying to his agent or his esteemed friend and fellow philosopher, dean of the American commissioners of peace. He wrote to Oswald on July 27, 1782:

> I know the correctness of my own conduct, and that it can stand every test. A French minister might not so easily be brought to understand the conduct of others. But those with whom you have particularly to treat, know too much of the parties incident to our Constitution, and

45. Sparks Mss., XL, 23–31. Franklin (Smyth ed.), VIII, 565–566 to Vaughan, July 11; 567.
46. Sparks Mss., XL, 29–31. Oswald to Shelburne, July 12, 1782.

of the violence and inveteracy occasioned by personal disappointment, to be easily misled by false assertions or newspaper comments.

That is, Franklin would understand why Fox was angry and know accordingly why Grenville had spoken as he had upon leaving Paris.[47]

To give further assurance, however, Shelburne continued that the King had granted him permission to release the despatch which had been sent to Carleton in America, dated June 5, conceding independence before the negotiations of peace. Oswald might show Franklin this "to satisfy his mind, that there never have been two opinions since you were sent to Paris, upon the most unequivocal acknowledgement of American independence." And, "to put this matter out of all possibility of doubt," wrote Shelburne, a commission would be forwarded immediately to Oswald with full power to make "the independency of the colonies the basis and preliminary of the treaty now depending and so far advanced. . . ." (It was advanced because of Franklin's eight points.) Shelburne hoped with Oswald that the articles called "advisable" would be dropped, and those called "necessary" alone retained as the ground for discussion. If that were done, the treaty might be "speedily concluded."

From this overture, Shelburne turned to his own conception of "federal union," and another hint to the American commissioners. Oswald knew well, said he, that he had "never made a secret of the deep concern" which he felt over the separation of the colonies from the mother country. They were "united by blood, by principles, habits, and every tie short of territorial proximity." But Oswald also knew that he had "long since given it up, decidedly though reluctantly." He was governed by the same motives, he said, in seeking now to lay a foundation that would "avoid all future risk of enmity." And to Oswald, but for Franklin, he wrote: "In this view, I go further with Dr. Franklin perhaps than he is aware of, and farther perhaps than the professed advocates of independence are prepared to admit. My private opinion would lead me to go a great way for Federal Union; but is either country ripe for it? If not, means must be left to advance it." One could hardly get into a single letter more of diplomatic reassurance, pledge, acceptance of terms under reservation and stipulation, and revelation of policy.[48]

47. Fitzmaurice, II, 167–168. This letter of July 27 is not in the Sparks Mss.

48. *Ibid.*, II, 168–169. Wharton, VI, 15–16, dated Shelburne's letter to General Carleton as June 25, 1782. But Shelburne himself referred to it as of June 5 (according to Fitzmaurice, II, 168).

Franklin understood. He accepted the commission which now came for Oswald. He scarcely bothered to scrutinize the document, when Oswald showed him a copy on August 7. He, too, hoped that "they should agree and not be long about it." But this was not yet the attitude of John Jay. He examined the commission with care. To him, if there were not two opinions "upon the most unequivocal acknowledgement of American independence," all Shelburne had to do was to make the acknowledgment; and this Shelburne had not done as yet. The commission still talked about the "Colonies." In Jay's opinion, therefore, Shelburne's sincerity remained "questionable."[49]

Benjamin Franklin was not mistaken. Neither was John Jay. Shelburne had told the truth of the matter. Both Fox and he were willing to grant "unequivocal acknowledgement." But he had not yet stated the whole truth. There was a difference of time and condition between Fox and himself. The whole truth appeared in the King's "Orders and Instructions" to Oswald four days after Shelburne's letter of July 27. When he grasped the meaning of these from his conversations with Oswald, Jay came over to the position of Franklin. And his determination exceeded Franklin's as he discovered that Vergennes was endeavoring to impede the negotiations. Franklin seems never to have perceived the intentions of Vergennes. If he did, he did not think that they were dangerous to the United States.[50]

Shelburne's Plan of "Federal Union"

HAVING heard that Franklin had expressed a "strong desire" to keep the treaties of peace distinct, the King ordered Oswald July 31 to confer with the American commissioners under whatever title they should choose and whatever authority they said they had derived from their superiors in Congress. He was to receive any ideas that would restore peace "with most speed and certainty" between "Our Kingdom and the said American Colonies." In case he found that the Americans were "not at liberty to treat on any Terms short of Independence," he was to declare to them that he had authority "to make that concession." For the King was disposed to purchase peace "at the Price of acceding to the complete Independence of the thirteen States. . . ."[51]

49. Sparks Mss., XL, 55, regarding Franklin. Oswald to Townshend, August 7, 1782. Wharton, V, 639. Jay to Adams, August 2, 1782.

50. See below, p. 77. Bemis, 210 ff., *Diplomacy of the American Revolution,* citing evidence 211 n. For Jay's view of Franklin's appraisal of Vergennes, see Wharton, VI, 15.

51. Sparks Mss., XL, 44–49.

Here it was, simply and exactly. Unless Franklin had been misinforming Oswald and Grenville all along, and his correspondents Hartley and Vaughan as well, the Americans would not be at liberty to discuss terms short of independence. Although he wished it were so, Shelburne knew that he could not get the American colonies back into the British Empire. France had accomplished her purpose. They were independent. And he had to have peace. He therefore would not obstruct the way to peace by refusing to acknowledge what was a fact.

But why then was he so slow about doing it? The answer appears in the ninth paragraph of these instructions of July 31, 1782, to Oswald. It reads:

> In regard to the Question of any National substitution for the dependent connection with Great Britain, you must in the first place seek to discover the dispositions and intentions of the Colonies by the Intimations and propositions of the Commissioners. And if it shall appear to you to be impossible to form with them any political League of Union or Amity to the exclusion of other European Powers, you will be particularly earnest in your attention and arguments to prevent their binding themselves under any engagement inconsistent with the Plan of *Absolute and Universal Independence* which is the indispensable condition of Our acknowledging their Independence on Our Crown and Kingdoms.[52]

Shelburne's plan no longer was to reconcile the colonies within the British Empire. It was to acknowledge the independence of the American States in order that he might break the relationship which they had developed with France during their period of revolution and, if possible, get them into a coöperative association with Britain against France and her European satellites. This might be founded, as Franklin had suggested and Jay was to urge, upon freedom of trade and navigation between the British Empire and the United States. And Oswald was to negotiate "an unreserved System of Naturalization" between "Our Kingdom and the American Colonies."

Shelburne could not yet drop the word "Colonies" from his vocabulary, but he was instructing his agent to deal nevertheless with independent States. There was desire still that those States should not unite too closely. But it was not unwillingness to admit that they were free now—independent and sovereign. It was determination to get them out of the clutches of France. If Oswald and Fitzherbert, Grenville's successor as minister to France, perceived that France and the other belligerents were attempting to frustrate

52. *Ibid.*, XL, 48.

the general treaty, Oswald was to persuade the American commissioners to deal separately

> in the hope that the concessions you are authorized to make, will appear
> to them to satisfy the interests and the Claims of their Constituents, as
> in that case they can have no justifiable Motive to persist in a War,
> which as to them will have no longer any object, and it is to be hoped,
> will not be inclined to lend themselves to the purposes of French Ambition.[53]

Lord Shelburne was given no chance, however, to show what success he himself might have had with the plan. Shipowners were too well represented in Parliament to permit concessions to American shipping. He was obliged to abandon the idea of free trade. Then the strange coalition of Lord North and Fox overturned his ministry soon after Oswald's preliminary treaty with the United States. He was not allowed to complete the "general peace." His "system of Naturalization" experienced a profound transformation, if it can be said to have survived at all. Certainly the practice of impressing Americans into the British Navy was a weird descendant, utterly foreign to American concepts of expatriation and naturalization. Nonetheless, the statesmanship which Shelburne advanced in 1782 to bring about peace with the United States and to divorce them from France was to govern in large part the course of events for those States throughout the next twenty years of their rise to maturity.[54]

The King's instructions of July 31 to Oswald are further revealing. In order to make the peace "more solid and durable," he was to cede the town and district of New York. And then, having removed the question of independence, he should not fail to look after the rights and interest of individuals—in particular, those who had been imprisoned for their loyalty to the King and those who had extended credits in America prior to 1775. These debts should be a matter for the "sincere Interposition of Congress with the several provinces." The Loyalists should be restored to all their rights and granted a general amnesty. Oswald was to offer a portion of the King's "ungranted Lands" in each province if the Americans, not satisfied with the cession of New York, asked further concessions in return for compensating the Loyalists.[55]

Legalities and ethical principles are clear in such matters of private rights. Financial obligations which had been honestly incurred with no relation to public affairs are matters of private honesty.

53. *Ibid.*, XL, 48, 49.
54. See below, pp. 131, 168–170, 191, 303–304.
55. Sparks Mss., XL, 46, 47.

But those who seek to resist Government when Government is establishing, or maintaining, itself do risk the loss of their lives and their property to Government. Their rights invariably become badly tangled with treason whenever sovereignty migrates from one party in power to another through successful violence. Defeated Loyalists are never popular. These problems of the American Revolution were not solved for another twenty years—not until Britain, France, and the United States had become involved again in conflicts of territorial ambition and sovereign power. And Tories then were rare as well as unpopular.[56]

56. See below, pp. 186–188.

IV

INDEPENDENCE AND EMPIRE:
JAY'S PART

A "Lasting Peace"

FROM the first of August, 1782, it was not Benjamin Franklin with whom Oswald had to talk about American independence and a "lasting peace," the commitments of the United States to France, and Britain's hope of separating them from their ally. While John Jay was recovering his health, Franklin became painfully ill with "the gravel" and unable to give himself to the negotiations as he had. But this did not make the difference. As Franklin expressed it, Jay was a lawyer. He had to be satisfied on points which did not bother Franklin. So Franklin deferred to Jay, although retaining his own confidence in Vergennes while he waited for his eight points, necessary and advisable, to work upon British minds, and Jay's too for that matter. But in addition, Franklin knew that Spain's affairs were confusing the situation of the United States between France and Britain. Jay understood those matters better than he. They were within Jay's special province.[1]

The independence of the several American States was no longer in dispute. Shelburne had yielded to Franklin on that point. The question was the manner in which Britain would recognize the fact and whether Britain would acknowledge that the American States were *united* in their independence. On this significant point, Jay's legal mind was to cause a delay that may have cost the States some territory, but it compelled more than recognition of their freedom from King and Parliament in London.

The question of a "lasting peace" was closely related. It worried Oswald. Vergennes had spoken of it in April. Franklin had used the phrase in almost every conversation. And here was Jay now on August 7 picking up the argument that independence was not to be the price for peace, talking at length on the younger generation in America and their enmity toward Englishmen, and using the very phrase again.

What it meant in one respect to Franklin, and possibly to Vergennes, had been revealed by Franklin's proposal on June 11 that

1. Sparks Mss., XL, 92, 75.

there should be a treaty among all the nations associated in war upon Britain to give aid to any one of them in case Britain should renew the war with that nation after the general peace. But it meant in another respect far more important to Franklin complete independence for the United States and reparations to them in the form of territorial domain. When he spoke of "Canada," he had in mind Nova Scotia, Quebec, and the western region above the Great Lakes from Nipissing toward the headwaters of the Mississippi, just as Congress had stipulated in the instructions of 1779 to John Adams.[2]

It is certain that Vergennes did not subscribe to this meaning on behalf of France. He had long since ordered Gérard to stop American action in the Floridas and to discourage the attempt to conquer Canada. He was on the point of indicating to the British minister in Paris, Fitzherbert, that he did not favor the immediate recognition of American independence. And he was about to send his secretary, Rayneval, to deal with Shelburne in London against the territorial and maritime interests of the United States.[3]

That John Jay did not accept the first meaning of "lasting peace" is apparent from his reply when Oswald asked what security would be effective. Jay would not "give a farthing for any Parchment security whatever," for treaties would mean nothing, said he, when any "Prince or State" found it convenient to break through them. He told Vergennes about August 15 that he considered "mere paper fortifications as of but little consequence."

The same thought applied to the American alliance with France. Oswald made it his business to find out what Jay had to say about that. Would the United States be obliged to stand by France? Yes, said Jay, but then qualified his answer with "unless unreasonable." It was clear that, although he would honor the commitments which had been undertaken to make the war and its peace and to guarantee French possessions and acquisitions in the West Indies thereafter, Jay was inclined no more than Franklin, probably not so much, to undertake any other obligations in the future to France.[4]

Oswald reported again at this time, August 7–9, that Franklin had freely declared on various occasions that the treaty with France would be at an end with the grant of independence. Even though this evidence comes to us from a British source only, it is not propaganda. It is a report of the British negotiator to his Government. It

2. *Journ. Cont. Cong.,* XIV, 958.
3. Bemis, *Diplomacy of the American Revolution,* 211 n. See above, p. 22, and below, pp. 81–83.
4. Sparks Mss., XL, 58–59, 61. Wharton, VI, 7–8.

is strong evidence that the "old Doctor" himself was abandoning the first meaning of "lasting peace" and coming over to the second, of reparations by Britain chiefly in territorial concessions. Vergennes had been none too enthusiastic about Franklin's proposal of a treaty among the enemies of Britain. Besides, Franklin had been among the earliest speculators upon the future of the American settlers in the Mississippi Valley. He had sooner sell his "street door" than give up American rights on the Mississippi. He still had faith in Vergennes because he knew that French policy was founded upon separation of the United States from Britain, and he valued the French alliance for its threat to Britain. But he felt with Jay that the United States must become independent of both Britain and France. Were they not indeed getting in position to "command" the general peace?[5]

Oswald thought so. He asked Jay for no direct explanation as to what he meant by a "lasting peace," but guessed that it meant some "unpleasant or unfavorable limitation on the Conduct of Great Britain." He feared that it would result in a dangerous check upon British sea power. This suspicion so preyed upon him that he wrote at length about it to his superiors in London. The American Confederacy, he said, could dictate peace to the European powers. The American commissioners would take "Superintendency over the General Peace" and stipulate terms "just and reasonable" according to their own views. The Congress was assuming the "right of arbitration" between Britain and her opponents; it might act the part of "Dictators to Great Britain"; it might take upon itself the "guarantee" of the general peace, believing that "the united Power of their Confederacy will be of such weight as to make it the Interest of either of the belligerent Powers to desist from War whenever they chose to interpose. . . ." Oswald's imagination ran on. He predicted that there would be "Swarms of Armed Adventurers" such as could force any commercial or colonial power to stop fighting any other: "This capacity in the American Colonies," he declared, "if admitted to exist at this time, must continue to increase and become more decisive from year to year, in proportion to the quick increase of Population in that Country: which abounds in every necessary material for the equipment of Shipping. . . ." And they would be, declared he, under no risk of attack from Europe. Oswald's thoughts are reminiscent for us of Kalb's report to Choiseul in 1767 and Vergennes' declaration to Montmorin at the close of 1778. They were prophetic of the future power of the American people on both land and sea.[6]

5. Sparks Mss., XL, 66. See above, p. 40, and below, p. 95.
6. Sparks Mss., XL, 59, 64–65, 68–69. See above, pp. 3–4, 26.

Another talk with Franklin within a few days greatly relieved Oswald's apprehensiveness for the moment. He wrote home that the design which he had attributed to the Americans was "unjustly imputed." Yet he left his thoughts in the despatch, to be "under the Eye of Government," he said, as this might well happen in the future. The Americans would discover "the expediency and benefit of resorting to it." He could not get out of his mind Franklin's "hint or caution" in the previous July that Britain should not force the United States "into the hands of other People." It was a hint which Shelburne and his secretary, Townshend, were taking very much to heart.[7]

Jay's negotiations with the Spanish ambassador, Aranda, also stirred Oswald's suspicions. He had sounded Franklin toward the end of July, and Franklin had said that Aranda had powers (which, as a matter of fact, he really did not have) to make a treaty of commerce and alliance with the United States like those with France. Franklin hesitated to say this, but he had done so. And Oswald had replied offhand that he knew it. Franklin threw out the remark "in the easy way of conversation." But Oswald had perceived that it was to be "properly marked and communicated," to speed British action toward correcting the "mistake" about independence as Fox left the Government and Grenville withdrew from Paris. When Oswald came now on August 15 to inquire of Jay, however, he heard something very different in tone and content.[8]

Rivals in the Mississippi Valley

JAY had conferred with Aranda by appointment in the first days of August:

> Opening Mitchell's large map of North America [reported Jay to Congress] he asked me what were our boundaries. I told him that the boundary between us and the Spanish dominions was a line drawn from the head of Mississippi down the middle thereof to the thirty-first degree of north latitude, and from thence by the line between Florida and Georgia.

Aranda at once had objected. Prior to the last war, said he, the Western country had belonged to France; after its cession to Britain it had been a distinct part of the British dominions until Spain had conquered West Florida and certain posts on the Mississippi and Illinois; even if Spain's right of conquest did not extend over it all, still it was possessed by free and independent Indian nations; certainly, it did not belong to the American States. Remembering that

7. Sparks Mss., XL, 73.
8. Ibid., XL, 50–52.

Floridablanca had never advanced this argument in any of their conferences, John Jay had noted it well. He would never for a moment admit it to serious consideration. But he had agreed to wait for the map which Aranda would send to show the tentative boundary which Spain desired east of the Mississippi. How vividly he must have recalled that discourse by the French minister, Gérard, after dinner in December, 1778![9]

When Aranda's map arrived it displayed in red ink a line drawn northward on the east side of the Flint River near the border of Georgia close to the Appalachians, crossing the Ohio River at the mouth of the Kanawha and proceeding westward near the shore of Lake Erie, northward by Huron and back around Michigan to Superior. Spain would exclude the American States from the Alabama country above the Floridas, the entire Ohio Valley, and the Illinois country on the west.

Accompanied by Franklin, Jay had taken this map to Vergennes on August 10. The French foreign minister was "cautious and reserved." But his secretary, Rayneval, had asserted that the Americans were claiming more than they had a right to ask. Franklin had joined with Jay in declaring that the Spanish idea was extravagant and that the Mississippi ought to be the American boundary. It was not merely a remark in passing, to affect Vergennes at the moment and perhaps to be explained away later. It was a direct statement, to be taken at its face value whether or not it might have some adverse effect upon subsequent relations with France. For Benjamin Franklin wrote to Robert Livingston, secretary of foreign affairs in Philadelphia, two days later:

> Mr. Jay will acquaint you with what passes between him and the Spanish ambassador, respecting the proposed treaty with Spain. I will only mention, that my conjecture of that court's design to coop us up within the Allegany Mountains is now manifested. I hope Congress will insist on the Mississippi as the boundary, and the free navigation of the river, from which they could entirely exclude us.[10]

This was Franklin's reply to the suggestion of Livingston, dated January 7, 1782, which Franklin had received in March. Among his comments on the terms for peace Livingston had written that the peacemakers might be willing to leave the country beyond the mountains to the Indian inhabitants. In that case, he said, it should enjoy its independence "under the guarantee of France, Spain, Great

9. Wharton, VI, 22. See above, pp. 31–33.
10. Wharton, VI, 23. Franklin (Smyth ed.), VIII, 576, 580.

Britain, and America, and be open to the trade of those whose lands border upon them."[11]

We might be unjust to Livingston at first glance, knowing as we do that there was a close relationship between La Luzerne, French minister, and Livingston, secretary to Congress. La Luzerne had met the wishes of Vergennes and persuaded Congress to accept French leadership in the peacemaking. Without doubt Livingston also had been influenced to a considerable degree, for on December 30, 1782, he took Jay to task for carrying his suspicions of France "too far."[12]

But in fairness to Livingston, we must read his letter of January 7, 1782, to Franklin with care. He proposed the four-power guarantee of the Indian country from the Appalachians to the Mississippi at a time when he was thinking that Britain might try to hold the region. He was aware of British intrigues among the Indians. He saw the power which Britain would possess from the Gulf of St. Lawrence to the Gulf of Mexico. He feared for the Southern States as that Western country filled with immigrants from Europe and from the American States—"a hardy race of people" who would be "inimical" to the Southern States and have "the savages subject to their command." It was not a preposterous fear. It might easily have become fact. We will see British policy working later to that very end. In the summer of 1782, however, British policy was devoted first to separating the United States from France as they gained their independence from Britain, and for that purpose British statesmen were willing to concede territory to them in the West.[13]

It happened, by coincidence or design, immediately after the conference of Jay, Franklin, Vergennes, and Rayneval over Aranda's map, that Oswald had waited upon Franklin to express the hope that Franklin's four "necessary" points would "pretty nearly end the Business," and that the four "advisable" points would be dropped or modified. The four "necessary" were not only independence, "full and complete in every sense," and fishing rights on the banks of Newfoundland but settlement of the boundaries between "Their Colonies" and the "Loyal Colonies," and limitation of Canada as it was before the Quebec Act of 1774. This could mean nothing else than willingness on the part of the British agent to favor the claim of the United States to the western country reaching from the line of Lake Nipissing to the Floridas and from the Appalachians to the Mississippi.

11. Wharton, V, 87–94. Franklin (Smyth ed.), VIII, 397.
12. See above, pp. 29–30. Wharton, VI, 173, Livingston to Jay, December 30, 1782.
13. *Ibid.*, V, 90. See below, pp. 135–137, 402–407.

Oswald had hoped. But Franklin had not replied. Oswald then had urged that they should stop hostilities on the sea, and he had mentioned the Loyalists. But Franklin was fixed upon the idea that the Tories were a problem "exclusively" for the several States. Oswald hinted that "private recommendation" might be made "to their countrymen," for he was aware that the King's "ungranted lands" would fall of necessity to the States quite as readily as court-houses and other public property. Again Franklin did not respond. The conference had closed, as Oswald found that it always did "upon like occasions," with Franklin touching once more upon the advisability that Britain should cede all of Canada.[14]

Then Oswald had come to Jay on the fifteenth to discover what he was doing with Aranda. He set Jay straight about the question of independence. Jay was gratified, he reported, upon seeing the fourth article of his instructions which declared the King's "earnest wish" to purchase peace "at the Price of acceding to the complete Independence of the thirteen States." He got in a word also against Jay's making a treaty with Spain like the treaties of alliance and commerce with France, and he heard what he longed to hear.

Jay replied that he had not proceeded far with the Spanish treaty. Unless Britain forced them into it, he continued, he did not see that the people of America "had any Business to fetter themselves" with such a treaty. Oswald could hardly ask for a more direct hint than that. Jay was not going to let Spain stand in the way of peace with Britain. But when Oswald sought to include France, mentioning "by the by" that, as soon as the United States were independent of Britain, they would be independent of all other nations, Jay was not ready as yet to broaden the hint. He merely smiled and said "they would take care of that."[15]

Oswald had now learned enough, however, to send the memoranda of his conversation to London and to state his conclusions. The "American Business," he said, was at the point where independence must be granted "absolutely and unconditionally" or his negotiations would cease, and Fitzherbert's with the French as well. The Americans had given up their demand for a separate declaration, under the Great Seal, that the United States were independent. They would be satisfied if such a statement were included in the treaty. Independence might stand as one article, but it had to be "absolutely and irrevocably" independent of other articles in the treaty and in no way dependent upon the 'event" of them.[16]

14. Sparks Mss., XL, 75–77, Oswald to Townshend, August 11, 13, 1782.
15. *Ibid.*, XL, 82, 84–85.
16. *Ibid.*, XL, 53–54.

As Oswald waited for Townshend's reply to this despatch of August 17, Jay's negotiations with the Spanish ambassador entered upon their third, and last, phase under the supervision of the French foreign office. Aranda insisted once more, on August 26, that the region beyond the Appalachians belonged to the Indians. Jay retorted that his nation claimed the right of preëmption from the Indians and sovereignty over them as against all other nations. Aranda was "very urgent" that Jay should mark on his map "some line or other to the eastward of the Mississippi" upon which they could agree. But Jay had discovered that the Spanish ambassador had no powers as yet to deal with him. And he himself had no intention of yielding anything "eastward of the Mississippi."

Rayneval accordingly intervened again, and by September 6 had submitted his views to Jay in writing. He proposed now that the territory west of the Appalachians should be divided. South of the Ohio, the Indian lands nearer the mountains should be put under American control, those to the west under Spanish authority; the remaining territory north of the Ohio should be left to Britain. And he urged Jay not to break off negotiations because Aranda had no powers. It might offend Aranda. These however, said Rayneval, were merely his "personal ideas."[17]

Jay did not return Rayneval's memorandum to him, nor make any comment except that he had received it and would send a copy to Livingston. He made no comment, either, in his report to Livingston upon the similarity between Rayneval's proposal and Livingston's suggestion of January 7 to Franklin. It is hard to believe that Jay did not know of the suggestion, note the similarity, and think that Livingston might be under the persuasion of La Luzerne. But he merely remarked upon Rayneval's effort to make it seem only his personal solution of the problem. As it came, however, from "the first and confidential secretary" of the French foreign minister, Jay was positive that it came with Vergennes' knowledge and consent. And when Rayneval left secretly for London, after another conference with Aranda, Jay was convinced that there was a scheme afoot to play Britain against the United States for the benefit of Spain and France.

The plan, he believed, was to limit the independence of the United States and their territorial domain, for Spanish interests in the Mississippi Valley and navigation on the Gulf of Mexico, and—as he wrote later—to divide the fisheries between Britain and France "to the exclusion of all others." Without consulting Franklin, who did not concur, as he knew, in his suspicions of Vergennes, Jay sent his

17. Wharton, VI, 24–28.

own confidential agent, Vaughan, to counteract Rayneval in London and to insist that the British Government must acknowledge American independence as the premise rather than the outcome of the peace. In this instance, even though he was not wholly correct in appraising Vergennes' intentions, John Jay was nearer the truth than Benjamin Franklin.[18]

The "United" States of America—Rayneval in London

JAY was ready now to broaden the hint to Oswald and include France among the powers from whom the United States would be independent. For he was sure that France as well as Spain wished to keep them out of the Mississippi Valley. He knew that the independence of the United States, confined to the Atlantic Seaboard without dominion beyond the Appalachians, would be more fancied than real. To make it real, they had still to rely upon their mother country. But before they could do that, her statesmen would have to recognize their union.

Townshend's reply to Oswald's report of August 17 arrived on September 4. The cabinet had considered the demand of the Americans that their independence must be acknowledged before the peace, and had come to agreement that this should be granted upon terms. For, as Grantham, secretary for foreign affairs, wrote on September 3 to Fitzherbert in Paris, the action would be disagreeable to France. The bond between her and the American States "would thereby be loosened before the conclusion of a peace." Townshend, therefore, commended Oswald for showing the fourth article of his instructions to Franklin and Jay. The King, he said, would grant complete independence. But it could not be "unconnected with a Truce or Treaty of Peace." It could not be a single, separate article to be ratified by itself. It might be the first, and an unconditional, article of the treaty. The King agreed to the "plan of Pacification" submitted by Franklin as "necessary." It was to be "understood and expressed," however, that the boundaries of Canada were to be contracted no farther than they had been before the Quebec Act of 1774. And, as the privilege of drying fish ashore had not been mentioned by Franklin, Oswald was to assume that it was not to be in the treaty.

The King, wrote Townshend, would be pleased to waive the "undoubted rights" of those merchants whose claims had accrued against American debtors prior to 1775, "for the salutary purpose of precluding all future delay." And he would waive, too, the claims of the refugees, although he hoped that the colonies would do some-

18. *Ibid.*, VI, 27–32, Jay to Livingston, November 17, 1782.

thing for those Loyalists. But if, regardless of these concessions, the Americans still would not proceed unless their independence were acknowledged without connection with other clauses in the treaty, Oswald was to get a declaration from them that they would be satisfied with an acknowledgment which rested upon the King's stipulations concerning the boundary of Canada, the fishing rights, the debts, and the Loyalists. If they would make such a declaration, then Oswald "in very last resort" might tell them that the King was willing to acknowledge "absolutely and irrevocably" the independence of the "Thirteen United Colonies," without relation to other parts of the treaty. But Oswald was to get that treaty.[19]

The major point in this intricate formula seems to have been great reluctance to concede that the American States were united as one nation in their independence. The argument that the cabinet was unable to make such a concession before approval had been given by Parliament was based on a mere technicality. The persistence in using the word "Colonies" was irritating, but it was not significant. If they were recognized as independent, they were in fact "States."

What the British ministers hoped was that they might concede independence to the several States, so as to bring the war to an end and destroy the *raison d'être* for the French alliance. Then, as revealed in the instructions of July 31 to Oswald, they might so construct the terms of peace that the States would abandon the alliance and return to their orbit within British international politics. And finally, they hoped that they might be able to leave those States disjointed, at the most but loosely confederated, so that they would be tempted individually to return to the British Empire whenever they became dissatisfied with conditions in America.

For this purpose, if no other, it was essential that Britain should remain on the North American continent. We should take note that, in spite of his concessions in regard to debts and Loyalists—"to preclude delay," the King did not instruct Oswald to discuss Franklin's constantly reiterated point on the advisability of ceding Canada to the United States. Nova Scotia and Quebec were kept distinct from the Western country above the Great Lakes and beyond Nipissing.

We may observe also that, whatever mistakes Jay made in suspecting that Vergennes was not trying to establish American independence, and whatever losses of territory he incurred by delaying the negotiations until after Britain had saved Gibraltar, John Jay did not blur the importance of compelling Britain to acknowledge formally in the Treaty of 1782 what Thomas Jefferson had so boldly

19. Bemis, *Diplomacy of the American Revolution*, 212. Sparks Mss., XL, 93–96.

proclaimed in the Declaration of 1776—the independence of the
United States of America.

Oswald sent to Franklin and Jay the first part of Townshend's
letter of September 1, stating that the King would grant to America
"full, complete, and unconditional independence, in the most explicit manner, as an article of treaty," and he argued with Jay that
it was he now who was delaying the other treaties with France,
Spain, and Holland. Franklin was persuaded. He wrote to Rayneval
that they were ready to proceed and that he hoped "Mr. Jay will
agree to this." But John Jay would not budge. Rayneval had gone
to England. Jay replied to Oswald on behalf of the United States:

> . . . until their Independence was acknowledged, absolute and uncon-
> nected with the Treaty, they were as nobody; and as no People. And
> France could tell them so, if they were to pretend to interfere; having
> failed to acquire that Character, for which they had jointly contended.
> And therefore they must go on with France until England gave them
> satisfaction on the point in question.[20]

The hint which Oswald had sought on August 15 was broad
enough now. If Britain put her acknowledgment of the independence of the United States beyond the reach of France, Jay would
feel that they were no longer obliged to "go on with France." But
he had sufficient experience in diplomacy to surmise, if he did not
know, that there were reservations in this letter from Townshend
which Oswald had not shown to him. Had Jay seen what we have
just seen, he would have known.

Oswald still tried to save "time" by reading the second article of
his instructions of July 31 from Townshend, in which he had been
authorized to deal with the American commissioners under whatever
title they chose and whatever authority they said they derived from
their superiors. But Jay insisted that Oswald had no authority except in the King's commission. He might get a new commission. This
one, said Jay, could be "applied to the People you see Walking in
the streets as well as to Us." He would concede a point, however, if
Oswald got such a new commission authorizing him to make a treaty
whose preamble described Jay's constituents as the "Thirteen United
States of America"; he would no longer insist that Britain must
recognize American independence prior to the treaty. Oswald sent
this information to Townshend on the tenth of September.[21]

But Oswald did not tell Jay of the concessions which Townshend

20. Franklin (Smyth ed.), VIII, 590. Franklin to Rayneval, September 4, 1782. Sparks
Mss., XL, 97–98. Oswald to Townshend, September 10, 1782.
21. *Ibid.*, XL, 101, 100. For Jay's report on this episode, see Wharton, VI, 18–20.

had just authorized in regard to the debts and the Loyalists; instead, he followed up Jay's hint concerning France. For there came into Jay's hands on the same day a letter which Marbois had written in Philadelphia and which the British had intercepted. In it Marbois urged that France should oppose the American claim to the fisheries! After all, why should you offer concessions to Jay when you could accomplish the same purpose at less expense? The vital thing was to separate the "Colonies" from their ally. You could make those concessions later, if you had to do so in order to save Gibraltar.

Besides, it was strongly evident now that John Jay of his own volition was coming over to the side of Britain. And it was unmistakable after Oswald's new commission arrived, for they began to talk about sending the British troops in New York to recapture the Floridas from Spain and to retake British possessions in the West Indies from France. As for the effort of France to "saddle" Britain with her private engagements to Spain, by October 2 Jay had declared to Oswald in so many words that he would allow "no such thing."[22]

Marbois' letter concerning the fisheries was discredited then as a British forgery. But the copy to be seen in the French archives today proves that it was genuine. What Jay suspected was true. The French interest comprised not merely separating the American States from Britain and satisfying Spain with Gibraltar and the Mississippi Valley. It included also maritime rights for France herself in the North Atlantic, particularly the fisheries, that training school for naval power. She had no obligations to help the United States regain those rights for themselves. She had rather, as Vergennes had written to Montmorin in 1778, a strong desire that "the new republic which is rising" should not be "exclusive mistress of this whole immense continent." Vergennes, like Oswald, feared the strength of the American people on the sea. Ample proof of this is available in the record of Rayneval's mission to London.[23]

Vergennes' "private and confidential" secretary conferred with Lord Shelburne and his ministers from the thirteenth to the eighteenth of September. They examined the problems of armed neutrality and free commerce, of Holland, Spain, Gibraltar, and Minorca, commercial arrangements, Dunkirk, Africa, the East Indies, the West Indies, the fisheries off Newfoundland, and American inde-

22. Sparks Mss., XL, 130–138. For the English text of the Marbois letter, see Wharton, V, 238–241.

23. Bemis, *Diplomacy of the American Revolution*, 220–223. Doniol, *Rayneval*, in *Rev. d'hist. dipl.*, VI (1892), 62–89. *Corresp. George III*, VI, 123–129.

pendence in its most important aspect now, the extent of the American domain.

Rayneval explained the "system" which France would like to establish for the fisheries of Newfoundland. It should be a new arrangement "according to which each nation would fish exclusively in the part which would be assigned to it." To this Shelburne agreed in principle, but said that without doubt the Americans also would lay claim to the fisheries. He hoped that the King of France would not support them. Rayneval replied that he did not know the views of Congress. And possibly he did not, although he must have known what Franklin thought about the matter. Nevertheless, he stated his belief that he could take it upon himself to assert that "the King would never protect unjust demands." That division of the fisheries between Britain and France which Rayneval sought would indeed have made virtually any "demands" of the United States "unjust."

When they came next to discuss the secrecy which they should observe in case they succeeded in establishing "preliminaries," Rayneval matched Shelburne's fears of "the Americans and the Hollanders" with assurance that France would guard the agreement faithfully. This was going far from the pledge of the American alliance to make peace together. But Rayneval went farther. He reported to Vergennes: "I said besides that there would be means to baffle them, principally in leaving them ignorant of the state of the negotiations between France, Spain and England." This object, said Rayneval, "my lord Shelburne" held "extremely to heart." What, may we ask, would Franklin have thought, if he had overheard?[24]

As for the extent of the United States, Shelburne had "foreseen that they would have much difficulty with the Americans." They would make as much trouble, he said, on account of their boundaries as on account of the fisheries of Newfoundland. But he hoped that the King of France would not support their "demands." Rayneval replied that he had no doubts of the eagerness of the King to restrain them within "the bounds of justice and of reason." Shelburne then wanted to know what were the pretensions of the Americans. Rayneval supposed that they would stress their charters and lay claim from the Atlantic to the "South Sea." This was an insinuation which Shelburne did not miss, for he responded that the point about the charters was "nonsense." Rayneval carried the discussion no further, he reported to Vergennes, because he did not wish either to sustain the American pretension or "to annihilate it." But he did urge Shelburne's thoughts to go on. He remarked that "the English ministry ought to find in the negotiations of 1754 relative to

24. Doniol, *Rayneval*, 75.

the Ohio the boundaries which England, then sovereign of the 13 united states, believed ought to be assigned to them." Such a boundary would have held the United States out of the Northwest above the Ohio.[25]

Vaughan in London—Jay's "Few Acres"

THE course which Britain should follow in order to come between her rebels and her enemy was plain. It lay in the Mississippi Valley. Rayneval had asserted that the independence of the American States from Britain was to be "without restriction." That was a fact anyway. But the extent of their territory was a matter upon which their own ally did not agree with them, indeed was hostile to them and preferred agreement with their mother country.

Oswald's new commission went forward on September 24, still referring in irritating fashion to the American States as "Colonies," but authorizing him to negotiate with the Americans as commissioners "by and on the part of the Thirteen United States of America" as John Jay insisted. Vaughan had come on the heels of Rayneval with instructions from Jay to tell Shelburne that it was "the obvious interest of Britain immediately to cut the cords which tied us to France"; that it "would not be wise in Great Britain to think of dividing the fishery with France and excluding us"; that it "would not be less impolitic to oppose us on the point of the boundary and the navigation of the Mississippi."

The reasons could not have failed to impress Shelburne whose purpose had been all along to break the French alliance and to form a "political League of Union or Amity" with the American States, "to the exclusion of other European Powers," if he could not hold them within the British empire.[26] Jay had told Vaughan that if Britain would allow the United States to extend to the Mississippi and to the "proclamation bounds of Canada" on the north, and would consent to "mutual free navigation of our several lakes and rivers," there would be an inland system of transportation from the Gulf of St. Lawrence to the Gulf of Mexico which would supply the inhabitants north and west of the mountains with foreign commodities more easily than the ways from the ports on the Atlantic.

---

25. *Ibid.*, 80. For Franklin's letter to Livingston, October 14, 1782, saying that "different accounts" of Shelburne's "sincerity" induced the French ministry to send Rayneval to London and that he returned "quite satisfied," see Franklin (Smyth ed.), VIII, 614–616. Faÿ has followed this line of thought in his *Franklin, The Apostle of Modern Times* (p. 474), and declared that Rayneval was "only going to deal with French questions." For John Adams' contemporary opinion regarding fisheries and boundaries, see Wharton, V, 840.

26. Sparks Mss., XL, 123–127. Wharton, VI, 31–32. See above, pp. 50–51, 67.

This trade, said Jay, "would be in a manner monopolized" by Great Britain, as the United States would not insist that Britain should admit other nations to navigation of waters which belonged to her. But Britain should not try to keep any of that country, he continued, for it would not be in her power either to settle or to govern it. The United States would refuse to give her aid. The "utmost exertions of Congress could not prevent our people from taking gradual possession of it. . . ." If Britain should try, she would "sow the seeds of future war in the very treaty of peace" and "naturally lead us to strengthen our security by intimate and permanent alliances with other nations." John Jay had more faith than Robert Livingston in the loyalty of the American pioneers.[27]

Lord Shelburne knew now, after the visits of both Rayneval and Vaughan, what must be done in order to separate the United States from France. He had only to get news from Gibraltar to know how large his concession of Western territory to the United States would have to be. He learned on September 30 that the French and Spanish assault upon Gibraltar had failed. The garrison had been relieved by Howe's fleet. The siege was being raised.[28]

When Oswald's second commission came, phrased to meet his wishes, Jay drafted four articles of a treaty. And Franklin approved them. Although still trusting Vergennes personally, Franklin no longer felt obligated to tell the French minister all that he himself approved. The articles were not shown to Vergennes, as Jay said, "for very obvious Reasons."[29]

Britain was to acknowledge that the United States were "free, sovereign, and independent States." That would have suited Vergennes. But the boundaries which Jay proposed for them were to run from the northwest angle of Nova Scotia down the highlands to the Connecticut River, down it to the forty-fifth parallel of latitude, westward along that line to the St. Lawrence, then straight to Lake Nipissing, and then westward straight to the source of the Mississippi, down that river to the thirty-first parallel of latitude, then due east to the Chattahoochee River, down it to its junction with the Flint, then straight to the St. Mary's and down it to the Atlantic, thence northward sixty miles off the coast so as to include all islands between East Florida and Nova Scotia. Jay left the region from the mouth of the St. John River in the Bay of Fundy to the northwest angle of Nova Scotia open for further negotiation as Congress had

27. *Ibid.* See above, pp. 74–75.
28. Bemis, *Diplomacy of the American Revolution*, 213. Fitzmaurice, II, 191 n. *Corresp. George III*, VI, 138.
29. Monaghan, 206.

instructed. Such boundaries in the West could not have pleased a foreign minister whose "private and confidential" secretary had been pleading the case of Spain with Jay, and then insinuating to the British prime minister that Britain should retain the whole area southward to the Ohio River.[30]

Vergennes might not have objected to Jay's second article in regard to the cessation of hostilities, return of prisoners, withdrawal of armies, restoration of archives, records, and papers. But he most certainly would have been annoyed by the third, for it stipulated that the subjects of Britain and the people of the United States should continue to enjoy the fishing rights to which they had been accustomed on the banks of Newfoundland and elsewhere, with the shore rights too of drying and curing fish upon terms of equal privileges and hospitality. And Jay's fourth article would have displeased Vergennes equally. It provided that the navigation of the Mississippi, "from its source to the ocean," should forever remain free and open. Waterways, ports, and places belonging to Britain and the United States there and "in any part of the world" should be open to the merchants and commercial vessels of both parties on the same terms that each accorded to its own merchants and ships, excepting only the special privileges of the British chartered trading companies—as for example the Hudson's Bay Company—in which neither the subjects of Britain nor any of the "more favored nations" could participate.

Such an agreement would destroy Spain's control of the Mississippi for the greatest part of its length and put her authority over the remainder in jeopardy. What would be still more irritating to France, commercial relationships would be established between the United States and Britain which surpassed any undertaken with France in the Treaty of 1778. This prospect would be anything but happy for the statesman who had declared in 1778 that he did not desire "by a great deal" to see the new republic become mistress of the North American continent and attain economic self-sufficiency.[31]

Oswald agreed to Jay's four articles on October 8 and sent them to his Government. But the good news from Gibraltar had reached England and the ministry knew there was an increasing rift between the Americans and the French over the pretensions of Spain. John Jay was now planning ways and means with Oswald for Britain to retake West Florida. And Vaughan, who had reappeared in Paris to make the American commissioners' "first jealousies" of

30. Bemis, *Diplomacy of the American Revolution,* 228, map 4. Wharton, V, 806.
31. *Ibid.,* V, 806–807. See above, pp. 20–21, 26.

the Rayneval mission to London "subside and vanish," had reported
back to Shelburne on October 3 that Jay saw "no apparent obstacle" in the way of immediately framing a treaty. Jay had even told
Vaughan that "America would not upon such an occasion stand
for a few acres." The British cabinet, therefore, decided on October
17 to enter objections to Jay's articles for a treaty. There was no
need now for Britain to go so far. Shelburne met with Townshend
and Grantham on the following Sunday, October 20, to draft orders for another representative in Paris, partly to reprove Oswald
but more to check the territorial ambitions of Franklin and Jay.[32]

Sir Henry Strachey joined Oswald with these instructions: They
were to urge the British right to all backlands and insist that the
area of the American provinces had been limited by the Proclamation of 1763, in any case that the King had the right of soil however the charters were understood. They were to urge, as Rayneval
had insinuated, that the western boundary of Canada was the old
French line on the Ohio River, and that the eastern had been established by the Quebec Act of 1774. They were to do all this for the
purpose of obtaining some compensation for the Loyalists, either
by direct cession of territory in their favor or by half or some portion of the proceeds from the sale of the backlands, or at least by a
favorable boundary for Nova Scotia. They were to extend this line,
if possible, to include the province of Maine; if not so much, then
the province of Sagadahock; at the "very least" the district of Penobscot. And they were to urge "just boundarys" for West Florida.
What that meant becomes evident in the secret clause which was
added to the provisional treaty of November.[33]

But none of these matters were to stop negotiations. For Strachey
was instructed further that it was understood, "if nothing of this
can be obtained after the fairest and most strenuous trials," Oswald
might settle upon the basis of the American propositions. He was
to omit only the right of drying fish on the island of Newfoundland and the provisions in Jay's fourth article for reciprocally free
trade. He was to keep all that concerned the Mississippi River. In
other words, Shelburne and his colleagues felt that they had no
power to fix terms of commerce and navigation, except on the Mississippi. And indeed they would have met strong opposition in Parliament from the representatives of British shipping if they had
proposed any concessions to American commerce elsewhere. Shel-

32. MHS Proc., 2d ser., XVII, 410, Vaughan to Shelburne, October 3, 1782. Sixth
Report, Royal Comm. on Hist. Mss., Append. 403. Fitzmaurice, II, 192. *Corresp. George
III*, VI, 143–144.
33. See below, pp. 92–93.

burne's talk with Franklin about federal union in an economic sense had been no more than talk.[34]

Boundaries and Loyalists, therefore, were not to detain Oswald. It had only to "appear authentically" that every instance had been used to get the best terms possible in favor of the refugees and British creditors prior and subsequent to 1775. The refugees were "of great importance." But, if the Americans would let Maine go with Nova Scotia and would join the British in regard to West Florida, there were "resources" which might satisfy those Loyalists. The debts to British creditors, however, did require "the most serious attention." Honest debts should be paid in honest money. There should be "No Congress money." And finally, Strachey was to return to London as soon as possible. Manifestly Shelburne was eager to close with the United States now, upon terms of American independence and suspicion of France—and, we might add, before he lost control of Parliament to the coalition of Charles James Fox and Lord North.[35]

John Adams' Contribution

THE lines were written for the final scenes as Adams arrived from Holland on October 26 to resume his part. This was not to his liking. He had been commissioned in the summer of 1779 as the sole agent of Congress to make terms of independence, peace, and commerce with Britain. With such an ambitious program possessing his thoughts and affecting his behavior, he had discounted the implications of the alliance with France. He had advised, even ventured to dictate to the French foreign minister on the conduct of the war; he had presumed to interfere with the mediation of Austria and Russia. Vergennes, however, had not endured such presumption. He had rebuffed Adams sharply and ordered La Luzerne to impress Adams' shortcomings upon Congress.[36]

Adams had gone on to Holland to negotiate there for loans and a treaty of commerce as if the United States were an independent nation. But La Luzerne had succeeded with Congress. It had reconsidered its plan for negotiating peace. John Adams was to share his powers with Benjamin Franklin and John Jay, and with Henry Laurens and Thomas Jefferson when they should arrive in Paris. The commissioners were to insist that Britain must recognize not only the independence of the United States but also the validity of their treaties of alliance and commerce with France. And in regard

34. See above, pp. 61–62, 65–68.
35. Sixth Report, Royal Comm. on Hist. Mss., Append. 403.
36. Adams, *Works*, III, 298–299. See above, pp. 28–30, 43.

to boundaries and other matters, Congress ordered the commissioners to follow the lead of the French ministers. La Luzerne had contrived well. He was justified in reporting that the negotiations had been put in the hands of the King. The United States had given over their diplomatic independence at Paris to the French Government. Or rather, Franklin, Adams, and Jay would have done so had they followed their instructions.[37]

John Adams' inclination to ignore those instructions came in part from a sense of injury and pique; he did not call upon Vergennes after returning to Paris from The Hague until he was advised by Lafayette and Franklin that Vergennes was expecting him. But it is to be said in his favor that he had noted at once that Vergennes was dealing in secret with the British envoy, Fitzherbert. Adams quickly picked up the threads of the past negotiations. He quickly agreed with Jay that they should honor their obligations to France and be grateful, but should think and act for themselves. Adams' contributions to the settlement were real, and beneficial to the United States. For the establishment of their own credit, an honest people, quite as much as individuals, should pay debts which had been contracted in good faith. American fishermen would need privileges ashore near the fishing grounds if fishing rights were to be used effectively. The province of Maine did belong in the United States and not in Nova Scotia—if the rights of settlement, tradition, and American interest were served. Adams' errors were in diplomatic tact and judgment rather than in fact.[38]

To tell Oswald bluntly that every European nation would be "continually manoeuvring" to work the United States into the "real or imaginary balances of power," and that they were afraid of being made the tools of Europe, was the truth. But it was dangerously unwise at that moment. For they had not yet secured the treaty which would establish their independence of Britain and release them from all except specific obligations to France. Adams may not have known the exact purposes behind Rayneval's mission to London, but he did know enough of Vergennes' diplomacy to surmise that France would coöperate as readily with Britain as with Spain in restricting the power and the territory of the United States. At least he could see that the enemy and the ally were on the point

37. See above, p. 42. Doniol, IV, 605, 617–626, La Luzerne to Vergennes, June 13, 14, 23, 30, 1781. Jefferson declined the mission on account primarily of the health of Mrs. Jefferson. Jefferson (Ford ed.), I, 71. Laurens hesitated but finally came to Paris. See below, p. 91.

38. Adams, *Works*, III, 303–304. Wharton, V, 838–840. Adams to Livingston, October 31, 1782. Wharton, V, 845, Adams' journal, November 3, 1782.

of settling their own differences, and were doing it secretly. This was no time to antagonize both. It would have been better to hold his tongue and leave the truth unsaid. What appears to have saved his country from the evil consequences of such indiscreet talk was the determination of each to wrest the United States from the other. But then, probably John Adams knew that, too, and his indiscretion was deliberate.[39]

John Adams' appraisal of Franklin, however, cannot be called a mistake of judgment rather than of fact. It seems clearly to have been a mistake of fact. Franklin was not trying cunningly to divide the American commissioners. He was working with Jay. He was not wavering before Vergennes, unwilling to say yes and unable to say no. He was maintaining diplomatic courtesy. He had long since told Oswald, if no one else, that the French alliance would be at an end upon the establishment of peace between Britain and the United States. And three weeks before Adams arrived in Paris, Franklin had approved Jay's four articles, which had not been shown to Vergennes "for very obvious Reasons." But for equally good reasons Franklin, able opportunist that he was, continued to assert his faith in Vergennes personally. The independence of the United States did lie at the heart of French foreign policy. French money was still necessary to the American cause. Even if the French alliance should lose its *raison d'être* with the conclusion of peace and for all practical purposes come to an end, so long as it was not formally abrogated, its stipulation that France would guarantee the possessions of the United States on the continent, and they France's possessions in the West Indies, served as a threat to hold Britain in check. Britain would still be a North American power long after peace had been made, and the most dangerous menace to the future of the United States. It would be wise for them indeed to keep on as good terms as possible with France quite a while longer.[40]

John Adams analyzed his own opinion of Benjamin Franklin when he recorded how he himself enjoyed French flattery. More than one, said he, had told him that he was "the Washington of the negotiation." And he had replied: "You do me the greatest honor, make the sublimest compliment possible." "A few of these compliments," he wrote in his journal, "would kill Franklin if they should come to his ears." If they did—and doubtless they did eventually— they must rather have amused the "old Doctor," who could recall that for the second time now the diplomat from New England had

39. *Ibid.*, VI, 11, conversation between Adams and Oswald on November 18.
40. See above, p. 49.

required prompting before he seemed to realize that he should pay his respects to the foreign minister as soon as he arrived in Paris. Self-esteem and envy dulled John Adams' perception that Benjamin Franklin's purpose was the same as his own. In the words of his grandson, Charles Francis Adams: "Whatever Franklin might have been disposed to believe of the French court, his instincts were too strong to enable him to trust them implicitly with the care of interests purely American."[41]

But then psychiatrists may explain the whole of John Adams' attitude as a Puritan's aversion for dalliance—especially inasmuch as the recipients of the "old Doctor's" affection were either very much younger than he, or unmistakably frowzy. Adams' wife Abigail has left a portrait of Mme Helvetius, written two years later, which may tell as much about John as about Abigail:

> She entered the room with a careless, jaunty air; upon seeing ladies who were strangers to her, she bawled out, "Ah! mon Dieu, where is Franklin? Why did you not tell me there were ladies here?" . . . "How I look!" said she, taking hold of a chemise made of tiffany, which she had on over a blue lute-string, and which looked as much upon the decay as her beauty, for she was once a handsome woman; her hair was frizzled; over it she had a small straw hat, with a dirty gauze half-handkerchief round it, and a bit of dirtier gauze, than ever my maids wore, was bowed on behind. . . . She ran out of the room; when she returned, the Doctor entered at one door, she at the other; upon which she ran forward to him, caught him by the hand, "Helas! Franklin"; then gave him a double kiss, one upon each cheek, and another upon his forehead.

As they dined, Mme Helvetius sat between Franklin and Adams, "frequently locking her hand into the Doctor's, and sometimes spreading her arms upon the backs of both the gentlemen's chairs, then throwing her arm carelessly upon the Doctor's neck." Franklin had assured Abigail that she would see "a genuine Frenchwoman . . . one of the best women in the world." But Mrs. Adams had to "take the Doctor's word" for it. Abigail would have "set her down for a very bad one, although sixty years of age, and a widow." And after dinner Mme Helvetius "threw herself upon a settee, where she showed more than her feet." She had "a little lap-dog, who was, next to the Doctor, her favorite. This she kissed, and when he wet the floor, she wiped it up with her chemise." Abigail hoped she would meet other French ladies whose manners were "more con-

41. Adams, Works, III, 305–306, 309 (1782); 124 (1778). Ibid., I, 375.

sistent" with her own "ideas of decency." Else, said she, "I shall be a mere recluse."[42]

Final Bargaining

THERE had to be much last-minute haggling with the British representatives over boundaries, Tories, debts, fisheries, and the evacuation of New York. Strachey reported on November 8 that the Americans conceded the point about Newfoundland but insisted upon fishing in the Gulf of St. Lawrence and using the Magdalen Islands and the unsettled shores of Nova Scotia. Debts incurred since 1775, he said, were out of the question as illegal, but those prior to 1775 appeared to be safe. Nothing would be done for those refugees who were already under the protection of the British Army, and nothing for others except what the British ministry could offer in Canada. On account of their obligations to France, said Strachey, the Americans would not agree in advance to a quiet evacuation of New York, for they could not make a separate peace or truce. But they were confident that General Washington upon seeing the provisional treaty would not obstruct the withdrawal of the British forces.[43]

Franklin had even to threaten Oswald, Strachey, and Fitzherbert with specific claims for plundering and burning by the Loyalists and the British armies, before they would accept the American formula for the debts and the Loyalists. Both parties, however, surrendered their maximum claims to territory. The British abandoned the Penobscot and the Ohio. The Americans gave up the line from the forty-fifth parallel at the St. Lawrence to Nipissing and thence to the headwaters of the Mississippi. Henry Laurens arrived in time to insert the stipulation that the British troops should carry away with them no Negroes or other American property, and to sign the provisional treaty with Franklin, Jay, Adams, and Oswald on November 30, 1782.[44]

John Jay's contention was met. The treaty acknowledged that the independence of the United States was the very basis of peace between the two countries. Although it was still technically subject to change as France made her terms with Britain, there was no danger of alteration as long as the United States and Britain were sat-

42. Letters of Mrs. Adams, 199–200. For other ladies of Franklin's acquaintance, see Faÿ, Franklin, 456–469.
43. Sixth Report, Royal Comm. on Hist. Mss., Append. 404.
44. Franklin (Smyth ed.), VIII, 621, Franklin to Oswald, November 26, 1782. Wharton, VI, 87, 112. Adams, Works, III, 336.

isfied with their agreement. For France of all the combatants was now most in need of peace, and Spain could have no voice in the matter except through France or Britain. There was to be an effort in the following spring to establish something like the "federal union" of commerce and navigation between Britain and the United States which Shelburne and Franklin and Jay had conceived. But it came to naught, and the provisional treaty of November, 1782, became the definitive peace between Great Britain and the United States of America on September 3, 1783.[45]

The British had capitalized the friction between the Americans and the French, and the successful defense of Gibraltar, to thwart American pretensions to the western country above the Great Lakes from the St. Lawrence and Lake Nipissing to the Mississippi River. But except for that, Britain conceded boundaries for the thirteen States and their Western domain including the whole region east of the Mississippi from the Lake of the Woods and the Great Lakes down to the thirty-first degree of latitude, the Chattahoochee River, and a line drawn straight from its juncture with the Flint to the source of the St. Mary's River and along that stream to the Atlantic Ocean. And the Americans were assured that they should have the province of Maine eastward to the St. Croix River.

Britain gave fishing rights on the banks off Newfoundland and in the Gulf of St. Lawrence, with the privileges of drying and curing fish on the unsettled shores of Nova Scotia, Labrador, and the Magdalen Islands. It was agreed that creditors of both parties should meet with no lawful impediment to the recovery of the full value in sterling money of all bona fide debts heretofore contracted. The American Congress was bound to recommend earnestly that the legislatures of the several States should compensate the Loyalists. There were to be no more confiscations and prosecutions for participating in the war. The British armies were to be withdrawn, prisoners released, and no Negroes or other property of American inhabitants taken away. Both parties were to enjoy free navigation of the Mississippi from its source to the ocean. Territory conquered before the arrival of the provisional treaty in America was to be restored.

A separate and secret agreement accompanied the provisional treaty. It stated that if Britain were to retain West Florida as a result of her negotiations with Spain, the northern boundary of the province should be at the line from the Mississippi at the mouth

45. Miller, Treaties, II, 96–100, 151–156. Bemis, Diplomacy of the American Revolution, 249–251. Gutteridge, Hartley, 301 ff. For the "conciliatory propositions" and the "sketch of a provisional treaty of commerce" accompanying Hartley's letter to Franklin on March 12, 1783, see Wharton, VI, 288–291.

of the Yazoo eastward to the Chattahoochee River instead of the thirty-first degree of latitude, farther south. In other words, if Spain were to get back the Floridas, she would obtain a smaller area than Britain would have kept for herself.[46]

Adams, Franklin, Jay, and Laurens wrote to Secretary Livingston on December 14, 1782, to explain. Britain had insisted, they said, upon keeping the province of Quebec; and they knew that France and Spain opposed their claims to the Western country. So, having no reason to think that they could ever get lines more favorable, they had accepted the boundary of the Great Lakes and the St. Lawrence below the forty-fifth degree. But they had gained access to the northwestern region adjacent to Lake Superior for the United States. They had agreed to the provisions concerning debts and Loyalists from reasons of "both justice and good policy." In their opinion, no acts of government could dissolve the lawful obligations of individuals which had been contracted prior to the war. And no other arrangement for the Loyalists could have brought British ideas of honor so near reconciliation with the views of Congress and the sovereign rights of the several States. As for the separate and secret article, they valued it highly as an inducement to get Britain to join with the United States in stipulating that the Mississippi River should remain open to free navigation.

As they had reason to imagine, they said, that France was opposed to their views on the fisheries and the Loyalists as well as the boundaries, they had communicated none of these agreements to Vergennes until the respective articles had been signed. And not even then had they told him about the separate article. But they hoped that Congress would approve the considerations which had led them to deviate from the spirit of their instructions. Vergennes himself, they asserted, had appeared surprised, but not displeased that they had obtained so favorable a treaty.[47]

Vergennes' Injured Air—American Empire

THE foreign minister of France could not appear otherwise. He had to tell Franklin that the American commissioners had "managed well," and put his stress upon the fact that they had won recognition of American independence—as if that were "most apprehended as a difficulty in the work of a general peace." He had to maintain the semblance of British unwillingness to free the American States, even if he himself knew better and doubted that he really could deceive anyone. Vergennes did assume an injured air to Franklin

46. Miller, *Treaties*, II, 101 n.
47. Wharton, VI, 131.

when he learned that the American commissioners were sending their preliminary treaty home to Congress without waiting for France to conclude hers with Britain. He committed the question of the proprieties to Franklin's own integrity and threatened that further financial assistance would depend upon a satisfactory explanation. But he quickly thought better of this, and accepted Franklin's suave confession that the American commissioners had been guilty of "neglecting a point of *bienséance*." For he appreciated the meaning in Franklin's intimation that "the whole edifice" would sink to the ground immediately if he refused to extend further assistance because of a "single indiscretion" on their part.[48]

The "whole edifice" was not simply the separation of the American colonies from their mother country. It was their establishment as States removed from British influences and held close to France. This had to be done if France were actually to diminish British authority among the powers of Europe. There had to be a power friendly to France and potentially hostile to Britain in the midst of the British Empire. Vergennes did not want to make this new republic in America entirely free.

It would be a sad outcome indeed for France, if he set up and strengthened the United States, only to force them back upon intimate terms with the common enemy. Beyond expressing one's momentary irritation at the turn of diplomatic fortune, therefore, one must not go. Vergennes honored Franklin's request for additional funds with a loan of more than a million dollars and hoped, we may suspect, for the best to come eventually from a bad situation. He could do nothing else—except perhaps regret that he had not followed Turgot's advice in 1778. Rodney had won a devastating victory over the French fleet in the West Indies. The Spanish had failed at Gibraltar. The French Treasury was reaching the point of exhaustion. France could not continue financing war much longer, even for herself. France could only hope to make a peace which would not utterly ruin her prestige in Europe, to gain time in which to restore her finances and fleet, and keep the American alliance for future use.[49]

But there was little hope for France now in her alliance with the United States. Their statehood, as Jay had so stubbornly maintained, was already a fact. Their independence was acknowledged by Britain as well as by France. Their dominion over the back country all the way to the Mississippi River was conceded by Britain.

48. Franklin (Smyth ed.), VIII, 628, 634, Franklin to Livingston, December 5, 1782. Wharton, VI, 140, 143–144, December 15, 17, 1782.
49. See above, p. 13, for Turgot's opinions.

And Britain was the only power in position to dispute it with them, for Spain had lost whatever opportunity she may once have had to check the westward expansion of the United States. That had passed with Floridablanca's rebuff to Jay's original offer of a triple alliance among Spain, the United States, and France. The American States had reached their immediate objectives. They were not likely to go beyond, merely to oblige France.

Benjamin Franklin may have been right in still believing that those who wished to destroy the "good understanding" between France and the United States would do them "irreparable injury." It may have been true, as he wrote on December 26, 1782, that their "firm connection with France" gave them "weight with England, and respect throughout Europe," and that if they broke faith with France, "England would again trample us, and every other nation despise us." But this was looking at the situation too exclusively from the interest of the United States at the end of 1782.[50]

John Jay revealed the plight of France and the greater interest of the United States when he wrote to Secretary Livingston on December 14: "It is our policy to be independent in the most extensive sense, and to observe a proper distance towards all nations, minding our own business, and not interfering with, or being influenced by, the views of any, further than they may respect us." Jay himself was even beyond the stage now of wishing to fulfill the obligations of the alliance with France: he urged in regard to the West Indies that it would be "unwise to permit Americans to spill the blood of our friends in the islands, for in all of them there are many who wish us well." It was John Jay rather than Benjamin Franklin who forecast the American policy of the future. And Jay lived to participate in executing it to the distress of France on more than one occasion.[51]

We know that Jay was unduly fearful that American independence of Britain was still in doubt after August, 1782. Franklin was right in feeling that it mattered little thenceforth whether the British Government acknowledged that independence at the start of the negotiations or as a result of the peace. He was correct also in his estimate of Vergennes' sincerity upon that question. American independence had been the aim of the French foreign minister when he brought his country into the war between Britain and her colonies. He had expected to use it to diminish the power of the ancient enemy of France and to restore France to supremacy in Europe. He did not wish to see those infant States remain under

50. Franklin (Smyth ed.), VIII, 649, to Samuel Cooper.
51. Wharton, VI, 137. See below, pp. 141, 191–194.

the control of Britain. He wished to get them free and then to keep them "vigilant" and "uneasy," permanently under the protection and guidance of France.[52]

But the extent of the domain which the United States should have was an entirely separate question to Vergennes. The evidence is very strong indeed that Jay's suspicions were sound in regard to this matter. Gérard, under instructions from Vergennes to curb the American desire for Canada and the Floridas, had taken up and developed the case for Spain beyond the Appalachians. La Luzerne, his successor at Philadelphia, had contrived that final instructions to the American commissioners for peace should hold them under the supervision of the French Government. Montmorin in Madrid, although never giving any indication to Jay that France agreed with Spain on the point, nevertheless had admitted finally that Spain wished to modify American independence and to keep herself in position to mediate between Britain and the United States when they came to the general conference on peace. Gérard, Rayneval, and Vergennes himself all had supported the Spanish right to conquer British territory at the expense of American priorities based upon colonial charters, notwithstanding the fact that those priorities were assured by the spirit of the alliance between France and the United States.[53]

There is a loophole for France here. She was not obliged to guarantee until after the peace any conquests which the United States might make. But this strengthens the judgment that France, although renouncing for herself any portion of the British possessions on the North American continent and conceding the right of the United States to make conquests, insisted upon an equal right of conquest for Spain in the hope that the outcome of the competition for the Western country would be to the advantage of her European ally. It would be not only fair compensation to Spain for the risks which she had incurred in aiding France to humble Britain but also, for France, a powerful check upon the tendency of the American States to defy the rights and pretensions in the new world of all European powers, even those of their ally and benefactress. Vergennes was not overlooking the future interest of France when he wrote to Montmorin that he did not wish by a great deal to see the rising new republic get exclusive possession of the continent.[54]

52. See above, pp. 22–26.
53. See above, pp. 25–26, 54, 81–83.
54. See above, pp. 19–22, 73–78.

In any case, John Jay did not separate the American aims of independence and empire. He applied the principles of Thomas Paine's *Common Sense*. He saw to it that the United States should be as remote as then possible from the "wars and quarrels" of Europe. He may have erred in encouraging the British reconquest of the Floridas and the secret clause placing the northern boundary of West Florida at the line of the Yazoo if the Spaniards were not dispossessed. In the light of subsequent British activities, the risk was great. But subsequent events, too, were to prove that it had been worth taking in order to counteract the overtures of Rayneval to Shelburne in 1782. Britain's statesmen chose for the moment to leave the Floridas in Spanish hands so as to safeguard British interests elsewhere. When they came later to use the Floridas for their own purposes, they found that American pioneers were pouring into the Southwest and rapidly making the Gulf Coast untenable by any foreign power.[55]

It is true that Jay had missed a chance in the first days of September when Oswald received his second set of instructions from Townshend. Jay might then have pressed the Scot to disclose the whole of that letter and to negotiate a preliminary treaty upon that basis, before Rayneval got in touch with Shelburne, before the good news arrived in London from Gibraltar. It is possible that Oswald might then have made commitments to which Shelburne might have adhered later.

If such an agreement had followed Townshend's instructions verbatim, it would have said nothing about American rights to dry fish ashore; nor would it have acknowledged that the "Colonies" were the United States of America. But, to their advantage, it would have been silent also about their paying debts and compensating Loyalists, and it would have given them the territory above the Great Lakes from the St. Lawrence–Nipissing line westward to the source of the Mississippi.

The fact is, however, that Oswald did not reveal the whole of his letter from Townshend—as he had not revealed the contents of his memoranda from Shelburne in May to Franklin, nor his first instructions from Townshend in August to Franklin and Jay. And though it may be logical, it is not an inevitable conclusion that Shelburne would have adhered to such a treaty. He might not have done so—even if it had reached him before Vaughan arrived after Rayneval, to prove that the rift was widening between the French and the Americans, and before the news had come from Gibraltar,

55. See below, p. 548.

to relieve the British from having to make extreme concessions to the Americans in order to divert them from supporting extreme demands by the French and the Spaniards.[56]

After all of these things are considered duly, it would seem true to the facts to say that John Jay forced Great Britain to recognize the American States as one united nation—a significant achievement. And he as much or more than anyone else helped them to gain title to an imperial domain reaching from the Appalachians to the Mississippi and from the Great Lakes to the Floridas. He caused delay over what may look like technical details, and perhaps he lost an opportunity to acquire Upper Canada. But when we think of what might have been from Ontario to Huron, we should also think of what is from Michigan and Superior to the Mississippi and beyond.

It is not too much to declare that Jay's insistence upon American independence as a fact, his refusal to be directed by Vergennes, even his inaccurate appraisal of French motives, actually hastened the negotiations with the mother country to a practical conclusion in the fall of 1782—a conclusion which was highly advantageous to the United States of America. By encouraging the British ministry (already sympathetic with the American cause against their King) to exploit American distrust of France, John Jay eliminated the danger of a European agreement at that time such as Vergennes had in mind for keeping the young nation on the Atlantic Seaboard from expanding into "this whole immense continent."

56. Bemis, *Diplomacy of the American Revolution*, 212–213, 226–227.

V

CONFEDERATION OR SEPARATION

Title But Not Possession

THE American rebels had won. They were free from King and Parliament in London. They had their own governments and title to an imperial expanse beyond the Apalachian Mountains. But as we look back upon their situation from the relative security of our own time, it seems extremely precarious. There was little respect abroad for the United States as a nation. There was fear that they would become strong in the future. But there was scant belief then that the Confederation of American States had real power. And there was practically no confidence in the ministries of Europe that the American Government of 1783 could control internal affairs and meet the obligations of the States to the outside world at the same time.

Before the American leaders could expect favorable answers to their importunities abroad, they had first, as Franklin had observed in 1778, to put their own house in order. They had to establish authority over domestic issues, to turn undisciplined factiousness into the set channels of partisan effort, to erect a central government that could manage the affairs of the American people as a whole—if need be to the disappointment of local and sectional aims. When they could force obedience upon opposing factions, then only could they command the respect of foreign powers. For those powers would advance their own interests with little regard for the wishes of the American people until they were able to look out for themselves.[1]

France had stood by the American States until they got their independence; but that was what she had sought from the beginning for her own ends. Britain had formally acknowledged the success of their rebellion because she appreciated their worth as friends if they could not be retained as colonies; but she still held the military posts in the Northwest even though yielding claim to the soil. Spain had made her peace with Britain without recognizing American independence. France's effort to deny the American

1. Whitaker, *The Spanish-American Frontier*, is indispensable for this chapter. For Franklin's opinion, see above, p. 28.

claims in the Mississippi Valley had been stopped momentarily by the provisional treaty of 1782 transferring British title there to the United States. But the French interest in North America, even though officially renounced, was latent in the population of Quebec, Illinois, and Louisiana; and it was soon to rise again. And Spain, although seeming to acquiesce because she did not protest the northern boundary of West Florida as it was drawn in the Treaty of 1783, failed to do so only because she dared not delay the return of peace with Britain on that account.[2]

Negotiations with Spain—Dissension in Congress

SPAIN was in no way obligated to the United States by the Peace of Paris. Rather, she saw in the feebleness of their confederation opportunity for her own purposes east of the Mississippi. She would take under her protection the Creek, Chickasaw, Choctaw, and Cherokee Indians, natural enemies of the advancing American pioneers, and use them against those republicans to defend Louisiana, Florida, and Mexico. There were, besides, many Tories in the region who had cause enough to hate the patriots of Georgia. Outstanding was the half-breed chieftain of the Creeks, McGillivray, who by reason of his power among the Indians and his connections with merchants in London had sufficiently recouped his losses in the Revolution to live as well as any planter on tidewater. And means to accomplish Spain's purposes were at hand in the exchange of arms and supplies for furs.[3]

But there were weaknesses in Spain's own position. She herself did not have adequate sources of supply and facilities for trade. She would have to rely upon British goods and British trading companies in Florida. And, although she had the sea power to close the Gulf Coast to the United States, she could not close it to Britain if the British Government should decide to make the interests of her traders there a matter of national policy. In addition, American land companies, speculators, pioneers were forever pressing, scheming, dickering for new settlements regardless of Indian occupancy or Spanish claim. And so, the Government at Madrid tried also for an understanding with the American Congress in Philadelphia as Spanish officials on the frontier endeavored to hold the Indian area

2. The treaty between Britain and Spain made no mention of the independence of the United States. See Martens, *Receuil de Traités,* III, 541–553. Spanish recognition of the United States occurred when Charles III addressed Congress, September 25, 1784, in regard to the mission of Gardoqui. See Wharton, VI, 820, 824.

3. Whitaker, 37–39. *Can. Arch.* (Brymner ed.), 1890, xliii, 153. Pickett, *Alabama,* II, 30 ff.

against the American settlers, and probed the rumors that Americans of the "Western waters" might be persuaded, for certain considerations, to revolt from Eastern authority just as the Revolutionaries had thrown off King and Parliament. Gardoqui, with whom Jay had dealt so unsatisfactorily in Spain, came in 1785 to negotiate with him in New York upon instructions that might appeal to the maritime States of the Confederation.[4]

Gardoqui was not to open Spain's colonies to American commerce, but he might grant the privileges of the most favored nation in her home ports and in the Canary Islands. And he might arrange for a defensive alliance and reciprocal guarantees of territories such as Jay had offered so persistently in 1780–81. Had this been done, it might have obliged Spain to assist the United States in expelling the British from the posts of the Northwest.

In return for these concessions, however, Congress was to admit that the Spanish border on the east ran up the Flint River to its source, thence along a straight line to the Hiwasee, down that river and the Tennessee to the Ohio and down it to the Mississippi, thence up the Mississippi to British territory on the north. This line receded greatly from Aranda's ideas in 1782, but it still enveloped most of the Indian country in the Southwest, and it would have made the Mississippi a Spanish river as far to the north as the Ohio. Gardoqui was to keep the Mississippi closed to free navigation within Spanish territory. He might, however, let the Americans have St. Augustine in East Florida and he might alter the line in the Mississippi Valley somewhat.[5]

The Spaniards were really anxious now to have an understanding. But John Jay, who had returned to take Livingston's place as secretary of foreign affairs, was in a greater dilemma than he had been at Madrid when Congress had changed his instructions. He was caught between the interests of the seaboard and of the settlements beyond the Appalachians. And his situation was confused by the antagonism between the States having rights to Western lands from colonial charters and those which had none. To complicate it still more, Virginia reserved her "western counties," or Kentucky, when she ceded to the Confederation her claim to the lands north and west of the Ohio River. Accordingly, whereas Massachusetts was more concerned for her shipping than her Western lands, Virginia's interest now was distinctly less maritime than inland. The Mississippi river-system and outlets for Western produce were more important to her than the tobacco trade of her seaboard plan-

4. Whitaker, 33–46.
5. *Ibid.*, 68–72. See above, pp. 73–74.

tations, particularly since Spain restricted the importation of American tobacco. The most dangerous rift for Secretary Jay threatened to come, therefore, not between older communities on the seaboard and pioneering settlements in the back country, nor between States with Western claims and those with none, but between New England and Virginia which had been closely linked in revolt against their mother country. This gravely menaced the immediate fortune of the Confederation as well as the United States of the future.

After prolonged discussion with Gardoqui, and consultation with a special committee of Congress appointed at his request, consisting of Rufus King of Massachusetts, Charles Pettit of Pennsylvania, and James Monroe of Virginia, Secretary Jay submitted a plan on August 3, 1786, which he thought would best serve the whole Confederation. He should be authorized to negotiate a treaty setting the Spanish boundary along the thirty-first degree of latitude, as stipulated in the Treaty of 1783 with Britain, thus removing the Spanish claim from practically all the Indian territory south of the Tennessee River and west of the Flint. And Spain should agree to open her home ports and the Canary Islands to American shipping. In return, the United States would give reciprocal rights of trade in their ports and forbear using free navigation on the Mississippi for twenty-five or thirty years.[6]

Jay argued that such a commercial treaty with Spain at this time was of more importance, in respect to both politics and commerce, than any the United States had made or could make with any other nation. It would aid in holding France to the side of the United States, he said, for France was bound to Spain under the Family Compact. It would put a check upon Britain and her highly competitive shipping. And Spain, as a great consumer of American produce, would provide the gold and silver of which the United States had great need. Although he still believed, as he had in Madrid, that they should never surrender their right to the navigation of the Mississippi, he did not think that it was so important now. They could not enjoy its use immediately unless they fought for it, and they were not yet ready to make war: "Why therefore," Jay asked, "should we not (for a valuable Consideration too) consent to forbear to use what we know is not in our power to use?" They should consent, so that Spain would not join with Britain against them in the West.

The time was coming, as Jay had "often reminded" Gardoqui, when the Americans "would not submit to seeing a fine river flow before their doors without using it as a highway to the sea for the

6. *Journ. Cont. Cong.*, XXX, 323; XXXI, 467–484.

transportation of their productions." But this was not the time. Even if the "Spanish business" were removed, the situation of the United States would still be "seriously delicate" and "call for great circumspection both at home and abroad." Nor would this cease to be the case "until a vigorous National government be formed, and public Credit and confidence established." John Jay was anticipating the Constitutional Convention of 1787.[7]

But neither land speculators nor settlers chose to admit the distinction, if they saw it, which Secretary Jay had made between the use and the right of free navigation. On the motion of William Grayson of Virginia, Congress ordered Jay to submit without delay any information which he might have received concerning the sentiments of France in regard to "our right of Navigating the Mississippi" and the territorial claims of Spain "on the east side of the Mississippi." And Charles Pinckney of South Carolina addressed Congress at length on August 16 for the opposition, taking up Jay's argument point by point.[8]

Although conceding that an equal treaty of commerce with Spain would be more valuable than one with any other European nation except Portugal, Pinckney did not believe that the United States would gain much more than they already possessed, nor that the treaty really would be reciprocal. He declared that the New England States had a beneficial trade with Spain in fish, lumber, and other articles, whereas the great export crop of Virginia and Maryland, tobacco, was "expressly prohibited." And it was not necessary, in his opinion, to make such concessions to Spain in order to hold France to the side of the United States. France, if he understood her politics, was ambitious to be the "ruling power" in Europe, and was afraid of England. Therefore she would never risk a contest in which she would have to face both Great Britain and the United States, "merely to support Spain in the impolitic demand of shutting the Mississippi." And Britain was so interested in opening Spanish America to her own commerce, according to reports from John Adams in London, that "if any event should take place in which even a distant hope of accomplishing this object should offer," there could be "no doubt of her availing herself of it." Pinckney was confident that Britain would never take the side of Spain against the United States but would "importantly interfere in our favour." As for Spain's gold, the treaty proposed would give no advantage which the United States did not then enjoy.

Coming then to the right of navigation on the Mississippi, Pinck-

7. *Ibid.*, XXXI, 481, 484.
8. *Ibid.*, XXXI, 509–510, 935–948.

ney asserted that Congress had always considered the sale and disposal of the lands in the Western territory as the means for discharging the public debt. Their value depended upon the right to navigate the Mississippi. Emigration into that country had to have the support and protection of Congress. What would Congress do, he asked, if Britain made a similar request—that the United States forego the use of the Northwest and let her retain the posts and the fur trade for a given number of years? He doubted that members representing the States particularly interested would suppose themselves at liberty to assent without consulting their constituents. And yet one case was as strong as the other; the same policy should apply to both; for each involved the interest of the country as a whole. If they should not surrender their claim to the use of one, even though the British still held the posts, they should not surrender their claim to the use of the other, even though the Spaniards blocked the Mississippi:

> Is it not to be clearly seen by those who will see, that the policy of Spain, in thus inducing us to consent to a surrender of the navigation for a time is, that by having a clear and unincumbered right, she may use it for the purpose of separating the interest of the inhabitants of the western country entirely from us, and making it subservient to her own purposes? Will it not produce this? It will. Will it not give her influence the entire command of the numerous and extensive Indian tribes within this country? It will certainly have this effect. When once this right is ceded, no longer can the United States be viewed as the friend or parent of the new States, nor ought they to be considered in any other light, than in that of their oppressors.

Pinckney therefore would make no treaty at all with Spain at this time. But he agreed with Jay that the Government was "feeble and unoperative." Congress should have additional powers. Without them, said Pinckney, "we cannot exist as a nation." He too feared separation in the Union and looked forward to the Constitutional Convention of 1787.[9]

But James Monroe of Virginia took a quite different course in opposition. He had been chairman of the committee which had instructed the secretary on August 25, 1785, to make no treaty with Spain which did not acknowledge the territorial bounds and the right of navigating the Mississippi as stipulated in the Treaty of 1783 with Britain. In the following December Monroe learned from Jay himself that he had agreed with Gardoqui to subordinate the question of the Mississippi in their negotiations and that Jay

9. *Ibid.*, XXXI, 945, 948. For Pinckney's comment to President Washington, December 14, 1789, see Washington (Ford ed.), XI, 463 n.

wished to forego using the Mississippi for a period of twenty-five or thirty years in order to arrange advantageous commercial terms. This was frank. But when Jay asked Congress in May, 1786, for another committee to "instruct and direct" him, Monroe had written to James Madison as if there were something surprising and underhanded in the request. He talked of the "folly of our councils," the "vice of those who govern them in many instances," and criticized his fellows on the committee in particular. Pettit of Pennsylvania, he said, was a "speculator in certificates" with "impressions entirely Eastern" and an opinion that Virginia wished "to defraud the publick creditors." As for King of Massachusetts, he "hath married a woman of fortune in N. Y. so that if he secures a market for fish and turns the commerce of the Western country down this river he obtains his object." (Monroe too had just married a New Yorker; but his own "object" was not a "market for fish.") By June 16, Monroe had become "perfectly satisfied" that Secretary Jay "required no arguments to bring him into the same sentiment" with Gardoqui. And on July 16, Monroe had written to Thomas Jefferson: "I have a conviction in my own mind that Jay has manag'd this negociation dishonestly."[10]

Now, as it came before Congress in spite of his opposition, James Monroe poured out his feelings on August 12 to Patrick Henry, Governor of Virginia. Jay, said he, had long been "intriguing with the members" to get a commercial treaty with Spain first: "We found he had engaged the eastern states in the intrigue, especially Mass:, that New York, Jersey & Pena. were in favor of it & either absolutely decided or so much so as to promise little prospect of change." It was "one of the most extraordinary transactions" that he had ever known, "a minister negotiating expressly for the purpose of defeating the object of his instructions, and by a long train of intrigue & management seducing the representatives of the states to concur in it."

Jay's treachery was not the only "subject of consequence" which Monroe would call to Patrick Henry's attention. He was certain that "committees are held in this town of Eastern men and others of this State upon the subject of a dismemberment of the States east of the Hudson from the Union & the erection of them into a separate govt." In conversations where he had been present, he declared, he had heard Eastern people talk of including Pennsylvania, and sometimes, all the States down to the Potomac. What was the object of closing the Mississippi? It was, asserted Monroe, to break up the

10. *Journ. Cont. Cong.*, XXIX, 657–658. Monroe (Hamilton ed.), I, 131, 134–135, 137, 141. Monroe was attending Congress in New York at the time.

settlements on the "western waters, prevent any in future, and thereby keep the States southward as they now are—or if settlements will take place, that they shall be on such principles as to make it the interest of the people to separate from the Confederacy, so as effectually to exclude any new State from it."

These "Eastern people" wanted, he said, to keep the population in the East so as to "appreciate the vacand lands of New York & Massachusetts": "In short, it is a system of policy which has for its object the keeping the weight of govt & population in this quarter, & is prepared by a set of men so flagitious, unprincipled & determined in their pursuits, as to satisfy me beyond a doubt they have extended their views to the dismemberment of the govt. . . ." This was surprising commentary from a person who was at the same moment working up a "little plan" for himself, Madison, and their friend Jefferson in the lands along the Mohawk. But those who are swift in accrediting motives to others often are not thoroughly conversant with their own.[11]

What James Monroe himself was thinking about the preservation of the Union at this time appears in a letter to James Madison on September 3. Whereas there were but five States, from Maryland to Georgia, in opposition, there were seven States, from New Hampshire to Pennsylvania, supporting Jay's plan. (Delaware's representatives were absent.) Monroe worried about Pennsylvania. "A knowledge that she was on our side wo.ᵈ blow this whole intrigue in the air," said he; it was in the "Southern interest" to get Pennsylvania; if "dismemberment" occurred, Pennsylvania must not go to the East: "I have always considered the regulation of trade in the hands of the U.S.," he declared, "as necessary to preserve the Union. Without it, it will infallibly fall to pieces. But I earnestly wish the admission of a few additional States into the Confederacy in the Southern scale." That is, the central Government ought to have control of trade, but the Southern States must control the central Government, or else the Union could not be preserved. This future President of the United States was provincial, and young, and destined to remain so for some time to come.[12]

Whether or not the "Eastern people" were as villainous as James Monroe imagined, John Jay was cleared of his charges—by Monroe's own statements to Governor Henry. It was not dishonest to inform, in December, the chairman of the committee which had given you

11. *Ibid.*, I, 120, 139, 144–150, 169. To Jefferson, October 12, 1786. See also Madison (Hunt ed.), II, 231–233 and 257–268 at 265. To Jefferson, August 12, 1786. According to Madison's editor (II, 232 n.), Jefferson did not join in the enterprise.

12. Monroe (Hamilton ed.), I, 163. See below, pp. 178, 228–244, 529–542.

instructions in August, that you could not complete the negotiations upon the basis of those instructions. It was not underhanded
to explain to him the course which you were pursuing apart from
those instructions toward an eventual arrangement with Gardoqui.
Congress would still have the power to reject as well as to accept
the results of those negotiations.

Nor was it furtive to ask later in May that Congress should appoint another committee to instruct and direct you and that the
matter should be kept secret so that foreigners resident about Congress, particularly English and French, might not interfere. Jay
had only to recall the efforts of Gérard when he himself had been
presiding officer of Congress in 1779, and the subsequent activities
of La Luzerne, to value the aid of secrecy while formulating a national policy. But the fact is that Jay did not keep it secret from his
opposition in Congress. James Monroe himself was a member of the
new committee with which he consulted.[13]

As for the charge that Secretary Jay was busy lining up votes
in Congress for his plan, the answer is: No doubt he was doing so
—just as were Monroe, Pinckney, Grayson, and those on the other
side of the issue. But such procedure is not customarily considered
treason to a deliberative assembly, except in the minds of such as
James Monroe.

In any case, John Jay had submitted his plan openly and fully
to Congress before James Monroe had written to Patrick Henry.
This plan was to hold in suspense the right to navigation on the
Mississippi in order that they might maintain the international balance there while the older communities on the Atlantic Seaboard
brought their economy out of colonial conditions, particularly their
foreign trade, and strengthened their Union with a "vigorous National government." And, as ordered by Congress, he reported on
August 17 concerning the Spanish claim to territory east of the
Mississippi and the attitude of France toward American navigation
of the river.

Jay reviewed Aranda's attempt to draw the boundary close to
the Appalachians and the Great Lakes, and pointed out that Gardoqui was asking for much less now. He cited the efforts of Gérard,
La Luzerne, and Rayneval to support his opinion that France would
not admit the American right of navigation. And he referred to a
recent letter from Jefferson, who had taken Franklin's place in
Paris, as indicating that Vergennes would not consider this right
"within their Guarantee" under the terms of the Alliance of 1778
and the Treaty of 1783.

13. See above, pp. 29–33.

Jefferson had written, May 23, that he had sounded Vergennes on the obligation of France to guarantee the boundaries of the United States. They were discussing the fact that Britain was retaining the posts in the Northwest. Vergennes had said, of course, that the United States could always count upon the friendship of France; but he had added, significantly, that it would be necessary for them to "verify" those boundaries. Jefferson had answered that there was no question what those boundaries were, for the British had admitted that they were clear; but he had not pressed the question further, he said, "lest a reciprocal question should be put to me." Jefferson was thinking of the American guarantee in the French West Indies. But Jay construed this episode to mean that France would uphold Spain's argument against the United States on the Mississippi as her ministers had supported Aranda in regard to the boundary of the Southwest.[14]

Jay's explanations, however, did not change the alignment of the States in Congress. The committee of the whole reported his plan favorably on August 23, leaving blank the number of years during which the United States should forbear using the navigation of the Mississippi. But the representatives of the five Southern States, led by Charles Pinckney, still fought day after day for more than a month trying to convince the majority, led by Rufus King, that they should not allow their secretary of foreign affairs to proceed. The Southerners insisted that, under the Articles of Confederation, such a matter of policy could not be initiated by a simple majority in Congress. It had to have, they argued, the approval of nine of the thirteen States. They would not rely upon the provision in the Articles that no treaty could become binding upon the Confederation until it had the consent of nine States. And so Secretary Jay, even though he had the majority with him and legally could have pressed the negotiations toward the kind of a treaty which he had suggested, wisely never brought the matter to a decision. The opposition was too vehement and ominous.[15]

The Virginians, George Washington and James Madison, had not allowed their dissenting views regarding the navigation of the Mississippi to affect their agreement with Jay that a "vigorous National government" was necessary to the Union. But Patrick Henry was aroused by Monroe's suspicions of New Englanders and concerned for his own speculations in the lands of the Southwest. He alarmed his friends in Kentucky about the closure of the Mississippi and

14. *Journ. Cont. Cong.*, XXXI, 537–552. Jefferson (Ford ed.), IV, 229.
15. *Journ. Cont. Cong.*, XXXI, 554, 565 ff. See Articles of Confederation, Art. IX, para. 6.

opposed the new Constitution largely on that account, referring to it again and again in the debates of the Virginia convention: "This new constitution," he declared, "will involve in its operation the loss of the navigation of that valuable river. . . . If Congress should, for a base purpose, give away this dearest right of the people, your Western brethren will be ruined. . . . To preserve the balance of American power it is essentially necessary that the right to the Mississippi should be secured."[16]

Many of these "Western brethren" were threatening in fact to go much farther than Patrick Henry, if Congress did not match their eagerness with an ultimatum to Spain. They would quicken their departure from the States on the Atlantic and separate altogether. They might create another confederacy in the Mississippi Valley, independent perhaps, more likely under the control of Spain, but divorced at least from the Union of the seaboard. Charles Pinckney believed that they would separate if the Mississippi were closed as Jay suggested. Rufus King thought that they would if it were not. But John Jay, as he had at the end of his mission to Spain in 1782, sagaciously marked time and waited for stronger federal authority under the Constitution.[17]

Meanwhile the Spanish Government had decided to change its policy again. The aggressiveness of the American frontiersmen was as disquieting to Spain as to the Confederation. And there was always in Spain the fear that Great Britain would meddle with her colonies if given the slightest chance. Floridablanca proposed to avoid these dangers in three different ways. He might win over the American Congress with further concessions. Gardoqui was therefore instructed on September 5, 1787, to agree that the southern boundary of the United States should be, as Jay maintained in accordance with the Treaty of 1783, at the thirty-first parallel of latitude excepting the district of Natchez, which should be kept by Spain. Spain would thus drop her claim to exclusive jurisdiction over the Indians in the Alabama country; and she would accept a joint commission to determine the validity of the American right to free navigation of the Mississippi. But at the same time, Florida-

16. Washington (Ford ed.), XI, 41–42, 76–79. Correspondence with Henry Lee, June 18, October 31, 1786. For Lee's replies, see footnotes there. Madison (Hunt ed.), II, 253–256, to Monroe, June 21, 1786; 257–267, to Jefferson, August 12, 1786. For Madison's exoneration of Jay in the Virginia convention of 1788, see *ibid.*, V, 179–184. Henry (Henry ed.), III, 350, 351, 374–377, 379–380, 463–464, 475, 507, 518, 521, 522, 524–525. Whitaker, 49.

17. *Journ. Cont. Cong.*, XXXI, 944–945. Pinckney's Speech of August 16, 1786, is also to be found in AHR, X, 817–827. King (King ed.), I, 175–179. King to Gerry, June 4, 1786.

blanca looked further into the hints from James Wilkinson and others that a Spanish party might be fostered in Kentucky, and perhaps in the settlements on the Cumberland and the Tennessee southward, to rebel against Congress. As still another possibility, if either or both of these ways should fail, Spain might welcome the American pioneers and incorporate them in a growing province of her own behind the barriers of the civilized Indian nations and the Mississippi River.[18]

All three ways failed. Those immigrants who came into Spanish territory remained American in thought and behavior, resenting the petty despotism of local officials and clamoring for their rights of democracy and religion—their own conceptions of liberty. They would not incorporate themselves into the Spanish system. The faction headed by Wilkinson did not grow strong and lead the West on to a Spanish destiny. It succeeded only in keeping Kentucky uncertain. Wilkinson himself, though greedy for pay from Spain, was in the last moment of decision, during the famous conspiracy of Aaron Burr in 1806, an American. And Floridablanca's revised plan for a treaty was stopped by the very weakness of Congress, divided between East and South, seven States to five, with Delaware "absent."

Any hope that the rifts in the American Confederation would widen to impotent rivalries, however, was vain. Spain's opportunity faded as Gardoqui lingered in New York while Secretary Jay marked time. Instead of separating into two or more little confederacies subject to dictation from Britain, France, or Spain, the States were binding themselves more closely under a new federal authority of increasing power. Although geographic barriers, climate, economic circumstance might alter the American character beyond the Appalachians, change it greatly from that of the older communities on the Atlantic, they could never make it Spanish. Once those "men of the Western waters" got an effective voice in the Federal Government for their own interests, there was no chance that they themselves would break the Union, least of all to please some foreign power.[19]

British Desire

BRITAIN was far more dangerous to the United States than Spain, as they sought their place among independent nations, their rights in the Mississippi Valley, their share in the commerce of the world. John Adams went on from the peace negotiations at Paris to be

18. Whitaker, 80–85, 102–107.
19. See below, pp. 458–461, 468–470.

the first American minister to Britain. He obtained an audience with the King. How gratifying it must have been to stand before George III, representing in person the success of the Revolution! For Adams had been one of the most determined advocates of independence and no reconciliation with the mother country. We may let imagination play too upon inner thoughts of George III which have never been recorded in memoir or biography. But when Adams got to the real business for which he had come to London—the Northwest ports, compensation for the slaves which had been taken away with the British forces, the fisheries, and reciprocal agreements for shipping and goods—he met stubborn questions about those old American debts to British merchants and about compensation for the Loyalists, so many of whom now were refugees in England.[20]

Adams could make no headway against these obstacles. The truth was very near Jay's statement to him, November 1, 1786, that not a day had passed since the Treaty of 1783 on which some one of the States had not violated the fourth article stipulating that no legal impediment should be put in the way of the collection of bona fide debts. It was clear that no state legislature would consider any general plan for reimbursing Loyalists. It was equally clear that neither would Pitt come to terms with Adams. British shipowners would not care to see American merchantmen in English ports and the West Indies, nor would British shipbuilders welcome the sales of American vessels. British fur traders would prefer to have British troops protect them and look after the British obligations by treaty to the Indians of western New York and the Ohio country. And Pitt himself was soon, if not then, thinking of the British future in the Mississippi Valley, from the Great Lakes to the Gulf of Mexico, which Jay had portrayed for Shelburne in 1782 from quite a different point of view.[21]

It may have been wise for John Adams to stay in London as long as he did, merely to keep pressure upon the British Government. But there was no chance of his accomplishing anything else. His conference with William Pitt, however candid and engaging, had no tangible results. He was snubbed by the King after a time, and courtiers readily followed the royal example. The Government slighted his mission by failing to extend the same courtesy of appointing a minister to the United States. The British would not yield their immediate advantages of commerce and geographic position in America for the sake of other possibilities in the future.

20. See above, pp. 9–10, 91–93.
21. Jay, *Jay*, II, 191. Pellew, 240. See above, pp. 83–84, and below, pp. 135–136.

Why should they admit American shipping into competition with their own in British ports when, without doing so, they could obtain everything from America which they desired? Why defer to a union which was not actual? It was self-evident that Congress could negotiate no treaty of commerce which would bind the several States. These realities have been fixed in the legend that, when Adams announced himself as the minister from the United States, he was asked where were the other twelve. Irritated by his failure, he requested in 1787 that he be recalled, and on April 20, 1788, he returned to America. Any agreement with Britain would have to come at a later date and, it was to be hoped, out of more favorable conditions.[22]

Until these should appear, Secretary Jay urged that Congress should not make public Adams' remarks in his despatches of November and December, 1785, about the growing trade of the United States with the Orient—"lest it encrease the Jealousy," said Jay, with which those "Adventures" had already "inspired the Nations trading thither." Congress, he declared, could do nothing about "the restrictive and unfriendly System of Trade with Respect to America" for the moment. They could only recommend to the States. They had better not try even to do that—"lest non Compliance should diminish their Respectability, and impair the little Authority they possess." Britain would keep the Northwest posts, said Jay, "on Pretence of the Treaty of Peace having been violated by american Acts relative to british Debts and the Tories," and he warned Congress: "On this Point your Secretary can only repeat what has been suggested in other Reports viz.ᵗ, that what wrong may have been done, should be undone; and that the United States should, if it were only to preserve Peace, be prepared for War."[23]

It would have been good on general principles, for the sake of peace, to undo whatever wrongs had been done to British creditors and Tories. But it was much shrewder advice to get ready at once for war in the back country. For General Haldimand, Governor of Canada, had appreciated what the provisional treaty of November, 1782, would do to the fur trade by admitting Americans to the navigation of the Great Lakes and the portages west of Lake Superior. He knew how fiercely the Iroquois and their dependent tribes

22. Adams, *Works*, VIII, 240, 274, 302. For French comment upon British control over American commerce, see Bancroft (1882 ed.), II, 412, Otto to Vergennes, February 16, 1787. For the Jay Treaty of 1794, see below, pp. 184, 190–191.

23. *Journ. Cont. Cong.*, XXX, 243–244. May 8, 1786. For Adams' despatches of November 11 and December 3, 1785, see *Works*, VIII, 343, 350.

would resent the cession of the Ohio country which had been recognized as their own territory by the Treaty of Fort Stanwix in 1768. Haldimand had decided even before the definitive treaty of September, 1783, that Britain should not carry out those agreements if some excuse could be found for evading them; and by July, 1784, he had found it in the American treatment of the Loyalists. This was his "private opinion," so he told the American, Colonel Hull, who had come to arrange for the British evacuation of the posts on American soil. But it is almost certain that Haldimand had received the despatch from Lord Sydney in Pitt's cabinet, dated April 8, 1784, which ordered that the evacuation should be delayed on the ground that the United States had not "complied with even one article of the treaty." This procedure had been determined in London before the King had proclaimed the ratification of the Treaty of 1783, before the actions of the several American state legislatures had really begun to give provocation for doing so.[24]

Then Major Beckwith had come to the United States to observe and report to Haldimand's successor in Quebec, Lord Dorchester, who relayed the information to Sydney in London. There was general "contempt" for the Confederation, said Beckwith, but he did not believe that the convention at Philadelphia would draft any plan which would be approved by Congress or afterwards by the state legislatures. He thought at first that George Washington would not attend the convention, nor return to public life. And he suspected later that Washington had a "french bias." He was wrong about Washington and the Constitution. But he did observe the rapid migration to Kentucky and the Northwest Territory and remarked shrewdly that these people were friendly toward Britain. They were not averse to trading furs for British manufactures in Canada, he said, rather than by way of the Eastern States. He thought that the peculiar situation of Vermont—claimed by New York and denied admission into the Confederation—would be affected by the new "national government," very likely to the advantage of Britain. For the Vermonters "seemed determined to remain in their present unconnected situation." As Dorchester was dealing with Levi Allen at the time, this was significant comment. But Beckwith also noted that the retention of the Western posts was exciting passions not entirely to Britain's advantage.[25]

24. Bemis, *Jay's Treaty*, 4–11. Farrand, "The Indian Boundary Line," AHR, X, 787–788. McLaughlin, "Western Posts and British Debts," AHAR, 1894, 416–417.

25. *Can. Arch.* (Brymner ed.), 1890, 97–99, 101–106, 132 (State Papers), 188, 190. Bemis, "Vermont Separatists," AHR, XXI, 547–550. See also regarding Allen in London, AHR, VIII, 78–86.

Another report to Dorchester, from Detroit in June, 1788, told of the stir beyond the mountain passes in and about Pittsburgh whence the pioneers were moving down the Ohio to Kentucky and the Northwest Territory. The Kentuckians, said this agent, were inclined "to wish for Independency" and navigation of the Mississippi, apparently unwilling to wait for the "new proposed federal government." And the "adventurers" into the Northwest, he thought, might "prove favourable towards a harmonious understanding in point of Commercial interest between Great Britain and these rising settlements." He had already "received advances" from a certain General Parsons who was connected with the enterprise on the Muskingum River, and he had "strongest invitations" to go to Fort Pitt. What was Lord Dorchester's pleasure in these matters?[26]

The evidence is circumstantial, but it is clear, as to what Dorchester and his superior, Lord Sydney, in London desired. There was much that could be done for Britain among the pioneers in western Pennsylvania, Kentucky, and the Northwest. The Indians, too, were worth keeping in mind, and not merely as persons to whom the British Government had obligations by treaty concerning their ancestral lands. Lord Sydney was not sure that Britain should give "active assistance" just then. It might be "a measure extremely imprudent. . . . But at the same time," said he, "it would not become us to refuse them such supplies of ammunition as might enable them to defend themselves." He instructed Dorchester on April 5, 1787: "There cannot be any objection to your furnishing them with a supply, causing it to be done in a way the least likely to alarm the Americans or to induce the Indians to think that there is a disposition on our part to incite them to any hostile proceedings." Possibly Lord Dorchester did not "induce" them. But is it any wonder that, as the agent reported from Detroit, "Mr. McKee" on the Miamis River thereafter seemed "to possess an entire influence over the minds of the Western Tribes?"[27]

Far from restrained by official hesitance in London about starting military action on the American frontier, Dorchester felt encouraged to write to Sydney on August 27, 1789: "My Lord—The growing importance of the country west of the Apalachian mountains, requires that I should transmit to Your Lordship every material information respecting it." He "therefore" sent a "plan of the Colony of Kentucky," discussing its terrain, its distances, the loca-

26. Brymner, 99–100.
27. Bancroft (1882 ed.), II, 416. Brymner, 100.

tion of its settlements. He told the number of its inhabitants— sixty-two thousand according to a census taken in 1788—and described them as "soldiers and husbandmen." He estimated its available "militia" at ten thousand. He named leading citizens. He spoke of the eight hundred "congressional" troops under Harmar and their equipment. He said that the fortunes of western Pennsylvania and Virginia seemed to be inseparable from Kentucky. And he looked beyond to New Orleans which, said he, "must become, at no distant period, the great emporium of North America, and therefore highly worthy of the marked attention of the British Government, as a commercial and manufacturing kingdom." John Jay indeed was not stupid when he warned Congress to "be prepared for War," and favored a plan for the Mississippi which he thought would keep Spain from coöperating with Britain.[28]

French Ambition

THERE was greater peril from the French, too, than John Jay and Thomas Jefferson could have discerned in Vergennes' remark that the United States would have to "verify" their boundaries before France undertook to guarantee them. France had not reduced Britain's sea power. She had failed to get Gibraltar and Jamaica for Spain. But Spain had received Minorca in the Mediterranean and the Floridas along the Gulf of Mexico. And France had her West Indies again. Vergennes clung to the Family Compact and hope of restoring French dominance in Europe. For that purpose, those islands were to be closely interlocked with France. Only such traffic in produce from the United States should be permitted as they had to have. France would monopolize the rest of their commerce for her own shipping and goods in the best mercantilist manner. For the same purpose, Vergennes leaned to the side of Spain in America. Whatever made the Spanish King anxious there might weaken his devotion to his nephew in Europe. Besides, as Vergennes had said, France herself could not wish to see the United States appropriate the continent.[29]

France was in position still to take an active part in American affairs, against the interests of the United States if she chose. And it was likely that her ministers would so choose. As the Americans now had their "independence," they could look after it for themselves, provided they did not join with the British in doing so, or

28. *Ibid.*, 118.
29. See above, p. 26. For commentary upon the commercial policy of the "old régime" in its last, or liberal, phase, see Nussbaum, 11–36.

Britain did not try to take advantage of them. If otherwise they did not get on well, or quarreled among themselves, France would not care. On the contrary she would be rather pleased.

Of such a nature were the advices on August 30, 1787, from the cabinet at Versailles to Otto, chargé d'affaires in Philadelphia. Vergennes had died earlier in the year, but Montmorin had taken his place and there was no change of policy as yet with regard to these matters. Otto had suggested that in case of war France should seize Newport and New York to keep Britain from retaking those seaports. Montmorin replied:

> It appears, sir, that in all the American provinces there is more or less tendency towards democracy; that in many this extreme form of government will finally prevail. The result will be that the confederation will have little stability, and that by degrees the different states will subsist in perfect independence of each other. This revolution will not be regretted by us. We have never pretended to make of America a useful ally; we have no other object than to deprive Great Britain of that vast continent. Therefore, we can regard with indifference both the movements which agitate certain provinces and the fermentation which prevails in congress . . .

But as for their quarrel with Spain:

> I fear that the discussions in regard to the Mississippi will become serious, and that they will become embarrassing for us. Spain may misapprehend her interest; but that does not give the Americans the right to employ force against that power. The mouth of the Mississippi belongs to her; she has therefore the right to open it or keep it closed, and the Americans can obtain special favors only by means of negotiation. The court of Madrid would not be difficult to gain over if it had the same principles as ours in this matter.[30]

What were these differences of principle? Montmorin doubtless had in mind that France had relaxed her mercantilist theories in the West Indies, and was contemplating further concessions to American ships and goods in France also, whereas Gardoqui could not open the Spanish colonial ports to American commerce. But France had done so of necessity—to supply her islands with foodstuffs and other materials which she could not effectively provide, and not from any change of principle in regard to monopolizing her colonial possessions.[31]

As for principles involving the Mississippi, neither would the Spaniards have any regrets if "revolution" should dissolve the

30. Corwin, 358. Bancroft (1882 ed.), II, 438.
31. See below, pp. 122–123, 170.

American Confederation. Montmorin had got quickly out of touch with Spanish intentions since returning from Madrid if he believed that the orders to Gardoqui for negotiating a treaty with Jay in New York contained the only purpose of the Spanish Government. Or else, Montmorin was just writing diplomatic verbiage for Otto to soothe Jay while he kept the real contents of this despatch to himself. Whatever may have been the case, the French cabinet was far from taking a coöperative and friendly interest in the American ally as it struggled with its internal politics and its controversy with Spain over the Southwestern boundary and the navigation of the Mississippi.

John Jay sensed this fully and made an argument accordingly to Moustier, the new minister from France, that the alliance no longer subsisted. But this was going too fast and too far for Montmorin. He replied through Moustier on June 23, 1788, that the King and his council were "singularly astonished" at Jay's opinion. Jay had forgotten the terms in which the alliance had been conceived; he should reread the Treaty of 1778 and convince himself that it was perpetual. Moustier should assure him that the King regarded his alliance with the United States as "inalterable."[32]

Even so, both parties had abandoned their alliance for all practical purposes, it is fair to say, as soon as they had reached their common objective in American independence from Great Britain. Montmorin was but shrewdly holding on to what little remained of the old agreement, not to fulfill obligations to the United States, but for possible benefits to France. A new constitution for the American Union was now before the States. If it were adopted, who could foretell what effect it would have upon the foreign relationships as well as the domestic affairs of the American people?

There were Louisiana and the port of New Orleans, very much on the minds of all parties. Rumors were abroad in America that the province was going back to France, that Spain would receive a French possession elsewhere in return. Jay had inquired of Otto, and he had reported to Vergennes on April 23, 1786. Vergennes had replied, August 25, that there had never been any question of exchanging French possessions in the West Indies for Louisiana. "And, if it is again mentioned to you," said he, "you will formally deny it."[33]

This was precise. In fact, it was too precise. Vergennes could say it with absolute sincerity and still leave room for the retrocession

32. Corresp. Moustier and Montmorin, AHR, VIII, 728.
33. Bancroft (1882 ed.), II, 387. Lyon, 60, 66. Villiers du Terrage, 371. Fletcher, 375 n.

of Louisiana. France had other holdings besides her West Indies. There was Guiana on the coast of South America. And there were Dutch and British possessions in or near the Caribbean also, which Spain might prefer to Louisiana in accordance with her mercantilist ideas about colonies, and for which an international bargain working three ways might be arranged—with no respect for the United States. In view of such opinions as Lord Dorchester's regarding New Orleans, and the activities of British trading companies in the Floridas, it perhaps was not likely that Britain would enter into any bargain which gave Louisiana back to France. But the same could not be said of the Netherlands.[34]

Vergennes' denial that France would trade her West Indies for Louisiana did not mean that she did not want Louisiana. Those islands, particularly San Domingo, were held essential to her system in Europe. It was easy therefore to declare that they would not be exchanged for anything else. But Louisiana was desirable, too, for the very fact that its produce would release those islands from dependence upon the United States for supplies. With this in mind, we cannot say that France would not have exchanged Guiana or some other territorial pawn for Louisiana, even though Vergennes did leave the impression that she had no designs upon Louisiana at that time.[35]

Was France, as Vergennes seemed to declare, not interested in the American hemisphere beyond her West Indies? Was she merely concerned now with developing her commerce and maintaining the balance of power as it was—for the advantage of Spain and to check the growth of the United States? There is other evidence which may not be ignored.

The people of France had not particularly regretted the cession to Spain in 1762. But there had been great dissatisfaction in Louisiana, even rebellion against Spanish rule; and agents of the province had secretly approached the French minister at Philadelphia since 1779 asking that it be recovered. France had surrendered to Britain. But Frenchmen had been left behind to dream of the future in America. The Creoles of Lower Louisiana, devoted to the commerce and social life of New Orleans, the inhabitants of St. Louis and the Illinois country above the Ohio, individual planters, traders, trappers scattered here and there throughout Spanish provinces and Western districts of the United States thought and talked, hoped and despaired, of the day when France might return to the Mississippi Valley. The interest of France remained alive notwith-

34. See above, pp. 114–115.
35. Lyon, 54, 59–60. Fletcher, 368–369, 375.

standing the fact that she had solemnly renounced in favor of the United States all claims to the territory east of the Mississippi save New Orleans, and Vergennes had adhered with nicety to the pledges of the American alliance. Her statesmen in Europe might officially deny specific plans for the redisposing of North America, whatever may or may not have been their inner reservations or ulterior purposes, but officials in America caught the spirit of her people. And Moustier was soon to pour it into the minds of those who followed Vergennes in the foreign office at Paris.[36]

Was it not in Vergennes' thoughts, too, before his death? He had supported the claims of Spain east of the Mississippi. His secretary, Rayneval, had so presented them in 1782 that John Jay, for one, had been convinced that France was seeking to confine the United States within the Appalachians. Was this not done for the ultimate benefit of France?[37]

The famous *mémoire* pointing to this conclusion—alleged to have been found among Vergennes' papers, and written in 1778 when he made the alliance with Franklin—has been proved a fabrication of 1802. Presumably it was intended to supply Napoleon with a document which would show that he was carrying out the policy of the Bourbons, whereas, in reality, he was completing the American policy of the Girondist revolutionaries and their successor, Talleyrand, by that time his own minister of foreign affairs. Doubt has also been raised that Bourgoing, French representative at Madrid in 1790, sought officially to get Louisiana back for France. This doubt rests upon the facts that the French historian, Sorel, who made the statement, cited no sources for his information, and that a search among the papers in the French archives has revealed no document to support it.[38]

The continuity of French official policy, however, is not the same thing as the continuance of French interest in the Mississippi Valley. There is no doubt that Frenchmen in America retained desires bordering close upon expectations. It may as well have been that Frenchmen in France, Vergennes himself, regardless of breaks in policy announced for reasons of state, still lived on hoping for the return of France to empire in North America. Otto thought Vergennes sufficiently interested to hear of the rumors in America and Jay's inquiry about them. Vergennes' reply does not neces-

36. Lyon, 34–35, citing Renaut, 53–57. *Ibid.*, 45–54, 66. Dr. Howard Rice has given me much information on the French in the Mississippi Valley. See his *Barthélemi Tardiveau, A French Trader in the West*.
37. See above, pp. 74, 77–78.
38. Corwin, 9–13 n. Phillips, 30–32. Fletcher, 369.

sarily have to be interpreted as a disclaimer of interest in Louisiana on the part of France. It would have been more convincing if it had been less punctilious.

It is uncertain historical technique to conclude from silences that a positive policy lurks behind them. But that is no worse than to overlook the fact that they are often significant. Vergennes would hardly have wished to inform the party of opposing interest that there might be an international exchange of territories to its disadvantage. If he were anxious to get back Louisiana, certainly he would not wish to tell Jay before he had prevailed upon the Spanish Government to accept his offer. In the absence of definite proof that there was no such plan and that Vergennes had abandoned Louisiana forever—proof which will bear scrutiny for evidence unconsciously submitted by him—historians have no right to assume that he had less thought than any other Frenchman of France returning some day to Louisiana. The proof that the famous mémoire was a forgery in Napoleon's time and Vergennes' reply to Otto in 1786 are not sufficient grounds for such an assumption.

If, nevertheless, Vergennes himself did intend that his statement to Otto should be a sweeping disclaimer, it did not discourage the new minister at Philadelphia, Moustier, from taking up with the yearnings and ambitions of Frenchmen in America. Gathering in all the information he could obtain from every source, Moustier sent a voluminous report to Montmorin on March 10, 1789. It ran to more than three hundred pages carefully describing the geography of the Mississippi Valley; its economic future; the location and character of its settlements; the strategic importance of the Florida Coast; the reasons why Spain could be induced to return the country to France—chiefly so that the remainder of Spanish America might be protected from the frontiersmen of the United States; the key position of New Orleans near the mouth of the great river and close to other inlets from the sea, controlling the whole valley and providing the materials of life to free San Domingo and other French West Indies from dependence upon the Atlantic States; the likelihood that the men of the Western States would prefer French to Spanish authority in the mid-continent and might even be enticed into separating their country from the States east of the Appalachians. And finally, Moustier advanced the powerful argument that if France were not forehanded in redeeming her people and their possessions, either Britain or the United States or both would oust Spain and take the Mississippi Valley for themselves.[39]

This was looking into the future with keenest appreciation of

39. AAE CP EU Sup. 6, No. 33. Photocopy in Library of Congress.

coming realities. Moustier saw that whatever power won the great prize would have to break sharply with the statesmanship of the past. No mercantilist system would suffice. France should not attempt simply to restore the old régime of strong mother and feeble child. France, no more than Spain, could expect thus to hold a continental area in the Western Hemisphere against either British or American competition. Britain's strength upon the sea and possession of Canada close by gave her special advantages over France and Spain. The United States did not then have the naval strength of Britain, to be sure, but they were a maritime nation; they had potentiality upon the sea not to be disregarded; they had the materials and markets which the inhabitants of the mid-continent needed or desired as much as those of any other countries; and above all, the United States had the greatest advantages of immediate adjacency to the coveted valley and a restless people who were already crowding forward to take it.

If France were to regain her power in North America, she would have to supplant Spain at once along the Mississippi, welcome settlers into her domain with little concern as to their origins, accelerate the development of their economic enterprises, and create a populous, strong, and self-supporting inland state which would stand off Britain on the north and the United States on the east, preferably at the passes in the mountains, and look to France in Europe for its government. We may not assume from the tenor of Moustier's arguments that he peered so far into the future as to see an autonomous French state in the mid-continent, bound to France in Europe only by mutual concern in the political and economic affairs of the world, comparable to the British commonwealths of today. But that was the purport of his arguments. It had been the lesson which Turgot, France's great minister of finance, had foretold and which the American Revolution had given to the statesmen of Britain.[40]

What were the thoughts of the new minister of foreign affairs as he read these observations from Moustier? Did Montmorin recall Vergennes' letter to him in Madrid, of October 30, 1778, saying that the United States might be "self-sufficient before long" and "very certainly would make a very hard law" for other nations? Did he consult Kalb's warning to Choiseul in 1767, that the Americans would annex the possessions of the European powers on the North American continent as their population increased by birth and immigration from every quarter of Europe? What did he suppose would be Jay's reaction if Jay also were to see Moustier's re-

40. See above, p. 13, for Turgot.

port on Louisiana? Montmorin had long since met personally with Americans and American aims. He had watched Jay in Madrid —supported then by Franklin and later in Paris by Adams also— doggedly refuse to compromise the imperial pretensions of the United States in the Mississippi Valley. And now he had just been obliged to notify John Jay that the alliance with France, its obligations as well as its privileges, was still in existence. What indeed would the French foreign minister of 1789 have done about the plan of Moustier, had there been nothing else to absorb the minds and tax the powers of France's statesmen?[41]

Moustier's report arrived in France, however, as the Estates-General came into session for the first time in 175 years. Montmorin had no chance, if he would, to put a new policy for North America into execution. The mémoire lay idle in the archives of the foreign office while France herself was shaken to her foundations. But Moustier's ideas were not useless. The Revolutionaries of France took up his plan—although he became an émigré. It was good propaganda among the people to charge that the Bourbon King had let France's empire slip from his grasp. Revolutionaries deplored now that Louisiana had ever been given over to Spain, and vehemently set out to retake it. Such was the peril in America from France as the United States came through their period of confederation to the new order under the Constitution.[42]

Jefferson in France—The Treaty of 1788

THOMAS JEFFERSON, successor to Benjamin Franklin as minister in Paris, inherited much of the acclaim which had been lavished upon the great American, but actually accomplished very little more than John Adams in London or John Jay in New York. Jefferson did witness voluntary concessions to American ships and produce both in France and in her West Indies. The commercial treaty of 1778 had given to the United States the status of most favored nation and had declared that there should be "the most perfect Equality and Reciprocity." But it had by no means removed such monopolies in France as that of tobacco, nor the principle of mercantilism in regard to her colonies, nor the mass of specific prohibitions, special fees, and exclusive privileges such as those of the French East India Company. In 1784, however, a royal decree had opened certain French West Indian ports to enumerated goods so as to admit American ships with the foodstuffs and supplies which those colonies needed and to allow the export of the rum and mo-

41. See above, pp. 37–39.
42. See below, pp. 156–157, 194–195.

lasses which New England desired. In 1787 and 1788 other decrees loosened the restrictions upon American shipping and products further, both in France and her West Indies, particularly with regard to whale oil, codfish, rice, wheat, and flour. As Jefferson reported later when Secretary of State for Washington, these decrees opened markets for seven twelfths of the American whale oil and two thirds of the produce from the codfisheries.[43]

But all of these decrees were gratuitous. They were subject to local exceptions. They might be modified or withdrawn at any time. They were not a solid base for the development of commerce between the United States and France. Besides, the French merchants either could not or would not extend the long-term credits to American purchasers of French goods necessary to establish them in competition with the British. And to complete the uncertainty, the several States were vying with one another for the foreign trade. Beyond control by Jay, secretary for their Confederation, or persuasion by Jefferson, their minister to France, they were manipulating tariffs and tonnage duties, disregarding the most-favored-nation clause in the Treaty of 1778 and giving France provocation to retaliate.[44]

Under these conditions of divided responsibility and conflicting authority, it is not surprising that negotiations begun by La Luzerne in 1781, to protect French interests with rules for the conduct of trade and with consular courts, should end at this time in a special treaty. The agreement was reciprocal. Each party was to have a corps of consular officials in the territory of the other. There were to be American courts for American citizens in France as well as French courts for French subjects in the United States. But this mutual quality was more apparent than real. The shadow of extraterritorial rights lay more sinisterly upon the youthful republican States in America than upon the established monarchy in Europe.[45]

On the face of it, La Luzerne's plan had been reciprocal, but it was open to rigorous interpretation in the United States and to many exceptions in France according to preëxisting institutions and conditions there. It was part of the system for articulating the American States with France and against Britain, for subordinating them to French leadership, for holding them under a protectorate short of complete independence. The committee of Congress, of which Edmund Randolph was chairman, had entered objections

43. Woolery, 40. Bemis, *Jay's Treaty*, 21 n. ASP FR, I, 109 ff., 300. Jefferson (Ford ed.), V, 411–413.
44. Bemis, *Jay's Treaty*, 29. Woolery, 40–42.
45. *Journ. Cont. Cong.*, XXI, 792, 804 n.

immediately. Reciprocity was "tendered," but certain provisions were inadmissible as ambiguous or repugnant to the "spirit and genius of America." They were "in derogation of municipal law." To vest the consuls with a degree of criminal jurisdiction was an "improper interference with the usages of America; might excite great jealousy." The committee acknowledged, however, that the restrictions upon emigration conformed with the stipulations in the commercial treaty of 1778. Congress revised the plan to meet the objections of the committee and sent it to Franklin in France.[46]

When this returned as a convention signed by Franklin and Vergennes, it was found to have been revised again. It was still an agreement of subordination for the United States, not so much because of its phraseology and specific reservations in the text, for the word *respectively* appeared throughout, as by reason of the hindrances which it might put in the way of American interests. John Jay presented these clearly to Congress, July 4, 1785, and recommended that the convention should not be ratified. But as they had gone so far, he said, they should instruct Jefferson to reopen negotiations, stating their objections and assuring the King of their readiness to ratify a convention "made agreeable to the Scheme" which Congress had proposed in answer to La Luzerne.[47]

Jay's major objections were that the convention did not properly designate this country as the United States of America; that reference to the respective States raised question of their Union; that diplomatic immunity should not be extended to minor officers, as they were not immediate representatives of their sovereigns; that consuls should not be called upon to give evidence in a manner less formal and less coercive than were officers of the Government; that the consular chanceries would be an *"Imperium in Imperio,"* thus clashing with the "internal policy" of the States; that the power of the consuls to arrest passengers could be used to stop immigration; that even legal naturalization would be hindered; that there was no limit to the duration of the agreement. And this descendant of Huguenots feared that American Protestants would be denied freedom of worship in Catholic France.

Summing up these and other objections to the convention, Secretary Jay declared that it had three purposes, which America had no interest in promoting. They were: to provide against infractions of the French and American laws of trade, to prevent the people of one country from migrating to the other, and to estab-

46. *Ibid.*, XXII, 17, 25 n., 46.
47. *Ibid.*, XXVIII, 433 n.; XXIX, 505–515; XXXI, 725.

lish in each other's country an influential corps of officers, under one chief, for propagating mercantile and political views.

In other words, the United States had no interest in enforcing the laws of France, and they wanted no treaty enforcing their own. They had no reason to apprehend that their people would emigrate to France or her possessions, and if they wished to regulate immigration, they could do so for themselves. In France, where the people did not participate in the Government, said Jay, every measure to influence their opinions would be unimportant, and so the United States did not want a corps of officers there for political purposes. But in the United States

> a Minister, near Congress, Consuls so placed as to include every Part of the Country in one Consulate or other, Vice Consuls in the principal Ports, and Agents in the less important ones, constitute a Corps, so coherent, so capable of acting jointly and secretly, and so ready to obey the Orders of their Chief, that it cannot fail of being influential in two very important political Respects; *first* in acquiring and communicating Intelligence, and *secondly* in disseminating and impressing such Advices, Sentiments and Opinions, of Men and Measures, as it may be deemed expedient to diffuse and encourage.

And that was just what did happen later under the Convention of 1788.[48]

Jefferson reopened negotiations in Paris with a letter to Montmorin on June 20, 1788. The convention, he said, gave the consuls immunities under the law of nations which the laws of France herself did not admit. It extended other "preeminences" far beyond the law of nations. It did not contain the limit of duration which Congress desired. "As to ourselves," he told Montmorin, "we do not find the institution of Consuls very necessary. Its history commenced in times of barbarism, and might well have ended with them." Consuls would make "national questions" of all cases which arose, whereas simple "correspondents" in charge of the affairs of mercantile houses would tend to prevent such crises. But it was Rayneval—even closer than Montmorin to Vergennes through all of his efforts to restrain the Americans—with whom Jefferson had to deal.[49]

When their negotiations were closed, and the treaty signed, November 14, 1788, Rayneval had agreed to many of the changes which Jay had urged. For French relations with Britain were inse-

48. *Ibid.*, XXIX, 509. See below, pp. 156–157.
49. *Dipl. Corresp.*, II, 168–173.

cure as Sweden and Turkey fought with Russia and Austria; the French West Indies were dependent upon the United States; and there was as always the menace of the British fleet to French shipping. France still needed the United States as a friendly neutral, if not ally. And yet, for good cause, neither Jay nor Jefferson was satisfied that the treaty was the best that should have been obtained.

Rayneval had conceded among other revisions that consuls should not have the privileges of the law of nations but should be expressly subject, both in persons and property, to the laws of the land; that the right of sanctuary in their houses should be reduced to protection only of their chancery room and its papers; that their coercive power over passengers should be taken away, and over "deserters of their nation" save "deserted seamen only"; that the clause giving them power to arrest and send back ships be struck out; that the innovations in the laws of evidence should be done away; and that the treaty should be limited to twelve years. But in spite of this John Jay did not like it. He felt, as he had declared to Congress, that a sovereign power, such as he wished the United States to be under the new Constitution, should not allow foreigners to exercise civil authority, even so limited, within its own jurisdiction. And Jefferson, when reporting to Jay that he had signed the treaty, both expressed his regret and revealed his difficulty: "Convinced that the fewer examples the better, of either persons or causes inamenable to the laws of the land, I could have wished still more had been done; but more could not be done with good humor. The extensions of authority given by the convention of 1784 were so homogeneous with the spirit of this Government that they were prized here."[50]

Neither Jefferson nor Montmorin, who signed for France, then foresaw what would come of events in the very next year as the new Union in America began to harden under the presidency of Washington and the Estates-General precipitated revolution in France. However imminent, those forces were not yet at work upon the relationships of France and the Confederation of American States. But under any kind of stress, such a treaty was more likely to work hardship upon the States than upon France.

Thomas Jefferson came home in 1789 virtually as empty-handed as John Adams, his collaborator in England. The commercial concessions which France had made during Jefferson's stay abroad were good as far as they went. But they had been made not so much in recognition of American rights under the Treaty of 1778 as to

50. *Ibid.*, II, 193–194. For Jay's commendation of Jefferson, March 9, 1789, see II, 258. Monaghan, 261–262. For the text of the treaty, see Miller, II, 228.

meet French need in Europe and the West Indies. They were gratuitous. They were not incorporated in a treaty as were arrangements between France and Britain in 1786. They could be manipulated or set aside at any moment. And they were later—in order to penalize neutrals and not to promote reciprocal commerce—when Revolutionary France went to war with Britain. The consular treaty of 1788 was a liability, not an asset. And so it proved when Citizen Genet came in 1793 vaunting the mutual aims of the French Revolution and America, and seeking to turn the consular courts into prize courts for the disposal of captured British shipping. As for political concessions from France affecting Spanish claims in the Mississippi Valley or British forts on American soil, not only were there none, but the secret opinions and plans of her responsible officers, in France and in America, were as hostile to the United States as any in Britain or Spain.[51]

Legacies to President Washington

THIS commentary may seem too despondent. Representatives of the American Confederation had scored successes in Europe. Even before the treaty of peace in 1783, John Adams had obtained a treaty with the Netherlands upon the principles in the commercial treaty of 1778 with France. In 1783 Franklin had made a similar agreement with Sweden. And in 1785 Franklin, Jefferson, and Adams signed a treaty with Prussia for ten years, committing both parties to the principle that private property should be as inviolable at sea as on land; fixing between them the understanding that "free ships make free goods," in case either were a neutral while the other was a belligerent; and agreeing that if they should go to war with one another, they would not commission privateers to take or to destroy their respective vessels engaged in noncontraband trade.[52]

But without minimizing these achievements, we must note the similarity in position of these contracting parties. Both Sweden and the Netherlands were as subject to British sea power as the United States, and as dependent in large measure upon foreign trade. And the Kingdom of Prussia was virtually an inland state. It had few if any maritime interests to risk in such a compact with the United States. In fact, this treaty might well have become a makeweight in the European schemes of Frederick the Great with which Britain was necessarily involved.

51. Schmidt, Receuil, Index under "Etats Unis." For the Franco-British Treaty of 1786, see Chalmers, Treaties, I, 517 ff. See below, pp. 167, 172–175.

52. Miller, Treaties, II, 59, 123, 162 (particularly articles 7, 12, and 23).

The agreements with Sweden, the Netherlands, and Prussia were not settlements of controversies with those states, revealing European deference to American power and according prestige. They were assertions of a common interest in opposing the mistress of the seas. As for the treaty with Morocco in 1787 which grew out of the raids upon American commerce in the Mediterranean, Morocco alone came to an agreement without exacting tribute. In dealing with the other Barbary States, the American Confederation had to follow the European practice of purchasing peace.[53]

The situation of the American people was precarious in 1789. They had successfully revolted from their mother country with the aid of France, but they were by no means released from the dangers of British, Spanish, and French interest in the future of their continent. They had been spared so far the full violence of that counteraction which political philosophers anticipate in the experience of every revolutionary state. Perhaps because of their very weakness their Confederation was less likely to disintegrate than we are inclined now to think. Although they were pulling and hauling uncertainly against each other, there nevertheless was a great unifying force among them—that vision of their "rising empire" in the West which Washington saw so clearly and implored his officers at Newburgh in 1783 not to deluge in the blood of civil strife. But they had not yet gained mastery of themselves so that they could extend their authority with any sureness beyond the Appalachians. To ward off foreign threats alone, their need for reorganization under strong federal government was imperative. So precarious indeed was their situation that they could not change it immediately upon establishing the new government under the Constitution. The designs of France, Spain, and Britain in the Mississippi Valley were most dangerous legacies from the Confederation to President Washington.[54]

53. Miller, *Treaties*, II, 185–227.
54. Washington (Ford ed.), X, 170.

VI

WASHINGTON'S POLICY
UNION AND ISOLATION

The Major Object

GOVERNMENT under the Constitution began in the midst of great hazards. Spain was an intriguing neighbor across the Mississippi and below the Yazoo and St. Mary's. British officials were scheming with Vermonters and settlers along the Ohio, supporting the Indians in western New York and below the Great Lakes, taking full advantage of the economic dependence of the Atlantic States upon Britain and the weakness of their internal organization. And the French were no longer allies, regardless of Montmorin's protestations. The Estates-General met six days after George Washington took his oath as President of the United States, and spun France headlong toward war. Before Washington could make sure that the Whisky rebels in western Pennsylvania would succumb to his display of Federal authority, Revolutionary France had become a vicious reagent in America, to exploit the resources of the United States in her struggle with Britain if she could, and to rack the very structure of this country if that would serve her own ends.

The author of the Declaration of Independence might still think, as he had in 1787 of the Shays Rebellion in Massachusetts, that "the spirit of resistance to government" was valuable and that he would wish it always kept alive. Thomas Jefferson might "like a little rebellion now & then." But the leader of the American Revolutionary Army had been a conservative. And once he had seen the British troops depart from his country, George Washington took quite a different view on the matter. He greeted the uprisings in Massachusetts with "Good God! Who, besides a Tory, could have foreseen, or a Briton predicted them?" Washington set himself to making such disorders no longer possible in the nation which he had done so much to create. It was a task which would put under tremendous strain his great capacity for taking responsibility.[1]

1. Jefferson (Ford ed.), IV, 370. To Abigail Adams, February 22, 1787. Washington (Ford ed.), XI, 103. To Henry Knox, December 26, 1786.

The major object of immediate importance to President Washington was peace with Britain. Subordinate but indispensable to it was neutrality, even to the point of repudiating past commitments in the Alliance if France should go to war again with Britain. This had to be so, from the very situation of the United States. For Britain had retained large and contiguous areas in America. She was a rival now upon this continent; her own expansive forces would keep her in competition with the United States long into the future. The issues left by the Peace of 1783 were still heated. The problems of debts, Loyalists, and boundaries had been fixed by the formulas in the treaty, but actual solutions for them were yet to be found. The United States could declare that Britain had no legal right to hold the Western posts on their soil, but this did not answer her demands in behalf of creditors and Tories. And the United States had maritime interests beyond their naval strength, for the fleet which had protected their trade in colonial times was now the strong arm of a foreign power. Britain controlled the sea. A war between nations competing for empire, commerce, and international prestige was a very different matter from a colonial rebellion against remote authority to establish self-government. As he commissioned Gouverneur Morris to be his personal representative in London, therefore, George Washington wrote on October 13, 1789: "It is, in my opinion, very important that we avoid errors in our system of policy respecting Great Britain; and this can only be done by forming a right judgment of their disposition and views."[2]

Intimate Diplomacy

MORRIS arrived in London from Paris by way of Antwerp and Amsterdam on March 27, 1790, and had his first interview on the twenty-ninth with the Duke of Leeds, Pitt's secretary in charge of foreign affairs. The Duke was "very happy" to see President Washington's letter; he wished to cultivate a "friendly and commercial" intercourse with the United States; he vouched for the rest of the ministry as of the same opinion, and he listened pleasantly to Morris' comment: "We are too near neighbors not to be either very good friends or very dangerous enemies." But when Morris got to the several "points of the treaty which remained to be performed," Leeds either did not "exactly know the situation" or tried to change the conversation. As for sending a minister to the United States, it was hard, said he, to find "a man every way equal to the task, a man of abilities, and one agreeable to the people of America"; it

2. ASP FR, I, 122. Washington (Ford ed.), XI, 440, 441–443.

was "difficult"; it was "a great way off." Morris assured him that
Britain had such men, and he was certain there were many who
would be glad to accept. But the Duke seems to have displayed a
modesty not habitual with him at other times. He changed the
conversation again.[3]

Subsequent interviews with Leeds, and with Pitt, took Morris
really no farther. He called attention to British impressment of
American sailors and protested humorously that it was one privilege which the United States did not wish. Leeds observed as jocu-
larly that the Americans were being treated as the most favored
nation, like Britons themselves. But the ministers would consider
the possibility of honoring certificates of citizenship to save Americans from the British press gang. Morris discovered, however, that
Pitt was not so interested in the Treaty of 1783 as in making a new
one. He had to tell the prime minister that it would be idle to form
a new treaty until the old one had been satisfactorily applied.

Morris argued that the confiscation of American slaves by the
British Army notwithstanding the treaty had caused a decline of
productivity in the States and had thus hampered the payment of
the debts. But those debts, he said, would now be properly handled
as they would come before the new Federal Courts which had jurisdiction over obligations incurred by treaty. Meanwhile, Britain
should withdraw from the posts in the Northwest if she wished
peace. For they were a matter of "national honor" to the American
people. Those who had made the peace, said Morris, had been very
wise in separating the possessions of the two countries at the Great
Lakes. For many wars came from quarrels among borderers. And
Britain did not need to retain the posts to enjoy the fur trade. It
would "centre in this country," he asserted, "let who will carry it in
America." Pitt, however, did not yield to this argument, and Morris
had to end it with a threat: "We do not think it worth while to go
to war with you for these posts; but *we know our rights, and will
avail ourselves of them when time and circumstances may suit.*"

Pitt then asked if Morris had power to treat. Morris replied that
he had not, and that his Government "would not appoint any one
as minister, they had so much neglected the former appointment"
of John Adams. But, asked Pitt, would the United States appoint
a minister, if Britain did? Morris "could almost promise that we
should," but Britain would have to make the first move. Pitt, however, suggested that in the meantime he might deal with Washington
through one of the British consuls. Morris retorted that the United
States could not take notice of consuls or anything they might say.

3. Morris (Morris ed.), I, 310–311. *Dict. Nat. Biog.*, XLII, 288.

A letter from a consul of course would be received by the President, as Washington's introducing Morris to Leeds had been received, but no consul could hope to reach Washington in person. Pitt's "pride was a little touched at this," and he tried to argue away the point of "etiquette." It "ought not to be pushed so far," he remarked, "as to injure business." Morris was ready. He assured Pitt that

> the rulers of America had too much understanding to care for etiquette, but prayed him at the same time to recollect that they (the British) had hitherto kept us at a distance instead of making advances; that we had gone quite as far as they had any reason to expect in writing the letter just mentioned, but that from what had passed in consequence of it, and which (as he might naturally suppose) I had transmitted, we could not but consider them as wishing to avoid an intercourse.

William Pitt remonstrated. The British, he declared, were "disposed to cultivate a connection, . . ." But Gouverneur Morris had penetrated all of this talk to the heart of the matter. As he reported to Washington on May 29: "It is evident that the conduct of this Government towards us, from the time of my first interview with the Duke of Leeds, has depended on the contingencies of war or peace with the neighboring Powers; and they have kept things in suspense accordingly. When, therefore, they came a little forward, it proved to me their apprehension of a rupture." He epitomized the character of the whole British people as pride. "If they are brought to sacrifice a little of their self-importance," said he, "they will readily add some other sacrifices." So he let it be known through Richard Penn that he would not urge the appointment of an American minister to Britain. He held himself somewhat aloof and frequented the home of La Luzerne, now ambassador in London. "If I am not mistaken," he wrote in his diary, "it will be proper to be intimate at the French ambassador's, to a certain point." And he matched Pitt with insistence, humor, argument, and indifference. The time, in fact, was coming when the British would "add some other sacrifices" in America on account of conditions in Europe.[4]

But that was not then. The British ministers gave the personal agent of the American President many weeks in which to be intimate at the French ambassador's "to a certain point," to attend the trial of Warren Hastings, to get himself fitted with a new artificial leg, to write for the ladies dolefully awaiting his return to Paris gallantries which Benjamin Franklin himself might have envied.

4. ASP FR, I, 123–125. Morris (Morris ed.), I, 314, 326–332. For the repercussion in New York of Morris' "intimacy" with La Luzerne, see Hamilton (Lodge ed.), IV, 343–345. Hamilton to Washington, September 30, 1790.

Gouverneur Morris stayed at London well into September. But it was no use. He might as well have been in Paris. He could accomplish nothing more at that time with Leeds or with Pitt. He returned to Paris—where he did not have to write to the ladies.[5]

Navigation of the Mississippi?—"Let It Sleep"

PRESIDENT WASHINGTON's ultimate objective lay beyond the immediate necessities of peace with Britain and neutrality in the wars of Europe. It was that empire in the West which he had held before his disgruntled officers at Newburgh. If they could only remain in peace with Britain and neutral toward France, they would attain that empire at the expense of decadent Spain. For as he had observed in December, 1784: "The spirit of emigration is great. People have got impatient, and, though you cannot stop the road, it is yet in your power to mark the way; a little while, and you will not be able to do either. It is easier to prevent than to remedy an evil." It would have been hard indeed to get those people back into the Union, once they had separated themselves from it.[6]

Washington had disagreed therefore with John Jay in 1786 that the United States should forego using the Mississippi for a while. In his opinion, they should neither relinquish nor push their claim to the navigation. Instead, they should "open *all* the communications, which nature has afforded, between the Atlantic States and the western country, and . . . encourage the use of them to the utmost. . . ." For it was a matter of "very serious concern" to the States on the seaboard, he said, "to make it the interest" of the men in the West to trade with them. Their "ties of consanguinity" were weakening every day, and soon would be no "bond": "We shall be no more a few years hence to the inhabitants of that country," he feared, "than the British and Spaniards are at this day." Indeed not so much perhaps, for he felt that if the Westerners made commercial connections with the Spaniards, they would unite with them in other matters, and once so joined, they would be difficult to separate. For this very reason he did not want the navigation of the Mississippi to be conceded by Spain just yet. And here he disagreed also with his fellow Virginians, Patrick Henry and James Monroe, and with Charles Pinckney of South Carolina.[7]

George Washington, President for the American people, would not favor the men of Kentucky and Tennessee any more than those

5. ASP FR, I, 126–127. Morris (Morris ed.), I, 312.
6. Washington (Ford ed.), X, 424, 429, to Richard Henry Lee, President of Congress, December 14, 1784.
7. *Ibid.*, XI, 41, to Henry Lee in Congress, June 18, 1786. See above, pp. 103–109.

of the Ohio country. The way should be cleared before all pioneers moving into the West, both Easterners and Southerners. No one should be preferred or hindered by the Government in Philadelphia —lest the "ease" with which those frontiersmen "glide down stream" should give "a different bias to their thinking and acting." This gave him more concern than the resistance of Spaniards. Whenever the new States had become "so populous" and "so extended to the westward" as "really to need" the navigation of the Mississippi, he declared, there would then be no "power" which could deprive them of it. "Why then should we prematurely urge a matter," he asked, "which is displeasing and may produce disagreeable consequences, if it is our interest to let it sleep?"[8]

The President was much more concerned over the "restless and impetuous spirits of Kentucky" than "all the opposition that will be given by the Spaniards." He summoned Thomas Jefferson, well known in Kentucky, to take Jay's place in charge of foreign affairs at the head of the new Department of State as he made the lawyer, John Jay, Chief Justice of the Supreme Court in October, 1789. Jefferson had never questioned Jay's "honest intentions" as had Monroe; he had views that were more in keeping than Jay's with the President's desire to let the immediate issue with Spain "sleep." Thomas Jefferson had written to James Madison from Paris on January 30, 1787:

> I never had any interest Westward of the Alleghaney; & I never will have any. But I have had great opportunities of knowing the character of the people who inhabit that country. And I will venture to say that the act which abandons the navigation of the Mississippi is an act of separation between the Eastern & Western country.

Jefferson's vision of empire reached with Washington's to the Mississippi. It was to extend far beyond.[9]

There is no intention to imply here that George Washington's vision of empire stopped at the Mississippi. He too, as his Secretary Jefferson was soon doing, may have been looking beyond. For Washington wrote to Lafayette on August 11, 1790, that if Spain were "wise and liberal at once," she would easily remove "all causes of quarrels" with the United States; "at a future period," this might be "far from being a fact." But for the time, he had enough territorial problems within the acknowledged domain of the United States, and he set himself to the task of eliminating them. He worked steadily to dispose of all troubles with the Indians there, by negotia-

8. *Ibid.*, XI, 42.
9. Jefferson (Ford ed.), IV, 363. See below, p. 517 f.

tion where possible as in the case of McGillivray's Creeks, by force if unavoidable. In any event, tribal ownership was not to hold individuals from the land. His diplomacy, backed by preparations for war, kept the Northwest Territory in favorable suspense, and influenced those "restless and impetuous spirits of Kentucky." His show of force broke the uprising of white men in western Pennsylvania who resented his Federal authority. And his policy was rewarded. He saw two States beyond the Appalachians, Kentucky and Tennessee, abandon "separation" during his presidency and follow Vermont into the Union of the original thirteen on the Atlantic Seaboard.[10]

Blessed with the protective barriers of nature as well as the communications which it afforded, and profiting from the continuous strife among the nations of Europe which might otherwise have blocked the way, George Washington's countrymen were to advance his concept of American empire beyond the Mississippi with gigantic strides across the continent to the Pacific—a colonization of such magnitude and speed as the world had never seen. But, before this could happen the "wars and quarrels" of Europe had involved the United States again as Thomas Paine had feared in 1776. And, not only did it appear most unlikely that they would ever advance beyond the Mississippi; it was even uncertain that they would retain what they had acquired in the great valley. For another of those far-reaching European controversies was already brewing war as Gouverneur Morris conversed with Leeds and Pitt and President Washington wrote to the Marquis de Lafayette in the summer of 1790.[11]

Nootka Sound, New Orleans, Neutrality

GREAT BRITAIN and Spain clashed over a trading site on Vancouver Island far to the northwest on the Pacific Coast. The real matter at stake, however, was not Nootka Sound. It was nearer at hand. It was possession of the Floridas, Louisiana, and New Orleans. For William Pitt had in mind the "grand Plan" of the Venezuelan, Francisco de Miranda, and thought so well of the idea of a great state in Latin America that he gave money to this famous adventurer. Gower, British minister in Paris, busied himself learning how far the National Assembly would go with Spain under the Family Compact, and he found naval armaments in preparation. Leeds and

10. Washington (Ford ed.), XI, 495–498. For the treaty with McGillivray, August 7, 1790, see ASP IA, I, 81; Martens, IV, 510–516. Bemis, "Vermont Separatists," AHR, XXI, 547–560. For the Whisky Insurrection, see below, pp. 164–166.
11. See above, pp. 8–9.

Pitt in London, although yielding nothing to Morris for American shipping, and little else, had left him with the impression that Britain would pay some kind of a price for American neutrality in case there were war. And Dorchester in Quebec sent Beckwith to New York again, to watch military and naval activities and to find out what Washington would do. Beckwith was to suggest, cautiously, that Britain might help the United States open the navigation of the Mississippi. This, however, would have to be done very cautiously, for British merchants really preferred to compete with Spanish rather than American shipping in the Gulf of Mexico.[12]

Meanwhile another secret agent was reporting from New York. He sent news to London about an insurrection in Mexico; about the arrival of McGillivray to treat with the United States; the dissension in Congress between Northern and Southern members over Hamilton's proposal that the Union should assume the debts of the States; and the restlessness among Western settlers. He thought that many of them would join with Britain against the Union if they could get lands, employment, money, clothes, and above all that outlet down the Mississippi to the sea for their produce.

It was an excellent opportunity for Great Britain, if she could be sure that France would not come to the aid of Spain and that the United States would not support their old ally. By fostering Miranda's revolt from Spain, Britain might open a huge market for British shipping and goods. By seizing New Orleans and retaking the Floridas, or as Pitt spoke of them, the "Southern Farms," she might bring the whole Mississippi Valley, that "Granary of America," under her control, as a protectorate at the least.[13]

President Washington saw the great danger to his country. He had been hoping that it might gradually recover from the distresses in which the Revolution had left it and that it might patiently advance with its task of civil government, "unentangled in the crooked policies of Europe, wanting scarcely anything but the free navigation of the Mississippi"—which, he declared, "we must have, and certainly shall have as we remain a nation." He was counting upon the United States being "the gainers, whether the powers of the old world may be in peace or war, but more especially in the latter case." But if this quarrel over Nootka Sound came to de-

12. Robertson, *Miranda*, I, 90–119. Turner, "English Policy Toward America in 1790–1791," AHR, VII, 706 ff., 711–715. Miranda to Pitt, September 8, 1791. Manning, 427–430; Sorel, II, 94. ASP FR, I, 123–125. *Can. Arch.* (Brymner ed.), 1890, 143–145; Manning, 414–415. "English Policy" (Turner ed.), AHR, VIII, 78–86. S. Cottrell to W. W. Grenville, Whitehall, April 17, 1790.

13. "English Policy" (Turner ed.), AHR, VII, 717–719, 723–726.

cision by arms, he sensed that Britain would take back the Floridas. He had no doubt that she would attack the Spanish posts on the upper Mississippi and New Orleans from Detroit. And then: "The *consequences* of having so formidable and enterprising a people as the British on both our flanks and rear, with their navy in front, as they respect our western settlements, which may be reduced thereby, and as they regard the security of the Union and its commerce with the West Indies, are too obvious to need enumeration."[14]

It has since been found true that the British statesmen were not planning to send troops down the Wabash toward Louisiana. The attack upon New Orleans would have come from a fleet in the Gulf of Mexico. The military activities in Canada were caused by anxiety that Harmar's advance upon the Indians north of the Ohio would develop into an assault upon the British troops holding the posts in American territory. But Washington was alarmed by a report that the "Traitor Arnold" was in Detroit and had twice reviewed the militia of the neighborhood. He called upon his closest associates in the Government, August 27, 1790, to give him their opinions in writing. What should he say if the Governor of Canada asked permission to send troops across the territory of the United States? What if—and he thought it more likely—Dorchester should do so without permission?[15]

The replies came from men of very diverse experiences, aims, and personalities, but they revealed that certain common principles underlay the foreign policy of this nation then, which in large measure still govern its performance. Historians find in the discussion aroused in 1790 by fear of British encroachment, antecedents of the famous doctrine of American nationality which James Monroe later proclaimed to the world for its guidance. Doubtless Monroe heard ideas upon union and isolation in 1790 which influenced his utterances in 1823. His actions, though, immediately before the affair of 1790 and soon thereafter, would seem fitter subjects for irony.[16]

Advices for the President

SECRETARY JEFFERSON had already been thinking and talking over the possibilities in case Spain and Britain went to war. The United States should let both see that they were ready for it, but of course their own object should be to feed the belligerents and not to join in the fight. "If we are not forced by England," he wrote to Monroe,

14. Washington (Ford ed.), XI, 497 n., 497–498.
15. Bemis, *Jay's Treaty*, 72. Washington, *Diaries*, IV, 136.
16. Manning, 423. See above, pp. 104–107, and below, pp. 228–245.

"we shall have a gainful time of it." He knew well, however, that Britain would have designs upon Louisiana and the Floridas, and he feared that if she were successful there, she "would soon find means to unite to them all the territory covered by the ramifications of the Mississippi." "If Great Britain establishes herself on our whole land-board," he said further, "our lot will be bloody and eternal war, or indissoluble confederacy." That of Spain might be worse.[17]

Wishing to make the most of her sad prospects, Jefferson had drafted "heads of consideration" to be sent to Carmichael in Madrid. Spain would be much better off, to Jefferson's way of thinking, if she voluntarily ceded to the United States all territory on their side of the Mississippi, on condition that they guarantee all of her possessions on the western tributaries of the river. It would be safer, much safer, for Spain to have the United States rather than Britain as her neighbor. For conquest was not in their principles, so he said; it was inconsistent with their government; their interest was not "to cross the Mississippi for ages," and never would be "to remain united with those who do."[18]

So positive a declaration might lead us astray, if we did not observe that these were arguments for Carmichael to use in Madrid rather than assertions of personal conviction. Even so, it is to be noted that Jefferson qualified his statement in regard to crossing the Mississippi; the phrase "for ages," however reassuring, is indefinite. As for not remaining "united" with those who did cross the river, Thomas Jefferson, with all his imagination, simply could not comprehend in 1790 the sweep of the forces which were to carry the United States beyond the Mississippi and to transform the competition for the territory there, even before his death in 1826, into a struggle not between East and West, but between North and South.

After drafting the considerations for Carmichael, Jefferson had written to William Short whom he had left as chargé d'affaires in France. He had enclosed confidential papers which Short would keep to himself if there were no war between Spain and Britain. But if there were, he was to show them to Lafayette and consult with him as to how far they might be communicated to Montmorin. The French foreign minister should know that the United States would be among the enemies of Spain if she did not admit their "right to the common use of the Mississippi, and the means of using and se-

17. Jefferson (Ford ed.), V, 198–199. To Monroe, July 11, 1790; V. 230, for Carmichael, August 2, 1790.
18. *Ibid.*, V, 225–231. August 22, 1790. The first draft in Jefferson's papers was dated August 2.

curing it," and Montmorin should govern his course with that fact very much in mind. This implied that the United States were still friends and allies of France. But it also meant that, if France went to war against Britain for the sake of Spain and did not get for the United States what they wanted from Spain, France might find them fighting on the other side.

Short was furthermore to impress upon Montmorin that the United States must have a port of entry on the Mississippi under their own jurisdiction. Jefferson described to Short how the island of New Orleans was geographically separated from both Louisiana and West Florida and would serve admirably as an American possession. But the idea of ceding it would be too much for Spain "in the first step" and, Jefferson supposed, even for Montmorin. Short therefore was to get him to recommend "only in general terms" that Spain should transfer a port, with some adjacent territory, near the mouth of the Mississippi—and leave "the idea" of New Orleans "to future growth."

Jefferson knew that the idea might be too much for Montmorin. He had information since his return from Paris that Moustier had "conceived the project of again engaging France in a colony upon our continent." Moustier had "directed his views" toward the Mississippi, and he had sent "a good deal of matter on the subject to his court." Jefferson ordered Short to be on his guard. But he himself did not choose to think much of it. He hardly suspected, he said, that the French ministers "could be seduced by so partial a view of the subject as was presented to them." He suspected it less, "since the National Assembly has constitutionally excluded conquest from the object of their government." How fatuous it was to believe this, if he really did, Thomas Jefferson learned within three years, upon the arrival of Citizen Genet.[19]

Looking at the situation again from the angle of the British menace, Jefferson had conferred with Madison and submitted their joint considerations to Washington. If Britain took the Floridas and Louisiana, the United States, "instead of two neighbors balancing each other," would have one, "with more than the strength of both." Jefferson and Madison therefore favorably considered that the United States might take advantage of D'Estaing's suggestion and propose to Spain, through France, that Louisiana and the Floridas be established as independent states under the guarantee of all three—France, Spain, and the United States. This might get them into another war with Britain, but it would be a popular war.

As for direct dealings with Britain, Jefferson and Madison would

19. Ibid., V, 218–221. August 10, 1790.

have the President say to Beckwith that any treaty of commerce between them should be "founded on perfect reciprocity," and would therefore be its own price. A treaty of alliance would have to be for a manifest object and could not be inconsistent with existing engagements—that is, the obligations of the United States to France. And Beckwith should understand that, although the United States were disposed to be "strictly neutral" in the event of war between Britain and Spain, they would view "with extreme uneasiness" any attempt of either to seize the possessions of the other on their frontier, for they considered their own "safety interested in a due balance" between their neighbors.[20]

Now on August 28, in answer to the President's request, Secretary Jefferson declared his opinion that the United States ought to take part in the "general war" likely to happen—if there were no other way to prevent the "calamity" of Louisiana and the Floridas being added to the British Empire. But they should preserve their neutrality as long as they could and enter that war as late as possible. For this purpose, he had three separate proposals, constructed according to the time and manner in which Britain crossed American territory. If Britain should ask permission, they should avoid giving any answer. Britain would send her troops through none the less, and the United States could then accept apologies or "make it a handle of a quarrel hereafter, if we should have use for it as such." If Britain should force an answer early in the war, before the United States wished to take its hazards, they would have to grant the permission and compensate Spain by allowing her the same privilege. If the British should pass without so much as asking leave, Jefferson would express dissatisfaction to the British Government, keep alive an altercation, and wait for events to decide whether it was "most expedient to accept their apologies, or profit of the aggression as a cause of war."

Although the preference of the Secretary of State for France over Britain was evident, he appreciated the unquestioned superiority of Britain at the moment and realized that every advantage for the United States lay in retarding the issue. But Jefferson by no means felt that the United States should submit abjectly for long. "One insult pocketed," said he, "soon produces another." He knew that there were trying times ahead, but he believed that this young nation already had weight in the balances of the world. He was confident that it could play the European powers against one another for its own advantage.[21]

20. *Ibid.*, V, 199–203. July 12, 1790.
21. *Ibid.*, V, 238–239. August 28, 1790.

The Chief Justice gave his opinion to the President on the same day. John Jay examined the question in the light of international law more thoroughly than had Jefferson, but he reached the same conclusion—that the right of dominion gave the right to exclude foreigners. On the matter of policy, however, Jay was still so worried about the weakness of the country that he could not dare to think of war with Britain. And as a matter of fact, the country was no better prepared for such a war than it had been when he was secretary for the Confederation. He therefore counseled prudence. He would allow the British to march through American territory. That did not seem to him "to afford *particular* cause of complaint." The region, in fact, was still in Britain's possession. Once her troops reached the Mississippi, they would be entitled by the Treaty of 1783 to navigate it from source to mouth. And Jay even had rather allow the British to seize the Floridas at this time, as he had planned with Oswald in 1782, and disturb the balance of power—much rather—than "engage in a War to prevent it." The idea of maintaining such a balance might deserve serious inquiry later, Jay agreed, but it would be premature now.[22]

The Vice-President expressed his views on the next day. John Adams had no more wish to offend Spain than Britain. He, therefore, would refuse permission to Britain to cross the territory of the United States. But he would not turn to war if the British crossed without it. This people would not willingly support a war, he said; the Government did not yet have the strength to command the men or the money until the causes and the necessity for the war had become generally known and approved. Instead, Adams would remonstrate with the British Government; and, notwithstanding his own past discouragements at the British Court, he would press negotiations in hope of getting satisfaction eventually for the injury done to the United States.[23]

General Knox, Secretary of War, answered the President that same day with similar thoughts upon neutrality as the vital necessity of the United States. He went on to consider developments which might entangle them in spite of their need to stay out of war. France would be likely to keep the Family Compact and then, of course, would try to draw the United States into the conflict. It would be a grave question whether they could comply with the treaty of friendship and commerce with France and observe "an exact neutrality" at the same time. It hardly seemed possible that

22. Ford, 50–55.
23. Adams, *Works*, VIII, 497. August 29, 1790. For his Spanish policy as President, see below, pp. 316–318, 331–332.

either party would make it worth their while to abandon neutrality, and yet the United States might have to get into the war "to avert a greater evil." What that was, Knox did not specify. Nor did he reach definite conclusions in regard to what course the President should follow if the British advanced into American territory, except that he might summon Congress into session. It was vested with the right of declaring war. While it was discussing the matter, "the dispositions and designs of the contending parties," he said, "will unfold themselves, the terms of each side be known and estimated, and the United States better able than at present to judge of the exact line of conduct they ought to pursue."[24]

Alexander Hamilton, Secretary of the Treasury, submitted his opinion on September 15, 1790. He had been conferring with the British agent, Beckwith, before Jefferson took charge of the Department of State. He continued to do so, sometimes with Jefferson's knowledge, as often without it. There was a personal factor in this as well as variance of opinion in regard to affairs of state. For Beckwith reported Hamilton as saying to him:

> The President's mind I can declare to be perfectly dispassionate on this subject. Mr. Jefferson, our present Secretary of State, is, I am persuaded a gentleman of honor, and zealously desirous of promoting those objects, which the nature of his duty call for, and the interests of his country may require, but from some opinions which he has given respecting your Government, and possible predilections elsewhere, there may be difficulties which may possibly frustrate the whole, and which might be readily explained away. I shall certainly know the progress of the negotiation from the president from day to day, but what I come to the general explanation for is this, that in case any such difficulties should occur, I should wish to know them in order that I may be sure they are clearly understood and candidly examined; if none take place the business will of course go on in the regular official channel.[25]

The only acceptable justification for such an attitude is that the Government under the Constitution was new. Divisions between departmental responsibilities were not clear. The President's control over negotiations with foreign powers was not yet firmly established. The Cabinet was only then developing as a council of confidential advisers. Any and every member of the Government, whether in Congress or the Administration, assumed that if he felt himself called upon to do so he might discuss affairs with foreign agents as in the days of the Continental Congress. And yet, it would

24. Ford, 103–106.
25. *Can. Arch.* (Brymner ed.), 1890, 148–149. Hamilton (Lodge ed.), IV, 296–299. Bemis, *Jay's Treaty*, 76.

seem, Alexander Hamilton could not but have sensed that he was very close to betrayal of high trust. He did not stop, however, with the departure of the secret agent, Beckwith. When Hammond came as minister, he too found the Secretary of the Treasury meddling in the affairs of the State Department, and willing to talk upon matters as they were discussed in the Cabinet.[26]

Hamilton had already hinted to Beckwith that the United States would dislike "any enterprise on New Orleans." But he put a different stress from Jefferson's upon the facts of the situation. He did not think that the American people were ready for war. He saw that if war became general in Europe the price of money would rise and the United States could not place their loans upon so good terms. They could overcome that disadvantage best, in his opinion, by remaining at peace while the powers of Europe were increasing their debts in new wars. The United States would find themselves in a very favorable situation at the end of the general war.[27]

Hamilton, therefore, now advised the President to maintain peace with Britain even if he had to consent to the march of the British troops across American territory and the capture of New Orleans. If the British went through without giving him a chance to consent, there of course would be no alternative to war. Hamilton agreed on this point with Jefferson, that one insult taken produced another. Humiliation, said he, was "in almost every situation a greater evil than war." But Alexander Hamilton was in too close touch with Beckwith to worry much about that. Beckwith would let him know, and he would see that things were "clearly understood and candidly examined" in Washington's "perfectly dispassionate" mind.[28]

The Secretary of the Treasury reminded the President that, whatever their obligations of gratitude to France, Spain had "slender claims to peculiar good-will from us." The closure of the Mississippi in fact, declared Hamilton, threatened to separate the Western country from the United States; this was a greater menace to their future than Britain's retention of the posts in the Northwest; Spain, therefore, was the immediate enemy; war with her was more logical. As the United States did not want Canada so much as the Mississippi Valley, they should prefer Britain as their ally.[29]

It was true, Hamilton admitted, that the British would be dangerous in New Orleans. They would make it into a trading center

26. See below, pp. 183–184.

27. Hamilton (Lodge ed.), IV, 299–302, Hamilton to Washington, July 22, 1790; 302–312, 307, to William Short in Paris, September 1, 1790.

28. Ibid., IV, 313–342 at 342.

29. Ibid., IV, 324–325, for Hamilton's plan in 1798, see below, pp. 319–328.

for their shipping between the Mississippi Valley and their West Indies. The Atlantic States would suffer. The Southern States which now supplied Britain with tobacco and other commodities for her trade in European markets would also be injured. Indeed, whenever the United States could make good their pretensions, they should not leave New Orleans and control of the Mississippi with any foreign power. But at this time, said Hamilton, they should prefer to risk the capture of New Orleans by the British to its retention by Spain. His rationalization was: "Good or evil is seldom as great in the reality as in the prospect. The mischiefs we apprehend may not take place. The enterprise notwithstanding our consent, may fail." Besides, Britain might purchase American neutrality by ceding a part of the territory in question which bordered on the Mississippi and by guaranteeing the navigation of the river. If she did not, there was still his best point to rely upon. Britain's war with Spain would add millions to the British debt, while the United States by avoiding war would gain steadily in recruits, resources, and strength.[30]

Thus President Washington had considerations before him from very different points of view. What he actually would have done, however, if Britain had ignored the sovereignty of the United States and had moved her troops down the Wabash River without so much as asking leave, is as much a matter of speculation as what Montmorin might have done with Moustier's plan for the Mississippi Valley if there had been any chance. Judging from the cool tone toward the British in Washington's diary and his letters at the time, one may venture that he would have been much harder to incline toward Hamilton's views than Hamilton presumed. But Washington was saved by the Spanish and British diplomatists from having to make any decision. They were able to solve the problem of Nootka Sound before the militarists took charge of the next "general war" in Europe.[31]

The European Truce

IF Pitt and his colleagues were uneasy as the French Assembly endeavored to make the old Family Compact into a national policy, Floridablanca was dismayed by the rising popular dislike of monarchy in France. Those dreadful Republicans were north of the Pyrenees now, as well as east of the Mississippi. The interplay of Austrian, Prussian, Turkish, and other forces in European politics,

30. *Ibid.*, IV, 327, 337, 338–339.
31. Washington, *Diaries*, IV, 139, July 8, 1790; 143, July 14. Washington (Ford ed.), XI, 501, to Hamilton, October 10, 1790.

moreover, was so confused at the time that both Spaniards and British preferred settlement by diplomacy to war. Floridablanca exchanged pacific declarations with Fitzherbert on July 24, 1790. They reached agreement, October 28, upon terms for settlement. And although Floridablanca fell from power, Godoy completed the policy by alliance with Britain, May 25, 1793, against Revolutionary France; and made final settlement of the quarrel over Nootka Sound on January 11, 1794. Spain honored the British flag there, and then both parties abandoned the place—with, however, a mutual agreement to resist the pretensions of any other power in the vicinity.[32]

George Washington was spared in 1790 from having to make up his mind what the United States would do if William Pitt should disregard European complications, defy the United States, and turn Britain's sea power to constructing a new colonial domain in the Americas—centered upon New Orleans, reaching through the Mississippi Valley to Canada on the north and interlocking it with British possessions in the West Indies and Central America. It was well for the future of this country that Washington was not obliged to make the decision then. Neither Hamilton's wish that the British might fail to take New Orleans or to hold it if they did, nor Jefferson's assumption that the United States could soon get ready for such a war, had good foundation upon the evidence of the time. When eventually a British expeditionary force did come from the sea to take New Orleans, not Spain, nor France, but the United States were in possession of the city and its entire hinterland. That the statesmen of Britain, on the other hand, were wise not to disregard European conditions in 1790 and the potentiality of the United States, was more than supported by immediate events.

32. Martens, IV, 488–491, 492–499; V, 472–479. Manning, 405–406, 453–456, 468–471. See below, pp. 156, 162.

VII

REVOLUTIONARY FRANCE
OBSTACLE TO ISOLATION
Washington's Anxiety—Jefferson against Hamilton

STRIKING at royalist activities beyond their frontiers, the Republicans of France sent their King to the guillotine on January 21, 1793. Eleven days later they declared war upon Great Britain. They followed that on March 9 with a declaration against Spain. And forces were loosed which were not to be checked until Napoleon Bonaparte had been confined to St. Helena. The internal explosion of France shook the monarchies of all Europe as the French Republic abandoned the defensive for the attack. And part of that assault upon the existing order in Europe was to be the reëstablishment of French power in America according to the proposals of Moustier.

The news of war between Britain and France and the approach of a representative of these radicals in France stirred again the conservative instincts of the American President. He had written on March 23 to the minister in Portugal: "All our late accounts from Europe hold up the expectation of a general war in that quarter. For the sake of humanity I hope such an event will not take place; but, if it should, I trust we shall have too just a sense of our own interest to originate any cause, that may involve us in it." And now on April 12 to Jefferson, his Secretary of State, ". . . it behoves the government of this country to use every means in its power to prevent the citizens thereof from embroiling us with either of those powers, by endeavoring to maintain a strict neutrality." He required Jefferson to give mature consideration to the matter, for he had heard that privateers were already preparing in American ports. He set out the next day from Mount Vernon for Philadelphia where he arrived on the seventeenth. On the nineteenth he summoned his associates to consider a chain of questions which his Secretary of the Treasury, Hamilton, had prepared. What should be his plan of conduct? Should he issue a proclamation of neutrality? Should he receive a minister from the French Republic? Would the United States be compelled by good faith still to adhere to the treaties of 1778? His youthful country was in great danger of uncertain companionship.[1]

The Treaty of Amity and Commerce had declared that its obligations should be "perpetual." These included the pledges that the ships of war and the privateers of either party could take their prizes into the ports of the other party, and that it should be unlawful for any privateers of an enemy of either to fit their ships in the ports of the other. The Treaty of Alliance, although describing itself as a merely "defensive" alliance to maintain the independence of the United States, and practically designed for the period of the American Revolution only, nonetheless had stated that the United States would guarantee against all other powers from that time "and forever" the existing possessions of the Crown of France in America and such conquests as it might make of the islands in or near the Gulf of Mexico. In return, France had undertaken to guarantee the possessions and conquests of the United States. If these treaties still held in full force, President Washington might well be fearful whether the United States could keep out of the European conflict.[2]

The words *perpetual* and *forever* did not cause anxiety. No party could be bound indefinitely and irrevocably to a commitment which might drag it to destruction. The right of self-preservation was generally admitted then as now among nations to suspend if not to dissolve the obligation of an international contract, however explicit. There was no doubt in Washington's council that the United States could break such bonds as those words implied. But there was sharp division of opinion as to the course which they could follow in honoring their obligations to France and yet avoid the reprisals of Britain.

All came to an agreement that the President should issue a proclamation and receive the minister. Secretary Jefferson, however, insisted upon omitting from the document the word *neutrality*, and upon including the word *modern* so as to define the goods which the United States would consider contraband.

He wished to hold back the express declaration of neutrality "as a thing worth something to the powers at war." If they bid for it, he said, "we might reasonably ask a price, the broadest privileges of neutral nations." He had in mind Britain and her control of the sea. She might be led to an invaluable commitment.

His purpose in urging the use of the word *modern*—though he

1. Washington (Ford ed.), XII, 276, 278, 279–281. Jefferson (Ford ed.), I, 226.
2. Miller, *Treaties*, II, 5, 16, 17, 36, 38–40.

did not reveal it at the time—was to strengthen the principle of
"free ships make free goods," which had been established in the
treaty with France of 1778 and confirmed in the treaties with the
Netherlands, Sweden, and Prussia. Here he thought not only of
American shipping but of the supplies, not actually materials of
war, which France had already begun negotiations to purchase in
this country through her secret agent, Col. W. S. Smith, John
Adams' son-in-law.[3]

The Secretary of State would make the President's proclamation, if issued it had to be, one of benevolent neutrality toward the
old ally of the American States. But the Secretary of the Treasury
would give it just the opposite direction.

Hamilton did not wish to receive the new French minister, unless it were made clear that the United States had the option of
holding the treaties of 1778 in suspense. He wanted to believe that
they were null and void, inasmuch as they had been made with the
King of France and Louis had been driven from the throne. He
cited the authority of the famous writer upon international law,
Vattel, who had dealt with the idea that an alliance might be renounced if a change of government had made it useless, dangerous,
or disagreeable. But Hamilton knew very well that treaties subsisted between states and not between governments. At best the
Alliance of 1778 would only be voidable. Elsewhere in his disquisi-
tion, Vattel himself was not so apt in his treatment of the subject.
And so, Hamilton turned his argument at length to the stronger
position that the Government of France was not yet entitled to
full recognition. The counteraction in Europe, in fact, indicated
that its future was doubtful; a monarchy in some form might be
restored; everything was, as he said, *"in transitu."* Hamilton, however, did not question the obligation of the United States to meet
the payments on their debt to France regardless of the form of her
government. This implied for him no admission that the treaties
were still in force.[4]

The fact that France had taken the offensive against Britain and
Spain, Hamilton declared, had released the United States from the
guarantee in the "defensive" alliance of 1778. They had the choice
of staying out of the whole affair. If they did not use that option
they would pass from the state of neutrality to that of an ally;
they would authorize the powers at war with France to treat them

3. Jefferson (Ford ed.), VI, 315–316, to Madison, June 23, 1793; VI, 485, Opinion on
Neutral Trade, December 20, 1793. Bemis, *Jay's Treaty*, 148. For the treaties, see above,
pp. 18–21. For Colonel Smith, see below, pp. 152–154.
4. Hamilton (Lodge ed.), IV, 369–408, 385.

as an enemy. Here was the real determinant in all of Hamilton's reasoning upon the problem. The leading power at war with France was Great Britain, neighbor of the United States in North America and possessor of command over the seas. The United States were getting most of their manufactured goods from Britain, and collections from the duties on British imports sustained the American Treasury. His efforts to establish the national credit so essential to the independence of this country might fail, if it did not remain neutral and inclined to the side of Britain.

Hamilton's facile reasoning from the abstractions of authorities on international law to the substantives of world politics affronted the Secretary of State. On occasion Jefferson also could weave and ravel logic and practicality with skill. But in this instance his thinking was under the control of the facts of the contractual obligation to France, and of the possibility that France might still put pressure upon Britain and Spain in the Mississippi Valley for the eventual benefit of the United States there.

The Secretary of State had long since settled that matter of recognition about which Hamilton would make so much to-do. Jefferson had written Gouverneur Morris, minister to France, in the previous November that it accorded with our principles to acknowledge the rightfulness of any government formed by the will of the nation substantially declared. He had restated the matter in December even more forcefully:

> We surely cannot deny to any nation that right whereon our own government is founded, that every one may govern itself under whatever form it pleases, and change these forms at it's own will; and that it may transact it's business with foreign nations through whatever organ it thinks proper, whether King, convention, assembly, committee, President, or whatever else it may chuse. The will of the nation is the only thing essential to be regarded.

Again in March, with Washington's approval, he had reiterated those principles and advised Morris that the United States had resumed payment upon the debt, as information had come of the meeting of the National Assembly with full powers to transact the affairs of France. It was "even providential that monies lent to us in distress could be repaid under like circumstances."[5]

So, a line or two in Vattel's treatise on international law had for Thomas Jefferson no influence whatever upon the question whether the United States should recognize the new Government of France

---

5. Jefferson (Ford ed.), VI, 131, 149–150, 200. For Washington's confirming statement, see Washington (Ford ed.), XII, 269, March 13, 1793.

and receive its minister. But, on the other hand, neither did he assay at their proper value the financial policy of the Secretary of the Treasury and the dependence of this country upon peace with Britain for years, come what might in the meantime.[6]

The Secretary of State had no fear that trouble would arise from the clause in the Treaty of Commerce which gave French ships and privateers the right to use American ports and to bring in prizes captured from their enemies. The Netherlands and Prussia had countenanced this right in their own treaties with the United States. And Britain's last treaty with France, he said, had given the same privilege in British ports at the expense of the United States. Complaints, therefore, could hardly be in order if the United States permitted the French to use American ports even though the British had no such rights there by treaty.

As for the chance that France might attempt to fit out privateers within the territorial waters of the United States, Jefferson maintained that they were free to withhold the right. The specific denial of the privilege to the enemies of France, in the Treaty of 1778, did not mean that the United States had to concede that privilege to France. Rather, the United States were entirely free in their own interest to refuse the same thing to France which they had contracted to deny to Britain for the benefit of France. He anticipated that "a fair neutrality will prove a disagreeable pill to our friends," but he believed that it was the wisest course for the United States up to the last possible moment. Until then he would not renounce the treaties with France as the Secretary of the Treasury desired. To do so would be the real breach of neutrality. That would give France just cause for war.[7]

The guarantee of her West Indies to France, however, gave Thomas Jefferson pause. It was dangerous. But he insisted upon searching the caverns of probability and imminence. And in these he found nothing real. When and if they ceased to be merely conjectural, there would be time enough in self-preservation to declare the treaties null. In the meantime, surely the "forbearance" for ten years from calling upon France to guarantee the Northwest posts entitled the United States to some indulgence by France. If, on the other hand, failure at once to repudiate the obligations to France were to bring down upon them some terror "in the dark," presumably the wrath of Britain, "very well. Let Rawhead &

6. Bemis, *Jay's Treaty*, 138. Jefferson (Ford ed.), VI, 232, to James Madison, April 28, 1793.

7. *Ibid.*, VI, 223, Opinion on French Treaties, April 28, 1783; VI, 232, to James Madison, same date.

bloody-bones come, & then we shall be justified in making our peace with him, by renouncing our antient friends & his enemies."

In the very last resort, therefore, Jefferson would prefer as did Hamilton to risk a war with France rather than have it with Britain. But Thomas Jefferson would not scare at the mere suspicion of British reprisals. And to his great pleasure, he learned when the new French minister arrived in Philadelphia that France did not intend to hold the United States to the guarantee of the West Indies, until they could agree upon a new treaty binding both nations against those powers which monopolized colonial possessions to the disadvantage of foreign shipping.[8]

This was not so magnanimous on the part of France as Genet would have Jefferson believe. France did not want the United States Government to declare war on Britain, as it would have to do if it undertook to fulfill the guarantee. American neutrality was preferable—if it were benevolent toward France. Britain's superior navy had the French islands at her mercy. Ports were bombarded and troops were thrown ashore. There was a strong possibility that Britain would keep those islands whatever the outcome of events in Europe. But whether she would or not, American frigates and troops were not likely to be so effective against British forces in the West Indies as American money and foodstuffs under the guard of neutral rights. The United States were already the granary of the West Indies. Their supplies would be more important to France herself in Europe than their military and naval coöperation.[9]

The Proclamation of 1793—"Picking a Quarrel"

As the members of his Cabinet had unanimously agreed that there should be a formal statement, the President directed Attorney General Randolph to draft a proclamation. And on April 22, Washington made public the policy which the American Government would pursue during the war between Austria, Prussia, Sardinia, Great Britain, and the United Netherlands of the one part, and France of the other. The duty and the interests of the United States required that they remain friendly and impartial toward the belligerents. Their citizens were warned to avoid all acts and proceedings whatsoever that ran counter to this disposition. They were duly notified that if they rendered themselves liable to punishment or forfeiture under the law of nations by committing, aiding, or abetting hostilities against or carrying articles "deemed contraband by the *modern* usage of nations," to any of the belligerents, they

8. *Ibid.*, VI, 222–223; 260–261, to Madison, May 19, 1793.
9. Moore, V, 4407–4408.

would not receive the protection of the United States. Moreover, their Government would prosecute in its own courts all persons who should violate within such jurisdiction the law of nations with respect to the powers at war. Thus armed, President Washington awaited the representative of the new republican order in France.[10]

The proclamation omitted Spain, Russia, and Portugal from the specified list of belligerents among whom the United States would maintain that studied impartiality and friendliness. Was this omission deliberate? News of the French declaration against Britain, Holland, and Russia and of Portugal's declaration against France had appeared in the Gazette of the United States in Philadelphia on April 6, 1793. And on April 17, two days before the President's advisers met at his request, the Gazette had announced that there was a letter in town from Lisbon, dated the fifth of March, stating that France had declared war upon Spain.[11]

This report, to be sure, was inaccurate. France had not actually declared war upon Spain until March 9. And it is not likely that the Cabinet thought this news alone warranted any action in regard to Spain. But there is other evidence to suggest that the list of belligerents was not drawn carelessly. It may be that Russia and Portugal were left out because they were of little consequence in America's relations with Britain and France. And it is of course possible that all three were omitted because the United States had not yet received official confirmation of their status as belligerents. But this is difficult to accept as the sole cause for the omission of Spain.

In the previous autumn President Washington had learned of happenings in the Southwest which would lead him to suspect, if he did not know, that the Spanish governor, Carondelet, had outbid him for the good will of the Creeks under McGillivray. In fact, McGillivray was at Pensacola negotiating against the United States when he died on February 17, 1793. And on the twentieth, Col. W. S. Smith, confidential agent of the Girondists in France and intimate friend of Miranda, who was now in the French Army, had called upon Secretary Jefferson. Smith had left France in November with instructions, he said, to tell Washington that the French ministers would have nothing more to do with Gouverneur Morris; that they were going to send Genet with full powers to give the United States all privileges in their countries, particularly their West Indies; that they might even set those islands free during the next summer; that they proposed to emancipate South America,

10. ASP FR, I, 140.
11. Fenno's Gazette of the United States. Originals in the Harvard College Library.

and would send Miranda with forty-five ships of the line; that they wished to have the American debt to France paid in provisions, and had authorized Smith to negotiate such an agreement. The French attack upon Spanish America, said he, would begin at the mouth of the Mississippi and move southward around the Gulf of Mexico; they would have no objection if the United States incorporated "the two Floridas."[12]

It is not easy to determine how much of this was mere talk flowing from Colonel Smith's hobnobbing with Miranda, in whose schemes he was interested for years thereafter, or from his own eagerness to manage the payments on the American debt and the shipments of provisions to France. It may also be that Thomas Jefferson interpolated specific statements later, foreshadowing events after they had occurred. He himself said that twenty-five years or more afterwards he gave a "calm revisal" to the "Anas" in which this episode with Smith was recorded. But this entry was supported in large part by evidence elsewhere at the time. The French minister at Philadelphia, Ternant, had received complaints from Lebrun about Morris and submitted them to Jefferson. Smith had been commissioned by the French ministers; he was negotiating with Secretary Hamilton in regard to the debt, and he was contracting for flour, grain, and salted provisions on the account of France. And Miranda himself had written to both Knox and Hamilton about his connection with France and his revived hopes for those "grand and beneficial projects" in South America. Washington had other sources of information besides Colonel Smith.[13]

Whatever it was that Smith did say to Jefferson on February 20, both the President and the Secretary of State had been impressed. With Washington's "approbation" in writing, Jefferson drafted a letter on March 23 to Carmichael and Short, American commissioners in Spain, telling them that France meant to send an expedition and offer independence to the Spanish colonies beginning at the Mississippi, and that she would not object if the United States took the Floridas. For these reasons, accordingly, they were to make no treaty with Spain which would bind the United States to guarantee the Spanish colonies against their own independence, nor indeed against any other nation. When he had suggested that the United States might guarantee Louisiana to Spain, wrote Jefferson,

12. Jefferson (Ford ed.), VI, 118, October 14, 1792, on Carondelet. Whitaker, "Alexander McGillivray," No. Ca. Hist. Rev., V, 181–204, 289–310. Jefferson (Ford ed.), I, 216–218.

13. Ibid., I, 155; VI, 193–194. Corresp. French Ministers, 170, 187. Hamilton (Lodge ed.), 418–420. Robertson, Miranda, I, 126–127.

in return for the cession of the Floridas to them, he had done so under the apprehension that Britain would seize Louisiana and encircle the United States with her colonies and fleets; but that danger had been removed by the "concert" between Britain and Spain. He felt now that "the times" would soon enough give "independence, & consequently free commerce to our neighbors" without the United States having to involve themselves in a guarantee and the risk of war with Britain.[14]

But this was not to be said in regard to war with Spain. Washington and Jefferson were deeply stirred by the reports of Spanish activity among the Indians on the Southwestern frontier. By June 14, Washington had ordered Secretary Knox to spare no reasonable expense in obtaining information about the Spanish forces in the Floridas and "troops lately arrived in New Orleans." Jefferson wrote on the twenty-third that war with the Creeks was inevitable; no one of the President's advisers, he said, doubted that it would lead to war with Spain. And indeed if the insults of Spain's agents at Philadelphia, Viar and Jaudenes, truly indicated the policy of Spain, there was likelihood of war between the United States and Spain in the summer of 1793.[15]

In either case, whether through caution or through design, the exception of Spain from the proclamation of neutrality on April 22 had left the United States entirely free to profit at the expense of Spain from the French plan of attack in America. They would not be obliged to alter their statements in order to save their faces as they took the Floridas. But more important than that, the exception of Spain left a great loophole for individual citizens of the United States through which, until their Government expressly closed it, many found their way into the service of France—bound for adventure beyond the domain but not the aspirations of the American people.

There were the British, however, to be taken into account. And although Washington and Jefferson agreed upon what to expect of Spain and what they should do if they had only her to consider, they soon differed upon the course which they should pursue in handling Britain with France and Spain.

As he witnessed the popular enthusiasm for the new French minister, and realized that Britain would make no concession to American shipping to get a declaration of neutrality, Jefferson came to

14. Jefferson (Ford ed.), VI, 206.
15. Washington (Ford ed.), XII, 297–298. Jefferson (Ford ed.), VI, 315–316. ASP FR, I, 263–269, for the letters of Viar and Jaudenes, and Jefferson's to Carmichael and Short, June 30, 1793, about them.

speak of the proclamation as pusillanimous, in his confidential correspondence with Madison. But it was not expedient to oppose the proclamation altogether, "lest it should prejudice what was the next question, the boldest & greatest that ever was hazarded, and which would have called for extremities, had it prevailed." This was to take advantage of the war between France and Spain. "Spain," said he, "is unquestionably picking a quarrel with us."[16]

Even after that Jefferson allowed himself to encourage Genet in thinking that the American Government would not interfere with those citizens who joined a French enterprise against New Orleans, provided their rendezvous were "out of the territories of the United States": "I told him," said Jefferson, "that his enticing officers & souldiers from Kentucky to go against Spain, was really putting a halter about their necks, for that they would assuredly be hung, if they commd hostilities agt. a nation at peace with the U.S. That leaving out that article I did not care what insurrections should be excited in Louisiana." And he gave Genet for his agent, Michaux, a letter of introduction to Governor Shelby of Kentucky. Jefferson wrote it first to describe Michaux "only as a person of botanical & natural pursuits." But when Genet said that he wished the Governor to view Michaux "as something more, as a French citizen possessing his confidence," Jefferson took the letter back and wrote another.[17]

May we conclude that Jefferson meant to say that things would be different if the United States were not at peace with Spain, and that he hoped they would not long remain so? That such officers and soldiers would not be stopped in advance? That if all turned out well for the United States as those persons succeeded in their enterprise, their contributions to the American cause would be gladly received? But if they failed, and other events proved distressing to their country, that they would have to pay for their sins?

Genet seems to have reached conclusions something like these, for he reported to Paris on July 25:

> Mr. Jefferson appeared to me to sense quickly the usefulness of this project but declared that the United States had begun negotiations with Spain on the matter of granting a port of entry to the Americans below New Orleans and that so long as this negotiation was not broken the considerateness of the United States would not permit them to take part in our operations. Nevertheless he gave me to understand that he thought a little spontaneous irruption of the inhabitants of Kentucky into New Orleans could advance things. He put me in touch with many representatives from Kentucky and notably with Mr. Brown who, im-

16. Jefferson (Ford ed.), VI, 259, 316. May 19, June 23, 1793.
17. *Ibid.*, I, 236–237. July 5, 1793.

bued with the idea that his country would never flourish so long as the navigation of the Mississippi was not free, has adopted our plans with as much enthusiasm as an American can show. He has indicated to me the ways of operating with success, has given me the address of many safe men, and has promised to apply all of his influence to the successful outcome of our projects.[18]

If Secretary Jefferson believed in the summer of 1793 that France would generously share the spoils of victory in Spanish America and that Britain would stand idly by and permit all this to happen, if he had forgotten his fears of British encirclement, President Washington had not, nor was Washington overlooking British activity behind the Indian war parties in the Northwest Territory. Washington read the times and conditions differently. He did not know yet that Godoy and Fitzherbert, now titled Baron St. Helens, had signed a treaty on May 25 requiring Spain and Britain to come to the aid of one another in case either should be "attacked, molested, or inquieted, in any of their States, rights, possessions, or interests, in any time or manner whatsoever. . . ." He did not need to know it. After all, Spain and Britain were at war with a common enemy; and in such a crisis the United States, in his opinion, could not separate one from the other. Their "concert," far from being a safeguard for American interests in the Floridas and the Mississippi Valley, was a menace.[19]

At the very first news of war in Europe, Washington had thought of strict neutrality. Then he had approved Secretary Jefferson's plan to modify it somewhat in favor of France, because of the commercial interests of his own people; and he had not been averse, at least, to excepting Spain from the proclamation, because of the grave situation in the Southwest. Perhaps he too, for a while, entertained hope in regard to the Floridas—"the boldest & greatest that ever was hazarded." But Washington returned to his first determination that the United States must be strictly neutral toward every French endeavor, even those against Spanish America, as he listened to the arguments of Secretary Hamilton, felt the constant pressure of the British minister, Hammond, and observed the irritating behavior of the new minister from France.

The Plans of Genet—"Liberty Warring on Herself"

CITIZEN GENET had arrived at Charleston, South Carolina, on April 8, aboard the frigate *Embuscade*. Although expressly instructed by his Girondist superiors to do nothing which would question the new

18. *Corresp. French Ministers,* 221.
19. Martens, V, 472–479. ASP FR, I, 277. See above, pp. 136–140.

constitutional régime in the United States, and warned by Lebrun that the American character was cold and that he should put his "entire confidence in the sentiments of President Washington and Messrs. Jefferson, Butler, and Madison," this professional diplomat of the old Monarchy, turned fiery son of the Revolution, felt in no way obliged to restrain himself until he had been presented to the American President and personally accepted as the minister of France.[20]

He had been ordered to base his diplomacy upon a new treaty which should establish an "intimate concert" with the United States for extending the "Empire of Liberty," guaranteeing the sovereignty of peoples, and punishing those powers which maintained exclusive commercial and colonial systems. After that had been done, he was to develop the plans for liberating Spanish America, opening the Mississippi River, delivering "our ancient brothers of Louisiana from the tyrannic yoke of Spain," and perhaps uniting the "fair star of Canada" to the American constellation. But was he to wait for the treaty? Had he not also been told that reports of conditions in France might make the American ministers follow an irresolute and timid course? And until the American Government should decide to make common cause with France, was he not "to germinate the principles of liberty and independence in Louisiana and other provinces of America adjacent to the United States," to maintain agents in the West, and to use the Kentuckians, who would "probably second his efforts without compromising Congress"? Citizen Genet was not going to wait for such a treaty, if he could get on with the real business for which he had come.[21]

The *Embuscade* had been held by adverse winds from sailing directly into the Chesapeake, so his report implied, but Genet saw no point in remaining aboard as she went on to Philadelphia. Instead, he negotiated with Governor Moultrie, who coöperated heartily with him at first and won his acclaim as a "sincere friend of our revolution." He began at once to refit the prizes taken by the *Embuscade* as privateers for France. He interpreted the consular powers in the Treaty of 1788 as allowing him to establish admiralty courts in this country for disposing the prizes captured by the French cruisers and privateers. He put the French consul, Mangourit, to work upon the plans for commissioning Americans and inciting Indians to attack Spain in the Floridas and Louisiana. And then, he set out through the countryside on a grand approach to the Government of the United States, luxuriating in the fraternal wel-

20. *Corresp. French Ministers*, 201–211; for Lebrun's warning, see 215 n.
21. *Ibid.*, 204, 205.

come of "the good American farmers" and their offers of grain and
flour to France.[22]

Genet was quick to sense, and to appropriate for his uses, the
popular resentment against the President's proclamation of April 22
and the enthusiasm which greeted his arrival in Philadelphia on May
16. He was as quick, and as indiscreet, in scorning the reserve and
the dignity with which he was received by the President. "Old
Washington," he said, did not "forgive him for his success," would
hinder him "in a thousand ways." But "true Republicans" would
triumph. He would encourage democratic societies on the model of
the French political clubs, and before long he would have a working
majority in the Congress. Even Secretary Jefferson warned him that
the Federal executive now controlled the management of foreign affairs. And this should have given Genet thought. But had not
Gérard, La Luzerne, Marbois before him operated directly, and
with success, among the members of Congress? If need be, he would
appeal over the President to the people, to the real sovereigns in
America.[23]

He would discuss the question indefinitely, but he would not stop
equipping the privateers in American ports. He would urge that the
Treasury advance payments on the American debt to France—in
"assignments" to dealers in produce so that the money might be
spent in this country—and this he would do ostensibly in order that
he might continue sending relief to the French West Indies. But
he would find better uses for the proceeds—in privateers to capture British shipping, expeditions to the Floridas and Louisiana, uprisings among the French Canadians.[24]

Genet's plan was to send the French fleet to destroy the British
fisheries in Newfoundland, retake St. Pierre and Miquelon, raid the
British convoy coming out of Hudson's Bay, and burn Halifax, then
to pick up a force of American and French volunteers in Virginia,
strike in passing at the Island of Providence, "lair of all English
privateers," and take possession of New Orleans in coöperation with
George Rogers Clark who was to come down from Kentucky. The
French fleet, under a command which had little sympathy with

22. *Ibid.*, 211–213. Genet's report from Charleston, April 16; 215, from Philadelphia,
May 18. For Moultrie's afterthoughts, see ASP IA, I, 310. For the Treaty of 1788, see
above, pp. 123–126.

23. *Corresp. French Ministers*, 217. Jefferson (Ford ed.), VI, 323, to Monroe, June 28;
338–339, to Madison, July 7, 1793.

24. *Corresp. French Ministers*, 216, 223; 232–233, Genet's report, July 31, 1793. Jefferson (Ford ed.), VI, 252–259, 273–289, 294–315, 329–330, 339–345, 363–366. ASP
FR, I, 141–167. Hamilton (Lodge ed.), IV, 417–432.

Genet, did not coöperate. But it appears that he was supported by Governor Clinton of New York.[25]

This "démagogue enragé," whom Catherine of Russia had found too much for her royal Court, was so absorbed by these purposes within his instructions that he lost sight of the essential requirement upon which they had been based. Genet did not strive first to win the confidence of the American President. Whether he could have succeeded in doing so before the news arrived that his party had been driven from power in France is very doubtful indeed, but that is another matter. He did not pay heed to the deeper meaning in Secretary Jefferson's remark about the rendezvous of Kentuckians beyond the territories of the United States. Whatever such lesser Americans as Moultrie and George Rogers Clark, whatever even Thomas Jefferson might say or do, the fact was that the American President had a strong hold upon the loyalty of his countrymen. "Old Washington" could not be ignored. And Thomas Jefferson himself began to resent Genet's behavior toward Washington and to deplore that the American people might not distinguish between the French minister and his nation.[26]

The President's advisers had agreed that the installments on the debt should not be paid in advance. Although Jefferson personally favored making the payments if the Treasury could do so conveniently—and did not like Hamilton's thought of declining curtly without explanation—he admitted that it was the right of the United States under the law to reject any change which would be disadvantageous to them. They would have to pay a higher rate of interest for new domestic loans in order to meet Genet's demand. Moreover, Jefferson saw the force in the argument that this régime in France might not last; the next Government of France might insist that the payments had been made to an illegal government and that the United States still owed France the amount which had been advanced.[27]

Decision was made as readily to deny the use of American ports for equipping French privateers. The governors of the States were called upon to aid the Federal Government in maintaining the neutrality of the Union. Secretary Jefferson answered Genet's protests with letters of painstaking explanation and insistence upon

25. *Corresp. French Ministers*, 234–235. August 2, 1793. Treudley, 117–119.

26. Jefferson (Ford ed.), VI, 338–349, to Madison, to Monroe, July 7, 14, 1793.

27. *Ibid.*, VI, 287–289, to Washington, June 6, 1793. Hamilton (Lodge ed.), IV, 418–420. Miller, *Treaties*, II, 115–121, contract of February 25, 1783, regarding the debt to France.

the legal right of the United States under the treaties to pursue in detail the general course which had been laid down by the President's proclamation of April 22. And finally, port officials received exact instructions from Secretary Hamilton. They were to distinguish prizes, ships of war, and merchantmen which had been armed for defensive purposes from privateers. They were directed to bring all violators to the attention of the governors and the district courts for prosecution.[28]

The end to enduring Citizen Genet came as British cruisers concentrated upon the American Coast and British sailors brawled with Frenchmen in the streets of New York. Growing desperate in his effort to coördinate the naval expedition into the Gulf of Mexico with the enterprise of Clark and others in the back country, Genet dared in the middle of July to send the privateer *Little Democrat* to sea, after he had promised Jefferson that he would not. There was now no doubt in the President's council that he should be dismissed. It was only how this was to be done.[29]

General Knox alone wished at a meeting on August 1 to send off Genet at once. All finally agreed that a full statement worded so as to require his recall should be sent, together with his correspondence, to the Executive Council of France. Jefferson brought his draft of the statement to conference on August 20. He met no opposition to any part except his allusion to Genet's conduct as threatening to add still another nation to the enemies of his own country and to draw upon both the reproach of "liberty warring on herself." The President took no exception to this. In fact, he liked it. But as Hamilton and therefore Knox, and even Randolph, attacked the phrase, Washington let it be struck out. The final draft was approved on the twenty-third, and dated August 16 to conform with the last accompanying document. A special messenger was soon on his way to France.[30]

Before this, however, a savage reprimand to Citizen Genet, written on July 30, had left France for America. The Girondists had lost control of the National Convention, in part because they advocated a federal organization similar to that of the United States. It was a plan to decentralize government so as to relieve the provinces from domination by the city of Paris. But it took on the aspect of treason to the Republic as the provinces were increasingly suspected of royalist sympathies; and the defection of General Dumouriez quickened those fears. Barère proposed to the Convention

28. Jefferson (Ford ed.), VI, 307–312. Hamilton (Lodge ed.), V, 19, August 4, 1793.
29. Fenno's *Gazette of the United States*, June 15, August 24, 1793.
30. Jefferson (Ford ed.), I, 252–259; VI, 397.

on June 2 that Brissot, Lebrun, Clavière, and others be arrested. Brissot was accused of causing the war with Britain, then of plotting to restore the Monarchy, and finally on October 31 sent to the guillotine. The Girondists had fallen. The Jacobins were in power.[31]

Their ministry of foreign affairs recoiled furiously from Genet's reports. He had been sent, wrote Deforgues, "to treat with the *Government* and not with a *portion of the people.*" He had alienated from himself the only person who could be the spokesman of the American people to the French ministry. His expedition from Philadelphia by sea against New Orleans would violate American neutrality openly and make him odious to the Government. And there was more, to the same grim effect. Far from stirring resentment, therefore, against the United States when it arrived in Paris, Washington's demand for Genet's recall only set the Jacobins more vehemently against him. They despatched orders for his arrest with the minister to replace him. The guillotine would surely have awaited Genet, *"pour la cause de la liberté et de l'égalité,"* as it had most of his faction, if President Washington had delivered him to punishment. But Washington would not do so. He had made up his mind to dismiss Genet before the news began to arrive in Philadelphia of the demands of the "Club of Cordeliers" that all "Brissotins" be summarily executed, of the rioting in the National Convention, and Barère's proposal on June 2.[32]

These facts did not make Washington's decision. They appeared in the *Gazette of the United States* on August 3, 7, and 24 as he and his advisers were discussing and completing their statement to the Executive Council of France. Nor did it matter to him that Genet wrote directly to insult the President of the United States, declaring himself a "true republican," questioning Washington's principles and asserting that he had betrayed France to her enemies. Secretary Jefferson could attend to that by publishing Genet's letter and replying, as he did, in the press that it was not proper for Genet to have direct correspondence with the President. It was of no importance, either, that Genet persisted with his intriguing among the people after he had been told of his dismissal. He had been repudiated in France. There was now no danger from him as an official French agent. The President therefore instructed his Attorney General to tell Genet's successor that the United States had demanded

31. *Gazette of the United States,* Philadelphia, August 24, 1793. Ellery, *Brissot de Warville,* 346 ff.

32. *Corresp. French Ministers,* 228–231, July 30, 1793; 287–294, October 16, November 15, 1793. The excerpt in French is from the original instructions to Genet where his devotion to the "cause" is extolled. *ibid.,* 202.

only that he be recalled. Whether or not it might anger the Jacobins, George Washington would not have Citizen Genet sent back to France. He was allowed to remain with his American wife, daughter of Governor Clinton, safe in New York and political oblivion.[33]

Governor Shelby of Kentucky—The Law of 1794

THE President turned sharply, however, upon the Kentuckians. He had not yet seen William Short's despatch of August 20 from Madrid containing the text of the alliance which Godoy had made with St. Helens on May 25—obtained by Short from a person whom he was "not at liberty" to mention, and supposed still to be secret. But Washington was not going to let Western ambitions and fears develop a war with Britain so long as he was President. (That privilege was destined to be Madison's in 1812.) Washington took the "boldest & greatest" question "that ever was hazarded" out of his Secretary's hands. He ordered Jefferson to request that Governor Shelby be particularly attentive to the enterprise against Spanish dominions in the Southwest, that Shelby take legal measures to prevent it and warn the Kentuckians of the consequences if it occurred. This Jefferson did on August 29, commenting in addition that not only the peace of the Union but the special interests of Kentucky were involved as the negotiations with Spain were under way to the eventual opening of the Mississippi.[34]

Governor Shelby replied on October 5 that there was no attempt then to move against Spanish authority down the Mississippi, and promised his best effort to stop it when it should appear. Kentucky, he declared, had "too just a sense of obligations to the General Government" to countenance any such thing. Jefferson wrote again on November 6 naming and describing four Frenchmen whom Genet had sent to Kentucky. Michaux was not among them. Nor did Jefferson refer to his letter of introduction. Instead, he hoped that the citizens of Kentucky would not be "decoyed" into the proposed attack upon New Orleans. The "surest dependence," he said, would be upon regular measures by the "General Government," the "united authority" of all of the States.[35]

The Governor of Kentucky responded to this in a different mood on January 13, 1794. The President should be "full and explicit"

33. For Genet's letter to Washington, August 13, and Jefferson's reply, August 16, see Fenno's *Gazette of the United States,* August 24, 1793. Washington (Ford ed.), XII, 402–403 n., to John Adams, January 8, 1794. For John Adams' comments to Mrs. Adams on Washington's disregard of the Jacobins, see *Works,* I, 458–462.

34. ASP FR, I, 277, 455. Short's despatch of August 20; Jefferson's letter to Shelby, August 29.

35. *Ibid.,* I, 455.

as to what he would require. Clark evidently was preparing to do something, but Shelby doubted that he himself had any legal authority to restrain or to punish until that something had actually been done: "I shall, upon all occasions," he declared, "be averse to the exercise of any power which I do not consider myself as being clearly and explicitly invested with, much less would I assume a power to exercise it against men whom I consider as friends and brethern, in favor of a man whom I view as an enemy and a tyrant." If Washington were at all sensitive, and he was, he could have taken this to mean himself.

"I shall also feel," continued Governor Shelby, "but little inclination to remove the fears of the minister of a prince, who openly withholds from us an invaluable right, and who secretly instigates against us a most savage and cruel enemy." (The closure of the Mississippi and Indian war parties were indeed powerful stimulants to disloyalty beyond the Appalachians.) Shelby reserved the right to his private opinion "as a man, as a friend to liberty, an American citizen, and an inhabitant of the Western waters." But even so, he would stick at all times, he said, to his "duty to perform whatever may be constitutionally required of me, as Governor of Kentucky, by the President of the United States." Even so, too, it looks as though Shelby was reaching for his gun when Washington beat him to the draw.[36]

The President's first retort to the Governor of Kentucky was made to order for him by the Jacobin successor to Genet. Fauchet issued—somewhat reluctantly as it proved—a proclamation on March 6, 1794, revoking the commissions which Genet had given and forbidding violation of the neutrality of the United States. This came just as Clark was about to descend the Mississippi and armed forces were gathering on the Georgian border to attack St. Augustine.[37]

The second retort was Washington's own proclamation of March 24 warning all citizens and ordering the courts, magistrates, and officers of the United States to put strictly into execution all lawful means to prevent foreign enlistment. The third was a carefully prepared reply on March 29 to Shelby's letter of January 13. It was sent by Edmund Randolph as Secretary of State. For Thomas Jefferson was at last in the retirement of Monticello where he had long wished to be, away from the constant interference of Secretary Hamilton in the affairs of the Department of State. Randolph told Shelby that, on grounds of personal liberty, individuals of course

36. *Ibid.*, I, 456.
37. Mangourit (Turner ed.), 569–679, 629.

might take arms and provisions and leave the country. But, they would be held to acount nevertheless if their intent, when they did so, was to enter a foreign service against another people at peace with the United States. The President wished the Governor to do no more than the laws permitted, said Randolph, but the President had "consigned" measures to the Governor's discretion and execution. It would be well for him, therefore, to think over his sentiments as a friend of liberty, an American citizen, an inhabitant of the Western waters, and see how they harmonized with his duty as Governor of Kentucky. Randolph assumed that Shelby would coöperate.[38]

Washington's final retort to the Governor of Kentucky came with the Act of Congress approved on June 5, 1794. It expressly fixed the penalties of fines and imprisonment for accepting commissions in a foreign service, for enlisting and recruiting others, for equipping ships of war, setting military expeditions on foot to depart from the country, and similar crimes against the United States. It empowered the district courts to take cognizance of those crimes and authorized the President to use both military and naval force, Federal and State militia, if necessary to suppress such enterprises and to compel any foreign ships to leave the ports of this country. The speculations of the Governor of Kentucky upon jurisdiction and legality had become merely academic.[39]

The danger from French intrigues with American frontiersmen was thus reduced, but Federal authority was still very uncertain in the West and conditions there now took a curious turn. The old Spanish conspiracy, in which the notorious Wilkinson played the leading part, came to life as the plot against Spanish control of the Mississippi subsided in Kentucky. And the revived conspiracy with the Spaniards in New Orleans was linked now with the uprising of the "Whisky Boys" in western Pennsylvania.

President Washington looked upon the insurrection in Pennsylvania as the "first *formidable* fruit of the Democratic Societies" instituted "by their father, Genet," to shake the Government "to its foundation." But the Spanish commissioner in Philadelphia, Jaudenes, saw it quite differently. He reported to Madrid, October 31, 1794, that an emissary had come to him from the Whisky mal-

38. Richardson, I, 157. Jefferson (Ford ed.), VI, 101–109, to Washington, September 9, 1792; 206–207, to Short, March 23, 1793; 360–361, to Washington, July 31, 1793; 488–489, to Martha Jefferson Randolph, December 22, 1793. ASP FR, I, 456–457.

39. Folwell, *Laws of the United States of America* (1796), III, 88. See Hyneman, *The First American Neutrality,* for analytical presentation. Consult also Thomas, *American Neutrality in 1793* and Fenwick, 15–30.

contents, claiming connection with the "secret committee of correspondence of the West." Jaudenes had given this "M. Mitchell" a hundred dollars and a promise that Spain would treat with interested parties concerning the navigation of the Mississippi if they would declare their independence of the United States. "Mitchell" had returned later, said Jaudenes, with detailed memory of a letter from the "secret committee." This he set on paper as the letter had been destroyed. It proposed an independent inland state including the Ohio Valley from the eastern watershed to the Illinois River and from the Great Lakes to the Tennessee River on the south. This state would enter into an offensive and defensive alliance with Spain.[40]

We can make too much of so startling a proposition from mysterious and inconsequential persons. But Jaudenes thought enough of it to report it carefully to Godoy and to send in "M. Mitchell's" paper. And he delayed negotiations on the treaty which he had been instructed to obtain with the United States. One plausible explanation is that he did so until he could get a response from Godoy to the appeal of "M. Mitchell." Another more likely, however, is that Jaudenes had learned of Thomas Pinckney's appointment to Madrid and therefore realized that it would be useless for him to try to negotiate further in Philadelphia until Washington had heard from Pinckney.[41]

In either case, if Washington did not know of this latest intrigue and its curious twist—and there is little reason to suppose that he did—he nevertheless did know how grave the crisis was in Pennsylvania. It could spread sedition like fire among the explosives of Western discontent. He went in person with Federal troops drawn largely from his native Virginia, and with his old lieutenant, Dan Morgan, to suppress the revolt: "If this is not done," he declared, "there is an end of, and we may bid adieu to, all government in this country, except mob and club government, from whence nothing but anarchy and confusion can ensue." Besides, the power of Britain in America was behind those turbulent counties. There was, as Edmund Randolph said, no "proof" that British influence had been "tampering" with the people of Kentucky and in the neighborhood of Pittsburgh, "to seduce them from the United States." But this had been "boast of by them" and an "expectation" might have

40. Washington (Ford ed.), XII, 453–455. To Henry Lee, Governor of Virginia, August 26, 1794. Bemis, *Pinckney's Treaty*, 245–247, with map. See also Whitaker, 196–197, who names the secret committee from Carondelet's correspondence as Wilkinson, Innes, Sebastian, and Murray.

41. Bemis, *op. cit.*, 248. Whitaker, 202. See below, pp. 213–221.

been "excited in the breasts of some." Chief Justice Jay on extraordinary mission to London had not yet obtained Grenville's pledge to evacuate the posts and to maintain peace. General "Mad Anthony" Wayne had only just broken the British spell over the Indian warriors in the Northwest Territory.[42]

42. Washington (Ford ed.), XII, 469–471, to Morgan, October 8, 1794. Randolph, *Vindication* (1795), 83, as of August 18, 1794. For Wayne and the Treaty of 1795, see below, pp. 211–213.

VIII

TRUCE WITH BRITAIN

Britain at War

WHILE President Washington repressed French designs upon New Orleans that might involve the United States with Britain, his Secretary of State withdrew to his home in Virginia, asserting that he was out of politics and interested henceforth only in a farmer's life. But Thomas Jefferson was also confessing that he missed the newspapers of Philadelphia and, as he heard of events, his letters grew more hostile toward Britain, until he finally declared that the United States should interpose "at a proper time" and fulfill their guarantee of the French West Indies as stipulated in the Treaty of 1778.[1]

It did not appear to matter greatly to Jefferson that the National Convention of France had anticipated Britain early in 1793 with decrees authorizing interference with neutral vessels which carried foodstuffs to British ports. But the Convention had done so notwithstanding the stipulation in the Treaty of Amity and Commerce of 1778 that "free Ships shall also give a freedom to Goods." And it had manipulated its successive edicts in such a way as to honor the protests of Gouverneur Morris superficially while continuing to violate American property. Morris had appreciated the significance of these decrees. They broke the Treaty of 1778. They could be made to justify the United States accordingly in abandoning their guarantee to France. It rankled more in Jefferson's mind, however, that Britain had been satisfied with the Proclamation of 1793, with the neutrality of the United States in fact, and had seen no point in conceding anything to American shipping for a statement of that neutrality in words.[2]

The British were not fearful of the United States in 1793. They perceived no great danger in delaying a while longer the settlement of those old issues which had been left by the Peace of 1783. As the Americans would not compensate the Loyalists and pay debts con-

---

1. Jefferson (Ford ed.), VI, 453–454, 455, 495, 497, 498, 500, and 501–503 to Madison, April 3, 1794. Bemis, *Jay's Treaty*, is the authority on the subject of this chapter.

2. ASP FR, I, 373–375, Morris to Jefferson, October 10, 1793. For details of the French treatment of such American vessels, see *ibid.*, I, 244 ff. and Moore, V, 4412–4413.

tracted prior to the Revolution, the British would not pay for the Negroes taken away with their troops. Least of all, would they evacuate the forts which they still held on the American side of the Canadian border. From their point of view, the military preparations of the United States against the Indians south of the Great Lakes and the St. Lawrence appeared, as in 1790, to have those forts as the ultimate objective. And Genet's efforts to rouse the French Canadians increased the misgiving. But on the other hand, the uncertainty of these movements alone was excellent reason why they should construct that Indian buffer state which their officials in Canada wanted so much between the province and the United States.[3]

Foremost in British minds, however, was the necessity of beating down Revolutionary France. If this caused new difficulties with the United States, self-preservation would justify them. That the United States should stop the equipping of French privateers in their ports, and withhold protection from their citizens who dealt in contraband, was pleasing indeed to Britain. But she would give no compensation for such services to her. She would follow the lead and extend those restraints. She would stretch the meaning of contraband and choke all trade with the French West Indies. As for sailors, the rule with slight exception should be: Once an Englishman, always an Englishman. The Royal Navy needed men. The press gang therefore should not hesitate then to take them, even from the decks of American ships. The civil authorities could make explanation, and amends if need be, later.

So it happened that just as he got the situation better in hand along the Spanish border, President Washington was compelled to face the threat of a war with Britain from other causes, and with even more dangerous possibilities as there rose with it the peril, grave enough in itself, of the Whisky Rebellion.[4]

Neutral Rights—Reprisal

BRITISH naval officers had been impressing American sailors at the time of the crisis over Nootka Sound. Gouverneur Morris had protested then on his own responsibility, and had received a humorous apology. He had suggested that the admiralty courts of America should provide American sailors with certificates of citizenship in the future, and Pitt had approved the idea. But Morris had been on special mission as a personal agent for President Washington to

3. Simcoe (Cruikshank ed.), II, 35, McKee to Simcoe, August 22, 1793. See below, pp. 206–207.
4. See above, pp. 151–156.

discuss the problems left by the Treaty of 1783, the appointment of a British minister to Philadelphia, and a commercial treaty. Both parties were much more interested in sparring over those matters and their chances in case Britain were to go to war with Spain. The issue had not been clearly drawn in 1790 respecting the right of an individual to transfer his allegiance from one state to another by emigration and naturalization.[5]

It had been left for Secretary Jefferson to establish that principle, insofar as it applied to citizens of the United States, three years later when demanding the recall of Genet. They were free, he said, to divest themselves of their obligation to this country and to become subjects of another power. But of course they could not do so by an act of treason; the laws did not admit that the commission of a crime amounted to a divestment of the character of citizen. In other words, those who accepted Genet's commissions without first having formally renounced their American citizenship, and thus released the United States from responsibility for them, could certainly not expect immunity from the penalties of the American law.[6]

Jefferson, however, did not attempt before he left office to force this principle upon Britain with regard to those Americans who were now being impressed into service against France. And instead of using it as a cloak for the former subjects of Britain who had chosen to become American citizens, either by their rebellion or by subsequent naturalization, the American minister in London tried to develop the plan of Morris and Pitt. Thomas Pinckney accepted the duty of proving to the British press gangs that some of their victims, at least, were exempt because of their birth. Such certificates gave immunity from service in the British Navy. But they gave equal evidence of Britain's authority over foreigners ashore and within her territorial waters. And it was a sad occasion for any American who ran afoul of a British press gang without having a proper certificate of birth with him. It was hopeless for King George's former subjects who now prided themselves upon their citizenship in the land of the free.

Pinckney thus yielded to the British Government in regard to the rights of expatriation and of jurisdiction within the British domain. But he tried throughout his residence in London to stop the practice of impressment on the high seas. It was not a proper exercise of the belligerent's right of visit and search under international law, he argued. British municipal laws concerning citizenship had no place

5. Morris (Morris ed.), I, 326–327. See above, p. 131.
6. Jefferson (Ford ed.), VI, 381, August 16, 1793.

on the seas, except aboard British ships; the British Government was usurping authority beyond the limits of its jurisdiction.

To this argument Britain's statesmen gave no heed. They continued to assert the right of impressment, and to indulge in the practice, so long as Britain was at war with France and the United States did not have the physical strength to discourage them. In justice we must note, however, that through the whole period many a British subject who had never become a naturalized American used the pretense of American citizenship to evade serving his King.[7]

Britain's treatment of American commerce had been more exasperating. Her steady refusal since 1783 to entertain any proposals for a commercial treaty that would admit American ships into the ports of the British Empire on a competitive basis had brought Secretary Jefferson to the point where he was ready to apply legislative reprisals regardless of consequences for the American Treasury and the chance of war with Britain. He had reported in 1791 upon the value to the United States of the gratuitous French *arrêts* of 1787 and 1788. Seven twelfths of America's whale oil, he said, went to France and two thirds of its codfish to the French West Indies. Therefore he had suggested that Congress should grant some exemption to French shipping from the tonnage duties of the Acts of 1789 and 1790 so that these French concessions would be tied to reciprocal legislation under the most-favored-nation clause of the commercial treaty of 1778.[8]

But more significant than the favor to France had been the implicit purpose of discriminating against Britain. Madison had prepared resolutions for Congress. Then the plan had been dropped as the British Government at last sent an accredited minister to the United States. But whatever the American expectations of Hammond, nothing had come of his mission to the advantage of American shipping.

Instead, after war began again with France in 1793, an order-in-council had appeared on June 8 declaring that it was Britain's right to detain vessels carrying foodstuffs to any port in France or any port occupied by the armies of France and to divert those cargoes from the French by purchase. When Jefferson heard of this early in September, he instructed Pinckney to request explanations immediately and to obtain its revocation. A neutral nation had the right, he declared, to judge for itself what market suited it best; it had the right to trade in any commodities except implements of war; this

7. Zimmerman, 30–61. Bemis, *Pinckney in London,* 228 ff.
8. Jefferson (Ford ed.), V, 266. ASP FR, I, 109–110.

order manifestly violated the law of nations. And certainly interference with neutral merchantmen carrying grain had not as yet become one of the generally accepted prerogatives of belligerents, even though the French Convention had anticipated the British Government in trying it.[9]

The second part of the British order, moreover, distinguished the United States from Denmark and Sweden with regard to attempts to enter blockaded ports. No doubt Britain had obligations to them by treaty which she could not set aside with a mere order-in-council. But as Jefferson asserted to Pinckney, this section of the order did exactly declare that the vessels of the United States would be lawful prize. When therefore Hammond notified him of the order on September 12, Jefferson replied as courteously as he could that he had already heard of it and had taken up the question elsewhere. He did concede to Hammond that Britain's distinction of Denmark and Sweden because of commitment by treaty was not unfriendly toward the United States. But that was a principle which could work both ways. The United States, too, had obligations by treaty. We need only recall their commitments to France to appreciate the readiness with which Jefferson made the concession on that point.[10]

Pinckney was to see what he could do with direct negotiations in London, but Secretary Jefferson was not at all hopeful. This order of June 8 was so determined and ruthless. Furthermore Hammond continued neglecting to answer his letter of May 29, 1792, about Britain's violations of the Treaty of 1783. And finally, Jefferson had information that Britain had sponsored a truce between Portugal and Algiers which would leave American shipping open to raids in the Atlantic as well as the Mediterranean. Church, American consul at Lisbon, had written: "I have not slept since the receipt of the news of this hellish plot—pardon me for such expressions. Another corsair is in the Atlantic. God preserve us." Church bemoaned the high price for "protected vessels." And he noted that one of the Algerine frigates was "a very late present from the British King." Humphreys vitiated this report in large part by another from Gibraltar that the British consul at Algiers had made this truce "without authority" from his Government. But Jefferson was not appeased. He had gone back to his opinion of 1791 that the only escape from the British dragnet lay in reprisal upon British shipping.[11]

9. ASP FR, I, 240.

10. Jefferson (Ford ed.), VI, 412–416, to Pinckney, September 7, 1793; 431, to Hammond, September 22.

11. Ibid., VI, 7–69, letter to Hammond, May 29, 1792. ASP FR, I, 288 ff., 296. Jefferson (Ford ed.), VI, 488–489, to Martha Jefferson Randolph, December 22, 1793.

As he cleared his desk in the Department of State before retiring to Virginia, therefore, Jefferson sent to Congress, December 16, 1793, an elaborate statement of the foreign restrictions upon American commerce and this time an explicit recommendation. Dismissing the fact that the great bulk of the country's trade, both export and import, was with Britain and her possessions, and ignoring French depredations upon American ships, Jefferson stressed the greater lenience of France toward American commerce. He proposed that the United States should match discrimination with discrimination. "Free commerce and navigation are not to be given," he declared, "in exchange for restrictions and vexations." If other nations wished American commodities, they should unload a fair proportion of them from American ships. The development of this country's shipping was essential to its defense. Thomas Jefferson seems not to have appreciated the changes which were coming over French policy at that very time. Or, if he did, he was determined that they should not bend his course from reprisals upon Britain.[12]

Jacobin Policies in Relation to America

A TRANSFORMATION nevertheless was taking place in France that was to alter her relations with the United States fundamentally. The Jacobins had done more than oust the Brissotins from office and repudiate Genet's actions in America during the summer of 1793. They had turned the system of France from free trade toward protection, from dependence upon foreign shipping to reliance upon her own, from a colonial policy which allowed the United States specific favors to a plan for combining the colonies with France and excluding all foreign interests uniformly.[13]

The Girondists had opposed the old mercantilist theory of kingdom and colonies, had furthered the commercial policy of Vergennes in its last phase, and had advocated even greater freedom of trade in which the colonies should grow prosperous by direct intercourse with foreign countries. They had adhered to the principle of free ports with special privileges, as part of their program of federalization. The city of Paris, the provinces, and the colonies, while enjoying exceptional privileges in some instances, should all be parts of the whole French State—as against the British Empire. The Girondists had not opened the West Indian ports to American shipping and produce solely because France was at war again with Britain and wished to employ American neutrality to get by the

12. *Ibid.*, VI, 470–484. ASP FR, I, 300 ff.
13. Nussbaum, *Commercial Policy in the French Revolution*. Brissot de Warville's *The Commerce of America with Europe*.

British fleet. They thought also of economic union with the United States against Britain, a sort of international mercantilism. From this had come the instructions to Genet to make a new treaty with the United States which should punish those nations monopolizing their colonies to the exclusion of foreign states.[14]

There had been two great obstacles to the success of this program, and the Jacobins saw them clearly. The Girondists were too optimistic in their disregard of Britain's sea power. Their ambitions in the Mississippi Valley put France in opposition to the United States whether they would or not. Possibly, though, they might have passed the first obstruction if they had not created the second in largest part for themselves.[15]

American statesmen saw these as clearly as the Jacobins, and shaped the policy of the United States accordingly. Recognition of Britain's control of the sea and her strategic position on the Great Lakes and in the Floridas, though they were Spanish in name, led straight to the assertion and enlargement of American neutrality —the development, as it were, of a counternationalism. This the Girondists could never have reconciled with their international mercantilism, never at least so long as they endeavored to operate in the Mississippi Valley for themselves. Realization of this ulterior purpose not only supported and intensified American recognition of British sea power but generated as well a spirit of competition in America with the "antient ally" herself—as Thomas Jefferson's own reflections will amply bear witness.[16]

The Girondists evidently could not see that the admission of American shipping into the French West Indian trade would not compensate the American people for interfering with their expansion into the Mississippi Valley. But it could not so compensate when both commerce and Westward expansion were inseparable from fear of Britain. British reactions might vary in form for each case, but they would be the same in effect upon the growth of American nationality. Few American statesmen were then so provincial as not to appreciate that the interests of the United States in the West Indies and in the Mississippi Valley were interdependent—as much so as the interests of Britain or France, though in other ways. Jefferson differed from Washington only in preferring to hazard more on the side of France against Britain, as Hamilton went to the other extreme on the side of Britain against France. All three were Ameri-

14. *Corresp. French Ministers,* 202, 204.
15. See below, pp. 405 f., 452 f., 494 f., for Napoleon's careful preparations concerning British seapower in the Caribbean.
16. See above, pp. 137–139.

cans and nationalists first, partisans and sectional leaders thereafter. The Jacobins came to power, it would seem, determined to keep themselves out of such a mess as the Girondists had made of relations with the United States, but in no way to sacrifice French interests in America while doing so. They observed how Britain used her merchant marine to get what supplies she wished from the United States for herself and her colonies, to carry a large share of their trade with the rest of the world besides, and still managed to keep American shipping out of her ports as she pleased with her navigation laws. They saw the United States adopt tonnage statutes and set up tariff barriers to foster their own industries and give themselves economic self-sufficiency in time. And the Jacobins were impressed. They planned a system for France upon these British and American models that would combine and improve the best features of both.

They opposed free ports and particular exemptions from the national law. They desired to incorporate the colonies in the French nation, with no tariff barriers of any sort between them and the homeland, with produce and supplies carried back and forth in French ships. They were for letting the grain trade virtually take care of itself, with France buying directly in the best market and carrying in her own merchantmen. They demanded a straight French nationalism—with no real international coöperation, however much they would do lip-service to the treaties with the United States, excoriate Genet, and apologize because their war with Britain led them into administrative errors when dealing with American ships carrying British goods.

To these ends, therefore, the Jacobins were turning France away from the Bourbon policy of Vergennes' last days, when concessions had been made to American shipping in the West Indies and Rayneval had made the treaty for reciprocal trade with Britain in 1786. They were chiefly responsible, before they had driven the Girondists from power, for the Navigation Act of March 1, 1793, denouncing the Treaty of 1786 and excluding English goods from France. They reversed the Girondist decrees which had opened the West Indies to American commerce after the declaration of war upon Britain. And they began in July, over the protests of Gouverneur Morris, to forbid American ships in the direct trade between France and her colonies. This they may have had a legal right to do, as much right as the Congress of the United States to make tonnage laws and erect tariff barriers. But the fact remains that they had begun to do so before the United States had given any provocation to them by conceding rights to the British cruisers on patrol in the West Indies.

France had altered her colonial policy, as she had violated the principle *free ships make free goods,* before Thomas Jefferson left office in January, 1794.[17]

Whether Jefferson realized it or not, the Jacobins had turned France to protection, nationalism, and direct hostility toward the United States in the summer of 1793. The long quarrel over the "Bordeaux Embargo" resulting from their decrees may have ended eventually with adequate reimbursement of the American shipmasters. But other quarrels arose as the Jacobins and their successors continued the practice of issuing decrees and counterdecrees with respect to American shipping, piling up millions of reclamations to be paid back to Americans, or in confiscations for the French Treasury—unless they stuck to private hands on the way. And although they talked vengeance upon Genet and high regard for Washington, the Jacobins, too, were looking at the Mississippi Valley through the eyes of Moustier.[18]

Debate in Congress—Hamilton's "Reveries"

ALTHOUGH the reports from Morris concerning French seizures of American ships had arrived, and had influenced Jefferson and Washington to reduce somewhat their cordiality toward France in the President's message to Congress in December, 1793, Jefferson preferred to think that the confusion of decrees in France came from internal disorders rather than a change of policy in regard to the United States. He sent another statement to Congress on December 30 as requested, giving such decrees as had come to the Department of State; but he stressed that he had received no official communication of them from France. While Jefferson retired to Monticello, Madison reintroduced his resolutions of 1791 aimed at Britain. Even after Morris' later reports of October, 1793, concerning the Jacobin decrees in regard to trade between France and her West Indies and the "Bordeaux Embargo" were available to Congress, the Jeffersonians did not cool toward France but strove still to enact their nonimportation bill against Britain. And Jefferson talked of honoring the guarantee of the French West Indies "at a proper time"—that is, of going to war with Britain.[19]

17. Nussbaum, 63. ASP FR, I, 243–246, 312, 362, 374.

18. ASP FR, I, 320, 373–378. *Archives Parlémentaires,* LXXIII, 350, 690, decrees of September 3, 11, 1793. For subsequent actions regarding the "Bordeaux Embargo," see ASP FR, I, 748–758. For Talleyrand and confiscations, see below, p. 285. For Moustier, see above, pp. 120–121, and for influence upon French policy, see below, pp. 295–298.

19. Washington (Ford ed.), XII, 349–358. Jefferson (Ford ed.), VI, 453–454, 456 n.–459, 460–462, 491–494, statement of December 30 to Congress. ASP FR, I, 310–313, 320–322, 374–378, 423–424, Morris' reports and Randolph to Congress, January 28, March 2, 1794. Jefferson (Ford ed.), VI, 502, to Madison, April 3, 1794.

To contradict Jefferson's statement of December 16, and Madison's resolutions, Secretary Hamilton had brought out the statistics and interpretations which he, too, had prepared in 1791. With them at his command, Representative Smith of South Carolina made a good case on January 13 that the British Parliament had not been so discriminatory as the Jeffersonians contended, nor France, except in her own interest, so liberal. France, in fact, actually was discriminating, he said; for the French Government's monopoly of tobacco was injuring the American industry. He pointed out that the export of American flour was greater to the British than to the French West Indies. He showed that even though the British were carrying American products to other parts of the world, in a great many cases Britain was the natural intermediary for the trade, and the result was extension rather than hindrance of American commerce. Wherever the United States had the natural advantage, he said, American goods went abroad in American vessels. Besides, the trade with Britain was indispensable to the revenues of the Treasury. But most telling of all of Smith's arguments was this: "Deficient in capital ourselves, it has been very useful to us to find a country which could nourish the industry, the agriculture, and the commerce of this country, and to advance its growth." French merchants were either unwilling or unable to extend credit to their American customers. The British could and did. Therefore, "Why should this young country throw down the gauntlet in favor of free trade against the world? There may be spirit in it, but there will certainly not be prudence."[20]

That very argument, however, was infuriating to those who held agriculture to be the life of the land and who looked forward confidently to the time when foreign states might be in debt to this country for distributions from its bountiful store of natural resources which they themselves did not possess. Why should traders, investors, capitalists, forever be safeguarded and preferred? Producers too, endured hardships, took risks, toiled, had rights to be considered and protected. The anger of the debate between Republicans and Federalists ran higher through February into March, embittered as before and since in our history by the essential conflict of interest between the mercantile seaboard and the agrarian communities of the interior. Then came news that impelled even Federalists to protest against Britain and to think of ways to be prepared for war.[21]

American ships were being confiscated and crews mistreated un-

20. Hamilton (Lodge ed.), IV, 199–224, Hamilton to Jefferson, January 1, 1792, and outline for Smith's speech. *Annals* Third Cong., 174 ff., 190, 207. January 13, 1794.
21. Beard, 275 ff.

der a new British order-in-council. Instructions had been issued on
November 6, 1793, to bring in as prizes all ships carrying supplies
to or produce from any French colony. The British reason was that
France had opened her West Indian possessions to American carriers,
as an act of war upon Britain. According to her "Rule of 1756"
Britain would not allow an enemy in time of war to permit what
it had itself not allowed in time of peace. But the truth was that
the Government of France had in practice opened colonial ports to
American shipping and goods prior to 1793, and recently, with the
advent of the Jacobins, was trying to exclude American shipping
for the advantage of French.[22]

Hamilton himself on March 8, 1794, submitted to President
Washington "some reveries" which "occupied his imagination." The
critical situation, he said, demanded measures "vigorous, though
prudent." They should fortify the principal ports in the several
States. They should raise 20,000 auxiliary troops. And they should
vest the President with the power to lay an embargo, partial or general, and to stop the export of commodities. It was a reminder of
colonial boycotts and a foretelling of that Jeffersonian plan of 1807
against which the Federalists of those days were going to rage. Hamilton also thought that Washington might consider participating in
some concert of neutral powers for common defense.[23]

Representative Sedgwick of Massachusetts, faithful Hamiltonian,
introduced the resolutions in Congress for a new army and an embargo which would keep all vessels, foreign or native, from leaving
the ports of the United States. It was intended directly to stop the
shipment of food to the British Army operating in the French West
Indies. For the moment both Jeffersonians and Hamiltonians were
belligerent. Days later Hamilton still grew heated when conversing
with the British minister about the order of November 6. But his
"reveries" had long since been dissipated. The Federalist counselors
were now very anxious not to let the quarrel grow into war.[24]

On March 10, Senators Ellsworth, Cabot, Strong, and King met
to confer on the wisest course to pursue. They agreed that Ellsworth
should go the next day to President Washington and advise him to
put the country in a posture of defense, but more important, to send
an agent to the West Indies for the purpose of discovering the true
situation of American property there and assisting in its legal defense, and above all, to despatch an envoy extraordinary directly

22. ASP FR, I, 430.
23. Hamilton (Lodge ed.), X, 63.
24. Bemis, *Jay's Treaty*, 202, citing Hammond's report to Grenville, April 17, 1794.
For Sedgwick's resolutions and statement, see *Annals*, Third Cong., 500–501.

to Britain to require satisfaction and to prevent war. For this post, Ellsworth was to tell the President that "Col. Hamilton was the character whose qualifications afforded a very commanding preference." When Washington expressed doubts as to Hamilton's political fitness, King persuaded Robert Morris to use his influence with the President in his behalf.[25]

The embargo was laid for a month and renewed for another. By that time Hamilton's desire to go in person to England had given way to the wisdom of President Washington. Such an appointment would have been most inexpedient in the face of active investigation by the Jeffersonians into Hamilton's conduct of the Treasury, his relations with investors in the public debt, his leaning toward foreign creditors. However much he wanted to go—or those British statesmen who had been reading the despatches from Beckwith and Hammond since 1789 wanted to have him come—Hamilton knew that for Washington's peace of mind at least he had better stay home and be content instead with fixing the policy for the President to follow. Hamilton framed in largest part the official instructions for the envoy, and gave the confidential advices as to what he might yield when the right moment for concessions came in the bargaining with the representative of the British Government. In all these preparations Edmund Randolph, Secretary of State, had scarcely more than the rôle of copyist.[26]

It therefore was not Alexander Hamilton, Secretary of the Treasury, but John Jay, Chief Justice of the United States, who set out on May 12, 1794, assured that Washington's administration would not permit his negotiations in London to be hampered by the measures before Congress for sequestering debts due to British creditors and for commercial nonintercourse until Britain should compensate American shippers, pay for the Negroes, and evacuate the Northwest posts. But it took the deciding vote of Vice-President John Adams in the Senate to defeat the nonimportation bill of the Jeffersonians.[27]

They railed at the appointment of Jay as acidly as they resented the suggestion of Hamilton but they were unable to stop it. James Monroe tried to show that, while secretary for the Confederation, Jay had yielded to the British on the point that the American States

25. King (King ed.), I, 517–519.

26. Hamilton (Lodge ed.), V, 97–131, to Washington, April 14, 1794. Washington (Ford ed.), XII, 412, 414, to Hamilton, to Monroe, April 8, 9, 1794. *Ibid.*, XII, 419, to Randolph, April 15.

27. Beard, 274. Madison (Hunt ed.), I, 292. Marshall, *Washington*, V, 547. Washington (Ford ed.), XII, 424. For the debate in the House, see *Annals*, Third Congress, 535 ff.

had broken the Treaty of 1783. But Monroe's motion was voted down. Aaron Burr failed as completely to convince the Senate that the appointment of a member of the Federal judiciary to a diplomatic mission was against the spirit of the Constitution, mischievous, and bad policy.[28]

Meantime the British Government had replaced the irritating order of November 6, 1793, with another on January 8, 1794. It was perhaps a bit difficult in good conscience to argue, without the support of the well-established instruments of contraband and blockade, that American ships might be seized and condemned for carrying supplies to the French West Indies. Britain returned therefore to the principle of June 8, 1793, that she might detain vessels, pay the freight, and preëmpt their cargoes of foodstuffs. French property aboard American ships, of course, was another thing entirely. The British statesmen were by no means ready as yet to accept as international law the American precept *free ships make free goods*. Nevertheless, there was encouragement in this new order. It was moving in the right direction for Federalist shipowners. It might in fact have had rather pleasing effects upon American opinion, if it had not been enveloped in alarming news from another quarter.[29]

Into the midst of the debate over reprisals upon British shipping and the reaction to the order of November 6, there had come the report that Lord Dorchester, Governor of Canada, had declared to the Indian chieftains on February 10, 1794, that the King would soon be at war with the Americans, and the Indians and the British would then redraw the boundary of 1783 to their own liking. If this were a true statement of the purpose of the British Government, no effort to avoid war even by Jay's extraordinary mission could succeed. But although Hammond could not manage at all well the problem created by the order of November 6, he was equal to this occasion. He admitted "what he had not been willing should be supposed to be the Fact." Dorchester's secret address was genuine, he said, but it had not been authorized. His inference was obvious: the American Government should have no fear that the British would support Dorchester. And in fact he was given a reprimand in July, as part of the British plan of negotiation with Jay.[30]

28. King (King ed.), I, 522, April 18.

29. ASP FR, I, 430–431, Pinckney to Jefferson, January 9, 1794, giving Grenville's statements.

30. Bemis, *Jay's Treaty*, 176, 234. Washington (Ford ed.), XII, 408, to Governor Clinton of New York, March 31, 1794. Text in *Annual Register*, 1794, p. 250. McLaughlin, "Western Posts," 438. ASP FR, I, 462, Hammond's acknowledgment. King (King ed.), I, 524, conversation with Hammond, April 7, 1794.

The situation notwithstanding was extremely tense in the Northwest. For after Dorchester's remarks there came definite knowledge that Governor Simcoe of Upper Canada not only held the forts strongly but had moved farther into American territory and established an outpost on the Maumee River to cover Detroit. It seemed to confirm all that Congress had read between the lines of the papers which Washington had submitted in December. British intrigues were behind every Indian outrage upon American settlers.[31]

As the President sent commissioners to treat with the Iroquois in western New York, kept close watch for seditious activities along the Spanish border, and marched upon the Whisky Rebellion, he could wish to believe that all of these problems were separate and distinct from that of peace with Britain. But he knew better. He could only hope, instead, that military skill and diplomatic shrewdness would not desert "Mad Anthony" Wayne as he approached the Indian war parties under the guns of a British fort on American soil and that somehow or other John Jay would succeed in London as neither John Adams nor Gouverneur Morris nor Thomas Pinckney had been able to do before him.

Jay's Mission to London

JAY arrived in England on June 12, 1794. He came to press the demands of the weaker party in dangerous controversies of long standing. He represented a small neutral dealing with a great belligerent who controlled the seas and possessed a commerce vital to his own country. Although he had scarcely anything to offer in return that Britain did not already enjoy, he was to seek concessions for American shipping in the West Indies where Britain had one quarter of her own commerce, and where two thirds of her enemy's commercial interests were centered upon San Domingo. He was to defend the position in regard to American debts which he had already compromised when conducting the foreign affairs of the old Confederation and the injustice of which he had virtually acknowledged as one of the signers of the Treaty of 1783. He had to negotiate with a man who was soon to learn Jay's chief handicap to success directly from the most influential person in the American Government next to the President.[32]

---

31. ASP IA, I, 340 ff. To the Senate, December 4, 1793, regarding commissioners to deal with the Iroquois. Washington (Ford ed.), XII, 459. To Jay, August 30, 1794. For Dorchester's order to Simcoe to establish the post on the Maumee, February 17, 1794, see Michigan Pion. and Hist. Soc., Collections, XXIV, 642.

32. Turner's introduction in Corresp. French Ministers, 8. See above, pp. 92, 111.

In a way, his judicial temperament, his candor, his great personal pride—some called it self-esteem—unfitted John Jay for such undertakings. They may have made him an effective antagonist of Floridablanca at Madrid in 1780 and of Vergennes at Paris in 1782, but they could hardly make him a powerful advocate with Grenville at London in 1794. In another way, however, Jay's dignity, his judicial mien, even his susceptibility to compliment served the major purpose for which Washington had sent him abroad. It mattered not so much that he should obtain at once all his Government desired as that he should increase its prestige and make arrangements which would avoid war while the controversies between the two nations moved on to eventual settlement.[33]

Lord Grenville, minister of foreign affairs, had not known until but a few days before the arrival of the American envoy that the situation in the United States had become so critical. The letters of the Canadian authorities and Hammond's despatches from Philadelphia telling of the Congressional debate over discrimination, the new army and the embargo, Dorchester's address to the Indians and Simcoe's new fort on the Maumee, had been delayed in crossing the Atlantic. Grenville had been absorbed in the war upon France, with maintaining the European coalition and preventing another league of armed neutrality such as had complicated the last struggle with France during the American Revolution. He had let American affairs slide, putting off final responses to Thomas Pinckney and trusting to Federalist sympathies with Britain to keep Republican irritation from reaching the explosive point. He had been justified in feeling somewhat secure as he observed that France also was violating American neutral rights on the sea. But there were anxious moments now as the British ministers wondered how far the effects of this outburst from America, in which even Federalists were raucous, would extend. The United States were Britain's best customer. The British Navy could not be divided for sea duty on both sides of the Atlantic for long without endangering its control of the sea. Britain could no more really afford war in America at this time than could the United States.[34]

On second thought, however, Grenville must have realized that the coming of Jay in itself should allay as soon as risen any fear that the United States would go to war. Surely, the Jay mission bound President Washington to a policy of waiting. Congress might possibly get out of hand and declare war; but Congress could not ac-

33. Washington (Ford ed.), XII, 419, to Randolph, April 15, 1794, stating Washington's objects.

34. Bemis, *Jay's Treaty*, 218–221. See above, p. 167.

tually make it; Washington was commander-in-chief. Grenville had more perception than Genet of the changes which the new Constitution had made in America. The President's personal agent, Gouverneur Morris, was saying to the Committee of Public Safety in Paris, that the American military preparations were to check the Indians and to put the Government in position not to fear an attack by Britain. There was reassurance for Grenville in that negative, the report of which came to him privately from a British agent in Italy.[35]

A concession or so to the American Chief Justice, some of which had already been decided upon, would be in order. Dorchester should be set down for his remarks to the Indians. Appeals of the seizures in the Caribbean should be had from the admiralty courts in the West Indies to higher courts in England. And Britain would agree to evacuate the Northwest posts at a time to be decided, and upon conditions. The order-in-council of June 8, 1793, as it applied to the preëmption of neutral cargoes of grain bound to France, was withdrawn on August 6, 1794. With these points clear, negotiations could proceed in easy fashion.[36]

As Grenville viewed the situation, the longer they took the better. A victory like Howe's over the fleet of Villaret on June 1, 1794, was hopeful, even though the convoy of supply ships from America had eluded the British patrol and reached the French port. Spain's restlessness in the coalition against France was disturbing, but Russia and Prussia this time could be counted upon the British side. So long as Jay could report home some progress, there was little chance of war with the United States—unless of course something unforeseen or unpremeditated should happen in the back country of America, or possibly this league of neutrals, talked among Danes, Swedes, and Americans at the instigation of Frenchmen, should develop into a real instrument of force. That Lord Grenville would much deplore.[37]

Notwithstanding, therefore, the flurry caused by James Monroe's arrival in Paris with fervid greetings from the United States Senate, and his ostentatious acceptance of the fraternal kiss of the President of the French Convention, Grenville and Jay had accumulated in exchanges of opinion by September 13 a significant list of objects for a treaty. They agreed in principle that there should be: evacuation of the posts, a commission to settle the northeast boundary, compen-

35. Dropmore Papers, II, 537. Francis Drake to Lord Grenville, April 7, 1794. For Genet, see above, p. 158.
36. Bemis, Jay's Treaty, 232–235.
37. Mahan, Sea Power and the French Revolution, I, 122–161.

sation for damages to both parties, compensation for the British creditors, immunity for private debts and securities in time of war, admission into the British West Indies of limited American shipping, freedom of ports, sharp restrictions upon sales of prizes, regulations for the ownership and disposal of land, protection of vessels or property within respective jurisdictions, and a reciprocal prohibition of impressment.[38]

But Jay had not been able to bring Grenville to final conclusions or to get him really down to the principles at issue concerning neutral rights of commerce. He therefore decided to submit the draft of a treaty which would comprehend the points in the interest of the United States. This he did on September 30. By that time Grenville, however, had learned from Hammond what he was very pleased to know. The American Government, no matter what Secretary Randolph had put into the instructions of John Jay, would have nothing to do with the rumored league of armed neutrality toward which Denmark and Sweden were so feebly maneuvering.

Among Alexander Hamilton's "reveries" on March 8 had been the idea of concerted action by neutrals. No American statesman had forgotten the contribution of the European league in 1780 to the success of the American Revolution. With little more than that memory, and no knowledge that Russia was now on the other side, Secretary Randolph had instructed Jay to sound the ministers of Russia, Denmark, and Sweden upon the probability of an alliance to support the principles of armed neutrality—for, said he, they "would abundantly cover our neutral rights." But on July 8, 1794, the Secretary of the Treasury begged leave to inform the Secretary of State of his opinion: "Denmark and Sweden are too weak and too remote to render a cooperation useful; and the entanglements of a treaty with them might be found very inconvenient. The United States had better stand upon their own ground." Hamilton admitted that his impression had varied, but the foregoing, he announced to Randolph, was the "final result of full reflection."[39]

Then, usurping the prerogative of the Secretary of State to negotiate with representatives of foreign states, the Secretary of the Treasury again indulged himself, as he had since 1789, and told the British minister the same thing, with elaborations: "It was the settled policy of this Government in every contingency, even in that of an open contest with Great Britain, to avoid entangling itself with European connexions, which could only tend to involve this

38. Bemis, *Jay's Treaty*, 237–238.
39. Hamilton (Lodge ed.), V, 135.

country in disputes wherein it might have no possible interest, and commit it in a common cause with allies, from whom, in the moment of danger, it could derive no succour."[40]

Jay himself was about to write to Washington—much as he had asserted to Montmorin at Madrid in 1780: "As to a political connection with any country, I hope it will never be judged necessary, for I very much doubt whether it would ultimately be found useful; it would, in my opinion, introduce foreign influence, which I consider as the worst of political plagues." Jay's behavior may easily have given a similar impression to Grenville at this time. But that is quite a different thing from deliberately stating the results of the discussions in the cabinet of the Administration to the minister of the opposing country. Hamilton's remarks to Hammond have been properly designated since then as statesmanship pioneering before the Monroe Doctrine of 1823. When they were made, they were nothing else than the betrayal of a state secret.[41]

Hammond reported at once to Grenville, August 3, 1794. Grenville received the despatch on September 20. The draft of a treaty which Jay presented ten days later was subjected forthwith to ruthless excision, and he was left in the dilemma of sending home what it pleased Grenville to give him or virtually nothing at all. And yet, conclude the authorities on this period, and in historical perspective quite rightly, John Jay nevertheless signed on November 14, 1794, a treaty of great importance in his own time and of still greater value to the future of this nation.[42]

Terms of The Jay Treaty

THIS new contract to maintain peace with Britain is best appraised by its provisions concerning the West, the boundaries of the British domain, the claims of both parties for damages, their maritime commerce, the rights of neutrals, and the interests of France.[1]

Britain agreed to evacuate her posts on American soil on or before June 1, 1796. The date was set ahead in order to allow time for her traders to withdraw from the Indian country or adjust themselves

40. Bemis, *Jay's Treaty*, 246.
41. Bemis, *Jay's Treaty*, 248. Jay (Johnston ed.), IV, 59. For Jay to Montmorin in 1780, see above, p. 38.
42. Bemis, *Jay's Treaty*, 269–270, discussing the variant opinions of Henry Adams and Admiral Mahan.
1. Bemis, *Jay's Treaty*, chaps. xii, xiii. Miller, *Treaties*, II, 245–274. For contemporary Republican criticism, see Madison (Hunt ed.), VI, 238–257, draft of a letter, August 23, 1795; 263–295, speech in Congress, April 6, 1796.

to the laws of the United States either as citizens or alien property holders. Safeguards were established for the continuance of British trading with the Indians below the international boundary, and reciprocal rights were given to American traders above that line. But the whole domain of the Hudson's Bay Company to the north and west was to remain closed to them. Their advantages in British territory, therefore, were not comparable to those of British traders in the Western part of the United States. Permanent freedom of transit over the waterways and portages interlacing the boundary was assured to both parties, but there were provisions to prevent the entry of prohibited goods into the territory of either. Tolls and duties were to be reciprocal and no higher than those charged of natives. The Indians were to pass and repass freely with their proper goods and effects of whatever nature.

There were no declarations in the treaty, however, such as Jay had included in his draft: that Indian parties might not pass back and forth when they were at war with either party to the treaty; that both parties would abstain from political connections with the Indians and would restrain their respective Indians from war; and that they would make common cause against every future Indian war so far as to prohibit supplying arms and ammunition and to refrain from encouraging any tribes to join in it. Nor were there in the treaty the suggestions which Hamilton had made and Jay presented in his draft; that neither party should maintain armed vessels on the lakes and waterways of the boundary, and that they should enter into arrangements for reducing and withdrawing all military force from the borders.

Grenville's refusal to admit these clauses into the treaty was deliberate. He was working toward the plan for an Indian buffer state largely on American soil south and west of Lakes Erie, Huron, and Superior. Britain's statesmen would not be ready to abandon that hope until after the War of 1812.

The treaty included a provision for postponing determination of the northwest line from the Lake of the Woods to the Mississippi River, without prejudice to the interests of either party, until they could have a joint survey. Having learned from Hammond that the line of 1783 was geographically in error—as in all probability the source of the Mississippi was not to the west but to the south of the Lake of the Woods—Grenville had pressed Jay to concede that the acknowledged right of Britain to navigation on the Mississippi implied the right to approach the river entirely through British territory. This would have been advantageous in constructing the Indian state. But Grenville had other reasons. Secret agents had not been reporting about the "Granary of America" in years past with no effect. Britons, although their seaboard colonies were gone, still thought of great things to come in the Mississippi Valley.[2]

But John Jay, remembering the value which he and his fellow commissioners in 1782 had put upon the chance of American entry into the upper Mississippi Valley beyond Lake Michigan when they had given up pretension to the area from Lake Erie to Nipissing, had stuck to the argument of principle and intention. They had meant, he said, to draw the line due west to the Mississippi, not southward; the concept of free navigation did not necessarily include the possession of adjacent lands; otherwise, neither Britain nor America would have any basis for asserting, as they did, their right to use the Mississippi through Spanish territory to the Gulf.[3]

Grenville did not see fit to press harder upon the point at that time. This did not mean, however, that Pitt and he had resigned themselves to the loss of that territory. It meant that they would await developments after they had done with the war in Europe. Neither British nor Americans then realized that the future value of the minerals in the Superior country was greater than the fur trade. Neither had any conception how important a part those resources were soon to play in making the United States of America self-reliant, even disdainful toward the rest of the world. But postponement of the decision in 1794 marked a distinct gain for them.

The dispute over the northeastern line between Maine and Quebec and New Brunswick, on the other hand, was referred to a board of commissioners at Halifax chosen by both parties. It was to determine the identity of the St. Croix River which had been designated in the Treaty of 1783. The creation of a mixed commission so to arbitrate and settle an international quarrel was a significant achievement, but this departure in international procedure was more easily obtained than the solution of the problem for which it had been made. The St. Croix River was identified in 1798, but the northeast boundary was not finally drawn until 1842.

The Jay Treaty also provided that British creditors who had found legal impediments, contrary to the Treaty of 1783, in the way of collecting debts contracted before the peace, might present their claims to another mixed commission sitting in Philadelphia. The United States undertook to guarantee the payment of such awards as this commission should determine. For the very reason that

2. See above, p. 136.
3. See above, pp. 91–92.

legal impediments had stood in the way of their obtaining satisfaction in American courts, the treaty gave these British claimants direct access to the commission without having first to take their cases through the tier of American courts.

The Federal Court in the district of Virginia (chief among the offending States) had already declared valid in 1793 those bona fide debts to British creditors which had not been confiscated by the State while conducting her war upon Britain. There was pending an appeal to the Supreme Court concerning those debts which had been confiscated, for they involved the treaty-making power of the new Federal Government under the Constitution. Jay had sat on the bench at the second hearing before the circuit court. He was still Chief Justice of the United States. He knew that the Constitution contained the statement: "All treaties made, or which shall be made, under the authority of the United States, shall be the supreme law of the land; and the judges in every State shall be bound thereby, anything in the Constitution or laws of any State to the contrary notwithstanding." He might have insisted, therefore, that in the end the British creditors would obtain from the Federal judiciary of the United States the satisfaction to which they were entitled under the Treaty of 1783.[4]

But there was weakness in this procedure. The Constitution, although not adopted until 1788, was retrospective, to be sure, in that it declared all treaties which had been made under the authority of the United States to be the supreme law of the land. But Jay and his associates who had drafted the treaty with Britain in 1782 had written their pledge merely to read: "It is agreed that creditors on either side shall meet no lawful impediment to the recovery of the full value in sterling money, of all bona fide debts heretofore contracted." Was that, together with the retrospective force of the Constitution, strong enough to break down certain results of the revolution in the several States and to compel them to restore such debts as they had confiscated by right of their individual sovereignty?

It would seem so to us now, especially since the penetrating analysis and reasoning of the Justices on the Supreme Bench who in 1796 decided the case on appeal in favor of the British creditors against the State of Virginia. As Justice Wilson summed up the matter then, no State should have the power to confiscate debts: it was a disreputable proceeding, discountenanced in the law of nations; but even

4. Article VI. Jay's instructions took note of the fact that he had participated in the Virginia case as a member of the Court. See ASP FR, I, 473.

if Virginia had possessed the power to confiscate, the Treaty of
1783 had annulled her confiscation.[5]
Instead, however, of relying on that position, in advance of the
decision of the Supreme Court, and using the issue to enhance the
prestige of the Court while he was in London, Chief Justice Jay
had chosen rather to dispose of the question there under the strongest light which was then playing upon it. It was not then a judicial
question so much as a matter of international politics. Jay committed the United States to settlement by an instrument of international arbitration.

If the Senate were to ratify his treaty and the mixed commission
successfully to dispose of the claims of the British creditors, public
respect for the Federal Government which he had sponsored in close
association with Hamilton would be increased as effectively and far
more rapidly than by the obscurer process of judicial decision. John
Jay's use of the treaty-making power at this time is to be included
with Alexander Hamilton's contemporaneous demonstration of the
taxing power among the inhabitants of western Pennsylvania in
any discussion of the rise of Federal authority above the sovereignty
of the States.

Passing by the decision of the Supreme Court in 1796, the two
parties then proceeded with the organization of the mixed commission in May, 1797, as provided in Jay's Treaty. The first member
was chosen by lot, with the result that the commission was com-
posed of three British and two American representatives. The
American minority, however, would not listen to British opinion
that interest on the debts should have continued during the Revolution and that the property of Loyalists confiscated through attainder
should be restored. The work of the commission came to a stop, and
in retort the British Government withdrew its members from the
commission in London which was dealing with American claims.
This deadlock had finally to be broken by diplomacy.

In 1802, Rufus King negotiated a convention between the two
countries which determined that in the future no creditors on
either side should meet with any lawful impediments to the collection of debts and fixed the amount due British creditors on bona
fide debts contracted prior to the American Revolution at $2,664,-
000. It was appropriated by Congress and paid.[6]

5. *Ware v. Hylton,* 3 Dallas 199, as given in Curtis' *Reports* (1855), I, 164–229. For
Chisholm v. Georgia leading to Amendment XI and the *Brailsford Case,* also involving
Georgia, see Warren, *Supreme Court,* I, 91–104.
6. Miller, *Treaties,* II, 488–491. Moore, I, 278 ff. Gallatin's Report on Finances, *Reports Sec. Treas.,* I, 263. October, 1803. Bemis, *Jay's Treaty,* 318. For King's situation,
see below, pp. 511–514.

The third mixed commission, organized in similar fashion and seated in London, had taken charge of American claims resulting from interference with neutral commerce "under Colour of authority or Commissions from His Majesty," and also of British losses from the depredations of those French privateers which had been sent out from American ports at the time of Genet. In the case of this commission, however, the American claimants had first to seek justice in the British courts before they could appeal to the commission.[7]

Nowhere in Jay's Treaty was there any provision for compensating those Americans whose slaves had been carried away with the British armies. For reasons of sympathy with freedmen as well as of diplomacy, Jay had let the interest of American slaveowners go by the board. He justified this on the ground that the United States had gained compensation for the loss from the commercial clauses elsewhere in the treaty. Virginians, however, could hardly appreciate this benefit. Shipmasters might have some chance of reimbursement for damages to their commerce in the West Indies; but planters were now obliged both to satisfy their old creditors and to give up their claims for the loss of their property in slaves. Jay's Treaty was criticized in the mansions of the South as bitterly as in the counting-houses of the Northeast.[8]

The commission in London was organized on August 25, 1796, with three American and two British members. Their procedure was marred by disputes over technicalities in regard to their jurisdiction and the quarrels of the debt commission at Philadelphia. But after resuming its sessions in 1802, the commission at London completed awards of $143,428 to meet the British claims and of $5,849,082 to compensate Americans for the spoliations "under Colour" of the King's orders. Britain thus had not been directly confronted with any decision that its orders-in-council were invalid. Rather, it had been formally obligated by an international tribunal, in which it took part, to pay specific damages for what had been decided to be contrary to international law. It was a narrow but effective distinction.[9]

7. Miller, *Treaties*, II. 252, 253.
8. Bemis, *Jay's Treaty*, 260 n. Ogg, "Jay's Treaty and the Slavery Interests of the United States," AHAR (1901), I, 273–278.
9. Moore, I, 315. Bemis, *Jay's Treaty*, 320. Malloy, I, 596 n., states that the award to American claimants by the commission at London amounted to $11,656,000. Moore, I, 343, quoting from the *Autobiography* (p. 237) of John Trumbull, one of the commissioners, puts the figure at $11,650,000. But Bemis (p. 320), gathering up other statements in Moore's account (pp. 342–343), correlates them with the convention of 1802 (Malloy, I, 610–612), setting the rate of exchange at $4.44 to the pound sterling, to

The Jay Treaty endeavored to reduce the controversy which had persisted since the failure of John Adams' mission to London in 1788 over rival shipping and the trade between the United States and the British Empire. One article gave reciprocal rights of trade between the "Dominions of his Majesty in Europe, and the Territories of the United States." For a period of twelve years, the merchants and goods of both parties were to suffer no discrimination in tonnage and port dues or customs duties. This was a definite concession to American shipowners, even though existing laws in England made it extremely difficult to compete with the British there. Another article allowed American vessels of small tonnage to enter the British West Indies during the war with France and two years thereafter, but under the strict proviso that the United States would restrain American vessels from carrying molasses, sugar, coffee, cocoa, or cotton "to any part of the World, except the United States," either from those islands or from the United States. A third article gave the United States privileges of direct trading with British territories in the East Indies, under the restriction that American vessels should not engage in the coastwise trade there. But American vessels could sail from port to port in the British East Indies to leave goods in the transoceanic traffic, and it was agreed to have further negotiations after the close of Britain's war with France.[10]

Thus the envoy extraordinary for President Washington eliminated the Acts of Congress of 1789 and 1790 as means of favoring France, and destroyed the Jeffersonian program of economic reprisal upon Britain. In return, Grenville had conceded reciprocal rights of trade between British dominions in Europe and the United States, and had agreed to open the Oriental trade for the benefit of American shipping. The opportunity which he offered in the British West Indies, however, amounted to little, and the restriction which he maintained upon the export of cotton would impede a growing domestic enterprise of the American people.

Their cotton crop was expanding from a million pounds in 1789 to eight millions in 1795. Over six millions were shipped abroad that year. And by 1800 the production of raw cotton had reached thirty-five million pounds, its export nearly eighteen millions. The shipments from South Carolina alone had increased from $2,693,268 in 1791 to $5,998,492 in 1795. Cotton was chiefly responsible for this and most of it went to British mills. How much was carried in American vessels is hard to determine, but it is certain that the

put the amount of the award to American claimants at the figure, relied upon above, $5,849,082.

10. Miller, *Treaties*, II, 254, 255, 257, 264.

agreement between Grenville and Jay to confine the traffic to British shipping angered American shipmasters. And it hardly pleased the cotton planters to have such restraint upon their foreign trade. The Senate struck out this clause of the treaty.[11]

Jay had included in his draft a provision similar to that in the commercial treaty of 1778 with France giving the protection of the nationality of a ship to its cargo regardless of the ownership of the goods. "Free ships," he hoped, were to make "free goods." But Grenville would have none of it. The treaty continued the British practice; vessels suspected of carrying an enemy's property could be seized and detained, the goods confiscated. Jay's ideas upon contraband were rejected as well. He had attempted to establish a list of commodities such as textiles, metals, grain, flour, meats and other foodstuffs which should be noncontraband. He had to accept instead a clause permitting articles not generally considered contraband to be made so, provided only that they should not be confiscated but should be bought at full value "with a reasonable mercantile Profit thereon, together with the Freight, and also the Demurrage incident to such Detension."[12]

In short, although the United States reserved their general principles concerning neutral commerce and gained also a pledge for subsequent discussion and adjustment of views, they conceded to Britain that she must continue specific practices so long as she should be at war with France. Her cruisers would visit and search, detain neutral shipping, seize contraband, preëmpt noncontraband according to her own ideas on those matters—until that terrifying menace to herself and, in her opinion, to all correct principles of liberty and government, should be removed from the other side of the Channel. And more notable, perhaps, because Grenville had been willing in September to discuss the subject, the Jay Treaty was silent altogether upon the impressment of American sailors into the British Navy.[13]

The Interests of France—Fauchet's Appraisal

As for American relations with France, Jay's Treaty asserted in so many words that nothing in it should be "construed or operate con-

11. Woodbury, Secretary of the Treasury's *Report*, Ex. Doc. 24 Cong. 1 Sess., No. 146 (1836), pp. 7, 24, 75. Pitkin, *Commerce of the United States*, 50. Hammond, *Cotton Industry*, 232–233. Turner, *Rise of the New West*, 47, estimated the American cotton crop of 1791 at two million pounds and of 1801 at forty million but did not say what percentage went directly overseas in American vessels.

12. Bemis, *Jay's Treaty*, 303–304. Miller, *Treaties*, II, 259.

13. For other points in regard to limitations put upon neutral rights, see Bemis, *Jay's Treaty*, 260–261.

trary to former and existing Public Treaties with other Sovereigns or States." He had been given only two rigid instructions: they were to get admission of some sort into the British West Indies for American shipping and to make no agreements infringing upon American obligations to France. The inference is that he had not done so. And yet, this stipulation was not made in a separate article of the Jay Treaty, manifesting by its very position of equality with all other articles that its contents were comprehensive in their meaning and effect. It was made within the article which dealt with the reception of ships of war, privateers, and their prizes into the ports of the contracting parties. Did this imply, contrary to Jay's instructions, that there were to be no restrictions upon Britain in regard to any other matters which involved American commitments to France? It seems placed at least in such a way as to create ambiguity.[14]

The United States could declare, and did consistently, that they had violated no pledges in their treaties of 1778 with France. Their position was technically correct. The Jay Treaty left them still legally free to deny Britain the right to fit her privateers or to dispose of her prizes in American ports, as they had contracted with France in 1778. They were still obligated, if they should become belligerents, to respect the neutrality of French vessels, and cargoes excepting contraband, even if those vessels were carrying the goods of an American enemy. They were still bound, in case they went to war with France herself, to refrain from taking French goods from a neutral vessel.

They were not bound, however, and they never had been, as neutrals, to protect French goods aboard their own vessels by the use of force against an enemy of France. There was nothing in the treaties of 1778 obligating them, in case they were neutrals, to assume anything like the status of armed neutrality. They had a legal right still to the neutral ground of 1793 that they were under no obligation to participate on the side of France, unless France called upon them to guarantee her West Indian possessions; and they were therefore entirely free, so long as they did not violate any of their prior engagements with France, to make a treaty even with the enemy of France if that would make their own position as neutrals more secure.[15]

On the other hand, no candid person could have had any doubt then, or since, but that the Jay Treaty directly injured French interests to which the United States had been virtually, if not pre-

14. ASP FR, I, 474. Bemis, *Jay's Treaty*, 212, 260. Miller, *Treaties*, II, 262.
15. Miller, *Treaties*, II, 19–20, Article 22, Treaty of Amity and Commerce of 1778.

cisely, committed by the Alliance of 1778 against Britain in world politics. It restricted the application of the principle *free ships free goods* as general international law. The United States repudiated to a degree as neutrals what they had proclaimed as belligerents, and they did so to the disadvantage of their old ally in war. The inference from the contracts of 1778 with France, though not the legal requirement, had been that the United States would maintain their neutrality with force if necessary.

The Jay Treaty furthermore permitted Britain to resume her interference with the vital commerce of the French West Indies, without having to confine her cruisers to the narrow limits of ac-' cepted principles of contraband and blockade. It admitted British warships into American ports and gave their officers and men privileges ashore. This, of course, the United States had a right to do, but it afforded the British Navy practical advantages on the western side of the Atlantic close to the possessions of France. Such advantages might properly have been withheld at that time by a Government which was professing its friendship for France as well as its neutrality in the wars of Europe. This may readily be admitted without suppressing Alexander Hamilton's point that the United States had no obligation to guarantee the French West Indies inasmuch as France had taken the offensive against Britain. Jay's Treaty offended France, moreover, by submitting British claims for damages from the French privateers which had been fitted in American ports to an international body in which the British Government itself was represented. But above all, it flouted the old ally of the United States by including commercial agreements for the future with the common enemy of the past.[16]

From the French point of view it appeared that, for a trivial concession in the West Indies, nominal privileges in English ports, and a share in the carrying trade to the Orient, the United States had bound themselves to admit British shipping into their home ports over a period of years upon the same basis as the most favored nation; that is, upon equality with France. They had deserted the common cause of all those who were struggling to free the world from the monopolistic control of the British naval and mercantile system. They had dropped the strongest weapon for that purpose —their power to injure Britain heavily by discrimination—in order to gain a slight although immediate advantage for themselves. This, they had done covertly—hiding it, apparently, even from their own minister in Paris. How could it be anything to Frenchmen but a deliberate slap in the face of France? That neither Jay nor Hamil-

16. For Hamilton's argument, see above, pp. 148–149.

ton was reluctant to give it seemed clear from the reports of the French representatives in Philadelphia.[17]

In such an attitude as this, a mixture of disappointment and genuine grievance, Frenchmen and their friends in America turned over the incidents which had accumulated during Washington's administration to the climax in Jay's Treaty with Britain against the interest of France. They did not expend so much reflection upon the actions of the Government in France which in violation of the treaties of 1778 had been seizing American vessels laden with goods that were not contraband, had been reversing the colonial policy of the Girondists and nationalizing the direct trade between France and the West Indies at the expense of American shipping. Nor were they thinking much upon the activities of French agents within the United States other than Genet. There was plenty astir throughout this country, however, despite Fauchet's proclamation and the neutrality law of 1794, to give the American President not only cause for grievance but intense anxiety concerning the survival of the Federal Union and its territorial domain beyond the Alleghenies.[18]

Washington did not know it, of course, but Fauchet himself was appraising the likely contents of the Jay Treaty with notable accuracy, even before it reached America, and advising the French foreign office upon a policy to meet the new state of things in America. Prior to this he had conceived that the "system of conduct" dictated by the interests of France was simply to keep the United States in "a prolonged inertia" with respect to their relations with her powerful enemies until she should be freed from the major needs which she felt concerning her existence. Then, she could "attain a rank and establish an active system among the Foreign Governments." This he epitomized as a course of "wise delays and useful procrastinations." Of such a nature had been his renunciation of Genet's expeditions from Georgia and Kentucky into Spanish territory.[19]

But now, Jay's Treaty was destroying the *status quo*, and Fauchet proposed a "permanent system" for France to employ against the United States. Jefferson, he reported, had remarked: "The force of things surrenders the French colonies to us, France enjoys the sovereignty, we the profit." Her possessions in the West Indies were dependent upon the United States for their food supply. But to Fauchet, they did not have to remain so. There was Louisiana hold-

17. For the simultaneous mission of James Monroe to France, see below, p. 228 f.
18. See above, pp. 163–164.
19. *Corresp. French Ministers*, 560, 559–571. February 4, 1795.

ing out her arms; control of New Orleans would give France control of provisioning her West Indies. Far more important than that,
it could be the citadel of an empire in the heart of America—as
Moustier had written—which would soon include those Western
States and territories of America where there were so many friends
of the Revolution. Possessing New Orleans, what could France
not do at pleasure to quicken or to suspend the growth of those
Western settlements!

The revolutionary leaven in that part of the United States, asserted Fauchet, had been further strengthened since the repression
of the latest movement. (He was thinking of the Whisky Rebellion.) And the decision as to dismemberment of the United States
would so rest with France, said he, that France would surely be respected and courted by the Federal Government as soon as it had the
French for neighbors. So, Fauchet urged that his Government take
back Louisiana. This should be done by negotiation with Spain, but
he did not neglect to suggest also that "a small force sent in the
greatest secrecy from Europe or the Colonies, will land without
much resistance and will see itself forthwith enlarged by western
Americans won by the prospect of the advantages promised to
them."[20]

What if George Washington had read this despatch in 1795 as
he studied the Jay Treaty and wondered what next should be done?
Secretary Pickering was to see a copy of it, intercepted by the British and submitted to him several years later when reports first appeared that Spain had returned Louisiana to France. But again as
in 1793, Washington did not need particular evidence of a European
design. He sensed the situation as it was. He faced the severest test
of his statesmanship, and it was a highly personal matter.[21]

He, and he alone, sooner or later, had to make the decision whether
or not this country should accept the results of Jay's endeavors in
London. How widely and how deeply adverse influences had penetrated public opinion and divided its loyalty was the most alarming

20. *Ibid.*, 563–569. In using this document, Turner fixed attention upon its possible
relation to the Treaty of Basel in July, 1795, when France tried to force Godoy into
yielding Louisiana. See AHR, X, 266. Fletcher said that the instructions to the French
negotiator at Basel were framed after Fauchet's despatch had reached Paris. See MVHR,
XVII, 367–371. Whitaker, in *Journ. Mod. Hist.*, VIII, 7, corrects Fletcher's error regarding the evidence but shares the belief that Fauchet's despatch influenced the instructions
to Barthélemy. For other *mémoires* in the French foreign office regarding Louisiana
following Moustier's and prior to Fauchet's despatch, see AAE EU Sup. 7, Nos. 1, 2, 4–
6. Photocopies in Library of Congress.

21. *Corresp. French Ministers*, 568 n. For Liston and Pickering, see below, pp.
273–274.

uncertainty. The conditions upon which Britain had agreed that peace was to continue irritated him as much as anyone, but he knew that his country must not have war with Britain. That would be self-destruction. And yet, would the people submit to such a truce as Jay had sent home? Or, would they rage to the utter ruin of a national character so promising in its youth?

Ratification—Randolph Disgraced

THE treaty arrived from England on March 7, 1795, just after Congress had closed its session. The President called the Senate to return on June 8, and held the contents of the treaty in the meantime a close secret. Word got around, however, that it had reached the Department of State, and hostile speculations began to appear in the Republican press. Rufus King allowed Alexander Hamilton to read a copy. Other Senators were even freer with theirs. Fauchet tried to get the vote by the Senate delayed until his successor, Adet, should arrive on the thirteenth and reveal his instructions. Adet had nothing to offer, however, that could persuade Washington to withdraw the treaty from the Senate; and on the twenty-fourth the Senate concluded that the President should ratify. But it did so by the barest two thirds necessary and only after amendment striking out the provision which admitted American vessels into the British West Indies. The concession was too paltry, the accompanying restriction upon American cotton too exacting a price to pay.[22]

Adet wrote home that British gold, promises, and fear dictated the votes of the Senators; but he also reported that he himself had bought a copy of the treaty from a Senator. He then had arranged to get a digest of it into the hands of Benjamin Franklin Bache, editor of the Republican journal, *Aurora*, without Bache suspecting, so Adet said, that it had come from him. This move Adet expected to rouse popular feeling against the treaty and the "maneuvers" of the Government. He was informed, he said, that the Government intended to hold the treaty secret until Britain had passed upon the Senate's amendment.

The result of Adet's own maneuver was to force Secretary Randolph to put the official text of the Jay Treaty in his hands, and thus to lose great diplomatic advantage in dealing with him. Now, instead of listening to French approaches about a new commercial and consular convention with France, Randolph was in the humiliating position of having to look for concessions from France. Adet

22. King (King ed.), II, 10–11. Washington (Ford ed.), XIII, 59 n. Marshall, *Washington* (1807 ed.), V, 617–618.

also noted advantage in the fact that the Spanish representative was extremely piqued that Washington should have had negotiations in process at Madrid about the opening of the Mississippi at the same time that it was under consideration by Jay and the British cabinet. The Spaniard, remarked Adet, had become a French "instrument without his suspecting it."[23]

Then the complete text of the Jay Treaty reached the *Aurora*. Bache rushed it through the press and hurried off for New York and Boston to distribute copies at the mass meetings which would turn individual reaction into organized fury against terms with Britain. The alleged "town meeting" in Boston sent strong resolutions to the President. Hamilton was stoned when he tried to defend the treaty before a meeting in New York. A third gathering in Philadelphia listened to Republican harangues and adjourned to the house of the British minister to make a bonfire of the treaty.[24]

Organized animosity toward Jay and his treaty spread through the country. According to General Wayne:

> The *man of straw*, set up by a few *select* men of Boston, after running the *gauntlet* through all the cities and towns on the seaboard, from Portsmouth to Charleston inclusive, has recently been tossed over the Alleghaney Mountains into Kentucky, where the *poor fellow* has been unmercifully buffeted through every county, town, and village of that State by *heated mobs*, who, agreeably to fashion, have also resolved and addressed against Jay.

No riot anywhere, it would seem, was complete without hanging or burning John Jay in effigy. As the public became aware that the President would decide in the end to accept the treaty as amended by the Senate regardless of unsatisfactory features, Washington himself was vilified with rising epithet and indecency.[25]

So far Adet's scheme was working well. Such popular demonstrations were likely to give a "serious direction" to the next session

23. *Corresp. French Ministers*, II, 741–744. For Jaudenes' own report on the "bad faith" of Britain and the opportunity for Spain to keep France "hostile to Great Britain," see Whitaker in MVHR, 453–454.

24. The Republican Senator, S. T. Mason of Virginia, is credited with the honor of having given the text of the Jay Treaty to Bache. See Madison (Hunt ed.), VI, 258. Madison to Monroe, December 20, 1795. For Pickering's letter to John Quincy Adams in London, September 10, 1795, on those inspired meetings and countermeetings of "Merchants," see Upham, *Pickering*, III, 200–203.

25. *Ibid.*, III, 204. Wayne to Pickering, September 15, 1795. Madison (Hunt ed.), VI, 234–238. Madison to R. R. Livingston, August 10, 1795. For Washington's reaction to the accusations in the press and Bache's invective in particular, see Washington (Ford ed.), XIII, 220, 229, 244. For Adet on Washington and the people, see *Corresp. French Ministers*, 746 (July 17, 1795), 776–779 (September 2).

of the House of Representatives where "the patriots" who favored France were, he said, in a majority. Like Genet before him, he awaited expectantly a break between the Executive and the House of Representatives.[26]

Although possessed of a fiery temper, and very jealous that he should never be thought capable of stooping to faction and intrigue, George Washington set himself to ignore whatever might be said of him, to discount his personal dislike of the treaty, and to reach the decision which would best serve the country. He questioned his Cabinet officers about the proper method of ratifying. He called upon Hamilton, now withdrawn from the Government to the practice of law in New York, to advise him dispassionately upon the treaty, article by article and as a whole. He took note that Britain seemed again to be interfering with neutral rights under some kind of an order respecting provisions. And he wrote Secretary Randolph on July 22 from Mt. Vernon, where he had retired for the summer, that unless something had occurred since his departure which ought to be considered, he would ratify. But this would be on the condition that the new British order-in-council was not operating. It would be better to do so on this condition, and as the Senate had amended the treaty, he stated, than to leave matters unsettled. Meanwhile, he would respond to the protests of local committees, explaining carefully his position. He was watching such organized opposition closely. If it kept within a few localities, that would be one thing, but if it gave evidence of becoming "universal," that would be decidedly another. The French Government would make the most of the dissension; ratification of the treaty would then be a "very serious business indeed."[27]

We may be tempted by this remark to conclude that Washington might have come to think ratification inadvisable. But on the same day he wrote to Hamilton that the cry at the moment was "like that against a mad-dog"; the real temper of the people, he said, would appear later; he hoped that it would respond to the influence of such writers as Camillus in a New York paper which had come to his attention. Possibly he did not recognize in the lines of Camillus the familiar style of his old aide-de-camp and Secretary of the Treasury. In any case, he wrote to Randolph two days after that: "To be wise and temperate, as well as firm, the present crisis most eminently calls for." He realized, he said, that the preju-

26. *Ibid.*, 738–739.
27. Washington (Ford ed.), XIII, 59, 61–67, 68–72, 74, 79. Letters in June and July. For the new British order-in-council of April 25, 1795, see Newcomb, "New Light on Jay's Treaty," *Am. Journ. Int. Law.*, XXVIII, 685–692.

dices against the treaty were more extensive than he thought; but there had been the "most arrant misrepresentation of fact": American rights had not been neglected or sold; there were reciprocal advantages to the treaty; there had been no design to oppress France. And then poured out, for his pro-French Secretary of State to read, a revelation of what really underlay all of Washington's deliberation upon the course which he should follow: "If the treaty is ratified, the partisans of the French, (or rather of war and confusion), will excite them to hostile measures, or at least to unfriendly sentiments; if it is not, there is no foreseeing *all* the consequences, which may follow, as it respects Great Britain." He therefore would not quit the ground he had taken. He would hold the people to their own best interest, and he would press Britain to be better disposed toward the United States.[28]

Three years later, when angered by Monroe's charge that he had hesitated to ratify the Jay Treaty because of "shock" from the "general disapprobation" of the people, Washington wrote across the margin of his copy of Monroe's pamphlet:

A mistake, in *toto*. The *hesitation*, as mentioned on the other side, proceeded from the Provision Order, for it was obvious to the least discerning, that an opposition by the French party had been resolved on at all events, and had actually commenced before a single article of the Treaty was known; and the blaze, which he describes, broke out before it was possible to consider it, or a hundredth part of its opposers had ever read it.

Even so, this was relying too strongly on afterthought. His own letters in the summer of 1795 show that George Washington was anxious to discover how "universal" discontent among the people might become.[29]

As for the "Provision Order," ironically enough, it actually was not forbidden by the terms of the Jay Treaty. The British Government seems never to have bothered to explain it. Washington and Randolph believed that it renewed the old order for preëmpting foodstuffs owned by neutrals and bound to French ports. It has not been properly understood in this country until recently. But it was an order for the seizure of grain and provisions owned by the French Government. Neutral ships so laden were to be visited and searched; their cargoes, of course, were to be confiscated. The British knew that France was cashing the payments of the Amer-

28. Washington (Ford ed.), XIII, 76; 82, July 31, 1795.
29. *Ibid.*, XIII, 463, 472. For discussion of Monroe's *Conduct of the Executive,* see below, pp. 244–245.

ican Treasury upon the debt to France and buying supplies with the proceeds for delivery under the cover of American neutrality.[30]

Suddenly, however, as he had been endeavoring in the last days of July, 1795, to foresee "*all* the consequences" with Britain if he did not ratify, George Washington received a cryptic message from Timothy Pickering, Secretary of War, which closed his mind to further debate and brought him back to Philadelphia in haste. Pickering was in a state of "extreme solicitude" on the subject of the treaty "and for a special reason." He entreated the President to make no decision on affairs of state until he had returned.[31]

A British war vessel had captured despatches from the French minister to his Government. Fauchet's "No. 10" had been sent by Grenville to Hammond and handed by him on July 28 to Secretary Wolcott, Hamilton's successor in the Treasury. It involved the Secretary of State. How pleased Hammond must have been to have this parting shot at the man with whom he had been corresponding so acridly over the seizures of American vessels! Largely on account of that bitter exchange he was being recalled from Philadelphia. How amused within himself also! For he could never forget the many, many occasions when Hamilton had been as indiscreet in conversation with him, if not so clumsy. It was a perfect opportunity to cut the ground from under the only member of the Cabinet who still favored France. Randolph appeared to be more responsible than anyone else for the President's hesitation about ratifying the Treaty.

Timothy Pickering had pored over the despatch late into the night, aiding his scanty knowledge of French with a grammar and a dictionary to make a translation. He discovered statements and allusions to preceding despatches that displayed Randolph as having had conversations with Fauchet about the possibility of British collusion in the Whisky Rebellion, about Hamilton's desire to capitalize personally the Federal demonstration against the rebels, the wrangling between Jeffersonians and Hamiltonians, the President's inner feelings with regard to Britain and France—to the momentary advantage of France. There was a strong implication that Randolph's hand might have been out for French money. He had told Fauchet that there were "four men" who could "save" the country from the Whisky Rebellion, but they were indebted to English creditors and would be "deprived of their liberty" at the least step. He asked Fauchet: "Could you lend momentarily suffi-

---

30. Newcomb, 688, published in October, 1934. For the French purchases, see Rice, "James Swan," *N. E. Quarterly*, X, 464–486, September, 1937.
31. Upham, *Pickering*, III, 188, July 31, 1795.

cient funds to shelter them from English persecution?" Fauchet reported that he was "much astonished" at the request. But as George Washington read Pickering's translation of this on August 11, there must have risen in his mind the fact that Randolph was known among his closer associates to be in financial straits.[32]

It was a heavy blow to Washington. He had known Edmund Randolph in his own family for years. Randolph was the last of the original advisers whom he had gathered about himself as above all factiousness. Wolcott and Pickering, who replaced Hamilton and Knox, were obvious partisans, but he had counted upon Edmund Randolph. Yet he must have known that Randolph too had become a partisan, for he had been no more successful than Hamilton in concealing the development of his political views. The figure of Washington at this moment in his career is pathetic. He did not wish to believe what he could not but know was true: his nonpartisan ideal of government had crumbled. Party government was already there. Two things now were clear: they would ratify the Jay Treaty, they would give Edmund Randolph a chance to exonerate himself. But the second must not be involved with the first. Not the slightest connection with France was to taint the decision of the Administration.[33]

Keeping silent about Fauchet's letter, Washington brought the question of ratification before the Cabinet on the day after his return from Mount Vernon. They discussed the provision order once more. All, except Randolph, agreed that the President should ratify immediately and then send a strong protest to Britain about

32. For these despatches of Fauchet, see *Corresp. French Ministers*, II, 372, 411, 444. The quotations above are from the second despatch (p. 414). For Pickering's account of his procedure, written thirty-one years later, see Upham, *Pickering*, III, 215–219. For the question of Randolph's indebtedness to the Government, largely the product of his own carelessness about keeping vouchers for his payments when handling the funds of the State Department—ably supported by the particular zeal of his enemy, Timothy Pickering, who succeeded him as Secretary of State—and of the rule, since abandoned, that an official was liable for funds in spite of conditions beyond his control, see Conway's chapter on "The Fictitious Default," *Omitted Chapters of History*, 370–377; Trescot, *Diplomatic History*. . . . 1789–1801, 161 n.; and also *Senate Executive Documents*, No. 58, 50 Cong. 2 Sess. (1888–89).

33. Washington (Ford ed.), XIII, 89. To Wolcott, August, 1795. In his anonymous pamphlet, *Political Truth* (p. 20), published in 1796, Randolph asserts that he never divulged to the public his political sentiments until publication of his *Vindication* in 1795. He may not have made any public statements. In that respect he certainly was different from Hamilton. But the opinions of his contemporaries on record in published works, memoirs, biographies, and such documents as the *Correspondence of the French Ministers* show that, whatever may have been his intention, he did not succeed in withholding his political views from them. See the essay by D. R. Anderson in *American Secretaries of State* (Bemis ed.), II, 102, 300.

the order. Randolph maintained that, during the existence of the order, and during the war between Britain and France, they should not ratify. Washington ratified the Jay Treaty on August 18, 1795. In the presence of Pickering and Wolcott, the next day, he handed Fauchet's letter to Randolph.[34]

It was not a considerate way in which to do the thing. Washington certainly was well aware that those men were hostile to Randolph. It was not even fair, for Washington had known of the matter more than a week and had conferred with them about it while keeping it from Randolph. The Secretary of State was faced with accusers as well as an accusation, cross-questioned, and then asked how much time he would need to make his explanations. The only possible extenuation of Washington's performance is that he was overwrought—as he could be on occasion, hurt to the quick—as was also his tendency, half-convinced that Randolph was guilty. Perhaps there was also a trace of resentment from the knowledge within himself that Randolph had forced his hand while he still hung back, worrying whether or not the opposition to the treaty were "universal."

There seems to have been no curiosity recorded or thought taken upon the motives behind the transmission of the Fauchet despatch from Grenville to Hammond to Wolcott. One wonders how Washington would have acted in that dramatic moment if his beloved Hamilton—instead of his protégé, Randolph—had been standing there faced with one of Hammond's despatches transmitted from the French foreign office to Fauchet to Randolph—as easily the scene might have been staged with contemporary materials of fact.

Randolph of course withdrew to his quarters and resigned. If there had been in his mind only consciousness of his honor and integrity, he might then have stood quietly on his dignity, let the President have second thoughts on the affair, and his detractors bring forth evidence other than the insinuations of a foreigner who had been thwarted in his efforts to get money from the American Treasury. These had striking relation to those which Genet had made notorious. But Randolph had other things on his mind. He hurried to Newport after Fauchet before he should sail for France and got a statement; he gathered copies of other papers from Adet, Fauchet's successor; he reconstructed the events of the past months, informed Washington of his purposes, and published *A Vindication of Mr. Randolph's Resignation*.[35]

34. Marshall, *Washington*, V, 633.
35. Published by Samuel H. Smith, Philadelphia, 1795. Conway, 241–242. *Corresp. French Ministers*, 774–776.

By that time, however, ratifications of the Jay Treaty had been exchanged—on October 28, 1795. Washington had become angrier and angrier with Randolph's "insidious tendency" to see if he could involve the President in inconsistent replies, and had flatly written to him that there was no connection between the Jay Treaty and the details and suggestions which were in Fauchet's intercepted letter. Randolph, it may be, as Washington remarked to Wolcott, had developed the obsession that he had been "doomed to be a victim." Or perhaps he knew that he was being spied upon for Secretary Wolcott while he was in Newport. In any case, Washington was entitled to dismiss his *Vindication* as not a defense but an accusation. It labored over the story of the treaty and his mistreatment. Its explanation of the affair in which the suspicion of French money had appeared was held back until the later pages and then presented in altogether too vague and inconsequential terms. It was a Republican polemic, a partisan appeal to the people. It conformed too well with the spirit of the remark which Adet attributed to Randolph after his resignation: that, if the French would furnish the means for him to exonerate himself, the Republicans would carry the fight against the Jay Treaty into the next session of the House of Representatives.[36]

As for the question whether Randolph took part in any scheme for his own pecuniary advantage, we must leave it where it began and, in the absence of other evidence, where it should end—with the French minister in Philadelphia. Fauchet's despatches said that Randolph had suggested that France compensate certain other persons who would thwart the British intrigues with the Whisky rebels and thus would save America from civil war. Fauchet had not said that Randolph sought money for himself. In his certificate of exoneration for Randolph, he explicitly denied that Randolph had done so, or had received any such compensation. If there remain doubts as to the character or motives of this French minister—and well there may in other respects—it need only be said that Fauchet had no personal reason either to care for the American Secretary of State or to shield him. The French as well as the British minister had experienced much irritation in dealing with Edmund Randolph.[37]

The Republican party took the fight into the House of Repre-

36. Washington (Ford ed.), XIII, 109–111, to Wolcott, October 2, 1795; 125–127, to Randolph, October 25; 146, to Hamilton, December 22. Wolcott Papers, XXI, 47, William Ellery to Wolcott, from Newport, January 11, 1796. *Corresp. French Ministers*, 776, 783–785.
37. Conway, 247.

sentatives. They hoped that, as it must approve all money bills, they could withhold the funds necessary for the settlements provided in the treaty. Thus they might keep it from going into effect. But the President held stubbornly to his constitutional right; he had to share the treaty-making power only with the Senate. Washington refused to lay the papers concerning the Jay Treaty before the House, and the Federalist representatives rallied to the President. His position was so strong constitutionally, furthermore, notwithstanding the opinions of Jefferson and the arguments of Madison and Gallatin to the contrary, that the zealots, friends of France and foes of Britain, could not prevail upon the House to withhold the legislation which should accompany the treaty.[38]

Alexander Hamilton was victorious. Luckily no French cruiser had captured any British despatches to mar confidence in him. No distressing evidence of his revelations from the councils of the President was thrust into the hands of Washington. His betrayal of state secrets was not before the American public. President Washington, whether he thought so or not, had come to the position which Hamilton had taken in 1793: that American neutrality should lean to the side of the mother country, Britain, away from the ancient ally, France.

Bitter grievances still crowded the President's mind and his letters abroad: "If Lord Grenville conceives, that the United States are not well disposed towards Great Britain, his candor, I am persuaded, will seek for the causes, and his researches will fix them, as I have done." Gouverneur Morris would favor Washington if he told his Lordship so when they should again converse informally. Grenville's "researches" would then find, among other causes, "most atrocious depredations and violences on our commerce," insults by naval officers in *"our own ports,"* impressment of our seamen, "ungracious and obnoxious characters"—old Tories—sent among us as agents, instigations of Indian "ravages and cruel murders" of our frontier inhabitants.[39]

In spite of such infuriating things, however, Washington's policy still was to be peace with Britain. If Britain would not allow it to continue, then France of course would again be America's natural ally. He had instructed James Monroe, new minister to France, to keep all clear in Paris on that point. But if France obliged the United States to choose between war with Britain and the enmity of France leading possibly to war, they would have to take the risk of war

38. Jefferson (Ford ed.), VII, 41, to Giles, December 31, 1795; 68, to Madison, March 27, 1796. Adams, *Gallatin,* 158–166.
39. Washington (Ford ed.), XIII, 147–154. December 22, 1795.

with France; for there was to be no war with Britain at this time of their own choosing. The authorities of France may have thought that the American people were under "the new yoke of the English," as John Quincy Adams reported to John Adams from The Hague on December 30, 1796. But the Jay Treaty was a truce giving the United States further chance to grow strong before they had finally to come to conclusions with Britain about the Mississippi Valley. That to risk war with France was the wiser decision in 1795, far more productive of benefits near and remote, was placed beyond any doubt by immediate consequences both in America and in Europe.[40]

40. ASP FR, I, 668–669. Instructions for Monroe, June 10, 1794. J. Q. Adams, *Writings*, II, 66.

IX

BRITISH DEFERENCE AND SPANISH SURRENDER

Peace in North America

SO FAR as the British and American Government could maintain it officially, there was to be peace on the North American continent while Britain withdrew her troops from those forts which she had conceded in 1783 as lying within the domain of the United States. To have the British leave without being driven was a great advantage for the American Government. If Jay had accomplished nothing else at London in the summer of 1794, that in itself entitled him to credit rather than the abuse which he received so generally among his countrymen. But perhaps more surprising than their criticism of Jay was Grenville's willingness to remove those forces. As he had been in a position to yield just about what he himself pleased, it would seem that Grenville might have insisted upon more for Britain in the back country than he did. Why then was he so deferential to the United States? He did refuse to sign away the British right to deal separately with the Indians. He did insist upon navigation of the Mississippi River and tried to set the Northwestern boundary so as to leave a British thoroughfare down to its headwaters. Thus he retained the chance to establish an Indian buffer state in the Northwest at a later date. Why did he not make it then?

The answer is found largely in the changing conditions of Europe, for Spain was growing restive under her alliance with Britain and turning back to France. But Grenville now had Wayne's army in America as well to take into account. "Mad Anthony" had been closing in upon those Indian war parties before Simcoe's outpost on the Maumee below Detroit while Grenville conversed with Jay in London. Would the American general, if victorious, stop there? Grenville knew of course that success against Indians was not triumph over British garrisons. But if Wayne were only to try to prove the contrary, the instant effect would be war again between Britain and the United States. At another time Britain might welcome such an opportunity to advance her plans for the Northwest and the Mississippi Valley; she might drive the American Army from the field and redraw the line of 1783 along the

Ohio—as Rayneval had suggested to Shelburne in 1782, and as Dorchester, Simcoe, and lesser officials on the frontier were encouraging the Indians to expect. But not just then. It must not be forgotten here that British thoughts were engrossed in war to the death with the French Revolution—for self-preservation, maintenance of civilization, and free institutions, ends which were as emotionalized and distorted then as they have been since in another and more deadly struggle involving both European and American nations. And besides, Spain was in fact deserting Britain at Basel.[1]

Although Grenville knew from Hamilton, through Hammond, that the American Government would never join the proposed league of armed neutrals in Europe, he knew also that it was no time for even a little war with the United States. He had better prefer diplomacy with the Government at Philadelphia and continued intrigue among the American pioneers. For this purpose, it was fitting that Portland, in charge of the colonies, should send a "most private dispatch" to Lieutenant Governor Simcoe on October 24, 1795, just as ratifications of the Jay Treaty were about to be exchanged. Since Spain had made peace with France at Basel on July 22, Portland desired information from Simcoe whether the settlers of Kentucky and the Western country would coöperate with Britain in an attack upon Spanish America. Simcoe was to take into consideration the possibilites in using the Southern and Western Indians. He was to investigate the communications between Lake Michigan and the great river. But in the meantime, "Mad Anthony" Wayne had done much more than defeat the Indians in Ohio. He had altered radically the state of affairs in the whole Mississippi Valley.[2]

Wayne Against British Guns—News from Jay

THE raw levies upon whom Wayne had spent so many months of discipline had advanced in the morning hours of August 20, 1794, into the tangle of uprooted trees which a tornado had laid as a natural fortress for their enemies. Trailing their guns until they could lunge with their bayonets and then fire upon the backs of their foes, they had driven the Indians from the cover before Wayne's cavalry could get into action on the flanks as he had

1. Consider Edmund Burke's *Remarks on the Policy of the Allies with respect to France* (1793) and *Three Letters on the Proposed Peace with the Regicide Directory of France* (1796). For Rayneval, see above, p. 82 f. For Dorchester, see above, p. 179. Michigan Pion. and Hist. Soc., *Collections*, XXIV, 571, Brant to Simcoe, July 28, 1793. Simcoe (Cruikshank ed.), II, 332; III, 134, 318–324.

2. *Ibid.*, IV, 110. For Simcoe's reply in 1796, see below, pp. 267–268.

planned, and they had pursued the Indians to the very gates of the British outpost on the Maumee.

When he looked over the battlefield, Wayne saw white men with British muskets and bayonets among the dead. A Canadian taken prisoner testified that there were militia among the warriors. These were the notorious Detroit "Volunteers." That they had been sent under orders directly from Governor Simcoe cannot be asserted. It is most likely that they had received no official orders. But foraging parties of friendly Indians weeks before had reported to Wayne that they had seen three scarlet-clad officers keeping themselves at a distance behind the Indians who had attacked his position at Fort Recovery on June 30. The British agent, Colonel McKee, was reported also as having been in the field at Fallen Timbers, "but at a respectful distance, and near the river." There is no doubt that arms and ammunition had been distributed among the Indians out of the stores of the Indian department at Detroit—as Sydney had advised Dorchester some years before.[3]

If there is any uncertainty still about these matters, the papers of Simcoe himself should dispel it. He wrote on August 26, six days after the Battle of Fallen Timbers: "I am sorry that Lieutenant Colonel Caldwell was in the action, more so that he took so many men. I propose drawing some Militia from hence to reinforce his party." And on the following day: "Colonel McKee ought to be desired to use his influence with the Indians to detach to Wayne's Rear. He will bring up Cannon if he be not threatened. I shall hurry Brant. . . ." Three days after that Simcoe reported Wayne's victory to Dundas in London and asked for seamen on the Great Lakes. A seventy-four-gun ship, he said, "would probably preserve to his Majesty this encreasing Empire." On September 5 he wrote to Dorchester that, as the Canadian militia were being punished under the civil law for offending against the military act of the province, he had given a hundred guineas "to reward the meritorous conduct of the inferior classes of the community." And on the same day, he issued orders to arm for trouble with Wayne for "Ld. Howe's Victory and Major Campbell's judgment will not prevent a War, I hold it certain."[4]

Anthony Wayne, however, had no intention of settling the issue of the "Volunteers" on the spot. He drew up his army within range of the British post, but he did not move to attack. The British

3. ASP IA, I, 487–488, Wayne to Knox, Secretary of War, July 7, 1794; 491–494, August 28. McLaughlin, "Western Posts," 443. Bemis, *Jay's Treaty*, 181. For Sydney, see above, pp. 113-114.
4. Simcoe (Cruikshank ed.), III, 4, 7, 19, 40, 45.

commander had not given refuge within his stockade to the Indians. But neither could the British officer ignore a military force in battle array so close to his position. If he did, he would question his own right to be there. Major Campbell sent a stiff note to General Wayne. He demanded to know "in what light I am to view your making such near approaches to this garrison." He was aware, he said, of "no war existing between Great Britain and America." Wayne retorted in kind: "Were you entitled to an answer, the most full and satisfactory one was anounced to you from the muzzles of my small arms, yesterday morning. . . ." Nor was the American general aware of war between Great Britain and America, save from the British major's hostile act of "taking post within the well known and acknowledged limits of the United States."

Further explanations General Wayne would not give. But Major Campbell exercised his "judgment" and permitted not one shot from his guns as Wayne and his men rode about within pistol range and set fire to the house and stores of Colonel McKee, "principal stimulator of the war now existing between the United States and the savages."[5]

Leaving garrisons in the forts which he had thrown up in the heart of the Indian country and ruthlessly destroying the crops, Wayne withdrew to his winter base at Greenville, for, in spite of his great success at Fallen Timbers, it was possible that Simcoe and McKee would rally the Indians to another attack. Even if they could not, it would take time for those chieftains who now wanted peace with the United States to gain influence among all the tribes in the Northwest. Without general acceptance, it would be of little use to talk seriously of peace. Moreover, there was certain to be news of some sort before long from Jay's negotiations in London. And, although the President and Secretary Hamilton were overaw- ing the Whisky rebels with militia which had been called into the Federal service from the Eastern States, the rumors of British par- ticipation in that uprising near the headwaters of the Ohio River and his base at Pittsburgh were altogether too prevalent for Wayne's comfort. It was a time for the American Army to stand on guard rather than to be in the field.[6]

Wayne soon had word that Simcoe and McKee were hard at work in conference with the Indians near Detroit and that they had been joined by Brant, Iroquois chieftain, with promises of help from the Six Nations to the eastward. But, although Wayne could

5. ASP IA, I, 491, 493. Simcoe (Cruikshank ed.), II, 395–419, Campbell's corres- pondence, August 20–24, 1794.
6. See above, pp. 164–166.

not yet know it, or perhaps Brant either, the very day after Wayne
had heard through Indian channels of Brant's efforts in the West,
Timothy Pickering had made at Canandaigua in New York that
treaty of peace between the Six Nations and the United States
which President Washington had sent him to get. Brant was not
to have the support of his own people. Nor could the more belligerent chieftains near Detroit keep others from approaching
Wayne at Greenville and carrying valuable information to him.[7]

Wayne gave them fair welcome and safe return, but the ultimatum also that they all had to seek peace with the United States
and upon the basis of the treaty which St. Clair had made in 1789.
In short, the Indians had to abandon any hope of regaining the
lands down to the Ohio River which the British had led them to
think they might get back. They should see clearly, too, that they
could no longer rely upon the British against Wayne's army. Fort
Recovery stood secure upon the very site of St. Clair's disaster in
1791.[8]

Nonetheless, General Wayne was most anxious, for Congress
might become concerned now about his expenditures and so restrict appropriations that he would not be able to hold his "Legion"
up to strength. Then, he began to get encouraging information.

Captain Pasteur at Fort Knox on the Wabash reported what he
had heard from Kaskaskias in the Illinois country. Hostile Indians
were crossing the Mississippi every day into Spanish territory; there
was no withstanding the Americans, they said; they would go away.
The British concentration of Indian war parties, which had drawn
them even from beyond the Mississippi, was breaking in spite of
the efforts of Simcoe and McKee. Alexander Hamilton wrote to
Wayne on September 25 enclosing a part of a letter from Jay, dated
July 12, 1794. What the extract contained Wayne did not say when
he mentioned it to Knox, Secretary of War, on November 12, 1794.
But we know that Jay had forwarded to Hamilton on August 5 a
letter dated July 11 in which he spoke of favorable beginnings with
Grenville and remarked: "I fear the posts may labour, but they
must not be left. We must not make a delusive settlement; that
would disunite our people, and leave seeds of discord to germinate."
After such reassurance, the man who had held his temper when
taunted in the moment of victory by the British flag on American
territory could check his impatience and wait.[9]

7. ASP IA, I, 529. For Pickering's Treaty, November 11, 1794, see I, 545.
8. Ibid., I, 526–528. November 4, 1794.
9. Ibid., I, 550. November 3, 1794. Winsor, Westward Movement, 461. Jay (Johnston
ed.), I, 434.

In January, 1795, Wayne accordingly made a preliminary truce with the Indians, and summoned them to council as his guests at Greenville in the following June. By that time the movement for peace would have gained headway among the tribes which were sick of war; Simcoe and McKee might have failed to counteract the damage done to Indian friendship by Major Campbell's refusal to open his gates after Fallen Timbers; John Jay might even be home from London with a treaty.[10]

The tribes began slowly to assemble about Wayne's fort in the latter part of June. Some had practically to be forced to come, others demurred at the notice that they would accept St. Clair's treaty of 1789. Wayne, however, bided his time, and when he had present all the tribes which he thought necessary to make peace endure, he also had in his possession, at last, the text of the Jay Treaty.

On Friday, July 24, therefore, he read its articles, I and II, declaring that there would be peace between Great Britain and the United States and that the British would retire from the posts and places on the American side of the line as it had been drawn in the Treaty of 1783. Then he announced to the Indians that they, too, would have peace with the United States. The terms he would show them later.

For two days Wayne let sink into the Indian these facts: that his British friends had pledged themselves to get out of Mackinac, Detroit, Niagara, Oswego and other places from Lake Champlain to Superior; and that his chances of ever getting back the lands in the Ohio Valley were surely gone. On Monday, July 27, Wayne read to the counselors the details of the treaty which they were going to sign with him. There followed several days of discussion and some efforts at objection, but on August 3 the chieftains signed as he had said they should.[11]

Terms for the Indians—The Way to the Mississippi

WAYNE's treaty drew a line from Lake Erie up the Cuyahoga River across the portage to the upper Muskingum on the south, thence westward across the Miami so as to include Fort Recovery on a branch of the Wabash, then southwestward in a direct line to the Ohio at the mouth of the Kentucky River. All Indian claims to the land were relinquished to the east and south of this line. The tribes, however, might continue to hunt within the territory so long as they offered no injury to the people of the United States.

Beyond this line, to the west and north, Wayne forced the Indians

10. ASP IA, I, 559.
11. Ibid., 573; Little Turtle for the Miamis, 576; Sandusky Wyandots, 575.

to yield sixteen reservations strategically placed on waterways and portages. Among these specially notable were Fort Wayne, Sandusky, Detroit, Mackinac, Chicago, Peoria on the Illinois River, and another at its confluence with the Mississippi. These reservations were intended to be forts and trading posts. They soon became radiating points for further encroachment by white settlers upon Indian lands—causes for the wrath of Tecumseh, the Battle of Tippecanoe, and the War of 1812.

Wayne also required the Indians at Greenville to allow the people of the United States free passage by land and by water along this chain of posts. Besides the routes from the Ohio Valley to Lake Erie, he stipulated in particular the transit ways from Detroit and Lake Erie via Fort Wayne and the Wabash River to the Ohio and from Chicago down the Illinois to the Mississippi. The Indians were pledged to trade only with persons licensed by the United States through the superintendent of the Indian department northwest of the Ohio, and they were compelled to acknowledge expressly that they were under the protection of the United States and "no other Power whatever."

For the cessions of land, the United States agreed to pay in goods $20,000 and sums to the total of $9,500 annually to the Indians. It was also stipulated that, with certain exceptions such as the tract of George Rogers Clark, Fort Massac on the Ohio, the post at Vincennes and adjacent lands on the Wabash, Indian titles to which had already been extinguished, the United States on their part relinquished claim to all other Indian lands between the Ohio, the Mississippi, and the Great Lakes. The Indians could eject and punish any white persons who presumed to settle upon those lands.

This relinquishment lost much of its value for the Indians because of the accompanying provision that they could not sell those lands to any party but the United States. And although some of the chieftains had hoped that the American Government would undertake to maintain peace and order among the Indians themselves, the treaty obligated the United States only to protect them against all citizens of the United States and all other white persons. Indian wars upon Indians, which had given white men opportunity time and again to take their ancestral lands, could continue to make their cause more and more hopeless.[12]

The Treaty of Greenville was of the greatest importance to the United States. Wayne had cleared the Ohio country, nearly to the shore of Lake Erie, for white settlement without molestation by Indian war parties. Such an enlarged opportunity cut deeply, too,

12. *Ibid.*, I, 562–563, text of the Treaty of Greenville.

into Western resentments of whisky taxes, the Jay Treaty, and the hauteur and self-concern of aristocratic merchants in the East— feelings which could so easily have become fixed in determination to break from the Union. But more significant, Wayne had placed American military reservations in the West astride those ways of communication from Lake Michigan to the Mississippi which Portland wished Simcoe to investigate more thoroughly; he had driven an American wedge between the British merchants and the fur trade to which they had clung since 1783 despite the treaty; and he had pushed farther into the north and west British hopes of enveloping the United States. The achievement of an Indian buffer state was removed once more into the uncertainty of the future.[13]

There remained some chance that Britain might establish that barrier beyond Lake Michigan in the Minnesota country, and beyond the Mississippi. British agents did not cease working for it. But it was gone altogether from possibility along the Ohio, the Wabash, and in the Illinois country—unless of course Britain should endeavor to construct it and to guard it thereafter by force of arms. This the Government in London had no intention of attempting to do so long as Britain was at war in Europe with Revolutionary France, regardless of what subordinates on the frontier might urge.

Wayne had so altered the situation that nothing short of war between Britain and the United States could block the way before the American pioneers through to the Mississippi River. And now, while Wayne was putting the finishing touches upon the labors of Hamilton and Jay and Washington, another American general become diplomatist was bringing Spain to terms about those matters which had threatened "separation" in the Southwest and defied settlement ever since Jay had first appeared at Madrid in 1780.[14]

Thomas Pinckney in Madrid

As he kept watch upon frontiersmen near Spanish lands, the democratic clubs fathered by Genet, the Whisky Rebellion, and waited anxiously for results from the efforts of Jay, Wayne, and Pickering, President Washington grasped at the suggestion that he might send an envoy more befitting the pride of Spain than Carmichael and Short. Senator Pierce Butler of South Carolina who had been making himself a confidential adviser of Jaudenes and Viar rather hoped that he might be chosen. But Washington asked

13. Wolcott Papers, XXV, Wayne to Wolcott, from Detroit, September 4, 1796. Michigan Pion. and Hist. Soc., *Collections*, XXV, 104, Dorchester to Portland, October 26, 1795.
14. See above, p. 34 f.

Thomas Jefferson, then Patrick Henry, and then Thomas Pinckney, who could be spared from London so long as John Jay was there. The business in Madrid, said Randolph's instructions, would relate to the Mississippi; it would be temporary; "under present conditions probably not dilatory." Pinckney would hold to the same pretensions which Jay had maintained against Gardoqui in 1786.[15]

Pinckney arrived at Madrid on June 28, 1795. He found the Spanish Court still addicted to the wearisome habit of moving from Aranjuez to Madrid to San Ildefonso to San Lorenzo and back again. But Godoy's mood concerning discussions with a representative of the United States was quite different from that of Floridablanca from 1780 to 1782. Randolph had surmised correctly: negotiations were not to be dilatory this time. Whatever outward appearances, Godoy was eager for a treaty that would satisfy the United States. He was fearful. He, who as the Duke of Alcudia had signed the compact with St. Helens in 1793 binding Spain and Britain to mutual assistance and defense against Revolutionary France, was negotiating now for peace with France.[16]

Disillusioned by British destruction of the French ships and naval base at Toulon for which Spain could have had use, worried by the activities of the British fleet in the Caribbean, alarmed by the growth of republicanism among even the Spanish nobility threatening his own power, Godoy had come to fear his monarchic ally more than the republican foe. Besides, the troops of France were over the Pyrenees into Spain, and the Treasury could not carry the burden much longer. He therefore would chance the enmity of Britain and defend his doubling back to the traditional association of Spain with France by accusing Britain of avarice, interference with Spanish commerce, and bad faith. But just as he was hoping for a breathing spell, news had come of the American rebuff to Genet, and then of an American mission to London, and then of the Jay Treaty.[17]

Authorities disagree as to whether Godoy, Prince of Peace, knew the entire contents of the Jay Treaty before he came to terms with Thomas Pinckney. It really does not matter whether he did or did not, even though the Spanish Government constructed an argument later to excuse its delay in turning over the posts to the United States on the ground that Godoy had not known all there was in

15. Whitaker, 203. Washington (Ford ed.), XII, 453, 459 n. Bemis, *Pinckney's Treaty*, 238 n. ASP FR, I, 534. November 3, 28, 1794. See above, pp. 100–103.

16. See above, p. 34 f. Whitaker, "Louisiana in the Treaty of Basel," *Journ. Mod. Hist.*, VIII, 1–26.

17. Bemis, *Pinckney's Treaty*, 228. Whitaker, 183. Godoy, *Memoirs*, I, 458.

the Jay Treaty. It was general knowledge by this time that the previous agreement between Britain and the United States in 1782 had a secret clause disposing of West Florida to the injury of Spanish interests.

And Godoy would have been singularly naïve if he had relied upon even the official text of the Jay Treaty to assure himself that so ancient and honorable a move in the chess of diplomacy, in which he himself was adept, had not been used again at Spain's expense. The important fact was not what the treaty said in whole or in part—or what people said that it said—but that Britain and the United States had come to terms again. As Spain was leaving her alliance with Britain and returning to Britain's enemy, Britain was winning the United States from that enemy. Mother and children were becoming reconciled. Neighbors who had not been the best of neighbors had better be nervous. This realignment of international forces brought danger—especially for holdings far across the Atlantic, dominated by the British fleet, exposed to the sweep of American settlement down the Mississippi. Even before Grenville and Jay had completed their negotiations, the Prince of Peace had decided to take to cover.[18]

When he heard that an American plenipotentiary was on his way to London, Godoy had persuaded the council of state to send new instructions to Jaudenes in Philadelphia. He was to concede the boundary of West Florida and navigation of the Mississippi, if he could obtain a treaty of alliance and reciprocal guarantees of territories in the Americas. How John Jay would have mused over his table talk with Gérard, and his subsequent experiences in Madrid and Paris, had he seen this despatch to Jaudenes! Time indeed was playing the hand of his youthful country.[19]

Godoy had decided, in addition, that Governor Carondelet at New Orleans was to restrain himself. He was to explain that the recent treaty with the Indians of the Southwest was a measure for protecting the United States against attack without the consent of Spain, and not the first step toward war upon the American States across the Mississippi. He was to hold the intrigue with Wilkinson and his Kentuckians in suspense until Jaudenes had an opportunity to get that treaty in Philadelphia.[20]

When Pinckney arrived at Madrid, therefore, Godoy made the

18. Bemis, *Pinckney's Treaty*, 326–331. Whitaker, *Spanish–American Frontier*, 204–205, and his articles in MVHR, XV, 435–454; AHR, XXXV, 804–810; AHR, XXXIX, 454–476. In a letter to me, April 26, 1939, Mr. Whitaker put more stress on the argument of Spain. For the secret clause of 1782, see above, pp. 92–93.
19. Bemis, *Pinckney's Treaty*, 233. For Jay, see above, pp. 31 f., 34 f., 57 f., 73 f.
20. Whitaker, 198.

gesture of demurring until he had heard from Jaudenes. Meanwhile he himself would sound this American on the possibility of an alliance and reciprocal guarantees of territories and possessions in the Americas. Perhaps also they might negotiate together with France. This would have led straight to the old objective of Jay which Floridablanca had rejected in 1782 on the part of Spain. Godoy suggested a "triple alliance."

But times had long since changed. Now, the American would have none of it. It was vain, said Pinckney, to wait for an answer from Jaudenes. He had with him Jaudenes' letter of last March to Randolph. And he reiterated what Short had already been instructed to make clear to the Spanish Court: the United States would enter no alliance nor give any guarantees. This American envoy had come to talk about, and to get, a settlement regarding neutral commerce, the boundary of Florida, and navigation of the Mississippi, not to bind the United States with respect to Louisiana, or even Mexico and Peru.[21]

Godoy dropped the subject of alliance and guarantees, but not the negotiation, for he had made his peace with France at Basel on July 22. There was more reason than ever now for holding to the good will of the United States. France had pressed Spain hard to surrender Louisiana; Spain had been able to put off France for a while with the cession of Spanish San Domingo; but the French were still insisting upon Louisiana. The Prince of Peace had won for Spain not only the right to expect British reprisals for her desertion but the privilege of groveling to France. And he knew it. He had therefore to appease those driving Americans behind him, if he were to hold off the new enemy on the one hand and to withstand the pressure of the new ally on the other until he could get his price for Louisiana. Spain's grip upon her ancient empire in the Americas was slipping, but Godoy was not yet willing to let go of Louisiana without compensation elsewhere—Gibraltar, if that could be had.[22]

Pinckney wrote home on August 11, 1795, that the Treaty of Basel was generally known. In his opinion, this new position of Spain would induce her to come to terms with the United States. The King was ready in fact, he said, "to sacrifice something of what he considered as his right, to testify to his good will to us." And on

21. ASP FR, I, 534. Pinckney's report, July 21, 1795. Jefferson (Ford ed.), VI, 206. Jefferson to Carmichael and Short, March 23, 1793. See above, p. 34.
22. Turner in AHR, X, 266 ff. Sorel in Revue d'historique, XIII, 46 ff., 72. Whitaker in MVHR, XV, 437–438; in AHR, XXXIX, 456–459. For the Treaty of Basel, see Martens, Receuil de Traités, VI, 124. See below, pp. 295–296.

the fourteenth, the council of state formally decided to give way regarding the navigation of the Mississippi and the boundary claimed by the United States—without an alliance and guarantees of Spanish possessions.[23]

Godoy, however, was not so alarmed over Spain's new situation in Europe and the failure of her frontiers to hold back the pioneers in America that he would concede everything. He still fenced with Pinckney about the damages done to the neutral commerce of the United States, and that matter of the free navigation of the Mississippi. It did Pinckney no good to labor through the historical argument that the United States had inherited the British right derived from the Treaty of 1763 between France and Britain to which Spain had also been a party. Godoy did not concede the point. Nor would he yield as Pinckney wished the accompanying right of deposit for American goods without payment of duties pending transshipment, either on a space of ground ceded by Spain for a depot or in the customhouse under two keys, one held by the Spanish official and the other available for the American shippers.[24]

But the Prince of Peace was aware of the decisiveness in Pinckney's letter of October 23 saying that he could not sign the proposed treaty until it contained the general rules which he desired concerning the rights of neutrals; provision for those American vessels which had been seized by Spain; and, especially, a plan for regulating the navigation of the Mississippi in some one of the ways which he had proposed. Godoy more than understood Pinckney's request for his passports on the following day. They conferred. Three days later, October 27, 1795, Pinckney's treaty was signed.[25]

The Terms

SPAIN honored the pretensions of the United States in the Mississippi Valley. Their southern boundary was acknowledged to be, as Britain had conceded in 1783, the thirty-first degree of latitude, from the Mississippi eastward to the Chattahoochee, down that river to its confluence with the Flint, and thence straight to the St. Mary's and along that stream to the Atlantic. All settlements, garrisons, and troops of each party were to be withdrawn from the territory of the other within six months after the ratification of the treaty. Spain agreed that the United States should have free navigation of the Mississippi, and permitted their citizens to deposit their goods in New Orleans, for the period of three years, without payment of

23. ASP FR, I, 535. Bemis, *Pinckney's Treaty*, 314.
24. ASP FR, I, 538. October 1, 1795.
25. *Ibid.*, I, 545.

duties pending transshipment and exportation. In case Spain wished to withdraw the privilege at New Orleans, the treaty stipulated that Spain should assign an equivalent place of deposit elsewhere on the Mississippi. This, at least, was the American interpretation of the clause. The Spanish text, however, left some doubt as to the indefiniteness of the commitment. There were grounds for argument later that Spain had retained the right to withdraw the privilege of deposit entirely at the end of three years.[26]

Two stipulations only were similar in any way at all to an alliance and guarantee of territories, those safeguards which Godoy had desired so much for Spain at the beginning of the negotiations. The first was that there should be "firm and inviolable Peace and sincere Friendship." But with the merest change in times and conditions this would mean nothing. The other was a mutual undertaking to restrain by force all hostilities on the part of the Indians living within the respective territories and to make the advantages of the Indian trade "common and mutualy beneficial" on the basis of "the most complete reciprocity." This also could be ruined by inertia if not deliberate action. From the American point of view, however, Pinckney had handled well this problem of the Indians on foreign soil—much better than Jay. Spain was obligated to restrain the Indians within her borders. Britain had not been so bound by the Jay Treaty.[27]

Pinckney also had far better success than Jay in obtaining concessions to the United States as neutrals. Whether or not he proved to Godoy, as he thought he did, that "the amplest freedom given to neutral commerce is consonant to the true interest of Spain," Pinckney was able to write into his treaty many of the clauses in the commercial treaty of 1778 with France and the Treaty of 1785 with Prussia, but slightly modified, and in some instances improved. Spain not only agreed now with the United States "that Free Ships shall also give freedom to goods" excepting contraband, but also accepted a specific list which confined contraband to actual instruments of war, such as arms, ammunition, and armor. There was included also an express statement of noncontraband which named many commodities that could readily become useful in war. And all of these could be transported to an enemy of either except into places under blockade. There was furthermore to be reciprocal protection against other powers for the vessels of each within the jurisdiction of the other. And the two parties agreed that their subjects or citizens respectively who took service as privateers for another

26. Miller, *Treaties*, II, 318–338, 337. See below, pp. 447, 458, 468–471.
27. *Ibid.*, II, 319, 322–333. See above, p. 185.

power at war with either of them should be treated as pirates. They did not renounce the use of their own private ships in war against each other as had Prussia and the United States in their Treaty of 1785.[28]

There was among other provisions a mutual prohibition against seizure for crimes without authority of law and prosecution according to the regular course of proceedings. This was to become significant in the Cuban insurrection a hundred years later. And those claims for damages to American commerce for which Pinckney had threatened to break off the negotiations were to be referred directly to a mixed commission sitting in Philadelphia, much as the Jay Treaty had provided for the adjudication of American debts and British spoliations.[29]

President Washington and the Senate could have no quarrel with such concessions to the United States. Spain had capitulated almost completely. The Senate ratified the Pinckney Treaty unanimously on March 3, 1796. Ratifications were exchanged at Madrid, April 25, and the treaty was proclaimed on August 2, 1796. But by that time fulfillment had become a different matter to Godoy. He had decided to go the whole distance backward into alliance again with France and war upon Britain.

Having satisfied the envoy of the United States, the Prince of Peace had turned immediately to use Louisiana for other purposes more vital in the interest of Spain. It was an expensive possession. It was hard to defend. But in the eager grip of France it might even yet become a real barrier to American advance upon the treasures of Spain beyond the Sabine and the Red Rivers. Less than two months after he had signed Pinckney's treaty, therefore, Godoy offered to exchange Louisiana for the part of San Domingo which had just been ceded to France in the Treaty of Basel. But the French Directory thought that guarding the rest of Spanish North America was price enough for Louisiana, and delayed.[30]

After ratifications of the Pinckney Treaty had been exchanged, Godoy made a treaty with the French minister, June 27, 1796, to cede Louisiana for the restitution of Gibraltar and for fishing rights off Newfoundland. These were altogether too high a price for Louisiana, in the opinion of the French Directory. It declined, as indeed it might, for Britain would have much to say about Gibraltar and fishing in North American waters. So Godoy had to be content

28. ASP FR, I, 546. October 28, 1795. Miller, *Treaties*, II, 329, 330–331, 323, 328. See above, p. 127.
29. Bemis, *Pinckney's Treaty*, 336. Miller, *Treaties*, II, 324, 335.
30. Whitaker, "Spain and the Retrocession of Louisiana," AHR, XXXIX, 459.

merely with a treaty to make war upon Britain, August 19, 1796, and hopes. Whether happy or not, Spain was to wait upon the inclinations of France, not only with regard to Gibraltar but also the disposition of Louisiana and relations with the United States.[31]

Godoy's Reservations

THOMAS PINCKNEY had enjoyed no luck in the summer of 1795 with his plan for a commercial agreement. He perceived, he said, that the true interests of Spain did run counter to such a treaty. As a matter of fact, if Spain had given commercial privileges to the United States, she would have been liable under other commitments, or the pressure of other powers seeking like privileges, to throw open her colonial empire to the rest of the world. Mercantilist theory was still too prevailing in Spain for Godoy to consider such a concession to the United States, and stay in power. Therein to a great degree lies the explanation of why Spain was unable to develop Louisiana profitably while she had the chance.[32]

Spain wished, said Pinckney, "to reserve the commercial advantages they could offer as the equivalent for a guarantee of their American possessions." But with that idea he would have nothing to do. He could not have forgotten the furore in Congress only nine years before when Jay had proposed an arrangement hardly more restrictive upon Western ambitions, in order to obtain commercial privileges from Spain. Pinckney dropped his plan for trade.[33]

To forestall criticism at home because he had not secured everything, Pinckney reported to Secretary Randolph that he had got the most he could obtain by friendly negotiation. It required, he said, "some knowledge of the national character fully to conceive" of his difficulties: "The peace concluded between this country and France, and the pacific disposition (at least exteriorly) exhibited to Spain by the British cabinet, added to our critical situation with the last Power, rendered this negotiation more difficult than it might otherwise have been." So it may have appeared at the moment to Pinckney in Madrid, unaware of Wayne's achievements that summer in the Mississippi Valley, and uncertain as to what would be the ultimate reaction of his own countrymen to the Jay Treaty, which President Washington was accepting as he himself negotiated

31. Renaut, 211 ff. Martens, *Receuil de Traités*, VI, 255, for the treaty between Spain and France, August 19, 1796.
32. See above, pp. 100–102, 109–110.
33. ASP FR, I, 546. See above, pp. 102–109.

with Godoy.[34] Yet this opinion seems strangely oblique in the midst of the facts which Pinckney did know concerning the results of Jay's negotiation with Grenville, and the situation in England whence he had just come. He did not have, of course, the actual terms of the Spanish treaty with France at Basel; but he must have known from Short, who had taken part in Godoy's preliminary maneuvers, that Godoy for some time had been seeking re-entry into the good graces of France, not from a position of strength, but as the weaker party anxious for release from war. To be sure, Pinckney had to ask for his passports before he could bring Godoy to sign his treaty. But it is all that he did have to do—a move which no previous American diplomatist at Madrid had ever dared to use with any hope of winning.[35]

In reality, except for Godoy's resistance to a commercial treaty which Pinckney could go home without if he had to do so, Pinckney's only insurmountable obstacle was the argument of Spain that the United States did not already possess by previous contract the legal right to free navigation of the Mississippi River through Spanish territory. That the United States had this right, Godoy would not, and did not, concede. His surrender was not abject. Pinckney had to yield something.

The treaty did not read as Pinckney wished it: "It is nevertheless agreed, that nothing contained in this article shall be construed or interpreted, to communicate the right of navigating this river to other nations or persons, than to the subjects of His Catholic Majesty, and to the citizens of the United States." Instead, it read: "And His Catholic Majesty has likewise agreed that the navigation of the said River in its whole breadth from its source to the Ocean shall be free only to his Subjects, and the Citizens of the United States, unless he should extend this privilege to the Subjects of other Powers by special convention."[36]

Beyond mistake, therefore, Godoy granted—he did not acknowledge—the right of free navigation through Spanish territory. But, as Pinckney wrote Randolph, "the substance, however, appears to me not disadvantageous." Why indeed should he be a stickler for a right in the past when he had won the substance, the right henceforth? Realistically considered, the right derived from the Treaty of 1783 with Britain had only been a stubborn pretension to hold against Spain. Now, it was a contract with Spain.[37]

34. *Ibid.* October 28, 1795.
35. For Jay's threat to Montmorin, French ambassador in Madrid, see above, p. 38.
36. ASP FR, I, 540. Miller, *Treaties,* II, 321-322.
37. ASP FR, I, 545.

Riparian Rights and Neutral Commerce

It has been held that Pinckney's article on the free navigation of the Mississippi was a contravention of the article which Jay and Grenville had just made to reiterate the pact of 1783 between Britain and the United States. But even Jay, in spite of his many deferences to Britain, had not undertaken that the United States would insure Britain's right of navigation against Spain's wishes to the contrary. The Jay Treaty did not obligate the United States to look after the British interest in the Mississippi. They were committed only to respect it so far as they themselves were responsible.

However complicated international law on riparian rights may have been at that time, it did not automatically validate a contract between two parties to invade the interest of a third. Unless the third party were bound to both of the other parties by an agreement in common, it still had a right to distinguish between them. And until the Pinckney Treaty, Spain had not concluded any agreement with the United States concerning navigation of the Mississippi. Moreover, Britain was no longer possessed, strictly speaking, of true riparian rights on the Mississippi, for she had returned the Floridas to Spain in 1783 as she yielded the territory east of the Mississippi to the United States.[38]

But let us accept it as a fact that, even though Britain had returned the Floridas to Spain, she still retained her entire right to navigation on the Mississippi by reason of her treaty with France and Spain in 1763, confirmed in the Treaty of 1783. The United States were not therefore barred, by their pledges of 1783 and 1794 to Britain, from making a treaty of navigation with Spain in 1795. What if Spain did choose to place reservations in that treaty concerning the British right to navigate the Mississippi? Britain, on her own account, could take exception to such reservations; but she could not do so through the United States, for they had not undertaken in the Jay Treaty, nor the Treaty of 1783 preceding, to guarantee Britain's use of the Mississippi, except as against their own action. Recognizing Spain's right to restrict British use within her own jurisdiction if she chose was not denying the British right within theirs. Pinckney's agreement with Godoy on free naviga-

38. Bemis, *Pinckney's Treaty*, 334–335. For the treaties of 1783 and 1794, see above, pp. 92, 185. For the contemporary discourse by Vattel on the use of public ways of communication, right of toll, right of government, rivers separating two countries, rights of third parties, conflicting rights of navigation, primitive rights of passage, see his *Law of Nations* (American ed. 1796), pp. 103–104, 174, 181–182, 184, 207, 244, 248.

tion of the Mississippi was no infringement of the contract which Jay had made with Grenville.[39]

By the same rule of judgment, though he was to do so, neither had Godoy any right later to take exception to the fact that Britain enjoyed greater right under the Jay Treaty of 1794 to interfere with the neutral commerce of the United States than Spain obtained in the following year under the Pinckney Treaty. To cite the provisions of the American contracts of 1778, 1785, and 1795 with France, Prussia, and Spain respectively—all containing stipulations that "free ships" make "free goods" and defining contraband as closely as the American diplomatists could in each case—and to argue therefrom that the United States compromised themselves when they accepted a treaty of less ample terms in regard to neutral commerce from Britain in 1794, is to blur two facts that should be kept clear.[40]

One is that all of these treaties were merely bilateral agreements between the respective states in international society. The other is that the contracting parties in each case undertook to bind themselves with respect to their own actions when they were belligerents in case the other contracting parties remained neutrals. Not one of them undertook, either when belligerent or neutral, to defend the treaty-associate against interference with its neutral rights by another power. There was no multilateral obligation. There was no agreement to forbid making more, or less, favorable terms with a third power, as the first party saw fit, or found necessary in its own interest.

We must not lose sight of the fact that Thomas Pinckney had gone to Spain to get concessions, not to bind his country with obligations. He knew what was in the Jay Treaty. But that had been the exception to meet necessity. His treaty was to be in accordance with the normal interests of his country when dealing with any and every power except the mistress of the seas.

Much conjecture may rise from the question whether Godoy knew the exact terms of the Jay Treaty when he negotiated with Pinckney and whether he would have conceded this point or insisted upon that according to the amount he knew or suspected. It seems established now that he did have the text. But if he had not received it, he should have had strong suspicions that it must have contained terms concerning neutral rights on the seas which

39. For the treaties of 1762–63, see Martens, *Receuil de Traités*, I, 92 ff.; the British-Spanish treaty in 1783, III, 541 ff.

40. Bemis, *Pinckney's Treaty*, 347–348 n. See above, p. 191. For Godoy's protests through Irujo, see below, pp. 262–265.

he could not get Pinckney to accept. To put it another way, Godoy would have been stupid beyond belief if he had misunderstood Britain's inclination, regardless of all diplomatic professions. No European statesman needed to read the text of the Jay Treaty in 1795 to know that Britain had control of the sea, maritime interests of the greatest moment to her people, and every intention of maintaining them against her rivals around the world.[41]

Rather than to say that Godoy accepted the terms of the Pinckney Treaty concerning neutral rights because he did not know what was in or back of the Jay Treaty, or because he hoped to bind the United States to an agreement which would protect Spain from British interference, the best interpretation of his motives seems not far from his own afterthoughts, historically inaccurate and unreliable though his memoirs may be in most instances. This agreement with Pinckney, he said, "was not a mere treaty or alliance." It was "a formal pact of navigation." He had signed another bilateral contract regarding neutral rights, to widen the margin of safety in the future for all nations, particularly Spain, which might wish to remain neutral and keep out of the stream of recurrent war.[42]

Within a year, however, it happened that Spain was back in war, this time against Britain and on the side of France. Godoy wished then, of course, although he could hardly have expected, to use the United States under the Pinckney Treaty against Britain. But by that time he had better reason to anticipate renewed hostility from the United States, for he had yoked Spain with France.[43]

Important as these neutral rights of trade were to the development of the American empire, they should not divert us from Thomas Pinckney's greater achievement. He had advanced the most important interest of the United States. While Anthony Wayne cleared the Ohio country and forced the Indian buffer state of the British farther into uncertainty, he was signing the death warrant to a similar plan of the Spaniards below the Tennessee. The men of the "Western waters" may have been taking possession of the lower Mississippi for themselves regardless of his efforts. But he had sent home a treaty which ruined all hopes—either Spanish or British or French—that those frontiersmen could be enticed into rebellion against the Government in Philadelphia and separation of the Union. James Wilkinson would continue to intrigue, and to beg

41. Whitaker in MVHR, XV, 435–454, at 447, quoting Pinckney to Short, September 26, 1795.
42. Godoy, Memoirs, I, 458.
43. See below, pp. 265–266, 316–328.

compensation from the Spanish Treasury. But the opinion of Spaniards which Andrew Jackson was rapidly gaining would soon be the mood of the Southwest. The time was approaching, too, when Americans would no more endure the thought of Britons using the Mississippi than they now liked the rumor that Frenchmen were scheming to have Louisiana again.[44]

44. Whitaker in MVHR, XV, 450.

X

THE ANGER OF FRANCE

Washington under Criticism

THE first President of the United States was entitled to the repose of Mt. Vernon, secure in the gratitude of his fellow citizens. As part of his reward, even though he had taken responsibility on their behalf and continued for another term with genuine reluctance, George Washington was accused of wishing to make himself King. His policies were willfully misconstrued, his course maliciously obstructed as during his command of the Revolutionary Army. Indeed few of this country's leaders have received so bitter denunciation, though none endowed with as much temper and as little humor has borne personal onslaughts with more restraint. He had made mistakes, grave mistakes, when dealing with individuals, and he merited criticism on that account, but he had achieved great things for the American people as a whole.

Their institutions of Federal Government were established. Their domestic affairs were in order. Their neutrality was maintained between Britain and France in spite of their economic dependence upon the mother country and their obligations to the old ally. George Rogers Clark, and many others of their number under the spell of Citizen Genet, had been kept from precipitating a war with Spain, Britain's ally for the moment. A conqueror of the Indian war parties incited by the British in Canada had been found for them in "Mad Anthony" Wayne. The Ohio country was now open for their settlement. And beyond, their troops kept watch over the lines of communication from the Great Lakes to the Mississippi. Their envoy, John Jay, had won a truce with Britain that saved them from war, had decisive influence in Wayne's subjugation of the Indians, and made possible Pinckney's success at Madrid. Their first President was about to retire, leaving but one of their major affairs in disorder. And yet Bache's *Aurora* speeded his departure on March 4, 1797, with this blast, an example followed glibly ever since by commentators in the American press who care not so much to be honest as smart:

If ever there was a period for rejoicing, this is the moment—every heart in unison with the freedom and happiness of the people, ought to beat

high with exultation that the name of WASHINGTON from this day
ceases to give a currency to political iniquity, and to legalize corruption. A new aera is now opening upon us, an aera which promises much
to the people; for public measures must now stand on their own merits.

He had failed to achieve these things without antagonizing France.[1]

The Farewell Address

FROM his own experiences, and with the craftsmanship of his most
intimate adviser, Alexander Hamilton, to aid him, George Washington had drawn the principles which he believed should be funda-
mental with respect to both foreign powers and internal factions,
and had presented them to the American people on September 19,
1796. It was of infinite moment, he declared, that they should
properly estimate the immense value of their national union to
their collective and individual happiness. North, South, East, West
—all sections should feel an immediate and particular interest in
the Union. A government for the whole was indispensable. No
alliance, however strict between the parts, could be an adequate
substitute. And having in mind the dangers threatening from
France behind Spain, but by no means yet removed from the British quarter as well, Washington pointed out to Westerners that connection with any foreign power would be unnatural and intrin-
sically precarious.

In dealing with other nations, he said, the people of the United
States should observe good faith and justice toward all. They should
avoid permanent, and inveterate, antipathies against particular nations and passionate attachments for others. The great rule of their
conduct should be, in extending their commercial relations with
foreign states, to have with them as little political connection as
possible. Europe had a set of primary interests which had none or
very remote relations with those of the United States. They would
be unwise to implicate themselves by artificial ties in the ordinary
vicissitudes of European politics or the ordinary combinations and
collisions of European friendships or enmities. Why, by interweav-
ing their destiny with that of any part of Europe, should they entangle their peace and prosperity in the toils of European ambition,
rivalship, interest, humor, or caprice? It was their true policy to
steer clear of permanent alliances with any portion of the foreign
world. Taking care always to keep themselves by suitable establishments on a respectable defensive posture, they might safely trust
to temporary alliances for extraordinary emergencies. And they

1. Quotation taken from Bassett, *The Federalist System,* 148.

must, he said, keep constantly in view that it is folly in one nation to look for disinterested favors from another.[2]

Monroe's Mission to France—Paine's Influence

IT was in the spirit of this last principle that Washington had sent James Monroe to France in June, 1794, immediately after the departure of John Jay for England. The rule was reciprocal. France could not expect the United States to follow a course that involved a sacrifice of their own interests beyond their standing commitments to France, any more than they should look to France for disinterested favors. It was folly for French statesmen to expect otherwise. It seems very doubtful that they honestly did so. Washington's despatch of the Republican, Monroe, clearly indicated to them that France could count upon the United States to honor the treaties of 1778 to the letter, but no more. For it was equally clear, from the very fact that Washington had just sent an envoy extraordinary to Britain to disperse the chances of war, that the Government in the United States would cling stubbornly to the position that their contract with France was nothing but a defensive alliance.[3]

There was left for French statesmen only the possibility that they might reverse George Washington's policies by obtaining the election in 1796 of Thomas Jefferson, traditional friend of France. How far Jefferson actually was from that position has already been seen. What he really would do for France when he became President of the United States will appear presently.[4]

Monroe's acceptance of instructions from Washington in the spring of 1794 could not be interpreted by anyone, not even by Monroe himself, notwithstanding his known dislike of Britain, to imply that the American Government meant to have him nullify the simultaneous efforts of Jay in London. It could only be interpreted to mean that the United States proposed to keep on good terms with France while they continued upon the course of neutrality which they had taken in 1793. They would avoid so long as possible that distressing question whether they would guarantee to

2. See V. H. Paltsits, *Washington's Farewell Address,* for a facsimile, transliterations, correspondence and documents, the contributions of Hamilton and Madison, and other pertinent evidence.

3. Washington planned first to have Thomas Pinckney go over to Paris if John Jay would be willing to stay on as minister to Britain. If Jay would not, then Washington wished to send Robert Livingston to Paris. When both Jay and Livingston declined, he commissioned Monroe. Washington (Ford ed.), XII, 422–423 n. Monroe left Baltimore about June 18. Monroe (Hamilton ed.), II, 9.

4. See above, pp. 150–151, and below, p. 390 f.

France, with military and naval assistance, her possessions in the West Indies. Up to this time, France herself had not chosen to hold the United States to the obligation. The French authorities had seen the advantage of American neutrality as they fought the British. The American merchant fleet, loaded with foodstuffs and convoyed across the Atlantic by French warships, had more value than the aid of the United States in war—even if it could be assumed that the American Government would respond when summoned.[5]

That the United States would obey such a summons rather than break their pledge to France was an assumption which France's statesmen, regardless of party, seem never to have seriously entertained. Indeed those who were to confer with Monroe were to show him no real desire to have the United States get into the war against Britain. It might cause annoying complications in the peacemaking, especially with Spain.[6]

They professed in the end, however, to have expected that the United States would insist upon British acceptance of the principle *free ships free goods* and would punish Britain if she did not leave French goods unmolested when found in a neutral American ship. They became exceedingly angry when they discovered in the Jay Treaty that Washington had no intention of doing any such thing, and they resorted to reprisals upon American commerce in direct violation of their own obligation to the United States. Presumably the reasoning was that, if President Washington would not stretch the compact of 1778 to concede a favor to France even though it endangered his own country, France had some right to break the Treaty of 1778 on her own account to the injury of the United States. In extenuation it can only be said that starvation was coming altogether too close to the populace of France for her statesmen to have regard for logic which conflicted with their feelings. Moreover, as it receded the Reign of Terror left in exhaustion other capacities as well as fear.

Washington took his position on solid ground. The Treaty of 1778 did not obligate the United States to force a third party to abide by the treaty's stipulations. It obliged them to deny themselves the right to confiscate the noncontraband goods of France apprehended in a neutral vessel, when they should become a belligerent and France should be their enemy. The United States might strongly desire, inasmuch as they possessed a large merchant fleet and a feeble navy, that the nations of the world should all bind themselves, when they became belligerents, to obey as law the pre-

5. See above, p. 151.
6. See above, pp. 157, 161, and below, pp. 245–246.

230230 OUR RISING EMPIRE

cept that a neutral flag should protect an enemy's goods excepting contraband. But this was no obligation on the part of the United States, save to those nations with which they had made bilateral treaties to that effect. Britain was not among that company; nor was Jay able, even though he tried, to get Britain to join that company.[7]

Washington knew that the United States had no obligation to France to coerce Britain into obeying the rule *free ships free goods*. What Washington did not know was how French national policy might have been distorted by the sudden and ruthless working of the guillotine upon the men who were struggling with each other for control of the forces of the Revolution. To find this out was one of the purposes for which he sent Monroe to France.

Monroe's written instructions from Randolph were to make himself acceptable, but he was also to maintain the self-respect due to his own Government. Both Genet and Fauchet, he read, had declared that France did not wish the United States to leave their neutral position. If, however, he should be approached in regard to the guarantee of the West Indies, or alliance, or even a treaty of commerce, he was to "refer the Republic of France to this side of the water." He was to say that Jay had been positively forbidden to weaken the engagements of the United States to France, but he was to defend the right of the United States to give asylum to the French émigrés. He was to advise the French Government not to try Genet's method of operating upon the people rather than the Government of the United States. And he was to insist upon compensation for the spoliations of American property by France's cruisers since the spring of 1793. If the recent embargo of Congress were mentioned, he would explain that it had been aimed at Britain but made general in order to avoid being a "cause of war," and that it had been discontinued because it was injurious to France; and he was to counter with protests against the French embargo at Bordeaux. He was to seek France's help in persuading Spain to open the Mississippi—for Spain, said Randolph, might soon be making peace with France apart from Britain. But, of course, if the United States were to be in war "with any nation on earth" —specifically Britain—France should know that she would be America's "first and natural ally."[8]

Monroe was given discretion. Months, obviously, would pass before he could report and receive particular directions from Phila-

7. See above, p. 191.
8. ASP FR, I, 668. June 10, 1794. Monroe (Hamilton ed.), II, 1–9. Randolph knew, evidently, of Godoy's approaches through Short. See above, p. 216.

delphia. But he was explicitly told: "It is expected, with a sure reliance on your discretion, that you will not commit the United States, by any specific declaration, except where you are particularly instructed, and except too in giving testimony of our attachment to their cause." Passing over the first part of this sentence—which is precise—and fixing upon the latter as his guide—although in comparison with the first it is vague—the new minister to France was to cause plenty of trouble for his own Government before he returned to America.[9]

James Monroe did not read in his instructions—nor does it appear that he was elsewhere informed officially—that Jay was to seek a commercial treaty with Britain in addition to release of the posts and payment for spoliations. This silence has been construed often as indicating that Washington and Randolph were concealing things from Monroe. But Monroe himself had no right at the time to such an opinion. He had just engaged as a member of the Senate that spring in the heated debate over shipping rights and reprisals. He was present when the United States lifted the embargo against Britain. He voted on April 28, 1794, for the nonimportation bill, designed to punish Britain until she made amends for raiding American commerce; and he saw the bill defeated in the Senate by the casting vote of Vice-President Adams. In fact, Monroe wrote to Jefferson about the episode and stated that it might be "ascribed to an executive manoeuvre." He remarked further: "'Tis said that the Envoy will be armed with extr.ʸ powers, & that authority to form a commercᶜˡ treaty will likewise be comprized in his instructions."[10]

James Monroe was aware that his Government was trying both to keep the peace with Britain and to maintain good relations with France, while pressing both powers to respect the neutral rights of his country. Moreover, he knew that he was to take the place of the man who had been Washington's personal representative in England in 1790 and who was being superseded in France only because his sympathies with the monarchy and his activities in its aid had made him distasteful to the succeeding Revolutionary Government. If James Monroe did not understand all this as he set out to replace Gouverneur Morris, he was singularly unobservant. His actions lead to a different conclusion.[11]

The new minister to France was aware of these things. In spite of them and his written pledge to Washington's administration, he took his mission as a mandate not so much from the President as

9. Monroe (Hamilton ed.), II, 6. For the Bordeaux Embargo, see above, p. 175.
10. *Annals*, 3d Cong., 90. Monroe (Hamilton ed.), I, 292–294, May 4, 1794.
11. See above, pp. 130–133.

from the American people, or rather that portion of them who felt with Jefferson in the spring of 1794 that maybe the time was coming when they should honor their guarantee of the French West Indies. Monroe had opposed the appointment of John Jay to England on the ground that Jay had already yielded to the British. He thought of Jay as the man who ten years before had been willing— "dishonestly," he said—to sacrifice to Spain the interests of Westerners, and Virginians, for the advantage of the merchants of New York and New England. He thought of himself as the man who would now assure the French people that no pro-British habits would check the true interest of the great republics allied in battle for liberty against monarchic oppression. He overlooked Jefferson's statement to him on April 24 that Jefferson's own wish was for peace if it could be preserved with good faith and honor. He lost sight of the fact that even this guide and preceptor had elaborated the principles of American neutrality, benevolent toward France, to be sure, but nevertheless, neutrality.[12]

James Monroe received orders from a Government thinking first of the common interests of the whole American people regardless of section or party. George Washington was to discover that Monroe had gone to France quite in the manner of Genet who had come to this country assuming that he could deal directly with representatives of the people and ignore "old Washington." Robert Livingston declined to go because he was opposed to the Administration. James Monroe went, and when he got there, listened to Thomas Paine, enemy of the President, rather than to Gouverneur Morris, Washington's friend and personal representative abroad.[13]

Monroe found the author of *Common Sense*, *The Rights of Man*, and *The Age of Reason* in a French prison, seriously ill and enraged that Washington had not got him released at once because he was an American citizen. Paine was convinced that the President had not done so because of fear that Britain would be offended. Through either pity or indignation, it does not matter which, Monroe got Paine out of prison and took care of him in his own home. It does matter that he came under the influence of Thomas Paine, whose personal feelings blinded him to the fact that George Washington was following the admonition of *Common Sense* to stay clear of the "wars and quarrels" of Europe. Paine was so distraught with

12. Monroe (Hamilton ed.), I, 301–302. Monroe to Washington, June 1, 1794. For the Jay-Gardoqui episode, see above, p. 100 f. Jefferson (Ford ed.), VI, 506. For Jefferson on neutrality, see above, p. 147 f.

13. For Genet, see above, p. 156 f. For Livingston, see Washington (Ford ed.), XII, 423 n. For Morris, *ibid.*, 433.

his own imaginings, frustrations, grievances, or whatever they were, that he denounced Washington's administration at length to the world and closed the diatribe with: "And as to you, Sir, treacherous in private friendship (for so you have been to me, and that in the day of danger) and a hypocrite in public life, the world will be puzzled to decide whether you are an apostate or an impostor; whether you have abandoned good principles, or whether you ever had any."[14]

Monroe's Blunders—The French Design for Louisiana

ARRIVING in Paris just after the fall of Robespierre, James Monroe found the situation of the French Government tense and its officials uncertain whether to receive him, but he hit upon the idea of approaching the president of the Convention directly. He was received before that body with the fraternal embrace on August 15. His address was no more fulsome than the letters which he had brought from the Senate and House of Representatives, but it was in public. It proved to be his first blunder at the expense of his own Government, for his words reverberated across the Channel to embarrass the negotiations of his fellow envoy. After that, however, Monroe recalled his instruction to insist upon compensation for damages to American commerce and presented the American case exactly to the Committee of Public Safety.

There was a great difference, he said, between British and French treatment of American commerce. Britain could dispute the American interpretation that *free ships free goods* was the law of nations. France was "regulated by treaty." He might also have kept uppermost in his mind the fact that France had preceded Britain by some months in raiding the shipping of the United States; but he committed a second blunder and went on to say that he was not instructed to complain of the French decree or to request its repeal. Quite the contrary, if France got any solid benefit from the decree, although he asserted that it did not, "the American Government, and my countrymen in general," he said, would bear the departure from the Treaty of 1778 not only "with patience, but with pleasure."[15]

14. Those who prefer to consider Paine as the victim of Gouverneur Morris' antipathy, Washington as remiss, and Monroe less influenced, will find these matters treated at length from that point of view in Paine (Conway ed.), III, 150–252, presenting Paine's *Memorial to Monroe*, September 10, 1794, and *Letter to Washington*, July 30, 1796. The quotation above is from *ibid.*, III, 252.

15. ASP FR, I, 676–678. September 3, 1794. For French violations of American shipping, see above, pp. 167, 175.

Members of the Committee, as was only to be expected after such a surrender of his case, told Monroe some weeks later that compliance with the treaty would be detrimental to France. Then no less than three times they brought him to the question whether he would demand execution of the treaty. Each time he avoided the answer by saying that he had nothing to add to his previous statement. He suspected, at the moment, that the Committee would call upon him to execute the guarantee of the West Indies if he said "yes." But of course his instructions had already taken care of that; he was not to let such a demand enter into his negotiations at Paris, but to refer it to his Government in Philadelphia.

After thinking over the conference, Monroe decided that the Committee had only pressed the question in order to obtain a means of justifying themselves to the French public later when they might decide to comply with the American treaty—as in fact they did momentarily by a vote of the National Convention on January 2, 1795. For the public, wrote Monroe to Randolph, would consider such compliance as a favor to the British and a change in the French system of trade. The French Government had virtually a monopoly over commerce at that time. Monroe therefore concluded that it would be impolitic for him to demand compliance with the Treaty of 1778. A refusal, he said, would weaken the connection between the United States and France.[16]

Right there, Monroe failed to accomplish the major purpose of his mission to France. It was to foster respect for American independence and neutrality. His judgment of the Committee's motives was mistaken. Just a week after he had reported to Randolph, the Committee of Public Safety decreed, November 15, 1794, ostensibly that neutral ships might come and go unmolested, but actually that enemy merchandise was still to be seized by the cruisers of France until those enemies had declared French merchandise loaded in neutral vessels to be free and "not liable to seizure."

Another decree on January 4 following the vote of the National Convention did appear to meet the wishes of the United States. It declared that the naval commanders were not to seize enemy merchandise from neutral ships, excepting of course contraband. It seemed to recognize the obligation of 1778. But in reality it, too, was conditioned upon the "crimes of England" and action by the "cabinet of London" to alter their orders-in-council. It was not issued in acknowledgment of France's obligation to the United States regardless of what Britain might do. Both of these decrees indicated strongly that, in spite of what the National Convention

16. ASP FR, I, 675, September 15; 681–685, November 7.

declared, the French authorities based their respect for American neutrality not upon the Treaty of 1778 but upon performance on the one hand by Britain and on the other by the United States beyond the requirements of their contract with France.[17]

But James Monroe's own thoughts were not upon neutrality. Other letters to Randolph burst with martial ideas: Austria and Prussia as well as Spain were war-weary, he declared, and soon would be deserting Britain's coalition against France; Denmark and Sweden were joining their fleets to resist British interference with neutral commerce; and the Spaniard, Gardoqui, had written to open a way for negotiating peace with France. This might be bad, said Monroe, for the interests of the United States in the Western World; it would take the pressure off Spain in Europe unless she could be checked in some other way through France. But the Committee of Public Safety had hinted about an American loan to France; perhaps that, he said, might be made the check upon Spain.

The moment therefore had come, in Monroe's mind, for the United States to strike. They should make this loan to France and welcome the consequence of war with Britain. War would gain their end; France would guarantee American objectives at the peace-making. He had Randolph's letter of September 25; it made him glad to hear that his "idea of our situation with Britain and Spain was correct." The French, to be sure, had no "real wish" (he noted that) for the United States to get into the war; in fact, he was "persuaded they would rather we would not; from an idea it might diminish their supplies from America." Monroe might have persuaded himself, too, that they could have had other ideas, as indeed they had. But he had no mind to suspect the French. It was time for war with the British. Their order-in-council of November 6 was, he declared, "war, in *fact*." "We could not have asked from fortune a more seasonable opportunity. . . ."[18]

Why not seize it? One reason should have been sufficient in the light of his instructions. His superiors in Philadelphia did not want war with Britain. But that was not sufficient for James Monroe after he had been acclaimed before the Convention of France in August, 1794.

Secretary Randolph's letter of September 25 did have some phrases which were bound to encourage Monroe in Paris. Among other things he read: "You know how Mr. Jay is restricted. . . ."

17. *Ibid.*, I, 642, 752. Moore, V, 4414–4415. Bemis, in AHR, XXXIX, 253, 255, gives the dates of these decrees as November 18, 1794, and January 3, 1795.

18. ASP FR, I, 678, Randolph's letter of September 25; 679, Monroe's of October 16; 685, November 20; 687, December 2.

The courts of Madrid and London are "cordial in nothing but a hatred against the United States and a determination to harass them through the Indians. . . . I have no hope of the western posts. . . . keep the French republic in good humor with us."[19]

These comments have also been construed to prove that the President and the Secretary of State were not candid with Monroe. From that point of view, Randolph seemed here to imply that Jay had no authorization to deal with Grenville in regard to commercial matters. But what indeed if Randolph had not told Monroe everything about Jay's mission either in writing or in conference before he left for France? His superiors were entirely at liberty to withhold any statement from him which might interfere with the success of their negotiations with Britain, so long as they did not violate the pledges of the United States to France. Monroe had been given explicit instructions concerning what he was to do; and unless he had become infatuated altogether with his own ideas, he knew that his Government would settle at the same time all issues with Britain if they could be settled. He did in fact know just how restricted Mr. Jay was—not simply by instruction to honor the obligations of this country to France. He knew that Jay was to maintain as much as he possibly could of American neutrality while seeking release for the United States from the hindrances and pressures still kept upon them by their mother country. He knew also that Jay was impeded by their own weakness or unwillingness to meet British demands in regard, for example, to compensating the Loyalists.

There were other things in this letter from Randolph that should have arrested Monroe's attention, and shaken his thought of war with Britain. He read of the uprising in the West against the whisky tax and—hardly restrained between the lines—the fears which gripped the authorities at Philadelphia in those September days of 1794. Randolph had cause to be depressed as he wrote. But toward the end of the letter came a significant bit of news. Reports were in from the West that Wayne had beaten the Indians. If that were true, their exultation, said Randolph, might have fallen; they would soon be sick of war. And staring Monroe in the face, and for him the most important thing in the whole letter, was Randolph's statement that the depredations of the French cruisers upon American commerce were arousing violent expressions in his own country—"which you cannot quiet too soon by a proper adjustment." Monroe did not read that he might depart from his instructions in regard to this question.

However, it was already too late. The minister in Paris was sacri-

19. *Ibid.*, I, 678.

ficing that part of his instructions even while the Secretary of State was writing the letter in Philadelphia. Monroe paid no attention when he received it, but hammered away at his idea of war with Britain. Did it not matter at all that France had no "real wish" for American participation?

We know why the French Government had none. Its plans for settling Franco-Spanish affairs both in Europe and in America, even then—before the Jay and Pinckney treaties—were opposed to the interests of the United States in the Mississippi Valley. Those who had just overthrown Robespierre were soon to take up where Genet had left off. They tried to make Spain give over Louisiana and close the Mississippi as Godoy sought peace with them.[20]

Monroe, to be sure, was not aware of this at the time. But, granted that his belief in the value of the French alliance was sincere, he need not have been, at the age of thirty-six, so sophomoric about it. France could hardly be expected, at any time or under any conditions, to undertake in the peacemaking to get for the United States objects which she might be glad to have for herself. Monroe was making such sweeping observations of world affairs from his eminence in the capital of France and drawing such far-reaching conclusions, that he might well have shortened his range a bit, just to be sure, and scrutinized possibilities immediately before him. But he was infatuated with the thought of victory over Britain. The two republics would glory in the humiliation of monarchy. Would they divide the spoils?

On the very day when Monroe was writing to Randolph to expound further his plan for war with Britain, Randolph also was writing to him—in the "frankness of friendship." Now, on December 2, 1794, the Whisky Rebellion was crushed. The reports of Wayne's victory at Fallen Timbers had been verified. Pickering had made the treaty of peace with the Iroquois in western New York. Despatches had come from Jay which had not told much, but at least they showed that negotiations were proceeding. And so, Randolph could proceed with the minister in Paris.

Monroe's public demonstrations in the Convention had been a mistake; his instructions did not call for the "extreme glow" which he had displayed. The United States, said Randolph flatly, were neutral. Monroe had been given no discretion in regard to the French decree; he could not avoid raising the issue; Morris before him had already raised it. The American claims for compensation rested upon the very fact that the decree violated the Treaty of 1778. France had not requested the guarantee of her West Indies;

20. See above, pp. 216, 219. Whitaker in MVHR, XV, 437.

in fact, to that day the French Government had implied that its policy was not to do so. But if the new authorities had made the request, Monroe could have repelled it simply by obeying his instructions to refer the matter home.[21]

When Monroe had read this letter, and could reply on February 12, 1795, he stubbornly defended himself. But in the meantime he had committed other blunders—even more reprehensible if he really were the minister of President Washington in France. He had written a letter to the Committee of Public Safety, December 27, 1794, offering to acquaint them with the real dispositions of his countrymen. He had given the Committee to understand not only that Jay would make no treaty in London involving commercial matters but also that he himself would get directly from Jay the draft of the treaty which he did make and show it to them.[22]

Jay had written in November that he would send over the contents of the treaty confidentially in cipher. There was nothing in the treaty, said he, repugnant to the obligations to France; but, it would have to be ratified before it could be made public. Monroe, however, wrote back on January 17, 1795, that his own representative would come for the text, as the French Government had requested a copy of the treaty on their rights as an ally, and he had committed himself to supply it. Monroe felt especially obligated, no doubt, because of the vote on January 2 by the National Convention to comply with the Treaty of 1778. But Jay replied on February 5 with an exact and literal extract of the clause declaring that nothing in the treaty should "be construed or operate contrary to former and existing public treaties with other sovereigns or states." For the remainder Monroe, and the French Government, would have to wait.[23]

As the Constitution had placed the treaty-making power in the hands of the President by and with the advice and consent of the Senate, Monroe should have known that he had no right as a subordinate diplomatic officer to commit himself to reveal the terms of an agreement which was being negotiated by another subordinate officer; and that, even less, had any foreign government, ally or no ally, the right to demand the text of a treaty before it had been ratified and had become an agreement between the contracting parties. Absolutely nowhere in the treaties of 1778 between the

21. ASP FR, I, 689, Randolph to Monroe, December 2, 1794. Randolph took some of the edge from this in a more kindly letter on December 5 (690) but he still insisted upon American neutrality.

22. Bemis in AHR, XXXIX, 255 n. 12. Extract from the French Archives.

23. ASP FR, I, 516–517.

United States and France can be found the faintest statement or basis for inference that France had a right to demand participation in any diplomatic negotiations of the United States with a third power—though there were precedents enough from the days of Gérard, Montmorin, and La Luzerne for the French authorities to try it.[24]

Monroe complained to the Secretary of State that Jay had refused to let him have the treaty. Jay did send over his secretary, John Trumbull, to tell Monroe orally what was in it, but Monroe would not listen. His honor was pledged, he said, to the Committee of Public Safety.[25]

Finally, at the request of Trumbull, the major features of the Jay Treaty reached Monroe through a Mr. Hichborn, an American resident in Paris, and of course then reached the Committee—if they had not already done so through channels familiar to every foreign office, invariably quite accurate and speedy, if unofficial. Monroe resented this "most informal of all informal communications" by way of Hichborn, but he "thought it best to send the paper in by my secretary, Mr. Gauvain." When George Washington read this remark, he exploded. "Here is striking instance of his folly! This Secretary of his was a foreigner—it is believed a Frenchman.—Introduced no doubt to his confidence and Papers for the sole purpose of communicating to the Directory the secrets of his office."[26]

Attention had swung across the Atlantic to the Senate and Washington, to Fauchet, Adet, and Randolph, before James Monroe's grievance against John Jay had been fully aired. Monroe was left to occupy himself with an effort through Short in Madrid to further American pretensions in the lower Mississippi Valley; with the arrival of Thomas Pinckney en route to Madrid and a rebuff from the French ministers when he offered to have Pinckney take messages for them to the Spanish Court; with the problem of the Algerine corsairs; and one more letter on September 10, 1795, to the Secretary of State, arguing for war with Britain.[27]

Monroe still had not seen the text of the Jay Treaty. Nor was he aware of all that had been involved in the negotiations for peace

24. See above, pp. 29–33, 37–39.
25. ASP FR, I, 700, March 17, 1795; 701, April 14, 1795. Trumbull, *Reminiscences*, 180.
26. ASP FR, I, 702. Simcoe (Cruikshank ed.), IV, 360, Hichborn's letter to Monroe. Monroe (Hamilton ed.), II, 243. Washington (Ford ed.), XIII, 485.
27. ASP FR, I, 712–720. Discussion of the Algerine affair has been omitted as of minor significance in this narrative.

between France and Spain at Basel. Nevertheless, he wrote on: he would arouse France to full zeal and strike terror in England by seizing British property in the United States, by taking the posts, and even invading Canada. He would cut up England's trade with privateers. This would be a powerful diversion, he declared, in favor of France; it would promote a general peace. And indeed it might have—at the expense of the United States.[28]

In this mood, Monroe awaited word from the Secretary of State, Edmund Randolph. It was to be written two days later. It was not to come from Randolph. It was not to be at all to Monroe's liking.

Washington Insisting upon Peace—Monroe's Defense

PRESIDENT WASHINGTON had ratified the Jay Treaty, August 18, 1795, and the next day had put the despatch of Fauchet in Randolph's hands. The thankless office of Secretary of State—abandoned by Jefferson, now resigned by Randolph under accusations far beyond his deserts—had gone begging for some weeks, until Timothy Pickering, Secretary of War, found himself acting head also of the State Department.

It was Pickering who, with personal pleasure, wrote the letter to Monroe on September 12, 1795, but under the circumstances it came to the minister in France, with texts of the Jay Treaty, directly from the President himself. When Monroe opened it, he read blunt and honest statements. They were entirely justifiable. But they were certain to fill him with dismay, and to infuriate those Frenchmen who were still hoping to use the United States against Britain on the seas while they thwarted American aspirations in the Mississippi Valley under Monroe's nose.

The British were interfering with the neutral rights of the United States, said Pickering's letter, and it was the interest of the United States to stop that interference. But the British were within their rights in refusing to relax their rules in America's favor; and so, the United States had been obliged to let them continue. The United States, however, had not relinquished any neutral rights which they already possessed. In regard to the preëmption of provisions, Britain had insisted upon her right, and the United States had stood their ground. The result was a compromise: Britain would pay for the foodstuffs which she diverted from French ports. This, said Pickering, would work to the advantage of France, for it would encourage American carriers wishing to take foodstuffs to France to continue in the attempt.[29]

28. *Ibid.*, I, 721.
29. *Ibid.*, I, 596–598. Pickering to Monroe, September 12, 1795.

The argument was not merely specious. Those carriers could now be sure of some return on their investment even if the shipments were apprehended by British cruisers. Of course, they still ran the risk of losing the speculative profit in the French market, for no British court was likely to appraise their cargoes at French values. But many would escape the British patrols and reach France.

As a matter of fact, Washington's administration had gone farther in aiding the shipment of provisions and supplies from the United States than France really had a right to ask. Congress had authorized the liquidation of the debt to France in March. And in June, before the Senate had accepted the Jay Treaty, Oliver Wolcott, Secretary of the Treasury, had made arrangements with James Swan, American agent of France, to turn over bonds of the United States in complete payment of the debt to France. These bonds were to be sold in the American market, and the proceeds therefrom used to purchase supplies for shipment under the neutral American flag to France.[30]

There was nothing unneutral toward Britain in this. Those American ships which carried such property of the French Government were manifestly liable to capture and their cargoes to confiscation by Britain. The Jay Treaty did not protect neutral traffic in enemy's goods. And these very things Britain proceeded to do under a new order-in-council of April 25, 1795.

The British had foreseen that Wolcott's arrangements with Swan would follow the Act of Congress in March, and had prepared for them. But they neglected, it appears, to advise Washington properly as to the contents of the new order-in-council. He thought they were disregarding the Jay Treaty and resorting again to the seizure of American ships with cargoes of provisions privately owned. He came very near suspending ratification of the Jay Treaty on that account. Had not the exposure of Randolph occurred, he might perhaps have done so. After that, there was no question in his mind: Britain was behaving very badly, but France threatened to draw the American people into war.[31]

Pickering's letter of September 12, 1795, to Monroe insisted, therefore, that the obligations of the United States to other countries centered upon the principle that in any new engagements they should violate no prior undertaking. The United States had not, he declared, nor would they do so. But they were independent, they were not subject to dictation. France had gone into the American

30. Rice, "James Swan, Agent of the French Republic, 1794–1796," *N. E. Quarterly*, X, 474–479.
31. See above, pp. 199–202.

Revolution to diminish the power of Britain; and the interest of France now was to prevent the reunion of the United States and Britain—even of their interests and good will. Monroe acccordingly should give in France all the solemnity of truths to these points: The American Government had no predilection toward Great Britain. But, neither had it any desire for war with Britain. Settlement of the differences between the two countries over the Northwest posts, the Indian war, the fur trade, and the right of neutrals could no longer be delayed without danger of war. In comparison with such menaces to American safety, the question of a commercial treaty with Britain was subordinate. But even this, said Pickering, was not a new measure. And as a matter of fact it was not, for John Adams, then Gouverneur Morris, and then Thomas Jefferson had tried long since to persuade the British Government to consider it.

In short, James Monroe read that the Jay Treaty had been accepted. It was the prime interest of the United States to remain at peace. The President was bound to preserve peace. The United States were not going to war with Britain, whatever Monroe himself might think about it. He was, therefore, to avoid "every intimation which may invite the expectations and enterprises of the French Government, calculating on such an event." Finally, he was to make the French realize that the United States were still friendly toward France in spite of the performance of Genet.[32]

As could be expected of him, Monroe defended his course in reply and spoke of his own "delicate and embarrassing dilemma." But he now waked for a time at least to his first duty, that of representing President Washington in Paris, as he had given his word to do before he had left America. He faced down the assertion of Delacroix that the Alliance of 1778 was at an end. He prevailed upon the Directory—which had replaced the Committee of Public Safety in control of the French Government—not to send a special envoy to protest the Jay Treaty in Philadelphia, and he succeeded in getting France's grievances presented to him at Paris instead. He pointed out to the French minister that the European combination in support of the principles of armed neutrality had dissolved; the United States alone, therefore, could not compel, nor could be expected to compel, Britain to respect those principles. In fact, some of those European powers had since joined with Britain against France. He presented Pickering's arguments that the Jay Treaty had not changed the law of nations on contraband for the worse. He, too, asserted that British preëmption of foodstuffs worked in reality to

32. ASP FR, I, 598.

the advantage of France. And in the summer of 1796—before he had received his recall—he prevented the despatch of Mangourit to take the place of Adet in Philadelphia. Mangourit would have come, not as minister, but merely as chargé d'affaires; and the appointment would have been even more of an affront, for Mangourit had made himself unpopular in America by his part in the activities of Genet. But James Monroe did not really care for this work.[33]

As he thought over his grievances and heard of the tumult in America about Jay's Treaty, of Randolph's resignation, and the plan to defeat the treaty in the House of Representatives, Monroe came more and more to minimize his own blunders. He enlarged upon the value of his policies for his country, he persuaded himself that he represented not Washington but the American people. Then he dared to write political letters home to fellow Republicans. And he gave the distinct impression to the French Government that the American people would change things in the next presidential election—just what Adet on this side of the Atlantic was trying his best to accomplish with voice, pen, and money.[34]

Meanwhile, President Washington had become annoyed by continued evidence of his minister's insubordination, by his failure to press conclusively the American claims against France, by his indulgence in partisan correspondence. The President let Pickering have free rein for his skill in writing acid letters and sent Charles C. Pinckney, Federalist, to take Monroe's place in France.[35]

In the meantime also, the Directory abandoned further argument with Monroe. Delacroix asserted that the United States had broken their tacit agreement with France in regard to neutrality. He declared, with little respect for the facts, that they had deserted their obligations under what was now generally acknowledged as forming "the public law of all civilized nations." The Directory issued a decree, July 2, 1796, that France would "treat neutral vessels, either as to confiscation, as to searches, or capture, in the same manner as they shall suffer the English to treat them." And finally, to expand the inheritance of John Adams as he came

33. *Ibid.,* I, 727, December 6, 1795; 659–661, 730–741.
34. *Ibid.,* I, 741–742. Bemis in AHR, XXXIX, 256, citing Monroe to Delacroix, February 17, 1796. Monroe (Hamilton ed.), II, 454–460, Monroe to Pickering, February 17, 20, 1796. For Adet, see *Corresp. French Ministers,* 892–896, April 22, 1796; 972–973, November 22, condemning "the British faction." For bills and vouchers in the files of the French legation, showing expenditures upon articles in the *Independent Chronicle* of Boston and other printing, see AAE EU Sup. 19 ff., 329–332, 343, 348. Photocopies in the Library of Congress.
35. Washington (Ford ed.), XIII, 216 n., letter to Washington from Pickering, Wolcott, McHenry, Cabinet officers, July 2, 1796.

to the presidency, the Directory broke off diplomatic relations with the United States both in Philadelphia and in Paris. They obliged Pinckney to withdraw under insulting conditions—treating him as if he were a common stranger to whom a card of hospitality had been refused by the police, and then finally giving him official notice in writing to quit the territories of the French Republic.[36]

With the cordiality of Barras and the Directory to flatter him personally, though Barras' remarks were highly derogatory toward his Government, James Monroe took his official departure from France on January 1, 1797. But he remained in Europe and kept up unofficial relations with the Directory well into the spring. As John Quincy Adams observed him at The Hague in March, "his deportment evidently discovered an exasperated and strongly agitated mind, though his conversation was in every particular extremely guarded." Then he came home to put his grievances before the American people. He demanded a desk in the Department of State that he might revise his correspondence with the documents at hand, and he produced a work of some five hundred pages entitled "A View of the Conduct of the Executive in the Foreign Affairs of the United States."[37]

It becomes more astounding as one reads. It spins an elaborate self-defense without hesitation over faulty premises or contradictory facts. Both Thomas Jefferson and Robert Livingston had advised Monroe not to involve the President personally in his charges. Livingston had warned that he had better have in his possession evidence of duplicity in regard to Britain before he made the accusation. But Monroe wrote another partisan appeal with temper exceeding that of Randolph's "Vindication," and with by no means as much excuse for its publication. Randolph, at least, had a right to be provoked at the way in which he was faced with the President's disapproval. Monroe was warned early in the course of his activity; he was told in so many words that the United States were neutral, and yet he persisted in talking for war. Randolph resigned. Monroe had to be dismissed.[38]

One needs little imagination to reconstruct the scene at Mt. Vernon, those hours in the spring of 1798, as George Washington read James Monroe's "View of the Conduct of the Executive" and

36. ASP FR, I, 735, Delacroix to Monroe, July 7, 1796; 577, text of the decree of July 2; II, 10, reports of C. C. Pinckney, January 6, February 18, 1797. Moore, V, 4419.

37. J. Q. Adams, *Writings,* II, 151, to John Adams, March 30, 1797. Monroe (Hamilton ed.), III, 73 n., July 19, 1797; 74–75 n., Pickering's consent and defense of President's right of removal, July 24.

38. Jefferson (Ford ed.), VII, 177. October 25, 1797. Bond, 92. For Randolph, see above, p. 202.

set down these explosive commentaries in the margins with his firm hand: "unfortunate" appointment—"self-importance"—"party man," who got himself into his own "predicament" in Paris—the Jay Treaty was a "death warrant" to France's "hope of embarking this country in the war on the part of France"—"the French party in the U.S." began to criticize the Jay Treaty "before one article therein was known by those writers"—"Did the treaty with G.B. surrender any right of wch the U.S. had been in possession? Did it make any change or alteration in the Law of Nations, und^r which G.B. had acted in defiance of all the Powers of Europe?—Or did it give her any authority to sieze provision vessels contrary to that Law?—If none of these why all this farrago, but to sow the seeds of discontent, by imposing upon the uninformed?"[39]

Without a doubt George Washington was now prejudiced in defense of the policy of isolation which he had chosen for this country early in his administration. He had taken full and exclusive responsibility for it in the last critical moments of 1795 and 1796. He was not likely to reopen his mind to criticism of it in 1798. He was mistaken, to be sure, in thinking that France wished really to get the United States into the European war against Britain. For these French diplomatists had no desire to put themselves in another dilemma such as Vergennes' of 1782. Nevertheless historical judgment comes to rest upon Washington's opinions rather than upon the views of James Monroe.[40]

The French Government—despite rapid and bloody changes from Girondists to Jacobins to Committee of Public Safety to Directory—was following the advice of Moustier, the urging of Fauchet, the desire of the French people, to restore a colonial empire in America in rivalry with the United States. Although Pelet had explicitly assured Monroe at Paris that the agent of France negotiating with Spain was expressly instructed that he should use his utmost efforts to secure for the United States the points in controversy between them and Spain, Barthélemy was ordered to get the Spaniard, Iriarte, to concede at Basel just the opposite—the retrocession of Louisiana to France so that the Mississippi might be closed against the American pioneers.[41]

Even if a triple alliance could have been made in the manner of

39. Washington's copy of Monroe's "View," with the notes in Washington's handwriting, is in the Harvard College Library. The quotations above are from pp. lx, liv, lxi, xlv, xxxv, xlv. See also Washington (Ford ed.), XIII, 449–452, to John Nicholas, March 8, 1798, showing Washington's reaction against Jefferson as well.

40. See above, pp. 93–96.

41. ASP FR, I, 698, Monroe to Randolph, March 9, 1795. Whitaker, in MVHR, XV, 437; in *Journ. Mod. Hist.*, VIII, 8.

1780, as Godoy suggested to Pinckney—and this seems inconceivable for the reason that France now wished it no more than the United States—the United States would not have gained security. Such an alliance would merely have advanced French interests to the injury of their own. They most certainly would not have gained the major necessity of that time. Above all else they needed to remain at peace with Britain, their most powerful and menacing neighbor on this continent. Neither Spain nor France, nor both together in close alliance with them, could have assured this to the United States. It could be obtained only by persistent effort to hold Britain and the United States upon friendly terms while they ironed out their differences and conflicting interests.[42]

The statesmen of France appreciated this fact, if Monroe did not, and as they saw that *rapprochement* developing they realized its meaning: France must renounce the alliance with the United States and look after her own interests, make peace with Spain, force her back into the service of France, and for the loss of the United States, take compensation elsewhere.

There was Louisiana—and the back country of the United States stretching eastward from the Mississippi River to the Appalachian Mountains. Could those passes be defended by a new state in the Mississippi Valley against armies advancing from the Atlantic Seaboard? Fauchet had expressed optimistic opinions upon the susceptibilities of the American pioneers beyond the mountains. His successor, Adet, was sending General Collot to examine the terrain. The inheritance of John Adams had yet another complication. The emotion of France was not merely anger.

42. For Godoy to Pinckney, see above, pp. 215–216.

XI

JOHN ADAMS' DIFFICULTIES

The "Heir Apparent"

THE second President of the United States had been waiting his turn with much more respect for George Washington than he had shown for Benjamin Franklin in Paris. But he was fully as self-conscious. John Adams wrote to his wife on January 20, 1796:

> I am, as you say, quite a favorite. I am to dine today again. I am heir apparent, you know, and a succession is soon to take place. But whatever may be the wish or the judgment of the present occupant, the French and the demagogues intend, I presume, to set aside the descent. All these hints must be secrets. It is not a subject of conversation as yet. I have a pious and philosophical resignation to the voice of the people in this case, which is the voice of God. I have no very ardent desire to be the butt of party malevolence. Having tasted of that cup, I find it bitter, nauseous, and unwholesome.[1]

Political forces with which John Adams did not adequately reckon had been developing these seven long years while he presided over the Senate. His election was opposed, as he said, by the French minister and his henchmen. And "demagogues" about Thomas Jefferson were trying hard to defeat him, though Jefferson himself was deferring to his age and experience, his seniority in public life. But Federalists, too, had constructed an organization. It was not centered upon his personality, nor his political principles, least of all upon his ambitions. The Vice-President had long since ceased to take part in the President's counsel as he once had in regard to the affair over Nootka Sound. The Federalist system revolved about the ideas and the wishes of Alexander Hamilton; and Hamilton did not think that John Adams had the ability to succeed George Washington. Hamilton presumed rather to think that Thomas Pinckney, national figure because of his success in Madrid, would make a better President than Adams. Or perhaps it is more accurate to say, Hamilton thought that the Federalist clique would continue

---

1. Adams, *Works*, I, 485. Whitaker, *The Mississippi Question, 1795–1803*, is essential to this and succeeding chapters.

to run the American Government more snugly under Pinckney than under Adams.[2]

The French minister, Adet, made his calculations without proper consideration for the influence which George Washington still exerted upon the minds of the people in spite of all criticism. Far away at The Hague, young John Quincy Adams had much keener perception. He wrote to Joseph Pitcairn in Paris on November 13, 1796:

> There is a great ignorance of the character and sentiments of the American people in France among those who imagine that any manoeuvre of *theirs* could turn an election against the President of the United States.
> . . . France will find it more easy to go through five and twenty revolutions at home, than to root out that man's merits and services from the memory of Americans, or a proper sense of them from their hearts.

Adet's efforts to obtain the election of Jefferson served rather to strengthen the candidacy of John Adams, once it became known that George Washington preferred the New Englander.[3]

Hamilton, also, reckoned without due regard for the solidarity of New England and its feeling that it should follow Virginia in receipt of Federal honors. Eighteen electors in New England withheld their second votes from Pinckney, fearing that he might slip into the presidency ahead of Adams. Partisan management was soon to break through provincial lines and to steal the choice of the President from the electoral college, but not quite so soon as 1796. Hamilton's candidate ran third to Jefferson and Adams.[4]

Thomas Jefferson alone could take much satisfaction from the electoral returns, for he as the leader of the real opposition had missed the presidency by only three votes, and these could be traced to electors who had stood by Adams through personal loyalty. Jefferson wrote graciously to Adams that he "never one single moment expected a different issue," nor wished it. He was pleased that it was "impossible" for Adams to be "cheated" of his "succession" by a "trick worthy the sublety" of his "arch-friend of New York." Thus Jefferson turned Adams' thoughts upon Alexander Hamilton —while he himself "devoutly" wished that Adams might be able to "shun" war with France. For it would destroy "our agriculture, commerce & credit." If Adams could avoid it, the "glory" would be all his own.[5]

2. Jefferson (Ford ed.), VII, 91–92, to James Madison, December 17, 1796; 98–100, to Madison, January 1, 1797. See above, pp. 49, 89–91.

3. J. Q. Adams, *Writings,* II, 42.

4. Adams, *Works,* I, 493. Statement of C. F. Adams.

5. Jefferson, (Ford ed.), VII, 95–97, to Adams, December 28, 1796. Adams, *Works,* I, 507.

As for himself, Jefferson declared that he had "no ambition to govern men." It was "a painful and thankless office." But he must have meant that he did not have the ambition just then, for he replied to John Langdon, who notified him of his election as Vice-President, in regard to returning to office:

> If I had contemplated the thing beforehand, & suffered my will to enter into action at all on it, it would have been in a direction exactly the reverse of what has been imputed to me; but I had no right to a will on the subject, much less to controul that of the people of the U S in arranging us according to our capacities. Least of all could I have any feelings which would revolt at taking a station secondary to mr. Adams. I have been secondary to him in every situation in which we ever acted together in public life for twenty years past. A contrary position would have been the novelty, & his the right of revolting at it.

Nor did Jefferson suffer his will now to act in reverse. He informed Madison a few days later: "I have had occasion to write to Langdon, in answer to one from him, in which I have said exactly the things which will be grateful to mr. A. & no more. This I imagine will be shewn to him. . . ." Thomas Jefferson was biding his time as he took Adams' place in the chair of the Senate, and came actively again into the "politics" which he had told Adams in the previous February that he "never loved & now hate."[6]

John Adams nonetheless was President, even though by three votes only. And before he lost that high office to Thomas Jefferson in 1801, he had proved his ability to hold it on behalf of the American people, despite the continued opinion, and efforts, of Alexander Hamilton to the contrary.

The "Assaults" of France—Collot's Journey

THE victory of Adams over Jefferson in 1796 signified that Washington's attitude toward France would be maintained; and Adams' retention of the Cabinet as he found it gave double assurance. But this was, in fact, to make the difficulty more exasperating. Hamiltonian presumptions had been rebuffed in the election but not discouraged. Secretaries Pickering, Wolcott, and McHenry looked to the lawyer in New York for direction rather than to their superior in Philadelphia, and soon they were not even hesitating to ask Hamilton how they might thwart the purposes of Adams.

It was a mistake, however, for anyone to think that John Adams was unaware of his situation in all its complexities. Even before he was sure of his election, he had written to Mrs. Adams: "John

6. *Ibid.*, VII, 111, to Langdon, January 22, 1797; 115, to Madison, January 30; 56, to Adams, February 28, 1796.

Adams must be an intrepid to encounter the open assaults of France, and the secret plots of England, in concert with all his treacherous friends and open enemies in his own country. Yet, I assure you, he never felt more serene in his life." The British minister, for another, thought at the time that Adams had "firmness" of character sufficient to remove "all danger of his being *bullied* into measures" which he did not approve. Liston considered Adams' election "favorable to the interests of His Majesty . . . not because I perceive in Mr. Adams any partiality of sentiment towards Great Britain, but because he detests the principles and dreads the predominance of our enemies. . . ." But John Adams was to have need of all the firmness, serenity, and clearheadedness that he could command.[7]

General Victor Collot was back again in Philadelphia from his survey of the Mississippi Valley before Adams had become President. His tour beyond the Alleghenies, nevertheless, had created a problem for Adams. As the French Directory had broken off diplomatic relations, Adet sought a personal and unofficial conference with the new President on March 13, 1797, before returning to France. A certain Willcocks, he said, had just published a slanderous statement that he had sent a French general to revolutionize the States in the West and detach them from the Union. Covering his motives—so he said—and giving Adams a "half-confidence," Adet reported to the French foreign office that he was sure he had convinced the President that it was slander. Adams had replied that he wished to maintain the good understanding which had governed the relations of the two countries up to that time, and Adet was positive that he meant it; for, said he, Adams was not one who could "control his anger or other affections of his spirit." They gave him away "too strongly not to display themselves by signs or movements impossible not to perceive."[8]

But could this Frenchman be so sure that he had obscured his own actions as cleverly as he thought he had read Adams' behavior? Adet had thought himself good at making Jaudenes the instrument of France without the Spaniard's knowing it. Did it follow that he was equally good at covering his tracks so that Adams could not see? Adams remarked to his wife that the purport of Adet's visit was "to clear up his character"—but it "was of no consequence," and so he would not write about it. There is small chance

7. *Ibid.*, I, 495, December, 1796. Liston to Grenville, February 13, 1797. Liston Papers, Transcripts in Library of Congress.

8. *Corresp. French Ministers*, 1000–1001, March 26, 1797.

that John Adams was misled in March, 1797, concerning the journey of Victor Collot.[9]

Secretary Pickering had learned from the British minister, in January, of intercepted letters which showed that the French were planning an insurrection in Quebec. Their principal agent was David McLane, a citizen of Rhode Island; but Ira Allen and Vermonters were implicated. Jacob Oster (possibly Astor) was said to be responsible for the shipment of arms. The talk was of an invasion from the United States by twelve to fifteen thousand men. One would be too credulous if one thought that Timothy Pickering had not reported this to John Adams as soon as he could and that Adams had not taken note of it. It was enough to make him beware the "half-confidence" of the French minister about any rumor. But there was evidence also available touching directly upon the enterprise of General Collot in the West.[10]

At the time of Fauchet's return to France in November, 1795, and while they had James Monroe in hand, the Committee of Public Safety had instructed Adet to report all that he could gather upon the Western States, Louisiana, and the dispositions of their inhabitants. Even before that Adet had been busy in the cause. He had sponsored the activities of Elijah Clarke and others in East Florida —as an "insurrection" within Spanish territory, of course, and not as an "invasion" from the United States. The "neutrality" of the United States had to be respected! He had sent Samuel Fulton, one of Genet's American lieutenants, to investigate and report back upon the state of things; for a "number of inhabitants of East Florida" had petitioned him on July 18, 1795, begging the aid of France in throwing off the yoke of Spain.[11]

Then had come the news that France had made peace with Spain at Basel, and close upon it that Pinckney had reached a settlement with Godoy. Elijah Clarke and his men had been left for the time in their "critical situation," virtually as pirates on Amelia Island— unless they chose to follow their ammunition and arms into the service of General Laveaux in San Domingo. Adet, good at doing things without others suspecting it, had not permitted the distress

9. Adams, *Works*, VIII, 532. April 7, 1797. For Adet and Jaudenes, see above, p. 197.
10. Liston Papers, to Grenville, January 25, 1797. For documents showing payments from Adet's funds in Philadelphia to McLane, see AAE EU, Spt. 19, ff. 344–347, October, 1796–February, 1797. McLane died on a British scaffold. See AAE CP EU, XLVIII, f. 264, Adet's report to Talleyrand, September 22, 1797. See also Brymner, *Can. Arch.*, 1891, Note D, p. 62; State Papers, Lower Canada, p. 146 ff.
11. *Corresp. French Ministers*, 826, 928. For Monroe in November, 1795, see above, p. 233 f. For Fulton, see below, p. 259 f.

of Floridians under the yoke of Spain to obstruct his own view of the American scene.[12]

Adet knew the importance for France of Pinckney's treaty with Godoy. He realized that the new States beyond the Alleghenies would constitute "the riches, the strength, the power of the United States." He commissioned General Collot in March, 1796, and reported to Paris on June 21 that Collot was off to get the detailed information to complete the memorandum which he himself had long since been preparing on the necessity that France should re-enter Louisiana. When Collot had returned, said Adet, he would present in all its developments a project useful to his country, capable alone of checking the British upon this continent, and of "keeping the Americans from depriving us of the reward for the sacrifices which we have made for them."[13]

Victor Collot had stopped at Pittsburgh and looked about him. It would, he observed, "certainly become one of the first inland cities of the United States." But he had seen other things too. There were but three passes over the Alleghenies in Pennsylvania, a fourth in Virginia. In order to cross "with any other troops than light infantry, these defiles must be forced." The Whisky insurrectionists, some eight thousand men, he wrote, had not been soldiers; else they could have held these defiles against the Federal troops. These mountains were "destined, at some future period, to become the limits of the western states, and those of the Atlantic." There were only seven roads through this natural line of defense all the way from Niagara to the Bay of Appalache; only three points of attack, since the roads converged; and Pittsburgh at the head of the Ohio River was "the true Key of this frontier": "covered by mountains and passes without end, backed by the most astonishing navigation canal in the universe, by which all sorts of provisions and reinforcements can arrive, Pittsburg may truly be called impregnable."[14]

But the French general also talked in Pittsburgh. An unnamed informant, insinuating that Albert Gallatin was involved in the affair, had told Secretary Wolcott on May 19 of Collot's trip, and stated that he himself had seen Adet's instructions in writing. The expense, he said, was to be borne by the French Government with proceeds from the American bonds. Wolcott reported at once to President Washington. The informant returned on May 21 and

12. *Ibid.*, 826, 831, February 9, 1796. For Adet's dealings with "la Société populaire" of Charleston through the consuls, duPont and Fonspertuis, see particularly pp. 828–829.
13. *Ibid.*, 928–929.
14. Collot, I, 24, 28, 38, II, 265, 269.

made clear that he had been talking with Collot himself. Accordingly a secret agent had been sent after this general who was "too communicative for the service with which he has been entrusted." The agent reported back from Pittsburgh on June 15, 1796, that he had been in a long conversation with Collot. The general had remarked that France would not "quietly put up" with the Jay Treaty, that she might soon "get possession of Louisiana and both Floridas"; and he had asked: "If that should be the case, as there is great probability, what will become of the produce of your Kentucké, your western territory, indeed of all the country this side of the Alleghany mountains? You will be reduced to the necessity of throwing yourself into the arms of the French, and abandon the Union which cannot give you a market, &c., &c., &c." It is not surprising that in the meantime Washington's Secretary of War, McHenry, had written Governor St. Clair of the Northwest Territory to be on the lookout for a certain "De Callot" and associates and to get hold of their papers.[15]

The influence of these events upon Washington's farewell address to the people in September is certain. It is hard to believe that Secretaries Wolcott and McHenry did not make them known also to John Adams in the following March, if he had not already heard. If, however, Adams had need for any other sources of information about the aims of France in the mid-continent, there was a report to the Secretary of State from Monroe himself, at last on August 4, 1796, telling of the approaching alliance again between Spain and France and the chance that France would get Louisiana and the

15. Gibbs, I, 350–354. The defensive manner with which Gibbs presented these documents, in close relation with a selection from Jefferson's "Anas," dated March 27, 1800 (Jefferson, Ford, I, 287), indicates strongly that James Ross, Federalist rival of Gallatin in western Pennsylvania at the time, was Wolcott's informant and possibly the secret agent who followed Collot and talked with him at Pittsburgh. Jefferson recorded Judge Breckenridge's story of his conversations with Collot, who had "let himself out without common prudence" and had given Breckenridge his ideas how France might hold the passes and support them from New Orleans. According to Jefferson, Breckenridge had made notes of these conversations with Collot and had "lent them to Mr. Ross." Ross, "in breach of confidence," said Breckenridge, had given them to Washington "by whom they were deposited in the office of the board of war." Search in the archives of the Connecticut Historical Society at Hartford on August 19, 1938, turned up these memoranda by Wolcott, and the report of the agent from Pittsburgh, among the Wolcott Papers (XXI, Nos. 32, 33, 34). But there were no signatures to confirm the charge that Ross was the informant, nor the suspicion that he might have been the agent in Pittsburgh.

For documents from the French legation in Philadelphia, showing payments to Collot by James Swan, American agent managing the proceeds from the American bonds, and similar expenditures, see AAE EU, Spt. 19, ff. 327–328, 333, 341–342. St. Clair (Smith ed.), II, 395, 396.

Floridas. Adams' own son had written to Pickering from The Hague on October 16, reporting keen suspicions that the Directory of France had under consideration "sending a powerful armament to New Orleans." There was intimation also of an attack upon the British in Canada. It is impossible to think that Secretary Pickering kept from the incoming President news so much in line with his own feelings. Adet's personal assurances in March, 1797, though of no "consequence" to John Adams, did not lull him to sleep.[16]

Collot had gone on down the Ohio, taking soundings, noting all fortifications and determining their weaknesses, getting data for military maps, sizing up the people and their loyalties, moving steadily forward to escape "the persecutions with which we were menaced by General Waine, who had received orders to arrest us." At Louisville, he saw George Rogers Clark lying drunk, he said, in the street. And he observed with what great respect the "hero" of the West was treated even in that condition. Clark had been covered with a blanket "to preserve him from the contempt of the people." But evidently Collot did not linger to confer with that "person of great military talents," the "rival, in short, of General Washington," when he should become sober.[17]

Why, Victor Collot did not say. This French general, recently Governor of Guadeloupe, now in the United States on a British parole, might have had a very interesting conversation, and significant for us, with "that great man" about to be made a brigadier general of France. Within a year Clark was writing Samuel Fulton in Paris that he had his commission and was awaiting orders. He had just rejected an overture from the Governor of Canada, he said, that he enroll volunteers, lead an expedition of two thousand men against St. Louis, then move down the Mississippi, and advance across the plains to take Santa Fé. But Clark did not "love despots in general and the English in particular"; France could be certain that he would "make every effort to maintain the interests of the Republic in this province where they have always been considerable."[18]

Collot had not delayed to hear such things from Clark then. Perhaps he dared not, for fear that he would be overtaken by Wayne. There were other thoughts on his mind, however, which even George Rogers Clark might not have approved. Clark was

16. ASP FR, I, 741. J. Q. Adams, *Writings*, II, 31. For Washington's address, see above, pp. 227–228.
17. Collot, I, 132, 152–154. James, *Clark*, refers to Collot's journey (pp. 432–433) but not to this episode at Louisville.
18. Villiers du Terrage, 362–363, Clark to Fulton, March 2, 1797, from Louisville.

still waiting for his orders from the French Directory in June, 1798. Possibly the thoughts of Collot regarding the value of the mountain passes and the Ohio River for France, added to the proposals of Moustier, the urging of Fauchet, the memorandum of Adet, and the desire of Talleyrand had something to do with it.[19]

In any case, General Collot went on down the river, evading arrest until he arrived at Fort Massac near the juncture of the Ohio with the Mississippi. There Captain Pike stopped him. "I immediately showed him the whole of my manuscripts," Collot recorded. Perhaps he remembered from his experiences in Rochambeau's army that American officers did not read French.

These did not. They held council. They thought of sending his papers back to Philadelphia—Collot's real fear—but they decided that it would be cruel to detain him all winter until they could find out what was in the papers. And yet—he had been "indefatigable in taking the survey of the Ohio, and all of the Western States." Even so—he had done nothing contrary to the laws of the United States. Well—he might go along under escort while within American territory. And—they let him keep the papers![20]

Victor Collot reached the old French settlements on the upper Mississippi in August, 1796. He observed that their inhabitants were still loyal to France. He then made a trip into Spanish territory up the Missouri River as far as the Osage—without the knowledge of the Spanish commander, he said, as he "had taken the precaution to pass St. Charles in the night." He also took the precaution of returning to the American side of the Mississippi before he made public entry into St. Louis. There he surveyed the fortifications with great care and drew plans for defending the position—ostensibly for Spain against a British attack from Canada. But we may insert France in place of Spain. Meanwhile, according to his account, he had gone up the Illinois River toward Lake Michigan into American territory. And here we should recall that only in the previous year General Wayne had taken from the Indians military reservations upon the Illinois as well as the Wabash for the United States.[21]

When he came back from the Illinois, Collot heard bad news. The Spanish minister in Philadelphia had warned the Governor of Louisiana, Carondelet, in New Orleans about him. The American Secre-

19. AAE CP EU, XLVIII, f. 130. Clark to Fulton, June 3, 1798, from Philadelphia. See below, pp. 295–298.

20. Collot, I, 191–193. The American captain very likely was Zebulon Pike, later famous for his explorations.

21. *Ibid.*, I, 232–264, 278; II, 5 n. For Wayne, see above, pp. 211–213.

tary of State had issued orders for his arrest. Indians, he was told, were coming from Canada to assassinate him. It would be embarrassing to ask the Spanish commander—whom he had passed in the night—to let him continue his "researches in upper Louisiana." He had thought, so he declared later, that he might return by way of the Illinois, the Lakes, the Mohawk, and the Hudson to New York. And he would have learned much of military value if he had. But now, he would certainly be arrested at some American post or if he fell into British hands, he would lose his parole.

Collot decided that he would proceed down the Mississippi "at all events," as he had been originally directed. And while about it, he would examine the streams which flowed into the Mississippi from the west. He made a second journal filled with praises of Carondelet, "whilst the true journal was carefully concealed." Spaniards could read French. "This little stratagem will readily be forgiven me," he inserted afterwards, "since it saved me the disagreeableness of being sent to the Havannah, where I should probably have been detained a long time."[22]

The servants of the Spanish Crown in America were more determined than those at home to resist French schemes. Carondelet was waiting for Collot to arrive. On he came, observing that the mouth of the Ohio could not easily be defended on account of the height of the floods; that the Arkansas River, with the Osage, was the key to Mexico by way of Santa Fé; and that the American population, its spirit of enterprise and its location, was the greatest menace to Spain. Then the two Chickasaw Indians whom he had come upon shortly after leaving the Illinois country suddenly reappeared and wounded his companion, Warin, so severely that he died later in New Orleans. Who had instigated this attack Collot did not know, but he had strong suspicions.[23]

At Natchez in October, 1796, he noted the old Tories in the population and more recent elements discontented with the American Government. He startled the commandant, Gayoso, with the report which he had received from Lorimier, a French settler and Indian chieftain at Cape Girardot up the river. The British, said Collot, were preparing an expedition in Montreal of 2,000 regulars and 1,500 militia accompanied by Indians to invade Upper Louisiana; they had agents in Tennessee and Kentucky organizing an expedition to attack Lower Louisiana; and they had secured the governor of one of the American States.

Although inaccurate, doubtless, there was more in this story than

22. *Ibid.*, II, 1–4.
23. *Ibid.*, II, 13, 26, 35, 39, 53.

Collot may have interpolated. Just a year before, Portland had instructed Simcoe to look into using the Southern and Western Indians, to investigate the lines of communication from Lake Michigan to the Mississippi, and to discover whether the people of Kentucky would join in an attack upon Spanish America. Within the next six months, George Rogers Clark received his offer from the "Governor of Canada" to lead 2,000 men against St. Louis, Santa Fé, and down the Mississippi. And at this moment, the conspiracy of Chisholm and Blount was beginning in the Southwest.[24]

At the same time Collot appraised the military value of Natchez for his own purposes. He took note that it was in a stronger position than other towns above it, for there was no American river near upon which artillery could be brought directly. But all of these positions on the east side of the Mississippi, he decided, were far from covering Louisiana without the alliance of the Western States. This he found true of Baton Rouge also. He stopped for a visit with M. Boré, an ardent Frenchman, whose sugar plantation lay six miles above New Orleans. Then came the arrest which he should have expected from Carondelet notwithstanding his "little stratagem."[25]

Carondelet took a great interest in the papers of the French general, particularly those recording observations on the Missouri and Osage Rivers, west of the Mississippi, so much so that he neglected to return them when he finally allowed Collot to depart. But after keeping Collot virtually a prisoner in Balize at the mouth of the Mississippi for almost two months, Carondelet consented that he should return to Philadelphia, and at last he got away from Louisiana with most of his journals and a good memory of the rest. He managed also, despite his confinement, to gather information about Mobile from an officer, so he said, who had resided there for several years.[26]

24. Collot, I, 219; II, 11. See above, p. 207. Collot's reference to a governor brings to mind Blount of Tennessee, and leads one to think that the news of his conspiracy had already reached the Western frontier by October, 1796. But Collot's statement may have been inserted at this place in his narrative when he came to prepare it for publication. For he also declared that he heard of Chisholm's plan at Natchez and told Gayoso about it; whereas, internal evidence contradicts him. It is most probable that he did not get that particular information regarding British schemes until the following March when both he and Chisholm were in Philadelphia. Turner in AHR, X, 586, discussing Collot, II, 64–68.

25. *Ibid.*, II, 76, 98, 169. Cruzat, 314. For Carondelet's explanation to Adet, see Gayarré, III, 385; also Collot, II, 123.

26. Some of these papers were copied by a Major Guilmard. Others were summarized for Carondelet. The originals were sent after Collot, but were tossed overboard, May 20, 1797, to prevent capture by the British. Cruzat, 315. Collot, I, 278 n.; II, 534.

Collot, Fulton, DuPont, and Clark

SOON after January 1, 1797, Victor Collot was again at the capital of the United States and at work in the seclusion of the quarters of the French consul general, Létombe, drafting his maps and summarizing his conclusions. They were reported in cipher by Létombe, July 18, 1797, as if they were antidotes to British and American virulence—for the benefit of Spain. But this is what Létombe wrote:

> It is the opinion of General Collot that all half-measures, every palliative, will be insufficient, useless, that they will be able to retard for some time the loss of this colony, that of Peru and of Mexico, but will not save them. The General insists, consequently, upon this: that France acquire Louisiana and the Floridas by negotiation and take Canada by force, because he believes firmly that this is the only means of holding the United States within pacific bounds, of breaking their exclusive ties with England, of keeping our colonies—supplying them ourselves with the produce of our soil, and finally of recovering in the two hemispheres the preponderance which the nature of things gives to us.

They were at work now upon the topographical part of Collot's reports, Létombe adding in closing, right there "under his eyes," but the embarrassment would come when he tried to get the plans and maps to Paris. "The seas swarm with ships of war, corsairs, and the United States are full of ambushes." He awaited instructions.[27]

John Adams was not looking over Collot's shoulder with Létombe as the general worked upon his maps in Philadelphia, but the Administration was not oblivious to the situation in the West—nor uninformed. Captain William Henry Harrison wrote on May 22, 1797, of a certain Hamilton who was attempting to recruit settlers in Cincinnati for Spanish territory beyond the Mississippi; and on August 13, of a Mr. Jones, late chaplain in the American Army, now violently attached to France, who seemed to be on some mission related to the establishment of a French "Republic west of the Mississippi." Andrew Ellicott sent from Natchez, May 27, the perennial information that Spain was counting upon intrigues with the Westerners, in case there was a break with the United States. Ellicott named specifically Wilkinson and Sebastian among others. On July 28, Major Rivardi wrote from Detroit to Pickering upon

27. *Corresp. French Ministers*, 1048–1051, 1076. On October 27, 1797, Létombe wrote again that the general was correcting his work. All the maps drafted at Létombe's house would be ready toward the following January. The despatch of July 18 summarizing Collot's conclusions was received in Paris on November 3, 1797. For the negotiation of C. C. Pinckney, Marshall, and Gerry with X, Y, and Z for Talleyrand at that time, see below, pp. 281–292.

both French and British activities among the Indians, and again from Niagara on November 29. And during the following year Pickering and McHenry paid $2,560 with Adams' approval from the funds of the State Department for information about a plan of the French to incite the Southwest and Georgia to separate from the United States.[28]

As for Wilkinson's intrigue with the Spaniards, John Adams preferred to suspend judgment until there was more than persistent rumor. He rebuked his son-in-law, Col. W. S. Smith, for hastiness in pronouncing Wilkinson guilty of high crime. Adams took Smith to task at the same time upon the report that he was speculating for himself in the lands and claims of British subjects who were about to leave American territory under the terms of the Jay Treaty, while the public impression was that Adams had sent Smith "for ends of government."[29]

As for the French plan in the Southwest, papers concerning another younger American with personal expectations while on public service give us a very direct clue. Adet had instructed one Samuel Fulton, some twenty-five years of age, to make a tour of the South and West in the fall of 1795. He was to tell no one the object of his mission except Victor duPont, consul at Charleston; and he was to send all his letters to duPont, who would forward them to Adet. He was to find the disposition in South Carolina and Georgia toward "the insurgents of France," and their number, resources, and plans. He was to discover the attitude toward the Jay Treaty in the Carolinas, Georgia, and Kentucky. He was to learn what the inhabitants of Louisiana and Florida thought of an insurrection and subsequent "French domination." And he was especially to see General Clark and obtain all the details which he thought necessary.[30]

According to his expense account, Fulton visited Kentucky, Illinois, Tennessee, went from Knoxville to Natchez to Mobile, was ill thirty-five days, and passed through East Florida, Georgia, and South Carolina before reappearing in the spring of 1796 at Philadelphia. Then in May Adet sent him to Paris with despatches. A letter straight from George Rogers Clark to the Committee of Public Safety meanwhile had reported Fulton's arrival in Kentucky and the plan of attack upon Louisiana and the Floridas. If Fauchet only had not countermanded Genet, wrote Clark, "this territory would today be in the hands of the republic." A memorandum also found

28. McHenry (Steiner ed.), 263–265, 272 n. 2. Whitaker, *Mississippi Question*, 289 (103). Pickering Papers, XXI, 368.
29. Adams, *Works*, VIII, 567.
30. AAE CP EU, XLVIII, f. 300.

its way into the French files to show a list of officers of the "Légion révolutionnaire du Mississippi au Comité de Salut Public." The generals were to be G. R. Clark and Benjamin Logan. Among the colonels was Samuel Fulton. There was hardly a man in the Western country, it asserted, who would change his "love of France" for the "guineas of England."[31]

By October, 1796, Fulton himself was in Paris and reporting to Delacroix, minister of foreign affairs. He had now heard that France was about to get Louisiana from Spain without having to attack. He therefore had some "facts" for the minister upon the best season in which to take over Louisiana, upon the necessity of gaining the affection of the people in the Western States by sending a confidential agent to make them party to the "intentions" of France, for there was no doubt that the British faction would do everything in their power. Delacroix could count upon raising troops in the country to garrison the banks of the Mississippi; Clark's men were disposed to enter the service of the Republic; it would suffice to send arms, munitions, and such things from Europe.[32]

By this time also, General Collot had reached Natchez and had nearly completed his survey for France of inhabitants, conditions, and terrain along the Ohio, Illinois, Missouri, Mississippi, and Arkansas Rivers, from a rather different point of view. Adet himself arrived at Paris in the following summer with some of Collot's findings, and reported to Talleyrand on September 22, 1797. The remainder of Collot's charts and maps followed when they could get past British "corsairs" and American "ambushes." But Samuel Fulton stayed on in Paris, and when he heard in July, 1798, that Talleyrand had arranged for Spain to give up Louisiana and the Floridas, he offered his services again. If Talleyrand would assure his protection, Fulton would go and "secure for us a sufficient quantity of the best lands in the Country, as I know well whare the most valuable spots are situated."[33]

Whether Fulton and Clark or Victor Collot were to direct the fortunes of France in the Mississippi Valley, either plan if successful would play havoc with the interests of the United States there. But

31. AAE EU, Spt. 19, ff. 325–326, 334–340. *Corresp. French Ministers,* 828, 896. AAE CP EU, XLVIII, ff. 301–302, Clark's letter to Committee of Public Safety, and the "Legion."

32. AAE EU, Spt. 7, ff. 47–48, to Delacroix, October 21, 1796.

33. AAE EU, Spt. 28, ff. 26–34, 35, 40–41, 42, for Adet and Collot's papers. AAE CP EU, XLVIII, ff. 258–264, Adet's report to Talleyrand, September 22, 1797. For Fulton in 1798, *ibid.,* XLIX, f. 187. For Fulton once more in 1802, AAE EU, Spt. 7, f. 314.

the place to forestall such an event was not then on this side of the Atlantic. So long as France was at war with Britain, intrigues in America, if kept under close watch, would practically take care of themselves—provided negotiations could be reopened in Paris. George Rogers Clark was threatened with imprisonment, but upon "maturer deliberation," said he, was invited to give up his French commission, or withdraw from the United States. Seeing "clearly that English gold alone is the cause of it," he refused to surrender his commission, and withdrew to St. Louis to await news from Fulton. Adams' administration, however, did nothing for months about Collot. Pinckney, Marshall, and Gerry were fencing with Talleyrand in Paris. The exposure of Senator Blount, besides, was engrossing. It was not until John Marshall returned with the X Y Z papers that antipathies revived toward Frenchmen still in America.[34]

Timothy Pickering, having the alien law of 1798 temptingly at hand, then urged that he be allowed to deport Collot, and President Adams signed the warrant. Again there was delay for nearly a year as the Secretary of State kept this French general under surveillance while he ran down the report that another was here in disguise. It proved groundless. But Pickering was more eager than ever to expel that "bitter enemy of this country," Victor Collot, and return him to the jurisdiction of the British "where he could do no harm." Adams, too, was convinced that he was a "pernicious and malicious intriguer," and quite willing to execute the alien law upon him, notwithstanding the fact that negotiations were opening once more in Paris. If Pickering could get sufficient evidence against Létombe, he might deport him also.[35]

Meantime, Victor Collot had been living harmlessly in Newark and making no more disquieting excursions anywhere. There was no need. His charts and maps were finished, and ready for Létombe to get safely to France if he could. When the Secretary of State got to the business of deporting this French general, there was no need for that. He was gone. Either because he had got wind of Pickering's intention or because arrangement had been made at last with Britain for his exchange as a prisoner of war, Collot had returned to France.

34. AAE CP EU, XLVIII, f. 130, Clark to Fulton, June 3, 1798, from Philadelphia. See James, *Clark*, 511–512, for a transcript of this letter. See below, pp. 293, 332.

35. Adams, *Works*, VIII, 606, October 16, 1798; IX, 14. August 3, 1799. Pickering Papers, IX, 426, 453; XI, 524–525. For the mission of Ellsworth, Davie, and Murray, see below, p. 375. For echoes in Canada of Collot's activities on the Mississippi, see Michigan Pion. and Hist. Soc., *Collections*, XXV, 171, 187, 191, correspondence of Prescott, Russell, Brant, and Portland, October 1798–March, 1799. General Prescott believed that Collot had promised certain Indian tribes that he would return in 1799 to lead an attack upon Upper Canada.

There is left to amuse one who searches among the papers of Timothy Pickering a blank warrant signed by John Adams. It would be less humorous for us, if Napoleon had decided to keep the Peace of Amiens with Britain. Collot was at one time considered for command of the expedition which General Victor prepared to make to Louisiana.[36]

John Adams, however, had no time for chagrin. Other things were on his mind, and they were far more dangerous to the immediate interests of his country than what might follow eventually from General Collot's survey of the Mississippi Valley. French cruisers continued to raid American shipping, particularly in the West Indies. And there were the "secret plots of England." Again, as in 1790, suspicion was abroad of an attack upon Louisiana and Florida from Canada. The rumor would not separate from the Blount conspiracy, no matter how the British minister tried. There was also the threat that Spain would keep the posts in the Southwest in spite of Godoy's pledge to Thomas Pinckney.

Pickering, Irujo, and Godoy

IRUJO, successor to Jaudenes in Philadelphia, took up Adet's quarrel with Pickering over the Jay Treaty. France had broken off diplomatic relations with the United States, and Spain had now returned to war on the side of France. Spain accordingly would carry on for her ally. But Spain too had a grievance, in fact more of one. The Pinckney Treaty had come after the Jay Treaty and therefore appeared to be the more binding obligation of the United States. Irujo and his superior, Godoy, insisted that the United States were violating the Pinckney Treaty by allowing Britain to continue her interference with American "free ships" and confiscation of "enemy goods." They protested also the explanatory agreement which the United States had made with Britain on May 4, 1796, stipulating that Wayne's treaty with the Indians should not impair the rights which had been conceded in the Jay Treaty to British traders on the waterways of the international boundary. This pertained to the

36. Anderson, "Enforcement of the Alien and Sedition Laws," AHA, Rpt., 1912, 117 n. 10. For Talleyrand and Collet, March–May, 1798, chiefly concerning Collot's parole, see AAE CP EU, XLIX, ff. 244, 246, 258, 385–386. ASP FR, II, 518. See below, p. 400.

Collot prepared his maps and reports for publication in Paris at about the time of the Louisiana Purchase—with additional commentary reflecting the fact of American ownership of the country which he had surveyed for France in 1796. The work was not published, however, until 1826. Collot had died in July, 1805. There are sets of the original French and English editions of the narrative and atlas in the Harvard College Library. Another edition with the same pagination as the English edition was produced at Firenze in 1924.

Mississippi River. It, too, seemed to infringe upon the Pinckney Treaty. Irujo demanded explanations and amends.[37]

If the American Government did not give that satisfaction, the penalties were to be that Spain would withhold the right of deposit at New Orleans and would not evacuate the posts east of the Mississippi and north of the line of the Pinckney Treaty—although they would be retained, professedly, to guard against the British attack upon Upper Louisiana. Godoy countermanded his original orders to fulfill the Pinckney Treaty. And Carondelet was only too pleased to reoccupy those posts which he had not dismantled under Godoy's first instructions and to continue intriguing with Wilkinson and other American separatists up the river. For the Spanish Governor did not believe in the inevitability of Spanish retreat before the American pioneers on this continent, any more than he welcomed Collot's reconnaissance for France. And Gayoso at Natchez cleverly played upon the settlers' fears of the Indians, retaining control over that section in spite of the efforts of the American commissioner, Ellicott.[38]

Secretary Pickering retorted in kind to Irujo's accusation that the American Government had been "surprised" by Britain into a breach of faith with France and Spain. Pickering's argument was all the more exasperating because it could not be refuted. The fact that the United States had yielded more advantageous terms to British sea power previously did not break the subsequent contract with Spain. If the United States were to go to war and Spain were to remain neutral, as Pickering pointed out, the United States would be obligated to leave unmolested the goods of an American enemy aboard a Spanish vessel, excepting contraband. But that was not the matter at issue. Moreover, the United States had undertaken, if they should go to war with Spain herself, to respect Spanish goods and persons when found aboard a neutral vessel—excepting of course contraband, goods bound into a blockaded port, and soldiers in actual service. But neither were these matters at issue.[39]

The issue was whether the United States were obliged by their treaties with France and with Spain to compel Britain to stop interfering with American neutral commerce. And about this, there could be no question. If Spain used American neutral ships to cover her goods, she had to take her own chances with the British cruisers and prize courts. The United States had no obligation to any party

37. ASP FR, II, 14, 87, 96, 98. Miller, *Treaties*, II, 346–347.
38. Whitaker, *Mississippi Question*, 59–60. Ellicott, *Journal*, 46–72, correspondence with Gayoso and Carondelet, March 11–31, 1797.
39. ASP FR, II, 14, 16, Pickering to Irujo, May 17, 1797.

to force a third power to respect the principle *free ships free goods*. Pickering may have been personally insulting in his debate with Irujo, but he was correct.[40]

The subject, obviously, must be kept distinct from the obligation of the United States to protect Spanish shipping and goods within the territorial waters and jurisdiction of the United States. That obligation was expressly undertaken in the Pinckney Treaty.[41]

As for the explanatory agreement of 1796 with Britain concerning the navigation of the Mississippi, again the Spaniards were trying to make much out of little. They argued that it impaired the right of the Spanish King to open the Mississippi to whom he pleased. But it did no such thing. By it, the United States had only confirmed the British right of navigation so far as they could give it along their own frontier, and no farther. Britain may have had the right within Spanish territory beyond that line; but if she did, it was by reason of her own prior agreements with Spain and not by reason of the Jay Treaty or any other agreement with the United States. The United States could not grant to Britain what they did not possess.

The simple fact was that the United States were contending with Spain over the free navigation of the Mississippi for themselves. Just as Pickering put it, any declaration by the Spanish King alone to exclude other nations was quite immaterial to the United States.[42]

This clause in the agreement of 1796 with Britain—declaring that "no stipulations in any treaty subsequently concluded by either of the contracting parties with any other State or Nation" could derogate from the "rights of free intercourse and commerce" secured by the third article in the Jay Treaty—did not give Britain additional power with which to compel Spain to open the Mississippi River through Spanish territory to British use. It took not two but three to make a bargain binding at that time upon all the parties of interest in the Mississippi River. Rather, the clause was a safeguard for Britain against the United States. It stopped the American Government from employing the Pinckney Treaty with Spain as an instrument for closing the Mississippi against the British.[43]

There was no breach of legal commitments to Spain on the part

40. Miller, *Treaties,* II, 328–330, Article 15 of the Pinckney Treaty.

41. *Ibid.,* II, 323, Article 6.

42. ASP FR, II, 17. Miller, *Treaties,* II, 321–322, Article 4. See above, p. 222f., Pinckney's proposal and Godoy's stipulation. See Bemis, *Pinckney's Treaty,* 348, for discussion from the Spanish point of view. For Grenville on the effect of the Pinckney Treaty upon the British right of navigation, see Liston Papers, Grenville to Liston, December 12, 1796.

43. Miller, *Treaties,* II, 347.

of the United States, either in regard to neutral shipping or concerning the navigation of the Mississippi. It is hard to perceive how there was even failure to live up to a moral obligation to Spain, not to speak of France. But Irujo was not so minded. And like the French ministers before him, he seemed to think that a foreign plenipotentiary in the United States really did not have to defer to the Administration. He could appeal to the people if he saw fit, and manufacture public opinion to boot. His correspondence with Pickering and his utterances in the press became so flagrant, his dealings with the Republican party so obvious, that President Adams moved to have him recalled. The Spanish foreign office evaded with one excuse and another. Irujo remained in Philadelphia with his American wife and his profitable business of smuggling American goods into the Spanish colonies, until the election of 1800 had brought the Republican party to power and the Spanish minister back in favor with the American Government.[44]

In the meantime Spain had taken another sharp turn. Godoy had decided after all to comply with the Pinckney Treaty, evacuate the posts in the Southwest, and formally grant the right of deposit at New Orleans. Carondelet had already been facilitating trade in the lower Mississippi for purposes of intrigue. Godoy's reasoning appears to have been that it was better to concede a part than to risk losing the whole of the Spanish interest in North America. As he commented, October 20, 1797, on the margin of a report from Irujo, "You can not lock up an open field." So far he had been able to hold off France and to retain Louisiana for a price in Europe. But France was getting nearer and nearer to war with the United States. These Americans might join the British on the offensive; and if they did, their blows were sure to come down at once upon the ally of France.[45]

The conspiracy of Blount might have been interpreted as proving that Spain ought to get help from France in defending the Spanish empire in America. But with France far from eager to give aid, that British intrigue was more wisely to be interpreted as meaning that Spain had better act quickly in appeasing the American Government, or the Spaniards would be driven not only from the posts above Baton Rouge but completely out of Louisiana, New Orleans, and the Floridas. And then Mexico would lie wide-open to attack.[46]

Godoy was not yet willing, on the terms of France, to hand over

44. Whitaker, *Mississippi Question*, 205 (313).
45. *Ibid.*, 90, 179–183. Whitaker in AHR, XXXIX, 454–476.
46. Whitaker, *Mississippi Question*, 115.

Louisiana as a buffer state between American pioneers and Spanish provinces south and west of the Red River. It might be that he could hold the region at the Mississippi and the Florida line of 1795 a while longer until France paid his price—if he gratified the Americans as he had set out to do in 1795 through fear of France. Indeed one could not shut an open field to hostile neighbors, but those on friendly terms might be induced to respect it. Godoy fulfilled the Pinckney Treaty in 1798. John Adams must have drawn at least one breath of relief.

The Prince of Peace could not foresee, however, the outcome of European events though they were already taking shape. Napoleon Bonaparte was gaining great victories for France. By 1800 Spain faced at last the inevitable: New Orleans and Louisiana had either to go to the Americans or the British, or to the French regardless of price. By 1800 also the United States had won from France sufficient respect for their maritime power to let slip the last thread of dependence upon their "antient friends," and Thomas Jefferson had become more respectful of "Rawhead & bloody bones." Louisiana was not to remain for long in the possession of France.[47]

Britain's "Secret Plots"

WHEN he returned from Louisiana, General Collot did not explain to the Spanish minister how the passes through the Alleghenies could be defended for France. He gave Irujo the news with which he had startled Gayoso, that the British were going to attack St. Louis from Canada; then they would send one force by way of the Osage and Arkansas Rivers to pillage Sante Fé while another moved down the Mississippi upon New Orleans. He advised that St. Louis be strengthened according to the plans which he had drawn. He urged Irujo to insist that the United States look to their neutrality and guard those lines of approach from the Great Lakes. All of this he presented upon the authority of one who frankly had just seen the dangerous military situation with his own eyes, and assumed that France and Spain were looking out for the interests of each other as allies in war upon Britain. But Collot was thinking how France might soon have the Mississippi Valley for herself, and how Spain and the United States in the meantime would keep Britain out.[48]

47. See above, p. 150, and below, p. 490 f.
48. AAE CP EU, XLVIII, ff. 98–103, 104–105, 106–107, notes from Collot to Irujo of February 25, March 3, July 12, 1797. See Turner ed., "Documents on the Blount Conspiracy," AHR, X, 577, 580, 585, for notes from Collot to Irujo, dated March 1, 9, April 15, 1797, transcribed from AAE CP EU, XLVII, ff. 126–129, 130–131, 137–139.

Irujo was impressed. He protested verbally to Secretary Pickering and then declared in writing, March 2, 1797, that he had proof of the British intention to send troops down the Fox, Wisconsin, or Illinois River. The United States, he supposed, surely would be too jealous of their rights to allow so scandalous a violation of their territory. Within a few weeks the Spaniards and Frenchmen in Philadelphia had gathered in more information, and Irujo wrote again on April 21. Now he knew to a certainty also, he declared, that the British were negotiating with General Elijah Clarke of Georgia to attack Florida.[49]

Pickering was impressed too, but not as Collot and Irujo intended. The affair was to him one more bit of French and Spanish intriguing to becloud the issue in regard to American obligations under the treaties of 1778 and 1795, and to stir up trouble between the United States and Britain. He replied politely but stiffly on April 28 that he had notified the British minister of President Adams' declaration that foreign troops might not cross American territory. Irujo could presume, accordingly, that there would be no violation of American neutrality. As for General Clarke of Georgia, the district attorney would make inquiries. All unneutral designs would be frustrated. But Pickering was more afraid of France. He wrote to Rufus King on June 20 that France meant to regain Louisiana—"and to renew the ancient plan of her Monarch of *circumscribing* and encircling what now constitutes the Atlantic States."[50]

John Adams, too, was impressed, but with different reflections from those of his Secretary of State. Past experiences during the Revolution, the peacemaking at Paris, and his stay in London led Adams readily to suspect Britain of jockeying the United States into a tight situation. And he had very good cause now to be wary of British "secret plots."

Replying to Portland's instructions of October 24, 1795, that he should investigate the avenues of approach from Lake Michigan to the Spanish positions on the Mississippi and discover the temper of the American settlers in the West, Lieutenant Governor Simcoe had reported on May 17, 1796, that his source of information in Kentucky had been stopped. He had no knowledge about Kentucky but what was "theoretical," he said, and far less beyond. Wayne certainly had altered conditions along the Ohio. Simcoe, however, was not so discouraged that he intended to accept the stoppage as permanent. He himself left his post in Upper Canada, July 20, and

49. ASP FR, II, 68, Irujo to Pickering, March 2, April 21, 1797. For Liston's denial regarding Elijah Clarke, see below, p. 275.
50. ASP FR, II, 68–69. King (King ed.), II, 190–192.

returned to England—where he was given command of an expedition to San Domingo the following December. But before he left his province, he committed Portland's letter *"most confidentially"* to Peter Russell, who was to have charge of Upper Canada during his absence, and advised Russell as to the choice and instruction of the "Confidential person" who should obtain "all the Information possible, relative to the important objects therein mentioned." What came of Russell's efforts is not fully known. It was in the following March, 1797, that George Rogers Clark wrote Samuel Fulton of his offer from the "Governor of Canada" to lead a British expedition against St. Louis, Santa Fé, and down the Mississippi.[51]

Nor was Robert Liston, British minister in Philadelphia, as yet discouraged. Into the midst of his endeavors to keep track of Adet's plotting rebellion in Quebec and an attack from Vermont, there had come a certain Chisholm, native of Scotland, in the fall of 1796. Chisholm had recently arrived at Philadelphia from the Southwest accompanying a party of Indians to confer with the Government about their rights. He had come at the direction of Governor Blount of the Territory. He had taken advantage of the visit to present a petition for himself and other British subjects requesting citizenship in the United States. Getting no encouragement from Secretary McHenry, declared Chisholm later, he had gone to the British legation. There his ideas appeared as a plan for the "Recovery of the Floridas to Great Britain." Liston thought well of the proposal, although demurring somewhat. He reported it to his superiors in London, January 25, 1797, and informed General Prescott, who had taken Dorchester's place as Lieutenant Governor at Quebec and commander of the British forces in Canada.[52]

Chisholm's plan seems to have been to raise a force of old Tories living in the Southwest, some 1,500 men, and to add to them American frontiersmen from Kentucky and Tennessee, Creek and Cherokee Indians, Yankee traders, West Indian British, Indian chieftains such as Brant in the North, Canadians, speculators in land of any class or allegiance, and anyone else who wished to get into the venture. Then, supported by the British Government—a frigate and two or three armed vessels with a few fieldpieces—the main

51. Simcoe (Cruikshank ed.), IV, 267, 335. *Can. Arch.*, Upper Canada, 1891 (Brymner ed.), 71. For Simcoe's expedition to San Domingo, see Riddell, *Simcoe,* 298; and its significance for the United States, see below, pp. 287, 305, 354 f.

52. Turner ed., AHR, X, 576–577, 595–596. *Can. Arch.*, Lower Canada, 1891 (Brymner ed.), 62, 146, 149. For Liston to Grenville, February 13, 1797, giving further detail, see Liston Papers. Simcoe (Cruikshank ed.), IV, 307, Dorchester to Portland regarding Prescott, July 19, 1796.

troops would attack Mobile, Pensacola, and New Orleans. Another force, including "Brant and his Associates," and such frontiersmen as could be collected from New York and Pennsylvania, would attack New Madrid on the Mississippi and then move up the Red River to take the silver mines. Such an enterprise once in motion, of course, need not of its own accord stop at any particular point.[53]

As Liston appraised it, March 16, 1797, after several months of consideration:

> the Certainy which the last accounts from Europe convey of the farther Continuance of the War, the Probability of the Cession of Louisiana to the French by the Spaniards, and the serious consequences that must attend it, together with the Advantages which might acrue to His Majesty's Interests from even a temporary possession of that Country are Considerations that struck me as being of such Importance as to render it improper for me to discourage the Idea of his Voyage. I have therefore consented to Mr. Chisholm's Proposal and have paid his Passage to England, giving him hopes at the same time that the Expences of his Stay in London, and of his Return to this Country will be defrayed by His Majesty's Government provided the amount does not exceed the Sum of One Hundred and Fifty pounds.

Was this Scotsman turned Indian chieftain going to be another Miranda?[54]

The British minister saw that there were drawbacks to the scheme. American neutrality, perhaps, should be respected. It would be dangerous, he conceded, to enlist the Indians in such an enterprise, for the United States were obliged by the Treaty of 1795 with Spain to suppress Indian uprisings on their side of the border. But it might go well, he knew, if a quarrel between the United States and France should cause the United States to break with Spain also; then the Treaty of 1795 would not stand in the way.

Liston was not really concerned about American neutrality. The adventurers would not become an expedition until they were across the line and upon Spanish soil. Probably the enterprise would be able, he insinuated, to get along successfully without the Indians. Thus, in diplomatic language which left him, personally, a way out in case the scheme collapsed, the British minister urged his Government to take up the plan of Chisholm.

General Prescott replied to Liston from Quebec on February 16, 1797. He had waited, before answering some of Liston's inquiries,

53. Turner ed., AHR, X, 576, 595–601.
54. *Ibid.*, X, 582–583, Liston to Grenville. Also in Liston Papers. For Pitt and Miranda, see above, p. 135 f., and below, p. 316 f.

he said, until he could get the opinions of gentlemen long engaged in trade "between this Country and the Mississippi." From circumstances stated by a certain Mr. Richardson, Prescott concluded that it would be difficult to forward supplies "from this Country" for the "proposed Expedition against the Floridas" unless "the people of the States were inclined to favour the Enterprise":

> Were this the Case, or were we still in possession of the Posts on the South Side of the Lakes, I cannot doubt but the Conquest of the Floridas, and of the Spanish Possessions on the Mississippi might easily be effected; and in all Events I shall most readily co-operate, to the utmost of My Power, in furtherance of any Scheme of this Nature which You shall agree upon with His Majesty's Ministers.[55]

Two weeks later, at Louisville, Kentucky, George Rogers Clark was writing that letter to Samuel Fulton in Paris which all but confirms the opinion that Prescott or Russell or both had already gone beyond standing ready to "co-operate" with any "Scheme of this Nature." The authenticity of Clark's letter, preserved in the Archives of the French Ministry of War, is hardly to be questioned. The accuracy of Clark's report may not be denied merely on the grounds that he was seeking favor with the French Government.[56]

In this month of March, 1797, Chisholm appeared again at Philadelphia. He babbled in the taverns and quarreled with "Frenchmen" so noisily that perhaps he gave Collot at this time the information which Collot transmitted to Irujo on April 15 and later printed as if it had come to him while at Natchez in October, 1796. The more important matter, however, is that Chisholm had seen Liston again and persuaded the British minister to send him to England.

How Liston wished later that he had delayed until he had heard from his first report to Grenville on the plan! But he was too interested at that moment in its possibilities to think of caution. The project was of "so great importance" and "such easy execution." Brant's threat to lead his Mohawks with the French against the British Government in Canada, if he did not get their sales of land in Upper Canada approved, did not worry Liston very much. He began to have doubts only when he observed the effect of Irujo's clamor upon the American Government.[57]

55. Liston Papers, Prescott to Liston, February 16, 1797. Digest in Brymner ed., *Can. Arch.*, Lower Canada, 1891, 149. For Richardson's report, see Michigan Pion. and Hist. Soc., *Collections*, XXV, 136. February 6, 1797.

56. For Clark's letter of March 2, 1797, to Fulton, see Villiers du Terrage, 362–363. See above, p. 259 f. For other documents related to the question, see James, *Clark*, 511–515.

57. For Collot, see above, p. 256 f. AAE CP EU, XLVIII, f. 97, contains a letter of Chisholm, dated March 17, 1797, sent in by Collot to show evidence of the Chisholm

The Secretary of War had sent orders to the posts on the frontier that no travelers could pass or frequent the interior of the country except those British traders from Canada who had rights under the Jay Treaty. Chisholm might have some difficulty getting back and forth in his own section of the country. But even yet, to Liston's mind, it was a good project, for on May 10 he advised his superiors in London to send someone with or after Chisholm in whom they had implicit confidence, "who might in the first moment travel without suspicion as a Canadian Merchant, and afterwards act as circumstances might direct." It is unmistakable that the minister in Philadelphia wanted action, whatever his Government in London was deciding to do.[58]

"His Majesty's confidential servants" in the foreign office had reached their decision almost before Chisholm had left Philadelphia on his voyage across the Atlantic. Britain was not to be involved in this particular scheme for the Floridas. Grenville wrote to Liston on April 8, 1797, that, "exclusively of the inadequacy of the means to the end proposed," Liston's own objections to the plan were sufficient to counterbalance the advantages. The British Government would not wish to use the Indians. It would be improper also, declared Grenville, to incite an expedition within the United States in violation of American neutrality.[59]

Without scorning these professions, we must however take into account here the letter of instructions which Grenville had sent to Liston, January 27, 1797, before he had heard from Liston about Chisholm's proposal. In case a rupture between the United States and France should occur or appear highly probable, wrote Grenville, it was the King's pleasure that Liston should express willingness to afford naval protection to the commerce of the United States against the attacks of the "common Enemy."[60]

Pitt's foreign minister was not thinking merely of respect for American territory and the inhumanity of Indians in warfare. Maritime interests were at stake. The Dutch fleet, dominated by France, had yet to be broken at Camperdown, October 11, 1797. An offer to protect American commerce might result in disposing American naval resources to the advantage of Britain.[61]

plan. For Brant's quarrel with Russell over the Mohawk lands in Upper Canada, see Liston Papers, to Grenville, February 24, March 18, July 19, October 3, 1797; Russell (Cruikshank ed.), I, 180, 235–236; II, 166–171; III, 602.

58. Turner ed., AHR, X, 588–589. Also in Liston Papers.

59. Printed in Annals, 5 Cong., 2376.

60. Liston Papers, Grenville to Liston, January 27, 1797. Liston received it between March 17 and April 5. James in AHR, XXX, 49 n. and MVHR, I, 44–56, 51 n.

61. J. Q. Adams, Writings, II, 218, to Vans Murray, October 26, 1797. McHenry

Britain was still very much at war with France in the spring of 1797 despite negotiations for peace. Although Grenville and his counselors knew that France had cut off diplomatic relations with the United States, they did not yet know what would be the reaction of the American people to that news. They did know that the Jay Treaty had stirred a violent reaction against Britain. They knew that Washington had accepted that treaty by no means out of affection for Britain and acquiescence in her purposes among the Indians of the West. They knew of Wayne's victory at Fallen Timbers and the Treaty of Greenville, and the consequences for British interests in the mid-continent. They knew, from his previous career, that the elevation of John Adams to the presidency could mean no increased love of the British. And the return of Thomas Jefferson to public life with so strong an endorsement by the electoral college made it very wise indeed to wait and see how the "people of the States"—as Prescott remarked to Liston—responded to the plans for invading Spanish territory. After all, it meant an attack upon the interests of France, and there were many in America who still reacted with that Revolutionary hero, George Rogers Clark, both in loyalty to France and hostility toward the mother country.[62]

Pitt and Grenville anticipated that the United States might be drawn into coöperation against France, but they were waiting to see what events would bring forth. Grenville must have been very glad indeed that the decision was safely made before Chisholm had arrived in London. He was so closely watched there by agents of the American minister, Rufus King, that he could not have negotiated in any secrecy with the British authorities if Grenville had wanted him to do so. Moreover, his profligacy about town raised doubts that he could be relied upon as one of the "principal persons" or have any close connection with those who were at the center of the scheme.[63]

On this side of the Atlantic, one of those "principal persons," evidently the chief one, in the meantime had come to light. He was William Blount, now Senator for the newly admitted state of Tennessee. Many of its inhabitants had recently been intriguing with Spain. Some were still doing so, but most of them were eager to

(Steiner ed.), 285, from Vans Murray at The Hague, October 13, 1797. For Grenville's further instructions to Liston and the development of this overture to the United States in the following years, see below, p. 305 f.

62. J. Q. Adams, *Writings*, II, 68–211, letters to John Adams, December 30, 1776, and September 21, 1797, on the two peace missions of Malmesbury. Malmesbury, *Diaries*, III, 250 ff. E. D. Adams, *Influence of Grenville on Pitt's Foreign Policy, 1787–1798*.

63. Turner ed., AHR, X, 577. King (King ed.) II, 216–219, 236–237, 253–258. King protested Liston's conduct on August 28, 1797.

crowd the Spaniards out of the fertile river-bottom lands along the Gulf. Among these Blount stood foremost.

As he was obliged to return to Philadelphia for the special session of Congress called by President Adams to consider the situation with France, Blount put on paper, April 21, 1797, what he had intended personally to tell his friend Carey. Carey talked while intoxicated, it was said, to just the wrong person—with the result that Blount's letter was seized from him and taken to Philadelphia. President Adams had it by the middle of June. It seemed to confirm the very thought he had expressed to Mrs. Adams in the previous winter. Here was the British "secret plot"—no longer secret.

According to this letter, Blount wished to see Carey about Chisholm's business with the British minister. A "man of consequence" had gone to London. Blount appears not to have known that Chisholm himself had gone. If that person made the arrangements to be expected, said Blount, he was to have a hand and probably would take charge of the whole affair on behalf of the British.

We need follow the ramifications of the plot no farther into its tangle of parties and speculations in land, even though, fantastic as it may seem, at the fringes of the tangle will be found not only Liston but also the Spanish minister, Irujo. It was sufficient for John Adams to read that British intrigue implicated an American Senator in a scheme to use Creeks and Cherokees somewhere. There was an indication in Blount's comment that his friends might readily talk so as to throw the blame for the recent treaty with the Indians in the Southwest from himself "upon the late President." But wherever it was to happen, obviously it would threaten the peace of the United States. When he heard of this, George Washington was furious. It was "Nefarious conduct." Blount's defense, said he, would be conducted "with as much effrontery as art."[64]

Secretary Pickering let the British minister hear of the discovery before he should have to reply to official inquiries from the American Government. For Pickering, as Liston thought, was absorbed in believing that French agents were accusing Britain in order to cover the transfer of Louisiana. It is indeed very likely that Liston had put into Pickering's hands at just about this time those despatches from Fauchet which urged France to take back Louisiana, and which the British had intercepted. In any case, Liston flattered himself in his report to Grenville on June 24, 1797, that he had persuaded Pickering "with some degree of success" against making "the business

64. ASP FR, II, 76–77. Washington (Ford ed.), XIII, 400–401, to McHenry, July 7, 1797.

public." He wrote to Pickering on the twenty-ninth, officially repeating his remark in conversation that he had no knowledge or belief that any attack upon Spanish territory was contemplated from Lake Michigan. He had been informed since their talk, so he declared, both by the Governor General of Canada and by His Majesty's Secretary of State, that there was no such plan.[65]

Two days later, Liston received another letter from the American Secretary of State. Doubtless there was no British plan, it agreed, to advance from the Lake; but what about other projects with which Liston's own name had been connected? This letter was gracious, but it said nonetheless that the American Government was relying upon information, not upon suspicion. The British minister realized now that there was a mind other than Timothy Pickering's behind the pen of the Secretary of State. He might have persuaded Pickering, as he thought, but "the business struck the President in a different light."[66]

It most certainly did. John Adams did not suppress the evidence involving Blount as Liston wished to have done. Adams laid it, with other papers concerning Spain and the West, before Congress on July 3, 1797.[67]

To General Prescott in Quebec, this was a great indiscretion much to be deplored. It would encourage the party in the States which would gladly blame the British minister. To Oliver Wolcott, Secretary of the Treasury, the outcome of the matter now clearly would be that the British would not "support" Blount's project: "The advance made by our people shews, however," said Wolcott, "the profligacy of our patriots and the precarious tenure by which the western country is attached to the existing government" And to Liston himself it seemed that the President was playing politics in order to disgrace Blount because he was vehemently opposed to the Government, and to weaken the "democratick party in general." Liston had told Pickering on the previous day that he had been talking with certain persons and had reported to London, as was his duty; but he had declined to give further particulars and to name the persons who had talked with him. They might be enemies

65. These were Fauchet's despatches of February 4 and 16, 1795. Pickering's copies are now in his Papers, XLI, 190, 198. He wrote on the despatch of February 4: "Lent me by Mr. Liston, British minister, to read & return but it was forgotten," and a similar remark on the second. See *Corresp. French Ministers,* 559, 578. See above, p. 195. Liston Papers, to Grenville, June 24, 1797, received by Grenville, August 6; Turner ed., AHR, X, 589–590. ASP FR, II, 69, Liston to Pickering, June 29, 1797.

66. ASP FR, II, 70, Pickering to Liston, July 1, 1797. Turner ed., AHR, X, 592–594, Liston to Grenville, July 8, 1797.

67. ASP FR, II, 66 ff.

of Britain, he said, who were trying to involve his Government in trouble; or they might have meant him well, and therefore should not be betrayed. He was sure in either case, that none were hostile to the interests of the United States; the matter should rest, he thought, upon Grenville's official disavowal which he forthwith submitted to Pickering on July 15.[68]

John Adams' decision may have been compounded to a degree from all of these considerations. But to his way of thinking, it absolutely was not for the British minister in Philadelphia himself to decide whether certain Americans were or were not hostile to the interests of the United States; nor was their policy in regard to other nations to be shaped by any unauthorized individual, not even if he were a member of the Senate from that uncertain "western country" which Secretary Wolcott feared. Congress should examine the evidence regardless, and expose to full view whatever it found in the "secret plot" of Britain—while the President's special commissioners, Pinckney, Marshall, and Gerry went to France. "Our country" was caught once more, declared Adams, in a "critical situation" between the two great European powers. He consequently would not deviate from that independent course which he himself had helped to set at Paris in 1782. Whatever else may be said of his shortcomings as President, it must be conceded that, at a time when partisan feelings in this country were bitterly pro-British or pro-French, no one was more pro-American than John Adams.[69]

The Senate expelled Blount and the House impeached him. The resulting investigation disclosed other evidence to show that a British agent had offered Elijah Clarke of Georgia $10,000 for his services, whether or not the British minister knew anything about it—Liston denied that he did. Rufus King cornered Chisholm in London and drew from him a lengthy statement implicating many persons in a widespread plan of attack upon Spanish America from the territory of the United States—whether or not Britain's officials in Canada and in England had any connection with it. They would not have admitted the fact officially if they had.[70]

Chisholm left for America, but he did not report, as he promised,

68. Can. Arch., Lower Canada, 1891 (Brymner ed.), 155, August 31, 1797. Turner ed., AHR, X, 592–594, Liston to Grenville, July 8, 1797. ASP FR, II, 71. Annals, 5 Cong., 2376. Gibbs, I, 548, to Oliver Wolcott, Sr., July 4, 1797.
69. ASP FR, II, 66.
70. Ibid., II, 71. Annals, 5 Cong., II, 2404, 2413, 2373. Turner ed., AHR, X, 606, Thornton to Grenville, December 28, 1797. Liston Papers, Liston to Grenville, August 30, 1797, February 6, May 2, 1798. King (King ed.), II, 253–258 n. December, 1797. Turner ed., AHR, X, 595–605, the declaration of John D. Chisholm.

to the Government in Philadelphia. If he survived the voyage, and it is likely that he did so, he disappeared into the Cherokee nation, never again to seek attention in the white man's civilization. But his name, carried on by his son, still prevails in Kansas and in Oklahoma where the remaining Indians of the old Southwest were forcibly transported after 1830. Senator Blount evaded the Federal officers and returned to Tennessee where he continued to hold office under the protection of popular acclaim. And Robert Liston rested, though somewhat uncomfortably, upon Grenville's disavowal of the project, waiting for better times. He was to have cause to complain that his letters and British despatches were opened, that his messenger had been arrested in Pennsylvania for horse-stealing, his baggage rifled, and two letters to Peter Russell in Upper Canada examined. These, however, fortunately for him, commented only upon John Adams' West Indian policy.[71]

Better times did come for Robert Liston, as the mission to France of Pinckney, Marshall, and Gerry failed. The British were to get another chance at negotiating with Americans—and next time with men of rank close to the Administration itself. Their plan was to be developed again without proper estimate of the stubborn character or the statesmanship of John Adams.[72]

The First Mission to France

THE President's very first move on coming to office had been a nonpartisan effort to forestall the diplomatic break with France likely to follow Monroe's recall. Though undeceived by the French minister's "half-confidence," John Adams meant literally what he said to Adet: he did wish to maintain a good understanding between the two countries. He had proposed to Jefferson on the eve of the inauguration that he take another mission to France. If the Vice-President, however, felt that he should not be so far away in case of accident to the President, would not his close friend, James Madison, go with Elbridge Gerry of New England and Charles Cotesworth Pinckney of the South, thus representing three great sections and satisfying all parts of the United States?

Had Jefferson or Madison accepted the undertaking, neither would have damaged irreparably the Federalism of Adams nor their

71. Articles by White and Thompson in East Tenn. Hist. Soc. Pubs., 1929, Nos. 1 and 2, pp. 66 nn., 3–21 respectively. Ridings, *Chisholm Trail,* 15–17. Adams, *Works,* VIII, 658, 667, 668. Wharton, State *Trials,* 683. For Toussaint Louverture and Adams, see below, p. 363.

72. See below, p. 319 f.

own Republican leadership, even though the result might have been a complete reversal for the diplomacy of their protégé, James Monroe, now on his way home at last. But they both declined. Adams turned then to his Federalist secretaries for counsel, summoning Congress in the meantime to special session. And he wrote on March 31 to his son, John Quincy Adams, at The Hague: "America is not SCARED." Probably not, but the words do sound like whistling for one's own courage.[73]

Secretaries Pickering and Wolcott, however, opposed the President's ideas. Pickering wrote to Alexander Hamilton, arguing against a mission to France. Wolcott balked at selecting a minister from "the French party," although he appreciated that the alternative might be war. He found the plan for a representative commission intolerable—until he was brought up short by Hamilton.[74]

The former Secretary of the Treasury had expressed his opinions to George Washington and to Theodore Sedgwick, Federalist Senator, in January and February before John Adams had come to the presidency. There should be an extraordinary mission to France, said Hamilton, just as there had been in 1794 to England, but this time, it should be a group of three including a "man in whom the opposition has confidence." He proposed that Madison and Cabot of Massachusetts should join Pinckney. They should go to make explanations, to remonstrate, to ask indemnification for the raids of the French cruisers upon American commerce, "and perhaps to abrogate or remodify the treaty of alliance" while negotiating a new treaty of commerce. For Alexander Hamilton was uneasy about that guarantee of the West Indies in the Treaty of 1778: "In the future, and in a truly defensive war," said he, "I think we shall be bound to comply efficaciously with our guaranty. Nor have I been able to see that it means less than obligation to take part in such a war with our whole force." He did not care for treaties which were not executed. He liked less a war in which much was to be risked and little gained.[75]

Now on March 30, therefore, Hamilton wrote to Wolcott from New York: "I ought, my good friend, to apprise you, for you may learn from no other, that a suspicion begins to *dawn* among the

73. Adams, *Works*, I, 507–508, March 3, 1797; VIII, 537, to J. Q. Adams, March 31. Jefferson (Ford ed.), I, 272. *Annals*, 5 Cong., I, 48, proclamation of March 25, 1797.

74. Pickering Papers, VI, 249, March 26, 1797. Gibbs, I, 482, to O. Wolcott, Sr., March 29, 1797. Adams, *Works*, I, 508.

75. Hamilton (Lodge ed.), X, 231–235, 239–241, January 20, 22, February 26, 1797. Quotation from p. 240, second letter to Sedgwick.

friends of the government, that the *actual* administration is not much averse to war with France. How very important to obviate this!" Did the secretaries not observe that France was breaking through the coalition against her? Why the Czar of Russia was only lukewarm toward the allies; he would be hostile next; and "If England is left to bear the burthen alone, who can say that France may not venture to sport an army to this country?" They should exhaust "the expedients of negotiation" and at the same time "prepare *vigorously* for the worst."[76]

In reply Wolcott confessed the error of his ways and acknowledged the leadership of the lawyer in New York, but still he pled: "Is a direct mission to France, of which Mr. Madison is to be a member, in your view indispensable?"

Hamilton rebuked, if he did not shame, with this answer: "If Madison is well coupled, I do not think his intrigues can operate as you imagine. Should he advocate dishonorable concessions to France, the public opinion will not support. His colleagues, by address, and showing a disposition to do enough, may easily defeat his policy, and maintain the public confidence. Besides that, it is possible too much may be taken for granted with regard to Mr. Madison." Indeed it was—for one thing, that he would go at all.[77]

And so, John Adams was to have his way because it coincided with that of the great Federalist. A commission of envoys extraordinary should go to France. But the President had the final word about its membership. Instead of George Cabot as Hamilton wished, Adams first selected Francis Dana whom he personally admired. Dana had been eminent among the more conservative Revolutionaries; he had gained experience in European diplomacy when abroad with Adams for the Continental Congress; he was Chief Justice of the Supreme Court of Massachusetts.

As Madison was not to be persuaded, Adams discounted the necessity of having a member of the "opposition" and chose John Marshall of Virginia. He was already known as a lawyer of the first rank in his state—so much so that the famous Frenchman, Beaumarchais, had retained him as his counsel for claims against Virginia. Adams thought Marshall remarkably versed in the law of nations. When Dana declined the appointment, Adams came back to the idea of a bipartisan commission and named Elbridge Gerry of Massachusetts, in spite of remonstrance in the Cabinet.[78]

76. *Ibid.*, X, 248–249. Gibbs, I, 484.

77. *Ibid.*, I, 488, to Hamilton, March 31, 1797. Hamilton (Lodge ed.), X, 251–253, to Wolcott, April 5, 1797.

78. Beveridge, *Marshall*, II, 173, noting Beaumarchais' mortgage on Marshall's property; 218, concerning Adams. Adams, *Works*, VIII, 549, to Gerry, July 17, 1797.

Pinckney, of course, would head the commission. The French
Directory would have to realize at the start that it was dealing with
the representatives of a self-respecting Government. The group was
also pleasing to Adams from the point of view of national politics.
It represented the Southern, the Middle, and the Northern States
alike. It would be as far removed in temper as possible from the rancor of Federalist "Monocrats" and Republican "Jacobins." Gerry
was suitable, both as a supporter of Jefferson and as Adams' personal
friend.

The President then went before Congress on May 16, 1797, to
state his policy. He would make a fresh attempt to negotiate with
France, he said, notwithstanding the fact that the address of Barras
on Monroe's departure had disclosed sentiments "dangerous to our
independence and union" and a disposition "to separate the people
of the United States from the Government." John Adams did not
deny himself the use of words because an adversary was formidable.
That offered only greater temptation to his vocabulary: "Such
attempts ought to be repelled, he declared, "with a decision which
shall convince France and the world that we are not a degraded
people, humiliated under a colonial spirit of fear and sense of in-
feriority, fitted to be the miserable instruments of foreign influence,
and regardless of national honor, character, and interest." If in the
renewed negotiations it were found that the American people had
committed errors or had done injuries, they would be willing to
make amends. But in the meantime, Congress should provide for a
navy, reorganize the militia, arrange for an army, prescribe for
arming merchantmen in self-defense and convoying those which
were not armed, and should look to the fortification of their principal seaports.

John Adams would go even farther. It was very true, he said, that
they ought not to involve themselves in "the political system of
Europe." But if they would expose the "efforts" which were being
made to draw them into "the vortex," they must prepare against
those efforts "in season." To this end, he recommended that the
United States should renew the treaties with Prussia and Sweden.
"However we may consider ourselves, the maritime and commercial
powers of the world will consider the United States of America as
forming a weight in that balance of power in Europe which never
can be forgotten or neglected." A nation which was determined to
be neutral in such circumstances should consult with others of the
same purpose.[79]

The second President of the United States would maintain the

79. Richardson, I, 233-239.

neutrality of his predecessor. He would strengthen it, however, by those forces which already comprehended the interrelationship of American and European commercial interests but magnified the distance of European politics from American concern. It was too early in the development of this young nation as yet to talk strongly of excluding Europe from primary concern in the affairs of the whole Western Hemisphere. It was not too early to tell European statesmen that they were to have nothing to say in American affairs of the United States. Adams' instructions through Secretary Pickering to Pinckney, Marshall, and Gerry on July 15, 1797, therefore, sought changes in the contract with France that would release the United States from guaranteeing the French West Indies, that would put an end to those foreign tribunals which France had built within American jurisdiction upon the consular convention of 1788, that would prevent the sale of French prizes in American ports, assure compensation for damages in the past to American commerce, and would stop interference with the neutral trade of the United States, excepting of course that which was based upon accepted principles of contraband and blockade.

On the other hand, the instructions said little about the grievances of France beyond a wish to do justice. For Adams and Pickering assumed that the issue of Jay's Treaty was closed. If, however, the French should press for alterations in their treaty rights concerning contraband and enemy's property in neutral ships, they were to meet no difficulty in replacing the 23d and 24th articles of their commercial treaty of 1778 with the 17th and 18th articles of the Jay Treaty. That was to say, Adams and Pickering were willing to drop for the time being the principle of *free ships free goods* and the narrow definition of contraband for which the United States had been contending.

They might as well have been dropped. Britain had refused to accept the American views. The international league had failed to advance those neutral aims. France was showing no regard for them. And the United States alone could not maintain them against the opposition of Britain and the inertia of the rest of the world. The envoys to France, accordingly, were ordered to concentrate upon the more immediate desires of the United States. They were to pursue these with "inflexible perseverance" and "force of sentiment," although never letting "anything like warmth and harshness" give the French so much as a pretext to put the blame upon this country. For such finesse, however, it need hardly be said, they were not able to take as their model either Secretary Pickering or President Adams.[80]

John Marshall carried abroad the orders and instructions to young John Quincy Adams, minister in Berlin, for renewing the treaties with Prussia and with Sweden. But Elbridge Gerry took with him the experience of a special lecture from the President as to how he in particular should behave. John Adams, after reflection, must have had misgivings about the character of Gerry, for he admonished him upon the "utmost necessity" of harmony and unanimous action by the commission. It was probable, wrote Adams, that Americans, English, Dutch, and French all would try to arouse jealousies among the envoys. Some believed, although he himself did not, said Adams, that Gerry might display "an obstinancy that will risk great things to secure small ones."[81]

It was a prophecy. Gerry's initial enthusiasm for Republican France was to require this and that deference to her susceptibilities —only to delay significant decisions. Then, as he saw the situation of the envoys grow worse, his fervor cooled into dread of war with France and he became all the more anxious to avoid conclusions. One may recall Monroe's behavior in Paris before him. But Gerry's reaction to the thought of his country at war was not like Monroe's. Gerry had doubts of victory.[82]

Dealings with X, Y, and Z

PINCKNEY and Marshall arrived in Paris from the Netherlands, September 27, 1797, and Gerry came on October 4. They presented their credentials to Talleyrand, foreign minister for the Directory on the eighth, and learned that they would hear from him within a few days. Then on the eleventh Marshall received a call from Church, American consul at Lisbon, who came bringing advice from Thomas Paine. It was that the American commission should await events; the United States ought to remain in a state of "unarmed neutrality"—quite the contrary from Adams' proposals to Congress. Marshall and Gerry had their first disagreement. John Marshall wished offhand to relieve Tom Paine entirely of any illusion that he had influence with this American commission.[83]

80. ASP FR, I, 153–157, instructions to Pinckney, Marshall, and Gerry, July 15, 1797. For the Jay Treaty, see above, p. 184 f.

81. Adams, *Works*, VIII, 548–549, July 8, 17, 1797, to Gerry. For J. Q. Adams' treaty with Prussia, see below, p. 379.

82. See above, p. 235.

83. Marshall's Journal, October 11, now in the Pickering Papers, Miscellaneous, v. 51.

What Thomas Paine expected to do is revealed in the letter which he had written to Talleyrand on September 27. He had enclosed his "Letter to Washington," which had been made public while Monroe was in Paris, and said that he would send other thoughts on American affairs in a few days. In the meantime, he presumed that Talleyrand did not intend to assure Pinckney, Marshall, and Gerry anything at their first interview; it would be best, said Paine, to receive them with a *"civil signification of reproach."* Pinckney, he asserted, had committed himself in his correspondence with Pickering, which the Secretary of State had been foolish enough to publish. And did Talleyrand know Mountflorence, chancellor in the American consulate? If he visited the foreign ministry, Talleyrand would do well to keep him "at a distance," for Mountflorence was the "confidential intrigant" of Pinckney. Paine's subsequent thoughts were that Talleyrand should negotiate with the American commissioners a general convention for nonimportation, in which the nations should act as a whole against Britain, with France taking the lead.[84]

Thomas Paine seems to have had some influence with Talleyrand. His private secretary, Osmond, told Mountflorence on October 14 that the Directory were exasperated with President Adams' remarks to Congress: they would expect an explanation; the commissioners would probably not get an audience with the Directory until their negotiations with the foreign minister were finished; but certain persons might be appointed to treat with them and report to Talleyrand. In short, they were not to be received officially at once, if ever. Their negotiations were not going to be easy, and it was likely —not successful at all.[85]

At this turn of affairs, Marshall was for breaking through the "contemptuous" silence about the condemnation of American shipping in the prize courts. They should demand that the Directory stop the plunder then and there before negotiations went any farther. Gerry was of "a contrary opinion," however, and so Marshall and Pinckney deferred to him "to preserve unanimity." Then, news arrived on October 17 that the British had destroyed the Dutch fleet at Camperdown; Marshall suspected that the Directory would now be able to surmount "some of its strongest objections to peace with the United States." But another event of that very

pp. 539–657, Massachusetts Historical Society. ASP FR, II, 157 ff., "XYZ Papers" submitted to Congress April 3, 1798, and thereafter. Beveridge, *Marshall*, II, 254–255.

84. AAE CP EU, XLVIII, f. 268, Paine to Talleyrand, September 28, 1797; ff. 273–277, Paine's plan for nonimportation. For Paine and Monroe, see above, pp. 232–233.

85. ASP FR, II, 157.

day was soon to restore those objections. The Treaty of Campo Formio with Austria, October 17, 1797, following Napoleon's victories
in Italy, gave French pride and arrogance a tremendous lift. Spoils
of war were enriching a country which but two years before had
faced starvation.[86]

Before this news arrived in Paris, Talleyrand had begun that indirect play with the American envoys which was to win him fame
for avarice and misjudgment, but also to gain the time for France
which she had to have if she were to reach her objectives in America.
Adet had arrived and reported to him on September 22. Collot had
delivered some of his papers to Adet on April 11 before Adet left
America. These discussed the predicament of Spain between Britain
and the United States, the necessity that France should take Louisiana; they described the Ohio, the Wabash, the Illinois, the Yazoo,
and Mobile, the topography of Missouri, the plan for defending St.
Louis; and they contained general remarks upon all of the Indians
west of the Mississippi River. Létombe's despatch with Collot's conclusions reached Talleyrand's office later on November 3.[87]

On October 18, "X," identified as Hottenguer, a Swiss banker,
called upon Pinckney with what he said was a message from Talleyrand. (Obviously, if need arose later, the ex-Bishop of Autun could
disavow the whole affair and simply leave "X" as an insupportable
liar.) Hottenguer did not know, he said, what parts of the President's speech to Congress had been objectionable to the Directory;
but he did know that the American envoys would make a good
start if, according to "diplomatic usage," they provided a little
sweetening of 1,200,000 livres—approximately $250,000. And
there should be a loan by the United States to France. The amount of
the loan would be determined by their "ability to pay." In order not
to make England jealous or to violate American neutrality, said he,
the form of the loan would be an advance by the United States of
payments "contracted by agents of the French Government with
the citizens of the United States." Hottenguer himself, we know,
had connections with James Swan, agent for France in purchasing
supplies with the proceeds from the liquidation of the American
debt to France.[88]

The American envoys were expected to buy the right merely to

86. Marshall's Journal, October 15, 17. For a list of the American vessels captured
by French privateers in the vicinity of San Domingo, Guadeloupe, and condemned in
1796–1797, see AAE CP EU, XLVIII, f. 305. For French starvation, see above, p. 229.
87. These papers from Collot are listed in AAE EU, Spt. 28, f. 42. See above, p. 250 f.
88. ASP FR, II, 158. Marshall's Journal, October 18. Statement by Howard C. Rice
regarding Hottenguer and Swan. See above, p. 241.

present the matters upon which they had been instructed. In the process they could also seriously compromise their country's neutrality between the belligerents, France and Britain, by making a loan to France. Then, perhaps, they might be able to negotiate in regard to claims for damages to American commerce, release from guarantees, and such matters. Pinckney and Marshall in conference opposed Hottenguer's suggestions. But Gerry favored the idea of a loan.

Two days later "Y" or Bellamy, a merchant of Hamburg, appeared upon the scene. Of course he was "not a diplomatic character"; so he could express only his own opinions; but he was a "confidential friend of M. Talleyrand." The American commissioners could consider what that meant! They might also guess that Bellamy could be repudiated as easily as Hottenguer. But they listened to him. They would have to disavow Adams' speech to Congress, he said, and to make reparations for it. They could have a new treaty with France but it would have at least to put France back on precisely the same footing as Britain. And a secret clause in this treaty should provide for a loan to France. The essential matter remained. It was indispensable to further negotiation: *"Il faut de l'argent—il faut beaucoup d'argent."* No, even Talleyrand himself was not authorized, said Bellamy, to speak for the Directory. Bellamy, however, thought that Talleyrand thought he could prevail upon the Directory to receive them if the Americans accepted these propositions as the basis for the proposed treaty.

Bellamy was back the following morning at ten, having passed the earlier hours with Talleyrand. Hottenguer was also present. Bellamy now harped upon the exasperation of the Directory. M. Talleyrand and he were extremely sensible, he said, of the pain that the Americans were feeling, but they would have to comply. The Directory was determined upon reparation. If the Americans would agree, then their claims against France might be submitted to a commission appointed as under the Jay Treaty—with the exception of the claims rising from seizure of ships which lacked the *rôle d'équipage*. It was a notable exception, for practically no American ships were carrying this particular kind of ship's papers and the French courts were taking advantage of that fact to condemn American property. Merlin, while minister of justice, said Bellamy, had written a treatise opposing these claims; but anyway, the whole Directory were decided on the point.[89]

The American lack of rôles d'équipage must have been most gratifying to Merlin, for according to Hottenguer, he had been

89. ASP FR, II, 160. Marshall's Journal, October 20 and 21.

paid so well by the owners of the privateers that he was to take no part of the *douceur* of $250,000 which the American envoys were to provide for the Directory. Talleyrand himself appears to have received 2,000,000 francs or so as his share from confiscations of neutral ships captured by French privateers.[90]

When the Americans urged Bellamy to express his personal opinion as to the means by which they could make reparation to the Directory, he answered: Money. The Directory, said he, was so jealous of its own honor and the honor of the nation that it must be treated with the same respect which the Americans had shown for the King—unless they could find something more valuable than respect. And they could. "That was money." They could buy from France at twenty shillings in the pound 32,000,000 florins of Dutch rescripts, worth ten shillings in the pound.

Bellamy was certain that the Dutch Government would repay the United States after the peace. Ultimately they would lose nothing, so he said. But to us, perhaps there still would be a difference between a value of ten shillings and a purchase price of twenty. And the douceur of $250,000 was, of course, to be additional.

Pinckney, Marshall, and Gerry withdrew to another room to consider the matter for a moment by themselves, and to put their common decision in writing. Gerry argued with Marshall and Pinckney. But they came back to tell Bellamy that, although their powers to negotiate a treaty were ample, a loan, in any form, was not within their instructions. One of them, accordingly, they suggested, should return at once to consult their Government, provided that the Directory would suspend all further captures and all procedure against American ships detained.

Bellamy could not hide his disappointment. He declined to take a copy of the American decision, asserting that he was unauthorized. It was only his suggestion, not the Directory's, nor even Talleyrand's. The Americans said they understood perfectly; the form of the proposal was to be theirs, but the substance was the foreign minister's just the same. They rejected it.

Bellamy stayed to argue vehemently, and to intimidate if he could. They would not be received, he said; and he appeared to shudder at the thought of the consequences. Perhaps Gerry had sympathetic twinges, but Pinckney and Marshall replied that America had made every possible effort to remain on friendly terms. If France would

90. Marshall's Journal, October 27, upon Merlin. For Talleyrand's prize money, see introduction by Whitelaw Reid to Talleyrand's Mémoires (Broglie ed.), I, xlviii, citing the biography by Bastide, published in 1838. See Bastide, 216, for charges against Talleyrand as of 1798–1799.

not hear, but would make war, the United States would defend themselves. They stood ready to treat, to put France and Britain on the same footing. They rejected the excuse regarding the *rôle d'équipage* as a municipal regulation that could not alter the obligation of a treaty. They could not disavow the speech of President Adams. It was Constitutional. They had no power. Anyway, they could not change opinion one bit by disavowing the statement. It would make them ridiculous to try, they said, for all America was aware of the facts concerning Barras' remarks to Monroe as stated by the President. It is not on record how Bellamy received so typically an American retort to an insult to intelligence.[91]

Six days after that, October 27, Hottenguer came on the news of Campo Formio. Had not that materially affected the situation? It might have for France, replied the American envoys, but not for the United States. What if the French should now insist that "all nations should aid them or be considered and treated as their enemies"? Very well, was the answer, despite Gerry's inner qualms; the United States would fight in defense of their commerce, if they had to do so. Their commissioners, however, had come to negotiate. But, said Hottenguer, they did not speak to the point. It was money. They had not said whether—no, they had not—what was their answer? At this Pinckney blurted out his famous "It is no; no; not a six pence." But Gerry still had mental reservations. Well, persisted Hottenguer, they might pay the douceur "to interest an influential friend" in their favor? No? Why, did not General Pinckney know that was the way business was done here? He had been a long time in France and in Holland! The Americans had not supposed, Marshall interjected, that such a suggestion on their part would have been anything else than a deadly affront to France—like paying Indians or Algerines to keep the peace. Ignoring that thrust, Hottenguer declaimed once more upon France's strength which nothing could resist. Marshall rewarded this assertion with, "America is a great, and so far as concerns her self-defence, a powerful nation."[92]

It was not mere bravado. War would have been serious for the United States, but no less so for France. Americans with any experience at all knew, as Talleyrand and other French statesmen knew, that France was vulnerable in the Western Hemisphere. Her West Indian possessions were dependent on supplies from North America, and most of those came from the United States in American ships. True, Napoleon had beaten the Austrian Emperor and

91. ASP FR, II, 160–161.
92. Marshall's Journal, October 27.

had gained the Treaty of Campo Formio to enlarge French power and territory on the continent of Europe. But equally true, and far more significant in determining the course of events in America, the British had broken the Dutch fleet at Camperdown. Before he even thought of invading England, Napoleon would have to devise better ways than he had to meet Britain's power on the seas. Until he did, certainly the French West Indies were at the mercy of France's enemies, provided they could overcome also the natives and the more deadly resistance of yellow fever.[93]

So far, nevertheless, the negotiations with the American commission were going just about as Talleyrand wanted them. The issue was drawn. The Directory would not receive the Americans unless they made it financially worthwhile. And they would linger in Paris hoping to negotiate but refusing to proceed through the agency of informal persons, who could be repudiated. Nor would they discuss a loan further without getting specific instructions from Philadelphia. All of this would consume time, as Talleyrand desired. Days and months would pass, and no real change in the situation would occur. The courts meanwhile would go merrily on condemning American shipping. He would draw Gerry farther from his colleagues by confiding to him that the Directory wished really to deal with him alone, and to get rid of Marshall and Pinckney whom they considered as virtually British.

To this end, "Z" or Hauteval, confidant of Talleyrand, had already told Gerry of the foreign minister's disappointment that he had not seen the Americans frequently "in their private capacities"; and Gerry had gone with Hauteval to confer with Talleyrand apart from Pinckney and Marshall. This led eventually to Gerry's recall and great personal discomfiture. But in the course of his separate dealings he was able to get the evidence directly in conference with Talleyrand and Bellamy on December 17 which proved, in spite of all of Talleyrand's later denials, that he had made the suggestion through Bellamy regarding the douceur of $250,000 and the loan to France by way of the purchase of the Dutch "rescripts." Talleyrand had said to Gerry on this occasion that Bellamy's proposals were "just" and "might always be relied on." He had even written out the plan himself for the Dutch florins, and then burned the paper.[94]

93. Stoddard, *French Revolution in St. Domingo,* regarding Howe's expedition. For Simcoe, see above, p. 268.

94. ASP FR, II, 162–163. Hauteval and Gerry, October 22; Gerry and Talleyrand, October 28; Bellamy, Talleyrand, and Gerry, December 17. For Pickering's use of this episode, see *ibid.,* II, 230.

Meanwhile Hottenguer and Bellamy were returning again and again to persuade Pinckney and Marshall that they must consider the loan and the gratuity. Talleyrand did want something more than time. If he kept trying, he might yet find the crack in the armor of Marshall and Pinckney. Surely every man had his weakness. Talleyrand wanted money for himself.

Marshall's connection with Beaumarchais came to mind. On December 17, Bellamy suggested to Marshall that Beaumarchais would be willing, if his claim against the state of Virginia were established, to turn over a portion amounting practically to the gratuity. Thus, at no expense to the American Government, that preliminary fee would be paid and negotiations could proceed. But also, Marshall would have to win the case against his own State in order to provide the means whereby the Federal Government could bribe the officials of France. John Marshall did not step into that trap.[95]

Three days later a lady, who said that she was surely not in the confidence of M. Talleyrand, tried her skill with Pinckney. Why would they not make a loan to France? Had not France helped the United States? If they stayed six months longer, they would get no farther with their negotiations unless they made the loan. Then, said Pinckney, they had better go home at once. But, she retorted, that would lead to a break; they could not afford to risk that, for "we have a very considerable party in America who are strongly in our interest."[96]

Hottenguer had touched upon the same point when remarking that Aaron Burr and James Madison would have better pleased the American people as the envoys to France. It was very true that there was a strong pro-French party in the United States. Feeling was running high, so high that at times John Adams feared civil war. There was brawling between Federalists and Republicans, even on the floor of Congress. But any French statesman who expected enthusiasm for France in America to choke America's interest in itself had not yet discovered the facts.

The political divisions of the United States were not the product simply of quarreling over European friends. We must not forget the rivalries between New Englanders and Virginians, shipowners

95. Marshall's Journal, December 17.

96. ASP FR, II, 167. Beveridge, *Marshall*, II, 290–292. Austin, *Gerry*, II, 202 n. Other implications in this affair are more alluring. Talleyrand made use of them later in self-defense. See ASP FR, II, 225, "an anonymous publication . . . said to have issued from the French office of foreign affairs," contained in Gerry's letter of October 1, 1798. This publication belittled X and Y, and spoke of the "lady" as "known to be connected with Mr. Pinckney." Lyman (1828 ed.), I., 336–339, regarding Mme. de Villette.

and speculators in Western land, creditors and debtors. But in spite of these antagonisms, influential leaders in both Federalist and Republican parties had a great desire in common. They would possess the North American continent regardless of European friendships or enmities.[97]

The American commissioners decided again on December 18 that they would not negotiate with unauthorized persons. Instead, although Gerry was reluctant to do so, they would send a formal letter to Talleyrand in which they would state their objects in coming to France, discuss those matters just as if they had been officially received by the Directory, and then close with the request, virtually an ultimatum, that official negotiations should begin or they should receive their passports.

John Marshall made this letter a complete review of the American case against France for depredations upon American commerce since 1793. He reiterated Pickering's arguments in support of American neutrality according to the law of nations and the American view of contraband. He defended the Jay Treaty once more, restated Washington's position with respect to Monroe's mission in 1794, and even recalled the behavior of Genet. But Elbridge Gerry delayed so long over reading and approving Marshall's draft that the letter was not presented until January 31 although it was dated January 17, 1798.

Both Marshall and Gerry could have spared themselves all their labor. Talleyrand had no intention of wading through Marshall's argument to find a rebuttal. His secretary intimated on February 3 that long letters took too much time for what they were worth. He did not reply until March 18.[98]

Getting no official response immediately to their letter, the envoys had requested a personal interview with Talleyrand. They obtained it on March 2. Pinckney began with conciliatory remarks but Talleyrand brushed them aside. He complained not only of Adams' but of Washington's speeches. He was provoked with the coldness and distance of Pinckney and Marshall. He had expected to see them frequently as private persons. They should consider granting a loan. It could be arranged so as to become payable after the war had closed and thus not injure American neutrality. Surely they could appreciate the difference between an express prohibition

97. See King (King ed.), II, 192, Pickering to King, June 20, 1797. Also Beveridge, *Marshall,* II. 279–280.

98. Marshall's Journal, December 18, January 20, February 3. ASP FR, II, 169–182, 188–189.

and a mere silence in a set of instructions. He insisted that they could negotiate a loan.[99]

Then John Marshall took charge of the interview. The extraordinary mission was proof enough, he declared, that the United States wanted reconciliation with France. They moreover had "so long patiently borne the immense loss of property" inflicted by the policy of France in regard to neutral commerce. But to make a loan to France was something else. It not only was beyond the powers of these commissioners. It would injure their own country. Neutrality was of "the last importance" to the United States. A loan really payable after peace had returned to Europe could be negotiated after the war had closed. As for seeing the Directory, he personally did not care. He saw no reason for calling in public character even upon M. Talleyrand until they were received publicly as the commissioners of the United States.[100]

A second conference on March 6 altered the situation to no degree. In fact there was no conclusion possible except that there had been no change in the status of the American commission since October. But there had been a change in Elbridge Gerry's relations with his colleagues. That harmony and unanimity was gone which President Adams had virtually commanded him to maintain, and the semblance of which, at least, Marshall and Pinckney had tried to preserve. Gerry had confessed to them on February 4 that he was not at liberty to disclose his communications with Talleyrand. He admitted under pressure on March 1 that Talleyrand planned to dismiss them and negotiate with him alone. The former Bishop of Autun was getting on with his American policy—perhaps too far.

John Marshall was convinced now that it was Elbridge Gerry who had originated the idea of a loan payable at the close of the war. Gerry still seemed to think, wrote Marshall in his journal, that Marshall would eventually see the matter as he did; but "I told him that my judgment was not more perfectly convinced that the floor was wood or that I stood on my feet and not on my head, than that our instructions would not permit us to make the loan required." As Pinckney agreed with him, Marshall then urged that Gerry and he should return together and explain the situation to their Government while Pinckney remained in Paris. But Gerry's mind could not even consider such a move. Talleyrand had made sure of that.[101]

Elbridge Gerry was fidgeting between the hope that he might

99. ASP FR, II, 186.
100. Marshall's Journal, March 2.
101. Marshall's Journal, March 1 and 3.

negotiate successfully alone—though informally and without credentials—and the fear that if he did not try, the rupture would occur which he believed meant war. Talleyrand's reply to Marshall's formal letter had not met the American arguments on the points at issue under the law of nations. It had merely restated France's grievances that the American courts had taken jurisdiction over French prizes and that British vessels had been admitted into American ports. It protested the Jay Treaty. It complained of the invectives in American newspapers, and so on. The appearances therefore to Gerry were that perhaps he might gain something in further discussion. Had not Talleyrand said that the Directory was ready to treat "with one of the three" commissioners? And still, Gerry knew what President Adams had expected of him. It was not to be led by the nose. He told Talleyrand on April 4, when he finally consented to negotiate alone, that the effort would be "unavailing," "utterly impracticable." The truth seems therefore to be that he was afraid. Talleyrand had said that he could not leave France; so he believed that he could not; yet he knew that he should. Vans Murray put it very gently indeed when he observed that Elbridge Gerry was in a "thick fog of his own conjuration."[102]

The upshot of the quarrel within the American commission was that Gerry stayed at Paris in spite of plain words from Pinckney that his position was false. Pinckney withdrew to the south of France where he was permitted, on account of his daughter's illness, to remain as a private person. And Marshall sparred grimly with Talleyrand to get himself formally dismissed, while Talleyrand tried to make him leave on his own responsibility, asking his passport of an American consul like any other private citizen. It took the threat from Marshall that he would return by way of England, and the repeated intercession of Beaumarchais before Talleyrand would grant the passport which was due to any representative of a foreign power regardless of his personal acceptability. Marshall sailed at last on April 24 from Bordeaux for America, leaving this behind him for the French archives:

> John Marshall has the honor to acknowledge the receipt of the letter of the minister of exterior relations inclosing his passport & a letter of safe conduct.

> Tho' he had expected that the letter would have been more special yet he trusts that it will protect him & will prevent the vessel in which he

102. ASP FR, II, 188, 200, 205, Talleyrand to Pinckney, Marshall, and Gerry, March 18, 1798; Gerry to Talleyrand, April 4, 1798; Gerry to Pickering, October 1, 1798. AHA Rpt., 1912, 406, Vans Murray to J. Q. Adams, from The Hague, May 14, 1798.

may sail from being turned out of her course. In this confidence he embarks from one of the ports of France.

Talleyrand had met his match in irony. He had been compelled officially to recognize the American commission if only in negative fashion.[103]

103. AAE CP EU, XLIX, f. 323.

XII

HYSTERIA

The Adams Temper

FEELINGS were rising fast on this side of the Atlantic. Despatches from the American commissioners in France which had been written between October 22 and January 8 had arrived together on March 4, 1798. The last of these declared that they had no hope of being officially received. President Adams at once notified Congress of this opinion, and then read the deciphered reports of the goings and comings of Hottenguer and Bellamy. As a result, he had decided by March 19 to advise Congress that a settlement with France was not likely. Vice-President Jefferson greeted this as an "insane message"; but the President nevertheless sent orders for Pinckney, Marshall, and Gerry to come home unless in the meantime they had been received officially and allowed to negotiate with authorized persons. In no event should they pay a douceur to anyone or negotiate a loan to France. By April 3 John Adams had determined to spread all the papers before Congress and the public, withholding only the names of such individuals as Hottenguer, Bellamy, and Hauteval. As more despatches arrived from France, Adams accordingly sent them to Congress, on May 4, June 5, June 18—until he reached his climax on June 21. Then he announced that General Marshall had reached "a place of safety, where he is justly held in honor," and he vowed: "I will never send another minister to France without assurances that he will be received, respected, and honored, as the representative of a great, free, powerful, and independent nation." The Adams temper had almost ruined the President's intention to keep his country out of war.[1]

The Federalists in Congress were eager for a war. Just where it might have to be fought and whether it would really serve the interests of this country were questions to which they did not bend their minds. Albert Gallatin, leader of the Republican opposition in the House, took the unpopular course of reasoning upon such questions. Federalists seemed to think that the only alternative to war with France was a humiliating treaty with her. Gallatin saw an-

1. ASP FR, II, 150–153, 169, 185–199. Jefferson (Ford ed.), VII, 218, 221, to Madison, March 21, 1798, and to Monroe, same date.

other. The American people, he argued, did not have to face "surrendering by treaty" their "rights and independence as a nation." They could declare that it was not their "interest," in spite of depredations and losses suffered, to get into this European war; it was coming to a close; he had rather take those losses and avoid others which were bound to accompany war. To him, a foreign war was the only real danger for this country. He therefore steadily opposed any legislation which might lead to war with France. He would keep cool and wait.[2]

Congress—with even some leading Republicans fervent—swept over Gallatin and his adherents. Successive measures—many of them Alexander Hamilton's—were enacted to raise a provisional army, to equip the navy, to authorize attacks by both privateers and public vessels upon French ships found preying upon American commerce, to suspend commercial intercourse with France and its dependencies, to allow the arming of merchantmen in self-defense, to abrogate the treaties of 1778 and 1788 with France, and to raise a war loan of $5,000,000. Secretary Pickering wrote to Gerry on behalf of the President, June 25, 1798, that he should have withdrawn with Marshall and Pinckney, that he must now drop his effort to prevent a rupture, and come home.[3]

John Adams' fellow citizens were outraged, and they *were* "scared." The Philadelphia *Gazette* declared on June 29: "We are told that in addition to the immense armament collected at Flushing, gunboats and rafts of a peculiar construction are building in all the forts opposite to our eastern coasts." Rufus King at London wrote in March that the French Directory, inspired by the "success of their Enterprises in Europe" believed that they might "gain 'un point d'appui' in our Country, or upon its borders" and "easily make a fourth of September at Philadelphia!" King was thinking of New Orleans. George Washington at Mount Vernon wrote to Timothy Pickering in July: "If the French should be so *mad* as openly and formidably to Invade these United States, in expectation of subjugating the Government, laying them under contribution, or in hopes of dissolving the Union, I conceive there can hardly be two opinions respecting their Plan, and their operations will commence in the Southern quarter." The French consul

2. Adams, *Gallatin,* 200, discussing Gallatin's debate with Harper.
3. Jefferson (Ford ed.), VII, 242–243, to Madison, April 19, 1798, regarding the "vibraters" in the House and Giles, Clopton, and Cabell. For the Acts of Congress, see Stats. at Large, I, 552–608. List in Scott, 19–20. Also see *Annals,* 5 Cong., III, 3717–3795. ASP FR, II, 204, Pickering to Gerry, June 25, 1798.

general, Létombe, had quite a different reaction to the American spirit. When he reported to Talleyrand on April 18, regarding the war measures of Congress, he remarked: "Already there is talk of conquering Louisiana."[4]

Talleyrand's Plan for America

ELBRIDGE GERRY had dispersed his "fog" on the other side of the Atlantic before Pickering's orders arrived. One with political aspirations would always do well to evade such dilemmas; but a friend of the President, who sometimes followed the lead of the President's chief political rival, would do particularly well to get home again and see for himself just what was going on there. He had not been able to persuade Talleyrand to make any real proposals in line with his original instructions which he might relay to his Government. He consequently had no argument for lingering without further instructions. More convincing to Gerry was the new tone of the French foreign minister. Whereas Talleyrand had so recently been refusing to let him go he was now practically begging him to stay. It was hard to prove, even to oneself, that one had personally to remain at Paris in order to keep America out of war with France.

The foreign minister of France had as a matter of fact great plans to injure the United States but they did not include an immediate war. Talleyrand had seen America for himself in years past. And he had presented his views to the National Institute on April 4, 1797, before he became minister of foreign affairs for the Directory. He had recognized then that the American people were English in habit and material interest. Their commerce with England was continually increasing; they would naturally gravitate toward their mother country and away from the ally in their war for independence; they were even saying that France, after assisting in their separation, was trying now to keep them disunited. He had urged accordingly that France should build anew in the Western Hemisphere. Like Fauchet and others before him, Talleyrand had seen the opportunity for that colonial system in Louisiana. It had been French; its colonists were so still. He had not gone on to complete in detail the political thoughts which were in his mind. But it was not hard to draw from his academic remarks a broad hint that

4. James in AHR, XXX, 50 n., quoting the Philadelphia *Gazette*. King (King ed.), II, 294–295, to Vans Murray, March 31, 1798; 300–301, to Pinckney, Marshall, and Gerry, April 2. Washington (Ford ed.), XIV, 34, to Pickering, July 11, 1798. AAE CP EU, XLIX, f. 328, Létombe to Talleyrand, April 18, 1798.

Louisiana might easily become French once more, if Godoy were to
fall from power in Madrid.[5]

Previous negotiations with Spain had failed because France had
not found the right price to complete the transaction. Talleyrand
protested as foreign minister in August, 1797, that the restitution
of Gibraltar and the establishments on Nootka Sound had never
been regarded as "the conditions *sine qua non* of peace" in any
treaty, "open or secret," between France and Spain. In other words,
Spain should not think that France would be compelled to obtain
Gibraltar for her or else go without Louisiana. There were other
considerations which France might oblige Spain to accept as the
right price.[6]

The problem of France's new minister of foreign affairs was not
so much to find those compensations for Spain, as to get Louisiana
before the Government of the United States came actually into
support of the American pioneers who were already encroaching
upon Spanish territory beyond the Mississippi and below the line
of the Pinckney Treaty of 1795. Talleyrand had not given as much
thought as he should to a report from Otto, former chargé d'affaires
at Philadelphia, now an expert in the foreign office in whom he had
confidence with respect to other matters. Otto had warned in June,
1797—before Pinckney, Marshall, and Gerry had reached Paris—
that France was in danger. The Americans, he said, were "the greatest navigators of the earth"; and the policy of France was driving
these excellent seamen into the arms of Britain. They would join
with France's enemy, if France did not take care; then she would
have left only the regret that she had won American independence
in order to destroy her own commerce and colonies. The Americans really were aloof from European politics; and although they
applauded the French Revolution, they were determined to stay
neutral. Moustier, Genet, Fauchet, Adet, all had injured France's
interests, declared Otto, by trying to involve the United States
with Europe and to come between the American people and their
Government. Even Jefferson, he warned, suspected that France
intended to destroy the American Constitution.[7]

Talleyrand, to be sure, was not yet fully in control of the French
foreign office. The Directory was still keeping a hand in its affairs.

5. Talleyrand, "Mémoire lu à l'Institut," *The Pamphleteer*, IV, 463 (1813–1828),
followed by an "Essay on Advantages from New Colonies." For Talleyrand's letters to
Lansdowne from America, February–June, 1795, see Pallain, *La Mission de Talleyrand à
Londres en 1792*, pp. 421–454.
6. Pallain, *Le Ministère de Talleyrand sous le Directoire*, 15. See above, p. 219 f.
7. James in AHR, XXX, 45–47.

But he might have paid more attention to Otto and less to Thomas Paine in the fall of 1797. And he himself should have known that the Americans could not be played upon indefinitely without retaliating, especially when they had the means and the opportunity to do so in the French West Indies where Toussaint Louverture was already making the French Government uneasy. Talleyrand appears to have needed more experience with Americans, advice from others besides Otto, and less greed for money, before he could arrive at that realization.[8]

As Marshall and Pinckney prepared to leave Paris in April, 1798, Godoy lost control at Madrid, it is suspected through French influence. In any case, Talleyrand had seized this opportunity to renew the negotiations for Louisiana, while he intimidated Gerry. His instructions in May to Guillemardet, French ambassador at Madrid, declared that the Americans meant at any cost to rule alone in America and to exercise at the same time a preponderant influence in the politics of Europe. A "crimp" should be put in their ambitions; they should be confined "within the limits which Nature seems to have traced for them." (It is apparent that he meant the Appalachian Mountains.) Like Victor Collot, he too appreciated that Spain could not "do this great work alone." She therefore should let France take over Louisiana and the Floridas, and make them a "wall of brass forever impenetrable to the combined efforts of England and America."[9]

But for once, contrary to his usual perception, or luck, this churchman become politician, this refugee in America, then citizen of the United States, then politician in France again, was late. Spain was turning over Natchez and the posts in the Southwest to the United States, as Godoy had pledged to Thomas Pinckney in 1795.[10]

Talleyrand, seemingly unaware of the significance in that fact, was trying to keep his American policy from developing too fast. His purpose in holding Gerry, he stated in July, 1798, was to prolong negotiations in their "half friendly, half hostile" condition at his own pleasure. It was so profitable. The colonies of France were still being provisioned by the Americans, while the French privateers enriched themselves and officials in Paris from their raids upon that very trade. He observed also that the Spanish Court appeared less obstinate in regard to Louisiana, even willing to have

8. See above, p. 282, for Paine. See below, p. 315, for Toussaint.
9. H. Adams' Transcripts, French State Papers, I, 1. ff, May–June, 1798. For Collot, see above, p. 258.
10. Vans Murray to J. Q. Adams, July 10, 1798, AHA Rpt., 1912, 430. Adams, *United States*, I, 355–357.

French forces sent over to check the invasions which the English and the Americans, he said, were contemplating there.[11]

In no way did Talleyrand's American policy include a declaration by France of war upon the United States. That, he had told the Directory on June 1, would only let France into "an Anglo-Federalist trap." The thing to do was delay until the French party in the United States won the next election. What Talleyrand and the Directory had not yet learned—in spite of reports from Létombe and intercepted despatches to England which told of the rising war spirit—was that the Americans might not wait for the next election. Congress might declare war upon France.[12]

News arrived within three weeks to teach this fact to the French foreign minister and his superiors. Talleyrand's immediate reaction was to bristle. He added to his report of July 10, 1798, the assertion that the issue was changed: America was taking hostile measures; a war loan was complete; armed vessels of the Federal government were pursuing French ships. It was, he said, a veritable declaration of war. The Directory therefore should put an embargo upon American vessels in French ports and postpone every idea of accommodation with the United States. He did not hold to this opinion long for close upon the news about Congress came warnings which he could have heard in the retorts of Marshall and Pinckney months before, had he chosen then to believe his own ears.[13]

Victor duPont—whom President Adams had refused to accept in place of Létombe, perhaps for the very good reason that he had been intimately concerned with the enterprises of Adet—returned to France on July 3. He reported that the conduct of the French cruisers was one of the principal causes of the growing coldness toward France in the United States. They were not only preying upon American commerce in the West Indies; they were raiding even within the territorial waters of the United States. The feeling which they aroused served as the pretext for those "hostile measures which the Government of the United States has promised England to adopt against us." The violations of American territory, furthermore, were having an ominous effect upon "our friends."

11. Pallain, 307–309, 312. ASP FR, II, 211, Gerry to Talleyrand, June 10, 1798, asking passports; 214, Talleyrand to Gerry, June 27, urging him to resume "explanations."

12. Morison in MHS Proc., XLIX, 76 n. For the letter of Pickering to King, reporting the growing anger with France, and the evacuation of Walnut Hills and Natchez by the Spaniards, intercepted by the French, May 3, 1798, see AAE CP EU, XLIX, f. 346.

13. Pallain, 309–310. Vans Murray to J. Q. Adams, July 17, 1798, AHA Rpt., 1912, 433.

The Republicans, as much as the Federalist merchants, were "proud of their independence as a nation."[14]

DuPont had talked with Jefferson and others on the eve of his departure. They had all said repeatedly that "they and the liberty of their country were lost if the Directory did not choose a behavior as wise as that of the federal government was little." This opinion, suggested duPont, ought to have weight with the Directory and all in France who were friends of "liberty," especially with Talleyrand whose personal knowledge of the United States made him so able to judge the circumstances. If the Directory did not stop the French raiders, the United States would be obliged to reunite with England, "who in a few years would succeed in appointing one of her princes to the office of President."[15]

Talleyrand knew conditions in the United States well enough to give no consideration to an idea so wild as the last. DuPont was reporting accurately both the Republican profession of fear for American liberty and Republican pride in the independence of this nation. He was not correctly weighing that profession with the pride of independence. Adet had analyzed Thomas Jefferson and his kind more keenly in 1796: "Jefferson, I say, is American and, by that title, cannot be sincerely our friend. An American is the born enemy of all European peoples."[16]

We should also recall here Secretary Jefferson's advice to President Washington in 1790—at the time of the controversy over Nootka Sound. The United States should view uneasily, he had said then, any attempt by either Britain or Spain to take the possessions of the other on their frontier; for their own safety was concerned in a "due balance" between their neighbors. We should also remember Jefferson's willingness in 1793, at the time of Genet's mission, to drop "our antient friends" if need be to preserve the interests of the United States.[17]

Balance of power meant to Jefferson in 1798, as it had in 1790 and 1793, that the United States should be free from commitments to any foreign state—free enough at least to play one against another for American advantage in this part of the world, particularly on the continent of North America. There was an additional factor in 1798: the former Secretary of State was now the

14. Morison in MHS Proc., XLIX, 66–67, 71. DuPont to Talleyrand, in writing, July 21, 1798.
15. Ibid., 74, 75.
16. Corresp. French Ministers, 983, December 31, 1796.
17. See above, pp. 137–140, 150–151.

Vice-President, actively engaged in becoming President by the election of 1800. He and his party might indeed be "lost" if the irritation of America swelled to anger against France and other things Republican. Such was the real nature of that "liberty" for which Thomas Jefferson and his friends feared, if the Directory were to drive the United States into war on the side of Britain.

The Federalists in power would not be any less American, or any more willing than Republicans to accept an English prince as President. DuPont's notion could not influence one who had admonished Guillemardet that the Americans meant at any cost to rule alone in America. But Talleyrand could not fail to be impressed by duPont's reasoning that war with the United States would strengthen the British Navy with American sailors, would lay the French West Indies open to the new allies, would invite the population of the Western territory of the United States—"half warrior, half farmer"—to invade the adjacent colonies of Spain and deprive France of any chance of regaining Louisiana before Britain seized it. This would happen just as Talleyrand's negotiations with the Court at Madrid appeared to be making some progress. France simply could not allow the United States to get into the war.[18]

Talleyrand therefore informed Gerry on July 15 that France desired reconciliation. It was the United States, he protested, who were keeping up the friction by ordering attacks upon French men of war and breaking off commercial relations. As the "long suffering of the Executive Directory" could not endure, there would have to be a temporary embargo on American vessels in retaliation. But Talleyrand nullified this diplomatic threat with a diplomatic surrender. The Directory would wait until "irresistibly forced" into hostilities, he said, so great was their "repugnance to consider the United States as enemies": "Since you will depart, sir, hasten, at least, to transmit to your Government this solemn declaration."[19]

On July 22 Talleyrand wrote again, this time to plead that negotiations be resumed in Paris. There need be no loan to France, nor explanations about the speeches of President Adams; and France, he asserted, was already checking the violences in the West Indies upon American commerce and citizens. Then he announced to Gerry on August 3 that the Directory had decreed on July 31 that French privateers be sharply restrained in the West Indies; that no letters of marque be issued there except by the special

18. Morison in MHS Proc., XLIX, 73. AAE EU, Spt. 7, ff. 107–108, Guillemardet to the Spanish foreign minister, June 24, 1798. Lyon, 97–98.
19. ASP FR, II, 220.

agents of the Directory, and these would have to respect the vessels of neutrals and allies.[20]

But Gerry would stay no longer. In fact, he could not, for he had been peremptorily ordered to come home. So Talleyrand turned to the American consul general. Skipwith reported to Secretary Pickering on August 22 the Directory's decree of August 16 that the embargo on American vessels in French ports should be raised immediately. Those American seamen who had been arrested as Englishmen, wrote Skipwith, were being released from French prisons.[21]

In the meantime, William Vans Murray, American minister to the Netherlands, had learned of the French embargo from "a respectable authority at Paris," and had warned American captains to get their vessels out of Rotterdam and Amsterdam because they were under French control. Beyond that he had not been alarmed for he too was thinking about the French colonies in the West Indies: "though hunger makes a tyger dreadful," said he, "nothing so tames a man as very, very spare diet." Talleyrand was no tiger to Vans Murray.[22]

Timothy Pickering, Secretary of State, got a different view from Rufus King, minister at London, who wrote on August 17, "we should constantly remember that the Tiger crouches before he leaps upon his prey." Pickering in fact was so impressed that he used King's phrases word for word when he reported to Congress on January 21, 1799. And he was not persuaded by the latest news from Gerry and Skipwith that Talleyrand was earnest about reconciliation. Our resistance, said Pickering, had surprised France, and increased her resentment. She was determined "to fleece us." If Timothy Pickering was thinking of Louisiana as he had on June 20, 1797, when writing King that France meant to regain it and encircle the Atlantic States, he was much nearer the truth than Vans Murray. Whether man or tiger, Talleyrand did have control now over the foreign affairs of the Directory. He was not as uneasy about the safety of the French colonies in the West Indies as he should have been. His first purpose was to avoid war with the United States so that France might indeed "fleece" them in the Mississippi Valley.[23]

20. *Ibid.*, II, 222–223. Waite's State Papers, III, 370, decree of July 31, 1798.
21. ASP FR, II, 227–228.
22. Vans Murray to J. Q. Adams, July 17, July 20, 1798; AHA Rpt., 1912, 433, 436–438.
23. King (King ed.), II, 392, to Pickering. ASP FR, II, 229–238. See above, p. 273 and below, p. 333 f.

President Adams, once past his first anger at Talleyrand's scheming with X, Y, and Z, preferred to concentrate upon the dangers in a war with France which would necessarily involve the United States with Britain. He came over completely to the position of Albert Gallatin as successive letters from his son, John Quincy Adams, in Berlin, to Mrs. Adams and to Secretary Pickering and to himself, indicated with increasing sureness that the French Government wished very much to have no war with the United States. He soon had the telltale direct from another source for Talleyrand had not waited for his eagerness to seep through Gerry and Skipwith, to Pickering, to the President. William Vans Murray found himself talking confidentially at The Hague on July 17, 1798, with Pichon, the new secretary of the French legation, just arrived from Paris. Pichon had been secretary to Genet and Fauchet in Philadelphia, and more recently in the American division of the French foreign office.[24]

Murray had already written to John Quincy Adams on July 3 about this amiable and solicitous Pichon, and had sensed from their conversation that the French were afraid of a rupture with the United States. Murray believed then that they would go on "plundering as much and whine more." But now on the seventeenth came Pichon with the copy of a letter from Talleyrand, dated July 9, deploring that Gerry would stay no longer. (We should not forget that by this time Victor duPont had conferred with Talleyrand.) Talleyrand's desire to avoid a break was so obvious, and Pichon's acknowledgment that the United States had real grievances and a right to prepare for defense was so frank, that Murray hastened to get this information across the Atlantic to John Adams himself as fast as possible.[25]

The French, reported Vans Murray, were "deeply alarmed." America's "energetic measures" had "stunned them." He did not "write to government" through Secretary Pickering, he said, because the letter might possibly not have come from Talleyrand. Besides, there were too many persons looking over the correspondence in the Department of State; and, for all he knew, he might be venturing beyond purposes of the Government which had developed since his last instructions. But he personally was certain that it had come from Talleyrand.[26]

24. J. Q. Adams, *Writings*, II, 263, 275, 283, 303, 310, 361, letters from February 25 to September 14, 1798. AHA Rpt., 1912, 463, Vans Murray to Pickering, September 1, 1798.

25. Vans Murray to J. Q. Adams, July 3, 1798, *ibid.*, 426–427. As early as April 17, in fact, upon hearing from Pinckney in Paris that Gerry was staying, Murray had reasoned that France dreaded a "rupture." To J. Q. Adams, *ibid.*, 395.

26. Adams, *Works*, VIII, 680–684, Vans Murray to John Adams, July 17, 1798.

John Adams received this private despatch at his home in Quincy, Massachusetts, on October 9, 1798. It was deciphered by Secretary Pickering at Philadelphia and returned to the President on October 18. Here was the key to the problem: the United States could stop French meddling with American commerce without going to war. They could risk waiting for Louisiana. Timothy Pickering did not believe so, but John Adams needed only to be formally assured that France would negotiate upon the basis of his declaration of June 21 to Congress that the United States were "a great, free, powerful, and independent nation."

And Talleyrand? The French minister may have supposed that he was getting on nicely with his American plan, but he was too slow. Spain had surrendered the posts east of the Mississippi and north of the line of the Pinckney Treaty. And, according to a report to the British foreign office after the exposure of the Blount conspiracy, some two thousand American families in Kentucky and Tennessee has accepted the Spanish offer of four hundred acres for each head of a family and two hundred for each male child, with immunity from taxes for a period of years, and had crossed over the Mississippi into Louisiana.[27]

British Purposes—Impressment and Coöperation

JOHN ADAMS had very good cause to prefer Albert Gallatin's reasoning to Timothy Pickering's belief. Britons, too, were reluctant to treat the United States as great, free, powerful, and independent. Liston's intrigue with Chisholm had been shattered by publicity. But British commanders continued to interfere with American shipping in the West Indies. The mixed commissions of the Jay Treaty which were supposed to adjust American debts, British spoliations, and the dispute over the St. Croix River bickered, delayed, and kept the two countries on edge. And, although the British foreign office still pursued the idea which Grenville had begun with Hammond in May, 1794, and renewed with Liston in January, 1797, that the United States might be led into naval coöperation against France, Britain kept on impressing American seamen.[28]

27. Liston Papers, Thornton to Grenville, December 5, 1797. This despatch was received by Grenville on January 2.

28. See above, p. 186 f. Liston Papers, to Grenville, June 27, 1797, on the debt commission; Chipman to Liston, October 23, 25, 1798 regarding the St. Croix; Grenville to Hammond, May 10, 1794; Grenville to Liston, March 18, 1796; November 18, 1796. For Gouverneur Morris in London during March, 1796, see Morris (Morris ed.), II, 158–162. Letters to Washington and Hamilton concerning French and British relations with the United States.

A series of British actions intensified American feelings about sailors and ships, though it must be said that the United States could not avoid all blame. The populace was aiding and protecting numerous British deserters. Captain Mowat of His Majesty's *Assistance* notified Liston that his sailors were escaping into the American woods, and he threatened: "I tell you, sir, that I have not got an American Subject on board, but I will not say how long it will be so." Admiral William Parker expressed himself as opposed to having Americans on British ships. But Admiral Sir Hyde Parker stopped *habeas corpus* proceedings in Jamaica and had those Americans flogged who complained to the American agent. A British squadron finally went so far on November 17, 1798, as to take part of the crew from the American man of war *Baltimore*. President Adams thereupon ordered all American commanders "to resist every future attempt of the kind to the last extremity." Sir Hyde's retort was that he would not govern his conduct by political motives; mischiefs resulting from the President's order, he declared, would have to be "laid to the charge of the American Government." Even though Grenville was half-apologetic in his explanation that the *Baltimore* had been a merchantman and her captain had not obtained the proper commission from the President, Adams had to be content for the future with no more than the assurance that a repetition of the affair was unlikely.[29]

The arrogance of British naval officers reached its height, or depth, as you prefer, in 1799 with Captain Jones of His Majesty's packet boat, *Chesterfield*, moored at the wharf in Philadelphia. The steward's "lump of beeswax" was missing, and he got into such an altercation with the native truckman about it that a constable came aboard to arrest him. Captain Jones tried to toss the constable off the gangplank into the water, but he did not succeed. He then attempted to defend his ship with "half-pikes" against the constable and his posse. He failed again. Then he struck his colors and threw his mail pouches overboard. Robert Liston thought that the "Jacobin faction" had staged the affair to cause trouble between Britain and the United States, but he went in person to see John Adams. They solved the problem finally with an "earnest wish to give satisfaction," but with an agreement also that the United States were hardly so much "enemies" of Britain as to warrant Captain Jones's dumping his mail pouches overboard to prevent

29. Liston Papers, correspondence with Mowat, Grenville, March, 1797–October, 1797; with Grenville about the *Baltimore*, January–June, 1799. King (King ed.), II, 553–555, King to Grenville, March 11, 1799. Pickering to King, January 8, 1799, in *Instructions to Ministers*, V, 49, Department of State.

capture—at the wharf. President Adams must have thought this British seadog an ass. Suspicion lingers that the British minister shared the opinion.[30]

Britain's move toward naval coöperation with the United States appeared to American observers in Europe as the logical outcome of France's refusal to deal with Pinckney, Marshall, and Gerry. Such a proposal might have been advantageous to this country, if it had been designed to be an alliance between equals for the single purpose of defeating France. But it was not. The British Government was willing, very willing indeed to protect certain parts of the commerce of the United States against the "common enemy." Grenville had made his overture depend, however, upon compensations that would have subordinated the United States to Britain at once. There were contingents also which might have wrecked their hopes of empire in the future.[31]

The British fleet was to protect American shipping, provided American seamen were put under the command of British officers. That is, the United States would have to acknowledge Britain's superior position by giving away authority over their own citizens. A better example of subversion of sovereignty could hardly be asked. Convoys would be supplied to American merchantmen, excepting those which came from the ports of the enemy. That is, all maritime interests of the United States were not to be protected by their ally. Only those would be in which Britain herself took an interest—such as the direct trade between the United States and Britain. Britain reserved to herself to decide what American commerce was permissible. It was not to be a coöperative enterprise between the navies of two independent nations.[32]

Grenville coupled this plan also with the designs which Britain still had upon the French island of San Domingo in spite of the fact that her forces under Howe, and then Simcoe, had failed to overcome the Negroes and yellow fever. If the United States would approve of these designs, Grenville implied, Britain might go so far as to countenance their obtaining New Orleans and the Floridas from Spain. Certainly the latter suggestion was calculated to allure all Americans save the most provincial of seaboard merchants who clung to the old traffic with the West Indies as preferable to every other interest of the American people.

30. Liston Papers, to Grenville, March 4, 1799. Pickering to King, March 6 in *Instructions to Ministers*, V, 76.

31. J. Q. Adams, *Writings*, II, 260, to Gerry, February 20, 1798. AHA Rpt., 1912, 383–384, Vans Murray to J. Q. Adams, March 12, 1798.

32. Liston Papers, Grenville to Liston, January 27, 1797.

Grenville's whole proposal rested upon a presumption that fairly shouted: Beware. The American Government had to realize, of course, that Britain reserved the right to make peace with France, when and in what manner she herself saw fit as developments occurred in Europe. Naturally enough, Britain would do this unless bound in close alliance to the United States, possibly even then. But there was an even more dangerous insinuation in this reserved right. Before the summer of 1797 had passed, Grenville's agent, Malmesbury, had been instructed, when negotiating peace with France, to get New Orleans and adjacent territory, if he had the opportunity. Which was the more genuine, the offer of Louisiana to the United States or the effort to get it for Britain herself? In view of Pitt's previous interest and subsequent actions, it would seem that Britain's interest in Louisiana for herself took precedence.[33]

Liston set out to develop the plan as he had been directed, taking care that the United States might not now compromise the Jay Treaty while endeavoring to restore good relations with France. In April he notified those whom he knew to be "friends" that the British commanders would protect American merchantmen, especially those bound for the British West Indies. He found Secretary Pickering "much pleased" and "one of the most violent Antigallicans" he had ever met. But meanwhile he had also got himself so entangled with Chisholm and Blount that he had to use the discretion which Grenville had allowed. When Liston reported in July, therefore, he had not yet presented his memorial to the American Government upon the British interests in the dispute with France. Grenville approved this delay, as very well he might, considering Liston's embarrassment by the exposure of Senator Blount; but he ordered Liston in September to keep watch "with utmost vigilance" and to employ "every exertion" in behalf of Britain as the negotiations progressed at Paris.[34]

John Adams had been thinking over these questions for himself. He had arrived at a decision while the Senate was still hearing the testimony against Blount, even before Marshall's reports had begun to come from Paris. Following the example set by Washington, Adams asked his Cabinet officers, January 24, 1798, for their opinions as to what should be done if the mission to France failed; in the process, he made perfectly clear what was his own attitude toward Britain.

33. Guyot, 409–410. Malmesbury, III, 384–385. See below, p. 402 f.

34. Liston Papers, Grenville to Liston, April, 1797; Liston to Grenville, April 18; to Grenville, July 13; Grenville to Liston, September 9. See above, p. 271 f.

Would it not be the soundest policy, wrote Adams, even in case of war between the United States and France, for the United States to remain silent toward Britain and wait for her overture? Even then, would it not be imprudent to connect themselves in any manner that might keep them from "embracing the first favorable moment or opportunity to make a separate peace?" They could expect no benefits from Britain, he said, which her own interest would not impel her to extend to them without prior stipulation. What if Britain were to fall from the dangerous precipice on which she stood? Would not "shaking hands" drag the United States down also?[35]

No evidence has to be distorted to support that hypothesis. If France had broken through Britain's power and had forced William Pitt to negotiate in defeat, the French invasion of America for which Collot had just done the groundwork and which Talleyrand was then contemplating, would have played havoc with the interests of the United States beyond the Appalachians and their enterprises in the West Indies. But this, of course, could have happened without any connection between the United States and Britain.

The Secretary of War, James McHenry, immediately forwarded the President's queries to Alexander Hamilton, and then incorporated Hamilton's opinions almost verbatim as his own in the report which he submitted to Adams on February 15, 1798. McHenry—that is Hamilton—opposed declaring war upon France but favored a "mitigated hostility" still leaving "a door open for negotiation." He outlined military and naval legislation much like that which Congress subsequently passed after the X Y Z papers had arrived. He agreed that there should be no formal arrangement with any other nation but proposed that they sound Britain for a loan, convoys, perhaps ten ships of the line, and "a cooperation in case of open rupture, pointing to the Floridas, Louisiana, and the South American possessions of Spain." It was to be assumed that in all probability the Spanish alliance with France would draw Spain into war with the United States.[36]

McHenry revised Hamilton's estimates as to the size of the provisional army and militia, inserted the points with regard to a loan, convoys, and ten ships of the line, and specifically designated New Orleans "to be ours in case of conquest." Hamilton had written that "all on this side the Mississippi must be ours, including both Floridas." Important for us to note at this point—as essential to

35. Adams, *Works*, VIII, 561–562.
36. *Ibid.*, VIII, 562 n.

an understanding of his subsequent actions—Hamilton also said to McHenry that he thought the overthrow of England and the invasion of the United States very possible, so much so that the Government must make its calculations upon those assumptions. But Hamilton wrote further:

> As to England, it is believed to be best, in any event, to avoid *alliance*. Mutual interest will command as much from her as Treaty. If she can maintain her own ground, she will not see us fall a prey—if she cannot, Treaty will be a public bond. Should we make a Treaty with her & observe it, we take all the chances of her fall. Should France endeavour to detach us from a Treaty, if made, by offering advantageous terms of Peace, it would be a difficult & dangerous task to our Government to resist the popular cry for acceptance of her terms. 'Twill be best not to entangle.

This amounted to no less than Adams had already said on January 24[37]

The Attorney General, Charles Lee, did not seek the advice of Hamilton before replying to the President. He gave his own opinion to Adams on March 8 while the first reports from Pinckney, Marshall, and Gerry were being deciphered. Lee wished to avoid an intimate connection with Britain but he would declare war upon France. He would open American ports to British privateers, arm American merchantmen, prohibit all trade with France; and if Spain followed France, he would send an army to take New Orleans. This was the straightforward counsel of a Virginian Federalist, brother of "Light-Horse Harry," devotee of Washington, opponent of Monroe, close friend of Marshall. We must admit that there was a great deal to be said in support of it, knowing as we do the real purposes of Talleyrand.[38]

Secretaries Pickering and Wolcott, it appears, did not answer the President's queries in writing. But Timothy Pickering wrote two letters to Hamilton on March 25—sending the lawyer in New York information out of John Marshall's reports that were still a state secret. As Pickering put it, he did so of himself "without the privity of anyone." In the light of this information, what should they say to the British Government? Their opponents, wrote Pickering, were insinuating that they had made an offensive and defensive alliance, but the truth was that not a word as yet had been sent to Rufus King. As for himself, he would wish to send

37. McHenry (Steiner ed.), 291–295. Hamilton to McHenry in February, 1798.
38. Adams, *Works*, VIII, 563 n. See above, p. 295 f.

"provisional orders" to King for that purpose. Hamilton's ideas on the subject would be highly acceptable. In addition, what should they do in respect to Louisiana? He had just heard from Humphreys in Madrid that Gayoso had been ordered to evacuate the posts in accordance with the Pinckney Treaty.

"Perhaps these orders," said Pickering, "may have resulted from Spain's seeing or fearing the necessity of ceding Louisiana to France, and hence concluding that she might as well do a grateful thing to us before surrender." But his mind did not linger over gratitude. He went right on to tell Hamilton how easily Louisiana could be defended with troops commanding the Mississippi at its mouth, others halfway up to New Orleans, and others at the entrance from the sea into Lake Pontchartrain. "The Spanish force in all Louisiana is small," said he, "probably not rising to a thousand men, from the Balize to the Missouri." It requires no imagination on our part to appreciate what Timothy Pickering wished that day to have done about Louisiana.[39]

Hamilton's ideas were forthcoming by return post. He reiterated what he had said to McHenry, and in a previous letter to Pickering as well on March 17: that the independence of the United States had to be maintained. But his thoughts were developing under reflection as they had in 1794 when there was danger of war with Britain. He now qualified his opposition to an alliance. He did not favor making it immediately; public opinion was not prepared for it; it might embarrass acceptance of offers from France that were satisfactory. No, he would not send provisional orders to King. He would wait. In the meantime it would be desirable to get Britain engaged, as he had suggested to McHenry. Britain should lodge powers with her minister in Philadelphia equal to exigencies that might arise. It would be good, too, if she could be persuaded to send "a dozen frigates to pursue the directions of this government." So it would have been, indeed, if Grenville's purpose had not been quite the reverse of letting the American Government direct the British fleet.

As for Louisiana, Hamilton did not at this time take up with Pickering's hint that the United States should seize and defend against France. Rather, Hamilton would accept it "absolutely" if Spain would cede or, if Spain would not, he would take over with an engagement to restore to Spain. In any case, however, it was evident that he would miss no chance to anticipate France, and

39. Hamilton Papers, XXX, 4212. Pickering Papers, VIII, 241, 536. Hamilton (Hamilton ed.), VI, 272, 276.

Britain too, in that quarter. There is no question but that Alexander Hamilton had the vision of empire.[40]

Supported by Hamilton again as in 1797—although he may not then have known it and after the bitterness of defeat in 1800 could not perceive it—President Adams made his decision of January 24, 1798, the basis for the policy of the United States on the one hand with respect to Britain, her overtures, and interests in the western world and on the other, with regard to France and her dependent, Spain. Instead of the "provisional orders" which Pickering wanted to send, this significant instruction went to Rufus King in London on April 2, 1798, from the Secretary of State: "In the first place, threatening as is the aspect of our affairs with France, the President does not deem it expedient at this time to make any advances to Great Britain. The interest of her own commerce will on some occasions lead her to afford convoys to ours."[41]

If the affairs with France came to actual war, the instructions continued, there were abundant causes for the United States, in quest of their own security, to fight "as long as the respective interests of Great Britain and the United States should require it." No offensive and defensive alliance, however, would be necessary to assure that. Instead, the two governments should agree from time to time upon such operations as circumstances made necessary. The United States would guard Britain's colonies with their troops. To aid in this, however, they would like six ships of the line. The inference was that these would be under the direction of the American Government. They had been satisfied in the past to have Spain as their neighbor in Louisiana. But if war came, Spain as ally of France would have to suffer, for they would find it "expedient, perhaps necessary" to seize Louisiana and West Florida. These were the "Key to the Western World" without which the waters of the Mississippi and its branches would "lose more than half their value" to the United States. Pickering admitted that arms were scarce, and he ordered King to secure them abroad. But within a year, he declared, they would be manufacturing their own cannon.

John Adams, then, would join with Britain in case of absolute necessity. His country was not strong enough as yet to take a completely independent course. It was not to be many more years before his son, John Quincy Adams, with his eyes upon the Far West and the Pacific Coast, would assert that the United States

40. Hamilton (Hamilton ed.), VI, 269, 278, March 17, 27, 1798, to Pickering. Hamilton (Lodge ed.), X, 280.
41. Adams, *Works*, IX, 268, 293 (1809); X, 147 (1815). *Instructions to Ministers*, IV, 256–264, Department of State.

should not "come in as a cock-boat in the wake of the British man-of-war." But in 1798, the American minister in London had to be instructed to urge that Britain should authorize her minister in Philadelphia "to concert with us such measures of cooperation." There had followed immediately, however, this very significant reservation "for the part *we* shall take in the war will be confined to this side of the Atlantic." (One principle in the famous doctrine of 1823 was already taking shape.) And then had come an insinuation—which Rufus King might perhaps use as a counterstroke to any British argument that the United States ought to be afraid of an invading French army: "The safety of the British colonies on the Continent," declared his instructions, "may depend on the military aid of the United States."[42]

Notwithstanding the excitement and the rumors of the time in both America and the British Isles, the two governments could have had no genuine fear that there would be French military operations on this side of the Atlantic until France had first broken Britain's control of the sea. Liston reported on April 2 the rumor that the French flag was flying at Pensacola. There was much talk of a French invasion of the British Isles and interest in the Irish Rebellion. It may have been good propaganda. Vans Murray wrote in March that he considered the French invasion of England, "to be made and to fail," the great event which was to "change the tide" and "settle the destiny of Europe for ages." But Napoleon in reality was off for Malta, Egypt, and Britain's routes to India and the Orient.[43]

If France found it difficult to invade Britain, how much more so would it have been to reach America and to maintain French forces here against the British fleet! There was, of course, the very great possibility on the other hand that Britain would make peace with France and leave the United States to look to their own defenses. This is just what did happen, before Napoleon turned to complete Talleyrand's plan for America.[44]

Louisiana and San Domingo

JOHN ADAMS was ready in the spring of 1798 to help Britain protect her continental colonies in America from French invasion, for that would defend the United States themselves at the same time.

42. J. Q. Adams, *Memoirs*, VI, 179, November 7, 1823. *Instructions to Ministers*, IV, 256–264. King (King ed.), II, 296–297.

43. Liston Papers, Liston to Grenville, April 2, 1798. Murray to J. Q. Adams, March 12, 1798, AHA Rpt., 1912, 384. James in AHR, XXX, 50.

44. See above, p. 295 f., and below, p. 405 f.

He had other thoughts about French and British rivalry among the islands of the Caribbean. Aid given to the great Negro, Toussaint Louverture, would be an effective blow at France. San Domingo was one of her richest possessions; its Creoles were wealthy and influential in Parisian society. Moreover Adams was as aware as Talleyrand of the importance of American commercial interests in the West Indies, and determined to protect them against France even with arms, much as he feared the consequences of war. He knew that Britain, too, was opposed to American trading in the Caribbean. And he was of no mind to increase the opportunities of British commanders and admiralty courts by helping Britain to oust France from San Domingo, least of all to create a British monopoly of West Indian commerce.

When therefore Robert Liston endeavored to exploit the rising war spirit of Congress in May, 1798, and establish the plan for naval coöperation, he found the Administration as a whole thinking that a rupture with France was "almost unavoidable" and the "American Ministers"—Pickering, Wolcott, and McHenry—fixed, he said, on "the conquest of the Floridas and Louisiana for themselves and the acquisition of St. Domingo (if not of the other French Islands) by Great Britain." But the President, though angry with France, was not so sure of a "cordial reception in England." The Administration feared that Britain might make a separate peace with France and permit the Directory to give its whole attention to vengeance upon the United States. The Administration was vexed with British interference with American commerce particularly in San Domingo at the Mole St. Nicholas. It had a third grievance over the British exercise of visit and search upon vessels while under the convoy of American ships of war.[45]

Grenville answered this report on June 8 as soon as it reached London. He too expected war between the United States and France, though France, he knew, would not be the one to declare it. Rufus King was seeking war materials and had suggested naval coöperation as he had been instructed in April. Grenville saw difficulty in the American plan for recruiting sailors and placing British ships in the American service. He would not yield in regard to visit and search of merchantmen under convoy. Britain could not depart, he said, from usages long established. The American apprehension that there might be a separate peace was "certainly solid and well founded," for, if the French invasion of England failed, or France abandoned the scheme, it was "by no means improbable that some offer of Peace may suddenly be made." Britain would accept it,

45. Liston Papers, to Grenville, May 2, 1798, received June 7.

"if free from all engagements to other powers." The United States
had better hurry, therefore, and make their agreement with her.
She would unquestionably fulfill engagements previously contracted. She would view American conquest of Louisiana as a
"matter of satisfaction" instead of "jealousy" provided it were
counterbalanced by her own acquisition of San Domingo. Grenville would investigate the admiralty court at the Mole St. Nicholas and have it discontinued, if it were irregularly established.[46]

Here was a startling turn of affairs. Did it mean frankly that
Pitt and Grenville were prepared now to abandon Pitt's interest
in the Mississippi Valley, that "Granary of America," and the Floridas, his "Southern Farms," if the United States would undertake
a war with France in order to secure for Britain those West Indian
islands which they had guaranteed to France in the Treaty of 1778?
At first glance it may appear so. If other events then feared, such
as the French invasion of England, had come in proper sequence,
it might possibly have happened so.

We must not, however, overlook variables in the problem at the
time, which, far from making New Orleans appear inconsequential
to Britain, on the contrary made it more important to her as a lure
for American support. The thought of France in control of New
Orleans was the one thing which was likely to rouse hysteria against
France among Republicans as well as Federalists in the United
States. The loss of New Orleans by Spain and France would weaken
the hold of both Latin powers elsewhere in this hemisphere, particularly upon the coast of the Gulf of Mexico and the islands about
the Caribbean. If Britain could not gain New Orleans for herself,
her chances would improve in other quarters through its falling
into the hands of the United States.

It did not have, necessarily, to do that, or to remain in their
hands if it did. Britain's tentative offer in 1798 was predicated
entirely upon an American break with France and agreement with
Britain to guarantee her expansion into San Domingo. If the United
States did not fulfill their contract, Britain need not worry about
failing to complete hers. Besides, it was linked with the notice which
Grenville gave with equal frankness that Britain would hold herself free to make her own peace with France. This could mean
terms between them in regard to New Orleans and the Mississippi
Valley that would make the United States very unhappy. Nations
which have come into a situation for professed reasons, finding
themselves in command of it because of subsequent events, unforeseen or not stipulated, have often remained for quite a different

46. Liston Papers, Grenville to Liston, June 8, 1798.

set of motives. Filipinos would understand this today perhaps more readily than ourselves. Pitt and Grenville did not abandon the British desire for New Orleans in 1798. They merely set it to one side.

Even before Grenville's reply had reached him, Robert Liston had discovered that John Adams sensed as much. Liston wrote on June 12 that, to his surprise, the ideas of the American Government had changed. Whereas the "Ministers" had given him the impression in May that they favored Britain's acquiring San Domingo, he now heard Pickering talk about a "plan" for the blacks. Liston demurred that if they were free and independent they would have dangerous influence upon the neighboring British colonies and the Southern States of America. Pickering argued that they could never be returned to slavery under either Britain or France, and they had better be free and independent than free and under the rule of France. He did not discuss the point of their freedom under Britain.[47]

This was a matter which should not be delayed as the United States prepared that summer for war with France. The British minister visited the President in September at his home in Quincy. He found John Adams, he said, with "little or no reserve in talking of political subjects." Adams told him that his own mind was made up. He himself would enter into engagements "without scruple and without loss of time." But he had to wait, for "publick approbation"; the people were "meditating"; "it would not perhaps be wise to disturb their meditations."[48]

This picture of the American people quietly reflecting upon alliance with Britain while furious with France in the summer of 1798, does not seem to have properly amused and informed Liston. He agreed with Adams that they should not disturb the meditation. He would be ready, he said, when Adams was ready, to establish the plan of American and British coöperation upon a footing of "perfect reciprocity."

The President, though voluble on "political subjects," was not so inclined to speak of their details. He would listen, said Adams, "with attention and candour." He wished Britain to make the overture. Liston complied eagerly. The United States would provide the seamen, and Britain the ships. War with France was inevitable. Spain was likely to remain neutral, and the French Directory might

47. Liston Papers, to Grenville, marked confidential, June 12, 1798 received July 11.
48. Liston Papers, two letters to Grenville, September 27, 1798, from Boston, marked received November 26; another from Philadelphia, January 31, 1799, received by Grenville on March 9.

think it wise to keep her so. But this ought not to stop the United States—that is, Liston hoped it would not, as he came to the real point at issue: San Domingo in return for Louisiana.

So far Adams had listened with "attention and candour." Now he replied to Liston with "candour," revealing specifically what he had thought as long before as 1783. The geography of the West Indies made their dependence upon the North American continent natural. They had to have its provisions. This meant that ultimately they would come under its economic domination. Moreover the French Revolution had given a new turn to political opinion in America. The prevailing conjecture now was that the large islands at least would become independent. They might still be connected with Europe by alliance and friendship, but they would not be in subjection. In short, America opposed Europe's "exclusive" mercantile and colonial systems. Adams admitted that freedom and independence for Toussaint Louverture's blacks in San Domingo would endanger slavery in the Southern States of his own country. But he chose for the moment to play upon the British minister. As France could not supply the islands, and Britain seemed to be abandoning them, he said "it was natural that they should throw themselves into the arms of America."[49]

Liston reported immediately to Grenville that there were "speculative politicians in this country." He might have added that the American President, for one, was not permitting anger with France to confuse his "meditating" upon the vital interest of his countrymen in the trade with San Domingo and their need for peace with Spain at this time, if they were to reach their ultimate goal in the Mississippi Valley.

John Adams knew that he was handling explosives as he intimated that the United States might enter into some agreement with Toussaint and his blacks. He assured Liston that apprehension lest he give offense to Britain, which appeared to have other views on San Domingo, had kept him from adopting the measure. And he was quite right. When Grenville heard in July of Secretary Pickering's remarks to Liston, he had expressed "horror" to Rufus King that the American Government "might be disposed to countenance the establishment of a Republic of Blacks in St. Domingo."[50]

John Adams had taken part in too many European negotiations before this not to understand the meaning in diplomacy of the word "horror." He let the matter rest just as it was upon his conversa-

49. *Ibid.* Treudley, 95. Adams, *Works,* VIII, 79, to Robert Livingston, July 3, 1783, from Paris.
50. King (King ed.), II, 367–368, King to Pickering, July 14, 1798.

tion with Liston at Quincy, and awaited developments. Liston continued trying to get the plan of coöperation under way, and succeeded in having the guns which were to be lent to the United States from the British stores at Halifax given to them outright. Pickering kept in touch with affairs in San Domingo, Toussaint's approaches to the United States, the British evacuation of the Mole St. Nicholas, the raids of British cruisers upon American commerce, and protested to Rufus King "of how trifling consequence to the *British nation* but how pernicious the effect on the public mind in the United States!" Grenville complained that American citizens had not responded with "members" of their Government to the "equally beneficial" plan of coöperation, and nursed his "horror." But he was not to shudder for long. Other events were surely coming which were to modify John Adams' conception of the best policy for the United States with regard to the West Indies in their relation to Louisiana.[51]

One in fact had already occurred. The great adventurer, Francisco de Miranda, was no longer in the French Army. He was again upon the British scene with his "grand Plan." Whatever his inconsistencies, Miranda was certain of one thing always. He would be on the opposite side from Spain in every enterprise. The British Government was intrigued again as at the time of the quarrel with Spain over Nootka Sound.[52]

"We Are Friends with Spain"

MIRANDA's plan for revolutionizing Spanish America attracted William Pitt. British ships and goods would be welcome in Latin American republics as they were not in Spanish colonies; uprisings would injure the enemy through her ally; and Pitt knew well that French statesmen were maneuvering toward Louisiana. The restoration of a French empire of the first magnitude in America could not but worry the possessor of Canada, Jamaica, and the Bahamas. For the same reason, Miranda's program might appeal to the United States—particularly at a time when their relations with France were going from bad to worse as their commissioners met insult and rebuff. Besides, Britain should on general principles keep affairs in that quarter of the world closely in hand for the future

51. Liston Papers, to Grenville, November 7, 1798; to Grenville, June 12; Wentworth to Liston, July 24, August 10, November 23, 1798, from Nova Scotia Archives, v. LII; and Grenville to Liston, January 19, 1799. *Instructions to Ministers,* Department of State, V, 7, Pickering to King, December 15, 1798. Liston Papers, Grenville to Liston, December, 1798, draft of No. 20.

52. Robertson, *Miranda,* I, 161–187. See above, pp. 135–136.

advantage of the British Empire. Pitt, therefore, gave Miranda another hearing in the latter part of January, 1798, and soon put the American minister in touch with the situation.[53]

Rufus King reported to Secretary Pickering, February 7, that "the prospect of our being engaged in the war has renewed the project that on more than one occasion has been meditated against South America." The objective would be "the complete Independence of South America to be effected by the co-operation of England and the U.S." All of this was true, and it was accomplished years later in large part by Britain and the United States working in virtual coöperation. But it was not the whole truth in 1798, as King learned almost immediately.[54]

Britain was interested in South America, but more involved in the affairs of Europe. Pitt saw that if France overthrew the Spanish Government and took Portugal, Britain herself would be in greater danger. There might really be an attempt to invade the British Isles. There had just been a mutiny in the British fleet. Ireland was on the verge of rebellion. The members of the British cabinet therefore deliberated upon Miranda's plan with these things facing them. They came to two conclusions and notified the American minister.[55]

Rufus King, accordingly, had two very significant facts to report to Secretary Pickering on February 26, 1798. First: "if Spain is able to prevent the overthrow of her present Government and to escape being brought under the entire controul of France, England (between whom and Spain, notwithstanding the war, a certain understanding appears to exist) will at present engage in no scheme to deprive Spain of the possession of Sth. America." But if France overpowered Spain, Britain would take up with Miranda's plan and would act upon the second decision of the cabinet—which was to propose then to the United States at Philadelphia that the two nations coöperate in putting Miranda's ideas into execution.[56]

Again on April 6, King reported that Britain had informed Spain that "she will not countenance or assist the Spanish Colonies in becoming independent, but that she will join her in resisting the endeavours of others to accomplish it, provided that Spain will oppose the views of France against her own Dominions and those of Portugal." He notified Pickering also that Ireland had been put

53. Robertson in AHA Rpt., 1907, I, 318–321.
54. King (King ed.), II, 278–281.
55. See Pallain, 310–321, for Talleyrand on Spain and Portugal. Rose, 339–364, for the Irish Rebellion.
56. King (King ed.), II, 283–286; III, 561, King's diary, February 15.

under martial law and preparations were being made to meet the French invasion.[57]

Here was evidence enough, when it reached the Department of State, that the United States would be unwise to count upon British coöperation in attacking Spanish America. But John Adams had already mistrusted British "secret plots" and preferred to build upon the good will of Thomas Pinckney's agreement with Godoy in 1795. Britain's coöperation on the seas was one thing, in the mid-continent of America quite another. Her agents had not ceased their intriguing among the Indians of the Northwest after the Jay Treaty, Wayne's victory at Fallen Timbers, and the Treaty of Greenville. Nor was the influence in the West of such a hero as George Rogers Clark to be forgotten. Clark denounced the Government in Philadelphia at this time and crossed over the Mississippi into Spanish territory rather than surrender his commission in the French Army.[58]

In view of these circumstances, it was preferable to make immediate capital of Spain's withdrawal from the posts in the Southwest, her grant of the right of deposit for American produce at New Orleans, and her permission to survey the boundary along the thirty-first degree of latitude—those desires of the men of the "Western waters" which, if gratified, would transform their dangerous tendency to separate from the Eastern States into loyalty to the Union. Proposals came straight to the President of the United States from Miranda in London, nicely timed to catch John Adams on the rise of popular fury against France. But he curtly dismissed them with: "We are friends with Spain. If we were enemies, would the project be useful to us? It will not be in character for me to answer the letter. Will any notice of it, in any manner, be proper?" Clearly Adams doubted it. No notice was taken.[59]

It was transparent that Pitt and Grenville had set their propositions before Rufus King upon the definite understanding that Spain would have to succumb in Europe first before Britain would strike at France with Miranda in South America. This fact was strangely obscured to Rufus King in London, either by his Federalist disgust with Gerry's diplomacy and bitterness toward France for plotting disunion in the United States, or by his belief in the report that

57. *Ibid.*, II, 304–306.
58. Adams, *Works*, VIII, 583–587, Pickering to Adams, August 21, 1798, forwarding King's reports of February and April and other information regarding Miranda. See above, p. 261.
59. Adams, *Works*, VIII, 569, 581; 600, to Pickering, October 3, 1798. But see Robertson in AHA Rpt., 1907, I, 332, for a different view.

a British expedition and arrangements at Trinidad were going ahead anyway to prepare for eventualities, or because he was afraid that France would succeed in revolutionizing Spain and would then force its iniquitous "System" into the Americas.[60]

King reported accurately to Pickering, but he himself did not think the problem through. There was no conjecture in his reports that France might prefer to slip into the place of Spain in Louisiana by diplomacy, rather than stir British anxiety over Canada or American fears about the Mississippi Valley. And for whatever reason, he did not tell Miranda of the reservations and provisos by the British cabinet.[61]

Instead, King encouraged Miranda to get in touch with Alexander Hamilton and Henry Knox, to send over his special agent, Caro, and appeal directly to President Adams. King himself became so enthusiastic in his letters to Pickering and Hamilton that he lost sight of the fact that the plan of Miranda could never succeed without the full coöperation of Britain. He wrote to Hamilton on July 31, 1798: "The Destiny of the new world, and I have a full and firm persuasion that it will be both happy and glorious, is in our hands. We have a right and it is our duty to deliberate and act, not as secondaries, but as Principals." To Miranda on the following day, he declared that his advices from home exhibited "a fine Picture of what France has not yet seen; a nation of freemen rising with scorn and arms against her!"[62]

It was true the United States would appropriate the "Destiny of the new world" before long, and within King's own lifetime. But in 1798, Britain and France were still the "Principals." It was because they were unable to live at peace with one another in Europe that the United States were rising to superiority over them in this hemisphere. The United States at that time had still to have grave reckonings with both. As for his confidence in Miranda, Rufus King might have given more thought to Grenville's remark to him on August 16 that "none but Englishmen and their Descendants knew how to make a Revolution."[63]

Hamilton's "Plot"—"Energy Is Wisdom"

JOHN ADAMS would not answer Miranda, but Alexander Hamilton did. When he first heard again in the spring of 1798 from that

60. King (King ed.), II, 300–301, 305–306.
61. King (King ed.), III, 563–564, King's diary, March 23. Robertson in AHA Rpt., 1907, I, 324.
62. King (King ed.), II, 375. Robertson, *Miranda*, I, 179.
63. King (King ed.), II, 392, to Pickering, August 17, 1798.

roaming zealot with whom he had talked in 1784 about the libera-
tion of Spanish America, Hamilton dismissed the idea as absurd.
He wrote across Miranda's letter of February 7, 1798: "I shall not
answer because I consider him as an intriguing adventurer." In
May, Hamilton protested to King against Britain's "abusive captures of our vessels." Why was the British Government doing it!
What could be gained "to counteract the mischievous tendency of
abuses"? But the fear that France would attack this country gripped
Hamilton more and more strongly as news came of Talleyrand's
play upon the American commissioners in Paris; he soon found
interest in the proposed adventure and got better control of his
irritation at Britain. With misgivings that Britain might fall and
America suffer invasion, there also came over him a fascination.
This could be a great opportunity for his country, and for himself
—the chance for the military fame to which he had always aspired.
Four years before, when there was fear of war with Britain, he
had declared that "wars oftener proceed from angry and perverse
passions, than from cool calculation of interest." His behavior now
belied this observation as the rule of his own conduct.[64]

What Alexander Hamilton did in the months that followed has
been called a plot comparable to the affair for which Senator Blount
was impeached. And there is the worse implication that Hamilton
pursued his own ends even to the overturn of the American Government. John Adams said: "this man is stark mad, or I am. He
knows nothing of the character, the principles, the feelings, the
opinions and prejudices of this nation. If Congress should adopt
this system, it would produce an instantaneous insurrection of the
whole nation from Georgia to New Hampshire."[65]

To look at the matter through Hamilton's personal ambition,
however, is to minimize significant actions on his part and, in
consequence, to misjudge both his motives and his object. He would
indeed direct the President, if he could, through his own henchmen in the Cabinet, for he did not scruple to do things behind
the back any more now than when he had been dealing with Beckwith and Hammond to Jefferson's discomfiture. He would change
the judicial system, even amend the Constitution. Alexander Hamilton was without question a partisan leader. He was self-seeking.
He set out upon a course which thoroughly entitled the man who

64. Hamilton Papers, XXX, 4202–4203. Hamilton did not record the date when he
received this letter. Hamilton (Lodge ed.), X, 283–284; V, 99, to Washington, April 14,
1794. See above, p. 177.
65. Adams to H. G. Otis, quoted from Morison, Otis, I, 162. For Blount, see above,
p. 273 f.

was President to rail at him. But he did not pursue that course beyond the limit of the interest of their country. Nor did he defy John Adams' counterdecisions.[66]

When Hamilton heard again from Miranda, Congress had passed, with the approval of Adams, the measures preparatory to war which Hamilton had suggested through McHenry and Pickering. The break with France had become all but complete. Hamilton himself, notwithstanding Adams' displeasure, was organizing the army, as virtually Washington's chief of staff. It was generally expected that he would be the real commanding officer, inasmuch as Washington would not take the field. Because of these developments, therefore, his reply to Miranda on August 22, 1798, through King at London, was very different from his opinion of the preceding spring.[67]

Now, Hamilton wrote to King that he wished the enterprise "much to be undertaken." He would be glad, however, if the principal agency should be in the United States, "they to furnish the whole land force if necessary." The command in that case, he remarked, would "very naturally fall" upon him, and he hoped he should "disappoint no favorable anticipation." The sum of the results to be accomplished would be "the independence of the separate territory under a moderate government, with the joint guaranty of the cooperating powers, stipulating equal privileges in commerce."

To make it certain that those in the British Government with whom King conversed should appreciate this equality between their country and the United States, Hamilton asserted that Britain alone could not "insure the accomplishment of the object." The United States, he conceded, were not yet ready for the undertaking, but they would "ripen fast"—if an "efficient negotiation" were started upon the terms which he outlined. In the accompanying note to Miranda himself, Hamilton said expressly that Britain should supply the fleet and place a "competent authority" with someone in the United States. Miranda's presence here too would be "extremely essential."

Then Hamilton declared to Miranda, in so many words, what surely was not necessary to tell King, minister for John Adams, but what we must not overlook if we would keep clear Hamilton's

66. Adams, *Works*, I, 514 ff., narrative by C. F. Adams. Hamilton (Lodge ed.), X, 278 ff., successive letters to Pickering, Wolcott, others; 329–336, to J. Dayton, on Constitution.

67. Hamilton Papers, XXX, 4219–4223, Miranda to Hamilton, April 6, 1798. Adams, *Works*, I, 529. Gibbs, II, 71, Pickering to Wolcott, July 11, 1798.

course in regard to the enterprise: "I could personally have no participation in it unless patronized by the government of this country."[68]

This statement alone completely distinguishes Hamilton's "plot" from the schemings of Chisholm and Blount, of Wilkinson and his associates, and even from the actions of George Rogers Clark—although Clark had some justification in the fact that the Alliance of 1778 with France had still to be abrogated properly notwithstanding the Act of Congress on July 7, 1798. There are no grounds for doubting the honesty of Hamilton's declaration to Miranda. If the suspicion persists that he had some subtle reason to be insincere with Miranda, one has only to read the letter which he wrote to his henchman, Timothy Pickering, Secretary of State, just a week later. Should President Adams hold out against his appointment as second to Washington in command, said Hamilton, "in the last resort, I shall be inclined to have much deference for his wishes."[69]

The correct interpretation of Hamilton's conduct lies in the fact that he believed that France sooner or later would so act as to make war inevitable. He therefore would be prepared with a national army. War would jeopardize further the interests of the United States on the seas; it would cause internal friction, possibly violence; it would threaten ruin to their future in the West. He felt that the spirit of the nation would be equal to this ordeal, for he declared in his letter to King on August 22: "The indications are to my mind conclusive that we are approaching fast to as a great unanimity as any country ever experienced, and that our energies will be displayed in proportion to whatever exigencies shall arise." He wrote this in the face of rising opposition to the new Federal taxes and the Alien and Sedition Acts of Congress.[70]

From Alexander Hamilton's point of view, a war which gave opportunity to seize the Floridas and Louisiana would subdue if it did not silence. It would check the enthusiasms for France among those who were also personally interested in Western lands and settlers. Whatever their immediate connections with Spaniards in New Orleans, it would soon bind the men of the West to the Union. It would push into the background local friction over taxes and stringent legislation by Congress. Hamilton would never forget how

68. Hamilton (Lodge ed.), X, 314–316. Other letters from Miranda, August 17, October 19, 1798, and October 4, 1799, are in the Hamilton Papers, XXXI, 4397; XX, 220; LVI, no number.

69. Hamilton (Hamilton ed.), VI, 355, to Pickering, August 29, 1798. For the Act of Congress, see above, p. 294.

70. Hamilton (Lodge ed.), X, 314–315.

the Whisky Boys had been dissuaded from local rebellion against national authority.[71]

As for his own ability to mold opinion and then to direct the Government into and through this crisis, Hamilton saw that the threat of war with France had brought the Cabinet more than ever under his influence. The reaction of the President himself to the X Y Z papers seemed to indicate that Adams' ideas, too, had come more into line with his own. Proper developments might lead them still farther. His friends in the Federalist party dominated Congress. General Washington had "resumed his station at the head of our armies." That he had long since become susceptible to the influence of him who was now "second in command," Alexander Hamilton was fully aware. "A noble career," "great destinies," he declared, were before this country.[72]

Hamilton could not avoid perceiving, however, that war with France would lay the United States open to British manipulation. But could not Britain's own interests in Canada, the West Indies, and Latin America be counted upon, even so, to assure naval support and protection against European armadas? Would not this happen, if for no other reason than that such cover was necessary while the land forces of the United States broke down the French and Spanish barriers to the expectations of Britain herself in the western world?

Evidently, Hamilton was quite positive Britain would begin that "efficient negotiation" and send that person with "competent authority," for the very reason that Britain alone could not accomplish the object. But he did not take into consideration that Britain might not even try, unless conditions radically changed in Europe. Had he not seen King's despatches in cipher to Pickering? It indeed would have been highly improper if he had. But if he had—and both Pickering and he had given out confidential information as they saw fit before this—Hamilton did not examine his judgment, any more than King himself had done, in the light of King's reports to the Secretary of State that the British would take no part with Miranda unless the French seized Spain. That was a very uncertain factor.

Nevertheless, there were many developments in the summer of 1798, to make Alexander Hamilton confident that his were the accepted principles of American statesmanship. What he could not

71. Whitaker, *Mississippi Question,* 126–127. Hamilton (Lodge ed.), X, 325–327, to H. G. Otis, December 27, 1798.

72. Hamilton (Lodge ed.), X, 316, to Miranda, August 22, 1798; 321, to King, October 2, 1798.

know were the inner thoughts of that man who appeared to be fretting so childishly at his home in Massachusetts over the interference with his choice of officers to serve under Washington. In addition to such peevishness, and terrible anxiety as Mrs. Adams lay critically ill for months, John Adams was giving himself to careful study of the international situation from every angle and of the particular significance in the news which had begun to reach him from Europe. About matters which involved his country with both Britain and France, he would not allow himself to be hysterical.

Until the President should take decisive action, Inspector General Hamilton moved on exuberantly. He betook himself to Philadelphia to aid Secretary McHenry. He conferred with General Washington and General Pinckney about the new army of the "black cockade." He wrote to General Gunn of Georgia, December 22, 1798, that he looked forward to offensive operations: "If we are to engage in war, our game will be to attack where we can. France is not to be considered as separated from her ally. Tempting objects will be within our grasp." Harrison Gray Otis, chairman of the House committee on defense, asked if the President should be authorized to take the French West Indies as indemnity for the spoliations of American commerce. Hamilton replied on January 26, 1799:

> As it is every moment possible that the project of taking possession of the Floridas and Louisiana, long since attributed to France, may be attempted to be put in execution, it is very important that the Executive should be clothed with power to meet and defeat so dangerous an enterprise. Indeed, if it is the policy of France to leave us in a state of semi-hostility, it is preferable to terminate it, and by taking possession of those countries for ourselves, to obviate the mischief of their falling into the hands of an active foreign power, and at the same time to secure to the United States the advantage of keeping the key to the Western country.

It was "essential to the permanency of the Union."[73]

Hamilton would attempt even to detach South America from Spain in order to thwart France's "pursuit" of "universal empire." He was so absorbed in the future of the old Spanish domain that he neglected to answer Otis' inquiry about the French West Indies. Although his reply did show him fully aware that negotiations might be renewed with France, it revealed also that he did not be-

73. Hamilton (Hamilton ed.), V, 142. Hamilton (Lodge ed.), VII, 45; X, 338. Morison, *Otis*, I, 158.

lieve Talleyrand and the Directory had abandoned their policy of "semi-hostility." It may be that Timothy Pickering had not passed on the information from Skipwith and Vans Murray as he had from Marshall![74]

Even after President Adams had decided to try diplomacy again, the "second in command" and adviser of Cabinet officers wrote as late as June 27, 1799, to Secretary McHenry: "It is a pity, my dear sir, and a reproach, that our administration have no general plan. Certainly there ought to be one formed without delay. If the chief is too desultory, his ministry ought to be more united and steady, and well-settled in some reasonable system of measures." There should be a "precise force," naval and military, adequate for "eventual security against invasion," and besides "we ought certainly to look to the possession of the Floridas and Louisiana, and we ought to squint at South America."[75]

Alexander Hamilton had become so eager by this time that he disregarded the sudden transformation in Rufus King's counsel from London. King had written on September 23, 1798, to Hamilton in New York: "You will have no war! France will propose to renew the negotiation upon the basis laid down in the President's instructions to the envoys. At least so I conjecture." King had learned through French papers of Nelson's victory on August 1 at Aboukir Bay over the French fleet supporting Napoleon in Egypt.[76]

Hamilton discounted this, presumably, because King had subsequently reported on October 20 that the British Government approved the plan as Hamilton had outlined it in his letters of August 22. If Hamilton did so, he ignored the previous British warning that no action would be taken with Miranda unless France overturned the Government of Spain. But then, why should he not try? Here was King saying now that he had delivered Hamilton's enclosure as directed and that "things" were in London "as we could desire": "there will be precisely such a cooperation as we wish the moment *we are* ready." Rufus King was enthusiastic once more over "the glorious opportunity." It was up to Hamilton to get the United States "ready."[77]

There was one fact which the "second in command" could not ignore. "The chief," however "desultory," did have a "general

74. See above, pp. 301, 308.
75. Hamilton (Lodge ed.), VII, 97. Whitaker, *Mississippi Question*, 128–129.
76. Hamilton Papers, XXXII, 4482. This letter was forwarded to Philadelphia, but no record was made as to when it was received.
77. Hamilton (Hamilton ed.), VI, 368. King (King ed.), II, 454–455.

plan." It was not confined to military action. It was not tied to a hope that Britain might coöperate with her fleet. It did not commit the United States to a quarrel with Spain because Spain was allied to France. It did not disregard the fact that Westerners were satisfied at the time with the situation in the Mississippi Valley. It did not minimize the strife between "Jacobins" and "Monocrats," Republicans and Federalists, Virginians and New Englanders, threatening to destroy the Union. Nor did it overlook the designs of France upon Louisiana. It comprehended settling all difficulties with France without recourse to war upon any country, though Hamilton was afraid that it would involve the United States on the side of France.[78]

In fairness to Alexander Hamilton, we must note that when John Adams finally made his decision, Hamilton kept his word as he had written to Miranda. More than that, he used his influence among his own followers in support of the decision. His critics may say that he did so because he dared not then resist public opinion which he perceived to be on the side of the President for the moment, or because he would not surrender his ambition to lead an army to conquest and personal glory and he still hoped either that he could direct or oust John Adams from power. It is true that Hamilton did continue to cherish his military plan. It is true that he did work to drive Adams from the presidency. But it is also true that, by the time of Adams' message to Congress on December 8, 1798, Alexander Hamilton, with all his eagerness to conquer, had sensed that some sort of a change was coming over French policy toward the United States.

In the same letter to General Gunn about offensive operations against Spain, Hamilton had also written that it appeared to him inadvisable to increase the army beyond the provisions of existing laws. This was not simply because little had been done toward raising the force already voted, or because serious discontent existed in parts of the country with regard to particular laws, but because "a prospect of peace is again presented by the temporizing conduct of France." Although Hamilton's letter to Otis on January 26, 1799, breathed the very spirit of aggressiveness, it also declared that his plan would accelerate any measures of accommodation which France really desired to bring about.

This should arrest attention. The offensive which Hamilton had proposed to Gunn and to Otis was primarily to anticipate and to block the real purpose in Louisiana which Talleyrand, whether

78. Hamilton (Lodge ed.), X, 356, to Washington, October 21, 1799.

Hamilton knew it or not, was at that moment most anxious to accomplish.[79]

Hamilton's far sight was keen. The sensitiveness of Talleyrand and the Directory in the preceding July to the report of Victor duPont upon American retaliation, coupled with Talleyrand's instructions to the French minister in Madrid, proves that the French statesmen were anxious to reconcile the United States so that France might have a better chance to get Louisiana again, before the American people swept across the Mississippi and made the restoration of her empire in North America forever impossible. And Hamilton's judgment of future consequences was sound. If the Floridas and Louisiana had fallen into the hands of an "active foreign power" in 1799, to remain there for any length of time, it would have been a dangerous menace to the "permanency of the Union" of the Western States with those on the Atlantic Seaboard.

What he did not properly observe was the very great importance to the Union of Western contentment at that time. Spain was fulfilling the obligations of the Pinckney Treaty. War just then would not have been at all popular among the Americans beyond the Appalachians. Neither did he consider, as he should have, the immediate danger in the "coöperation" with Britain upon which his whole plan relied. Hamilton would have denied that it would have gone beyond the "temporary alliances for extraordinary emergencies" which, in the "Farewell Address," Washington—and Hamilton himself—had told the American people they might safely trust. But, as Hamilton should have remembered, they had also told the people that it was folly for one nation to look for disinterested favors from another. The fact was that Britain's statesmen were expecting to use the United States, not to be used.[80]

To Alexander Hamilton, conditions nevertheless were right in 1799, and the time had come, for the United States to throw their weight upon the European balance, to force themselves into world politics, so that they might turn events to their own advantage in the Americas. To John Adams, those conditions were far from right and the time certainly still far off, if it ever were to come, when the United States should undertake any save neutral commitments to European power. They would be better able to advance their own interests by their own independent efforts, even though slow and uncertain for years. Before many months had passed Ham-

79. See above, p. 295 f.
80. Whitaker, *Mississippi Question,* 127–128. For the Farewell Address, see above, pp. 227–228.

ilton was to hear this very opinion from Rufus King and even to take that position himself. But to accept the President's statesmanship was not to endorse John Adams personally.[81]

Alexander Hamilton was a militarist. He was partisan and self-seeking. Yet at one and the same time he was loyal to the authority and the institutions of the American Government which, in fact, he himself had done so much to create. If his critics will allow him to speak for himself:

> You have mistaken a little an observation in my last. Believe me, that I feel no despondency of any sort. As to the country, it is too young and vigorous to be quacked out of its political health; and as to myself, I feel that I stand on ground which, sooner or later, will insure me a triumph over all my enemies.
>
> But in the meantime I am not wholly insensible of the injustice which I from time to time experience, and of which, in my opinion, I am at this moment the victim.
>
> Perhaps my sensibility is the effect of an exaggerated estimate of my services to the United States; but on such a subject a man will judge for himself; and if he is misled by his vanity, he must be content with the mortifications to which it exposes him. In no event, however, will any displeasure I may feel be at war with the public interest. This in my eyes is sacred.

It held him inexorably to deference and support of decisions by a man whom he did not respect—so long as that man had authority. It urged him on as relentlessly, even into political intrigue, to remove that man from power—if his judgment would not bend to his own wishes.[82]

This was the character of Alexander Hamilton's "plot." It was designed to speed the approach of empire. As he wrote to C. C. Pinckney in 1802, upon the news that Spain had returned Louisiana to France: "I have always held that the *unity of our Empire*, and the best interests of our nation, require that we shall annex to the United States all the territory east of the Mississippi, New Orleans included. Of course I infer that, in an emergency like the present, energy is wisdom." Little did he realize that the policy of negotiation which he decried, rather than war, was to acquire for the United States within six months not only New Orleans but the whole expanse of territory from the Mississippi River to the Rocky Mountains.[83]

81. See below, pp. 348–349.
82. Hamilton (Lodge ed.), X, 363–364, to Henry Lee, March 7, 1800.
83. Hamilton (Hamilton ed.), VI, 551–552. Hamilton (Lodge ed.), X, 444–446, to Charles Colesworth Pinckney, December 29, 1802. See below, pp. 508–511.

XIII

CREEPING

Peace for Empire—"Close-Fisted Americans"

MEDDLING from abroad and insubordination at home affronted great vanity, hammered an explosive temper. But the second President of the American people would not let such irritations, or his own shortcomings, distract him from the essentials in the interest of this country. They were independence and peace. They had been acknowledged in Europe and maintained for more than twenty years, but they were still in grave danger. Europe at war ravaged neutral commerce, fomented disunion between the States on the Atlantic and those over the Appalachians, interfered with the construction of new Territories in the region which had been granted to the American people, and threatened to prevent their growth as a nation beyond the Mississippi. Spain was again in the grip of France and weakening under the demand that she give back Louisiana.

Like Franklin, Jay, Hamilton, Jefferson, and others, John Adams sensed the future of the American people in the Floridas and Louisiana notwithstanding his attachment to the maritime interests of New England. It was no complete afterthought in 1811 when he wrote to Josiah Quincy, who was opposing the admission of the State of Louisiana on behalf of provincial New England:

> The Union appears to me to be the rock of our salvation, and every reasonable measure for its preservation is expedient. Upon this principle, I own, I was pleased with the purchase of Louisiana, because, without it, we could never have secured and commanded the navigation of the Mississippi. The western country would infallibly have revolted from the Union. Those States would have united with England, or Spain, or France, or set up an independence, or done anything else to obtain the free use of that river.

The framers of the Constitution, he declared, had foreseen the necessity of conquering the Floridas and New Orleans.[1]

To John Adams in 1798, the peace and independence of the United States were more important than Louisiana. They would

1. Adams, *Works,* IX, 629–632, February 9, 1811.

fall to ruin if the battles of Europe were fought again in North America. The one safeguard lay in keeping them neutral among all powers which were bellicose, or even likely to become aggressive toward one another. As Spain was now meeting her obligations under the Pinckney Treaty of 1795 despite Irujo's quarrel with Pickering, Adams would further that neutrality by cultivating her friendship regardless of her relations with France. He would have nothing to do with Miranda's project. Louisiana and the Floridas for the present should remain in Spanish hands. It did not matter that he responded, whether he knew it or not, exactly as Godoy desired.[2]

In the case of Britain, Adams would protest all impositions. He would not retaliate with force, because he well knew that she could strike hard on both sea and land. The United States were more open to her attack than to that of any other power. There were British troops in Canada; more could be placed there for all that American sea power could do to prevent it; and Britain would not always be at war with France. Even so, Adams knew also that he could accomplish much by exposing British "secret plots." After all Britain was at war with France. Her statesmen were as aware as he that the United States could injure her interests on the American continent and in the West Indies. Britain would not be so stupid as to force them back in desperation upon France, their old ally and Britain's deadly foe.

John Adams, accordingly, rebuffed the British plan of coöperation in 1798 and expressed sympathy with the idea of independence for the West Indian colonies of France. But he made no final statements. He awaited events. He remonstrated the treatment of American sailors and shipping, but persisted in settling the matter of American claims for spoliations, like those of British creditors and Canadian boundaries, under the plan of the Jay Treaty for mixed commissions. He recognized the fact that the British naval officers had grievances against the American populace for aiding deserters; but he would not attempt to solve the problem of impressment as Liston wished by a reciprocal agreement for the return of such persons. The right of immigration and naturalization was as much one of the first principles of American citizenship to John Adams as to Thomas Jefferson.[3]

As for France, Adams prepared to fight in self-defense. But even this, if he had his way, would be no more than malevolent neutral-

2. See above, pp. 219–221.
3. Liston Papers, to Grenville, May 12, 1797, October 28; September 5, 1799. Pickering Papers, XIII, 205, to Adams, February 20, 1800. See above, p. 169.

ity—sharp naval reprisals, if necessary to stop French raiding upon American commerce. It would not be war. He agreed that Congress should put an embargo upon supplies from the United States to France and its possessions—particularly San Domingo where France was most vulnerable. He agreed that Congress should take advantage of the situation and formally declare all the treaties of alliance, commerce, and consular agreements at an end. He dismissed Létombe and other French consuls. But, in spite of his anger and doubt that France would respond in good faith, he was ready for further negotiation to reëstablish the peace which France had broken, if it were based upon a new covenant of mutual obligation which acknowledged the sovereignty and independence of the United States without any question whatever.[4]

Timothy Pickering might be afraid in the fall of 1798 that the "tiger" was crouching, but John Adams knew that France could not strike directly at the United States. She could hardly put an army ashore on the Atlantic Coast, least of all keep it there. He would send the American Navy against France in the West Indies; but, in his opinion, the American people did not want a large army "without an enemy to fight." Recruiting naturally was slow, he said, for men of common sense would not enlist for five dollars when they could have fifteen at sea or in ordinary work on land. Now that it had been decided who was to be second in command to Washington, let the generals go ahead themselves and select the officers of battalions. In short, there was no need for Hamilton's army of the black cockade. "At present there is no more prospect of seeing a French army here, than there is in Heaven," Adams said on October 22. Possibly he too had been informed of Nelson's victory over Napoleon's fleet in the "Battle of the Nile" on August 1.[5]

With regard to Louisiana and the Floridas, that question which stirred Alexander Hamilton to such activity, John Adams held his ground upon the simple declaration, "We are friends with Spain." For the time being, the United States would have to take the risk that they might be transferred from Spain to France. This did not mean that President Adams had any intention of aiding and abetting such a change of ownership in the mid-continent.[6]

When Rufus King reported from London that duPont de Nemours was coming in the guise of a scientist, but for the purpose

---

4. See above, p. 294, and below, p. 375 f. Richardson, I, 270, proclamation regarding Létombe and others, July 13, 1798.

5. Adams, *Works,* VIII, 612–613, October 22, 1798. See above, p. 324.

6. See above, p. 318.

of making "an establishment without the limits of the United States, and within the boundaries of Spain high up the Mississippi," Adams declined to be "guilty of so much affectation of regard to science as to be willing to grant passports to duPont de Nemours or any other French philosophers, in the present situation of our country." It was not essential to decide whether King's interpretation was true. Adams wrote back to Pickering: "Mr. King judges correctly of the American Government, that it has no disposition to give any encouragement to the mission of the Directory. I hope he conjectures equally well of the English." The American Government had been troubled quite enough by Adet, Victor duPont, Collot, Létombe, and other Frenchmen, without admitting any more, even if this one was only a scientist and philosopher.[7]

We know now that duPont de Nemours expected to use his rôle as "savant-voyageur" to get other things for France. His letter to Merlin, President of the Executive Directory, in regard to his nomination said: "I shall be charged to collect the funds dispensed long ago to the United States, to draw them from the close-fisted Americans, to unite them with others which belong to the Swiss and the Batavians; and, diverting everything from England's trade, to turn it to the advantage of that of France and in favor of the greatest influence of our Country."[8]

By the fall of 1798, John Adams had summarily dismissed the proposals of Miranda—to the disappointment of Rufus King and Alexander Hamilton. He had repelled the British offer of co-operation—to the great displeasure of Federalist merchants, particularly in his own Massachusetts, who considered French interference with their shipping an atrocity, but looked upon quite similar action by British cruisers as a mere annoyance. He had encouraged Toussaint's ambition to rule in San Domingo as an effective weapon against France—to the sorrow of the British minister, Liston, and the horror of Grenville in London. He had insisted upon treating the quarrel of the United States with France so far, as purely and simply an affair of the United States. It might prove impossible, of course, to keep it so. He would know in time enough for co-operation with Britain if that had to be. Meanwhile, although irritated exceedingly by Hamilton's determination to be the ranking general in the army and by the subservience within his own Cabinet

7. Pickering Papers, XXXVII, 335, Pickering to Adams, September 11, 1798. King (King ed.), II, 367–368, King to Pickering, July 14, 1798. Adams, Works, VIII, 596, Adams to Pickering, September 16, 1798.

8. AAE CP EU, XLIX, f. 232, March 14, 1798; ff. 233–234, for an extract from the records of the National Institute, September 26, 1797, concerning de Nemours' proposed visit to America.

to that end—the "intrigue in this business with General Washington and me"—John Adams determined to put Hamilton's activity out of his mind, if he could. He would count upon the loyalty of his departmental heads to his own purpose of bringing France to terms without going beyond naval reprisals and economic pressure. This, he was becoming convinced, could be done. This is what was eventually accomplished.[9]

News about France

LETTERS from John Quincy Adams to his mother were reporting that France did not want war with the United States. Elbridge Gerry came in person during the first part of October to relate his experiences at Paris, and he said that Talleyrand was now sincerely anxious for reconciliation. Within the next ten days Adams received the first two of Vans Murray's private despatches. He was greatly impressed. He sent them to Pickering to be completely deciphered, and ordered him to keep them "within his own bosom." When he had them back again, by October 29, he read of two developments most important to his decision.[10]

One was that the moderates in the Netherlands, knowing their financial and commercial dependence upon peace with the United States as well as their political distress under the domination of France, were planning to offer mediation between the United States and France. If Britain reacted properly to this double-edged maneuver, Dutch holdings of the American debt and trade with the United States would be safer; the Netherlands might be freed from France. The idea of mediation by the Netherlands made little appeal to Adams, but the interest which Britain would necessarily have in such a turn of events in the Netherlands was significant to him. His purposes would be served without committing the United States to Britain.

The other development reported by Murray was that he had been approached by Pichon, the new French secretary of legation. Here was a messenger, evidently direct from the French foreign minister, asserting also that Talleyrand wished to continue negotiations even though Gerry would stay no longer, and admitting that the United States were quite right to defend their commerce against privateers, French as well as any others.[11]

9. Adams, *Works*, VIII, 587–589, to McHenry, August 29, 1798.

10. Adams, *Works*, I, 532–533; VIII, 677 n.; 614–615. For J. Q. Adams' reports, see above, p. 302.

11. Murray's letters to John Adams, July 1, 17, 22, August 3, 20, October 7, 1798, with enclosures, are printed in Adams *Works*, VIII, 677–691. For the situation of the Netherlands from Grenville's point of view, see King (King ed.), II, 399–401, King to Pickering, August 20, 1798.

Harrison Gray Otis came to the President's home on October 28 with a letter from Otis' close friend, Richard Codman, dated Paris 26 August 1798. It spoke of the change in the conduct of France, which Codman believed had resulted from the advices of Victor duPont, Volney, and others lately returned from America. Codman declared:

> I hope to God that on the arrival of the dispatches which Mr. Skipwith sends, by the Vessel that carries this, no declaration of War will have taken place or alliance made with Great Britain, if not & the desire for Peace still continues with our Government I think they may count on an equal desire on the part of France, & a reconciliation yet be brought about, which ought to be desired by all true friends to both countries.

He went on to tell how Dr. Logan, the friend of Jefferson who had taken it upon himself to go to France without authorization from the American Government, had informed the Directory and Talleyrand that France could count upon no party in America; that every American would rally to the Government and resist foreign invasion.[12]

Another close associate of Otis, Joseph Woodward, recently arrived from Paris, brought President Adams on November 1, 1798, a copy of the memorial which Dr. Logan had presented to Talleyrand. It pressed the American case, but in it there was also a suggestion that the French should be just to the Americans in order to "leave the true American character to blaze forth in the approaching elections"! John Adams' thoughts turned into himself. Could it be that the friends of Jefferson were playing politics in sending "embassies to foreign nations to obtain their interference in elections"?[13]

He had received, too, a third letter from Murray, written on July 22, which threw his mind back upon the situation as it had been before Gerry left Paris, before France raised her embargo and issued the order checking the privateers in the West Indies. Murray reported in this letter that he had heard nothing further from Pichon and, more discouraging, that "in the meantime *no act* on their part assures us of sincerity." Was the "President of three votes only"

12. Morison, *Otis*, I, 168–170 n. For Washington's coolness toward Logan upon his return, see Washington (Ford ed.), XIV, 130 n., November 13, 1798. For the "Logan" Act of Congress, see Stats. at Large, I, 613.

13. For the authorship of this memorial, and Otis' discomfiture in this situation, see Morison, *Otis*, I, 165–167, 170–173. Adams, *Works*, VIII, 615–616, Adams to Pickering, November 2, 1798. *Annals*, 5 Cong., 2619–2625, text of Logan's memorial.

going to be caught between the proverbial devil and the deep blue sea, while the French made sport of his naïveté?[14]

Codman, unmistakably a Federalist, had praised Dr. Logan, and soon that gentleman himself came to talk with the President at Quincy. We do not know whether Adams on this occasion regained the confidence in Logan's "candor and sincerity" which he declared years later he possessed. He made no record then which has been published. He had placed the interest of his country again before his own, however, by the time that he arrived in Philadelphia toward the end of November. He was determined to reopen negotiations if genuine overtures should come from France. The advices of Gerry, Murray, and Codman had indicated that such assurances might already be on their way to him. It was very likely. As a matter of fact, they were.[15]

Even before he had known the entire contents of Murray's first despatches, President Adams had written a letter to the Secretary of State which must not be overlooked by anyone wishing to get to the bottom of the famous grudge of the Hamiltonians in the Cabinet and in the Senate. They bitterly avowed later that John Adams had no mind of his own, that he had betrayed the Federalist party in order to win support elsewhere for his reëlection. Historians have been influenced by this charge. But Adams had directed Pickering in this letter of October 20, 1798, to obtain the advice of the departmental heads upon these questions: first, whether the United States should declare war if France had not already done so; and second, whether any further proposals of negotiation could be made "with safety." He had recalled his statement of June 21 to Congress, that he would send no more ministers to France until given assurance that they would be received and honored as representatives of an independent nation. He still held that opinion, he said, but it might be wise for him to state in his next annual message to Congress that he would be ready to send a minister to keep open the channels of communication if he did obtain "satisfactory assurances" from the French Directory.[16]

It is manifest that John Adams even then preferred the second course to a declaration of war, for he went on to mention as possible appointments Patrick Henry and others who had given no public speeches offensive to France; the Federalist, Robert G.

14. Adams, *Works*, VIII, 686, Murray to Adams, July 22, 1798; 629, Adams to Charles Lee, March 29, 1799.

15. *Ibid.*, VIII, 615–616 n.; IX, 244 (1809).

16. Adams, *Works*, VIII, 609–610.

Harper, and others who had; and finally, from those already representing the United States, King, Smith, and Murray himself.

Instead of following the President's direction as it was obviously intended, Timothy Pickering and his associates in the Cabinet feared "the instability" of Adams' resolves and proceeded to frame a message for the President which, according to the biographer of Secretary Wolcott who wrote the draft, "left no loophole for retreat." There is strong indication that Hamilton also, and perhaps others who were not members of the Cabinet, took part in its deliberations. Hamilton was in Philadelphia about this time for the conference with Washington and Pinckney on the problems of the new army. Disregarding the news from France, and King's letter to Hamilton saying "You will have no war!" the Federalist ring about General Hamilton were determined, it would seem, to get a field of operations for him along the Mississippi, even if they had to make a war.[17]

Secretary Pickering had defied the President point-blank on November 5, when Adams had requested that he make public the letter of explanation which Gerry had written in answer to his published comments upon the X Y Z affair. Contempt for Gerry, however, had become such an obsession with Pickering that he replied to Adams: "I shall go further, and display not his pusillanimity, weakness, and meanness alone, but his *duplicity* and *treachery*. . . . I verily believe, Sir, that his conduct would warrant his impeachment. . . . If Mr. Gerry should insist on the publication of his letter, let him publish it himself. I shall then take such notice of it as *truth* and the *honor of my country* require." To comprehend the personality of Timothy Pickering, one has only to couple this with his refusal later to resign as Secretary of State because he needed the salary of the office, he said, for the support of his family.[18]

Was John Adams so blinded by his own conceit that he assumed, as a matter of course, that his subordinates would be loyal to his administration once he had spoken? If this were the whole of it, the wonder is that he did not in this case dispense immediately with such insubordination. But Adams' self-esteem was not fatuous. He could be candid and shrewd.[19]

The truth lies near the evidence in the letter which he wrote to Gerry on December 15 after he had delivered his annual message to Congress. Gerry could decide if he wished, said Adams, to publish his explanation for himself since Pickering had refused to do so; but

17. Gibbs, II, 168–171; 186–187. For King's letter of September 23, see above, p. 325.
18. Adams, *Works*, VIII, 610, 614, 616; IX, 54, May 12, 1800. Pickering Papers, IX, 565; XIII, 499.
19. Gibbs, II, 212–214.

Adams hoped that he would not—"because things stand at this time well enough." He himself was satisfied that Gerry's conduct had been "upright and well intended." But General Marshall had left his journal with Pickering; it revealed that Gerry had held "separate and secret conferences with Talleyrand" and had advocated a loan to France after her war with Britain had closed. Marshall and Pinckney would attest to the correctness of the journal, and they would be believed. "Indeed," wrote Adams, "I do not know that there is anything in it that you would deny." Then he requested of Gerry: "At least, I wish you to wait until you see the communications I shall make to Congress. I hope all will be still and calm; I should hate to have any dispute excited about what is past." That is to say, Gerry would please accept without retort the criticism of what he really had done, and stand by until the President could reach the objective which they had in common for their country.[20]

Let it be said for Elbridge Gerry in passing that he honored the request. Thomas Jefferson wrote a smooth, beguiling, but unsigned letter on January 26, 1799, telling Gerry how many principles they shared and urging him to present his story to his "fellow-citizens" with "full communications and unrestrained details, postponing motives of delicacy to those of duty." But Elbridge Gerry was not James Monroe. Gerry published no "View of the Conduct of the Executive." He did not even put his story in writing for his friend, Thomas Jefferson, until after his friend, John Adams, had reached the last days of his administration, and the controversy with France had subsided to a mere question of ratifying the treaty which Adams' second mission to France at last had obtained from Napoleon.[21]

Federalists "Thunderstruck"

THE President accepted the greater part of the message which Secretary Wolcott had drafted, but he would not have the statement in it that no necessity existed for sending another mission to France. Adams' own draft, of which Pickering certainly was in-

20. Adams, *Works,* VIII, 617. For Marshall on Gerry's "prevarications," see Pickering Papers, XXIII, 306, Marshall to Pickering, November 12, 1798. Lodge, *Cabot,* 175–177, 181–183, correspondence of Cabot and Pickering, October 31, November 10, 1798, concerning Marshall, Gerry, and the administration.

21. Jefferson (Ford ed.), VII, 325, at 334. Jefferson asked Gerry to destroy "at least the 2d & 3d leaves." They would be "galling to some" and expose himself to "illiberal attacks." *Ibid.,* VIII, 40, to Gerry, March 29, 1801, regarding Gerry's letters of January 15, February 24, 1801. See below, p. 385.

formed, declared that he was prepared to send another envoy or to receive one from France duly commissioned and accredited by the French Government. He had not yet obtained those assurances from France which he had made requisite in his vow of June 21. The martial preparations of the United States in the meantime were not to be deprived of their value for his purposes. So, the annual message, as President Adams read it to Congress on December 8, 1798, announced to the world:

> Hitherto, therefore, nothing is discoverable in the conduct of France which ought to change or relax our measures of defense. On the contrary, to extend and invigorate them is our true policy. We have no reason to regret that these measures have been thus far adopted and pursued, and in proportion as we enlarge our view of the portentous and incalculable situation of Europe we shall discover new and cogent motives for the full development of our energies and resources.
>
> But in demonstrating by our conduct that we do not fear war in the necessary protection of our rights and honor we shall give no room to infer that we abandon the desire of peace. An efficient preparation for war can alone insure peace. It is peace that we have uniformly and perseveringly cultivated, and harmony between us and France may be restored at her option. But to send another minister without more definite assurances that he would be received would be an act of humiliation to which the United States ought not to submit. It must therefore be left with France (if she is indeed desirous of accomodation) to take the requisite steps.[22]

Adams reiterated to the Senate on December 12 that he had seen "no real evidence" of change in the disposition of France; and obviously alluding to Dr. Logan, he condemned "officious interference of individuals without public character." Nevertheless, it was apparent that he stood ready to act upon any overture from France which took up with his declaration to Congress on June 21, 1798.[23]

It seems unreasonable today that anyone could have thought otherwise at that time. But disappointment does amazing things to the minds of politicians. Pickering, Wolcott, Sedgwick—Federalists —irked because they could not dictate a policy that would lead to war, reserved the right to be completely thunderstruck within a very few weeks, when Adams had received that overture and had called upon the Senate to approve a new envoy to France. Thomas Jefferson—leader of the opposition—willed to believe on January

22. Richardson, I, 272–273. Pickering Papers, IX, 659, Pickering to Adams, November 27, 1798; X, 39, Pickering to Murray, December 11, 1798. Adams, *Works*, IX, 131 n.
23. *Ibid.*, I, 277. See above, p. 293.

3 that the President's speech, "so unlike himself in point of moderation," had been written by "the military conclave, & particularly
Hamilton." Adams came out "in his genuine colors," said Jefferson,
when he referred to Dr. Logan; the President was holding back
Gerry's correspondence with Talleyrand, which contradicted "some
executive assertions," in order to get the war measures through
before he produced "this damper."[24]

The Vice-President wrote these comments to his colaborer in
politics, James Madison, in spite of the fact that at the very moment
he himself knew of Murray's report to Adams that the French
were "sincere in their overtures for reconciliation." Either John
Adams or Timothy Pickering had not kept Murray's letters "within
his own bosom." A pigheaded Secretary of State might perhaps be
expected to miss his superior's reaction to the significant news from
Murray, and from Nelson at Aboukir Bay. It is hard to think the
same of the astute Republican leader. Thomas Jefferson was making
good political capital of the President's trials within his party.[25]

On January 15, Adams requested Secretary Pickering to draft a
plan for a new treaty and consular convention "such as in his
opinion might at this day be acceded to by the United States, if
proposed by France." He wished Pickering to take the advice of
all of the departmental heads, but to hold it in "inviolable confidence" and to complete the work as soon as possible. On Friday, the
eighteenth, Adams sent Gerry's reports to Congress, and the next
day answered orally Pickering's objections to the changes which he
had directed Pickering to make in his counterreport. Adams would
not yield to Pickering's opinions; but as he had promised to do so,
he allowed the Secretary to send his report to Congress on the following Monday, January 21. There is little indication that Timothy
Pickering was working as strenuously upon the draft of a treaty
for the President as upon his charges against Gerry. But that made
no great difference to Adams. The evidence meantime had arrived
from France for which he had been waiting.[26]

Another despatch had come from Murray in November to counteract his discouraging letter of July 22. He had written on August
3 that the Government of the Netherlands, having taken pains to
ascertain the point from motives of self-interest, was sure of the
amicable disposition of France toward mediation. Moreover Pichon

---

24. Liston Papers, to Grenville, February 22, 1799. Jefferson (Ford ed.), VII, 313.
    25. See above, p. 333. For Gallatin's understanding of Adams in December, 1798 and
comment on Murray's ambition, see Adams, *Gallatin,* 221–228, letters to his wife.
    26. Adams, *Works,* VIII, 621–623. Gibbs, II, 187. Liston Papers, to Grenville, Janu-
ary 30, 31, 1799. Pickering Papers, X, 245, to Adams, January 18, 1799.

had admitted, as proof of France's sincerity, that an American war would be very unpopular in France, and that if it occurred, it would endanger the French colonies. Then on January 21, while Pickering was having his day in Congress, Adams received still another despatch from Murray, written on August 20. It enclosed a copy of Talleyrand's reply to the Dutch minister that the Directory of the French Republic had received his offer "with satisfaction." Murray believed that it proved the anxiety of France. Finally, on or about the first of February, there came the despatch from Murray which settled the entire question for Adams.[27]

It had been written on October 7, 1798. It told of Pichon's departure for Paris on September 24, after Murray had "repelled the idea that 'the assurances' declared by you, Sir, in your message in June, had been given in any of Mr. Talleyrand's letters that I had seen." Murray had impressed upon Pichon, he said, that "nothing but a formal and explicit assurance of respectful reception worthy the minister of a free, independent, and powerful nation," just as Adams had said in June, would be acceptable; and that it was not to come as a favor, but as a right due to an equal power, "necessary to the dignity of the American Government and nation." Then Pichon had gone to Paris, and this evening, October 7, the French military postmaster had brought Murray the original of this letter from Talleyrand to Pichon which Murray now enclosed. It was not quite the public and solemn statement, said Murray, which he had demanded; but there it was, such as it was, for the President to read. As John Adams read the words of Talleyrand, dated September 28, 1798, he came to this statement, acceding literally to his ultimatum of June 21: "You were right in asserting that every plenipotentiary whom the government of the United States will send to France, to terminate the differences which subsist between the two countries, would undoubtedly be received with the respect due to the representative of a free, independent, and powerful nation."[28]

This was sufficient for John Adams, provided it were confirmed. He did not have to see the letter of October 2 from Joel Barlow to Washington, which had arrived at about the same time and which Washington had forwarded to him on February 1. Adams did need, however, the letter from Washington accompanying Barlow's. Although he had little confidence in Barlow, said Washington, or Barlow's information about France's change of heart and specific intentions, he himself was ready to obey orders from the President if negotiation would lead to the restoration of peace with France upon

27. Adams, *Works,* VIII, 686, 688.
28. *Ibid.,* VIII, 691. ASP FR, II, 239.

honorable terms. That was "the ardent desire of all the friends of this rising empire." It is a letter which should be read by all who think that Washington had become a rabid Federalist after his experiences with Randolph and Monroe.[29]

Assured of George Washington's support, John Adams dismissed the services of Joel Barlow as "a more worthless fellow" than Thomas Paine, but moved to decisions that were based upon the conditions quite as Barlow had reported them. Adams had already decided not to employ the mediation of the Netherlands. They were subject to France. He decided now that it would be better not to wait for France to send a minister to the United States. As the affront to the American nation had occurred in Paris, amends preferably should be made there. Without consulting his departmental heads further, he sent to the Senate on February 18, 1799, a copy of Talleyrand's letter to Pichon, to show why he had made the decision, and named Murray as envoy extraordinary and minister plenipotentiary to the French Government.[30]

Indeed, why should Adams bother to consult Pickering, Wolcott, and McHenry further? He had already sought their opinions and found them set against his own. They were his subordinates. His was the ultimate responsibility. He had only to follow the precedents established by Washington in assuming it. The "thunderbolt" struck, nevertheless, among the Federalists.[31]

Vice-President Jefferson, looking on from his eminence as the presiding officer of the Senate, wrote at once to his lieutenants, Madison, Pendleton, and Monroe, about this "event of events." The President, he thought, must have had that letter from Talleyrand for some time, and have held it until near the end of the session so that the Federalists could "go on with all the measures of war & patronage." They, however, were "graveled & divided"; they were dismayed; they did not know what to do. "It silences all arguments against the sincerity of France," wrote the Republican chieftain, "and renders desperate every further effort towards war." That is, it should have—according to Jefferson's views of the reasonableness of things. But the little Federalists were not reasoning. They were raging.[32]

One may learn the suppleness of epithet from the letters of

29. Washington (Sparks ed.), X, 398. For Barlow's letter to Washington, October 2, 1798, see *ibid.*, XI, 560.

30. Adams, *Works*, VIII, 624–626, to Washington, February 19, 1799. *Instructions to Ministers*, V, 57, Pickering to Murray, February 1, 1799. Also in Pickering Papers, X, 301–303. Richardson, I, 282–283.

31. Gibbs, II, 189. Adams, *Works*, IX, 241 ff. (1809).

32. Jefferson (Ford ed.), VII, 361, February 19, 1799.

Pickering, Cabot, Higginson, and Wolcott. But the language of Theodore Sedgwick exploded: "Had the foulest heart and the ablest head in the world have been permitted to select the most embarrassing and ruinous measure. . . ." Murray, said he, was "feeble, unguarded, credulous, and unimpressive"; and Adams, governed by the "wild and irregular starts of a vain, jealous, and half frantic mind." Except that the nomination must somehow be postponed, Senator Sedgwick did not know what should be done about it, so he wrote posthaste on February 19 to the guide of all true Federalists, the lawyer-general in New York. The Senator got his orders. They were not what he evidently had expected.[33]

In the crisis, the great Federalist considered the public interest as above personal ambition and all else. Alexander Hamilton stood by the principle of John Adams:

> The step announced in your letter [Hamilton replied to Sedgwick on February 21], in all its circumstances would astonish, if any thing from that quarter could astonish. But as it has happened, my present impression is that the measure must go into effect with the additional idea of a commission of three. The mode must be accomodated with the President. *Murray* is certainly not strong enough for so immensely important a mission. I will write tomorrow if my impression varies.

He did not write on the morrow.[34]

The Federalist Senators sent a committee to accommodate with the President. They found him determined to have a mission to France but quite willing to enlarge it to a membership of three; and before they could get farther with their hostile report to the Senate, he sent in the names of Chief Justice Ellsworth and Patrick Henry to be Murray's associates. The Senate approved—amusingly enough with unanimous consent only to the nomination of Vans Murray.

Theodore Sedgwick, Timothy Pickering, and their faction consoled themselves that they had softened the measure "by throwing it into commission," that the Cabinet had nothing to do with it, that Ellsworth and Henry would not leave the country until "direct overtures" should come from France. It was poor consolation. The President himself had first put in the reservation that Murray should

33. For Pickering, see Lodge, *Cabot,* 221; Hamilton (Hamilton ed.), VI, 398; Pickering Papers, X, 403, 427. For Cabot, see King (King ed.), II, 551; Lodge, *Cabot,* 224. For Higginson, see Gibbs, II, 230; AHA Rpt., 1896, I, 833–835. For Wolcott, see Gibbs, II, 462, December 31, 1800, regarding Adams' "hidden wisdom." For Sedgwick, see Hamilton (Hamilton ed.), VI, 396, February 19, 1799; V, 216, February 22.

34. Hamilton (Lodge ed.), X, 345–346. For Hamilton's pamphlet on Adams, published in 1800, see *ibid.,* VII, 309–364.

not negotiate until Talleyrand's letter to Pichon had been officially confirmed. Adams had not side-stepped the opposition in his Cabinet; he had ridden over it. He had no objection to the idea of a commission of three. In fact, it would serve much the same purpose as his first commission of Pinckney, Marshall, and Gerry in representing the sections of the country. Oliver Ellsworth was a New Englander and Patrick Henry, a Virginian.[35]

The British minister seems to have been one of the very few who was honestly not aware that the President would prefer reconciliation with France to coöperation with Britain, in spite of the Cabinet's resistance. Liston had observed the cooling effect upon the Administration and younger Federalists in Congress of Nelson's victory over Napoleon; but he had missed its significance, as he had the point of Adams' remarks at Quincy in September that, although he personally would enter engagements "without scruple and without loss of time," he must wait because the people were "meditating." Liston apparently still counted upon joint action against France, even though he knew that Nelson's victory had diminished the risk which the United States would take in standing alone; for he was writing to Grenville on the very day that Adams sent the nomination of Vans Murray to the Senate: "Mr. Adams from the time of his being placed at the head of the Administration of this Country has uniformly endeavoured to strengthen and increase its political connections in Europe, and has combatted on all occasions the erroneous and impracticable theory maintained by some speculators here, that America is sufficient to herself, is independent of the rest of the world, and ought to reject foreign treaties and negotiations of every sort." If Liston was not caught unaware, so complete a misconstruction of John Adams' declared policy of neutrality in European politics but commerce with Europe can only be ascribed to an overweening desire that the United States should coöperate with Britain against France, and a belief that Pickering, Wolcott, and their associates in Congress were more powerful than the President.[36]

Robert Liston learned, so he said, "with no small surprize" that he was mistaken about John Adams. The "federal party were thunderstruck"; this was "calculated to damp the ardour of the nation," and check the preparations for war which were expedient even if "pacifick negotiation" were planned; it was an "obnoxious step." The "federal men" were forming a committee so as to give

35. Hamilton (Hamilton ed.), VI, 398, Pickering to Hamilton, February 25, 1799. See above, p. 279.
36. Liston Papers, to Grenville, January 29, February 18, 1799. See above, p. 314.

the President time to reflect upon what he had done, and to listen to the remonstrance of his friends. They lamented that the condition of Mrs. Adams' health deprived the President of her counsel. He was in a "state of dotage," they said—though of this Liston could "discover no marks." He thought that John Adams had been driven to his "hazardous resolution" by the accounts which he had received from his son. He had frequently heard Adams say with "apparent despondence and grief," after letters from John Quincy Adams, that little or nothing could be expected from the "Sovereigns on the Continent" in opposition to France. So Adams, in desperation, had made the nomination of Murray only as a "counterpart" to the "insidious professions" of the French Government. Adams had "no faith" in their sincerity, Liston said.

The British minister quickly gathered up his wits and proceeded with his hopes. These "federal men" would do more than give the President time to listen to their remonstrances. Adams would suffer political losses. The "object of the friends of Government" was "to defeat the measure altogether." This might "possibly be in effect obtained," for the French Directory would not be "mean enough" to submit to the insult of the *Constellation's* victory over *L'Insurgente*. Liston might still be able to keep San Domingo for the British, and work out a plan for American coöperation.[37]

"Every Real Patriot"

THE rage of the little Federalists was annoying to a man of irascible nature, particularly to one who was conscientious and proud of his conscientiousness. John Adams, however, was not obliged to listen solely to their abuse. There were men with greater records in serving their country and superior influence who expressed approval of his decision.

In reply to Adams' letter of February 19 explaining why he had nominated Murray on the previous day and why he gave no weight to Barlow's letter, George Washington wrote on March 3: "I sincerely pray, that in the discharge of these arduous and important duties committed to you, your health may be unimpaired, and that you may long live to enjoy these blessings, which must flow to our Country, if we should be so happy as to pass this critical period in an honorable and dignified manner, without being involved in the horrors and calamities of war."[38]

It was a reserved statement, for Washington had just received

37. *Ibid.*, to Grenville, February 22, March 1, 4, 11, 1799. See below, p. 354 f.
38. Adams, *Works*, VIII, 624–626, to Washington. Washington, (Ford ed.), XIV, 156–157, to Adams.

CREEPING 345

Pickering's letter of February 21 declaring that the nomination of Murray was dishonorable to the country and disastrous to the prospects of the treaties with Russia and Turkey which Britain had urged the United States to make. But it was a sincere statement to President Adams, for Washington replied to Secretary Pickering on the same day that, although he was surprised "not a little" by the nomination, and by further information that there had been "no *direct* overture" from the French Government, he was not acquainted with all the information and the motives which induced the measure, and so he might have taken a "wrong impression." He would "say nothing further on the subject at this time." George Washington had returned to the command of the American Army in order to defend his country from invasion, not to be a party to the Hamiltonian plan of aggression upon Spain in Louisiana and the Floridas.[39]

President Adams soon had encouragement from another source almost as gratifying. John Marshall, so recently acclaimed the Federalist hero for defying Talleyrand, had declared his approval of Murray's appointment in a private letter to his friend, Charles Lee. The Attorney General, who had supported Adams against Pickering and the others, took particular satisfaction in forwarding this letter, even though it was "entirely of a private nature," and pointing out that Marshall had expressed his view before he had heard of the change to a commission of three.[40]

Henry Knox wrote to assure Adams that, in spite of factiousness among those Federalists who had been equally virulent against the Jay Treaty, the "great body of the federal interest" would support the President. Patrick Henry, although obliged to decline the mission because of critical illness, wrote that nothing short of absolute necessity could induce him to withhold his aid from Adams' administration. John Jay, now Governor of New York, whose own experiences had caused him great misgivings about French statesmen, gave his support nonetheless to Adams. Jay replied on March 29, 1799, to Senator Goodhue of Massachusetts, cousin of Timothy Pickering, who had advised Jay upon affairs in Philadelphia:

Much might be said, but not to much purpose; for whatever remarks may be applicable to the origin, progress, and present state of this perplexing affair, *it is as it is.* Nothing therefore remains but to make the best of the situation into which we are carried. . . .

I am for aiding and adhering to the President, and for promoting the

39. Washington, (Ford ed.), XIV, 154, to Pickering. Also in Pickering Papers, XXIV, 124, received March 8. Pickering Papers, X, 403. See above, p. 319 f.
40. Adams, *Works*, VIII, 628-629.

best understanding between him and the heads of the departments. Notwithstanding what has happened I hope his real friends will not keep at a distance from him, nor withhold from him that information which none but his friends will give him. Union, sedate firmness, and vigorous preparations for war generally afford the best means of counteracting the tendencies of insidious professions, and of too great public confidence in them.[41]

Though it pained him to have to do so, Secretary Pickering sent Murray's commission as Adams directed on March 6, 1799, and instructed Murray to notify the French minister of foreign affairs that the other members of the mission were not coming to France until direct and unequivocal assurances had been received in this country that they would be received by the Directory, and a minister or ministers of equal powers appointed to treat with them. To these instructions Pickering added that the President opposed any more indirect and unofficial communications whatever in the controversy with France; if that Government really wanted reconciliation, it would have to follow the course indicated.

This was a rather ungrateful stricture upon Murray's dealings with Talleyrand through Pichon. But Adams let it stand. Perhaps it was necessary to console Pickering a bit; probably Murray would not be offended very much. Adams himself wrote into the instructions the clause permitting the Directory, if they preferred, to send a minister plenipotentiary to the United States. After all, it did not matter where the negotiating took place if it eased relations which had been dangerously tense ever since Genet had come to America in 1793.[42]

Timothy Pickering could not very well relieve his mind to Murray in this letter of official instructions, but at the first opportunity he did. Murray had written on April 23 to tell of the great impression which had been made in Europe by the victory of the American *Constellation* over the French frigate *L'Insurgente* in West Indian waters on February 9, 1799, and to report the effect of President Adams' last speech. This was unexpected in Europe, wrote Murray, as the United States was supposed to be seeking war. Their position, now one of strength, was better for negotiation; France was in a bad military situation and her ministers discontented.[43]

41. Ibid., VIII, 626–627. Henry, (Henry ed.), II, 624. Patrick Henry died on June 6, 1799. Jay, (Johnston ed.), IV, 256, and also 274, to Theophilus Parsons of Massachusetts on July 1, 1800.

42. Pickering Papers, X, 445. Murray acknowledged these instructions on April 13. *Ibid.*, XXIV, 222.

43. Pickering Papers, XXIV, 236. Maclay, I, 177.

Pickering replied on July 10. He was sorry but he had to disagree. The French did not endure American defiance because they
respected the strength of the United States; the French were just
too busy elsewhere. Murray should know that the President's appointment of another mission was as unexpected in the United
States as in Holland; in fact, "every real patriot" here was "thunderstruck." Why! the President had not had the least consultation with
the Cabinet. He regretted, said Pickering, that he should have to
make these statements, but he had been forced to it by the sentiments in Murray's letter.[44]

So he wrote, and perhaps so he believed. But one marvels. Just
how could even Timothy Pickering convince himself that the Secretary of State was in duty bound to advise the very minister whom
the President had chosen that the President had dismayed "every
real patriot" with the appointment, and that the mission should not
proceed? Even in those days, before the precedent was fully matured
that all Cabinet officers hold their positions at the pleasure of the
President, there was no alternative for Secretary Pickering, if he
would maintain his own integrity, except to resign. It would be the
purest charity to say that Timothy Pickering lacked a sense of
humor.

The truth, of course, is that Pickering and his confrères of the
"black cockade" were playing politics now with a vengeance, and
no sense of humor. The idea was permeating that John Adams was
soon to be shelved. It would have driven the little Federalists utterly
frantic if the revelation had come as well that, in the election of
1800, their party was also going to lose the presidency and control
of the Federal legislature to those hated "Jacobins." All that saved
them from complete hysteria in the spring and summer of 1799
was the fact that the Federalist party had done rather well in the
Congressional elections of 1798, and the knowledge that when the
new Congress assembled in December, 1799, Theodore Sedgwick,
one of their select group, would move over from the Senate to high
command in politics as Speaker of the House of Representatives.
Before then, however, John Adams had grievously undone them
once more.[45]

"Snails Are a Wise Generation"

THE President held to his policy of creeping. Critics may insist, as
Hamilton believed, that Adams was letting slip a fair opportunity

44. Pickering Papers, XI, 407, 411.
45. Liston Papers, to Grenville, December 10, 1799. See below, p. 370.

to get Louisiana and the Floridas at once. They may contend that the United States could have broken then and there both French and British resistance on the North American continent. It does not seem so if we take adequately into account the vehement dissensions among the American statesmen themselves, the deep suspicions and animosities between Virginians and New Englanders as shown by the Virginia and Kentucky Resolutions in retort to Federalist administration of the Alien and Sedition Laws, the sharp antagonisms still prevailing between the mercantile interests of the seaboard cities and the agrarian interests of the back country, and even more significant to us, in this study of American empire, the great power which Britain still possessed in the Western Hemisphere in spite of her prolonged struggle with France.

About these forces General Hamilton was altogether too careless. President Adams was quite right in fearing that if pressure were put upon them by the Government, they might destroy the Union. His Federalist opponents came sooner or later to contradict their violent personal criticisms by acknowledging the wisdom of the course which he pursued, although they did not cease trying to deprive him of the presidency.

Jonathan Mason reviled Adams to Harrison Gray Otis as a deserter of his party, because he wished to negotiate further with France. But Mason declared in the same letter:

> We are not yet Nationally cloathed. Our Country & Govermt is yet assuming & accustoming themselves to National Features. Time is wanting to give these Features, stability. Great Britain well disposed, & France prostrate—we could creep along in our Navy, in our Army, in our Fortifications, in our Commerce—& all our permanent establishments, all of which would be opposed by the one or the other of these nations, & obstructed with success, were it not for the present irregular state of things in this Country & Europe.[46]

Rufus King still hoped in March, 1799, that something would yet come of Miranda's plan, and thought of war with France; but he wrote to Hamilton that all their conjectures, "explained and confirmed by everything we see, enjoin us to look for safety only in our own courage and upon our own continent." Certainly this would give no room for coöperation with Britain. Finally Hamilton himself declared to Theodore Sedgwick on February 27, 1800: "I observe more and more that by the jealousy and envy of some, the miserliness of others, and the concurring influence of *all foreign powers*, America, if she attains to greatness, must *creep* to it. Will it

46. Morison, *Otis*, I, 171–172, February 27, 1799.

be so? Slow and sure is no bad maxim. Snails are a wise generation."
Nonetheless President Adams should not be reëlected.[47]

The Government of the United States did not have sufficient control over the nation's strength to challenge the competitors in this hemisphere. It could not stop the transfer of title to Louisiana from Spain to France if Spain chose to consent—especially with so uncertain a friend in commercial relations and so domineering a neighbor on the north as Britain was then demonstrating herself to be. The policy of creeping was best for this country during John Adams' time. It was a fair legacy to Thomas Jefferson.

47. Hamilton Papers, XXXVI, 5054, King's comment on a pamphlet by Christopher Gore entitled "The Present State of the United States," in which Gore favored a more intimate connection with Britain "so far as a common enemy renders necessary to the safety of both." See *ibid.*, XXXVI, 4944, Gore to Hamilton, February 27, 1799, from London. Hamilton, (Lodge ed.), X, 362–363.

XIV

NAPOLEON'S TERMS

Government by Correspondence

JOHN ADAMS knew that the Federalist clique would try to keep Oliver Ellsworth and Patrick Henry from going to France. He had told Sedgwick early in February that they wanted to appoint a general over the President. And he wrote from Quincy on March 29 to his Attorney General, Charles Lee, that the nomination of Murray had produced "the real spirit" of the parties in this country and "laid open" characters to him:

> Some of these will do well [he said] to study a little more maturely the spirit of their stations. But vanity has no limits; arrogance shall be made to feel a curb. If any one entertains the idea, that, because I am a President of three votes only, I am in the power of a party, they shall find that I am no more so than the Constitution forces upon me. If combinations of senators, generals, and heads of department shall be formed, such as I cannot resist, and measures are demanded of me that I cannot adopt, my remedy is plain and certain. I will try my own strength at resistance first, however. This is free, and *entre nous*.

He threatened to resign and leave the presidency to Jefferson— either from peevishness, humor, or appreciation that nothing could more quickly sober Cabinet officers who loved their jobs and salaries. But he felt no compulsion to act in the spring of 1799. Instead, he returned to Quincy as soon after the close of Congress as he could, to be with his beloved Abigail who was still in very uncertain health.[1]

Had not George Washington absented himself at long intervals from the seat of government? The departmental heads could send on to Quincy whatever needed the President's decision or signature; there was nothing but routine to require attention, until they should hear from Murray that the French Government had sent the official assurances. Patrick Henry could not accept the mission? Then Governor Davie of North Carolina should take his place as the representative Southerner. General Forrest was fearful? He

---

1. Hamilton, (Hamilton ed.), VI, 394, Sedgwick to Hamilton, February 7, 1799. Adams, *Works*, VIII, 629. Liston Papers, to Grenville, March 11, 1799.

hinted that during the President's absence the departmental heads might come under the influence of men "filled with a certain kind of ambition," who believed that with some other person as chief magistrate they would have more power than at present? John Adams dismissed the fear and the hint with, "They give me no anxiety." Why, he could not take Mrs. Adams South before the "violent heat of the summer shall be passed."[2]

George Washington, however, had returned to Philadelphia in the heat of the summer of 1795 at once upon receiving a letter from Pickering that had been hardly more of a summons than General Forrest's. Mrs. Washington, to be sure, had not been critically ill. But here was Forrest reiterating to Adams practically what Adams himself had already said to Lee. There were men in the Government, as Forrest declared, who—"not satisfied with their proper share of power and who, getting yielded to them more than is their due, increase in their own consequence and claims, until they fancy themselves exclusively entitled to direct."[3]

This letter was not written by Timothy Pickering. It was about him. If the thought entered Pickering's mind to compare the shortcomings of Edmund Randolph with his own behavior, it did so only to be scorned. It nevertheless cannot be so treated by us. Could John Adams have seen at that time the private letter of July 10 from his Secretary of State to his minister at The Hague, he might have prepared the Federalist party for a change in his administrative personnel much sooner, and with less damage to his chances of re-election in 1800. But no, regardless of his own perceptions, and advices from General Forrest, John Adams would stay in Quincy until time to return before the next session of Congress. Even matters that were not routine could be handled by correspondence until then.[4]

The "Black Cockade"—Fries, Traitor

TODAY such a case as that of John Fries and his followers in Pennsylvania would seem too trivial for as much notice as it received in its time, even more so for inclusion in a narrative having primarily to do with foreign affairs. So it would be, had not the Federalist enemies of the President in and out of the Administration fiercely raised the "black cockade" and made of these trials for treason a vicious reagent to turn public opinion against Adams and his policy with regard to France.

2. Adams, *Works,* VIII, 637–638, April 28, 1799; 645–646, May 13.
3. *Ibid.,* VIII, 638. For Washington and Randolph, see above, p. 200 f.
4. See above, p. 347, for Pickering to Murray.

To them, Adams' performance in the case of Fries was one more proof of his erratic self-esteem. They used it to defeat him in 1800. Other Americans, however, then and since, as devoted to this country and susceptible themselves at no time in their careers to the charge of treason or sedition, have been grateful for the pardon of John Fries and, if this was the product of vanity, glad that John Adams was vain.

The Whisky Boys of western Pennsylvania had resisted the Federal excise tax. These malcontents of 1798 were opposing the tax on houses and lands, levied to provide the funds which General Hamilton and his Federalists of the black cockade desired for the new army and navy to make war upon France. At first the followers of Fries thought this tax illegal, and themselves loyal to George Washington. They confused Adams' supporters with neighbors who they believed had been Tories, and they detested assessors who came among them from other places. They forcibly released their friends from the custody of the Federal marshal and flaunted the tricolored cockade. The red, white, and blue was not then to Federalists so much the symbol of this country as of the French Revolution.[5]

Fearful that it might be another Shays or Whisky Rebellion, but aroused more by the conviction that these people were under the spell of a clergyman recently arrived from Europe with radical ideas, Secretary Pickering and Justices Iredell, Peters, and Chase pounced upon the affair as treason to the United States. It did not matter to them that all the acts which might be called treasonable had ceased after the President's proclamation had denounced them as such; that the performance of the alleged insurrectionaries had been strongly mixed with alcohol; that after his "treason" Fries had returned with amusing simplicity to his daily job as a public auctioneer; that at the first appearance of the Federal troops he leaped from his barrel and fled into a brier patch in a near-by swamp, only to be ignominiously uncovered by his own dog, Whiskey.[6]

Nor did it matter to Federalist dignitaries that the followers of Fries were mostly humble German folk who used the English language with great difficulty, save the profane and the indecent; and were so ignorant that they knew little more of the meaning of their resistance than that they liked neither taxes nor Tories. Fries and others were roughly handled by troopers of the black cockade,

5. Davis, *The Fries Rebellion*.
6. Liston Papers, to Grenville, March 14, 1799, reporting that it was "nascent insurrection" and that the clergyman had the "modern principles of illumination and anarchy."

rushed into court, and put on trial for their lives—all in disregard of the precedent that a strong government is lenient, which President Washington had so wisely established just four years before upon the collapse of the far more dangerous Whisky Rebellion. George Washington's Federalist disciples ignored his teaching. They smelled the taint of foreign radicalism, and screamed for the blood of traitors.[7]

Robert Liston thought that Fries would not be found guilty, but he did not realize how hysterical opinion had become. Timothy Pickering wrote to Adams that conviction was "anxiously expected by the real friends to the order & tranquillity of the country & to the stability of its government." The Secretary of State was taking "calm & solid satisfaction" in the prospect. John Fries failed of sentence to death after his first trial only because one of the jurors had declared, before voting, that Fries ought to be hanged.[8]

Reputable Federalists, including Judge Peters, held that this juror was within his rights. Justice Iredell, to the "surprise and chagrin" of Pickering, and against his own "wishes, bias, and inclination," was compelled by the "irrefragable" evidence to think otherwise. Peters "acquiesced," but not without declaring: "although justice may be *delayed*, yet it will not *fail*, either as it respects the United States, or the prisoner."[9]

A juror's indiscretion thus saved John Fries the first time from miscarriage of justice. Before his second trial began, Justice Chase presented his views of the law on treason to the jury in so high-handed a fashion that the defendant's lawyers withdrew from the case, and Fries stood trial without counsel. Chase then entreated him to "look up to the Father of Mercies, and God of Comfort," advised him that "there is no repentance in the grave," and sentenced him to death.[10]

The President surveyed these results from Quincy. He was not convinced by the reports of Secretaries Pickering and Wolcott. He corresponded with Attorney General Lee to assure himself as to the proper interpretation of the law on treason. He considered the argument of Fries's counsel that resistance to a tax law was not the same as resistance to a militia law. He sought to discover whether there really were *"great men"* involved in the affair, whether Fries

7. Pickering Papers, X, 528, to Adams, March 30, 1799.

8. Liston Papers, to Grenville, May 9, 1799. Pickering Papers, XXXVII, 417, May 10, 1799.

9. Pickering Papers, XI, 110, to Adams, May 18, 1799. Iredell, II, 575, to Mrs. Iredell, May 19, 1799. Liston Papers, to Grenville, May 29, 1799. Carpenter, 209; 45 (in appendix).

10. Wharton, *State Trials,* 612–625. Carpenter, 203–204.

were a native or a foreigner, industrious or idle, sober or intemperate, and whether these alleged insurgents in Pennsylvania had any connections with similar spirits in other States.[11]

John Adams had a good memory still—of committees of correspondence in his own Revolutionary days. He did not discover that influential men had given anything more than sympathy to the cause of Fries, and legal aid in his defense. But he did find that even the Attorney General, who had long since proven his loyalty to the President and his independence of the Hamiltonian clique, believed that Fries was guilty of treason; and Adams let his own view of the affair be clouded somewhat by irritation with Dr. Priestley who was scoring his administration for the Alien and Sedition Laws.[12]

In spite of these feelings, the President held to the precedent set by Washington's proclamation in 1795. He completed that policy with regard to the Whisky Rebellion by pardoning David Bradford, one of its most reprehensible leaders who had fled before Hamilton's army out of the United States into Spanish territory. He distinguished forcible resistance to a Federal law from treason to the state, and when the time came he exercised his Constitutional power to undo the work of Justice Chase. Putting aside the belief of his Attorney General, he took upon himself full responsibility for pardoning John Fries on May 21, 1800.[13] Whether from conceit or good sense, John Adams would not confuse the actions of the French Directory with a local uprising against taxes.

Britons and Toussaint Louverture

THE President stayed in Quincy throughout the summer of 1799 although handling another problem that was not mere routine. The British foreign ministry, worried by Liston's reports that the President of the United States so much as thought of independence for San Domingo, had moved to keep West Indian affairs in British hands as French power declined before Toussaint Louverture.[14]

Lord Grenville's diplomatic "horror" did not stiffen to inaction. General Maitland, successor to Simcoe, had already made an agree-

11. Adams, *Works*, VIII, 644, 648, 650, 653. Wharton, *State Trials*, 646–648, points which Lewis and Dallas intended to use for the defense in the second trial.

12. Adams, *Works*, IX, 15, 21, August 14, September 2, 1799; X, 154, Adams to James Lloyd, March 31, 1815.

13. Adams, *Gallatin*, 137–138. Pickering Papers, XII, 35, to Adams, September 9, 1799, opinion of Secretaries and Attorney General against pardon. Adams, *Works*, IX, 59–61.

14. See above, p. 314. Treudley, 106. Pickering Papers, X, 45, to Vans Murray, December 12, 1798.

ment for withdrawing the British troops from the island that would retain some measure of British influence with Toussaint; and had gone back to England for instructions. Rufus King had protested Maitland's agreement as likely to facilitate renewed depredations upon American commerce by the Dominican or French privateers. Also, it would favor the British merchants, he said, at the expense of the Americans. Pitt and Grenville at once assured him that Britain desired to work in concert with the United States; and they sent Maitland back on February 6, 1799, to reach an understanding in Philadelphia before he came to final terms with Toussaint in San Domingo.[15]

It was perplexing to know whether the Negro chieftain would or would not remain loyal to France in his war upon the mulatto, Rigaud, as the Directory gave way to Napoleon in France. But the British statesmen were more afraid that France would use Toussaint to incite a slave insurrection in Jamaica which would result in the destruction of all European colonial systems in the Americas. Unrestricted trade with San Domingo would *"open* this source of Ruin," said Grenville, and threaten the Southern States of America as well. It was a good argument to make in Philadelphia. At the same time, the British were hoping to have the West Indian market for manufactured goods to themselves, if they could, and as much of the carrying trade as possible for their own shipping.[16]

The instructions to Maitland, accordingly, proposed that there should be a trading company organized by the British and American Governments. This corporation would be given a monopoly of all commerce with that part of San Domingo which was under Toussaint's control. Britain would provide the manufactured goods, the United States the produce and live stock, and all other countries would be excluded. As the two powers made arrangements to Toussaint's satisfaction regarding shipments of flour and other supplies, he would be bound rigidly to prevent the passage to and from the island of persons who might cause trouble among the inhabitants of the Southern States of America and the British possessions; and he would have to stop the raids of Dominican privateers upon American commerce. If the plan worked, Toussaint would have power, whether or not he had an independent state; he would hold his fellow Negroes to their native soil, content with their own freedom;

15. Tansill, 29–30. King (King ed.) II, 483–485, correspondence with Dundas, December 8, 9, 1798. Liston Papers, Grenville to Liston, December 11, 1798, received by March 12. Pickering Papers, X, 565, Pickering to Adams, April 4, 1799.

16. Liston Papers, Grenville to Liston, January 19, 1799. King (King ed.) II, 499, 511, to Pickering, January 10, 16, 1799.

Americans would sell foodstuffs; Britons, their goods; and British ships would have the carrying trade.[17]

Even if the interest of New England's shipowners had not been in the way, strong views upon the Constitutional limitations to such an exercise of Federal authority would have made it politically impossible for Adams' administration at that time. Jefferson and Madison had just issued their Kentucky and Virginia Resolutions. They were aimed at the Alien and Sedition Laws, but they would apply with greater force to an attempt to enlarge the Federal treaty-making power so as to create an international corporation monopolizing trade. Pitt argued with King in London that, in a case of so much danger, Congress could find adequate power in the Constitution. General Maitland and Robert Liston appraised the situation in Philadelphia accurately. They concentrated their efforts upon obtaining from the American secretaries as free a hand as possible for Britain alone to deal with Toussaint in San Domingo.[18]

Adams and Pickering had already chosen as consul general and special agent Dr. Edward Stevens, early friend of Hamilton, long a resident in the West Indies, and thoroughly conversant with the complex internal conditions of San Domingo. Liston had reported to Grenville on March 12 that Stevens would try to persuade Toussaint that he should encourage cultivation and trade, establish free intercourse with the United States, and stop preying upon American commerce, that he should close his ports to the armed vessels of France and open them to American ships of war. Liston reported again on March 30 that he had conferred with Stevens himself. The American agent had recognized the danger in the independence of San Domingo, he said, but had believed that it was too late to check the movement; he had used the argument, prevailing in American minds at the time, that free Negroes under French control would be more dangerous to their neighbors than under Toussaint's rule. Stevens had been certain that Toussaint would soon overcome Rigaud and make himself master of the island—regardless of any public gestures to imply that he was still subordinate to the Directory in France. Stevens believed that he would make the Negroes work the soil; in other words, that there would be little danger of their spreading rebellion elsewhere in the West Indies, once Toussaint had full control in the island.[19]

17. Liston Papers, to Grenville, April 20, 1799. King (King ed.), II, 499, 511.
18. Ibid., II, 501.
19. Hamilton (Hamilton ed.), VI. 395, 398, Hamilton to Pickering, February 9, Pickering to Hamilton, February 20, 1799. Pickering Papers, X, 368; XXIV, 65, 103. Hamilton (Lodge ed.), X, 342, 343. Liston Papers, to Grenville, February 18, March

This all might be true, but Robert Liston was not one to count upon such safeguards to British interests, particularly when they were not within British control and they might easily result in a diminution of British trade to the advantage of the United States. Besides, he had just received copies of Maitland's agreement for evacuating in the island, the preliminary assurances to King, and orders to treat that agreement as of "a very secret Nature," confining himself strictly to the explanation of it which he found in these papers.[20]

With Maitland on April 3, now came to Liston full powers for negotiating with the American Government and instructions that Maitland and he were to conclude an agreement which, if it did not embody the actual "minute" respecting a trading company as submitted by Grenville to King, would rest solidly upon the restrictive principles of that plan. Then General Maitland, accompanied by a representative of the United States, should go on to San Domingo and execute there an agreement with Toussaint.[21]

Both the American idea of free trade with San Domingo and the British plan for a corporation, accordingly, had to be dropped before Liston and Maitland completed their negotiations in Philadelphia. It was agreed subject to President Adams' approval that, even though there could be no formal treaty among Britain, Toussaint Louverture, and the United States, Dr. Stevens was to act as intermediary between General Maitland and the Negro chieftain. Stevens would bring the two parties together and see to it that provisions taking care of American interests were included in the agreement which they should make.[22]

Liston's report of April 20 to Grenville clearly indicates a definite understanding at Philadelphia that such restrictions as the British fleet might find necessary to inflict upon commerce bound to and from Dominican ports, because of war with France, should not keep from Toussaint the supplies which he had to have; nor should they deny American shipping access to the island under the international law of the time. The implication was that Britain, although maintaining her rights of blockade and seizure of contraband bound to French forces, would actually withhold the blockade and permit goods to enter Toussaint's part of San Domingo, even in neutral

12, 30, 1799. *Instructions to Ministers,* V, 74, Pickering to Toussaint on Stevens, March 4, 1799. King (King ed.), II, 557–558, Pickering to King, March 12, 1799.

20. Liston Papers, Grenville to Liston, December 11, 1798, received by March 12, 1799.

21 Liston Papers, Grenville to Liston, January 19, 1799. Pickering Papers, XXXVII, 405, Pickering to Adams, April 5, 1799.

22. Liston Papers, to Grenville, April 20, 1799. Pickering Papers, XXXVII, 408, to Adams, April 23, 1799.

American ships which at any other time or under other conditions would be intercepted.

At the bottom of all this was the fact that, even though Toussaint had not yet ceased completely to be an enemy of Britain, he was no longer completely loyal to France. Favors would be extended to him with respect to foodstuffs and possibly certain military supplies. Naval equipment was to prove quite another matter to the commander of the British fleet.

Liston took care, moreover, that all vessels from the United States should have to get passports from the British envoy here, specifying ship, captain, passengers, and cargo. This requirement in regard to passengers might protect Toussaint against the return of the old ruling class, the Creoles. The purpose of that concerning cargoes, as Liston wrote to Grenville, was to give preference to British ships in transporting manufactured goods.

He had thought of stipulating that British goods should be carried only in British vessels, but this would have made an unfavorable impression, he said, in the United States. And Pickering had pointed out that American vessels would deal in contraband British manufactures anyway, despite British efforts to prevent it. After all, the principal profit from that trade would center in England.

On his part, Toussaint, according to the negotiators at Philadelphia, would have to submit to British control over the coastwise trade of the island. This they hoped would confine it strictly to British and American vessels and suppress native coasting entirely. The natives of San Domingo should stay on the land. And Toussaint would have to stop the migration of persons dangerous to order in neighboring communities.

If this could really be accomplished, Liston and his superiors in London would be satisfied then to let some supplies reach Toussaint's army in American ships; for even that would have its value, as the United States would be drawn closer to Britain. It would be worth the risk of diminishing British trade in the West Indies for a while. But although Liston complained at the moment that the British commanders in West Indian waters were not coöperating properly with him in Philadelphia, it could not have been very far from his calculations that they should harass the American competitors of British shipping. That, at least, is what they did.

Secretary Pickering, on the other hand, looked forward with keen anticipation of profit and a capital advantage from this concert in the West Indies with Britain. As Liston reported his achievements to Grenville, Pickering wrote to Dr. Stevens that the direct commerce of the United States to and from San Domingo would suffer no interruption from British cruisers. Two days later he wrote almost as exultantly to Rufus King in London his "strong expectations" that Toussaint would declare the island independent. Pickering was concerned because the Secretary of the Navy could get no more copper from the English dealers. This would cause immediate embarrassment, he said; but it would compel the Americans to explore their own mines, and soon they would have a supply. They were manufacturing their own muskets now from Massachusetts to Maryland, at thirteen dollars apiece.[23]

The President of the United States was by no means as sanguine. John Adams had not considered it essential that he should return from Quincy to confer with General Maitland. Whatever his real wishes had been in the previous autumn when he had made Liston nervous about the independence of San Domingo and perhaps other European possessions around the Caribbean Sea and the Gulf of Mexico, Nelson's victory over the French in the Mediterranean and successive events in Europe since then had altered Adams' perspective upon the interests of the United States even in this quarter of the world. He had obtained those "assurances" which he had demanded of Talleyrand, and had made his decision to send another commission to France.[24]

It was no time to adopt a course in the West Indies that would rouse France against the forthcoming negotiations, particularly if that course led to the independence of a French possession. Those guarantees in the old alliance of 1778 had long since ceased to be real, but they had yet to be officially abrogated. Nor was it now the time—if it ever would be—to alarm other European nations about the enthusiasm of the United States for the spread of their republican principles and the expansion of their imperial domain. It was certainly no time at all to seek commercial empire in the region where Britain had long held sway. If she were estranged at this moment, the reaction in France would be to obstruct the settlement which Adams desired. And it was no time to try going alone with Toussaint. Britain might turn to playing the game for France against the Negro chieftain. It was time just to let all things slide along easily under prevailing pressures, and wait.

Pickering had written to Hamilton in February, after the nomination of Murray, that the President would certainly do nothing to encourage Toussaint to declare the island independent, although doubtless he would reopen commercial intercourse if Dr. Stevens

23. *Instructions to Ministers*, V, 101, Pickering to Stevens, April 20, 1799; 106, to King.
24. See above, p. 293.

certified that Toussaint had stopped the privateering. But Pickering himself continued to think that the independence of the island would be an advantage for the United States. The Secretary of State was no more persuaded of the President's good judgment about San Domingo than of his wisdom in sending another mission to France.[25]

John Adams, nonetheless, was weighing these matters carefully. When he received King's reports of his conference with Pitt and Grenville on a British-American corporation to monopolize the trade of San Domingo, Adams wrote to Pickering, April 17, 1799: "The whole affair leads to the independence of the West India Islands; and although I may be mistaken, it appears to me that independence is the worst and most dangerous condition they can be in, for the United States." He was not sure, but he strongly suspected that they would be less dangerous all together under the government of England, France, Spain, or Holland, and least so under the same powers separately as they were then.[26]

This idea of a trading company made Adams wary. It would be most prudent for the United States to have nothing to do in the business. But if they were going to "meddle," they should leave the matter of independence absolutely to the inhabitants of the island themselves; and if this were not the "sense of the English," he said, the United States had better "leave the whole management of the affair to them." The United States might adhere to the treaty which the English would make with Toussaint, within two or three years; but they ought not to do so until it had been determined that they were to have no effective negotiations with France. The Secretary of State, however, should consult with the heads of the departments upon all these points; and, if other principles were more agreeable, the President would be "disposed to concur in any rational expedient" that might be "concerted with Mr. Liston."[27]

The President took no exception to the understanding which Liston and Maitland reached with the American secretaries. General Maitland went on to make an agreement in San Domingo with Toussaint, under the watchful eye of the American agent, Dr. Stevens. It proved for Stevens not so much a problem of keeping his eye on the British general as of getting Toussaint Louverture to accept Britain as a "party in the business."[28]

25. Hamilton (Hamilton ed.), VI, 399.
26. Adams, *Works*, VIII. 634–635.
27. *Ibid.*
28. Pickering Papers, XI, 67, Pickering to Adams, May 9, 1799; XXXVII, 425, to Adams, May 29. Liston Papers, to Grenville, May 29, 1799, received in London, July 30.

The Negro general was angry because Britain had made public his agreement of 1798. He was hesitant to let British shipping into his ports for fear of a premature rupture with France. He preferred to have British merchandise come under the American flag. He was irritated because the British had not delivered the flour from Jamaica which they had promised; and he was angry with the British commander, Sir Hyde Parker, for having stopped a vessel which had his passport. In reporting these matters to Grenville, Liston remarked that the commanders of that squadron were frequently wanting in the spirit of conciliation "which is called by the temper of the times."[29]

When John Adams heard of this hitch in proceedings and learned that his departmental heads in Philadelphia were debating whether they should renew commercial relations with San Domingo without the concurrence of Britain, he wrote to Pickering that his judgment went along with theirs: the American Government had better wait for further information.

Adams was afraid, he said, that the jealousy and avidity of the English would do injury to themselves as well as to American interests. But the United States could not prevent it. His own opinion was that if the powers of San Domingo would not admit British ships of war or commerce into their ports, the British Government ought to be content when sufficiently assured that the island would remain neutral during the war between Britain and France, "and not insist on defeating the connection between the United States and St. Domingo": "It is my earnest desire, however, to do nothing without the consent, concert, and cooperation of the British government in this case. They are so deeply interested that they ought to be consulted, and the commerce of the island is not worth to us the risk of any dispute with them." Upon this basis Pickering should inform Dr. Stevens without delay as to the course which he was to take in San Domingo. In the meantime, Toussaint and Maitland had found terms satisfactory to both parties, and to Stevens on behalf of the United States.[30]

It was agreed that Toussaint should have "greater facility." In deference to the nominal authority of France over the island, therefore, Colonel Grant, who had come with Maitland, was not to stay as British agent. Nor was there to be any other openly accepted. The understanding seems to have been that Stevens would act in that capacity. Maitland promised besides that upon his arrival in

29. *Ibid.* Pickering Papers, XXXVII, 428, to Adams, June 7, 1799; XI, 315, June 22.
30. Adams, *Works*, VIII, 657–658, to Pickering, June 15, 1799. Pickering Papers, XXXVII, 428, to Adams, June 7. Treudley, 130 ff.

Jamaica three vessels of provisions would be sent over to Toussaint; and Stevens assented to this although the arrangement in Philadelphia had been that commercial intercourse should be withheld to a later date.[31]

With these matters settled, Toussaint then signed the secret convention on June 13, 1799. It opened the two ports, Cap François and Port au Prince, to British and American ships, admitting the British under flags of truce and requiring that both British and American should have passports not only from consuls of the two nations but also from Toussaint; otherwise, they would be confiscable. He was determined to keep all Frenchmen out of the island. The check upon the "émigrés" then in the United States, who might wish to return to San Domingo, is apparent.

As for the coasting trade, Toussaint got concessions in return for pledging himself to suppress the privateers within his domain. This trading was to be confined to merchandise, restricted to small vessels, kept close to the shore, and forbidden beyond the point where Rigaud's control began on the south. All ships which did not conform would be confiscated. The British cruisers were to continue their patrol, to see that the vessels had the proper flags according to the secret treaty, and for their own part to see that no native coasting vessels slipped away toward Jamaica and other West Indian ports. But Toussaint reserved for vessels of state under his own orders the exclusive right to transport provisions along the coast.

This presumably did not disturb the British negotiators, for the coasting trade in provisions would more likely have been American; and Stevens seems also to have had no great objection. Both Maitland and Stevens, indeed, could be satisfied without participation in this trade if Toussaint lived up to his promise to allow no expeditions against either the United States or British possessions. They knew that the Directory in France had sent orders to launch such an attack, but they also knew that Toussaint had Roume, the French representative, helpless in his power. It all depended upon the good faith of Toussaint; because there were advantages to him personally if he kept his word, they had confidence that he would.[32]

Question as to shipping the naval stores and munitions which Toussaint wanted for his campaign against the mulatto, Rigaud,

31. *Consular Letters,* Cape Haitien, September, 1797–October, 1799, Department of State, "Convention Secrete," June 13, 1799, enclosed in Stevens' letter to Pickering, June 23, 1799, and marked as received September 4. The text of this letter is printed in AHR, XVI, 74–76, Jameson ed. Liston Papers, to Grenville, July 6, 1799, received August 10.

32. AHR, XVI. 77, Stevens to Pickering, June 24, 1799.

was something else. It was not certain what the British naval commander on the West Indian station, Sir Hyde Parker, would do when that came to decision. Perhaps he would prefer to have Toussaint and Rigaud fight to a draw, as the best way to make sure that neither had a chance to lead that expedition to Jamaica which the French Directory demanded. Under the Jay Treaty naval stores were to be treated as contraband.[33]

Having determined to leave the Dominican affair to the British regardless of effects upon American commerce there, President Adams did not take up the direct overtures from Toussaint. It seemed to him that Toussaint had "puzzled himself." Instead, Adams issued the proclamations necessary to put into operation the agreement of the Negro chieftain with Maitland insofar as it concerned American shipping, and to modify the position of the American Government as that became appropriate under changing conditions in the island. He left to diplomatic protest and negotiation the confusion of controversies persisting with Britain over her interception of American vessels in West Indian waters, and gave his mind to the political struggle within his own administration as the final assurances came to America that his envoys, Ellsworth, Davie, and Murray, would be officially welcomed in France. To Adams, regardless of the knots still to be unraveled, Toussaint's future in San Domingo was no concern of the United States. He closed that issue with a finality which may have caused anguish among the shipmasters of his own New England—where there was interest also in selling Toussaint munitions—but which could not have escaped admiration elsewhere for its statesmanship.[34]

While the British commanders interpreted to suit themselves the law on contraband laid down in the Jay Treaty, handled Dominican ports in similar fashion, as closed or not closed, when they visited and searched American vessels, and in November climaxed their performance by seizing Toussaint's fleet of six ships with artillery and stores which had been sent to invest Rigaud's position in the

33. Miller, *Treaties*, II, 259. See above, p. 191. Liston Papers, to Grenville, August 2, 1799. *Instructions to Ministers*, V, 210, Pickering to Stevens, September 5, 1799, on Jay Treaty.

34. Adams, *Works*, VIII, 661, to Pickering, July 2, 1799. Pickering Papers, XI, 180, 192, to Adams, May 30, June 1, 1799, on letters of Toussaint and proclamation; XXV, 12, Adams to Pickering, July 5. AHR, XVI, 66–67, 81–82, Toussaint to Adams, November 6, 1798, August 14, 1799. Liston Papers, to Grenville, December 31, 1799. Pickering Papers, XIII, 492, Pickering to Adams for the Cabinet, May 9, 1800, on revocation of restraints upon commercial intercourse with San Domingo. AHA Rpt., 1896, I, 825–828, 829–830, Higginson to Pickering, September 20, October 3, 1799, to Messrs. LeRoy, Bayard, and McEvers, October 28, regarding shipment of arms to Toussaint.

south, Secretary Pickering advanced from displeasure to fear that "this bad policy of the British" might injure the commerce of the United States. It was ascribable, he said, to "individual rapacity— perhaps to insidious views that the two Chiefs may destroy each other." And the American frigate, *General Greene*, helped Toussaint out of the difficulty. Under cover of reprisals upon France, she bombarded Rigaud's forts for Toussaint and thus aided in the fall of Jacmel on February 27, 1800. But President Adams had solved the riddle long since and told his Secretary of State that American commerce in the West Indies was not worth a quarrel with Britain.[35]

Britain's officials would argue technically that the agreement between Toussaint and Maitland in regard to coasting by native vessels did not permit such an expedition and then offer, as they did, to pay an indemnity. They were not going, however, to let him have what he wanted—ships and guns. Their idea of "greater facility" was not to let him destroy Rigaud, take over the whole island including the part which had been ceded by Spain to France at Basel in 1795, and put himself in position to fulfill French expectations in Jamaica for his own benefit, if he should so decide. They would take the side of France in the West Indies before they did that. They did not share Stevens' faith in Toussaint.[36]

John Adams understood this, if Timothy Pickering did not. Adams saw the close connection between letting the British handle Dominican affairs as they pleased and succeeding with his second mission to France. He knew that such a policy was essential if he would keep the United States in competition with Britain on the one hand and France on the other for New Orleans and the Floridas. Although Alexander Hamilton could not appreciate the fact, John Adams too had the far vision of American empire. But he would not let it bewitch him into overlooking the immediate perils infesting the waters of San Domingo. He would defer to British power but would not obligate the United States to Britain. He would defy France's power but stand ready to accept her overtures.

Federalists, "Jupiter," and France

THIS was more poise than the followers of Hamilton in the Cabinet could endure. Ignoring the obvious warning from Grenville through Liston that Britain might make peace and leave the United States to confront France alone, and reiterating again and again until it became an obsession that Talleyrand's assurances to Murray were

35. AHR, XVI, 91, Stevens to Pickering, January 16, 1800. *Instructions to Ministers*, V, 300, Pickering to Rufus King, March 7, 1800. Treudley, 137. Allen, 180. Tansill, 73.
36. AHR, XVI, 91–92.

insincere, the Hamiltonian Federalists came to open conflict with the President's decision that Ellsworth and Davie should go abroad.

The official declaration of the Directory that the envoys would be received was followed by news in the summer of 1799 that Talleyrand had been removed from the French foreign office, that the Directory's power was crumbling, that there was good chance of monarchy being restored in France. The Hamiltonians accordingly worked upon Ellsworth, and soon had him so vacillating that he was in danger of compromising his honesty with the President. Hamilton brought himself into the affair by informing Liston that he had advised Lafayette not to come as the French minister to the United States, and spreading his opinion that the envoys should not go to France on the eve of a possible counterrevolution. But John Adams stayed at Quincy and directed the execution of his French policy by mail.[37]

He checked the Secretary of State's desire to make an insult out of Talleyrand's "impertinent regrets" in his official letter to Murray on May 12. Adams would take no notice; the letter itself was authentic; diplomatic verbiage did not matter; he was positive that the French really meant to negotiate. "Their Magick," he said, "is at an end in America." He gave it straight from the shoulder to Pickering that he expected the "Cooperation of the heads of Departments":

> Our operations and preparations by sea and land are not to be relaxed in the smallest degree. On the contrary, I wish them to be animated with fresh energy. St. Domingo and the Isle of France, and all other parts of the French dominions, are to be treated in the same manner as if no negotiation was going on. These preliminaries recollected, I pray you to lose no time in conveying to Governor Davie his commission, and to the Chief Justice and his Excellency, copies of these letters from Mr. Murray and Talleyrand, with a request that, laying aside all other employments, they make immediate preparations for embarking.[38]

He might personally have "little confidence in the issue of this business," but he would "delay nothing" or "omit nothing" that would bring it to success if possible. He reminded Pickering that all

37. ASP FR, II, 243–244, Talleyrand to Murray, May 12, 1799. Pickering Papers, XXIV, 246, Murray to Talleyrand, May 18, 1799. For the pressure put upon Ellsworth, see Lodge, Cabot, 224, 233–250; Gibbs, II, 265–266; Brown, Ellsworth, 273–278; Flanders, II, 226–229, 236–238; King (King ed.), III, 91–92, 101, 110–114, 134–136. Liston Papers, to Grenville, June 17, 1799, received July 30, on Lafayette and Hamilton.

38. Pickering Papers, XXV, 80, Adams to Pickering, August 6, 1799. Adams, Works, IX, 10–12. Compare with Gibbs, II, 250.

the points of the proposed negotiation had been "minutely considered and approved" before he had left Philadelphia; there only remained the task of putting them into form. Pickering would therefore do so as promptly as possible, lay his draft before the heads of departments, receive their corrections, and send the papers on to the President. John Adams' mind was "well made up" concerning the kind of instructions to go with Ellsworth, Davie, and Murray. That their mission would succeed was another matter. He had his doubts.[39]

The Hamiltonians made as much as they could of this personal misgiving. They argued that the President did not know his own mind, that he was erratic. They presumed to say to each other that he was governed only by his own vanity, irascibility, and caprice. They did not conceive how he could balance one uncertainty against another and arrive at wise conclusions in regard to the more likely event. They forgot the courage, the forcefulness, the shrewdness that had marked his career before, during, and after the Revolution. They knew of Abigail Adams' influence upon her husband, but they discounted altogether too much now her balance, discernment, and intuitive wisdom.

The Secretary of State obeyed his orders as to preparing the instructions, but did not feel otherwise obliged to meet the President's expectations with regard to "Cooperation." The result was that Adams received a personal note from Secretary Stoddert, written August 29, urging not only public considerations such as the possible change of conditions in Europe at the last moment, but "those which relate more immediately to yourself," as reasons why the President should join his departmental heads in Trenton before the mission left for France. They were in Trenton because of the annual visit of yellow fever to Philadelphia.[40]

Perhaps self-esteem governed John Adams' reply to the Secretary of the Navy. Possibly it was mere stubbornness, after having refused to heed Forrest's warning some weeks before. As likely, it was that Puritan quality of scrutiny and frank self-appraisal, with a tinge of self-sacrifice, which has made many sons of New England strong, but uncongenial with other men.

In any case, Adams replied to Stoddert on September 4:

> For myself, I have neither hopes nor fears. But if I could see any public necessity or utility in my presence at Trenton, I would undertake the

39. *Ibid.*
40. Adams, *Works,* IX, 18–19. Liston Papers, to Grenville, October 7, 1799, on yellow fever in Philadelphia and New York.

journey, however inconvenient to myself or my family. 1 would not, indeed, hesitate, if it were only to give any reasonable satisfaction to the "best disposed and best informed men." But you must be sensible that for me to spend two or three months at Trenton with unknown accommodations, cannot be very agreeable. Alone, and in private, I can put up with any thing; but in my public station, you know I cannot. The terms of accommodation with France were so minutely considered and discussed by us all, before I took leave of you at Philadelphia, that I suppose there will be no difference of sentiments among us. The draught will soon be laid before you. If any considerable difference should unexpectedly arise between the heads of department, I will come at all events. Otherwise, I see no necessity for taking a step that will give more *éclat* to the business than I think it deserves. I have no reason nor motive to precipitate the departure of the envoys. If any information of recent events in Europe should arrive, which, in the opinion of the heads of department, or of the envoys themselves, would render any alteration in their instructions necessary or expedient, I am perfectly willing that their departure should be suspended, until I can be informed of it, or until I can join you. I am well aware of the possibility of events which may render a suspension, for a time, of the mission, very proper.

He knew that France was a "pendulum." He feared that the extremest vibration had not yet swung. He wished Stoddert to communicate confidentially by every post, for he was determined to keep the French from dividing the American people.[41]

As we know that Adams was thinking at the same time of Collot and Létombe and their activities in the country beyond the Appalachians, and was ready to deport them regardless of the stage of the renewed negotiations with the Government in France, we can understand that he meant just what he said. He was willing to suspend the mission of Ellsworth and Davie for a time, should that be advisable in meeting a new situation abroad. But he was inwardly resolved to go ahead over any obstruction at home, if that would advance the interest of this country.[42]

Secretary Stoddert's further argument on September 13 brought the President into action. Stoddert wrote that Adams must be among his Cabinet officers before he decided to suspend the mission to France, or otherwise. It would be a great measure either way, Stoddert declared, and "attended with consequences in proportion to its magnitude." England was looking on "with jaundiced eye," affected by the effort of the United States to treat with France and

41. Adams, *Works,* IX. 19–20.
42. For Collot and Létombe, see above, p. 261.

irritated by the prolonged controversy over the article in Jay's Treaty regarding the debts to English creditors; the British commissioners at Philadelphia had acted almost as if they wanted war; and Liston, on this subject, seemed far from "mild and reasonable." If Stoddert could have seen the comments about the American officials in the letters from Liston to Grenville at this time, he would have been less gentle in describing the behavior of the British minister. He said enough, however, to rouse President Adams as he went on to remark: "We have a right to make peace with France without asking the permission of England, and we are not to submit to unreasonable and unjust constructions of the treaty for fear of her resentment." Then Stoddert brought Timothy Pickering to mind, without direct accusation: "It may not be believed that the instructions to the ministers will wear exactly the same complexion if you are at Quincy, when they are delivered, as they would have done, had you been on the spot." And then, he put salt in the wound: "I have been apprehensive that artful designing men might make use of your absence from the seat of government, when things so important to restore peace with one country, and to preserve it with another, were transacting, as to make your next election less honorable than it would otherwise be."[43]

Between these letters from Stoddert, President Adams had received one from Secretary Pickering, submitting his draft of the instructions for the American envoys and reporting that he had sent a copy to Chief Justice Ellsworth. This caused Adams to look again at the "portentous scenes" opening as the Directory fell and rumors spread that France would return to monarchy. He replied to Pickering on September 19 that he was worried; his "ambassadors" might have to treat at a "Congress for general pacification"; it was an "awful question" what chance they would have; there might be another "reign of terror." Adams seemed to doubt the expediency of sending them abroad at that time.[44]

Stephen Higginson, Bostonian, dealer in munitions for Toussaint, member of the Federalist clique, reported Adams' uncertainty to Oliver Wolcott on September 16. He had visited the Adamses at Quincy. He found their "language" directly opposed to their attitude. They were surprised, he said, by the reports in the newspapers.

43. Adams, *Works*, 25–29, September 13, 1799. Liston Papers, to Grenville, March 9, August 4, September 30, December 30, 1799; Grenville to Liston, July, October 21, 1799, regarding American personalities and the debt commission.

44. Adams, *Works*, IX, 31–33, to Pickering, September 19, 1799. Pickering Papers, XII, 36, to Adams, September 10, 1799.

This was perplexing to him. He could not reconcile Adams' words with his intention to send the envoys. But Higginson presumed that they would go, "let us think as we may."

Why did John and Abigail behave so with Stephen Higginson? Was it that they were overcome with anxiety? Or were they waiting further news from France? Or were they piqued by the inquisitiveness and opposition of such as Stephen Higginson and George Cabot —who had presumed to tell them in the previous autumn what to do with Elbridge Gerry? Were they just determined now to keep these "friends" from meddling with the President's business? When George Cabot also came to persuade the President "to give up his projected negotiations," he was treated with "great kindness & hospitality," he said, but "every heart was locked & every tongue was *silenced*" upon the topics which he wanted "to touch." He was alone with "Mr. & Mrs. A." part of the time, but not with John, for Abigail never left the room.[45]

John Adams had Stoddert's second letter within two days after replying to Pickering. He read it "over and over again." There was "not a word in it to spare." It completed the decision. The envoys were going to France. Adams notified Pickering that he himself would be in Trenton between the tenth and fifteenth of October. He ordered Pickering to summon Attorney General Lee, for all must be together "to determine all the principles of our negotiations with France and England." He himself had been obliged in his time, he said, to leave for Europe in the middle of the winter. It would be "no misfortune" if the envoys were delayed so long as the thirtieth of October. Then to Stoddert, and to his own conscience, John Adams declared: "I have only one favor to beg, and that is that a certain election may be wholly laid out of this question and all others. I know the people of America so well, and the light in which I stand in their eyes, that no alternative will ever be left to me, but to be a President of three votes or no President at all, and the difference, in my estimation, is not worth three farthings."[46]

It may be too much to ask the reader to believe John Adams capable of so great self-effacement. But at least one can insist that he had the courage necessary to see it through. Neither British nor American politics were to block the course of his negotiations with

45. Gibbs, II, 262, Higginson to Wolcott, September 16, 1799. King (King ed.), III, 111, Cabot to King, September 23, 1799. For their efforts concerning Gerry, see Morison, I, 153; Lodge, *Cabot*, 168–173.

46. Adams, *Works*, IX, 33, to Pickering September 21, 1799; 33–34, to Stoddert, same day.

France, regardless of their effect on his chances of reëlection. As that could not happen until later, it was to be kept out of calculation until later.

Robert Liston, British minister, observed the revolt of the Secretaries, Pickering and Wolcott, with full appreciation. He reported to Grenville on September 30 that Adams' decision was not expected, nor approved, by the principal supporters of the Federal Administration. The President, said Liston, thought that he was obliged to make "unwilling sacrifices" to gain popularity. Agents of France in America had been at great pains to give publicity to Talleyrand's despatches. But Adams would be embarrassed, Liston was quite sure, by the fall of the Directory. His "ministers"—that is, Pickering and Wolcott—rejoiced to think that the negotiation would be delayed if not defeated. The Secretary of State, especially, was taking "peculiar satisfaction" in the thought; he spoke of the measure with "execration"; he hoped that, if the President hesitated on the question of "procrastination," Chief Justice Ellsworth would be "induced to decline proceeding" to France. Liston noted, however, that others judged from Adams' "pertinacity" that he would resolve to send the mission in spite of the "advice of his best friends."[47]

The others were correct. While Liston was visiting in Greenwich, Connecticut, on October 7, he learned that the President had gone through the town within an hour en route to Trenton. He made haste to report the fact to Grenville.[48]

Once in Trenton, Adams disregarded the presence of Alexander Hamilton and his arguments about the chaotic state of Europe. He slighted the contrary views of Pickering, Wolcott, and McHenry. He brooked no discussion in the Cabinet upon the question. Relying upon Secretary Stoddert and the opinion of Attorney General Lee that there were no "sufficient reasons" for suspending the mission, Adams made the last arrangements for the voyage of Ellsworth and Davie, and sent them off to Europe. If they did find when they arrived that the Bourbon was again upon the throne of France, they could deal with his ministers. Robert Liston reported to his Government that the hopes of the Federal Administration were "finally and totally disappointed." The "friends of good order" feared that it would mean the withdrawal of support from John Adams and the election of Thomas Jefferson.[49]

47. Liston Papers, to Grenville, September 30, 1799, received November 19.
48. *Ibid.*, October 7, 1799, received December 2.
49. Lodge, *Cabot,* 248, Pickering to Cabot, October 22, 1799. Hamilton (Hamilton ed.), VI, 414. Hamilton (Lodge ed.), X, 356, to Washington, October 21, 1799. Mc-

What indeed had happened to the man who had led Pickering to believe in February that he accepted the appointment "from the necessity of preventing a greater evil," and in September that "there is nothing in politics he more detests than this mission, and nothing in nature he more dreads than the voyage across the wide Atlantic"?[50]

John Adams had written to Oliver Ellsworth on September 22, the day after deciding the mission should go, to say that the convulsions in Europe would "certainly induce" him to postpone it "for a longer or shorter time"; but he had not said that he would abandon it entirely. He had advised the Chief Justice to continue with his duties until requested to embark, but also to anticipate departure between October 20 and November 1. That, Adams had written, was all he could say "at present."

Ellsworth had sent this letter, in part, to Secretary Pickering on September 26, and Pickering had quoted it to Cabot on the 29—blaming Adams for not having consulted "us in the origin of this humiliating business," and for not first acquainting his secretaries that he had in mind "a suspension or abandonment of it." The latter was Pickering's own wishful interpolation. Adams had not told Ellsworth that he thought of abandoning the mission. He had said: "I should be happy to have your own opinion upon all points. We may have further information from Europe."[51]

On his way to Trenton the President had stopped at the Chief Justice's home in Windsor, Connecticut, and they had talked over the situation. Ellsworth seems to have given Adams no intimation that he had been in correspondence with those who were opposing the mission, or that he had let Cabot know through Governor Trumbull that he thought as they did "on the general merits"; and he did not tell Adams then that he himself was planning to appear at Trenton. After Adams had gone on, Oliver Ellsworth thought better of his reticence. He wrote to the President on October 5 that he, too, was coming to meet Davie in Trenton. He would then accompany Davie eastward, he said, in case Adams were "inclined to

Henry, (Steiner ed.), 418. Adams, *Works*, IX, 38, Lee to Adams, October 6, 1799; 39, Adams to Pickering, October 16. For Adams' recollection in 1809 of his severe illness at this time, his conversation with Ellsworth and Davie about the Bourbons, and his interview with Hamilton, see *ibid.*, IX, 252–255. For Hamilton's version in 1800, see Lodge ed., VII, 340–347. Liston Papers, to Grenville, November 4, 1799, received January 10, 1800.

50. Lodge, *Cabot*, 224, 237, Pickering to Cabot, February 26, September 13, 1799.

51. Adams, *Works*, IX, 34–36, to Ellsworth, September 22, 1799. Lodge, *Cabot*, 243, Pickering to Cabot, September 29, 1799.

such suspension of our mission, as, under present aspect, universal opinion, I believe, and certainly my own, would justify."[52] It was feeble, but it was honest. Ellsworth regretted, he said in closing, that he had not consulted Adams at Windsor upon the propriety of his visit to Trenton; but if he erred, experience had taught him that Adams could excuse. So John Adams could, especially when he had reached a decision, and wished to use the man who might have erred. Thomas Jefferson, however, was soon recording gossip in his diary that Ellsworth looked beyond this mission to the President's chair.[53]

There is no mistaking that Adams' decision to send Ellsworth and Davie abroad set the Federalist clique at once to the business of throwing the President out of the party. Prophesying that Jefferson, Gallatin, and Madison would come to power, Pickering wrote to Cabot on October 22 that there was only one way to prevent it. Adams should announce publicly at the close of the next session of Congress *"that he will retire."* Then the Federalists, agreeing upon one man, "might yet save the country from ruin." Wolcott declared that the United States were "governed as Jupiter is represented to have governed Olympus," and he felt that Adams' administration would end in "a transfer of the powers of the government to the rival party." Cabot lost his night's sleep, so he said, when he heard the news from Trenton, but he did not think Adams would take the hint. He "flattered" himself that "the great Washington" would again "come upon the stage."[54]

Pickering had already complained to Washington on the twenty-fourth that Adams' decision was "fatally erroneous" and had put his hopes on "the interposition of Providence to save our country." McHenry wrote more broadly to Washington on November 10 that Adams' administration was a "sinking ship," that there was danger to "order and good government"—and had asked what should be done. Finally on December 9, Gouverneur Morris, once personal agent for President Washington in Europe, wrote to inform him that "leading characters, even in Massachusetts, consider Mr. Adams as unfit for the office he now holds," that his predecessor was "wished for and regretted," and that if Washington declined "no

---

52. Lodge, *Cabot*, 242, Cabot to Pickering, September 23, 1799. Flanders, 229, Ellsworth to Pickering, October 5, 1799. Adams, *Works*, IX, 37–38, Ellsworth to Adams, October 5, 1799.

53. Jefferson (Ford ed.), I, 282, January 2, 1800.

54. Pickering Papers, XII, 260. Lodge, *Cabot*, 248, Pickering to Cabot, October 22, 1799; 253, Wolcott to Cabot, November 4; 249, Cabot to Pickering, October 31.

man will be chosen, whom you would wish to see in that high office."[55]

To Pickering and to McHenry, George Washington replied in such a manner as to reveal dismay at the course of Adams, but nonetheless to leave hardly a doubt that he himself would remain loyal to the Administration, as he had assured Adams in the previous spring. To Gouverneur Morris there was never to be a reply. What Washington would have said and done, we can only surmise from what he had already said and done through the past year. He had told Alexander Hamilton in September that he decidedly did not approve the plan for concentrating a large force at Natchez, "as it would excite in the Spaniards distrust and jealousy of our pacific disposition." It would end in producing "the *thing* which was *intended* to be *avoided*"—hostility. He had not given in to Alexander Hamilton's ambition to have war with Spain in spite of the President. He had upheld the decision of the Government. It is as probable that he would not have risen to Gouverneur Morris' plea against John Adams. In any case, the little Federalists, counting upon "the great Washington" to oust John Adams and keep Thomas Jefferson from entering the new White House, were very sad men at the close of the year, 1799. George Washington died on December 14.[56]

They were in despair. "Our good and great General Washington" was gone. He had left without even a rallying cry against "Jupiter." Their fond hope of shattering John Adams and discomfiting Thomas Jefferson was lost. But they did not cease hunting some other leader who might do so. It was not to be Oliver Ellsworth, although effort was made among "moderate Federalists" in the fall of 1800 to promote his nomination. He was "distasteful" to the Hamiltonians. He had overcome his abhorrence of the mission and his dread of the Atlantic. Nor was it to be John Marshall, although Theodore Sedgwick recognized that he had "great powers" and much "dexterity" in applying them, and George Cabot said that

55. Washington (Sparks ed.), XI, 572, Pickering to Washington, October 24; 573, McHenry to Washington, November 10 (also in Steiner ed., 419). Sparks, *Morris,* III, 123, Morris to Washington, December 9. King (King ed.), III, 141–142, Troup to King, November 6, 1799, reporting that an attempt would "certainly be made by the best friends of the government" to get rid of Adams.

56. Washington (Sparks ed.), XI, 468 n. (excerpt), Washington to Pickering, November 3, 1799. Washington (Ford ed.), XIV, 215, Washington to McHenry, November 17; 204–209, to Hamilton, September 15. For Federalist moaning over the death of Washington, see Gibbs, II, 310; King (King ed.), III, 162, Sedgwick to King, December 29, 1799; 170, Troup to King, January 1, 1800, describing Gouverneur Morris' "funeral oration" in New York, its failure to stir feeling.

he was "virtuous & certainly an able man" who "seems calculated to act a great part." The trouble with John Marshall was that he should have been educated "on the other side of the Delaware." He had "the faults of a Virginian": "He thinks too much of that State, & he expects the world will be governed according to the Rules of Logic." It was to be General Charles Colesworth Pinckney of South Carolina for he stood next to Washington and Hamilton in the army of the "black cockade." He had been in France on a very different mission for his country. He was a Southerner but no Virginian. He would save the land from Adams, Jefferson, and "ruin."[57]

Cabot had described President Adams as a "Simple Individual." Sedgwick railed at his "miserable jealousy" of those "best entitled to the public confidence." Hamilton scored his "perverseness," "capriciousness," and "vanity." But there was more to the hatred of the Federalist clique for their President than personal animosity. They were afraid, to the point almost of madness, that if their country did not go to war with France, it would have to fight Britain.[58]

Hamilton told Washington that his "trust in Providence, which has so often interposed in our favor," was his "only consolation." Cabot wrote to King that he feared British action, and to Wolcott that Britain was very likely to treat those powers who traded with France as her "accomplices." Fisher Ames said to Pickering that he found no reason in "public principles" for Adams' "astonishing measure." It would "embroil the peace of the nation with England."[59]

Even Rufus King, who was so close to the British ministry that he should have known better, hurried to Lord Grenville to communicate "without preface" the information which he had received from his friend, Cabot, that the mission to France had been suspended, probably "never to be revived." King begged that Britain now should curb her naval officers, stop impressment and depredations on American commerce. He was not happy over Grenville's diplomatic fencing in reply. He was less so when he learned from Secretary Pickering that he had "been mistaken." King, however, did not criticize himself for having acted upon information from

57. King (King ed.), III, 170, Troup to King, January 1, 1800. Brown, *Ellsworth*, 311. Wharton, *State Trials*, 39. Van Santvoord, 284. King (King ed.), III, 162–163, Sedgwick to King, December 29, 1799; 182–184, Cabot to King, January 20, 1800.
58. King (King ed.), III, 101–102, Cabot to King, September 7, 1799; 145, Sedgwick to King, November 15; 173, Hamilton to King, January 5, 1800.
59. Hamilton (Lodge ed.), X, 356, October 21, 1799. King (King ed.), III, 144, Cabot to King, November 9, 1799. Gibbs, II, 323, Cabot to Wolcott, February 28, 1800. Pickering Papers, XXV, 243, Ames to Pickering, October 19, 1799 (also in part in Ames, *Works*, I, 257).

merely private sources. He expressed his fear, instead, that both Britain and Russia would retaliate upon the United States if their envoys succeeded in France. He believed that France would "embroil" them with Britain. It was some time before Rufus King recovered enough of his natural optimism to write to his friend Troup that he did not "disapprove of the Mission," although it would not strew his own path "with roses."[60]

All of these Federalists should have known that they were howling at a bugaboo. Fisher Ames himself made a point against them and for John Adams when he said, "France is our foe, and so is Britain. We must depend on ourselves." Possibly he did not know of Grenville's warning through Liston that Britain might negotiate her own peace with France. Let us presume that he did not. Fisher Ames certainly could have observed for himself that Britain would not wish to reëngage in war with the United States so long as she was at war with France. The British had not forgotten the American Revolution. They had no assurance that the French another time would stand to one side while they fought it out alone with the American people. They would have no war with the United States unless it were forced upon them. As for Alexander Hamilton and Rufus King, both should have realized that Britain's refusal to take up with Miranda's schemes in Spanish America unless France gave cause in Spain did not mean necessarily that Britain would attack the United States. Perhaps they did.

Meanwhile John Adams had gone on with the problem of his next message to Congress and the routine of his office while he awaited the results of his second mission to France. And Thomas Jefferson was minding his political fences and the choice of presidential electors in the state legislatures. Others besides Federalists knew the game of partisan politics. Others were not fighting among themselves.[61]

The Second Mission to France

THE instructions to Ellsworth, Davie, and Murray laid down certain ultimatums to France. There should be established a board of claims to determine what the French Republic had to pay for damages to the property of American citizens, particularly those vessels

60. King (King ed.), III, 150–153 King to Pickering, December 2, 1799; 165, to Pickering, December 31; 186, to Troup, January 24, 1800. For Cabot to King, October 16, 1799, see *ibid.*, III, 134–135.

61. Pickering Papers, XXV, 241, Adams to Pickering, October 18, 1799; XII, 359, Pickering to Adams, November 20. For Jefferson's activity, see Jefferson (Ford ed.), VII, 383–403 August, 1799–January, 1800, political letters to Madison, Randolph, Callender, S. T. Mason, Nicholas, Charles Pinckney, Monroe.

coming from England and her possessions and those seized for lacking the *rôle d'équipage* which France had demanded without right. Inasmuch as Congress had declared on July 7, 1798, that the treaties of 1778 and 1788 were null and void, all engagements were to be put into a new treaty; that is, the French Government was to acknowledge that the action of Congress was valid in international practice. The American envoys were to make it explicit that they would consider no sort of an alliance with France, nor guarantee of the whole or any part of France's dominions.[62]

Thus Toussaint Louverture was at liberty, so far as the United States were concerned, to make San Domingo independent. The loophole here for Adams' conscience was that the Treaty of 1778 had never guaranteed France's West Indian possessions against domestic insurrection or rebellion. Other French islands, too, might free themselves. But if the American contention was sound that Congress had a right to abrogate the treaties with France, it was also possible now for Britain to seize those French possessions, without any protest or action by the United States becoming necessary on behalf of France. A carefully chosen set of papers relating to the affair with Toussaint therefore was prepared for Ellsworth and Davie. Needless to say, that secret agreement which the British general, Maitland, had made with Toussaint on June 13, 1799, under the eye of the American agent, Dr. Stevens, did not appear on the published list. Adams and Pickering would not expect Ellsworth, Davie, and Murray to explain everything to France. It must have been apparent by this time to Toussaint as well that neither had President Adams any intention of helping him against Britain.[63]

The instructions to the American envoys further stipulated that France should be promised no financial aid or loan in any form whatever, such as Talleyrand had tried to get from Pinckney, Marshall, and Gerry. These envoys were to approve no undertaking which would be inconsistent with the obligations of a prior treaty. Secretary Pickering, when telling Robert Liston confidentially about their instructions, had been "pleased" to assure him there would be no grant interfering with the Jay Treaty. Pickering instructed King to say in London that, by her "outrages," the French Republic had lost "the priority of privileges" assured to her in Article 24 of the Jay Treaty with regard to foreign privateers in American ports.[64]

62. ASP FR, II, 306, October 22, 1799. Flanders, 236–238. For *rôle d'équipage*, see above, p. 284.
63. Miller, *Treaties*, II, 39, text on guarantees of 1778. Treudley, 139. ASP FR, II, 306, list of papers on San Domingo taken by Ellsworth and Davie.
64. Liston Papers, Liston to Grenville, November 4, 1799, received January 10, 1800.

Ellsworth, Davie, and Murray were also to deny the privilege of the consular courts which had been provided in the Treaty of 1788, on the ground that it was incompatible with American sovereignty. The treaty which they should make was to last "at the furthest" for twelve years, excepting the agreements upon debts, invested funds, and compensation for contracts and past injuries to the United States.[65]

The results of "Eighteenth Brumaire" were complete before Ellsworth and Davie reached Lisbon, November 27, and joined Murray in Paris on March 2, 1800. There was no Directory, Bourbon King, nor "reign of terror" again as the Federalists had feared. There was the First Consul. And Talleyrand was back in the ministry of foreign affairs. The news of his return to office made Federalists expect insults for Ellsworth, Davie, and Murray such as Pinckney, Marshall, and Gerry had received. They did not grasp the meaning for the United States of Napoleon's *coup d'état;* they saw only the prospect of another scandalous and futile bout with the notorious ex-Bishop of Autun. They did not understand Talleyrand's real intentions in America.[66]

The envoys of the United States obtained an immediate and cordial reception from Talleyrand on March 5, and an audience with Napoleon on the eighth. The instructions to the French negotiators, Joseph Bonaparte, Fleurieu, and Rœderer, were adjusted with little delay to meet the wishes of the Americans that the powers of the respective commissioners should be exactly equal. Then, after Joseph Bonaparte had recovered from illness, they began the argument which the Americans might fully have expected.[67]

The French denied that the Congress of the United States had any right to make the treaties of 1778 and 1788 null and void by simple legislative act. And there is much to be said for their argument under the Constitution of this country as well as international law. Treaties may be spurned, violated, broken by one party, but they cannot be abrogated without the consent of all parties. The treaty-making power under the Constitution had been given to the Executive and the Senate. A share in that power had not been expressly granted to the House of Representatives. And, as the Constitution did not specify any other process for invalidating treaties and other international contracts, it was a wide-open question whether Congress had any power, even with the consent of the

King (King ed.), III, 142, Pickering to King, November 7, 1799. For the French "priority" comprehended in the Jay Treaty, Articles 24 and 25, see Miller, *Treaties,* II, 262.
65. ASP FR, II, 301–306.
66. See above, p. 295 f.
67. ASP FR, II, 307 ff.

President, to cancel the obligation of a contract with a foreign state. Certainly that was the case in 1800 before the Supreme Court got its interpretation of the "supreme law of the land" under way with the decisions of John Marshall.

Congress, however, did have power under the Constitution to declare war, and thus to break the obligations of an international contract. Attorney General Lee gave it as his opinion that maritime war did exist, by authorization of both France and the United States—on their part by reason of the war legislation which Congress had aimed at France. Neither President Adams nor Secretary Pickering wished to accept such an opinion. They held to the fact that Congress had not actually declared war. If their commissioners were to admit that Congress had virtually done so by its legislation against French interests, France too might be released from her obligations under previous contracts with the United States. To Adams and Pickering, this should not be. Americans had claims for damages to be acknowledged, and paid, by France. The edge of war does indeed cut both ways.[68]

The French negotiators on the other hand insisted not only that the treaties of 1778 were still in existence but also that they were "anterior" to all other obligations of the United States to foreign powers. There was at least moral strength in their argument. Anyone who studies the growth of the United States from rebellious colonies into statehood must admit that the help of France had been indispensable. If the United States had not broken their obligations to France by war upon her—a possibility which had been anticipated in the treaties of 1778 themselves—the United States were still bound by those obligations. The French negotiators furthermore "anxiously insisted" upon the right of asylum for privateers and prizes, in particular, as a prior obligation of the United States to France which could not be compromised by any subsequent agreement with an enemy of France without the consent of France. This, they said, the United States had done in the Jay Treaty of 1795 with Britain.[69]

Technically, of course, the United States could still maintain that the Jay Treaty was inoperative as to the right of asylum for privateers, on account of the saving clause in its own Article 25 which

68. For the war legislation, see above, p. 294. Opinions Attys. General, I, 84, August 21, 1798.

69. For the rights of French privateers in American ports under the Treaty of 1778, and Article 25 of the Jay Treaty, see Miller, *Treaties*, II, 16–17, 262. For the divergent opinions of Hamilton and Jefferson in 1793 concerning the "defensive" alliance with France, see above, pp. 147–151.

said that it should not "be construed or operate contrary to former and existing Public Treaties" with other states. But Secretary Pickering was not doing that. He was arguing that France had deprived herself of her "priority of privileges."

The French, moreover, took a keener interest now in the maxim *free ships free goods*. It was to the advantage of France, although indulging herself at her own pleasure in raids upon American shipping, to hold the United States to any obligation, whether legal or not, that might be derived from the treaties of 1778. Britain should not be allowed to have preferential rights, by reason of the Jay Treaty, in dealing with neutral American commerce. Napoleon was thinking of another coalition of "armed neutrals" against Britain's power on the sea in 1800 such as had been attempted in 1780. France, therefore, did not want to be released from the obligation of *free ships free goods*.[70]

The American envoys, on their part, were not interested in renewing this obligation, for after so much trouble with France, Spain, and Britain over this matter, the American Government had adopted the plan of John Quincy Adams. He had suggested that he should agree to the formula *free ships free goods* in his negotiations with Sweden and Prussia only *"provided the enemy of the warring power* admitted the same principles and practiced upon it in their Courts of Admiralty; but if not, that the rigorous rule of the ordinary law of nations should be observed."[71]

Secretary Pickering had found this proposition "wholly unexceptionable," and President Adams had agreed. The instructions to Ellsworth, Davie, and Murray, accordingly, were reticent on the subject *free ships free goods*. As they were to maintain that the treaties of 1778 with France had been rendered null and voil by Act of Congress on July 7, 1798, the mutual commitment of the United States and France in this respect was to be left in the discard. Nonetheless the American envoys were to press the claims for damages to American neutral shipping prior to July 7, 1798, under the obligation of those old treaties and after that date, under the law of nations.[72]

These conflicts of opinion regarding the Act of Congress, the

70. See above, p. 21.

71. J. Q. Adams, *Writings*, II, 285–288, to Pickering, May 17, 1798, Pickering's reply, September 24. ASP FR, II, 253–254, Prussian demurrer; 244 ff., the Treaty with Prussia of July 11, 1799, submitted to the Senate, December 6, 1799. For its text, see Miller, II, 433–456, particularly Article 12 (441–442) modifying J. Q. Adams' plan. For similar instructions, May 1, 1799, to King regarding his negotiations with Russia, see *Instructions to Ministers*, V, 136, Department of State.

72. ASP FR, II, 301–306.

privateers, and neutral shipping were sufficient cause for delay. Besides, Napoleon was away on his Italian campaign; the battle of Marengo did not occur until June 14; and before he returned to Paris, little could be done that was final. There was another vital reason why the French commissioners marked time. Secret negotiations in Spain were approaching the achievement of what had so long been a major purpose of French statesmen. Spain, at last, was going to turn Louisiana back to France.

This event, so ominous for the future of their country, was not known to the American envoys in France—nor to anyone in America, for that matter, however strongly suspected or feared. James Monroe had finally awaked to the fact that France wanted Louisiana, and had reported to his Government. Adams and Pickering knew about Moustier's work and Collot's journey. They had heard also from Rufus King on June 4, 1799, that the French Government had been trying to get Louisiana. But there had been no official news of these latest efforts on the part of Talleyrand for Napoleon. Even if there had been, the instructions to Ellsworth, Davie, and Murray and their negotiations hardly could have, or would have, been different. What the United States needed most at that time were peaceful relations with every power in Europe having interests or aspirations on the North American continent—and then, settlements for damages done to American commerce, if those could be obtained.[73]

The French were ready by August 11 to present alternatives. They still argued that even war itself could not have annulled the treaties; and there had been no war made, they said—at least by France. The two parties therefore could acknowledge that the old commitments of 1778 and 1788 were still valid, and "anterior" to the Jay Treaty. If they did so, France would agree to reciprocal indemnification "for injuries mutually sustained during the existence of the misunderstanding." She would pay for the damages to American individuals, and the United States would pay the national claims of France arising from their violation of the treaties of 1778 when they made the Jay Treaty with Britain.

Or, the two parties could acknowledge that there had been a war between them which had wiped out all claims for damages during the period of its existence. They would then conclude a formal treaty of peace, and make a new agreement, nullifying the treaties of 1778 and 1788 and placing France upon an equal basis with Britain. France would freely relinquish the rights which she had ac-

73. Department of State, England, IX, No. 31, King to Secretary of State, March 21, 1799, received June 4. See also King (King ed.), II, 584.

quired, but she would never acknowledge the right of another power that had been founded upon the destruction of her own. Napoleon's real purposes were beginning to show through the words of his plenipotentiaries.[74]

The Americans made a counter-offer on August 20. They could not abandon the demand for indemnities, but they might go outside their instructions and suggest that the old treaties should be renewed and confirmed as if no misunderstanding had intervened. It would have to be provided, however, that the rights of privateers and prizes of the one party could be reduced "to those of the most favored nation" by the other party upon payment of 3,000,000 francs in seven years. It would have to be stipulated that the guarantees in the alliance of the two parties were limited and specified —on the part of France to furnish at her own ports military stores to the United States, limited to the amount of 1,000,000 francs; and on the part of the United States, when French possessions in America were attacked, to furnish at their own ports a like amount in provisions. It would have to be optional, besides, for either party to free itself "wholly" from its obligations to the other, in regard to guarantees, privateers, and prizes, by paying the sum of 5,000,000 francs in seven years.[75]

Other details are not necessary to reveal adequately the nature of the American offer. It is apparent that Ellsworth, Davie, and Murray knew exactly the obligation of the United States to Britain in the Jay Treaty, particularly the commitment with respect to privateers and prizes—that while Britain and the United States continued in amity, neither of them would in the future make any inconsistent treaty.[76]

This was a direct attempt on the part of the American envoys to buy release for the United States from those restrictions in the treaties with France which had become so obnoxious to American neutrality since the overturn of the French monarchy and the outbreak of war between Revolutionary France and Britain in 1793. It did not apply to the American claims for damages by French raids on American commerce.

The French negotiators demurred. They did not want that kind of a financial offset. France would still be liable for those spoliations, and the American claims were likely to run well over the 5,000,000 francs which the United States would pay to be "wholly" released. But that is not what they said. Instead, they offered on August 25

74. ASP FR, II, 331–333.
75. Ibid, II, 334.
76. Miller, Treaties, II, 262.

to confirm the treaties and to have commissioners appointed to liquidate the claims, provided the United States would agree, practically speaking, to rid themselves within seven years of their obligation under the Jay Treaty to admit Britain's privateers and prizes into their ports. If the United States did not succeed in doing so, then France would not have to pay for the spoliations. Moreover, the United States would have to do this regardless of whether Britain and France were still at war. If they should make peace before the end of the seven years, this new obligation of the United States to France would fall due within the life of the Jay Treaty, for it had stipulated that its article concerning privateers and prizes should endure for twelve years. We should note, too, that with respect to the treaties of 1778 the French did not repeat the American formula of "renew and confirm," but used simply the word "confirm." The purpose in insisting upon the priority of these treaties is unmistakable.[77]

The French negotiators presented a change also in the American suggestion as to the guarantees. It should be revised, they said to a "promise of succor" in the amount of 2,000,000 francs; and the price of redemption should be 10,000,000 instead of 5,000,000 francs. The Americans were now the ones to demur. Whatever the price, they dared not take up with a proposal from France that would endanger the Jay Treaty with Britain.

Further exchange of opinions advanced the negotiations no farther toward a settlement. The French were still arguing on September 13 that if the old treaties were to be abandoned, indemnities should be abandoned as well. That was to say: if France could no longer enjoy the whole guarantee by the United States of her possessions in the West Indies and the superior privilege for her privateers and prizes in American ports, while Britain's were forced out, France would not pay indemnities for having raided American shipping, no matter whether it had been done in violation of her obligations to the United States under the Treaties of 1778.[78]

Then the American envoys tried another way around the obstruction. They proposed that the issue over the treaties and indemnities be postponed for the time and that meanwhile the two nations should abstain from all unfriendly acts and resume commercial intercourse. They should merely permit all debts to be recoverable. There should be no further condemnations of property. Any confiscated between the signing of the agreement and the exchange of ratifications by the two Governments should be restored.

77. ASP FR, II, 335. Miller, Treaties, II, 264.
78. ASP FR, II, 338.

The negotiators came to terms upon this basis and signed a "convention," September 30, 1800. The word "treaty" was carefully avoided, in order that there might be no ground upon which to place a subsequent argument that the old treaties had been affected one way or another. France was left with something of a case in behalf of the old treaties, and the United States could hold that they were not operative, if they did exist.[79]

The Convention of 1800

BEYOND restoring peaceful relations and postponing decision as to the treaties of 1778 and 1788 and the indemnities due to or claimed by each party, France and the United States pledged themselves to release all public ships which had been taken; to return upon proof of ownership property captured but not yet condemned, or which should be captured before the exchange of ratifications; and to treat debts as if there had been no misunderstanding. They further agreed that citizens of neither party should have to pay any greater imposts or duties, of whatever nature, than required by the other party of the most favored nation's subjects or citizens. Each party was to have the right to trade with the enemy of the other—both directly and in its coastwise commerce—except in contraband goods and where the places or ports were actually under blockade.

The contraband list to which both parties subscribed was confined to the traditional arms, ammunition, and armor. Unlike the Jay Treaty, this agreement omitted naval stores as such from the list. It was expressly stated, moreover, that the ship apprehended with contraband, and the residue of its cargo, were not to be confiscable as "infected by the prohibited goods." Insofar as the Convention of 1800 could give it, therefore, the United States got protection against practices by France which Britain had been using upon American neutral vessels laden with contraband. France would receive the same protection, in case the United States were to become a belligerent and France were to be a neutral trading with the enemy of the United States.[80]

A separate article in the Convention of 1800 stipulated that "free ships shall give a freedom to goods." The next as expressly determined that an enemy's ship made all goods aboard confiscable, except such as could be shown as having been loaded before the dec-

79. *Ibid.*
80. Miller, *Treaties*, II, 457–479, particularly 467–468 for contraband. For the Jay Treaty on naval stores as contraband see *ibid.*, II, 259. Other clauses in the Convention of 1800, having to do with reciprocal rights of citizens and goods, properties, commercial agents, passports, and details, are not essential to this narrative.

laration of war, or within two months thereafter without knowledge that war had been declared. The two parties reciprocally engaged not to allow under the protection of their convoy any ships
which were carrying contraband to an enemy. Finally, the ships of
war and privateers of each party were to be admitted with their
prizes into the ports of the other, under the same conditions as those
of the most favored nation.[81]

Within these terms may be seen a design to assure France equality
with Britain. But this was no achievement. It had not been the position which France had held and which her Revolutionary statesmen
had tried to maintain. France had once been the most favored nation. Now she was accepting the fact that, since Jay's negotiations
with Grenville, it was Britain that enjoyed the privileges. The principle *free ships free goods*, to be sure, had been reiterated in this
treaty, even though the United States now were not so eager to
assert it. They were bound as before, in case they were at war, to
respect the neutrality of France and the cargoes of her merchantmen, excepting contraband. But there was a great silence in the
Convention of 1800 upon a matter which had made Frenchmen
rave. There was no statement that the United States—if they were
neutral and France were at war— would have to defend French
shipping against violation of the principle *free ships free goods* by
an enemy of France. France, too, would be reciprocally free as a
neutral from such an obligation to the United States. That, however, was not the point under the circumstances of the time.

The United States were neutral and France was at war, struggling
to maintain her colonial empire against Britain's might upon the
seas, while fighting at the same time to break Britain's hold upon
the coalition in Europe and to establish French supremacy there. Under such circumstances, the important fact was that France had
countenanced the Jay Treaty, permitting British cruisers to ignore
the rule *free ships free goods* and to seize not only French but neutral property according to Britain's own conception as to the immunities of neutrals, contraband, and enemy goods. Without a naval
arm to match the strength of the British, France could never hope
to employ the advantages of equality with Britain which the United
States solemnly assured in the Convention of 1800.

Whatever Napoleon's hopes of another league of armed neutrality
in 1800, his representatives signed an agreement with the envoys of
the United States which, by its very silence on this matter, admitted
the obligation of the United States to Britain under Jay's previous

81. *Ibid.*, II, 468 (Article 14), 469 (15), 473, (19), 477 (24).

agreement with Grenville. If this conclusion seems too strong, it must be conceded, at least, that the Convention of 1800 obliged the United States no more than they had ever been to defend their neutrality by sacrificing it in resistance to the British fleet.

When Napoleon let this convention go to the United States for ratification, he abandoned what was left—if anything substantial was left—of that coöperative structure which Vergennes and Franklin had raised in 1778 against the "common enemy." Doubtless Napoleon and Talleyrand no longer had use for the American alliance. Certainly they had other plans.[82]

The first reaction of Thomas Jefferson, old "friend of France," to the treaty which Davie brought home in December, 1800, was that there had been "a bungling negotiation." But it was not very long before he was realizing that the benevolent neutrality which he had tried to foster when Secretary of State was not the desire of the American people, nor even his own. France was coming into Louisiana.[83]

Those Federalists, too, were to learn a lesson, who raged because they had not been allowed to join with Britain in a real war upon France, and now were in a frenzy lest they would have a war with Britain on that account. They might have learned it before, from the frankness of Lord Grenville, or the shrewdness of John Adams, or even from the wisdom of their own Alexander Hamilton as it flowed through "the farewell address" of President Washington. One nation should not trust another beyond the limit of its interest. Britain also was soon coming to a truce with Napoleon and France.[84]

With Vice-President Jefferson in the chair, the Senate ratified the Convention of 1800 on February 3, 1801, but under the conditions that the second article, which referred to the claims and the treaties, should be expunged and that the life of the agreement should be restricted to eight years. Thus the claims for spoliations would be maintained and their eventual settlement merely postponed. The inference of the Convention that the treaties were still in existence, though not operating, would be replaced by the implication that their complete abrogation was only delayed. President Adams did not favor the Senate's changes, but he ratified the Convention and left the appointment of the new minister to France for Jefferson as he became President on March 4.[85]

82. See above, pp. 15–21.
83. Jefferson (Ford ed.), VII, 471, to Madison, December 19, 1800.
84. See above, pp. 227–228 and below, p. 405 f.
85. Miller, *Treaties,* II, 458–459 (Article 2); 482–487, note by Miller on James A. Bayard's refusal to go as minister to France.

Napoleon took characteristic action. He would not ratify the convention with the Senate's provisos, unless both parties renounced their "respective pretentions" in that second article. If the United States would not adhere to their obligations of 1778 and 1788—not that he cared much for those obligations—their citizens should get no indemnities from France for spoliations. Napoleon did care about spending French money as he pleased. Vans Murray had no authority to meet this situation, but he took responsibility for exchanging the ratifications in Paris on July 31, 1801, believing that the matter would have to go again to the United States Senate. And so the Convention of 1800 came across the Atlantic once more, this time with Napoleonic cleverness poured over it.[86]

Here was an amusing turn of affairs. It was as irritating to Republicans as to Federalists. If the Republicans, now controlling the Senate, approved this arrangement for restoring friendly relations with France, they would in reality endorse the Federalist repudiation of the French treaties by Act of Congress on July 7, 1798. And Republicans had roundly protested that Congress had no right to do so. Federalists, however, had to watch their claims for damages go overboard also, as they got rid of those treaties. There was no happy prospect that the Republican administration would compensate them out of the public treasury as France was released indefinitely, if not forever, from her responsibility.[87]

President Jefferson evaded the question whether Napoleon's "retrenchment" were part of the agreement. He merely commented on December 11, 1801, that the First Consul's ratification was not "pure and simple in the ordinary form," and requested another consideration by the Senate. The Senate resolved on December 19 that the Convention was fully ratified. Two days later the President proclaimed it to be "a law of the land."[88]

Retirement

JOHN ADAMS, denied the honor of succeeding himself in the White House at Washington, had "trotted the bogs five hundred miles" back to Quincy, to contemplation of seaweed as manure for his

86. AHA Rpt., 1912, 697–703, Murray to J. Q. Adams, May 18, June 10, July 15, August 8, 1801. ASP FR, VI, 137–147. Miller, *Treaties*, II, 481–482, Napoleon's "retrenchment"; 483–484, note by Miller.

87. Hill, *Leading American Treaties*, 71–74. Scott, *The Controversy over Neutral Rights between the United States and France, 1797-1800*, 92–94, Act of Congress in 1885; 227–293, *Gray v. the United States*, May 17, 1886.

88. Richardson, I, 332.

farm land, and Horace's satires as "having much good matter" applicable to himself:

O you who have never spoken falsely to any man, you see how I am returning home, naked and in need, as you foretold; and there neither cellar nor herd is unrifled by the suitors. And yet birth and worth, without substance, are more paltry than seaweed . . .

This is what I prayed for!—a piece of land not so very large, where there would be a garden, and near the house a spring of ever-flowing water, and up above these a bit of woodland. More and better than this have the gods done for me. I am content. . . . Here no wretched place-hunting worries me to death, nor the leaden sirocco, nor sickly autumn, that brings gain to hateful Libitina. . . .[89]

There was humor in him, but it was wry. His second mission had gone to France, and it had succeeded. There was peace with France, and there was no war with Britain to destroy, nor coöperation to humiliate. The scheme of Federalist enemies for drawing out George Washington had been stopped by Washington's own loyalty to the Government, and by Fate. Alexander Hamilton had been left to mourn the certainty that, whoever would now be head of the army, it would not be "the next in command." And then John Adams had learned other things beyond the intimations of Stoddert and what he had observed for himself about his Secretary of State.[90]

Vans Murray had endured Timothy Pickering's personal correspondence throughout the summer and fall of 1799, until upbraided for the manner in which he had addressed Talleyrand as he opened the way for the mission of Ellsworth, Davie, and himself. That was too much. Murray had retorted to his superior: "Sir, you have been angry at the thing itself & no *manner* of success could have pleased you." He added, in the iciness of the third person, that if Colonel Pickering had given out his opinion of Vans Murray, Mr. Murray might see fit to join the "publishing gentlemen" who set forth with documents their opinions of superiors in Philadelphia.[91]

The idea that he should imitate James Monroe and Edmund Randolph was distasteful to William Vans Murray, but he was angry enough to threaten. He spread his feelings before John Quincy Ad-

89. Adams, *Works*, IX, 580–581, to Samuel Dexter, March 23, 1801. Horace, Fifth and Sixth Satires, Second Book, translation by Fairclough.

90. King (King ed.), III, 175, Hamilton to King, January 5, 1800. Also in Hamilton (Hamilton ed.), VI, 416.

91. Pickering Papers, XXVI, 23, Murray to Pickering, August 28, 1799; XII, 141, 278, Pickering to Murray, October 4, 25; XXV, 296, Murray to Pickering, December 1.

ams in Berlin, and he explained the matter in a letter to the President. What John Adams thought of Murray's account has not been published. Whether it had anything to do with his discharge of Pickering is conjecture. But just as Pickering was becoming heartily sick of the affair with Murray, and wished "the whole correspondence to be buried in oblivion," the President had dispensed with the services of Timothy Pickering, as well as of James McHenry, and called John Marshall, who had approved the second mission to France, to be Secretary of State.[92]

Timothy Pickering had finished out the day—"working hard" in self-conscious virtue but contemplating a "bold and frank" exposure of John Adams, still writing furtively to Alexander Hamilton, and suspecting Charles Lee of prying, because Lee happened to glance at a letter from Hamilton in Pickering's mail. As he was taking over the Department of State temporarily, Lee had opened the letter in the presence of the clerk. He stopped as soon as he realized that it was personal. But, said Pickering to Hamilton, "half a minute was enough to read yours."[93]

Alexander Hamilton and his Federalists of the "black cockade" —with Oliver Wolcott still undetected in the Cabinet to gather evidence which might be used against the President—had continued their campaign of undermining their own administration. Guided by Wolcott's letters, they could denounce John Adams to each other as crazy and their old associate, Oliver Ellsworth, as feebleminded, for having made such a treaty with France. They could plump for Gen. Charles Cotesworth Pinckney in the electoral college. They could even defeat the President. They could not undo the work, however, in which he was later to take most pride. John Adams had come to the end of his public career, indeed responsible as much as any one man for the fact that the United States were entering upon the new century free from the old alliance with France on the one hand and from subordination to Britain on the other. Though he thought there were no others in America, John Adams had the right to say of himself that he was an American.[94]

92. AHA Rpt., 1912, 629, 631, 632, Murray to J. Q. Adams, December 6, 13, 24, 1799. Murray's letter to John Adams, December 16, is in the Adams Mss. For J. Q. Adams' replies see his *Writings,* II, 443–447, December 10, 15, 20, 1799, and January 6, 1800. Pickering Papers, XI, 62, Pickering to Murray, May 8, 1800. Adams, *Works,* IX, 53–55, to Pickering, May 10; Pickering to Adams, May 12; to Pickering, May 12.

93. Pickering Papers, XXXVIII, 23, to Hamilton, May 15, 1800.

94. Gibbs, II, 313, Wolcott to Ames, December 29, 1799. Pickering Papers, XLVII, 199, Wolcott to Hamilton, September 3, 1800; XXVI, 231, Wolcott to Pickering, December 28, 1800. Adams, *Works,* X, 113, to James Lloyd, January, 1815, giving an epitaph for himself; IX, 582–583, to Stoddert, March 31, 1801.

Nevertheless, there was plenty of trouble waiting his successor. On the very day after Ellsworth, Davie, and Murray had signed the Convention of 1800 with France, General Berthier obtained the signature of Urquijo for Spain upon a secret agreement at San Ildefonso. Louisiana was going back to France. On March 27, 1802, Britain made the Peace of Amiens with Napoleon.

XV

JEFFERSON'S POLICY
PEACE AND EXPANSION

The Inaugural

THOSE dreadful "Jacobins" had broken through the rift in the Federalist party. They had successfully exploited the reaction among the American people against war, the repressive Alien and Sedition Laws, the concentration of authority in a class which had profited most from the funded debt and the Bank of the United States. It was therefore to be expected that they would reverse policies and repeal legislation obnoxious to the common run of men. But Thomas Jefferson knew that internal hatred too long sustained would be good for neither the peace nor the unity of the nation. He would soften animosities as soon as he could, and he would have individuals turn to their own affairs as he adjusted governmental expenditure to the level of frugality. He hoped to restore freedom of opinion, balance between Federal and state authority, peace with all foreign nations. "To take part in their conflicts," he said, "would be to divert our energies from creation to destruction." He would reduce the army and the navy, and stop accumulating by taxation "that treasure for wars to happen we know not when," for he believed that it was likely to cause them. He accepted the Convention of 1800 with France. He was glad to see lapse the possibility of coöperation with Britain on the seas. He welcomed the chance to restate the cardinal principles of Washington's Farewell Address.[1]

President Jefferson phrased those admonitions against partisanship at home and ties abroad:

> . . . every difference of opinion is not a difference of principle. We are all Republicans, we are all Federalists. If there be any among us who would wish to dissolve this Union or to change its republican form, let them stand undisturbed as monuments of the safety with which error of opinion may be tolerated where reason is left free to combat it. . . .
> Equal and exact justice to all men, of whatever state or persuasion, re-

1. Lyon, Louisiana in *French Diplomacy, 1759-1804*, is essential to this and succeeding chapters.

ligious or political; peace, commerce, and honest friendship with all nations, entangling alliances with none.

This came from the American who was supposed to be the "Friend of France."[2]

To conclude from such words, however, that the third President of the United States was a complete isolationist and uncompromising pacifist is to miss the realism and calculation in Jefferson's statesmanship. He cut down martial expenditures. He finished the dispersal of the army of the "black cockade" which Adams had begun. He withdrew the frigates from the seas. But he would use forcible resistance. He was willing like Adams before him to fight. His provisos were, however, that the area of war should be strictly limited, the chances of success large, and the cost relatively slight.

The little war with Tripoli enforces this point. Jefferson brought it to a close very shortly in 1805, and virtually by purchasing peace. The United States had just obtained Louisiana. Europe had gone back to war. His country was perilously near becoming involved because of its maritime interests. He could be sure of neither the scope nor the outcome of this war regardless of whose side the United States should take or who won. Jefferson therefore stopped the affair with Tripoli and strove to maintain American rights on the seas against both Britain and Napoleon by diplomatic protest and economic pressure without using war.[3]

Recent commentators, as well as his Federalist contemporaries, have criticized Jefferson's policy of replacing the frigates with gunboats to patrol the American shore, especially in the light of his and Madison's subsequent collisions with British power and Napoleonic craftiness in the West Indies and in European ports. But the frigates would not have been equal in any case to such a task. His policy was in fact statesmanship of the first order. The United States were not then strong enough to contend alone with any other power overseas, except perhaps the pirate states of northern Africa.

It had been one thing to revolt from the mother country on this continent and by the aid of France to win political independence, or even to take the offensive against French warships and privateers in the West Indies behind the protection of the British fleet while Britain also fought with France. It would be quite another to challenge any power at this time to combat on land or sea. Both Britain and France still were so entrenched in the Western Hemisphere that

2. Richardson, I, 321–324, First Inaugural, March 4, 1801. For compliments on this address from duPont de Nemours, see Malone, 30.
3. Jefferson (Ford ed.), I, 305, Jefferson on the price of peace with Tripoli, May 26, 1804. For the text of the treaty, see Miller, *Treaties*, II, 529–556.

if only they would keep peace in Europe with one another, either could strike at the possessions, not to speak of the pretensions, of the United States in North America. Thomas Jefferson knew this, knew it well, and he was determined to make those pretensions realities. The United States were fast growing strong. They were, as he remarked, doubling their population in twenty-two years. But they dared not yet risk war as an instrument to accomplish their aims.[4]

It was wisdom for another reason to conserve their money and their energies. Influential Federalists in the Northeast were not taking their ejection from the seats of government in the mood that all were Republicans, all were Federalists. They were scolding Jefferson's dismissals of Federalist officeholders, reviling the "corruption" in his administration, railing that the repeal of the Judiciary Act of 1801 was "unconstitutional," and muttering soon to one another that New England, and possibly New York if Aaron Burr could be persuaded, might be withdrawn from the Union to form a new confederacy under the wing of Britain.[5]

This was very dangerous for Jefferson's hope that he might keep the United States in "honest friendship with all nations, entangling alliances with none," while they grew to the full stature of the British pledge in 1783, a nation reaching from the Atlantic to the Mississippi. But within three months of his inauguration he learned something even more alarming. France was on her way back to the Mississippi Valley. If he did not search the files of the Government for evidence that French agents had been trying to raise formidable obstacles on American soil to the authority of the United States, he had only to look again into his diary of March 27, 1800, where he himself had recorded the fact of General Collot's activity in the West. He had only to recall what was common knowledge, that George Rogers Clark had accepted a French commission in defiance of the Adams administration at Philadelphia in 1798. He could strongly suspect, notwithstanding the rapidly changing character of the Western population, that the interest of France once restored upon the continent was not likely to confine itself within Louisiana across the Mississippi. It was most likely to press eastward to the mountain passes before Pittsburgh where once had stood Fort Duquesne.[6]

4. Richardson, I, 327, First Annual Message, December 8, 1801.
5. Lodge, *Cabot,* 319–348, correspondence with Wolcott, Gore, King, Pickering, 1801–04. See also Warren, I, 206–222, citing opinions of Bayard, Hamilton, Hillhouse, Troup, Ames, Gouverneur Morris.
6. See above, p. 252. Jefferson (Ford ed.), I, 287, March 27, 1800.

Westward Expansion—Carondelet's Observation

FRANCE had withdrawn in 1763, but Frenchmen remained in Lower Louisiana and New Orleans, St. Louis, and the Illinois country above the Ohio. The King of France had renounced in favor of the United States all claim to the territory east of the Mississippi excepting New Orleans, and his ministers had kept that promise. But their Revolutionary successors had felt no such obligation, and Genet had come armed with commissions for Clark and other leaders among the Americans of the West. Their objective was to be, so they professed, New Orleans outside the limits of the United States and beyond the area which France had renounced in 1778; if Canada were taken from the British, they said, it might be added to the United States. Here was offered a reassuring glimpse of a North America divided between France and the United States.

Genet had no such proposal to make about the Floridas. France's renunciation of them had been weakened by the United States themselves in 1783; for they had acknowledged that the title of Spain to the Floridas had been fixed by recapture from Britain. This was a technical loophole for French enterprise, but it was one nevertheless. And there had been no pledge given to the Government in Philadelphia that France would refuse if the Americans of the West should choose to cast their lot, and their homes, with the new French state of Louisiana on the Mississippi after they had helped to reëstablish the authority of France there. Nor had France seemed to care if Americans got into armed conflict with British along the Northwestern frontiers. It was all too apparent that the Girondist plan to enlist the services of American citizens without so much as asking by-your-leave of the Government in Philadelphia had contained no genuine respect for the jurisdiction of the United States beyond the Appalachians.[7]

Then had come Fauchet's double-dealing in Philadelphia while the representative of France at Basel tried to get Louisiana as well as the Spanish part of San Domingo. Then, Adet's meddling with the ratification of the Jay Treaty and the election of the next President of the United States. And then, Collot scouting over the mountains, along the Ohio, Missouri, and Illinois Rivers, down the Mississippi to New Orleans, and back to Philadelphia to rouse the Spanish minister against the British. There was danger indeed in the Mississippi Valley for both Spain and the United States, but it was quite as much from France as Great Britain. In the meantime, Tal-

7. See above, p. 157. See also Turner in AHR, X, 257–258.

leyrand had been developing his policy of secret pressure upon Spain for Louisiana as he trifled with Pinckney, Marshall, and Gerry about the French raids upon American shipping and sought bribes for his colleagues and himself.[8]

All of this Thomas Jefferson could not have known in detail; but he had witnessed enough, and heard of more, to make him certain that the French were out to get Louisiana from Spain, either by diplomacy or by war. It did not perplex him whether their motives were commercial or political. Whether France acquired Louisiana to keep it or only to use it for bargaining with some other power, Louisiana in any other hands than those of declining Spain would mar the promise of American empire. Britain, too, could not wish France, even momentarily, to take back Louisiana. But it was not simply a matter of drawing straws to see which of the Anglo-Saxon powers on this continent would undertake the business of excluding the Latin for the benefit of both.[9]

Jefferson knew also that Britain herself had designs upon the trans-Mississippi country, for economic exploitation from Canada if not for eventual government. She had not yet given up hope that she could maintain an Indian area within the boundaries of the United States. Such a region south and west of the Great Lakes would be a protective zone between British America and the states of the Union which were rising in the middle region upon the river-system of the Ohio, Cumberland, and Tennessee. And Britons still enjoyed the trade in the Floridas on the south and with the Indians up those rivers within American territory, even though the Floridas had been returned to Spain and American settlers who had never been Tories were beginning to take charge in local affairs. If Britons had their way, Americans beyond the Appalachians would be held in an Indian vise from the south and from the north gripped by His Majesty's Government.[10]

It would never have done, therefore, to give Britain a free hand in settling the problem of the Mississippi. It would have been hazardous even to let her coöperate. If the United States had permitted this, they would have had trouble obtaining their own share without severe restrictions. From their point of view, their proper share would have been the Floridas and New Orleans, but Britain would hardly have considered these proper without compensation else-

8. See above, p. 281 f.

9. Lyon, 81–89, 96 n. Whitaker in Hisp. Am. Rev., XI, 485–487. Fletcher in MVHR, XVII, 376. Fugier, I, 27. Guyot, 233, 237. Renaut, 23.

10. See above, pp. 100, 136, 206.

where—particularly in the West Indies as Grenville had suggested through Liston in 1798 with respect to San Domingo.[11]

In that case, the shipping interests of the United States would have had to face permanent losses. And New England was far too disgruntled with the political outcome of 1800 to accept any such sacrifice for the benefit of the whole country. The situation of Thomas Jefferson in 1801 was much as John Jay's had been in 1786. One difference was that Jay had been assailed with threats that Virginians would break the Union if he did not further this interest in the Mississippi. Jefferson had to worry about New England. He would have been happy if things could have been left exactly as they were for a while—with feeble Spain in nominal possession of both Floridas, the isle of New Orleans, and the trans-Mississippi country, and with Europe at war—until the Western States of the Union could grow stronger.[12]

They were doing so with astounding speed. The estimated white population of the Northwest Territory in 1790 had been only 3,000, but there were some 15,000 by 1795; and the census of 1800 revealed a population in Ohio alone of 45,365. The numbers in Georgia, then a frontier state, increased from 82,548 in 1790 to 161,414 in 1800. Kentucky's population rose from 73,677 to 220,-955. Tennessee increased from 35,691 to 105,602. In comparison, the estimate for West Florida and Louisiana under Spanish rule in 1800 was but 45,000. East Florida was said to have only 4,445 in 1804. The American West already outweighed the Spanish, and besides the American pioneers were not stopping at the Mississippi River. Land grants by Spain in Upper Louisiana for 1801 showed American names in excess of all others.[13]

Some European onlookers appreciated what this meant. Carondelet, Spanish Governor of Louisiana, had reported in November, 1794, upon "the unmeasured ambition of a new and vigorous people, hostile to all subjection, advancing and multiplying in the silence of peace and almost unknown, with a prodigious rapidity, ever since the independence of the United States was recognized until now." He had realized that it was political as well as territorial expansion: "Their method of spreading themselves," he wrote, "and their policy are so much to be feared by Spain as are their arms. Every new

11. See above, pp. 311–316.
12. See above, p. 100 f.
13. Century of Population Growth, 1790–1900, United States Census. Whitaker, *Mississippi Question*, 8, 10, 36, 276–277. Lyon, 114. Marbois, *Louisiana* (Am. ed. 1830), 210–212.

settlement, when it reaches thirty thousand souls, forms a state, which is united to the United States, so far as regards mutual protection, but which governs itself and imposes its own laws." He was inaccurate about the actual provisions in the Northwest Ordinance of 1787 as to numbers, but his perception was sharp. This colonial system did generate local patriotism without necessarily destroying loyalty to the central government of the Union.

Carondelet had talked of the chance that these Westerners might separate from the Easterners and associate themselves with Spanish America against the States on the Atlantic Seaboard. But he really had not expected this to happen, for he had strenuously urged his Government to take a strong defensive position, conceding the trans-Mississippi country above the Missouri, perhaps, to "this prestigious and restless population" and relying for protection of Lower Louisiana upon the Indians to the east of the Mississippi. The Choctaws, Chickasaws, Creeks, and Cherokees, "fearful of the usurpations of the Americans," said he, "will be disposed to make the most destructive war on them whenever incited by presents and arms."[14]

Within twenty-five years there had been such a wave of colonization as Europe had not seen happen in three centuries. Thornton, British chargé at Philadelphia, reported in February, 1802, that there were 900,000 inhabitants now beyond the Alleghenies. The American people were fast taking the great valley for themselves. Soon no other Government could dispute it with theirs, if only foreign rivalries in it continued a while longer, and their own Government stood by them.[15]

Would it not do so? It was now in the hands of those who had opposed Hamilton's plan of attack upon Spain and France, and his followers were ranting that these "Jacobins" would ruin the country. The Federalists could not conceal how eager they were to win over the Americans of the West and return themselves to power in Washington. But they were sadly mistaken if they actually believed Thomas Jefferson so devoted to the old ally, or so politically obtuse, that he would give them this easy chance to drive him from office. They erred, too, if they thought that he had any intention of sacrificing the future of the American people which he had perceived as long before as the quarrel between Spain and Britain over Nootka Sound in 1790.[16]

14. J. A. Robertson, ed., *Louisiana*, I, 294–300.
15. Lyon, 114.
16. See above, p. 137 f.

Policies Concerning France and Britain

JOHN QUINCY ADAMS had correctly appraised the "Friend of France" in 1796 when speculating whether Jefferson would be elected instead of his father: ". . . if Jefferson is elected, I speak with confidence in saying that he will inflexibly pursue the same general system of policy which is now established." Nor had the French minister Adet been deceived in thinking Jefferson "the born enemy of all European peoples" because he was an American. Jefferson would have been even less a "friend" had he known of all the intrigues in which Adet was participating at that moment. Jefferson himself, while opposing war with France in 1797, had gone on record as explicitly for "the great American interest." It was represented, said he, by "persons attached to republican government & the principles of 1776, not office-hunters, but farmers, whose interests are entirely agricultural." It required "gratitude to France, justice to England, good will to all, and subservience to none."[17]

President Jefferson was not long in sending his views on foreign policy straight to a person in France who had been very close to Talleyrand and the French foreign office, at least in times past. Jefferson informed Thomas Paine on March 18, 1801, by the courier who took back the Convention of 1800 with the Senate's reservations:

> Determined as we are to avoid, if possible, wasting the energies of our people in war and destruction, we shall avoid implicating ourselves with the powers of Europe, even in support of principles which we mean to pursue. They have so many other interests different from ours that we must avoid being entangled in them.—We believe that we can enforce those principles as to ourselves by peaceful means, now that we are likely to have our public councils detached from foreign views. The return of our citizens from the phrenzy into which they have been wrought, partly by ill conduct in France, partly by artifices practised upon them, is almost extinct, and will, I believe become quite so.

It was to be understood that the new administration was not going to be hotheaded. But there were principles which it meant to pursue, and it had a policy of peaceful enforcement which it expected to bring results.[18]

Jefferson declared to Paine that the new plenipotentiary, Robert R. Livingston, would not leave this country until the courier had

17. J. Q. Adams, *Writings,* II, 42, November 13, 1796. For Adet, see above, p. 196 f. *Corresp. French Ministers,* 983. Jefferson (Ford ed.), VII, 169–170, September 1, 1797.
18. *Ibid.,* VIII, 18.

returned with the French ratification of the Convention of 1800. This meant that France was expected both to approve the Senate's reservation that the American claims were suspended for eight years only and to acknowledge as well that the treaties of 1778 and 1788 were abrogated. Regardless of the change from Federalists to Republicans, the American Government was going to hold to the advantage, however slight, which had been gained from Talleyrand's assurance to John Adams that France honestly wished reconciliation with the United States.

But it was Britain which would require the most constant attention. James Madison, incoming Secretary of State, had written to Jefferson on January 10, before they took office, to indicate the policy which they might adopt. He was discussing the debate in the Senate over the Convention of 1800 and the chance that Britain might be irked by the equality which this agreement accorded to France, especially concerning prizes in American ports. He observed that

> G. B., however intoxicated with her maritime ascendency is more dependent every day on our commerce for her resources, must for a considerable length of time look in a great degree to this Country, for bread for herself, and absolutely for all the necessaries for her islands. The prospect of a Northern Confederacy of Neutrals cannot fail, in several views, to inspire caution & management toward the U. S. especially as, in the event of war or interruption of commerce with the Baltic, the essential article of naval Stores can be sought here only. Besides these cogent motives to peace and moderation, her subjects will not fail to remind her of the great pecuniary pledge they have in this Country, and which under any interruption of peace or commerce with it, must fall under great embarrassments, if nothing worse.[19]

The shrewdness with which this policy was conceived and presented may seem likely to make it more effective than John Adams' balancing between French and British forces had been. It did have more finesse. Republicans were to be ministers to France and to Spain. But the Federalist and New Englander, Rufus King, peculiarly fitted because of such political and social relationships to maintain the understandings with Grenville which John Jay had begun, was to stay on at London to settle the old claims of English creditors and the spoliations of American commerce. Thus the Virginians in power assumed an attitude toward Britain which appeared national rather than local and partisan. But Jefferson and Madison were not to have for their policy of good will to all and subservience to none

19. Madison (Hunt ed.), VI, 414–415.

so secure a foundation as Adams had enjoyed in spite of his unde-
clared war with France on the sea. After eight years of exhausting
struggle, Britain and France were approaching peace. Although it
was to prove but momentary, it was extremely dangerous to the
United States while it endured.

The British had already struck at Toussaint in San Domingo by
intercepting the fleet which he had sent against Rigaud. They had
done this for their own protection, but it had also been to the advantage of France and injury of American commerce. Whatever
misgivings they might have about France retaking Louisiana, the
British seemed to be preparing for this in order that their interests
elsewhere, in the Mediterranean, on the European continent, in
Africa and India, might be reinsured against Napoleon. What Jefferson had hoped to accomplish by "peaceable coercion" of Britain
and France at war was checked by the return of peace to Europe,
and of France to action in America. Jefferson learned on May 25,
1801, from King in London that the French plan for Louisiana,
which he had previously reported, had "in all probability since been
executed." This addition to the news of 1799 came upon critical
events both in Europe and in the West Indies.[20]

For one, there had been a change of government in England.
Rufus King had been administering the Adams policy of nonaggres-
sion in Spanish America rather well despite his own enthusiasm for
the schemes of Miranda. He had urged upon Grenville that New Orleans was virtually a port of the United States, even though it was
Spanish and therefore subject to a British blockade. He had shown
that it was the depository of an increasing domestic commerce between the Atlantic States and those on the Mississippi and its tributaries. He had exposed the pretenses upon which British cruisers
were interrupting that traffic, and had requested that they should
not treat any article which was bona fide American property as contraband. Grenville had answered that he saw no objection to King's
request, provided that New Orleans were not a place of equipment
for Spanish privateers. A basis for agreement accordingly was being
established when Pitt and Grenville both resigned on the issue of
emancipating the Catholics in Ireland, to which they had been
pledged as a condition for the union with Ireland. Although this
affair had little or nothing to do with their American policy, their
withdrawal from the Government had broken the continuity of negotiation which was so important to the United States. As Hawkesbury took Grenville's place in the foreign office, Rufus King had to

20. State Department, England, IX, No. 8, March 29, 1801, received May 25. See
above, p. 380.

r again with the process of educating British officials in
n points of view.[21]

nother, France had made a second agreement with Spain
ng the return of Louisiana. Lucien Bonaparte had agreed with
doy at Aranjuez on March 21, 1801, that the kingdom of
Etruria would be exchanged for Louisiana and Elba. Jefferson and
King did not yet know this. But Jefferson had before him King's
statements that influential persons in France thought nature had
marked a line of separation between the people of the United States
living upon the two sides of the Appalachians; that the cession from
Spain to France was intended to have injurious effects upon the
Union; and that Louisiana and the Floridas might be given to French
émigrés as Britain had once thought of colonizing those lands with
American Tories. King had reported also that General Collot was
about to head an expedition of disaffected Englishmen, Scots, and
Irish to the United States. It was a "matter of mere conjecture,"
said King, whether this had any relation to the cession of Louisiana.[22]

We, however, may see in the Library of Congress today a pho-
tographic copy of Collot's "General Observations" upon the problem of taking over Louisiana. Rufus King's English informants
were more accurate than he knew. These observations had been submitted to Talleyrand just six days before King wrote his despatch to
Madison.[23]

Rufus King had proposed that the United States send a "minister
of talents" who should make a "plain and judicious representation"
on the subject of Louisiana to the French Government. Victor Collot advised his superiors that he should be sent in diplomatic character to the United States, after the inauguration of the new President, "solely out of confidence and for the sake of pure courtesy,"
to tell Jefferson that France was taking possession of Louisiana and
making provisions for governing the colony.

Collot would do this in order to prevent the "Anglo-Americans"
from spreading alarm among credulous folk by insinuating that if
the French had good intentions, they would not make a mystery of
the affair. He insisted upon this procedure because "we will be
able to maintain ourselves in this colony only by the sustained
friendship of the Americans." Neither Talleyrand nor Napoleon
seems to have been impressed by this point. Collot was not sent to
tell Jefferson. The information was not imparted in confidence or

21. *Ibid.,* IX, King's Nos. 1, 2, February 6, 9, 1801.
22. Martens, *Receuil de Traités,* VII, 337. ASP FR, II, 511. State Department, England, IX, King's No. 8, March 29, 1801.
23. AAE EU Spt. 7, ff. 162–166, March 23, 1801.

courtesy before Jefferson and his colleagues had found out for themselves. Nor was Victor Collot, in fact, ever to see the Mississippi
Valley again.[24]

Anxiety

RUFUS KING's despatch, received on May 25, caused Jefferson and
his Secretary of State to reconsider their policy. The very day after
it arrived, Jefferson wrote to his protégé, Monroe, that there was
"considerable reason to apprehend" the retrocession of Louisiana
and the Floridas. It was a move, he said, very unwise in both Spain
and France, "and very ominous to us." On July 13 he sent a "private
& confidential" letter to the new governor of the Mississippi Territory, Claiborne, about his relations with the Spaniards in New Orleans. The United States, said Jefferson, were "sincerely amiable
and even affectionate" toward Spain. They looked upon her possession of adjacent territory as "most favorable to our interests."
They would see "with extreme pain" any other nation take her
place. Then came this instruction to Claiborne: "Should France get
possession of that country, it will be more to be lamented than rem-
edied by us, as it will furnish ground for profound consideration
on our part, how best to conduct ourselves in that case. It would of
course be the subject of fresh communication to you."[25]

It is a mistake to assume, as has been done from the softness of
these remarks to Claiborne, that Jefferson was not alarmed by the
news of May, 1801, and that he did not become exercised until
nearly a year later. His phrases "very ominous" and "extreme pain"
themselves would point to the contrary, if we did not also know
of other matters interwoven with the return of France into Louisiana that were giving him and his Secretary of State anxiety at the
same time.[26]

Secretary Madison had written about these matters on July 10 to
their intimate political associate, Senator W. C. Nicholas of Virginia.
They felt that the retrocession of Louisiana was probable, as France
would use it to counteract the pro-British sentiment in the Atlantic
States and to allay the fear aroused by the Blount affair that there
was "some combined project" to throw the region into the hands of
Britain. France would shape her policy in Louisiana to conciliate
"the minds of the Western people." They had it also "directly as-

24. *Ibid.* See below, pp. 432, 446, 452.
25. Jefferson (Ford ed.), VIII, 57–58, to Monroe, May 26, 1801; 71, to W. C. C.
Claiborne, July 13.
26. Lyon, 148–149.

serted by a consul just returned from San Domingo that Toussaint will proclaim in form the independence of that island within 2 or 3 weeks." The importance of this to the United States, as well as to other nations, said Madison, would not escape Nicholas' eye.[27]

Here was a third circumstance very dangerous indeed. If Toussaint did as predicted, it was certain to mean to those "other nations" at least, that he really intended to build for himself the Caribbean empire between the American continents which Dr. Stevens had advised him it would be "folly" to try. Britain, if France could not, would never let him do that. If they joined forces to prevent it, not only would American commerce suffer heavily in the West Indies while they did so, but the United States might have to witness changes there reaching toward the shores of the Gulf of Mexico, no one could tell how far.[28]

Most nerve-racking of all was the speculation as to what Britain would do about Louisiana on her own account. Would she forego the opportunity to make peace with France in Europe and seize New Orleans before the French could take possession? Would she, "intoxicated with her maritime supremacy," disregard her dependence upon the trans-Atlantic "commerce" of the United States and the "great pecuniary pledge" which her subjects had in this country? Madison stated precisely the situation which she would create for the United States if she did, when he replied to King on July 24, 1801:

Should Great Britain interpose her projects also in that quarter, the scene will become more interesting, and require still greater circumspection on the part of the United States. You will doubtless be always awake to circumstances which may indicate her views, and will lose no time in making them known to the President. Considering the facility with which her extensive Navy can present itself on our part, that she already flanks us on the North, and that if possessed of Spanish countries contiguous to us, she might soon have a range of settlements in our rear, as well as flank us on the South also, it is certainly not without reason that she is the last of Neighbours that would be agreeable to the United States.

It will be agreeable and may be useful for you to know that the Seasons on which our summer harvests depend have been unaccountably favorable, and particularly the crops of Wheat throughout the United States are estimated to exceed by one half the produce of any preceding year, at the same time, the quality is uncommonly excellent.[29]

27. Madison (Hunt ed.), VI, 425 n.-427 n.
28. AAE CP EU, LIII, ff. 324–332, Pichon to Talleyrand, October 9, 1801, from New York, received November 18, reporting Stevens' remarks to Pichon.
29. Madison (Hunt ed.), VI, 435.

What could the Government of the United States do? One could still wish that the British might be lured by American wheat. But suppose they ignored the American Government? One would have a very hard job to control the export business of the whole American people, east and west of the Appalachians. Once in Louisiana, the British were likely to get as much wheat as they wanted, and in defiance of the American Government. All that could be done, then, was to cling to the policy of "peace and persuasion," keep one's eyes on Britain as well as France, speak sharply to neither just yet—and wait.

In view of what we have observed of British schemes and actions in the Northwest and the Southwest on acknowledged American soil, there can be no doubt that Jefferson and Madison were very anxious, and also extremely cautious how they approached the problem of stopping the return of France into the Mississippi Valley. This behavior came from no love for "our antient friends."[30]

Lessons for Hawkesbury

ON the other side of the Atlantic, Rufus King, Federalist, was as uncertain and as alert even before he received the letter of July 24 from his Republican superior, Secretary Madison. Into the midst of the perennial conversations about British interference with American shipping in European waters and depredations in the West Indies, impressments of American seamen, and the mixed commissions on debts and spoliations, King heard the new foreign minister inject an offer, May 30, 1801: British ports and supplies would be available for the American squadron operating in the Mediterranean against the Barbary States. Then Hawkesbury introduced the subject of Louisiana. He "unreservedly expressed the reluctance" of Britain to have France return to Louisiana. This, he said, would undo the work of the Seven Years' War; France would "extend her influence and perhaps her dominion up the Mississippi and thro' the Lakes even to Canada"; besides, the Floridas were so close to the West Indies that "England must be unwilling that this territory should pass under the dominion of France."

King did not report what his Lordship would have Britain proceed to do. Perhaps he did not give Hawkesbury chance to say, for he could not mistake, said King, his Lordship's object. It may have been one of those occasions when you should not let your opponent have further chance to talk. King had been forewarned somewhat on the twenty-fourth preceding by a hint from the new prime

30. See above, pp. 208–210, 266–276.

minister, Addington, concerning supplies for American frigates at Malta, Minorca, and Gibraltar, and his inquiry whether it would not benefit England to send an ambassador with a large salary to the United States. In any case, King did not hesitate to accompany his thanks to Hawkesbury for the friendly offer in regard to the frigates with a forthright though private statement upon Louisiana:

> I had no difficulty nor reserve in expressing my private sentiments respecting it, taking for my text, the observation of Montesquieu "that it is happy for Trading Powers, that God has permitted Turks and Spaniards to be in the world, since of all nations they are the most proper to possess a great Empire with insignificance." The purport of what I said was that we are content that the Floridas remain in the hands of Spain, but should be unwilling to see them transferred except to ourselves.

This despatch was written on June 1. It reached Madison on August 6, 1801.[31]

The pronouncement from the American minister to the British minister has the merit of frankness. It places King for us, if we have not already observed, among those seekers after empire—Franklin, Washington, Jay, Hamilton, Jefferson. At the time it must have appeared to Jefferson and Madison as a dangerous bluff, which might possibly work, but which might as readily become a boomerang in international politics. What if Britain, as Adams had feared, and Grenville so candidly admitted through Liston, should decide to end the war with France without any regard for the interests of the United States?

Negotiations for peace were in fact already past the stage of overture, as King himself was reporting. They were completed that very autumn as the threat of a French invasion of England, however unlikely, absorbed more and more of the talk in London. Beyond terms in regard to Egypt, Malta, Denmark, and other European matters, there was an understanding that the British fleet should let Napoleon move against Toussaint in the West Indies.

The Floridas, however, were going to be kept distinct in British minds. Hawkesbury had told King in August, when taking up his request concerning the domestic trade of the United States through the island of New Orleans, that, "having reason to be satisfied that Spain has ceded the Floridas, including New Orleans, to France, they could not, without disregarding their own security, consent to the proposed Article concerning our Trade to that Island." King

31. State Department, England, IX, King's No. 20.

soon witnessed further transformation in the attitude of the British ministry. John Adams' fear of Britain was justified.[32]

King reported to Madison on October 2 that the preliminaries of peace between France and Britain had been signed the night before in Hawkesbury's office. A week later he declared that it was the real peace. The forthcoming negotiations at Amiens, he said, would be "mere ceremonial"; and he had a very good idea of what to expect for the United States in this settlement. If France had retained Egypt, her commercial and colonial outlook would have been upon the Mediterranean; but presumably she had not, so now France would turn to San Domingo, and perhaps Louisiana. By the end of the month, King had learned of the proposed expedition to San Domingo, and anticipated correctly what that meant. American commerce would "experience fresh embarrassments" in the West Indies. And the next move of France woud be toward the Mississippi River.[33]

By November 20, the British ministry had seen fit to give a copy of Lucien Bonaparte's agreement of March 21 with Godoy to Rufus King, proving that France had made the secret treaty of October 1, 1800. King hurried it to Washington, where it arrived on February 18, 1802, and he reported that he had hopes also of obtaining soon a copy of the first treaty so that they could find out whether New Orleans and the Floridas were included in the transaction.

"It is not a little extraordinary," he continued, "that during the whole negotiation between France and England, not a word was mentioned on either side, respecting Louisiana, though this Government was not ignorant of the views of France in this quarter." He was positive now that there had been a definite understanding between the two concerning the expedition to San Domingo. And he was correct. The prime minister, Addington, had assured Otto, representative of France, on or about October 23 that both Governments were interested in destroying Jacobinism and the blacks in San Domingo. The ministry did not care, so Otto reported Addington as saying, how many troops went to San Domingo. Addington wanted only to know how many ships were gathering at Brest, that

32. King (King ed.), III, 502–504, King to Madison, August 24, 1801. For Treaty of Amiens following, see Martens, *Receuil de Traités,* VII, 404–414, March 27, 1802. For John Adams' fear, see above, pp. 310–312.

33. State Department, England, IX, No. 36, October 2, 1801, received between December 16 and January 14, 1802. No record on the document. King (King ed.), III, 523, to Madison, October 9, 1801. State Department, England, IX, "private" despatch of October 31. No date of receipt recorded. See also King (King ed.), IV, 6.

he might reply to the party of opposition. Here was the spectre of the French invasion of England.[34]

Lord Hawkesbury then granted King an interview on November 25. After the usual discussion of debts and spoliations under the Jay Treaty, King went straight to the questions: Did Britain approve of the French expedition to San Domingo? What about Louisiana? Hawkesbury admitted that there was an understanding in regard to the expedition—but became vague concerning Louisiana. Nothing, he stated, had been said during or since the negotiation with France about it: "he would not speak positively and what he did say was confidential, but he should rather conclude that no part of the Expedition now preparing was destined for Louisiana. Spain had certainly ceded Louisiana. But he did not exactly comprehend the Territory included under that Term."

His lordship did not indeed! This from the man who had been explicit so recently as August about the danger to Britain if France regained Louisiana, and the vital importance of the Floridas to the British West Indies, could hardly be attributed to lack of information. But it suited Rufus King's diplomatic situation to presume so and give his lordship a lesson in geography:

> I said by Louisiana without other words one would understand only lands west of the Mississippi; but we apprehended the Floridas and New Orleans likewise to be ceded. We then turned to a map and I pointed out to L. H. the boundaries of Louisiana as I understood them making the Mississippi on the East and the River Norde on the West the limits. He asked where New Orleans was and I pointed it out to him and also explained the ancient claim of the Limits of Louisiana and such as was advanced before the 7 years' war. . . .

He then enlarged upon the importance of Louisiana to France if New Orleans and the Floridas were included. Hawkesbury "seemed to have never considered the subject," and remarked that "it must be a very long time before a country quite a wilderness could become of any considerable value."

Apparently—if he really thought so—his lordship was not valuing very much the British traffic in furs with the Indians upon the upper reaches of the Missouri, nor the trade along the rivers flowing through the Floridas from American territory above. But Rufus King had not finished with his lesson. He told Hawkesbury that the United States viewed the matter in a different light. They wished the country to remain in the "quiet hands of Spain." And perhaps

34. State Department, England, IX, King's No. 42, received February 18, 1802. AAE EU Spt. 7, ff. 159–161, copy of Treaty of October 1, 1800. Lokke in AHR, XXXIII, 326, citing Otto to Talleyrand, October 23, 1801.

remembering his lordship's statements on May 30 and again in August, King asked if Britain would coöperate at Amiens with Spain and the United States. Would Britain use her influence upon France to restore the country to Spain, if the United States should employ what influence they had with France, and Spain also should continue to desire it?

Lord Hawkesbury would give no direct answer. He repeated that Britain had taken no notice of the retrocession, and said "he would not think that it would soon become of importance."[35]

We should suspect from such evasiveness that there was a French and British understanding about Louisiana, in addition to that on San Domingo and Toussaint—Hawkesbury's lapse into ignorance was so quick. From August to November was a very short time in which to forget the location of New Orleans and the value of the Floridas. We do not know, as King did not, that there was such an understanding. The British minister of foreign affairs nevertheless had as good as declared to King that Britain would not interfere with the ceremony of peacemaking at Amiens for the sake of either Spain or the United States. And the promise of Louisiana to some other power, if Britain did not take it for herself, had been an instrument of British diplomacy before this.[36]

If, however, there was no understanding with France about Louisiana, there certainly was determination on the part of the British Government, for in spite of Lord Hawkesbury's apparent ignorance of conditions in the Mississippi Valley, Britons as well as Spaniards and Frenchmen had felt the power in the American settlements advancing toward the river. And heretofore Britain had not been looking for opportunities to clear the way before the United States—as the experiences of Washington and Adams could testify. It was not likely that British statesmen would begin to do so now as they came to terms with Napoleon. If it could be restrained and balanced, French power in the interior of America for a while might possibly serve British interests there by obstructing the aims of the United States.

A French State in America?

WHILE Rufus King tried in vain to persuade the British Government that it should keep France from New Orleans, Victor Collot was striving in Paris to get under way the great plan which he had prepared in 1796. He was not sure whether he really would be in

35. King (King ed.), IV, 17–19, King's memorandum, November 25, 1801.
36. See above, pp. 312–314, for Grenville and Liston to Adams' Cabinet officers.

command of the expedition to Louisiana, or even be allowed to go along as a subordinate, but he endeavored to keep himself in the minds of Talleyrand and Napoleon. He submitted more "observations" on November 6, 1801, in regard to "this precious colony."[37]

He had seen how the British had taken advantage of the "error" in the Treaty of 1783 with the United States about the sources of the Mississippi River. They had placed forts and trading posts in Spanish territory below the Lake of the Woods on the Red River, the Des Moines, and other streams so as to control the trade with Sioux, Mandans, Poncas. He thought that this usurpation was one reason why Spain had gone to war with Britain. The treaty to be made at Amiens, therefore, should provide for commissioners to arrange the boundaries definitely between the British dominions and Louisiana; and the United States should be invited to send an envoy to look after their interests.

Collot then examined the strength and the spirit of the Indians in Upper Louisiana. They had been "most affectionate," he said, toward France in the old days, but had become so detached by British intrigue and "our long absence" that they had scarcely preserved the memory of the French name. It must be reawakened and those reattached who knew the French no more than by tradition. If this were done, he was certain that they would be effective aids to France. As for those Americans who were "coming annually with more force towards Louisiana," Victor Collot had this shrewd comment for Talleyrand. It was of the greatest importance to encourage them, said he, but "with wariness" that they did not fast become too numerous: "In a word, such a proportion must be observed, between emigrants from the United States and our French settlers, that they are forced *to combine with us, and not we with them.*"[38]

Louis Vilemont, former captain of a regiment in Louisiana, submitted his views upon the situation in the Mississippi Valley at length to Talleyrand on June 6 and July 3, 1802. He, too, was exuberant over Louisiana's great riches in soil and minerals. He, too, observed the "astonishing increase" of the American population west of the Appalachians, noting especially the new American trade with the Indians below the Great Lakes in competition after the Jay Treaty with the merchants of Montreal and Quebec. Nevertheless, like Collot, he believed that the French could win over the Indians, at least those beyond the Mississippi, and divert their trade down the river to New Orleans where he thought it belonged. The "grand point to gain," declared Vilemont, was control over these natives of

37. AAE EU Spt. 7, ff. 174–176, November 6, 1801.
38. *Ibid.*

Louisiana; the way to do it was to introduce agriculture among them. President Jefferson well knew this necessity, for he had been able to maintain peace with many tribes on the west bank of the Ohio only after shipping agricultural implements among them. (This was a remarkable forecast of the very thoughts which Jefferson was to put before Congress in the following January as he proposed the expedition of Lewis and Clark into the far Northwest.) And, continued Vilemont, there was only one way to defend the country until France could establish her "new order." There were not enough white people in it. The necessary standing army was lacking. These "savages" would be the only forces which France could throw against the "irruptions" which were bound to come upon her property in "the new continent." Louis Vilemont did not then go on to explain how she could expect any better luck with setting the Indians upon the American pioneers than Britain had met in the Ohio country. He did not discuss Wayne's victory at Fallen Timbers, nor analyze the Treaty of Greenville.[39]

Could France, notwithstanding the American advance, have created a French state in the heart of North America as Victor Collot and Louis Vilemont proposed, to supplement and to make secure her insular empire in the Caribbean? Collot had made the topographical survey and submitted plans for defense. Talleyrand had all but completed the diplomacy with Spain. There remained for the Government, as Collot stated, the business of populating the Louisiana country with those who would be loyal to France. Success, however, would have come not so much from the will of the French Government as from enthusiasm among the French people; and of that, in comparison with the zeal of the "Anglo-Americans," there was great doubt. Moreover, as Collot did not explain, the plan depended altogether upon whether France could get, and keep, Mobile and Pensacola with New Orleans, to protect the entrances into the Mississippi Valley from the Gulf of Mexico. New Orleans would be helpless without such littoral defenses.

The acquisition of Mobile and Pensacola was lagging as Napoleon's ambition collided with the desires of the Spanish Crown in Italy behind which lay British interests and fears. Britain's statesmen were as concerned about the future of the Floridas as about Malta. That they would have stood by through all the years necessary to establish Vilemont's "new order" in America, merely for the purpose of thwarting the aspirations of the United States, is as open to doubt as the enthusiasm of the French people for extensive colon-

39. AAE EU Spt. 7, ff. 186–200, June 6, July 3, 1802. See above, p. 207 f. For Jefferson on the Lewis and Clark expedition, see below, p. 461 f.

izing or the assumption that those Americans whom Collot would admit into Louisiana, "with wariness," would break with their friends and relatives in the United States and become citizens of Louisiana, both loyal to France and hostile to the Government of their native country.

As Napoleon better understood the nature of this westward migration of Americans and their Government's determination to keep pace with them, and as his attempt to reconquer San Domingo failed, he soon preferred to let the United States have Louisiana. They would build the continental empire in this hemisphere which would check British power, and he would raise his "Continental System" upon the ruins of Britain's trade and influence with the neighbors of France in Europe.

But that was not yet the idea, not even with Napoleon, in France. Frenchmen continued a while longer to plan ways and means of getting Louisiana, and possibly the Floridas. There was much left still to be lost in the Mediterranean and the Caribbean before Napoleon and Talleyrand awoke from their dream of American empire. Jefferson and Madison, too, had many anxious moments ahead of them thinking things over, before they dared to put any pressure anywhere.

American commerce was involved with the affairs of Toussaint in San Domingo. There was the question of American claims left by the Convention of 1800 for Robert Livingston to settle in Paris if he could, while he tried also to prevail upon France to transfer New Orleans and the Floridas to the United States—unless they happened still to remain within the province of Charles Pinckney at Madrid. As Rufus King's despatches came from London, there was, for Jefferson and Madison above all, that fearful misgiving about Britain's designs upon New Orleans and the Floridas, growing to conviction that the United States must not break completely with the tradition of friendship toward France. Besides, one had the Federalists always at home, ready to capitalize any mistake one might make with American interests in the Mississippi Valley, even though many of their own number were already afraid of the increasing political power in the States of the West.

A Direction to Conquest

THOMAS JEFFERSON had appreciated the complex relationship between American trade and French possessions in the West Indies when he had conferred with Vergennes as American minister at Paris in 1785. The United States were in debt to the monarchy of France for their independence; there was the specific guarantee to

defend her West Indian colonies, and this was bound with her favor
to American shipping. "Doubtless," he had written at that time
to Secretary Jay, "it has its price." The United States might purchase entry into the French West Indies, just as Holland had bought
protection, by paying the price of "aid in time of war." But even
at that early date, when popular sentiment for France was still
high, Jefferson had questioned whether the trade would be worth
it.[40]

In 1790, as the National Assembly of Revolutionary France was
trying to control both homeland and colonies, Thomas Jefferson,
as Secretary of State, had seen the opening for American trade in
those colonies, if their "clamors and arms" should silence the "clamors of the Bordeaux merchants." This time, the price which the
American representative in Paris, William Short, might offer had
been full payment of the American debt, not only arrears of principal and interest but also the balance not yet due, for Congress,
wrote Jefferson, had authorized it. But either the French National
Assembly had not wished to frame the new constitution for the colonies so as to open their ports to American commerce at the expense
of the merchants in Bordeaux, or else Washington's administration
had thought better of paying off the debt to France in that way at
that time. Perhaps the matter was too closely linked with the quarrel between Britain and Spain. This had arisen over Nootka Sound
on the Pacific, but it involved New Orleans and the Gulf of Mexico. And it endangered the hopes of the United States themselves
in the Mississippi Valley, which Jefferson for one was already stress-
ing.[41]

In any case, Washington and his Secretaries had not been obliged
to wait long to perceive that Revolutionary France correlated West
Indian commerce with the Mississippi Valley. Citizen Genet had
come in 1793 unmistakably bent upon directing American energies into the Floridas and Louisiana for the benefit of France, while
American ships continued supplying the French islands under the
cover of neutrality. Secretary Jefferson had not been reluctant to
have war upon Spain in the Southwest, if it benefited the United
States. He had been reluctant, if it were to aid only France, and
to get the United States into trouble with Britain besides. Jefferson, as well as Hamilton, had opposed paying off the debt to France
any sooner than the bond required. He had even been ready to abandon the "antient friends" and the guarantee of the West Indies,

40. Jefferson (Ford ed.), IV, 117, 129–130, sent to Jay, January 2, 1786. Treudley,
96–104.
41. Jefferson (Ford ed.), V, 236, to Short, August 26, 1790.

should that be necessary to keep the country out of war at that time with Britain.[42]

Then, as the leading opponent of the Federalist administrations, Thomas Jefferson had watched critically the failure of the Monroe mission to France under Washington and had played politics while John Adams struggled through the X Y Z affair, Federalist intrigues, the second mission to France, and negotiations with the British over San Domingo. Now in 1801, as President himself, Jefferson found it quite desirable to carry on the commercial policy of his predecessor, modifying it only to meet the changing situation of Toussaint Louverture as Britain became more and more alarmed for the safety of Jamaica, vexed with American aid to Toussaint, and willing finally to make terms with France.

John Adams had not shared the exuberance of those "speculative and enterprising" Americans whom Liston suspected of imperial visions in the Caribbean. Instead, he had sagaciously recoiled from the opinion that the independence of San Domingo would be a good thing for the United States—after hearing of Nelson's victory over the French at Aboukir Bay. He had come finally, as the Ellsworth mission reopened negotiations in Paris, to the view that independence for Toussaint would be the worst of all possible solutions for the United States. Their interests elsewhere were in fact superior to those which could profit from Toussaint's success.[43]

With this point of view Thomas Jefferson fully agreed. Ten years before he had written to William Short for consumption in France: "Whenever jealousies are expressed as to any supposed views of ours on the dominion of the West Indies, you cannot go farther than the truth in asserting we have none. If there be one principle more deeply rooted than any other in the mind of every American, it is that we should have nothing to do with conquest." Had he meant then that the United States were not interested in expansion anywhere or in any manner? It looks as though he might have. But it would be gullibility itself to lift such a statement out of its historical environment and treat it as if it were an absolute term. It was not. It was highly relative to the kind of constitution which the French National Assembly was then drafting for the colonies in the West Indies, and it was intended to have some influence upon that construction. Other evidence has shown that Thomas Jefferson had the expansion of the American empire very much on his mind at the time.[44]

42. See above, pp. 150–151, 159.
43. See above, pp. 315–316, 360.
44. Jefferson (Ford ed.), V, 363–364, to Short, July 28, 1791. See above, pp. 137–140.

It is true, whatever else had happened in the intervening years to remold Jefferson's thinking upon the attitude which his country should take concerning European nations in the Western Hemisphere, that nothing had as yet occurred to change his opinion that the United States should not defy those powers in the West Indies —certainly not Britain, nor even France. Spain might be different. But neither was Spain just yet to be pressed too hard overseas. It was not until after he had acquired Louisiana that Thomas Jefferson talked of having Cuba in connection with reprisals in the Floridas for Spanish intrigues in the West. Even then he expressed it in this smooth manner: "Probably Cuba would add itself to our confederation." Still he could declare that the United States were not interested in conquest, although fewer would believe him.[45]

Pichon's Warnings to Talleyrand

TALLEYRAND, as well as Robert Liston, British minister, had been keeping an eye upon John Adams' behavior toward Toussaint and San Domingo. As Ellsworth and Davie came to France, Talleyrand had urged that a new consular agent be sent to the United States— to "fathom what is going on with respect to our colonies." So Pichon, who had been in this country years before and more recently had negotiated with Vans Murray at The Hague, was soon on his way. He landed at Norfolk, Virginia, in March, 1801, and proceeded at once to Washington. He came ostensibly to further the new policy of conciliation following the Convention of 1800. Underlying that were more significant purposes. He was to break any resistance there might be in the American Government to the French recovery of San Domingo and the other islands, and he was to discover what the new Administration was thinking about Britain and Louisiana.[46]

By April 21 Pichon had not been able to find out what was in the treaty which Maitland had made with Toussaint under the guidance of Stevens, but he had been officially told that Stevens' successor would have to be chosen carefully or the United States would get into trouble with Britain and lose all the commerce of the island. He had concluded that "one continues to regard Toussaint therefore as independent," although "one" said that the United States wished only the trade of San Domingo. He reported that the American commanders were not coöperating in the Spanish part

45. *Ibid.*, IX, 124–125, to Madison, August 16, 1807.
46. Lokke in AHR, XXXIII, 323 n. AAE CP EU, LIII, Pichon's first report to Talleyrand, March 12, 1801. For detailed study of Jefferson's policy in regard to Toussaint and San Domingo, see Tansill, *The United States and Santo Domingo*, 70–109.

of the island, which had been ceded to France in the Treaty of Basel.[47]

He informed Talleyrand on May 1 that Britain would have need of American shipping "more than ever"—to do what the "armed neutrality" of the North would keep British ships from doing, transport provisions to Britain's ports on the Baltic. And he announced that the news of the retrocession of Louisiana to France had arrived. The rumor was already spreading that the French fleet was coming to Guadeloupe or San Domingo. If this had taken place, said Pichon, it was "one of the most delicate operations" that France could attempt as it had "neither surety nor advantage" for her. He gave two reasons: the Americans wanted the freedom of the port of New Orleans, and they had their eyes on the Floridas, at least one of them. He had treated the news with "indifference," he said, and to one inquiry had replied that it was "a thing extremely unlikely." But he had not thought it so much so himself that he neglected to submit his opinions to Talleyrand. The foreign minister of France was well advised of American hostility toward French re-occupation of New Orleans long before Robert Livingston arrived at Paris in the following November.[48]

Then Pichon went to New York to see for himself what was the nature of American dealings with San Domingo, and he "fathomed" what was going on. He reported to the ministry of marine and colonies on June 3 that Toussaint's project of independence had been deranged somewhat by the reconciliation of the United States and France but had not been abandoned. The American vessels which came daily from San Domingo guarded "an absolute silence" upon what was occurring there. He attributed this to Stevens' orders and called it "intervention." At the same time, he heard Edward Livingston say—without his having revealed what was on his own mind—that the United States would quarrel with France if she took over Louisiana, and he reported this at once to Talleyrand.[49]

Back again in Washington by the middle of July, Pichon carried the matter of San Domingo straight to Secretary Madison and the President himself. Madison reiterated that the United States wished nothing except to continue their trade with the island, but he also said that the Administration did not want to risk a quarrel with Toussaint; "that is to say," they were prepared for a declaration

47. AAE CP EU, LIII, ff. 104–105.
48. Ibid., LIII, ff. 115–118.
49. Ibid., LIII, ff. 135–140, 146–149.

of independence. Then to reassure Pichon, Madison added that he thought Britain did not favor this any more than the United States. As Pichon was about to withdraw, he remarked further that they had heard from London of the retrocession of Louisiana; he surmised that it had been a project of the late "misunderstanding" between France and the United States—either "hostile" or "to put the French colonies out of dependence upon the United States." "One would hope," he concluded, "that with the reestablishment of peace, France would abandon the ideas. . . ."

Madison recalled the old order, the pledges of 1778, and declared that the two countries could not live so close together without trouble. The United States had to have the navigation of the Mississippi. Their Western settlements were growing. They were accustomed to Spain, but disliked her "absurd system of prohibitions" at New Orleans. This was a "peaceful Government," he said; but his insinuation, though easy, was as direct as Pichon's protests in regard to Toussaint.

Pichon pled his ignorance of the retrocession, but argued that Louisiana had not been included in the French renunciation of 1778, and reported immediately to Talleyrand. This event, he declared, would "embarrass" the Administration "more than any other." It was the "germ of a new misunderstanding." Talleyrand also should add to his "information" the facts, said Pichon, that fifteen years before Kentucky had only 60,000 inhabitants, whereas now there were 250,000; and they exported by way of New Orleans, all the time, millions of dollars of produce.[50]

Two days later Pichon accordingly reported his conversation with the President. He had found Jefferson "very communicative" on the subject of Toussaint where Madison had been reserved. It is evident that there had been time for Jefferson to confer with his Secretary of State since Madison's talk with Pichon. Pichon had nothing of significance to relay to Talleyrand concerning the President's views on the French occupation of Louisiana. But he did, in regard to American relations with Britain.

Thomas Jefferson did not approve of the schemes of Toussaint Louverture. The President had stated frankly that he could not risk adverse public opinion by attempting to stop the trade with the Negro chieftain. Besides, this would only throw him into the arms of the British—a consequence which the French could hardly enjoy. But, if France made peace with Britain and then took action, the United States would be able to help "without difficulty": "Then

50. *Ibid.*, LIII, ff. 169–174.

nothing would be easier," said Jefferson, "than to supply completely your army and your squadron, and to starve Toussaint."

Pichon was glad to hear this. He was as pleased with Jefferson's declaration that he did not wish San Domingo to become "an Algiers" in the seas of America. It was a telling phrase which Napoleon used later to get his understanding with the British in regard to Leclerc's expedition and its supply from Jamaica; and by so much Thomas Jefferson helped to create the distressing situation in which Rufus King found American interests in the following October after the preliminaries of peace had been signed in Lord Hawkesbury's office. Pichon was not so happy about Jefferson's comments upon the "armed neutrality" of northern Europe against Britain.

There was little hope that the United States would join the league. Jefferson's "neutrality" was "passive"—for many reasons; but they all came down to the one basic fact of Britain's power on the sea. He would "certainly approve" the principles of the Coalition of the North, but he did not think that an armed league could force Britain to accept those principles. Only a concert, he said, of all commercial powers, suspending all communications with her, was likely to succeed. Pichon wisely concluded that for such coöperation America was too far away. Moreover, he was keen enough to perceive that in a crisis America was altogether too likely to make a "counter-league with England."[51]

All of these observations by Pichon had reached Talleyrand before Livingston arrived as Jefferson's minister to France. Yet Talleyrand chose to minimize their direct and ominous bearing upon the return of France to Louisiana. He answered Pichon on October 27, 1801, in the optimism of the truce which had just been made with Britain: "The information which you give me upon the favorable disposition of the United States towards France acquires a new degree of interest." But he did not discuss Pichon's due warning that the cession of Louisiana would cause a "new misunderstanding" with the United States. He merely told Pichon to hold himself to generalities in his conversations upon Louisiana "but nevertheless reassure always the federal government upon the effect that our neighborhood would have for it in case that we would have some establishment upon the continent of America." That Secretary Madison had already said Americans would dislike such neighbors did not appear to catch the attention of the foreign minister. But this ex-bishop was not thick. He was overconfident.[52]

Pichon, however, was not. He continued sending home astute

51. *Ibid.*, LIII, ff. 177–184.
52. *Ibid.*, LIII, ff. 349–354.

advice and sure prophecy. He wrote on October 2 that Livingston was coming to obtain explanations of the occupation of Louisiana as well as to press the American claims for spoliations, to prolong the "immense commerce" of the United States with the French colonies, and give explanations about Toussaint. He reported on the twenty-fifth that the Americans were angry with Spain for her seizures of their shipping and her declaration that Gibraltar was under blockade. They accordingly might "aim at" Louisiana before "we are there." Spain, he said, must be careful or "we will lose this possession before we have it." He urged that France should send her naval expedition directly to New Orleans, before her "project upon St. Domingo."[53]

He analyzed the evidence in the census of 1800 for Talleyrand on November 15. It was significant, he declared, for its revelation of the "spirit of adventure" in a warlike people. The white population had increased in thirty years from one-and-a-half to four millions. Maine was on the way to statehood. Tennessee, but ten years old, had 100,000 inhabitants. The Indiana Territory was already a "scion of a State." The Americans were now realizing what had been in 1787 only "a dream." The Mississippi Territory was the "cradle" for new states; people looked from Natchez as its capital toward New Orleans. And the Federal Government was more and more attentive to the lines of communication cross-country:

"All these developments, citizen minister, surpass imagination. . . ." wrote Pichon, "and these wildernesses, hardly known thirty years ago, are already so peopled, sensing already so much their importance as to attract the attention of their neighbors and of the general Government. These considerations, citizen minister, are worthy of our attention." [54]

On November 25 Pichon warned Talleyrand again. News of the truce with Britain had arrived. It was happy for the world. But it was "anything but welcome here" to the merchants, for it came "across their speculations." Six days later he wrote that Louisiana was very much on American minds. And the President was anxious, although he professed to be reassured that France had given up trying to exchange Parma for Louisiana. "This," said Pichon, "is the last opinion on this subject." Talleyrand would know better than he if it were "correct"! Other persons, however, were discussing which of Spain's possessions would be more desirable for the United States. "People of the West," said Mexico and Louisiana. "Merchants," said Cuba, "where one goes by boat from the Flori-

53. *Ibid.*, LIII, ff. 316–321, 343–345.
54. *Ibid.*, LIII, ff. 374–382.

das." Pichon remarked that it was just as if, ten or fifteen years before, one had talked hypothetically of their sharing the trade of San Domingo with France. That had become fact. So might these. "This people here," said he, "make a way in ten years."[55]

Finally on December 3, 1801, Pichon reported that a pamphlet had appeared near-by in Alexandria inviting the United States Government to seize Louisiana. He had seen the President at once about it. Jefferson had replied that it was "nonsense," deserving no attention. Then he had added that the United States would possess Louisiana by the force of things; for the moment, they had more land than they needed. What did this mean? Pichon was hardly deceived. It did not mean that Thomas Jefferson had no thought of acquiring Louisiana when he sent Robert Livingston to France. Quite the contrary. It meant that the President was not yet ready to make this an issue, least of all to say that he would fight for Louisiana. There were in this problem other very uncertain factors beyond the intentions of France.[56]

"The Last of Neighbours That Would Be Agreeable"

ALTHOUGH he may not have told Pichon so, Thomas Jefferson had begun to hear of the negotiations for peace between Britain and France, from King in London, before he had informed Pichon in July that he would aid in breaking Toussaint's hold upon San Domingo. He had learned, too, of the probable retrocession of Louisiana and had expressed his "extreme pain" to Claiborne ten days before. Could it have been that Jefferson was thinking that the restoration of France in San Domingo could be kept distinct from her reoccupation of Louisiana? It does not seem logical that he could have been reasoning so. Yet there is evidence that he had grounds.

Lord Hawkesbury had been very explicit to Rufus King in May. He was so again in August, about the British interest in the Floridas. The British understanding with France in October had only to do with San Domingo, and Britons were thoroughly aroused when French activities took on a wider range later. Moreover, if Hawkesbury was vague about Louisiana, he was positively mute concerning the Floridas when King gave his lordship's geography an overhauling in November.

It is plain that the British Government was determined not to hamper its peacemaking with France for either Spain or the United States. This does not signify that it could have had no ultimate

55. *Ibid.*, LIII, ff. 408–409, 433–436.
56. *Ibid.*, LIII, f. 437.

scheme of its own to thwart the aims of Napoleon in the Caribbean beyond San Domingo and upon the adjacent coasts of the Floridas. By the time Jefferson had promised to help France destroy Toussaint, Britain's statesmen more than likely had distinguished, in their purposes with respect to France, the arrangement for Louisiana to the west of the Mississippi from the disposal of the Floridas eastward from the island of New Orleans. This was unmistakably the case later. Jefferson had right in July, 1801, therefore to presume that something other than American anxiety might come between Napoleon's reconquest of San Domingo and his ambitions in Louisiana.

Whatever else Jefferson and Madison were thinking and planning to do, or not to do, as they conferred with Pichon in the summer of 1801, as they wrote letters to Monroe and Claiborne, read King's despatches, and prepared for Livingston's mission to France, they were probing for the British factors in every phase of the complex problem. There might be some profit for the United States, possibly even for their commerce, if France and Britain made peace. Privateering at least would stop. There might be some advantage, too, if Britain allowed France to break Toussaint Louverture and restore her authority in the West Indies. But what if Britain allowed France to come too far, come back into Louisiana? Or worse, what if Britain did not make peace with France, and put her own troops ashore at New Orleans?

It is not surprising that Jefferson, having to meet such apprehensions, made one statement to Pichon on San Domingo, wrote in another vein to Claiborne about the Mississippi, and had Secretary Madison instruct Rufus King at London in yet another. Through the maze, one thing is clear: Thomas Jefferson wanted neither France nor Britain as the neighbor of the United States on the Gulf of Mexico and the Mississippi River. If only the European balances would swing uncertainly a while longer, the United States would have not even Spain as their neighbor at New Orleans and in the Floridas; and the problem of the West Indies would take on a very different aspect soon thereafter. The United States would have consolidated their territories and established their control over both sources of supply for European possessions in the Caribbean —both the Atlantic Seaboard and the great Valley, which Pitt's secret agent had so aptly described as the "Granary of America." It was discernment rather than fear which delayed the voyage of Robert Livingston to France until the Convention of 1800 should return again to the United States with Napoleon's ratification. It was discretion rather than timidity which seasoned Livingston's instructions about damages to American shipping, the retrocession of Louisiana, and the Floridas with deft assurances of continuing good will toward France and desire for peace; it was keenest appreciation of the dynamic in peace for the American people at this moment.

XVI

LIVINGSTON'S EFFORTS IN FRANCE

French Pleasure, Federalist Sarcasm

THE appointment of the Chancellor of New York as minister to France may have come from maneuvering within the Republican party, and the fact that he did not wish to be Secretary of the Navy. It was an astute choice nevertheless for its influence upon French opinion. He would be welcome because of the partiality which he had shown to France when in charge of foreign affairs for the old Congress of the Confederation. He had tried to counteract John Jay's suspicions of Vergennes at Paris during the peacemaking of 1782. He had then opposed Washington's policy at the time of Jay's mission to England in 1794, had declined the accompanying mission to France, and had favored James Monroe upon his recall from France in 1797. But he was not involved with the friends of Monroe in France who had been displaced by the *coup d'état* of Napoleon Bonaparte. Robert Livingston would appeal to those like Victor duPont who had arrived at Havre de Grace from New York in February, 1801, with official despatches and private information for the minister of foreign affairs. DuPont wrote ahead to Talleyrand about the "happy revolution" in the United States, complimenting Talleyrand for his share in preparing it and for knowing how to extract "so great a part for the political and commercial interests of our country." Victor duPont was still a Frenchman as in the days of his consulship at Charleston, notwithstanding that he had removed to the United States and established himself in business here.[1]

On the other hand Livingston's past record made for caustic remarks by old Federalists. Robert Troup ridiculed the Chancellor's deafness and his aristocratic manners: "At Buonaparte's table his situation must be delightful to himself and the company. One of his sons will be obliged constantly to sit alongside of him and cry out, Mr. Livingston—Mr. Livingston—Mr. Livingston! Citizen sans culottes speaks to you! . . ." And again, on Livingston's voyage

1. Jefferson (Ford ed.), VII, 462, 466, to Livingston, December 14, 1800; 484–485, to Madison, February 1, 1801; 492–493, to Livingston, February 16; 499, to Livingston, February 24. For Livingston's previous career, see above, 74 f., 228, 232, 244. AAE CP EU, LIII, f. 8, Victor duPont to Talleyrand, February 4, 1801.

to "the Jacobinical paradise," "Report announces, and I believe truly, that the headquarter gentleman wished him to go in a merchant vessel: but with true democratic spirit he replied that he would not go at all if they did not send him in a government ship. When he went on board the other day to reconnoitre the accommodations the frigate afforded, it was generally doubted whether he heard the honorable voice of the guns. . . ."[2]

Neither Robert Livingston's deafness, nor his foibles, nor his leaning toward France were to impede his efforts for his country. He proved to be as American in his vision of empire as any who had gone abroad before him in quest of it.

The Issues

LIVINGSTON received a long letter from President Jefferson, before official instruction from the Secretary of State. It is highly significant both for its bearing upon what had happened in the days of Washington and Adams and for its relation to the mission which Livingston was about to undertake. Rufus King had reported on March 26, 1801, that the British Parliament was debating the rights of neutrals on the seas. Both the ministry and the opposition had denied the right of *free ships free goods*. The British fleet had just sailed for the Baltic. The expectation in London, said King, was that Denmark and Russia would soon be detached from the League of Armed Neutrality. Nelson's victory at Copenhagen occurred on April 2.[3]

Jefferson therefore wrote on September 9 that Livingston would not be instructed upon the great question of the maritime law of nations. Even this letter, said Jefferson, was only the unofficial opinion of himself; should the time come when it was expedient for the United States to coöperate in establishing the principle *free ships free goods,* Congress as well as the President and his Constitutional advisers would have to express its opinion. As for himself, he believed that the principle would "carry the wishes of our nation." The practice among others was different; the principle was not yet the law of nations; it was based only on special treaties; it was the exception, not the rule. And however friendly themselves toward the principle, the United States, "having no treaty with England substituting this instead of the ordinary rule," would never go to war to establish it.[4]

2. King (King ed.), III, 409, 459, 526–527, Troup to King, March 23, May 27, October 14, 1801.

3. *Ibid.,* III, 411–413, to Secretary of State, March 26, 1801.

4. Jefferson (Ford ed.), VIII, 88–92, to Livingston, September 9, 1801.

In short, Thomas Jefferson now endorsed the past policy of George Washington and Timothy Pickering denying that the United States were obligated under the Treaty of 1778 to use force in protecting French goods aboard American neutral ships from seizure by Britain's cruisers. Although not saying so expressly, Jefferson upheld the Federalist argument concerning the Jay Treaty; it had broken no commitment to France in regard to enemy goods in neutral vessels. In like manner, he repudiated the attempt which Monroe had made as minister to France in 1794–97 to get the United States into war with Britain on the side of France. Jefferson would in fact notify France that the United States did not concede the validity of her national claims against them on account of the principle *free ships free goods*. "Unforeseen circumstances," he told Livingston, "may perhaps oblige you to hazard an opinion, on some occasion or other, on this subject, and it is better that it should not be at variance with ours."[5]

As for the future, the President's great worry was not so much what France might attempt in the Mississippi Valley, after starving Toussaint in San Domingo, as what Britain was about to do. Until he had surer knowledge of that, Thomas Jefferson was going to make no moves likely to stir trouble with her over old issues or new. The United States were not to swing back from war with France into hostility toward her enemy, only to discover that the enemy had made her own peace with France and left them to face two strong opponents on both land and sea.

Then Secretary Madison cautiously instructed the new minister to France on September 28, 1801. Livingston was to assert the traditional friendship for France. He was to uphold the claims for damages to American shipping, as the Administration chose to believe that they had merely been postponed by the Convention of 1800. (Napoleon's "retrenchment" upon the Senate's reservations had not yet reached Washington.) Above all, Livingston was to impress upon France, as Charles Pinckney upon Spain, the "momentous concern" of the United States in the reported change of neighbors on their western and southern frontiers. He was to remark that the frequent recurrence of war between France and Britain endangered the western settlements of the United States with military expeditions from Canada and Louisiana. And he was to point to the unrest which would occur among the slaves in the Southern States, for they had been "taught to regard the French as patrons of their cause." He was then to state—with no gloss here of friendship—that a French neighbor might turn the thoughts of

5. *Ibid.* For Washington, Pickering, and Monroe, see above, pp. 240–241.

Americans toward a "closer connection" with Britain. Should he discover that the cession had or certainly would take place, he was not to irritate "our future neighbors" unnecessarily, nor to check "the liberality which they may be disposed to exercise in relation to the trade and navigation through the mouth of the Mississippi."

Besides smoothing the way for American trade down the Mississippi, Livingston was then to try to get France to hand the Floridas over to the United States, at least West Florida so as to include the Mobile River. Its importance to the United States, wrote Madison, recommended "the prudent use of every fair consideration" to obtain it. If Livingston found that France did not have the Floridas, he was then to enlist her aid in getting them from Spain—possibly in return for abandoning the claims of the United States on account of damages to their shipping.

As for Toussaint and San Domingo, Livingston could explain, if Pichon had not already done so, that the President had sent Tobias Lear to replace Edward Stevens. This was intended to confirm the information that the interest of the American Government in Toussaint's future was at an end. (But Lear was going to have a very hard time proving this to Leclerc when the French expedition arrived to subdue the blacks.) [6]

Thomas Jefferson was at work once more, as in 1790, upon the principle that the balance of power between Britain and France in America could be managed for the benefit of the United States. Critics have scored him again and again for frailties ranging from naïveté to cowardice. His greatest opponent, however, confirmed his judgment. Napoleon Bonaparte played eventually into his hand.

First Negotiations—Hope in Amiens

ROBERT LIVINGSTON arrived in Paris on December 3, 1801. He picked up the rumor that Spain had given back Louisiana in exchange for the Spanish part of San Domingo, and went at once to Talleyrand. The minister of foreign affairs tried to evade his question but admitted under pressure that Louisiana had been a "subject of conversation." Livingston withdrew after this strong hint: . . . "perhaps both France and Spain might find a mutual interest in ceding the Floridas to the United States." He as quickly discovered that his negotiations were not to be easy. By December 12 he knew that, if France had the territory, Talleyrand would never part

6. State Department, Despatches to Consuls, I, Instructions to Livingston, September 28, 1801. For Livingston's request for an interview to receive instructions on May 31, 1801, at Washington, see State Department, France, VIII. For Lear and Leclerc, see below, p. 489.

with it on the terms which he then had to offer. As another French official expressed it, none but spendthrifts paid debts by selling land —and added after a short pause, "but it is not ours to give."[7]

This information reached the State Department at Washington on February 26, 1802, just eight days after King's despatch from London enclosing a copy of the agreement which Lucien Bonaparte and Godoy had signed on March 21, 1801. Jefferson and Madison knew very well now that, practically speaking, the French did have Louisiana, New Orleans, and in all probability the Floridas. It was quibbling to say that they did not possess the country because the transfer was not complete. There was good chance, to be sure, that something might yet happen to prevent a part or even the whole of the region from actually passing to France. Godoy on other occasions had proved stubborn and slow. And Britain's interest in the Mississippi was decidedly to be taken into account. Jefferson and Madison meanwhile had to assume that France was in full possession until they got proof to the contrary. The news from Livingston and King was most discouraging, for, as Collot had remarked to Talleyrand, one's friend can hardly be considered for long a friend if he makes a "mystery" of some action which may injure one's own interests.[8]

Livingston also had to assume that France had acquired the whole area of Louisiana and the Floridas, and to proceed, moreover, on his own responsibility, since he was destined to receive no further word from his superiors in Washington until far into March of the following year. Undaunted by the rebuff from Talleyrand, he set out to gain every bit of information and to use every approach that might bring him to the first objective of his Government—New Orleans and at least West Florida. Frenchmen in Paris quickly had it demonstrated to them that the ways of this old "friend" were far more like those of his Federalist opponent, John Marshall, than of his fellow Republican, James Monroe.[9]

Livingston wrote on December 30, 1801, to tell King across the Channel what the situation was in Paris and to raise questions. He expected that part of Leclerc's fleet which had sailed for San Domingo would go on to Louisiana if Toussaint offered no resistance. Collot, he said, originally intended for the governorship, was

---

7. State Department, France, VIII, Livingston's report, December 10, 1801, postscript December 12, received February 26, 1802. See also ASP FR, II, 512. Livingston announced his arrival in France to Talleyrand from L'Orient on November 13, 1801, AAE CP EU, LIII, f. 373.

8. For King's despatch, see above, p. 405; for Godoy, p. 297; for Collot, p. 400.

9. See above, pp. 233–234, 290.

at present again out of favor. Spain, no longer a "free Agent," undoubtedly had made the cession. What did Britain think? Did the British not see that Spain in a "perpetual state of pupilage" under France would grant every advantage commercial and political to France, to the exclusion of Britain? Did they not realize that Americans in the West, the French in Canada, the Indians might be turned against Britain? Might King not induce the British ministry, with these "hints" and others which would occur to him, to stop "a final settlement of this business" about Louisiana?[10]

When Secretary Madison saw this letter, he reprimanded Livingston on March 16, 1802, for putting the United States in danger: Britain might abuse this "confidential resort to her" for the purpose of "sowing jealousies in France" to thwart "our object." Within a few weeks President Jefferson had thought better of it, and had sent the famous open letter of April 18, 1802, by duPont de Nemours to Livingston, declaring that if France took possession of New Orleans, the United States might have to marry themselves to the British fleet and nation. The reprimand lost all significance.[11]

Meanwhile, completely out of touch with his Government in Washington, Robert Livingston had pressed ahead with his idea —regardless of the chance that Britain might not rise to the "hints," and in spite of his own misgivings that the evil which the United States had suffered from the break with France was not to be calculated. He personally, he said on January 13, still saw more value in the old French pledge of American independence than danger in the commitment which the United States had once taken to guarantee the French West Indies. He regretted that France could no longer be held to her renunciation of the Floridas. He was affected by the assertion that France would have no claim to the Floridas if the United States had renewed the old treaties instead of abrogating them in the Convention of 1800. And he was disturbed by the suspicions in Paris that the United States themselves had designs upon the French islands. Officially, therefore, Livingston felt obliged to state "upon all occasions" that so long as France conformed to the Treaty of 1795 between Spain and the United States, respecting the Mississippi and the boundary, his Government did not consider itself as having any interest in opposing the transfer of Louisiana to France. He felt no personal obligation to stop trying to change conditions so that France would see the light, accept

10. State Department, France, VIII, Livingston to King, December 30, 1801.

11. ASP FR, II, 514, Madison to Livingston, March 16, 1802. Jefferson (Ford ed.), VIII, 143–147, Jefferson to Livingston, April 18, 1802.

his overture, and hand over New Orleans, and maybe the Floridas, to the United States.[12]

Rufus King's reply, too, was disheartening. He reported to Livingston on January 16, 1802, what he had learned from Addington and Hawkesbury during the preliminary negotiations of peace between Britain and France in October. They were greatly concerned, so they had said, over the cession of Louisiana; nevertheless, they were compelled to silence about it for reasons "affecting the equilibrium of Europe, and the welfare of Great Britain." King believed it was true that nothing had been said to France about the retrocession. Livingston could be sure, furthermore, that "not a word has been or will be said upon the subject at Amiens." Their only hope, as King saw it, could be that Britain, although using no open measure nor any other that would give France an excuse for involving her in new difficulties, still would put obstacles of some kind in the way of the French expedition to New Orleans.[13]

It was very scant hope. But Livingston clung to it, and to King's agreement with him that France still might be made somehow to feel the danger of throwing the United States to the side of Britain. He now forced upon Talleyrand, February 20, 1802, a formal expression of "concern" at the "reserve of the French Government" in regard to the cession of Louisiana. He was done with listening to informal talk about the value of Louisiana to France as an outlet for her "turbulent spirits"—buttered with assertions that France did not possess it. King had sent him a copy of the understanding between Lucien Bonaparte and Godoy. He therefore asked Talleyrand point-blank to say whether East and West Florida, or either of them, were included in the cession by Spain to France. He demanded assurances such as would prove "satisfactory" to the United States in regard to the limits of the Floridas and the navigation of the Mississippi River. He ended upon this note:

> If the territories of East and West Florida should be included within the limits of the cession obtained by France, the undersigned desires to be informed how far it would be practicable to make such arrangements between their respective Governments as would, at the same time, aid the financial operations of France, and remove, by a strong natural boundary, all future causes of discontent between her and the United States.[14]

12. State Department, France, VIII, Livingston to Madison, January 13, 1802.
13. King (King ed.), IV, 57–59.
14. State Department, France, VIII, note to Talleyrand of February 20, 1802, enclosed with Livingston's report to Madison dated February 15, 1802. For Marbois' remark to

It would be easy to treat Robert Livingston here as a novice at diplomacy who, from lack of experience abroad, or for want of something else to do while waiting out a lull in opportunities, blundered into the very situation which he should have delayed as long as possible. Talleyrand immediately framed a sarcastic rejoinder in which he did not even refer to Louisiana. It gave vent to the ex-bishop's power of smooth insult, but it was not really devastating enough. He did not send it. In its place three weeks later, casually linked with acknowledgment that he had received Livingston's several notes about the debts and the captures of American vessels, and had reported upon them to the First Consul, Talleyrand sent the American minister this piece of utter condescension: "Do you doubt, sir, that the questions which concern the United States, the determination of which may affect their relations with France, will be examined with equal interest and attention?"[15]

This was humiliating, but it should not make us forget other things. Livingston was not at loss as to what he would try next. He was obliged to play a bold and extremely uncertain game. He had little to risk, save his own prestige, if his formal expression of "concern" slithered, as it did, into the discard. He had long since, when in charge of foreign affairs for the Confederation, gained experience in the deviations of European diplomatists. He had been close to the realities in the peacemaking at Paris in 1782, even if at long range from Philadelphia. His bold thrust now at Talleyrand had failed, to be sure, but not completely. The fact that the American minister in Paris had demanded of France a statement satisfactory to his Government could not be entirely overlooked by the negotiators at Amiens, even if the French statesmen as well as Rufus King might have heard that Britain would make nothing of the cession of Louisiana on that occasion. They could not be too sure. Livingston knew that.

In spite of King's discouragement in January, Livingston had written again on March 10, three days before Talleyrand's reply to him, urging upon King once more the reasons why Britain should rouse herself to the danger to her own interests in North America. With the resources of Spanish Mexico as well as Louisiana at France's disposal, and the power of France in Europe to be considered, who could tell the extent of the sway which France would have "in and over America?" Britain had better look to the safety

Livingston on France's "turbulent spirits" see ASP FR, II, 513, Livingston to Madison, December 31, 1801.

15. Lyon, 157–159. State Department, France, VIII, note from Talleyrand of March 13, 1802, enclosed with Livingston's despatch to Madison, March 15, 1802.

of her colonies in the West Indies as well as Canada: "If any opening is given for pressing the business of Louisiana," wrote Livingston, "I will meet you at Amiens at any time you will appoint to forward it."[16]

Again it was bold play into the face of discouragement. But again, Livingston was no amateur at diplomacy. Nothing was to come of his effort, for Britain would not allow even her interests in the West Indies and Canada to interfere with the final arrangements at Amiens in the spring of 1802 for the peace which had been agreed upon at London in the preceding October. But Livingston was sticking to the one course which could avoid disaster for his country until it had grown powerful enough to defy both France and Britain in this hemisphere. The United States were most certainly in competition with both. Until they could swing off upon their own course, they had to throw their weight first to one side, then to the other, always against whichever of those European rivals came too close to encroaching upon their own aspirations in the Mississippi Valley. Immediate disappointments and humiliations therefore were to be considered as nothing in comparison with the ultimate gain which might be had from time in which to grow strong.

On March 24, 1802, Livingston answered the first letter which he had received from Secretary Madison since arriving in France. There was left but one hope, he said, of defeating the cession of Louisiana. That was in alarming Spain and Britain. He still believed that Britain might be persuaded to force the issue at Amiens. He was wrong about this, for the Treaty of Amiens was signed the next day, March 25, with no reference to Louisiana. But he was not mistaken in other perceptions which he reported to Madison. Talleyrand, he said, was "decidedly unfriendly" to the United States; the French authorities anticipated that the United States would be hostile, so they meant to take possession of Louisiana with as little notice given as possible; they expected, by commanding the trade of New Orleans, "to have a leading interest in the politics of our western country." He shrewdly observed that it was Napoleon himself rather than the French people who was eager to get Louisiana. The people were far from desiring any foreign colony which they considered "a weak point and drain for the population and wealth." He informed Madison that the French Government was listening to advices on the use of the Indians against the United States. We should note particularly that he suggested that Congress ought to take steps to establish Natchez or

16. State Department, France, VIII, Livingston to King, March 10, 1802.

some other place up the Mississippi as an American port to which shipping could enter without having to touch at New Orleans. This was months before the Spanish Government, to the satisfaction of Talleyrand, withdrew the right of deposit at New Orleans and caused the uproar which led to the second mission of James Monroe to France.[17]

The trend of Robert Livingston's thought in March, 1802, is clear. If France were determined to keep New Orleans and were expecting, by means of it, to dictate the politics of the Western country, she might find that she had succeeded only in making the navigation of the Mississippi a dangerously international issue—and without any great injury to the trading facilities of the United States. It would be an issue in which Britain too might take a very active hand by reason of her treaties with both Spain and the United States conceding free navigation of the river to her. Such an outcome would not be altogether happy for the United States, but neither would it be anything like a pleasure for France in Louisiana. Livingston's observations upon Talleyrand, Napoleon, the French people, and Britain's interest in the Mississippi not only determined his own subsequent procedure in Paris; they provided evidence to support the plans for the Indians of the Southwest and the Lewis and Clark expedition into the far Northwest which President Jefferson presented to Congress within a few months.[18]

Rufus King's Ideas

MEANWHILE Rufus King had been pondering how else they might stop the French expedition to New Orleans since he had no hope at all that Britain would do anything about it at Amiens. He expressed his thoughts to Livingston on March 23, the day before Livingston wrote to Madison. They had left the means of "Iron and Gold." The first was out of the question, said King, notwithstanding the example of almost every other nation. This must be agreed without dispute, for the United States had neither the military nor the naval strength at that time to take up the war with Napoleon as Britain laid it down. As for "Gold," King knew that no "set of claims," no "balancing of accounts," no "prospect of future advantage" for France would ever make the sale. There had to be "actual money and a great deal of it." Federalist memories of

17. *Ibid.*, VIII, Livingston to Madison, March 24, 1802. No record of date received. For the Treaty of Amiens, see Martens, *Receuil de Traités*, VII, 404–414. See below, pp. 447, 458.
18. See below, p. 461 f.

the trials of Pinckney, Marshall, and Gerry, with X, Y, and Z were still vivid. But King's thoughts were not solely upon the ex-Bishop of Autun. He was thinking also of taxpayers at home. And he was not guessing. Many of his Federalist friends in New England, though they might have rallied with Timothy Pickering to Hamilton's plan of attack upon Louisiana, deplored spending money to get it.

Nevertheless, Rufus King warmed to his idea as he considered the great benefits to the United States if they should gain New Orleans, the entire eastern bank of the Mississippi, and advance their frontier to the Gulf of Mexico. Said he: "It cannot be denied that economy is wisdom in States as well as individuals; but by the former as well as the latter, it requires to be rightly understood, not to become a vice instead of a virtue." In other words people at home might grumble at the burden of expense, but it could be made more attractive for them. King knew how. Livingston might persuade France to accept payment in supplies for her West Indian fleet.

Indeed it does seem that Federalist shipowners and merchants in New England might have come to look upon that kind of expenditure for New Orleans and the Floridas as virtuous rather than vicious. It is quite apparent, too, that Rufus King had no more affection for Toussaint and his fellows in San Domingo and Guadeloupe than John Adams or Thomas Jefferson.

As for Spain, King reasoned that occupation of New Orleans and the Floridas by the United States "would deserve to be received with favour in Madrid," because it offered "the only means of sparing the Spanish Treasure in America." Spain, therefore, may one ask, should not mourn the loss of New Orleans? And may one presume from this reasoning that Spain should never fear that the American people would "squint" at Santa Fé and the silver mines of Mexico? Had Rufus King forgotten so soon his own enthusiasm for the sweeping plans of Miranda and Hamilton? But whether he had or had not does not really matter now.

The American minister to Britain closed this letter to the American minister to France with a reflection which was already stirring in the mind of Robert Livingston and which had more weight in the balances of Europe than the immediate threat of American "Iron" or the use of American "Gold": "No policy in my opinion," wrote King, "has so often proved to be pernicious as that of shutting our eyes upon what we cannot avoid seeing, and of putting off exertions to prevent injury, and thereby leaving the public welfare either to the government of chance, or in the hands of the adversary. . . ." France, he declared, must be "openly opposed." But, as she was "one of the Great Powers which influence and in some sort control the affairs of the whole earth," he would not oppose her with force. He would use instead that "moral resistance which consists in the frank explanation of the injuries we foresee and apprehend, and the declaration beforehand of what we conceive to be our own Rights and Duties, should it become necessary to assert and perform them." "The Truth," said he, "should not be disguised from ourselves or others; that we are the first Power in our own hemisphere; and that we are disinclined to perform the part of the second."[19]

That it was the "Truth" may have been the sheerest presumption in March, 1802, but Robert Livingston proceeded to act upon it, always keeping Britain in mind. To take the offensive against France as Britain came to peace with France would make precarious business even more so. There was no certainty what the British might not try in order to serve their ends elsewhere—and to check the United States in America, for they had a strong interest in doing that too. But there were other encouraging facts to be taken into account.

Britain could not really wish to see France back in Louisiana, least of all in the Floridas which had so long been considered essential to the needs and defenses of the British West Indies. Those islands seemed as dependent upon the Floridas as were the British dominions in the Orient upon Egypt. Nor, to be sure, would Britain like to have the United States take the Floridas. But Livingston knew that she should have no immediate fear of an American attack upon her West Indies from Mobile and Pensacola. She might leave that problem entirely in charge of her fleet for some time to come, as she certainly could not if the French were established there. The chance with her displeasure, therefore, was worth taking, in the hope that the United States would be able to reassure her in regard to her use of the Mississippi and continental sources of supply for her islands.[20]

Livingston decided to take the chance. He reported to Madison, April 24, 1802, that General Bernadotte with five or seven thousand troops would leave shortly for New Orleans, "unless the state of affairs in St. Domingo should change their destination." He urged Congress, therefore, to make Natchez a rival of New Orleans

19. King (King ed.), IV, 86–90, to Livingston, March 23, 1802.
20. Fugier, I, 193–194. Browning, 28–29, 37, 41, 60, 87, 128, 154, showing that the British ambassador in Paris, Whitworth, was watching the Floridas almost as closely as Malta.

immediately. If Congress did so, and if the situation in San Domingo should require these troops, there would be time still "for gold to operate here." Taking up King's opinion, he stated that it would have to be "plentifully and liberally bestowed," not merely in assuming French debts, but in "active capital, afforded in supplies, to aid their armaments in the islands." He begged instruction as to the "utmost amount" that he could offer, for he was sure that France had obtained the Floridas, in spite of the fact that Pinckney had just reported from Madrid that they were not included in the cession.[21]

On May 28, Livingston wrote Madison again to report that Collot was going as second in command and that Adet was to be prefect. The expedition had been postponed, however, until September for reasons which Talleyrand had not explained to Bernadotte, but which Livingston suspected had arisen from Spain's resistance to including the Floridas in the transfer. If he did not hear from Madison soon, he said, he would present a "pointed memorial to this Government," in which he would state "fully and candidly our objections to their taking possession of the Floridas, and demanding security for the rights we had originally, and by treaty with Spain."[22]

Livingston then turned to the Spanish ambassador in Paris for a statement about the Floridas, asserting that the United States would protest if Spain had made a "naked cession" to France without protecting the rights of navigation and deposit which Spain had acknowledged in the Pinckney Treaty of 1795. On June 2 Azara replied: Certainly a treaty ceding Louisiana to France had been made, though it was his opinion that the Floridas had not been included.[23]

Both France and Spain now had been smoked out of their pretense that there was no retrocession of Louisiana. On June 8 Livingston forwarded Azara's reply to Madison and reported conversations held separately with Collot and Adet. They admitted that they were going to Louisiana; that was certain; and Pensacola and Mobile, they said, were given to France; but as to West Florida, they could not say. Livingston could. He had not a doubt that France so intended. France did what she willed in Europe, and it would "require firmness and exertion to prevent her doing so in America."[24]

21. ASP FR, II, 515–516, Livingston to Madison, April 24, 1802.
22. Ibid., II, 518.
23. Ibid., II, 518.
24. Ibid., II, 519, Livingston to Madison, June 8, 1802.

The "Truth"

THE American minister to France was fully launched upon the aggressive course of his own inclination, with King's timely encouragement from London. Happily there now came from home instructions more than ample to counteract Madison's reprimand for having approached Britain through King. DuPont de Nemours arrived with Thomas Jefferson's open letter of April 18, 1802. Its contents were to be impressed upon the Government of France. There would have been no point in trying to keep them from British onlookers in Paris. Thornton, chargé at Washington had already reported upon their general nature to his Government.[25]

In this famous letter, President Jefferson declared:

> The session of Louisiana and the Floridas by Spain to France works most sorely on the U. S. On this subject the Secretary of State has written to you fully, Yet I cannot forbear recurring to it personally, so deep is the impression it makes in my mind. It compleatly reverses all the political relations of the U. S. and will form a new epoch in our political course. Of all nations of any consideration France is the one which hitherto has offered the fewest points on which we could have any conflict of right, and the most points of a communion of interests. From these causes we have ever looked to her as our *natural friend,* as one with which we never could have an occasion of difference. Her growth therefore we viewed as our own, her misfortune ours. There is on the globe one single spot, the possessor of which is our natural and habitual enemy. It is New Orleans, through which the produce of three-eighths of our territory must pass to market, and from its fertility it will ere long yield more than half of our whole produce and contain more than half our inhabitants. France placing herself in that door assumes to us the attitude of defiance.

New Orleans might have remained quietly in the hands of Spain, said Jefferson, as Spain's feebleness induced pacific relations with the United States and concessions to American commerce; and perhaps not before very long, Spain would have found the cession to the United States worth-while. But "not so can it ever be in the hands of France." France and the United States could not continue long as friends, he declared, if they met in so irritable a position. The day that France took New Orleans would mark the union of the two nations which could hold exclusive possession of the sea. Thenceforth the continents of America would be sequestered "for the common purposes of the united British and American nations."

25. King (King ed.), IV, 124, King confidentially to Hamilton, May 7, 1802, regarding Thornton's reports of his conversation with Jefferson.

This was not a state of things, protested Jefferson, which the American nation either sought or desired. But Livingston and duPont de Nemours were to make it clear that this "change of friends" would necessarily involve the United States "as a belligerent power in the first war of Europe." France would have New Orleans only during the interval of peace. The United States would take it at the outbreak of the next war. France should understand that the United States did not oppose the return of France into Louisiana because of fear, "for however greater her force is than ours compared in the abstract, it is nothing in comparison of ours when to be exerted on our soil." Here was support for the presumption of King and Livingston, up to the hilt.

However there was a way, suggested Jefferson, in which France might ease her situation somewhat. If she considered Louisiana indispensable, she might cede the island of New Orleans and the Floridas to the United States. "It would at any rate relieve us from the necessity of taking immediate measures for countervailing such an operation by arrangements in another quarter." In other words, he would not approach the British Government at once. But still, New Orleans and the Floridas would only be considered "as equivalent for the risk of a quarrel with France produced by her vicinage." That is to say, it would not be comfortable to have France as a neighbor, even beyond the Mississippi River: "Every eye in the U. S. is now fixed on this affair of Louisiana. Perhaps nothing since the revolutionary war has produced more uneasy sensations through the body of the nation."[26]

Why was it that Thomas Jefferson made so bold as to talk about marrying the British fleet and nation, in spite of the fact that Britain had come to terms with France in the preceding October and at this moment was completing the ceremony of peacemaking? Ratifications of the Treaty of Amiens were exchanged by Britain and France on April 18, 1802, the very day of Jefferson's letter to Livingston. Had he been influenced, notwithstanding Madison's reprimand to Livingston, to think that Livingston's plan for coöperating with the British at Amiens might have succeeded? Or was he more affected than one would expect offhand, by the rumor which Pichon was giving currency at Washington in April, 1802, that the French fleet was "expected hourly on our coasts"? The dread of foreign invasion was still close to the surface; it had not been four years since George Washington had thought a French invasion quite possible if France made peace with Britain. Or was it that Jefferson surmised, even though the British would do nothing

26. Jefferson (Ford ed.), VIII, 143–147, to Livingston, April 18, 1802.

at Amiens, that they were sure to put more than verbal obstacles in the way of France when they saw the plans of Napoleon and Talleyrand for Louisiana expanding into the Floridas? One so self-destined as Napoleon would hardly stop of his own volition with the subjugation of San Domingo. And the British would never welcome him upon the Gulf Coast from Mexico to the Keys of Florida opposite Cuba. It is likely that Thomas Jefferson sensed before the Peace of Amiens was complete that it could not endure.[27]

Had there been no rivalry in the Floridas, there was trouble enough in sight over Malta and the Mediterranean to make that conjecture strong. If it were true, there was certainly no time for the United States to waste before they put in their own claim to New Orleans and West Florida. They could not expect Britain, at war again, to hesitate over seizing New Orleans, now that Spain had returned it to France. In view of his long-established desire for New Orleans, and his anxiety about Britain's intentions, this may have been the decisive factor in Jefferson's thinking.

Perhaps Pichon was even nearer the sources of Jefferson's decision when he sent Talleyrand this excerpt from the New York *Commercial Advertiser* of March 12, 1802: "The United States will either take possession of New Orleans, in order to be master of the navigation of the Mississippi, or our western territory on the banks of the Ohio and the Mississippi will separate from us and join those who will be in possession of the navigation of this latter river, for it is their only outlet to the sea and they cannot do without it." A way to get it for them, and to hold them in the Union besides, was to threaten France with a British alliance and attack upon New Orleans the very instant war broke again in Europe. France might thus be influenced beforehand to cede to the United States. If she were not, they would not have to wait long for another war in Europe.[28]

In any case, President Jefferson saw fit to anticipate eventualities following the Peace of Amiens, whether it be "long or short." He asked his friend, duPont de Nemours, virtually to present an ultimatum to the Government of France. And the gentleman who had been willing to undertake a political and financial mission to the United States in 1798 for the French Directory, who had then established his family in this country, was now pleased to make

---

27. Martens, *Receuil de Traités,* VII, 404–414. For Pichon, see Bayard Papers in AHA Rpt., 1913, II, 153, April 19, 1802. For Washington, see above, p. 294 and Washington (Ford ed.), XIV, 7, to Hamilton, May 27, 1798; 109, to Pickering, October 18, 1798.

28. Lyon, 150–151.

the subject of Jefferson's letter the principal aim of his voyage to France.

But duPont de Nemours had not yet become so much American that he had lost interest in the political and financial welfare of France. He did not like Jefferson's reasoning that Louisiana could remain French only to the next war. Napoleon, "a young soldier whose ministers kept their places only by flattering his military pride perpetually," he replied on April 30, would be much more "offended than moved" by the suggestion that the American Army would take Louisiana. Napoleon would be advised that the United States, and even their President, displayed an ambition for conquest that he ought to repress. He would be told that they were not bothered by the presence of Spain in Louisiana; they did not respect Spain; they looked upon "this colony of the Mississippi" as a stopping place and a magazine necessary to the army with which one day they expected to conquer Mexico. He would be reminded that it was precisely for the purpose of keeping Mexico in greater security that Spain had ceded the colony to him. "That your nation in general, Mr. President, and above all the ambitious of your nation, think of conquering Mexico," wrote duPont de Nemours, "is not questionable."[29]

Jefferson, too, said duPont, should give that some thought, for if it happened, he would have much to lose, as a philosopher, friend of humanity, and patriot. The victorious army of the United States would be corrupted forever, and those who remained in the conquered territory would form a redoubtable neighbor, with which the United States would be in a state of permanent strife. As it was aroused by revolution, as it was brought to the height of American civilization by the citizens of the United States who stayed there, Mexico would become more poisonous to liberty, peace, and prosperity in the United States. And Jefferson should beware the English and a passing alliance to ravage Spain. The English, declared duPont, hated and always would hate the second, even the third powers on the sea. Only France wished the United States to be a sea power. Only England feared this.

President Jefferson therefore should begin, urged duPont de Nemours, by agreeing with France that the United States would never wish to cross the Mississippi River—because it was to the interest of France, Spain, and the United States alike, said he, to discourage the temptation to the United States some day of conquering Mexico. He hinted that they should offer to help France

29. Chinard, 48–54. For de Nemours' previous activity and John Adams' opinion of him, see above, pp. 331–332.

get back Canada. He chided Jefferson, though mildly, for seeming ready to unite with Britain "against us." DuPont de Nemours knew better than to hope that he could turn Jefferson from his objective entirely; and so he proposed that they make an offer for what Jefferson wanted from France. Powers of the first rank were always poor, said duPont. France, therefore, would be susceptible to cash. But she would ask, of course, "the most possible." The offer should be large enough to persuade her before she took possession of the country; otherwise, governors, prefects, commercial companies would obstruct the bargaining for their own interests. "The longer you bargain and make a bad bargain," warned duPont, "the worse would be the break."[30]

This gentleman from France was still very much a Frenchman. He wrote Jefferson again on May 12 before sailing from New York to urge that a "liberal and generous estimate" would impress the French Government. "Agreement on the price," said he, "is the main thing." Perhaps to keep his friend, Thomas Jefferson, just a bit in hand, he remarked, that Leclerc might have discovered that secret treaty between Toussaint and Maitland which had been made under the eye of Dr. Stevens with the approval of the Adams administration. He expected, said duPont, to find bitterness in France on account of the aid which had come to Toussaint in San Domingo from the United States. Finally, he commended his sons' gunpowder mill to Jefferson. They would be able to make for him with greatest speed a powder superior to the best in Europe: "But, my excellent friend, do not burn it against us. Sell it sooner in our colonies."[31]

The accusation that the American people intended to conquer Mexico raises the question whether Jefferson himself, as duPont de Nemours intimated obliquely, thought at this time of acquiring the trans-Mississippi country between the British dominions on the north and Spanish America on the southwest. Jefferson noted the accusation, and wrote about it to duPont de Nemours and to Livingston. The letter to the former is not available, and Jefferson's comment to the latter is so brief that we cannot be sure. Yet he said to Livingston that duPont de Nemours had "received false impressions of the scope of the letter" of April 18. He did not say that duPont de Nemours had a mistaken idea of his thoughts.[32]

We cannot prove from this sort of evidence that Jefferson had such expansion of the United States in his mind when he sent his

30. Chinard, 53.
31. *Ibid.*, 55–58, to Jefferson, May 12, 1802.
32. *Ibid.*, 54, Jefferson to Livingston, May 5, 1802.

famous letter to Livingston in care of duPont de Nemours. Neither may it be said that Jefferson had no thought of the possibility because he did not say explicitly that he had none, or because he had remarked, in general terms only, to duPont de Nemours and to others that he wished the "present order of things to continue" on this continent. We must not forget the allusion in his letter of April 18 to the time when Spain might find it worth-while to sell Louisiana to the United States.

It was good diplomacy to profess that the United States wanted only New Orleans and the Floridas. This was the first step. It did not mean that others would not follow. The suspicion remains that the idea was very near if it was not yet within the consciousness of Thomas Jefferson. Events within a year uncovered full comprehension of it with remarkable speed.

Two things can be stated with certainty. Thomas Jefferson did have in mind then, regardless of the Peace of Amiens, to throw the weight of the United States into the balances of Europe for what he could gain for them on this continent—New Orleans and control of the Mississippi River first of all. The other is that Robert Livingston now had complete authorization to proceed in hope that his policy of pressure upon France, a nice mixture of "Gold" with the threat of "Iron," and the "Truth," would bring results. Secretary Madison also wrote to him on May 1, requesting that he ascertain the price which France would ask for New Orleans and the Floridas. DuPont de Nemours had that much influence upon the Administration. Madison directed Livingston to warn the authorities of France that a "neighborhood" with the United States could not be friendly. They should know, said Madison, that if they took possession of the mouth of the Mississippi, the "worst events" were to be "apprehended."[33]

Livingston replied to Jefferson's letter of April 18 on July 30, 1802. He was positive that France and Spain did not understand each other on the subject of Louisiana. There was a stiffness in the Spanish ambassador, which he proposed to foster so long as it did not interfere with any prospect of buying the Floridas directly from Spain. He stressed that the French still thought of Louisiana as extending across the Mississippi toward South Carolina and up to the Ohio country. The expedition to Louisiana, he reiterated, was being postponed, probably because of the misunderstanding with Spain over the Floridas. Meanwhile he was pressing the French to cede the Floridas and New Orleans to the United States in order to forestall the British. If he accomplished this, he did not fear that

33. ASP FR, II, 516, Madison to Livingston, May 1, 1802.

any colonies which France might establish on the far side of the Mississippi would be strong enough to injure the United States. He found the French, however, anxious to have the ports of Pensacola and St. Augustine, for fear that the United States would gain command of the Gulf. He would not care, said Livingston, if the French did retain Pensacola and St. Augustine, provided they sold West Florida and New Orleans to the United States. What the British would think about that does not seem to have disturbed him.[34]

If indeed the United States got New Orleans and outlet to the sea, with Mobile and the intervening territory on the east to protect the transit of their western commerce, they would attain their most important objective in the mid-continent. With that secure, they could leave adjacent regions and related questions to adjustment in time, confident that those matters would hardly be disposed to any great disadvantage for themselves. There was a genuine cause of misgiving for the American Government, though it was greatly lessening as the population of the West swelled with immigrants from the Atlantic Seaboard and their communication with the East improved. This was still in 1802 as it had been in 1786, that these "men of the Western waters" might shift their allegiance from the Government of the United States to whatever authority, through control of the mouth of the Mississippi, had power to choke their economic enterprise.[35]

This danger may appear to us now as having all but ceased to exist, for the schemes of Wilkinson, Innes, and others in Kentucky had come to naught. Ohio was about to be admitted to the Union as a State. And the plans of Liston, Blount, and Chisholm in the Southwest had been frustrated. Our knowledge, too, of the subsequent failure of the grand scheme of Aaron Burr and Wilkinson, whatever it was, minimizes for us the danger that the Westerners would break with the Government of the United States. But this could have by no means appeared so to Thomas Jefferson and Robert Livingston in 1802. Moreover, they were right in fearing British, as much if not more than French, penetration into the Mississippi Valley.

The British wished to control the outlets to the Gulf of Mexico. We must not forget that their hopes did not subside until after the War of 1812, yet to come for James Madison's discomfiture as President. By that time the "men of the Western waters" had become for the greatest part ardent Americans. Nonetheless it was not so much their patriotism as Napoleon's devastation in Europe

34. *Ibid.*, II, 519–520, Livingston to Madison, July 30, 1802.
35. See above, pp. 108–110, 133–134.

that saved New Orleans and the Mississippi from Britain. When her opportunity came at last to settle accounts with the United States in the mid-continent without the possibility of France coming to the aid of the United States, Britain was war-weary to the point of exhaustion. By that time, also, and perhaps the really determining factor, this youthful nation had grown too strong to tempt Britain into a war of conquest. She was not going to relish then even the task of holding on to her western domain which lay athwart the imperial ambitions of the United States.

Britain "Very Sour"

LIVINGSTON presented his "pointed memorial" to the French Government in August, 1802. He argued that France did not have the capital to spare at home with which to finance new colonies abroad. He asserted that French goods would not find really profitable new markets. He demonstrated that the trade of the French West Indies would gain no advantages in the Mississippi Valley better than they already had with the Atlantic Seaboard. He declared that in the next war the British fleet would surely bottle the French in New Orleans, and with American aid. But they would suffer before that. American capital already dominated the trade of New Orleans, he said; and if France took possession, the United States would withdraw their business, establish Natchez as a port up the river, and reduce the value of New Orleans to nothing. It would be far better, then, for France to transfer New Orleans to the United States on the pledge that they would keep it a free port for the French colony west of the Mississippi. If France did this, her rivalry with the United States would cease. Livingston's warning was emphatic, though not expressed, that their people in the West would take great exception to any other authority than their own along the Mississippi River. He did not explain how their shipping would get past New Orleans from Natchez to the sea if the French chose to block the river.[36]

This memorial seemed to have no effect and Livingston soon knew why. Spain had come nearer to accepting the Italian estates for the King of Tuscany in return for ceding the Floridas to France. And France was going ahead with the expedition to Louisiana. Talleyrand told Livingston "frankly" on August 31 that every offer from him was premature before France had taken possession. It was obvious that Napoleon had his heart set on it; and Livingston knew that Napoleon was "everything" in France. But

36. AAE EU, Spt. 7, ff. 323–336. See also ASP FR, II, 520–524. Lyon, 159–161.

he was not alarmed. He had every reason to believe now, he wrote home, that the Floridas really were not in the cession. Although no one dared tell Napoleon so, "every reflecting man about him," said Livingston, was opposed to "this wild expedition." They all knew now that their islands were calling for more than they could ever supply.[37]

News from San Domingo, evidently, was already foreshadowing the disaster on the way to Leclerc and his army. Livingston prophesied that the whole affair would end in France relinquishing the Louisiana country, and transferring New Orleans to the United States. Did he mean that France would release the whole territory west of the Mississippi to the United States? He did not say. Possibly that speculation had not yet entered his mind. But his prophecy of September 1, 1802, was accurate nonetheless.

Robert Livingston had yet to experience many dark moments before he was elated by his interviews with Talleyrand and Barbé Marbois in April, 1803; and had still to think of stopping short of the far goal. But he had observed in September, 1802, that Britain was "very sour." "The extreme hauteur of this Government to all around them," said he, "will not suffer peace to be of long continuance." He had sensed the opportunity before the United States as Europe went again to war. The breach of the Peace of Amiens in fact had already begun. Britain was holding Malta notwithstanding her pledge to evacuate. Napoleon was keeping troops in Holland despite his promise to withdraw them. He may have been intending, as he professed, to use them for replacements in San Domingo and for the expedition to Louisiana; but Englishmen could think again of invasions coupled with uprisings in Ireland. And Godoy, for Spain and Britain too perhaps, was blocking the transfer of the Floridas to France. When the King of Spain finally did give the order on October 15, 1802, to transfer Louisiana, the Floridas were not included.[38]

Florida or Louisiana?

EPISODES were occurring which make us suspect that Napoleon had been influenced by the arguments and the temper of Livingston and his superiors, at least so far as to consider them in the event of contingencies, although he made no sign of heeding and continued on his course toward Louisiana.

DuPont de Nemours emerged from his conferences with the

37. ASP FR, II, 525, Livingston to Madison, September 1, 1802.
38. Lyon, 125–126. Fugier, I, 193–194. Whitaker, *Mississippi Question*, 184, 307 n. 18.

authorities of France to make a definite proposal on October 4. It reached President Jefferson December 31, 1802. It was that the United States buy New Orleans and the Floridas from France for $6,000,000. France would retain Louisiana "absolutely" west of the Mississippi, and the right of free navigation. The French would share equal rights of trade in New Orleans and the Floridas with the Americans, and without paying any duties. The United States would allow no other nation to have these advantages.

He did not despair of success, said duPont, if Jefferson were willing to go so far. He did not think that the feelings aroused over San Domingo would then interfere. It would certainly be better than "to throw back your people, so justly proud of its independence, under the claws of the British leopard," said he, displaying the French interest without dissimulation. He added, with more indirection but the same purpose: "and to make you the instruments of the power of vengeance of your oppressors, who will never be to you but false, deceiving, and disdainful friends."[39]

It was a counter to Jefferson's threat to marry the British fleet and nation. But it also betrayed anxiety on the part of Napoleon's henchmen, if not Napoleon himself, that the United States might coöperate with Britain in the next war. DuPont de Nemours did not say that he had talked over this suggestion with Napoleon, Talleyrand, or anyone else in the Government. Neither did he say that he had not. It came with such definiteness from contact with authority that it had the marks of a proposal for serious consideration.

Then Robert Livingston had a conversation with Joseph Bonaparte. It was casual, but one to stir much reflection. Livingston's report of it to the President was written on October 28; but for some reason the despatch was delayed after subsequent reports and did not get into Jefferson's hands until February, 1803. Joseph Bonaparte had replied to Livingston's inquiry whether he had read Livingston's memorial on Louisiana by saying that he had, and moreover that he had talked about it with Napoleon, who had also read it with attention. The First Consul, of course, was his own counselor, said Joseph; but they were good brothers; he often had opportunities to turn his brother's attention to particular subjects.

Livingston seized the opening. Might not the only causes of difference between the United States and France, the claims against France and Louisiana, be removed "happily and easily" by returning Louisiana to Spain and giving New Orleans and the Floridas

39. Chinard, 63–65, duPont de Nemours to Jefferson, October 4, 1802.

over to the United States? Joseph Bonaparte replied by another question: "whether we should prefer the Floridas or Louisiana?" For that moment the answer was obvious, and it was given: "I told him," said Livingston, "that there was no comparison in their value, but that we had no wish to extend our boundary across the Mississippi, or give color to the doubts that had been entertained of the moderation of our views; that all we sought was security, and not extension of territory." Louisiana was indeed more valuable. But one should not overreach oneself.[40]

An idea had sprung from the conversation of one closest, if anyone were close, to the First Consul's inner thoughts. It took root in the mind of Robert Livingston. With succeeding events, it grew into a plan that had influence upon the eventual decision of Napoleon to sell the whole of Louisiana to the United States. When the affair was concluded, Livingston was positive that it had. As Joseph Bonaparte expressed it in this conversation on October 26, 1802, the First Consul "had nothing more at heart than to be on the best terms with the United States." As others might phrase it, the First Consul had nothing more at heart than to keep the British from getting what he could not be sure of keeping for himself —especially if he got paid for giving it up.[41]

At this point, Talleyrand saw fit to handle those waiting in his anteroom for conferences so as to slight the American minister. But he quickly found that he was not dealing with an Elbridge Gerry. Robert Livingston took the indignity to himself as offered to the United States, so reported to his Government, and made of the episode an opportunity to drop negotiations through the ministry of foreign affairs for a while and to follow the lead which had been given by Joseph Bonaparte. There might be more in it perhaps than Napoleon's brother then or ever conceived, possibly a great deal less; but it was worth exploring. Meanwhile Talleyrand, using accustomed devices, was trying to discredit Livingston at home through Rufus King who had come over to Paris. For King to see, Talleyrand wrote to his own private counsel and financier, Cazenove, that Livingston's resentment was due to his want of experience, to the fact that he had begun his diplomatic career late in life. Talleyrand "hoped that the Pr., whose knowledge of diplomacy he foresees, wd. see no reason to justify his minr." Again,

40. State Department, France, VIII, Livingston to Jefferson, October 28, 1802, not received until February 9, 1803. See Jefferson (Ford ed.), VIII, 210, to Livingston, February 10. ASP FR, II, 525–526. Guinness in MVHR, XX, 97.

41. See below, pp. 496–497.

Talleyrand, in spite of his own "experience" in the United States, did not know his Americans.[42]

Instead of taking the Federalist rôle which Talleyrand may have expected, Rufus King conferred with Livingston and blandly replied to Cazenove that he did not perceive that his interference "would be likely to prove beneficial." What else King talked over with Livingston in Paris during October, 1802, we may never know. We recall that in the previous spring he had given Livingston arguments and an aggressive vocabulary for use upon France. And we know what he said to Britain's prime minister in the following spring when Addington remarked that, if war should happen, one of Britain's first attempts would be to occupy New Orleans. King then interrupted Addington with:

> true it was we could not see with indifference that Country in the hands of France, but it was equally true that it would be contrary to our views, and with much concern that we should see it in the possession of England. We had no objection to Spain continuing to possess it; they were quiet neighbours, and we looked forward without impatience to events which, in the ordinary course of things, must, at no distant day, annex this Country to the United States.

Certainly this was no one for Talleyrand to count upon for help in undermining American opposition to his American policy.[43]

Nor did the French minister of foreign affairs know his Thomas Jefferson. As Talleyrand was affronting Livingston in Paris, the President was receiving Livingston's report of July 30 in answer to his letter of April 18 and replying:

> . . . we stand, compleatly corrected of the error, that either the government or the nation of France has any remains of friendship for us. The portion of that country which forms an exception, though respectable in weight, is weak in numbers. On the contrary, it appears evident, that an unfriendly spirit prevails in the most important individuals of the government, towards us. In this state of things, we shall so take our distance between the two rival nations, as, remaining disengaged till necessity compels us, we may haul finally to the enemy of that which shall make it necessary.

Although he had not yet received this letter from his superior, it was in just this way that Robert Livingston was keeping watch upon the rising enmity between Britain and France in the fall of

---

42. State Department, France, VIII, Livingston to Madison, November 2, 1802. King (King ed.), IV, 167–168, 555.
43. King (King ed.), IV, 241, report to Madison, April 2, 1803.

1802, and playing directly to the lead which Joseph Bonaparte had given him.[44]

Livingston reported to Secretary Madison on November 11, 1802, that France had "cut the knot" with Spain concerning the Italian estates, and the expedition to Louisiana would sail from Holland in about twenty days. He had been able to get no response to his notes upon the rights of the United States until Daniel Clark, American merchant from New Orleans, had drawn out the opinions of General Victor, who was to command in place of Bernadotte; these seemed to indicate that the French would do as they pleased once they got established in New Orleans. Then Livingston had succeeded in forcing assurance to himself that France would respect the rights of the United States under their treaty of 1795 with Spain.

This was unmistakably forced, so he urged Madison to expect that the first action of General Victor and his associates in Louisiana would be "the oppression of their people and of our commerce." Madison might then look for an "early attempt to corrupt our western people," and even an attack, said Livingston, upon Natchez "which they consider as the rival of New Orleans." Madison must be on his guard. "Above all" he must reënforce Natchez and give it every possible commercial advantage. The United States would win if they could only satisfy the needs of the Americans in the West and stand off the French forces. They might hope that "the dissatisfaction of inhabitants, the disappointment of officers, and the drain of money will facilitate our views after a very short time." Livingston would see Joseph Bonaparte again that day.

He had also to report that Napoleon had sent Beurnonville to Madrid to get the Floridas. There was no mistaking that it was a "favorite object of the First Consul." There was no misjudging "our prospects" if it remained so. But Livingston thought that it could be made less alluring to Napoleon. He referred to previous despatches in which he had urged "strengthening ourselves by force and ships at home, and by alliance abroad." No prudence, he declared, would prevent hostilities between Britain and France before long.[45]

There is significance in the fact that this report from Livingston of November 11, 1802, concerning Victor's expedition to Louisiana and Beurnonville's mission to Madrid, is recorded in the State Department as having reached Washington on January 3, 1803. This

44. Jefferson (Ford ed.), VIII, 172–174, to Livingston, October 10, 1802.

45. State Department, France, VIII, Livingston to Madison, November 11, 1802, received January 3.

was before President Jefferson sent his secret message to Congress about the Western frontier of the United States, the Indians and their lands along the Mississippi, and urged sending a party on a "literary pursuit" beyond the Mississippi into the far northwestern territory of Spain.[46]

Or did it belong now to France? Perhaps it was British. If the American President and his minister to France had their way, however, it was not going to remain either for long.

"Short Hints" for Napoleon

ROBERT LIVINGSTON in Paris had tremendous news from New Orleans almost as soon as it reached Thomas Jefferson in Washington. It was that on October 20 the Spanish intendant had withdrawn the right of deposit which had been conceded to Americans in the Treaty of 1795. This caused Livingston at once to take up the hint which Joseph Bonaparte had let fall on October 26, that the United States might prefer Louisiana to the Floridas. Possibly the time had arrived for them to cross the Mississippi. Perhaps France might not care so much for the whole of Louisiana as to risk losing it in the approaching war with Britain. Livingston gave Joseph Bonaparte a secret memorial, dated December 11, 1802, to be taken directly to Napoleon without the knowledge of Talleyrand.[47]

The citizens of the United States, declared Robert Livingston, would not stand for the withdrawal of the right of deposit at New Orleans. Did France have anything to do with this? Surely, France

46. See below, pp. 461–466.
47. Marbois stated in his *History of Louisiana* that this memorial was presented to Talleyrand. And in support of his opinion, the document on file in the French Archives, from which the photograph was taken for the Library of Congress, reads "To the Minister of Exterior Relations." But this document was not signed by Livingston. It may be a copy, and not the original draft made for Livingston. An error in transcribing when the memorial finally came to the foreign ministry, can account for such an address. It was the customary address. Livingston declared specifically to Madison that he had a "private memoir under the consul's eye" and that "the minister knows nothing of this." And after he had completed the treaty with Marbois in May, 1803, Livingston wrote to Madison that he had hinted at the sale of Louisiana "in my notes and in my letters to J. B." It was not until January 10, 1803, that Livingston broached the matter to Talleysand, not until after he had learned that Napoleon had informed Talleyrand about it. Therefore, in view of these circumstances, it seems correct to state that Livingston's memorial of December 11, 1802, went to Napoleon by way of Joseph Bonaparte and not Talleyrand as Marbois asserted. AAE EU Spt. 7, ff. 310–313, photocopies in the Library of Congress. Marbois (American ed.), 414. State Department, France, VIII, Livingston to Madison, December 20, 1802, postscript December 23. ASP FR, II, 566, Livingston to Madison, June 25, 1803.

ought to realize that she had only three objects in possessing Louisiana and the Floridas; they were to command the Gulf, to get supplies for the West Indies, to obtain an outlet for her people. She did not need all of Louisiana for these purposes. What was more, she could not control the whole country. She would never be able to hold Upper Louisiana against the British. She ought, therefore, to accept a treaty with the United States ceding to them Upper Louisiana above the Arkansas River and New Orleans with West Florida as far eastward as the Perdido River beyond Mobile. The United States would pay, and would accept settlement also of their commercial claims against France. France could keep the territory west of the Mississippi and south of the Arkansas, and East Florida beginning at the Perdido. These areas would provide the supplies necessary for her colonies in the West Indies, the desired control of the Gulf, and an outlet for surplus population—while the cession to the United States would put a barrier between French Louisiana and the British dominions. The United States would be satisfied with their access to the Gulf, and so they would remain friendly toward their traditional ally.

New Orleans, anyhow, asserted Livingston, was not much of a place. It would be nothing at all if the United States were to draw their "commercial capital" back to Natchez, as they undoubtedly would if France did not accommodate them. They moreover would aid "any foreign power" in expelling France from New Orleans when war came. "By grasping at a desert & an insignificant town," said he, France would throw the United States "into the scale of Britain" and "render her mistress of the new world" with Louisiana, Trinidad, and the colonies of Spain "at her mercy." France, therefore, should make this offer to the United States "gratuitously." But they were "not unwilling" to pay a price suited to the value of the cession and "to their own circumstances": "These short hints I flatter myself," concluded Livingston, "will serve to draw your attention to the subject; in which case I am satisfied many other reasons for the adoption of this Plan will suggest themselves to your reflection, reasons on which I do not from a respect to your time think is necessary to enlarge." It was good precedent for the more notorious Ostend Manifesto of a later date to Spain in regard to Cuba.[48]

"These short hints" drew "attention," indeed! But they did not produce the immediate action for which Robert Livingston yearned, and so he sent Joseph Bonaparte another note for the First Consul

48. *Ibid.*

within a few days, hammering upon the argument that France could not hope to retain the whole of Louisiana against both Britain and the United States. France should build another capital on the west bank of the Mississippi for her colony below the Arkansas and give New Orleans on the east bank to the United States. Something had to be done to appease them. Britain had found the Peace of Amiens no advantage. War was coming again. Britain would certainly attack Louisiana. No power in Europe would be able to oppose her force if she united Louisiana and West Florida with Canada. The "present feelings of the people of all parties in the United States" toward France would drive them into alliance with Britain. They resented a power which not only did not honor its obligations to them but formed colonies and held islands in their neighborhood. France had better seek to regain their esteem. The way to do it was to surrender a "distant wilderness" which could "neither add to her wealth nor to her strength."[49]

Robert Livingston reported to James Madison on December 20. He had found another channel to the First Consul as suggested. He had at that moment "some very strong memorials under his eye and some projects that appear to be well received." But he dared not reveal them in this letter to Madison. He would do so when he could get a "safe conveyance." Talleyrand, however, was behaving better now, probably because he suspected that Livingston had another approach to Napoleon. Florida seemed still to be in negotiation at Madrid, but France was likely to get it as Spain wanted Parma so much. Livingston begged instruction as to what he could offer. Nevertheless he would not be too sanguine, for only the day before Talleyrand had told him how infatuated Napoleon was with the plan for Louisiana. And yet, he himself had made so many converts that he would want to know how far he could go if favorable circumstances should arise. This peace in Europe would not last. Three days later Livingston added the postscript that his memorial had caused alarm, and requested that Madison begin negotiating with Britain about the northwestern boundary.[50]

It was a subject which, as a matter of fact, Jefferson had already broached with the British chargé, Thornton. For if France observed that the United States and Britain were settling that dispute over the source of the Mississippi which had remained in abeyance since Jay's negotiations with Grenville in 1794, and were settling it in

49. *Ibid.*
50. State Department, France, VIII, Livingston to Madison, December 20, 1802. Livingston's second memorial, undated, may be seen in ASP FR, II, 534.

such a way as to give Britain real access to the navigation of the Mississippi, there might result a decided advantage for Livingston's negotiations in Paris.[51]

This is just what Livingston had in mind; he fired a third time at Napoleon through Joseph Bonaparte on December 24, the day after his postscript to Madison. France, he insisted, had better consider his plan for an American buffer state across the Mississippi. If Britain came forward with payment of the American claims against her and then a proposition for adjusting the western boundary of Canada, there was likely to be a settlement which would place Britain upon the headwaters of the Mississippi, and then Britain would attack Louisiana from Canada as well as from the Gulf of Mexico. Although Livingston did not tell them, the French authorities could have known from their own informants in London that those old controversies between Britain and the United States over American debts and British spoliations, about which the mixed commissions under the Jay Treaty had wrangled so long, were indeed in the final process of settlement by diplomacy.

France, declared Livingston now, either should abandon her designs upon Louisiana altogether, or cover its frontiers by ceding the territory above the Arkansas River to the United States as he proposed. Otherwise, said he, France's conduct would speak "a language so painful to the feelings of the American Government" that they would not care about fixing their northern boundaries so as to protect the territories of France.[52]

Within two weeks, Livingston heard from General Bernadotte that Napoleon thought of sending him to the United States to negotiate upon the matters which Livingston had proposed through Joseph Bonaparte. This was personally irritating. Naturally, Livingston wished to finish what he himself had started. In addition, he sensed that it would mean delay just when things looked propitious. He knew that American traders would be furious over the withdrawal of the deposit at New Orleans. The Treaty of 1795 with Spain had been flouted. He wrote sharply on January 7, 1803, to Joseph for Napoleon to consider:

> I have examined the treaty: there is no pretense for this construction of it; and, as the right has been regularly exercised till now, it will be generally believed in the United States that this construction could only have been suggested by a wish on the part of France to get rid of the provisions of the treaty before she took possession. Now, sir, I will

51. King (King ed.), IV, 124, King to Hamilton, May 7, 1802.
52. State Department, France, VIII, December 24, 1802, third memorial for the First Consul, erroneously marked No. 4.

frankly confess to you that the United States will rather hazard their very existence than suffer the Mississippi to be shut against them. Of this you will easily be convinced when you learn that, when their numbers were but half of what they now are, and their means of defense infinitely less, their instructions to their Ministers that made the first treaty with Britain were, by no means to sign a treaty without securing the free navigation of that river. You will not, therefore, be surprised if this step of Spain should wind up the American people and Government to so high a pitch of resentment as shall lead them to a close and intimate connection with Britain, and perhaps to an immediate rupture with Spain.

He might have added, "and with France," but there was no need. It was obvious.[53]

Livingston did remark that General Bernadotte would be far happier if he arrived in the United States with a treaty to be put into execution rather than if he came to solicit one "in the face of a thousand intrigues and jealousies" of British agents and their friends among the citizens of the United States. He would have to answer vexing questions: Why had the claims not been paid by France? Why had the American minister received no sort of satisfaction on any subject for fourteen months? Why was France sending armies to the islands and taking possession of Louisiana and the Floridas? And so on. On the other hand, no chicanery, no crooked policy, rasped Livingston, would mingle with the treatymaking in Paris. Joseph Bonaparte might tell his brother, in short, that they could complete the treaty in a week. Talleyrand's countenance must have been ironic when he saw this letter, if he ever did see it.[54]

Joseph Bonaparte advised Livingston, however, that it would be better form to proceed through the regular channel of the foreign office; anyhow, Talleyrand had been told of his plan. So Livingston submitted an "outline of a treaty" to the foreign minister on January 10, 1803, and awaited developments—not too confidently. He was discouraged. It was indeed a long, long chance. But then, Britain was "very sour" and growing more so. He was sure at least of his argument that this American Government would swerve into alliance with Britain before it would let control of the Mississippi go to France without a fight. He wrote Madison on January 24 that Bernadotte was named minister to the United States; and he sent home, at last, copies of two memoirs showing his proposal to buy

53. State Department, France, VIII, January 7, 1803, Livingston's fourth memorial for the First Consul, erroneously numbered 3 and marked January 7, 1802, which internal evidence shows could not be so.
54. *Ibid.*

Upper Louisiana from France. There was no point longer in distrusting the mails. He had presented the matter to Talleyrand. This letter with the enclosed memoirs was marked as received at the State Department in Washington on April 25, 1803.[55]

The foreign minister seemed to wish well his project for Louisiana, said Livingston, but the First Consul was "immovable": "I confess to you I see very little use for a Minister here, where there is but one will; and that governed by no object but personal security and personal ambition: were it left to my discretion, I should bring matters to some positive issue, or leave them, which would be the only means of bringing them to an issue." For reasons best ascribed to his facile character, Talleyrand told Livingston on February 18 that the thought of selling Louisiana was out of the question. It was, he said, beneath the "dignity" of France. Talleyrand had just written also to Bernadotte, on the day after Livingston had submitted his proposal to buy Upper Louisiana, that France was pleased with the Spanish closure of New Orleans to American shipping. "The difficulty of maintaining it," he said to Bernadotte, "will be less for us than would have been establishing it."[56]

The "Chapter of Accidents"

NAPOLEON, First Consul of France, was not one to be stopped merely by the arguments or the threats of others, whether or not he kept them in mind for later reflection. While Livingston was making his attack through Joseph Bonaparte, Napoleon was ordering the minister of marine and colonies on December 19, 1802, to tell General Victor that he should get away for Louisiana as soon as possible before ice closed the harbor. Victor was to send an officer to the United States announcing the retrocession of Louisiana and giving reassurances to the American Government. He was to leave some of his troops in San Domingo and work in close relations with Leclerc, for their projects were intimate. He was to know how impatiently the French Government would await news from him, so that they could establish their own ideas about the pretensions of the United States and usurpations upon the Spaniards. And every time he saw the United States increasing their pretensions, he was to state that they had no knowledge in Paris of that particular matter, but that he would write and await orders.[57]

55. ASP FR, II, 531–532, Livingston to Talleyrand, January 10, 1803. State Department, France, VIII, Livingston to Madison, January 24, 1803, received April 25.
56. Ibid. AAE EU, Spt. 7, f. 315, Talleyrand to Bernadotte, January 11, 1803.
57. Corresp. de Napoléon I, VIII, 146, to Decrès, December 19, 1802.

It is clear that as late as December, 1802, Napoleon had no intention of yielding to the importunities of Livingston; but he was not ignoring what lay behind them. We cannot say that he was thinking then of letting the United States have Louisiana. Neither can it be said that he did not already realize what this American pressure upon his "favorite object" would mean, if he met with bad luck and things elsewhere did not develop as he planned.

Soon other events were not happening as Napoleon had designed. Transports could not be had in time to get Victor's expedition away before ice filled the harbor. Then Britain grew suspicious of those troops and ships concentrating in Holland and tightened her naval guard off the coast before the return of favorable weather. Replacements and money far beyond estimates had to be sent to Leclerc in San Domingo to overcome the "black rebels" and the ravages of yellow fever. Finally came the news in January, 1803, that Leclerc himself had died of the fever.[58]

As Beurnonville's efforts in Madrid began to be discussed publicly, Talleyrand noticed that Livingston had more to do with the British ambassador, Lord Whitworth. As a matter of fact, Livingston had told Whitworth that if France got the Floridas, the immediate effect would be to unite "every individual in America, of every party, and none more sincerely than himself, in the cause of Great Britain." Whitworth informed Livingston in February that Britain was "very averse" to the proposed exchange for the Floridas. With such encouragement from Britain, and with Livingston's support through Azara, the Spanish ambassador in Paris, Godoy and Cevallos were becoming too stubborn for Beurnonville at Madrid. Napoleon did appreciate the strength of Livingston's argument that New Orleans and the colony of Louisiana would be of little value to France without the supporting harbors and defenses of Mobile and Pensacola, especially Mobile, if a British fleet cruised the Gulf to blockade the mouth of the Mississippi, and the American population up the river were hostile to France.[59]

In addition, Napoleon's long conversation with Lord Whitworth in February came to naught. They talked for two hours about his grievances against Britain—Malta, protection of his enemies and personal abuse in the English newspapers, Egypt, invasion of England, his army and the British fleet, the alignments in Europe, the Algerians, Switzerland, Piedmont, and the little that he had to gain from war. Nevertheless, if Britain kept Malta, Napoleon seemed

58. Lyon, 193–194.
59. Browning, 37–39, 41, January 4, 7, 1803. ASP FR, II, 533–534, Livingston to Madison, February 18, 1803. Lyon, 191.

to be telling Whitworth candidly, it was war. Yet the British ambassador reported that the First Consul intended only "to frighten and to bully." The British Government made no concession regarding Malta. The ambassador reported to London again on February 28 that persons nearest Napoleon said it was war. Still Whitworth's second thought was that these men were "perhaps not most in his confidence."[60]

Then the First Consul had it straight from the American minister. Livingston's letter directly addressed to Napoleon spoke only of the claims, but his accompanying note to Talleyrand, dated February 24, 1803, wasted no words about New Orleans. It said: "There is unfortunately no medium, Sir, between a rupture and such declaration as shall satisfy the people of the United States, nor will the subject admit of delay." There was no use in waiting for Monroe, advance notice of whose special mission to France had arrived: "I have no doubt," declared Livingston, "that Mr. Monroe's instructions will be precise, and positive, & perhaps they may on that account be ill received here. If France really means to agree to our explanation of the Treaty, every reason of sound policy will rather direct her to do it as an act of good will, than as the result of any pressing measures on the part of the United States." Livingston asserted that this was not an official letter. But was it, notwithstanding, as good as an official warning? If it should prove to be the opinion of the American Government, backed by the American people, there would be more than argument and threat for Napoleon, arbiter of national destinies, to ponder—and in the very near future.[61]

Within the following month, then, if it did not happen sooner, the First Consul of France seems to have reached serious consideration of abandoning his plan to restore a French empire in North America. He gave General Victor no inkling. He insulted Robert Livingston. He kept up the impression that Bernadotte was going to America, even ordered him at the last moment to leave Paris for the port of departure. But Napoleon knew as well as Livingston that Britain was "very sour." Malta was still in British hands, to prove that if nothing else. The messages of the King to Parliament were becoming more strident. And the war spirit in Britain was rising. It would be hard enough in time of peace to take and to hold New Orleans out of the reach of the American people. But if

60. Browning, 78, February 21, 1803, Whitworth's report to Hawkesbury; 85, February 28.

61. AAE EU Spt. 7, f. 322, Livingston to Talleyrand, February 24, 1803. For accompanying letter to Napoleon, February 27, see below, p. 485 f.

war came again, France would have to fight the United States also, and this time it would be along the Mississippi as Hamilton, Miranda, and their co-workers wished to have it in 1798. That old "friend of France," Jefferson himself, was declaring as much, and here was his personal agent, duPont de Nemours, manufacturer of gunpowder in America, still in Paris to confirm it. All that Napoleon needed further to fix his decision was news straight from the United States of the uproar there over the withdrawal of the right of deposit and the reaction in Congress. This was soon forthcoming. Authorities maintain, however, that regardless of his change of mind about the Mississippi Valley, Napoleon intended still to reconquer San Domingo, that paradise for Creoles but not for Negroes, when he had done with the British in Europe.[62]

In spite of discouragements, notwithstanding insults, Robert Livingston was near his goal. As late as March 17, 1803, even after Napoleon's famous affront to him, the British ambassador was certain that Napoleon had no desire to go to war. There were no naval armaments, he reported to Hawkesbury, of any consequence "carrying on" in the ports of France. The Americans, said Lord Whitworth, were no longer fearful of the destination of the French fleet in the Dutch ports. They were sanguine enough to hope that they would hear no more of the exchange of the Floridas or even the projects on Louisiana. He was confident that Talleyrand had assured Livingston that those projects were deferred. So Livingston, said Whitworth, trusted to the "chapter of accidents for the rest." Within one month the situation was changed. If accidents they were, they had happened. Britain was on the verge of war again with France. And Robert Livingston was purchasing the whole of Louisiana from France—the territory above the Arkansas, the region below the Arkansas, the island of New Orleans, perhaps the Floridas, perhaps Texas.[63]

62. See below, p. 490. Treudley, 143, citing Roloff.
63. Browning, 128, Whitworth to Hawkesbury, March 17, 1803.

XVII

JEFFERSON'S PLANNING IN AMERICA

The Sweep of the Continent

THE President and his minister to France were not in touch for weeks on end. They did not need to be. Both were aware of the continental sweep beyond the Mississippi whence came the Arkansas and Missouri Rivers. They knew what lay to the southwest in the riches of Spain symbolized by Pensacola, Mobile, New Orleans, Santa Fé. They were Americans of common imagination and desire. They would buy from France at the expense of Spain, with American claims, "Gold," and the threat of "Iron" smoothly but surely pressed. They understood also what was on the north beyond the Indian barriers. The real competitor for this continent was neither Spain nor France.

Anglo-Saxons, not Latins, were the expansionists, the appropriators of their age. Frenchmen would never colonize in the manner necessary to put obstacles before the American pioneers. But it was not at all certain that Englishmen could not, if they had a fair opportunity. Britain and France might reach some agreement satisfying both in Europe, in the Mediterranean, the Orient, and leave each other free to work out her own plans for aggrandizement within her separate sphere in the Americas. If this happened, it would be the English who checked the advance of the American people on this continent.

There was little reason for Jefferson and Livingston to fear that Britain and France could set a common barrier against the United States. As the year 1802 progressed, it looked as though they had been able to agree upon San Domingo, and even that they might in regard to the Louisiana country beyond the Mississippi. But this was not likely concerning the Floridas. Britain's own interest in the Gulf of Mexico was too great for a common policy with France in that quarter. There was hardly a chance that the two could agree upon a single plan of operations against the United States.

But what if one of them proceeded without the other? If Britain alone crowded upon the United States, would the tradition of friendship and coöperation with the old ally be available? It was sadly frayed, but it was still there. If France herself tried to block this nation, would the threat of marrying "the British fleet and nation" suffice? John Adams had avoided it to the angry dismay of Federalists. Robert Livingston now advocated it and Thomas Jefferson had sent duPont de Nemours especially to flaunt it before the statesmen of his native country.

Jefferson and Livingston hoped realistically. If France encroached, the threat of alliance with Britain ought to be enough to persuade France that she should withdraw before the United States in North America and continue on friendly terms with them. Otherwise they would join with Britain to inflict greater damage upon French commercial and financial interests in the Caribbean and on the high seas. If Britain pressed too hard, revival of the Franco-American tradition should make her chary of her finances, commerce, prestige. But if hostilities had to come, the United States positively were not going to war with Great Britain. Although held back of the Lakes and the Illinois River since Wayne's victory at Fallen Timbers and the Treaty of Greenville, the British were still menacing on the north. And Britons were still active among the Indian tribes above the Floridas on the south even though the plans of Liston, Chisholm, and Blount had gone awry.[1]

Anxiety furthermore still remained that the "men of the Western waters" might not wait for the Government of the United States to follow after them into the Mississippi Valley. They might become so intermingled with Spaniards, French, English as to create another nation upon this continent. This anxiety was diminishing with the rapid increase of immigration from the older settlements on the Atlantic and with improving means of communication over the Appalachians. In its place rose concern that officials at Washington would lose their places if they did not gratify the desires of the West. The President's Federalist opponents were standing by eagerly. Westerners were indeed inclined to be Jeffersonian Republicans, but they might not long continue so if they had to suffer any denial, or even delay, of their ambitions.

For this reason if no other, Thomas Jefferson had to give particular attention to removing Indian titles to the lands along the river-bottoms of the country from the Appalachians to the Mississippi. That required a decided interest in the tribes and their activities beyond the river. The immediate security of the United States, caught between powers habitually at war, made it the matter of first importance to treat the Mississippi as if it were the front of the American defenses in an area where those powers were likely to contend. But that was not, could not be, the sole end in view for

1. Jefferson (Ford ed.), VIII, 228, to John Bacon, April 30, 1803. See above, p. 266f.

one who was presiding over the fortunes of both party and state. Use of the Mississippi required participation if not dominating influence in affairs beyond its channel. Jefferson had that full view of the problem, although he wisely did not proclaim it then for European or American audience. He knew that European onlookers were suspicious and that New Englanders feared for their political heritage from colonial times, but he also knew that American settlers were already crossing the river into Upper Louisiana and pushing on up the Missouri.

The "Western Mind"

WHEN news came that the Spanish intendant at New Orleans had withdrawn the right of deposit, Secretary Madison at once, on November 27, 1802, ordered Charles Pinckney to protest in Madrid and to demand reparation from the Spanish Government. He was to assume that the intendant had proceeded on his own responsibility. We know now that it was otherwise. Godoy and Cevallos had lost patience with American evasions and abuses of the treaty right. We know also that, even if the order had not originated with the French Government, Talleyrand was pleased with the intendant's action and thanked the Spanish authorities for it.[2]

Many in the United States instantly accused France of the move and raged accordingly. The President chose to wait and see. He would defeat his purpose of avoiding war if he should flare up now. He would be forced in reality to the side of the "British fleet and nation." That was to be held in hand as a threat, not made an instrument of action. Besides, he had not yet heard the result of duPont de Nemours' special mission. He had received no further word from Livingston since he had submitted his "pointed memorial" to Talleyrand in August upon reasons why France should not retain New Orleans and the Floridas, and had reported home that the French people were beginning to see the futility in Napoleon's colonial dream. Thomas Jefferson, too, appreciated that Britain was "very sour." It was no time to get excited, to antagonize France and to play into Britain's hand.[3]

The President merely indicated to Congress in his second annual message, December 15, 1802, that if the cession to France of Louisiana were effected, "the aspect of our foreign relations" would be changed, and the deliberations of Congress on the subject altered. He stressed instead the transactions with the Creeks and Choctaws

2. Madison (Hunt ed.), VI, 461–464. Whitaker, *Mississippi Question*, 189–199. Lyon, 167–175.
3. See above, p. 441.

in the Southwest and with the tribes about Vincennes in the Indiana Territory above the Ohio. They were giving up more lands for white settlement. These, he demonstrated, were essential as "an outpost of the United States, surrounded by strong neighbors and distant from its support." The intimate connection between Indian monopoly of land within the borders of the United States and the return of France into Louisiana may not have been apparent to Congressmen. It was to President Jefferson.[4]

Public clamor against France and Spain was so vehement, however, and his Federalist enemies so insistent, that Jefferson could not let the matter rest if he would, upon Pinckney's representations in Madrid and the protests to Spanish officials in New Orleans by the French chargé at Washington, Pichon, and the Spanish minister, Irujo. Nor could he leave it solely to Livingston in Paris. On December 17, Congress called for a report by the Secretary of State. Jefferson felt obliged to respond with a special message on the twenty-second assuring that he would "lose not a moment" in taking the proper steps to maintain the "rights of the nation."[5]

Happily for Jefferson, information arrived within the next twelve days to point the way for those steps. DuPont de Nemours' letter of October 4, 1802, reached him on December 31. It proposed that he offer $6,000,000 for New Orleans and the Floridas. And by January 3, the State Department had also received Livingston's despatches of November 11, telling of his confidential relations with Joseph Bonaparte. Livingston's letter of October 28, reporting the query from Joseph Bonaparte whether the United States had rather have Louisiana had not yet reached Jefferson. This did not come into his hands until February 9.[6]

These letters did not prove that France would wish in the end to sell any territory to the United States, but they showed that the matter was before persons high in the Government of France, even close to Napoleon. They gave Jefferson further reason for temporizing until Britain and France had drifted once more into war, and the United States had narrowed the gaps into their domain through the Indian lands along the Mississippi, the borders of Florida, and in the Northwest. If only he could persuade his countrymen of the West that he was attending to their interests, if only he could keep them from running after the Federalists, who were again demanding an attack upon New Orleans, seemingly with no thought for conditions in Europe, he might secure that permanent outlet to the

4. Richardson, I, 343–344.
5. Ibid., I, 346.
6. See above, pp. 443–444.

sea without going to war. He conceded that it would be worth, in the last resort, hazarding the very existence of the nation.

Jefferson took the steps. He nominated James Monroe on January 11, 1803, to be minister extraordinary and plenipotentiary to both France and Spain. He wrote on the eighteenth to the Governor of Kentucky to explain:

> . . . I have determined with the approbation of the Senate, to send James Monroe, late governor of Virginia, with full powers to him and our ministers in France and Spain to enter with those governments into such arrangements as may effectually secure our rights & interest in the Mississippi, and in the country eastward of that. He is now here and will depart immediately. In the meantime knowing how important it is that the obstructions shall be removed in time for the produce which will begin to descend the river in February, the Spanish minister, has, at our request, reiterated his interposition with the intendant of New Orleans.
>
> I inclose you a resolution of the House of Representatives on this subject, which with the measures taken by the executive, will, I hope, furnish new grounds for the confidence which the legislature of Kentucky is pleased to express in the government of the U. S., and evince to them that that government is equally and impartially alive to the interests of every portion of the union.[7]

It was a sagacious appointment. James Monroe had been known for nearly twenty years as the friend of the "men of the Western waters" and their rights to the Mississippi—ever since he had opposed the arrangement which Jay had made with Gardoqui in 1786 to close the Mississippi temporarily. He himself owned lands in the West. The Federalists in the Senate, now bidding for Western support, could not criticize him as he had argued against Jay and the special mission to England in the spring of 1794. His friends in France, to be sure, those members of the old Committee of Public Safety and the Directory, had long since fallen from power. He could make no special appeal to the officials about Napoleon. But that was not the point. The point was, as Jefferson had written to him on January 10, that the "western mind" had been thrown into a "fever" by the affair at New Orleans; and so, he was being called upon to make a "temporary sacrifice" of himself in order to prevent "this greatest of evils in the present prosperous tide of our affairs."

"The whole public hope," said Jefferson, would rest upon Monroe; he could not decline. On the thirteenth, after the Senate had con-

7. Richardson, I, 350–351. Jefferson (Ford ed.), VIII, 202–203, to James Garrard, January 18, 1803.

firmed his appointment, Jefferson made clearer to him that his mission was not only to hold the Westerners loyal but also to silence the Federalists who were clamoring for war in order to get themselves back in office. If anything more was needed to influence this Republican, Jefferson found it in: "But some men are born for the public. Nature by fitting them for the service of the human race on a broad scale, has stamped with the evidences of her destination and their duty." After that, how could a man of public zeal—and political ambition—decline? There was also in it a salary of $9,000 a year from the time of departure to the end of the mission with expenses paid. James Monroe accepted.[8]

The President was really in no great hurry to have the minister extraordinary and plenipotentiary leave for France, although he had told Monroe and the Governor of Kentucky otherwise. He had still to advance his plan for correlating the problem of the Indians east of the Mississippi with exploration of the Missouri country beyond. He had yet to prepare the reply which should go with Monroe to duPont de Nemours. The Administration had yet to win full control in Congress over the war policy of the country. Further assurances were necessary from Western leaders that they would await results from Monroe's mission. Arguments had to be matured with Secretary Madison that Monroe and Livingston should press upon Napoleon to show him why he had better sell New Orleans and the Floridas to the United States.

A "Literary Pursuit"—White Man's Sovereignty

JEFFERSON at once got to the matter of the Indians and exploration into French territory with a confidential message to Congress on January 18, just a week after his nomination of Monroe. The tribes within the United States, said he, had been growing more and more uneasy on account of the diminution of their lands; they were increasingly hostile to further sales on any conditions. This was dangerous to the safety of the United States particularly along the lower Mississippi where the Chickasaws, otherwise quite friendly to the Government, controlled the east bank of the river from the Ohio to the Yazoo. Their own habitations were not on the river, but even so they would not sell their hunting grounds there.

The thoughts in Jefferson's mind stand out. What indeed if France should try to enter vigorously upon the business of colonizing the other side of the Mississippi as Victor Collot and others urged? The United States would be extremely vulnerable at that

8. Jefferson (Ford ed.), VIII, 188, 190–192, to Monroe, January 10, 13, 1803. Sloane, "World Aspects of the Louisiana Purchase," AHR, IV, 518.

spot. Congress therefore must realize how important it was, declared Jefferson, to possess "a respectable breadth of country on that river, from our southern limit to the Illinois, at least," so that they could present "as firm a front on that as on our eastern border." This was the prospect which troubled him. The solution which he offered was simple in its conception but as far-reaching in its ultimate purposes as the most ardent of imperialists, even Rufus King or Alexander Hamilton, could have imagined.[9]

The Chickasaws and others, said Jefferson, were showing signs of wishing to turn from hunting to stock raising and agriculture. Therefore, they should be encouraged in that trend, and the way to do it was to increase the Government's "trading houses" among them so as to provide the "implements and comforts" of a higher standard of living in return for their products. Thus, they would be led to realize that they did not need "extensive but uncultivated wilds," and they would voluntarily release more and more land to the white men for settlement. In other words, the Chickasaws and their kind would then inevitably fuse into the general population, and those gaps along the Western boundary would close in the face of the French—if indeed it were to be the French who held sovereignty over the trans-Mississippi country.

But these government trading posts would ruin the business of the private traders who were now enjoying the traffic with the Indians. Thomas Jefferson's mind, with characteristic understanding of human nature, worked at once out of that dilemma to ultimate purposes. "It might be worthy the attention of Congress," he suggested, "in their care of individual as well as of the general interest to point in another direction the enterprise of these citizens, as profitably for themselves and more usefully for the public."

The Missouri country lay beyond. It was understood, said Jefferson, that the numerous tribes there furnished "great supplies of furs and peltry to the trade of another nation, carried on in a high latitude through an infinite number of portages and lakes shut up by ice through a long season." Such a commerce could not compete with trade down the Missouri and into the Illinois, the Ohio, the Tennessee, and other waterways within the "moderate climate" of the United States and connecting with the Hudson, the Susquehanna, the Potomac, James, or Savannah Rivers on the Atlantic Seaboard. Possibly too, there was but a single portage from the headwaters of the Missouri to streams flowing on the far side into the Pacific. Congress had only to send "an intelligent officer, with ten or twelve chosen men" to explore "the whole line, even to the

9. Richardson, I, 352–354.

Western Ocean, have conferences with the natives on the subject of commercial intercourse, get admission among them for our traders as others are admitted," and after making all other arrangements necessary, be back again "in the course of two summers."

What if Spain should object? Why, Spain "regarding this as a literary pursuit, which it is in the habit of permitting within its dominions, would not be disposed to view it with jealousy, even if the expiring state of its interests there did not render it a matter of indifference." Anyhow, the United States would only be seeking as other "civilized nations" to enlarge the "boundaries of their knowledge"—not yet the boundaries of their domain, we may interpolate.[10]

What if France, or Britain, took offense? Jefferson did not comment. But then, this was a confidential message to Congress, not an inquiry of those powers. The interest of France, presumably, could be left for the immediate future, and Monroe's mission, to determine. Just to be on the safe side, he later requested a passport for Lewis from the French chargé, on the ground that it was merely to be a scientific expedition. Pichon consented on that understanding, reporting to Talleyrand that it did not appear susceptible to "any other reflection."[11]

As for Britain? It was the trade of British subjects in the far Northwest which American citizens would take over for themselves. That problem, too, could be left for the present on the lap of the future. Meanwhile the British chargé, Thornton, gave a similar passport.[12]

We get here more than a glimpse of realities. The white man's sovereignty over the great stretches of the continent north and west of the Arkansas and the Mississippi Rivers was then but an assertion. It was the Indian's law that prevailed there, regardless of assumptions by Governments whether at Madrid, Paris, London, or Washington. The region was still too remote from Christendom for white men's governments to fear war with one another over it. It was still in the realm of private competition among Spaniards, Frenchmen, Britons, and Americans.

White men were then alive, however, who would bluster and threaten war between Christian nations over the division of that country according to their own conception of sovereignty. And white men of the next generation would ride those prairies and high plains in the uniform of the United States Cavalry trampling

10. *Ibid.*, I, 354.
11. AAE CP EU, LV, ff. 318–320, Pichon to Talleyrand, March 4, 1803.
12. *Ibid.*

the last efforts of Sioux, Cheyenne, Crow, and Kiowa to keep their ancestral rights. Such were the realities waiting upon the confidential message of Thomas Jefferson to Congress, January 18, 1803, with regard to "extending the external commerce of the United States."[13]

There is no intention to imply here that Jefferson had gone so far beyond immediate speculations. The recorded evidence does not show that at the time of this message to Congress concerning the Missouri country he had in his mind a scheme for acquiring all of Louisiana, or even what Livingston had already asked on the other side of the Atlantic. He did not get Livingston's letter of October 28 reporting Joseph Bonaparte's question about Louisiana until February 9. He did not receive Livingston's memorials showing his overtures to Napoleon through Joseph Bonaparte on December 11, 1802, and subsequent dates, offering to buy the territory above the Arkansas River, until after Monroe had gone to Europe. How the news of that offer might have affected his message to Congress in regard to the expedition up the Missouri and his instructions for Livingston and Monroe can only be guessed. It is fair conjecture nonetheless that if he had known, he might have matured more swiftly his long-range plans for trade with the Indians in the remote Northwest, and have sent instructions to Livingston with Monroe that would have put even more pressure upon France than Livingston was already applying with his aid and approval. And he might have been persuaded to set upon paper thoughts within himself which he had not yet cared to reveal.

We have no proof even that the idea of acquiring the trans-Mississippi country eventually for the United States was in the back of Jefferson's mind at this moment. We do not know that it was a motive of his plan to develop American trading on the Missouri in competition with the British. He stated to Congress that the plan was in order to consolidate the United States along the Mississippi. But, his profession to the contrary, we cannot be so sure that he was interested only in developing trade; that there was no thought of what might come to be thereafter, as he proposed to Congress, January 18, 1803, the expedition of his own private secretary, Meriwether Lewis—"an intelligent officer with ten or twelve chosen men."

We would like often to know what men think about before they speak and then do not say, or what they tell one another on unrecorded occasions, besides those studied thoughts which they commit to letters and to public utterances. What verbal *if-it-should-*

13. Richardson, I., 354.

happen-so's, for instance, had been exchanged between Robert Livingston and Thomas Jefferson in private conversation before Livingston took ship for France in 1801? Livingston was in Washington that spring. The chances are not good that we shall ever know. But it is altogether too easy to be satisfied with conservative conclusions from letters and statements which have been written for the eye of anyone in case that evidence should happen to reach the public —where the transition from critical friend to fellow partisan to honest opponent to unscrupulous enemy may be swift and ruinous.

Coincidences of time, similarities of attitude, identical language are not to be passed by without remark. Livingston wrote to Napoleon by way of Joseph Bonaparte on January 7 in Paris: "Now, sir, I will frankly confess to you that the United States will rather hazard their very existence than suffer the Mississippi to be shut against them. . . ." Thomas Jefferson in Washington wrote to duPont de Nemours on February 1: "For our circumstances are so imperious as to admit of no delay as to our course; and the use of the Mississippi so indispensable, that we cannot hesitate one moment to hazard our existence for its maintenance." This, of course, may have been the most fortuitous of coincidences. And then, it may not. No cable crossed the Atlantic in 1803.[14]

It is significant that Thomas Jefferson's plan for coördinating the problem of Indian holdings east of the Mississippi with exploration of the Missouri country beyond was conceived almost simultaneously with Robert Livingston's offer to buy Upper Louisiana. There is revelation, too, in the letter which Secretary Gallatin wrote to Jefferson about the Lewis expedition on April 13, 1803, before Livingston's report of his offer was marked as received on April 25 at the Department of State. Gallatin observed:

> The present aspect of affairs may, ere long, render it necessary that we should, by taking immediate possession, prevent G. B. from doing the same. Hence a perfect knowledge of the posts, establishments & force kept by Spain in upper Louisiana, and also of the most proper station to occupy, for the purpose of preventing effectually the occupation of any part of the Missouri country by G. B., seems important. . . .

With that in view Gallatin thought it advisable to ascertain the British communications with the Missouri from the Mississippi and, "still more in point," from Lake Winnipeg and the waters emptying into Hudson's Bay. Here were tasks for Meriwether Lewis beyond developing American trade with the Indians along the Missouri. Gallatin continued: ". . . whatever may be the issue of the present

14. See above, p. 451. Jefferson (Ford ed.), VIII, 203–205, February 1, 1803.

difficulties, the future destinies of the Missouri country are of vast importance to the United States, it being perhaps the *only* large tract of country, and certainly the *first* which lying out of the boundaries of the Union will be settled by the people of the U. States . . ." As a matter of fact, it was already being settled by them. But that is not the point for us just now. It is the revelation in Gallatin's letter of what was turning over in the minds of the statesmen who had sent Livingston abroad in 1801.[15]

First Things First

NOTWITHSTANDING the "vast importance to the United States" of the "future destinies of the Missouri country," and the wisdom of forestalling the British traders there, Thomas Jefferson was in no more haste to send Lewis and Clark on their adventure than to get Monroe off to France. He was more concerned to make sure that the outlets down the Mississippi and the rivers past Mobile and Pensacola stayed open while he cleared Indian lands for white settlement and consolidated the position of the United States upon the Mississippi. It would be good to have East Florida too, but that could wait. He sought first to control the war legislation of Congress and to prepare for the negotiations when Monroe should join Livingston in Paris. First things should come first.

Jefferson drafted his reply on February 1 to duPont de Nemours' letter of October 4, 1802, which had arrived on December 31. They were pleased to have duPont's proposal, but they could not meet it entirely. They were preparing modifications to which they could agree, he said, when the Spanish intendant at New Orleans, "unauthorized by his government," had suspended the right of deposit and thrown "our whole country into such a ferment as imminently threatened its peace." So, they were sending Monroe to aid Livingston "in the issue of a crisis the most important the U. S. have ever met since their independence & which is to decide their future character & career." France had better realize that she was as involved as she had been in the American Revolution. "The interests of the two countries being absolutely the same as to this matter," Jefferson suggested blandly, "your aid may be conscientiously given."[16]

After all that he had observed and learned of the French interest in the Mississippi country, Thomas Jefferson knew better than

15. Jefferson Papers, CXXXI, 22, 582, Gallatin to Jefferson, April 13, 1803. Photographed by permission of the Manuscripts Division, Library of Congress. Printed in Gallatin, *Writings*, I, 120–122.
16. Jefferson (Ford ed.), VIII, 203–208, February 1, 1803.

to think it "absolutely the same" as the interest of the United States. He meant to declare no such thing to the French authorities through duPont de Nemours. He meant what he went on to say, as it were in confidence to his friend, with the request that his letters be burned:

> . . . our circumstances are so imperious as to admit of no delay as to our course . . . the use of the Mississippi so indispensable, that we cannot hesitate one moment to hazard our existence for its maintenance . . . not but that we shall still endeavor to go on in peace and friendship with our neighbors as long as we can, *if our rights of navigation & deposit are respected* . . . it is peace alone which makes it an object with us, and which ought to make the cession of it desirable to France. Whatever power, other than ourselves, holds the country east of the Mississippi becomes our natural enemy. Will such a possession do France as much good, as such an enemy may do her harm? And how long would it be hers, were such an enemy, situated at its door, added to G Britain?[17]

Here was the identity of interest between France and the United States. Neither of them could afford to have the United States forced at that time into an alliance with Britain. That being indisputable, France would not expect the United States to offer much else. They were an agricultural country, said Jefferson, "poor in money, and owing great debts." Besides the Floridas were "barren sand" with only a few "rich bottoms," and those already "possessed by individuals." It was "peace alone" that interested both France and the United States. Monroe would come instructed on every phase of the problem with "a minuteness" that no written communication to Livingston could ever attain. There need be no delay, therefore, in completing the arrangements. DuPont de Nemours himself, "having a freedom of communication" which "diplomatic gentlemen" were denied "by forms," could smooth the way of "representations & reasonings which would be received with more suspicion from them."

It was all so clear to Thomas Jefferson. There should be no further delay, once the First Consul of France realized the "ferment" in the United States, and the menace therefrom to his own "peace."[18]

Jefferson wrote next to Napoleon himself, giving formal notice of Monroe's mission with power to join Livingston in bringing the negotiations to a close upon the basis of "our friendship." "And I pray God," said he in the usual diplomatic language, "to have you, Citizen First Consul, in his safe and holy keeping."[19]

17. *Ibid.*, VIII, 205–207.
18. *Ibid.*, VIII, 204.
19. AAE CP EU, LV, f. 272.

The American sense of humor may rise with remark that the First Consul would have need of it. But Napoleon and Barbé Marbois, his minister of the public treasury, seem to have felt more gravely the need of money. The letter from the American President to the First Consul came eventually to rest among the papers of the ministry of foreign affairs. And there is no comment upon it to reveal Gallic humor. It is a wonder perhaps that Talleyrand did not find a moment for some. But then he was very serious that spring, dealing with the stubbornness of Whitworth over the questions of Malta, Switzerland, the Netherlands, and with Robert Livingston's persistence. Despite all rebuffs, fancied or real, from his own Government and from the officials of France, Livingston was striving to put obstacles between France and Spain in regard to the Floridas, insisting that the United States would have control over the port of New Orleans in some way or other, threatening that they would side with Britain in the event of war. If humor was present, it was grim. France was on verge of war again with Britain. Frenchmen knew so well the full meaning of war.

Jefferson understood this too. He was glad to have his country stir, for the effect it would have upon France. But he was anxious that it should not move beyond the threat to war itself. His supporters in Congress were on guard that discretion should not be taken from the President as to the time and place of military action, while Monroe went to France with the letter to duPont de Nemours, instructions for Livingston and himself, and the good word for the First Consul.

New Orleans, Lock and Key

There was great need for a close watch. The Federalists were eager to force the President into action. Senator Ross, from western Pennsylvania, submitted resolutions with fiery speech. The United States had an "indisputable right" to free navigation of the Mississippi, he declared, and a convenient place of deposit in the island of New Orleans; neither the dignity nor the safety of this Union permitted so important a right to be held by a tenure so uncertain as the treaty with Spain; the President should be authorized to take immediate possession of such places on that island as he deemed fit; he should be authorized to call out the militia of South Carolina, Georgia, Ohio, Kentucky, Tennessee, the Mississippi Territory, to the number of 50,000; Congress should appropriate $5,000,000 for the campaign: "It is not difficult to determine," said Ross, "who will command and own the Floridas. They must belong to the master of Louisiana and New Orleans. Then the owners possess the lock and key of the whole Western country. There is no entrance or egress but by their leave." In other words, the United States should take what they believed ought to belong to them. It was their destiny.[20]

The struggle was on for the votes along "the Western waters." Gouverneur Morris, Senator from New York, supported Ross with an elaborate address on February 23. Once the personal representative of Washington in England and minister to the French Monarchy, then confidential agent in Europe for the British foreign minister, Grenville, Gouverneur Morris now proposed that the United States should take possession in New Orleans without consulting Britain, but declaring their friendship to France. They would explain that they had seized the mouth of the Mississippi River in self-defense. They would make amends to France by offering assistance in San Domingo and asserting that they had no obligation to Britain. They would do the same for Spain. To appease both, they would relinquish all claims for damages to their shipping by those powers in the past. They would reimburse their own merchants. This would be the way to buy New Orleans and adjacent territory. The price would be "paid to ourselves." (The idea would appeal to Federalist shipowners, hardly to Jeffersonian taxpayers.) If there was no result from these suggestions to Spain and France, said Morris, the United States should then tell them that this country would join Britain in conquering all French and Spanish dominions within reach. "Sir, this language will be listened to," he said.[21]

Indeed it might, particularly in Britain. Morris was not so reassuring on that matter. He admitted that Britain's price would be that the United States should stay in the war until peace were made by common consent. This, he had to concede, the United States should never do if they could avoid it. He was confident that the British fleet would be sent to aid the United States without the requirement of a treaty.

The inference was that the United States would be able to evade any commitment likely to block their territorial ambitions on the Gulf of Mexico east of the Mississippi River. But could they? Senators who were by no means subservient to the Republican administration could think not, decidedly not, and with good reason from knowledge of British aspirations in the Floridas so recently as the affair of Liston, Chisholm, and Blount.[22]

20. *Annals,* 7 Cong. 2 Sess., 91–95, February 16, 1803; 171–185, *183,* February 24. Marbois, 240.

21. *Annals,* 7 Cong. 2 Sess., 185–204, February 23, 1803. For Morris as British agent in 1795–1796, see Dropmore Mss., III, 87–88, 222, 224, 230, 258, 266.

22. See above, pp. 266–276.

The Administration answered Morris through his colleague, Senator Clinton of New York. Clinton recalled Morris' career as a Federalist in Europe and America and then asserted, without being wholly candid, that he was even more of an imperialist than the Republicans. He wanted not only New Orleans and the Floridas but all of Louisiana![23]

The Administration checked Ross with another set of military proposals from the West. Breckenridge of Kentucky, close friend of Jefferson, introduced amendments that would empower the President to call out and to arm 80,000 militia—but only when he himself should decide to do so. Ross's proposals failed on February 25 by a vote of 15 to 11. Breckenridge's then passed unanimously.[24]

It was no use for the Federalists to try further. The imperialists among them could not take the Western votes from the President and hurry the country into war. Alexander Hamilton's spirit did not permeate the West. And the Federalist party itself was not united in the cause. Representatives of New England's mercantile interests were not conspicuous in the debate upon Ross's resolutions. Those like Pickering of Massachusetts gloomed over the departed days when God's chosen had ruled America, before John Adams turned traitor, before infidels and rascals took over the Government. They were on the point of talking among themselves about a snug little New England Confederacy joined perhaps with Nova Scotia under the benevolence of Britain. They did not relish a war with France now. Further expansion of the United States would only add to the dominion of vile "democracy," only sink them deeper into subordination to the will of the American people. Why, Jefferson's friends would make him President for life![25]

Assured control over the war policy of Congress, Jefferson had now only to draft Monroe's instructions and get him off to France. At home, the West was well in hand; its uproar could do nothing but good for the United States when the news reached Europe. Under its influence, Pichon for France and Irujo for Spain were already bearing down upon the officials at New Orleans. The affair was dwindling to a quarrel between the Spanish Governor and the intendant. And word came in due time that the Government at Madrid had repudiated the action of the intendant. The right of

23. *Annals*, 7 Cong. 2 Sess., 246–254, Clinton's speech on February 25.

24. *Ibid.*, 255. The eleven Senators in favor of Ross's resolutions were: Dayton of New Jersey, Morris of New York, Hillhouse and Tracy of Connecticut, Olcott and Plumer of New Hampshire, Wells and White of Delaware, Mason of Massachusetts, Howard of Maryland, and Ross of Pennsylvania.

25. Lodge, *Cabot*, 337–341, Pickering to Cabot, January 29, 1804; 341–344, Cabot's wiser reply, February 14. See below, p. 545.

deposit was restored. It would not have mattered much then if Jefferson had known, as we do now, that the intendant had received his original order from Spain. Meanwhile, James Monroe was on his way, carefully advised to move with Livingston at Paris, and with Pinckney at Madrid, if that had to be, upon such a course as would take the United States into New Orleans and the Floridas, retaining if possible the tradition of friendship with France. If this really could not be done, Monroe was then, but only then, to play Jefferson's last card and seek that alliance with British fleet and nation. Hopes were strong, however, that it would never have to be played. His "good friend," duPont de Nemours, would see to that. Although Thomas Jefferson's confidence in the agents whom he had selected may have stumbled, his prescience as to the outcome was sure.[26]

Arguments to Impress Frenchmen

THE instructions of Secretary Madison to Livingston and Monroe, March 2, 1803, used more diplomatic language perhaps than Jefferson's letters of the previous April to duPont de Nemours and to Livingston, but the warning to France was as stern. "Hostile measures" toward the United States would "connect their Councils, and their Colossal growth with the great and formidable rival of France." This, wrote Madison, could never escape France's "discernment, nor be disregarded by her prudence."[27]

Prudence, indeed, could never disregard "Colossal growth." It might, however, examine size to discover whether it had also coordination and strength. So, Madison spun arguments to impress the statesmen of France. They were badly mistaken if they thought that they could command "the interests and attachments of the Western portion of the United States." In the first place, said he, those Westerners were bound to the Union by "ties of kindred and affection." This was an assertion of which Madison and Jefferson had serious doubts from the very recent past, but the time had come to will that the hope was fact. In any case, the French must think it so. If it were not yet quite so, Livingston and Monroe nonetheless were to make the French believe that the men of the West could not be won over. For, in the second place, they were held to the States on the Atlantic by "clear and essential interests." They, to be sure, had to have the outlet down the river by New Orleans for their own products, but they were as dependent upon the eastern

26. AAE CP EU, LV, ff. 274–281, Pichon to Talleyrand, February 13, 1803, with enclosures. Whitaker, *Mississippi Question*, 197–198, 205. Lyon, 175, 181–182.
27. Madison (Hunt ed.), VII, 9–30.

part of the United States for essential imports. Navigation ascending the Mississippi might improve, said Madison, but improvements would keep pace on the ways across the Appalachians from east to west.

James Madison did not then conceive of the railroad system which interlaces the Mississippi Valley with the Atlantic Seaboard today. But his vision did comprehend "improvements in canals and roads." By the time the steamboat had come to revolutionize the traffic of the Mississippi up and down stream after 1810, the whole valley was safely within the domain of the American people and out of the reach of all foreign powers except Britain. When the cleavage into warring sections did occur in the United States after 1850, it was not between East and West but North and South. European governments were very interested spectators of the Civil War, and they played dangerously near to the edge of participation, but they dared not intervene.

In addition, wrote Madison to Livingston and Monroe in March, 1803, if the Westerners were to form a separate state, they would lose their share of the revenues which were paid into the Treasury of the United States upon the foreign merchandise that would still have to come into their markets from the Eastern States. They would gain only the expense of maintaining a separate government. Besides, they would soon realize—and the French should ponder the evil thereof—that a "connection of the Western people" with France would cause a corresponding association of the Eastern people with Britain. "It is found from long experience," declared Madison, "that France and Great Britain are nearly half their time at War." So it would be with their allies.[28]

Here, James Madison had reached the heart of matter. Notwithstanding the old enthusiasms of George Rogers Clark, Samuel Fulton, and others, Westerners would quickly discover that France could give no protection to the outlet down the Mississippi "nearly one half of the time." They had better let the United States Government take full charge. France, too, had better do this, for it was the only way to keep the United States out of the wars of Europe on Britain's side. American interests, said Madison, already dominated the trade on the Mississippi, and would continue to do so "for ages." France's trade was even then subject to American power. She could only hope to preserve it, not by closing the river to the United States, but by accepting the protection there which the United States as a neutral would afford to her commerce upon the principle of the most favored nation.

28. *Ibid.*, VII, 13–14.

Madison's offer for New Orleans and the Floridas followed the suggestions of duPont de Nemours, but with explicit changes to fit his argument that France could save her commerce on the Mississippi and with the Floridas only by helping to establish there the Government of the United States. Whereas duPont de Nemours had proposed the sale on condition that the French have the right indefinitely to conduct their business in the ceded territory as freely as the citizens and vessels of the United States "without paying any duties," Madison stipulated now that, although there should be "free and common" navigation of the Mississippi from source to ocean, French vessels and citizens should enjoy equal duties with American below the line of thirty-one degrees of latitude, on the Mississippi, and in the ports of Florida on the Gulf, for only ten years. And the French should have the right of deposit free of duties at New Orleans, and other places in the ceded territory open to the commerce of the United States for only the same period.

Whereas duPont de Nemours wished to exclude all other nations from the commercial advantages which he sought to retain for France, Madison proposed that no other nation should be permitted to trade on either shore of the Mississippi below the thirty-first degree of latitude. And then, by unavoidable inference, he relegated France as well, at the end of ten years, to the same position with respect to the American side of the river. As for the gulf ports of the Floridas, he would assure France merely that she would never be "on a worse footing than the most favored nations."[29]

Robert Livingston's influence upon the instructions of March 2, 1803, from Madison to Monroe and himself appears most strongly in regard to the matter of the supremacy of American traffic and investment in New Orleans. Madison ignored duPont de Nemours' assertion to Jefferson before leaving the United States that New Orleans would always be "the *defacto* capital of the two Louisianas" and a French city because of its population. He took for granted instead that France would soon construct another "emporium" for its colony on the west bank of the Mississippi after New Orleans and the Floridas had been sold to the United States. It was according to Livingston's views that Jefferson and Madison worked out their ideas concerning the trade back and forth across the river below the thirty-first degree of latitude, fixing at only ten years the period in which preference would be given to France over other foreign states.[30]

Britain, of all other nations, was foremost in the minds of Jef-

29. *Ibid.*, VII, 18.
30. *Ibid.*, VII, 24.

ferson and his Secretary of State. The United States were obligated
to her in regard to free navigation of the Mississippi River by the
Treaty of 1783, confirmed and interpreted in the Jay Treaty of
1794 and the revised article of 1796. And this might be a distressing
fact, if they did not take care. In his accompanying "observations
on the plan," therefore, Madison made sure that Livingston and
Monroe thoroughly understood that the United States were not involved in any tripartite agreement—whatever France herself might
owe to Britain on account of the Spanish obligations which France
had assumed. The commitments of the United States were strictly
bilateral with Britain. The French Government was left entirely
"free to contest the mere navigation of the River by Great Britain,
without the consent of France."

In other words, the United States would not hinder, but neither
would they help France. Moreover, they themselves were free to
admit whomsoever they pleased into the navigation of the river,
save perhaps into that part below the thirty-first degree of latitude,
where they had possessed no claim to territory along the eastern
shore at the time of their treaties with Britain. The reality of this
Madison endeavored to gloss over by declaring that silence in the
French treaty of cession to the United States would be sufficient.
Britain, said he, had never asserted a claim on this subject against
Spain; and would not do so, he presumed, against France as she replaced Spain on the western bank of the Mississippi.[31]

Historians of the American people should note that Thomas Jefferson and James Madison, those Republican "friends" of France so
treasonous in the minds of their Federalist contemporaries, agreed,
in this case at least, with Washington, Pickering, and every other
who held that the United States were obliged to advance no interests but their own in the Mississippi Valley.[32]

DuPont de Nemours had suggested that the United States should
pay France $6,000,000 for New Orleans and the Floridas. Quite
naturally, Madison left blank the amount which Livingston and
Monroe were to offer. They were to buy as cheaply as they could.
But since the gross sum had "occurred to the French Government,"
that might be "as much as will be finally insisted on." Rather than
lose his main object, however, Jefferson had made up his mind "to
go as far as fifty—million of livres tournois." According to Madison's estimate this would amount approximately to $9,150,000.
They hoped that advance payment of the $2,000,000 which Con-
gress had authorized for Monroe's mission might speed ratification

31. *Ibid.*, VII, 21–23.
32. See above, pp. 222–223, 262–265.

of the treaty by France—in view of the "urgency of the French Government for money." It might also help to hold down the ultimate sum. For that purpose, Livingston and Monroe might even make the advance before the exchange of ratifications. Madison and Jefferson had sensed, more than Napoleon would ever admit, how tempting ready cash would be to him in the spring of 1803.[33]

The American plenipotentiaries were also to propose that the United States should take over the claims of their citizens against France. It was Gouverneur Morris' idea in very different surroundings but for much the same purpose. If this were done, wrote Madison, surely the French Government would "feel no repugnance" to having the United States designate the classes of debts and claims which they thought entitled to priority of payment.

Madison so designated them in these instructions. First should come those claims under the fourth article of the Convention of 1800 with respect to property captured and not yet condemned or which might have been captured before the exchange of ratifications of that treaty. Forced contracts or sales which had been imposed upon American citizens by the French authorities should come second. Third would be the voluntary contracts which they had not allowed the Americans concerned to fulfill.

The claims of French individuals against the United States, "founded upon antiquated or irrelevant grounds," declared Madison, had no connection with this negotiation. This disposed of Beaumarchais, that important intermediary in the days of the Revolution, more recently client of John Marshall and intercessor on his behalf with Talleyrand. But, said Madison, if stress should be laid on the point of Beaumarchais' claims so as to endanger the success of Livingston and Monroe, they could bind the United States for payment to his representatives of 1,000,000 livres tournois, "heretofore deducted from his account" against the United States; this, however, on the condition that the French Government declared "the same never to have been advanced to him on account of the United States."[34]

There were explosives in that proviso. The French would not want to say whether they had or had not. The use of funds on secret service is not often allowed to come to light in a court of claims. Jefferson and Madison must have been fairly confident that the claims of Beaumarchais would not be stressed in this negotiation.

Madison also carefully distinguished the claims of those citizens of the United States who had become creditors of the French Gov-

33. *Ibid.*, VII, 24–25.
34. *Ibid.*, VII, 25–27. Miller, *Treaties,* II, 459. See above, pp. 13, 288, 291.

ernment as its agents or appointees. He saw no obligation. If they could be included, however, without embarrassing the negotiation or affecting the demands of France, it would not be improper, he said, to admit them into the provision. Herein lay the expectations of such Americans as James Swan and his associates. During the recent war between Britain and Revolutionary France, Swan had been the agent of France in America, advancing money for the secret expenditures of the French legation in Philadelphia and purchasing supplies for shipment under the neutral flag of the United States. He had done much of this with proceeds from the bonds of the United States which Secretary Wolcott had turned over to him in 1795 as final payment of the debt to France of the American Revolution. But he had claims for reimbursement nonetheless.[35]

We may ask why Madison thought such an offer to take over American claims would appeal to Napoleon. The reports from Livingston up to this time had never indicated that there would be any "repugnance" to the suggestion. They showed, on the contrary, that Napoleon had no mind even to consider such claims, and his ministers had hardly been courteous on the subject. Jefferson and Madison must therefore have perceived that he would have no objection so long as the amount which he got from the negotiation was not curtailed. Was Madison, then, indulging himself in irony? His talk about feelings of repugnance in France would be so much diplomatic verbiage to Frenchmen.

It was not simply irony. It would have a strong appeal to Americans on the other side of the Atlantic and here. It would make Jefferson's plan for New Orleans and the Floridas more attractive in Federalist mercantile centers where French spoliations gave constant pain, where thoughts of Elbridge Gerry's performance in France were still bitter. And it might help Jefferson in the Senate. His followers had defeated the resolutions of Senator Ross by a vote of fifteen to eleven; but a sure two-thirds vote would be necessary to ratify any treaty which Livingston and Monroe might send home. It would be wise therefore to have a treaty return which salved particular grievances materially, even if it did so at the expense of the American taxpayers as a whole. We should note too, in deference to fact, that claims against France were not the exclusive pleasure of Federalists. Republican names were on the list given to the claims commissioners by Skipwith, American commercial agent in Paris, including that of Skipwith himself.[36]

There was accusation that Robert Livingston also had an interest

35. See above, p. 241.
36. Malloy, *Treaties*, I, 517–520. Miller, *Treaties*, II, 524–528.

in the claims against the French Government, through his connections with James Swan. Monroe was irate to Madison on this subject—after Livingston had practically closed the deal before Monroe could participate in it to his liking. But whether or not Livingston was personally interested in the claims, there is another story still to be told of his efforts before and after Monroe's arrival. He had been instructed from the beginning of his own mission to seek concessions in regard to both territory and claims. Until Monroe appeared, however, he had received no power to act. Naturally, he was displeased at the prospect of having to share the accomplishment with a man who had taken no part in the long and discouraging months of sparring with Talleyrand from December, 1801, to April, 1803. It was proper to think that Jefferson had sent Monroe to France more for political effect at home than for action in Paris. Monroe's previous associations and performances there in the days of the Committee of Public Safety and the Directory might even complicate and delay bringing Napoleon, First Consul, to satisfactory terms.[37]

Aspirations and Fears

WHAT were Monroe's reflections as he crossed the Atlantic and went up to Paris, minister extraordinary and plenipotentiary, into the company of Livingston and duPont de Nemours, other agents of the President but long absent from America? We can surmise a good part. In addition to the instructions concerning the Floridas, New Orleans, the Mississippi, Jefferson and Madison had surveyed the critical situation of France in Europe:

> The time chosen for the experiment is pointed out also by other important considerations. The instability of the peace of Europe, the attitude taken by Great Britain, the languishing state of the French finances, and the absolute necessity of either abandoning the West India islands or of sending thither large armaments at great expence, all contribute at the present crisis to prepare in the French Government a disposition to listen to an arrangement which will at once dry up one source of foreign controversy, and furnish some aid in struggling with internal embarrassments.

Here was food for confidence. This was the time for a smashing diplomatic victory, both to wipe out the disgrace put upon him, so unjustly he was convinced, by Washington and those Federalists of 1796, and to raise himself higher in the estimation of those Westerners who looked to him as champion of their interest (and his own)

37. See below, pp. 503–504.

in the lands beyond the Appalachians. It was an opportunity for a man of political ambition.[38]

How Monroe reacted to it is shown by his letter to Thomas Jefferson, mentor and patron, on March 7, 1803, from New York, two days before he went aboard ship. He had his instructions to study, but he was pondering Senator Ross's defeat. Those resolutions proved, he said, that the "federal party will stick at nothing to embarrass the adm^n, and recover its lost power." If, however, "the negotiation secures all the objects sought, or a deposit with the sovereignty over it, the federalists will be overwhelmed completely."

The Union would be saved, the Western people consolidated with the Eastern people, "republican principles confirmed," and "a fair prospect of peace and happiness presented to our country." On the other hand, if the "management of our great concerns in that river" were left to a foreign power, they could expect the public to disapprove. Monroe hoped that France would see that they would never allow another power "to tamper with our interior." If that was not France's purpose, said he, there could be no reason for declining "an accomodation to the whole of our demands." How different from the attitude of Washington's minister to France in 1794![39]

James Monroe, too, had been learning in the ways of American imperialism since he had called for war upon Britain in alliance with France regardless of consequences in the mid-continent of America. But he was no less self-important than before. He now accepted appointment with "ardent zeal to accomplish its objects." He took "much satisfaction from a knowledge" that he was "in the hands of those whose views are sound and attached to justice, and will view my conduct with candour and liberality" (perhaps a bit more of the latter). He embarked "with confidence." He was "fearless of the result as it respects myself personally."

This, however, did not include the chance that when he arrived he would find himself "in the hands" of Robert Livingston who had once advised him upon his return from France not to start a fight with George Washington unless he was sure of his footing. Since then, perhaps, Livingston had not retained his standing in the good company of those whose views were "sound." Monroe in any case soon forgot his pledge to be "fearless of the result." He was not long in placing Livingston before the Secretary of State as one who was not so "attached to justice."

It was ruinous to expectations of self-vindication and glory to

38. Madison (Hunt ed.), VII, 11.
39. Monroe (Hamilton ed.), IV, 4–8. See above, p. 228 f.

find, just as you arrived, that Napoleon too had penetrated the
maze in Europe; that the First Consul had assayed the real value of
American neutrality, if not friendship; that he preferred it to a
colonial area which he could not hold against both British fleet and
American pioneers, and had decided to let the Americans have more
than they had ever asked—for cash. And it was very hard upon
self-esteem and balance to discover that Livingston felt no need of
more than the mere authority to act which you brought to him.
This was in fact all that Livingston did need in April, 1803. Events
of the past few weeks had lifted him out of the long months of persistence but despair.[40]

James Monroe had also read in Madison's letter of March 2, 1803,
to him alone, that he was to go on to Madrid if he found the cession
of the Floridas depending upon Spain and not upon France. He
should get either or both of the Floridas from Spain, even if France
refused to cede the island of New Orleans.[41]

Actually, the Americans of the West could have managed without New Orleans for the time being, if they got West Florida from
Spain. Monroe took with him part of a very penetrating letter from
Gallatin to Madison, dated February 7, 1803, which reported upon
the relative ease with which the streams, inlets, and sounds connecting the Mississippi above New Orleans with Lake Ponchartrain
and Mobile Bay could be made navigable. "The advantage of american houses settled in an american *port* would soon give preference
over New Orleans to that port," said Gallatin.[42]

The legal right of deposit at New Orleans, then, was not so important in the realities as in the emotions of the time. New Orleans
was the object of aspirations, and fears. Madison was defining the
minimum only when he instructed Monroe to go on to Madrid for
West Florida if he could not get New Orleans in Paris. He was not
planning to curtail the aspirations of the Western people. New
Orleans was still their immediate objective—France and Britain being willing, particularly Britain. And herein lay their fears.

That Jefferson and Madison were still extremely nervous about
Britain as Monroe left for France is thoroughly shown by the letters
which Madison sent after him on April 18 and May 28. The first
letter spoke of Britain's anxiety "to extend her domain to the
Mississippi." It was probable that Britain would "connect with a
war on this occasion, a pretension to the acquisition of the Country

40. See below, p. 490 f.
41. Madison (Hunt ed.), VII, 30–34.
42. *Ibid.,* VII, 30 n.–33 n., Madison to Monroe, March 1, 1803. This was a third
and personal letter to Monroe before he sailed from New York. Gallatin's was enclosed.

on the West side of the Mississippi . . . or at least of that portion
of it lying between that River and the Missoury." This probability
was reason enough for Madison that the United States should not
press so hard upon France as to destroy what was left of the tradition of friendship and coöperation against Britain. Here is indication also as to why Jefferson had made his message to Congress confidential in January regarding the expedition up the Missouri, and
was in no haste to get Lewis and Clark on their way until the summer of 1803.

The letter of April 18 furthermore advised Monroe that, should
the French attitude oblige him to play his trump card of "recurring
to Great Britain," he himself was not to go if his special mission to
France had proved disagreeable to Britain. Livingston instead should
negotiate in England, and Monroe should take his place as minister
to France.[43]

The situation, however, had eased greatly by the time that Madison wrote to Livingston and Monroe on May 28, for the Spanish
Government had ordered the intendant to reopen the deposit at
New Orleans. And King's report of his pronouncement to the British prime minister had arrived. King had told Addington in April
that the United States would have Louisiana, and Addington had
replied that if Britain seized New Orleans, she would do so only to
exclude France. They would not mind, he said, having it belong to
the United States. Madison still feared that Britain might demand
compensations which would draw the United States into the war
"directly or indirectly," or ask some concession at the expense of
American commerce. He now wrote the ministers in Paris that the
Administration expected to get "better terms than your original
instructions allow." And the President was opposed now to any
arrangement whatever "that will not secure to the United States the
jurisdiction of a reasonable district on some convenient part of the
Bank of the Mississippi." Addington's manner with King had made
Jefferson "the more anxious also," said Madison, to concede as little
as possible to France on points that were "disagreeable to Great
Britain."[44]

How different this letter would have been if there had been a
cable across the Atlantic to inform Jefferson and Madison that an
arrangement had already been completed in Paris to give the United
States not merely "the jurisdiction of a reasonable district on some
convenient part" but the whole region west of the Mississippi as

43. Madison (Hunt ed.), VII, 37–43, to Livingston and Monroe, April 18, 1803.

44. *Ibid.*, VII, 48–51, to Livingston and Monroe, May 28, 1803. King (King ed.),
IV, 239–242, to Madison, April 2, 1803.

well as the island of New Orleans! It was the French authorities who had done the conceding, although for their own price. They had taken the lead in extending the "jurisdiction" of the United States so as to make Britons feel "disagreeable."[45]

Surprise?

JEFFERSON's plan for America had come close to realization much sooner than he dared to hope. It was still good international politics to be startled by the turn of events, and to seem cautious about exploiting them, for in spite of Addington's encouraging response to King, Britain had still to be taken into account. But was Thomas Jefferson really more startled than gratified by the news that the United States had acquired the whole of Louisiana?

We have evidence besides his stated reasons for sending Lewis and Clark into the Missouri country, besides Albert Gallatin's thoughts upon Upper Louisiana. It is in the manner with which Secretary Madison answered Livingston's complaint that Monroe had not brought instructions covering his offer to buy the territory above the Arkansas. Madison's reply was in an official, not a private letter to Livingston and Monroe. It was written on July 29, 1803, after the special messenger had arrived with the treaty of cession, but before it was known in Washington that France had ratified, and more important, before it was certain how the British Government would react to the news that the United States were acquiring the whole region beyond the Mississippi at least to the mountains, and strong pretensions as well to West Florida including Mobile.

The Secretary of State expressed in this public letter neither surprise that Livingston had conceived of such a possibility beyond his original instructions, nor pleasure that he had come upon such a happy idea. There was instead the simple explanation that Livingston's report and his memoranda for Napoleon had not arrived until after Monroe had left for France. This was supported by the comment that Livingston's own hopes of getting Upper Louisiana had weakened under the "decided neglect" of the French authorities. There was also the careful statement that President Jefferson desired to express "entire approbation" of Livingston's action "in concurring with the disposition of the French Government to treat for the whole of Louisiana." It was "justified by the solid reasons" which Livingston had given for it.

The President's approval, explained Madison, was not "precluded by the silence" in the instructions to Livingston and Monroe. When they had been drafted in March, the "object of the most sanguine"

45. See below, p. 493 f.

had been limited to the "establishment of the Mississippi as our boundary"; they had not presumed "that more could be sought by the United States, either with a chance of success, or perhaps without being suspected of greedy ambition"; and they had not "supposed that in case the French Government should be willing to part with more than the Territory on our side of the Mississippi, an arrangement with Spain for restoring to her the territory on the other side would not be preferred to a sale of it to the United States."[46]

Here is the telltale. It does not show that the Jeffersonian statesmen had no thought of a future for their countrymen beyond the Mississippi until Napoleon dropped the whole of Louisiana into their laps. It does not reveal that they had no hopeful expectations of crossing the line of 1783. It does not prove that they conceived only of a strong frontier at the great river, with the region beyond permanently in the possession of a weak and harmless European state—either returned to Spain by France or resold by the United States to some other, as even Livingston suggested when justifying the expenditure of so much money beyond the stipulation of the President.[47]

Madison's explanation does prove that the Jeffersonians were fearful of their immediate "chance of success." They were not "sanguine" that they could do more for the moment than establish the boundary firmly at the Mississippi and obtain control of New Orleans, and with it possibly West Florida. They were anxious to avoid the penalty of "greedy ambition." For they were still far from sure they would not find that the British had seized New Orleans, as a measure of war against France, before representatives of the United States could arrive to take over that "lock and key" to the North American continent beyond the Appalachians. Experience before this had proved that Britain could talk fairly in Philadelphia or London and come ruthlessly elsewhere between Americans and their interests. Jeffersonians had only to recall very recent actions of British seadogs in West Indian waters to appreciate that to the fullest extent.[48]

Finally, there is significance in the letter from Thomas Jefferson to duPont de Nemours on November 1, 1803—after ratification of the treaty had come from Napoleon, after financial arrangement had been made to his satisfaction through the Engish banking house of Baring and Hope, after the Senate had ignored the protests of

46. Madison (Hunt ed.), VII, 60–64, to Livingston and Monroe, July 29, 1803.
47. See below, p. 493.
48. See above, p. 363 f., for British treatment of Toussaint Louverture.

Federalists from New England and ratified, and also after it was certain that British forces were not ashore in New Orleans. Then Jefferson wrote to duPont de Nemours to thank him for his help and to say:

Our policy will be to form New Orleans, & the country on both sides of it on the Gulf of Mexico, into a State; & as to all above that, to transplant our Indians into it, constituting them a Maréchaussée to prevent emigrants crossing the river, until we shall have filled up all the vacant country on this side. This will secure both Spain & us as to the mines of Mexico for half a century, and we may safely trust the provisions for that time to the men who shall live in it.[49]

The idea is intriguing that the trans-Mississippi country was to be left to the Indians as a kind of constabulary who should hold the white emigrants back. It may seem to strengthen the opinion that even then Thomas Jefferson had no real desire for the Louisiana country. But the "until" repels mystery. Pioneers from the United States were already across the Mississippi and moving up the Missouri. Before white men had "filled up all the vacant country on this side," others would be far beyond. Those of us whose grandfathers were young at the time of the Oregon Treaty with Britain of 1846 and the Mexican War know that Jefferson could "safely trust the provisions for that time to the men who shall live in it"—that is, Americans, not Mexicans nor British.

Thomas Jefferson, however, could not keep himself from anticipating some of those "provisions." As information came to assure him that France and Britain really were going to fight it out on the battlefields of Europe and leave the Mississippi Valley to the United States, his ideas of what Livingston and Monroe had got for the American people rapidly expanded until he appeared to believe early in 1804 that, in addition to Louisiana proper and West Florida to the Perdido beyond Mobile, they had obtained the Texas country to the Rio Grande and all the territory lying northward to the British area above the sources of the Missouri, and possibly westward above the forty-second degree of latitude, to the Pacific Ocean. Immediately upon news that they had bought Louisiana, Madison had instructed Monroe, July 29, 1803, to say on his forthcoming visit to Madrid that the return of Louisiana to Spain for the Floridas was "inadmissible." There was "no equality" in their "intrinsic value." The western bank gave the United States now "the entire jurisdiction of the river." Besides, "We are the less disposed also to make sacrifices to obtain the Floridas, because their position

49. Malone, 78–79. See also Adams, *United States,* II, 254.

and the manifest course of events guarantee an early and reasonable acquisition of them."⁵⁰

In spite of their misgivings that they might not be able to buy even New Orleans, and their solemn talk about wishing Spain or some other power (but of course neither France nor Britain) to have the rest of the Louisiana country, we cannot believe that Jefferson and his Republican colleagues had not foreseen the opportunities beyond the Mississippi River as Monroe went abroad in the spring of 1803. Control of the river came first. Like Benjamin Franklin before him—who had said in 1780 that he would not "sell a drop of its waters," that a "neighbor might as well ask me to sell my street door"—Thomas Jefferson would "hazard their very existence" rather than permit the Mississippi to be closed to the United States. But, although it was the vital matter, it was only the first. Then would come trade beyond the Mississippi and up the Missouri. Then settlements. Then they could, indeed, safely trust the "provisions" for the future to the next generation. This was no feat at all for the man who had written in November, 1801, to Governor James Monroe of Virginia:

> However our present interests may restrain us within our own limits, it is impossible not to look forward to distant times, when our rapid multiplication will expand itself beyond those limits, & cover the whole northern, if not the southern continent, with a people speaking the same language, governed in similar forms, & by similar laws; nor can we contemplate with satisfaction either blot or mixture on that surface.⁵¹

50. Madison (Hunt ed.), VII, 53–60, 57, to Monroe, July 29, 1803. For the expansion of Jefferson's ideas, see below, p. 521 f.

51. Jefferson (Ford ed.), VIII, 105, to Monroe, November 24, 1801. For Franklin's letter to Jay in Madrid, see above, p. 40.

XVIII

LOUISIANA: PROFITS FROM WAR

The Opening

ROBERT LIVINGSTON had waited expectantly following his ultimatum of February 24, 1803, to Talleyrand, but with small confidence that there was any way short of a breach of diplomatic relations. There was too much evidence about that Napoleon was a law unto himself. Perhaps, as he thought, Livingston had made "converts" among the French ministers. Possibly even Talleyrand now favored restoring good relations by ceding Upper Louisiana with New Orleans and West Florida, as Livingston tried to believe; though it is doubtful that the ex-Bishop of Autun ever yielded to persuasions of the mind without substantive rewards for himself or for France, and little of that nature was in prospect here. If France withdrew from any part of the Mississippi Valley, she was likely to be ejected soon thereafter from the whole and without compensation. But quite apart from what Talleyrand might be thinking, Livingston had no intimation as yet from the First Consul that he took Livingston's plan at all seriously. Napoleon ignored the confidential memorials brought by Joseph Bonaparte. He had Talleyrand repel Livingston's direct address to him concerning American claims and the finances of France, American rights in New Orleans and the dangers from the Indians, the cession of the Floridas—the importance to France in short of America's friendship.

This Talleyrand had done on the eleventh of March. He suavely resented Livingston's "presumptions" that the French Treasury needed any release from the debt to American claimants, or the money which might be had from the cession of territory. The amount at which Livingston had set the claims of the United States was viewed with surprise. He was requested to prepare "an exact, certain, full, and verified statement of these debts." As for Louisiana, wrote Talleyrand, "the First Consul would have preferred that you had made it the object of a distinct and separate negotiation." For, with entire deference to Livingston personally, of course, the First Consul had decided, really, to have Bernadotte handle that matter in the United States. Thus Talleyrand indulged himself in that soft yet biting irony which he seems to have enjoyed so much when dealing with Americans. His sentences poured upon Livingston just after the American minister had learned that Monroe was coming to share his mission in France. This, added to the fact that Bernadotte was going to the United States, was enough to dishearten and to provoke a clumsy rejoinder. But, notwithstanding his skill in diplomatic fencing, Talleyrand had left Robert Livingston a good opening.[1]

The news of Monroe's appointment had already galled Livingston to the point of sending acid to Madison on March 3, and he had not blended it with the unction which Talleyrand used so neatly. He would try his best, declared Livingston, to prepare the way for Monroe, but he himself had established in Paris "a confidence which it will take Mr. Monroe sometime to inspire." As for whatever report Daniel Clark, merchant from New Orleans, had made of his conversations in the preceding fall with General Victor, and upon which Madison seemed to be relying so much for revelation of the "designs of this court, the prices, &c," Clark's ideas must have been derived from "his imagination only"; "the gentleman has a pretty warm imagination, and is liable to be deceived." General Victor himself, Livingston ventured to say, "knows less about what passes here than you do." Madison was left to decide whether or not that was complimentary to General Victor. It does not seem much of a puzzle.[2]

Having thus released his irritation, Livingston got back instantly to the business for which he had come to France in the first place. He told Madison that the Floridas were still in the hands of Spain; that he was using every exertion with the Spanish and British ambassadors to keep them so; and that Victor's expedition was still icebound in Holland. When he had Talleyrand's note on March 11, he read straight through the irony and the smooth disdain to the opening. Talleyrand had directly quoted Napoleon as charging him to say that the Convention of 1800 "in all its clauses" was to be "punctually and scrupulously executed." He had written further about the American claims: "You may rest assured, sir, that, after such a statement, every claim will be promptly and exactly paid."[3]

The minister of foreign affairs may have intended that this assurance should drop forever into the same endless irony with the rest of his sentences. Or he may have expected it to find bottom sometime upon Livingston's original proposal in 1801 that France

1. AAE CP EU, LV, ff. 324–335, Talleyrand to Livingston, March 11, 1803.
2. ASP FR, II, 537–538, Livingston to Madison, March 3, 1803.
3. AAE CP EU, LV, ff. 334–335.

settle those claims by ceding lands. There is circumstantial evidence that Napoleon had now begun to give to the "objects" which Livingston had in view the consideration which Talleyrand professed. War with Britain was coming nearer and nearer. It was but a few days after this, on March 12, 1803, that Napoleon indulged in his famous affront to Lord Whitworth: "I find, my Lord, your nation wants war again." But Livingston did not stop to speculate whether Talleyrand's promise for Napoleon was irony or offer. He announced it at once to the Americans in Paris who were interested in the claims—"in order to prevent the creditors," so he said, "from suffering by the speculations of those who were in the secret." But it would also shatter the pretense of Talleyrand and "publicly" commit the French Government, at least until it was "publicly" repudiated. And that would not be good for even Napoleonic prestige.[4]

Livingston replied to Talleyrand on the sixteenth, with double-edged praise of the First Consul. He was the "enlightened statesman" who after advancing his country to the "highest pinnacle of military glory and national prospects" had determined now to put its prosperity on "the firm basis of religion, good faith, justice, and national credit." That is to say, he was going to pay France's debts. Livingston let the matter rest there with this artful bit: "I am satisfied that, when the claims are brought forward, they will, as you have the goodness to declare, be promptly and fully satisfied." He went on to the question which, he was sorry to state, was of "a nature too pressing to admit of any delay."[5]

Bernadotte could attend to any new treaties, but there was the old question of the rights to the commercial depot at New Orleans and to free navigation of the Mississippi:

In what situation, sir, are we now placed? An armament is on the point of sailing for New Orleans; the port has been shut by the order of Spain; the French commandant will find it shut. Will he think himself authorized to open it? If not, it must remain shut till the envoy of France shall have arrived in America, and made the necessary inquiries, and transmitted the result of those inquiries to the First Consul. In the meanwhile, all the produce of five States is left to rot upon their hands. There is only one season in which the navigation of the Mississippi is practicable. This season must necessarily pass before the envoy of France can arrive and make his report. Is it supposable, sir, that the people of the United States will tranquilly wait the progress of negotiations when

4. ASP FR, II, 547, Livingston to Jefferson, March 12, 1803, reporting the scene in Mme Bonaparte's drawing room. See above, pp. 424–425.
5. ASP FR, II, 548–549, Livingston to Talleyrand, March 16, 1803.

the ruin of themselves and their families will be attendant on the delay? Be assured, sir, that, even were it possible that the Government of the United States could be insensible to their sufferings, they would find it as easy to prevent the Mississippi from rolling its waters into the ocean, as to control the impulse of the people to do themselves justice.

Livingston could not but flatter himself, sir, that the answer which the First Consul had given him referred only to such new treaties as would be for the mutual interest of France and the United States "early to negotiate." The question of Louisiana could not wait: "Louisiana is, and ever must be, from physical causes, a miserable country in the hands of a European Power."

Other words flashed before Talleyrand, including this sarcasm in closing: "I pray your Excellency to receive my thanks for the interesting manner in which you have made the communications of the First Consul." But Livingston did not need to expatiate upon what both understood. The United States now had the advantage, thanks to Napoleon's affront to the British ambassador. Outwardly there still appeared to be some chance that war might not come. As late as March 24, 1803, Livingston thought that there was a real desire both in the French Government and among the people to avoid it. But he learned from Rufus King in London that the British were preparing for it and expecting it. He knew that at last he had Talleyrand on the defensive, parrying the demands of the United States in hope that somehow the situation even yet might improve for France.[6]

Talleyrand's Last Gestures

MEANWHILE duPont de Nemours was still trying to serve both France and the United States; but his ideas as presented in a note to Consul Lebrun now leaned far to the side of France. New Orleans should be declared a free port for France and Spain, and their commerce favored to the exclusion as much as possible of the commerce of the five States of the West. The navigation of the Mississippi, said duPont, should remain free throughout its whole course to the three nations, "on the express condition that the United States shall exempt from every species of duty French or Spanish merchandise entering their territory by the Mississippi or Ohio."[7]

Livingston forwarded a copy of this note to Madison on March 11, but he was not worried by it. He himself had "hinted at making

6. *Ibid.* ASP FR, II, 549. King (King ed.), IV, 226–227, King to Livingston, March 11, 1803.

7. ASP FR, II, 547. Chinard, 69, duPont de Nemours to Jefferson, March 3, 1803, received May 21.

the island of New Orleans an independent State, under the Government of Spain, France and the United States" with the right of deposit for each and import duties which would not injure the American carriers nor France as the only manufacturing nation of the three. Such an arrangement might be made extremely advantageous, he said, to the Western people—if it had to be. The new nation would have always to feel its dependence upon the United States and respect their rights. He had taken the precaution of putting an "informal sketch" of the plan into the hands of Joseph Bonaparte. But he did not believe that it had to be. The chances were growing slim that the French would get the Floridas. If they did not, they would "put the less value on New Orleans."[8]

In the meantime also, as James Monroe, minister plenipotentiary and extraordinary, crossed the Atlantic, General Bernadotte, minister to the United States, was having his troubles in leaving port. British sails once more were clouding the horizon. The moment had all but arrived when Robert Livingston could tell the French foreign minster to his face that he knew that Talleyrand knew.

The great diplomatist, however, had one more gesture to make as if he still had the advantage. He had been on the very point of capitulating in regard to the debts, when word came from Pichon in Washington that the appointment of Monroe had "tranquillized everything." Talleyrand withheld the note which he had written and on March 21 presented another to Livingston in which he took the United States to task for viewing "the proximity of France with so unfriendly an eye."[9]

This disturbed Livingston not in the least. He replied with equally diplomatic language but with certain meaning: the United States did not want France on their Western frontier; if she came, they would resort to those "precautionary remedies" which "prudence justifies" and their situation "in the present state of Europe most peculiarly demands." It was the customary talk about "security." But it meant "co-operation" with Britain against France.

Talleyrand complained also that the Americans had helped the Negro rebels in San Domingo. It was the argument with which duPont de Nemours had tried to give his friend Jefferson pause. But now Talleyrand was only digging an old issue out of the quarrels of General Leclerc with the American consul, Tobias Lear, which Jefferson had long since buried under his promises to Pichon in regard to Toussaint Louverture. Talleyrand could make nothing

8. ASP FR, II, 545, Livingston to Madison, March 11, 1803.
9. *Ibid.*, 549–550, Livingston to Madison, March 24, 1803, enclosing the note from Talleyrand of March 21.

of it. Besides, Livingston knew that the British fleet was getting in Napoleon's way too rapidly for him to do anything except forget about San Domingo.[10]

Then came the day when, without receiving more than a shrug of the shoulders and a laugh, Livingston could tell Talleyrand that he knew. On Monday, April 11, the foreign minister suddenly asked if the United States would like to have the whole of Louisiana. Livingston responded, as he had to Joseph Bonaparte in October, 1802, that they wished only New Orleans and the Floridas; but he declared in addition, now, that the policy of France should dictate cession of the territory above the Arkansas River so as to put up a barrier against the British in Canada. Talleyrand, however, took up another point upon which Livingston had been drumming: the remainder of Louisiana would be of little value to France without New Orleans. What, he asked, would the United States give for the whole?

Livingston was deaf but he was not obtuse. He heard readily and understood thoroughly. It was time to be specific, receptive, but indifferent. The bargaining had begun—before James Monroe had arrived. (There was personal satisfaction in that.) He replied that he supposed they would not object to twenty millions, provided the claims were paid. Well they might not object. The bill of claims against France, as Livingston had already asserted, was close to that figure. It would have been a coup extraordinary if he had obtained the transfer of New Orleans and the entire Louisiana country in return for merely taking over the claims against France. It would have been no more than a favor to France on the part of the United States. Talleyrand remonstrated. The offer was too low. But still, would Livingston think it over and tell him tomorrow?[11]

Livingston thought it over, with speed and clarity. He was sure now what was happening. He had received Senator Ross's belligerent resolutions on the preceding Friday, April 8. He had sent them immediately to Talleyrand, expressing his "fear" that they might have been adopted by Congress. He had given a copy also to Bernadotte, and Bernadotte had gone at once to Joseph Bonaparte. Livingston was positive that the resolutions had been discussed "in council" on Saturday, and Talleyrand authorized to approach him.[12]

10. AAE CP EU, LV, ff. 345–348, Talleyrand to Livingston, March 21, 1803, and Livingston's reply, same date, regarding San Domingo; 349–350, Livingston to Talleyrand, March 23, regarding Louisiana and the Floridas. For Jefferson and Pichon, see above, pp. 413–418.

11. ASP FR, II, 552, Livingston to Madison, April 11, 1803.

12. *Ibid.*, 552. AAE CP EU, LV, ff. 374–375, Livingston to Talleyrand enclosing newspaper clipping in regard to Ross's resolutions, "Friday Noon," April, 1803.

So Robert Livingston returned the next day, Tuesday, April 12, "to press this matter further" with the foreign minster. He also presented an unofficial note urging Talleyrand to negotiate the transfer of Louisiana "completely" before Monroe arrived. The idea was that no time should be lost, if the United States were to be kept on the side of France in the approaching war. It would also be most gratifying personally if the transaction could be finished before the statesman from Virginia got upon the scene.[13]

Livingston found Talleyrand now as vague as he had been direct on the preceding day. He must answer evasively, he said, "because Louisiana was not theirs." Livingston smiled. Why, he had seen the treaty recognizing the fact; he knew that the Consul had appointed officers to govern the country; Talleyrand himself had told him that General Victor was to take possession. Bernadotte was going to the United States to treat on the very matter. But Talleyrand persisted. They had Louisiana in mind, he said, but as yet "had it not."

It was Livingston's turn now for alarm. The United States, retorted he, were "not disposed to trifle." He did not know what instructions Monroe might bring, but he was "perfectly satisfied that they would require a precise and prompt notice." In so many words, if France did not possess the region, Monroe and he would notify their Government of that fact, and advise it to take possession. They had cause enough against Spain to justify such a procedure. For a moment, Talleyrand must have seen the twenty millions glimmering. Livingston continued: he was fearful that his Government, he said, from the little progress he had made, would consider him a "very indolent negotiator." The tension was eased. Talleyrand laughed. On the contrary, said he, Livingston should have a certificate as "the most importunate he had met with." So they parted, with Talleyrand standing half-humorously upon ground which he had held at their initial conferences in December, 1801: France was thinking about Louisiana, but did not possess it![14]

That Talleyrand should attempt to do this was amazing to Livingston, but he did not have to wait long to learn why. For on the next day, Wednesday, April 13, after Monroe had arrived and they had gone over Livingston's papers, Barbé Marbois, minister of the public treasury, walked into Livingston's garden while they were at dinner. As he was a personal friend, this was not particularly strange, nor was it queer that he should come in for coffee and a chat. But he sauntered into another room with Livingston alone, where he learned of Livingston's last conversation with Talleyrand

13. *Ibid.*, II, 552. AAE EU Spt. 7, ff. 340–341, Livingston to Talleyrand, April 12, 1803.

14. ASP FR, II, 552–553, Livingston to Madison, April 13, 1803, at "midnight."

—as we may suspect he had already from Talleyrand or Napoleon. And he suggested that Livingston come to his home any time before eleven that night.

When Monroe had taken his leave, therefore, Livingston called upon Marbois, and found the clue not only to Talleyrand's relapse into evasiveness but also to the real purposes of Napoleon, First Consul. He "was disposed to sell." He "distrusted Talleyrand, on account of the business of the supposed intention to bribe"; at least so Livingston reported to Madison. He "meant to put the negotiation into the hands of Marbois, whose character for integrity is established."[15]

As no one could know the record of the ex-Bishop of Autun, or his plans, better than he himself, we may not wonder that he had become quickly evasive, even amused, in the conference with Livingston on the preceding day. Talleyrand must have known then of Napoleon's decision to reverse his cherished policy of stabilizing conditions in Europe so that France could rebuild her colonial empire in America. He must have known, too, that further negotiations with the United States were out of his hands; that, if any money was to be had from the Americans, it was all going into the treasury for Napoleon himself to dispose as he saw fit. His policy of state dropped, Talleyrand, fortuitist as always, carried on for France and himself with a shrug and a laugh. It was in the writ, however, that he would still be serving both when Napoleon had gone to St. Helena.[16]

Robert Livingston, though bold in speech to Talleyrand, was wavering in doubts and fears within himself. Was his course wise? Would his country be able and ready to pay? Might not Britain even then take New Orleans? Would the United States be forced at the last moment into challenging France, only to lose the object for which they had flung their defiance? Yet, the news of Ross's resolutions was encouraging; American troops might already be in New Orleans; if so, they would have to be driven out; and that would not be so easy for General Victor—if ever he got past the British fleet off Holland. Then came the thought of Britain again. He was constantly telling his French listeners that Louisiana would be worth little to them without the Floridas, and that Britain would never allow them to have the Floridas. But how much would Britain be willing to forego for the mere continuance of American neutrality, not to speak of coöperation against France?

Livingston could not know as yet, in the atmosphere of Paris.

15. *Ibid.*, II, 553.
16. See above, pp. 295–298, for Talleyrand's American policy.

He had not yet heard of Rufus King's pronouncement to Addington on April 2 and the British prime minister's reply that if Britain
seized New Orleans, it would be only to keep France from taking
possession. Livingston begged King not to leave his post in a moment
so critical. And he wrote to Madison on April 11, as he reported
that he had been offered the whole of Louisiana:

> I would rather have confined our views to smaller objects; and I think
> that, if we succeed, it would be good policy to exchange the west bank
> of the Mississippi with Spain for the Floridas, reserving New Orleans.
> Perhaps, however, I am too sanguine in my expectations: we will not,
> therefore, dispose of the skin till we have killed the bear.

But at Napoleon's instigation and with Marbois' help, Robert Livingston was soon killing the bear.[17]

Napoleon and Talleyrand's Plan

THE story leaves the despatches of Robert Livingston at this point
and turns to the account which Barbé Marbois dedicated years later
with "profound and respectful devotion" to His Royal Highness,
the Dauphin. As Marbois did not release this narrative until 1829,
it profited from afterthought, quotation out of reminiscence, and
omission. Talleyrand was still alive in 1829. Marbois' account nevertheless, if one is not charmed too much, gives the closest approach
to Napoleon's thoughts and reasons as the First Consul made the
decision in 1803 to abandon the North American continent to the
two Anglo-Saxon powers there and to seek destiny for himself and
France in the Old World.[18]

As late as April 1 Napoleon was still ordering Bernadotte to get
off at once for America. Did he think that there was yet a chance to
avoid a breach of the Peace of Amiens with Britain and to check
the ambitions of the United States? Was he still influenced by Talleyrand's grand scheme of defensive peace in Europe and colonial
expansion in America? Was he hoping against hope that Livingston's defiance and daring did not represent the mood of the American people as a whole? Or was it merely Napoleonic stubbornness
in the face of the inevitable? Whatever it was, within two weeks it
was abandoned. Instead of braving the British fleet on the Atlantic
as minster to the United States, to soothe, cajole, and block, Bernadotte was to cross the battlefields of Europe to the throne of Sweden.

And what of Joseph Bonaparte? According to the tale in Henry

17. King (King ed.), IV, 242–244, King to Livingston, April 8, 1803. ASP FR, II,
552.
18. Barbé Marbois, *Histoire de la Louisiane,* Paris, 1829.

Adams' famous history of this period, based upon the memoirs of Lucien Bonaparte, Joseph was angry with their brother for selling Louisiana, and the Napoleonic valet fainted as the First Consul scornfully flung himself back in his tub, drenching everyone. Lucien's feelings are easy to read. He had made the Treaty of 1801 with Spain, supplementary to the Treaty of San Ildefonso of 1800, for returning Louisiana. But, according to Robert Livingston's reports and memoranda from October, 1802, until July, 1803, Joseph Bonaparte had not only been most instrumental in bringing the realization to Napoleon that he should sell Louisiana to the United States; Joseph had "relished" the plan. Whether or not he was angry now, Joseph Bonaparte was in time to be King of Spain— but only for a time and without her vast domain in North America from British dominions to Texas, from the Mississippi to the Rockies.[19]

Barbé Marbois, minister of the public treasury, had observed the unusual reception which Napoleon gave to Livingston's complaints about the "prizes unlawfully made." "If one of the continental powers of Europe," said Marbois, "had dared to employ similar language, the invasion of its territory would have been the consequence." But there was the Atlantic Ocean, and "the first consul was cautious how he exhibited a resentment, which would have only manifested his own weakness."[20]

So Napoleon's resentment loitered while Talleyrand dealt with Livingston's importunities, and preparations went on for the expedition to Louisiana and completion of Talleyrand's plan for a French empire in America. It was a "favorite object" of Napoleon too—until the skies thickened.[21]

As Marbois read the political weather, the bad news of January, 1803, that Leclerc had died in San Domingo, severe as it was, did not check or alter Napoleon's purpose. Marbois interpreted with the shrewdest of comment:

> These armaments had only St. Domingo and Louisiana for their object; but nothing was farther from the habitual policy of Napoleon than half measures and timid efforts. There never had been an example, while the powers of Europe were at peace, of sending such considerable forces into remote countries. The anxiety of the English for their colonies in the gulf of Mexico might be easily justified. . . .

If France were once "great, strong, and powerful in those seas, who

19. Adams, United States, II, 33–39. Jung, *Lucien Bonaparte et Ses Mémoires,* II, 123–156. ASP FR, II, 533, Livingston to Madison, February 18, 1803. See above, p. 443 f.
20. Marbois (Am. ed.), 1830, 238.
21. See above, p. 451 f.

could answer for the future and guaranty Jamaica and the other British West India islands?" Who would, indeed! Not Napoleon. "Moderation rarely continues," said Marbois, "with a great increase of power."[22]

Here was one good reason why Napoleon persisted with his scheme for Louisiana. And here was the best of reasons why British statesmen gathered force to hold the French project merely to the recapture of San Domingo, why they worked to keep the Floridas in Spain's weak grasp, why they consented even that the United States should cross the Mississippi River although they wanted Louisiana for Britain herself.

These considerations, joined with mutual antagonisms over the execution of the Peace of Amiens, over Malta and the Italian States, rivalry in the courts of Europe, jealousies in Asia, Marbois saw making war become in the minds of both Governments inevitable. It was, then, not a question as to how they could prevent war. It was one of maneuvering so as to bring upon the other party the obloquy for causing it.[23]

Napoleon had looked upon war as certain, declared Marbois, before he heard of the English King's message to Parliament of March 8, calling for the militia of his realm. The First Consul, therefore, had stopped Victor's expedition not, as Talleyrand wished Lord Whitworth to think, in order to calm the uneasiness of the English King, but to prevent the capture of those ships and men by the British fleet. Also in consequence, Napoleon's famous outburst to the British ambassador on the following Sunday, March 13, however impulsive, even foolhardy, was not thoughtless or without calculation—even though Lord Whitworth thought there was in it "no traces of a great mind." Napoleon had decided who was going to have supremacy in Europe. Determination only remained as to whether he might not also accomplish his purpose in America in spite of the British. He would be "useful to the whole universe," Marbois quoted him years afterwards as saying, if he could "prevent their ruling America as they rule Asia." The determination came within a month of his affront to Lord Whitworth.[24]

There was a fact which Napoleon could not remove by wishing. France had not been able to land troops in Louisiana as he had ordered General Victor in December, 1802, so that he could leave the colony to take care of itself in the event of war. Britain's fleet

22. Marbois (Am. ed.), 249–250.

23. King (King ed.), IV, 253–254, memorandum by King, May 8, 1803.

24. Marbois (Am. ed.), 253–260. Browning, 116, Whitworth to Hawkesbury, March 13, 1803.

in the West Indies could occupy New Orleans with little effort. There were other facts which could not be ignored. The United States were more than distressed. Their President talked of marrying the British fleet and nation. Their minister in Paris was courting the British ambassador. Their Senate was discussing resolutions demanding seizure of New Orleans. And a special envoy and intimate of the President was arriving to follow up the overture which he had made through his friend, duPont de Nemours.

One could not know, but it was not hard to guess that James Monroe might have orders to go beyond Jefferson's insinuations through duPont de Nemours and cross the English Channel, if Livingston and he did not obtain satisfaction in Paris. If the First Consul lacked perception of the reactions possible in Americans, Talleyrand could tell of his own experience with John Marshall for Napoleonic reflection. If further admonition were necessary, there was the comment of Adet upon the Jefferson of 1796 still within recall.[25]

Other advices were not necessary. The time had come to face these facts, and to capitalize them in the grandest Napoleonic manner. Marbois was summoned into conference at St. Cloud on Sunday April 10, 1803, with Decrès, minister of marine and colonies. For Napoleon, "though full of confidence in himself," wrote Marbois so smoothly in 1829, "willingly consulted those who possessed practical experience, and he had too much reliance in his own powers to fear engaging in a discussion." Besides, "he was not above that paltry artifice, so common with many persons, who, though they ask advice, form beforehand an opinion which they desire to see triumph."[26]

The two ministers were acquainted with San Domingo, Louisiana, and the United States. Marbois had been secretary under La Luzerne in the French legation at Philadelphia, then intendant in San Domingo, and recently again in the United States as a consular officer. Decrès had served with the French forces during the American Revolution.

Napoleon told them of his expectation that he might lose Louisiana, and declared that the British should not have the Mississippi which they coveted. He was thinking, therefore, of ceding Louisiana to the United States. It would be "more useful to the policy and even to the commerce of France" in their hands than if he should attempt to retain it.

Marbois took the cue. They should not hesitate, he said, to sacri-

25. See above, pp. 286 f., 397.
26. Marbois (Am. ed.), 262–277.

fice what was about to slip from them. Or, in a more American translation, they should get out before they were thrown out. War with Britain was unavoidable. The United States threatened New Orleans. Once, they had been as feeble as Louisiana itself, but now they were powerful, and Louisiana was still in its infancy. It was open to the English on the north by way of the Great Lakes and on the south from the sea. But its conquest would be still easier for the Americans. They had only to enter the country to master it. If on the other hand Louisiana became a French colony, it would soon aim at independence. The more it flourished, the less chance France had of keeping it. Nothing, said Marbois, was more certain than the future in store for the European colonies in America. (This was particularly easy for him to see in 1829—after the revolt of Latin America from the Rio Grande to Cape Horn, and the assertion of the Monroe Doctrine.)

But why, interrupted Napoleon, had the French, who were incapable of succeeding in a continental enterprise, always made great progress in the West Indies? Marbois might have countered with: Had they?—and cited recent events in Haiti. But he chose to answer: "Because the slaves perform all the labour." Slavery was "the most detestable" of all of the scourges afflicting the human race, said he (in 1829?), and it had "given to Louisiana half her population." To occupy such a colony would occasion for France more expense, and trouble with the growing sentiment of the world for emancipation, than it would afford profit. Besides, there was "another kind of slavery" whose reign was almost over—the "exclusive system" of trade. France could not hope, he declared, to reestablish the mercantilist system in a country "contiguous to one where commerce enjoys the greatest liberty." In short, France would gain more from commerce with Louisiana in the possession of the United States than from attempting to monopolize its trade as a French colony. Finally, said Marbois, even though they were French in origin, the people of Louisiana had lost "the recollection of France." They would love only the princes who made them prosperous. This, Napoleon would not do so well as their neighbors above them on the Mississippi.

Decrès was of "a totally opposite opinion." He took the position which Talleyrand had constructed for the Directory in 1797–98, and upon which the secret Treaty of San Ildefonso had been made with Spain in 1800 as France and the United States closed their informal war on the seas. According to Marbois, Decrès said: "We are still at peace with England." The likelihood of war was no good reason why they should "despoil" themselves of Louisiana. They might avoid war with Britain. The political system of Europe was preserved only by "skillfully combined resistance of many against one." Napoleon did not have to submit to a tyranny on the sea. If Britain seized Louisiana, "Hanover would be immediately in your hands as a certain pledge of its restoration." France, deprived of her navy and her colonies, would be stripped of "half her splendour, and of a great part of her strength."

There was no more important single city on the globe, asserted Decrès, than New Orleans. "The Mississippi does not reach there till it has received twenty other rivers, most of which surpass in size the finest rivers of Europe." Once taken over and put to use, Louisiana would compensate the activity of the French for "the loss of India." And when "at the isthmus of Panama a simple canal should be opened," Louisiana would be on the new route to Asia. Its possession then would be "of inestimable value." So it was to prove, but not for France. After Napoleon III exploited the civil war in the United States only to fail with another French adventure in American lands, the United States gained supremacy in war with Spain, in diplomacy with Britain, and took Panama for themselves.

Decrès went on to explain how Louisiana would enrich France with a share in the commerce of America and Asia, how it would be an asylum for discontented elements in France, how it would replace San Domingo, how they would control the Indians. His argument recalls the memoranda of Collot and Vilemont. But Napoleon stopped the conference short "without making his intentions known."

At the break of day, however, Marbois heard these intentions as Napoleon handed him the most recent despatches from London, reporting that "naval and military preparations of every kind were making with extraordinary rapidity." Then Napoleon declared, according to Marbois: "Uncertainties and deliberation are no longer opportune. I renounce Louisiana. It is not only New Orleans that I wish to cede, it is the whole colony without reserving any part of it."[27]

Marbois was not to delay until Monroe had arrived. He was to see Livingston that very day. He was to get fifty millions, no less. For Napoleon required money to make war on "the richest nation of the world." Marbois could send his maxims about the sale of human beings, that "ideology of the law of nature and nations" to London, where they would be "greatly admired"—except when applied to "the finest regions of Asia." He himself wanted fifty millions, not in "souls" but in money. Marbois was to keep in touch with Talley-

27. Translation from Marbois (Fr. ed.), 298; (Am. ed.), 274.

rand, for the foreign minister alone knew Napoleon's intentions. Talleyrand did not entirely agree with them. If Napoleon "attended to his advice, France would confine her ambition to the left bank of the Rhine, and would only make war to protect the weak states and to prevent any dismemberment of her possessions." But Talleyrand now admitted, said Napoleon, that "the cession of Louisiana is not a dismemberment of France." So, in fact, Talleyrand admitted to Livingston that same day with his shrug and his laugh, in different words but with similar import.[28]

Was it that Louisiana was not a part of France because French officials had not yet actually taken possession? Or was it because the deal with Spain, in exchange for the Italian States, was not to be considered completely made until France got the Floridas as well? It does not matter which or what, except to those of us who would like to know every twist and turn in the rationalization of the ex-Bishop of Autun to the last deflection. Jefferson, Madison, and Livingston were not concerned whether it was a "dismemberment" of France, so long as the operation occurred, the United States got the section, and Britain did not interfere. Nor did they care either, when Spain complained of malpractice.[29]

Marbois' Offer—Monroe's Pique

BARBÉ MARBOIS saw Livingston, not on that very day, Monday, April 11, as he stated in his account, but after dinner on the Wednesday following. It was Talleyrand who spoke with Livingston on Monday. Here we must return to Livingston's version, for he wrote not in 1829 but immediately after he had returned from Marbois' home Wednesday at midnight. Talleyrand had started the bargaining, only to have Napoleon take it from him and put it in the hands of Marbois.

The First Consul, said Marbois, according to Livingston, had replied in the following manner to his expression of sorrow that there was any difference between France and the United States: "Well, you have charge of the Treasury; let them give you one hundred millions of Francs, and pay their own claims, and take the whole country." Napoleon had said fifty millions and no less, as Marbois remembered it in 1829. His recollection was accurate. One does not readily forget things which enhance one's own reputation.[30]

Livingston looked surprised, but Marbois continued. He had told the First Consul, he said, that the thing was impossible, that the

28. Marbois (Am. ed.), 274–277.
29. See below, p. 523 f.
30. ASP FR, II, 553, Livingston to Madison, April 13, 1803.

United States had no such means. The First Consul had then remarked that they might borrow. Livingston understood. It was clear that Napoleon wanted to sell, but also that it was going to be diamond cut diamond. He therefore replied to Marbois that the United States had no disposition to extend across the Mississippi River. No, he would not be pressed to name a sum. Whereas he had offered to close the deal with Talleyrand on the previous day, he now said that he would have to wait for Monroe. They would make an offer "after mature reflection." Marbois wanted him to mention a sum? Livingston replied with another question. As Marbois himself thought the First Consul's figure exorbitant, why did not he say what he thought reasonable?

Marbois was ready for this. He declared that if Livingston and Monroe would name sixty millions and take over the American claims to the amount of twenty millions more, he would try to find out if it would be accepted. The twenty millions was Livingston's own estimate of the claims in his note to Napoleon on February 27.[31]

Livingston balked, and turned to the old line of argument: France would throw the United States at the next election into the hands of men who were most "hostile"; this would "happen in the midst of war." Marbois urged him to try to come up to the mark. "Consider," he said, "the extent of the country, the exclusive navigation of the river, and the importance of having no neighbors to dispute you, no wars to dread"—as if Livingston had not been doing just that for months past!

Then Livingston yielded a bit. If there was a purchase, he asked, would France contract never to possess the Floridas? And would she aid the United States in obtaining them? Marbois agreed. So Livingston assured him that he would discuss the proposition with Monroe, and they would keep it secret; he requested that Napoleon should depute someone to negotiate with them who had more "leisure" than Talleyrand; and he went home to write to Madison until three o'clock in the morning. By that time he had decided: "We shall do all we can to cheapen the purchase; but my present sentiment is that we shall buy." They did, at Marbois' price.[32]

What of James Monroe and the instructions which he had brought with him? Robert Livingston had gone this far without even seeing them. He had shown his own papers, had told Monroe of his conversation with Talleyrand and his own preliminary hint of twenty millions, had explained Marbois' purpose in coming to his house. But he had then gone off to confer with the minister of the

31. See above, p. 485 f.
32. ASP FR, II, 553–554.

public treasury without taking Monroe with him. This was correct enough, for Monroe had not yet been presented to the foreign minister. But it irked Monroe, particularly as he had heard almost immediately from the American consul, Skipwith, that Livingston had been irritated by his appointment and was trying to accomplish without his aid the thing for which he had come all the way across the Atlantic.[33]

Monroe sat himself down to write Madison all about it on April 15. He was in the dilemma, he feared, of having to negotiate not only with the French but with his colleague; some pretext might be used to keep him from his audience with the First Consul until affairs got so far along that his country's interests might suffer— and he would be responsible. The insinuation all but broke through that Livingston might even then be making a mess of things. He did say that Livingston, even after learning that he was coming, had not abstained from topics entrusted to them jointly. It does not appear to have occurred to Monroe, as he poured out his misgivings to Madison, that he had only to withhold his signature from any agreement concerning those matters upon which he was jointly commissioned, in order to save their country, and himself, from such disasters as preyed upon his imagination.

There is another way of interpreting the situation. Livingston had been instructed nearly two years before to negotiate upon the claims and the Floridas. He had been very careful to distinguish between old and new treaties as soon as he heard of Monroe's appointment and Napoleon's intention to send Bernadotte to the United States. This meant that the treaties of 1795 with Spain and of 1800 with France were still within his diplomatic province. Monroe, apparently, had given no weight to this distinction, if he saw it, when he had gone through Livingston's papers. But Livingston did not lack authorization to confer alone with the French officials preparatory to agreements. He had a right to urge Talleyrand to settle the issues. He simply lacked, until Monroe arrived, power to close such agreements, and instructions with respect to the price which they might pay.

In justice to Monroe, he did remark when closing his letter to Madison that he knew of no real injury likely to happen to the object of his mission from what had as yet passed. This was honest on the face of it; but it also leaves one feeling that he hoped something might go wrong so that he could then straighten matters out and return to America in personal triumph. The man who once before could not keep himself from playing politics at home while on

33. Monroe (Hamilton ed.), IV, 9–12, to Madison, April 15, 1803.

diplomatic mission abroad was again in Paris. James Monroe seems to have learned very little from his experiences with "A View of the Conduct of the Executive" in the time of George Washington. He was to do much the same thing at the expense of James Madison, to whom he was then writing, but a few years later when disappointed that Jefferson did not send to the Senate the treaty which he had made with William Pinkney in England.[34]

The situation of Jefferson's protégé at Paris in April, 1803, was not as woeful as he made it out to be. Livingston had come to him the very day after the midnight conference with Marbois, had told him about it, and taken him forthwith to Talleyrand. Livingston, to be sure, had been provoked when he read their instructions that day and discovered that his own commission for the impending negotiations might be so construed as to make him inferior to Monroe. He wrote a frank complaint to Madison on the seventeenth. He was equally provoked that Madison had not mentioned his plan to get Upper Louisiana. He did not then know that his memoranda of the overture through Joseph Bonaparte to Napoleon had not reached Washington before the instructions were written and Monroe had left. But Livingston talked over these matters with Monroe. Monroe had his chance to demur. He decided with Livingston to proceed.[35]

Perhaps the French might overlook the fact that the Americans were not instructed to go beyond the Mississippi. We know that they well understood the fact, and did not care. They wished now to be rid of the whole territory. They cared only to get as much money as soon as they could.

The Bargain—British Money

LIVINGSTON and Monroe came upon Barbé Marbois in the office of Talleyrand on the afternoon of the fourteenth. We do not have to guess that he was there for purposes other than merely to keep in touch with Talleyrand because Napoleon had so ordered. He got at once to bargaining with the Americans. Livingston pressed instead for an immediate audience with the First Consul for Monroe (a point we should note which Monroe neglected to stress in his outpouring to Madison on the following day). Marbois soon departed. So Monroe and Livingston returned home to discuss what they should do. Just to make sure, Monroe pledged Livingston "to hold

34. Gilman, 101–102. Monroe (Hamilton ed.), V, 24–35. ASP FR, III, 173–183. See above, pp. 244–245.

35. ASP FR, II, 554–555, Livingston to Madison, April 17, 1803.

no further communication with Marbois or any other person" until he himself was recognized and someone regularly appointed to treat with them. Livingston proved to Monroe's outward satisfaction, whatever his inner feelings and his professions to Madison, that he had been recognized by Talleyrand and that Marbois had been regularly appointed to deal with them. So Monroe agreed on the fifteenth (when he was not writing to Madison) that they should offer fifty millions including the claims; but first, they would mention only forty millions. James Monroe was really getting on, despite his qualms and his complaints.[36]

Accordingly, Livingston offered forty millions to Marbois later that same day. Whereupon Marbois expressed "grave sorrow." He was sure that sum would not be accepted; perhaps "the whole business would be defeated"; the First Consul did not now seem "quite pleased" that Marbois had lowered the original price of a hundred millions excluding the claims. But, protested Livingston, the First Consul had agreed to pay the claims. Then, said Marbois, he would go that very day to St. Cloud, if Livingston wished. Livingston did wish, and he sought Marbois out the next day, the sixteenth, to learn the result. Marbois still had only to reply that the First Consul had been very cool; Livingston might consider the matter as withdrawn from his hands, he said, for he had received no further instructions from Napoleon. Was it quite true?

It was not. That very evening while Livingston was dining with Lebrun, Third Consul, who should happen to drop in but Marbois! The plan to sell Louisiana, he said, seemed to be relinquished; but if Livingston had another proposition to make, he might state it. Obviously the plan was not given up. It was merely Livingston's move. He therefore raised the offer to the fifty millions upon which Monroe and he had agreed. Marbois was still doleful. But he said he would try. And Robert Livingston went home "to rest a few days upon our oars"—and meantime to send a few lines on his own account to James Madison.[37]

It would be a while before they knew how to estimate Monroe's worth, wrote Livingston on April 17. When Monroe had been in Paris before, he had been compelled to keep in well with the party then in power, "now detested by the present ruler." Moreover, Talleyrand had "imbibed personal prejudice" that would "induce him to throw every possible obstruction" in Monroe's way. Did Robert Livingston, too, know how to play politics at home? Or was

36. Monroe (Hamilton ed.), IV, 12, to Madison, April 15, 1803. ASP FR, II, 554.
37. *Ibid.*, II, 554.

it simply personal irritation because he had been given a commission inferior to Monroe's?[38]

Even James Monroe decided finally that they could proceed without a formal audience for him with the First Consul. It was time to make an end of the chase about town after casual remarks. It was time to bring the negotiations down to propositions spread upon paper. Marbois reported to Talleyrand on April 21 that Livingston had said he would approach the terms which Marbois proposed if Marbois had authority to treat; and Monroe had come much farther than he had at first conceived; he was approaching the point where Livingston had stopped. Although he had conversed with each separately, said Marbois, he was certain that they were "entirely in agreement."[39]

Did this mean that Livingston and Monroe had surrendered to Marbois? Neither in his letters home made any direct reference to this episode. It is possible that both had been lured beyond their first intentions. But this did not mean, either to them or to Marbois that they had bound themselves to accept whatever he chose to offer. Such a conclusion is disproved by the negotiations which followed and the treaties which all three of them signed.[40]

Marbois came with Livingston on April 27 to Monroe's lodgings, because Monroe was ill, and opened the conference with a project ostensibly from Napoleon himself. Whether it bore any of the marks of Talleyrand's handiwork is hard to say. That it was compounded of Marbois' initial suggestions to Livingston and of duPont de Nemours' conversations among the French authorities during the past year is more readily suspect. Whoever did make this plan for Napoleon seems to have been very familiar with the maps and experiences of Victor Collot, if not with the extensive memoir of Moustier.

The First Consul would have a hundred millions from the United States for the whole of Louisiana and leave the claims of their citizens to them for settlement. In addition, not only for France but for Spain, he would have rights of entry and perpetual navigation of the Mississippi River, three places of deposit on the west bank —at the mouths of the Red, Arkansas, and Missouri respectively— and two on the east bank at the Illinois and Ohio Rivers. There would be local agents for each country in those stations.[41]

Livingston and Monroe must have recoiled as they thought of

38. *Ibid.*, II, 555.
39. AAE CP EU, LV, f. 395, Marbois to Talleyrand, April 21, 1803.
40. See Lyon, 221–222, for different stress.
41. *Corresp. de Napoleon*, VIII, 289, April 23, 1803. See above, pp. 120 f., 252 f.

their own instructions. They were to end French traffic on the Mississippi after ten years and put the British right of navigation as well upon a very different basis from that which had been guaranteed in the Jay Treaty even as amended in 1796. But this project was only a bluff. Marbois hardly took time to enjoy its effect before admitting that he thought it "hard and unreasonable." He submitted another "which he called his own."[42]

It was plain that Napoleon wanted quick money, not perpetual trade on the Mississippi. Marbois said his own plan lowered the demand to eighty millions including the claims. But Livingston clung to Napoleon's promise that France would pay those claims. Marbois had to wind about the point for some time before reaching a statement which virtually declared that this would be the way Napoleon kept his promise or not at all. It assumed, of course, that the negotiation would not fail; if it did, Marbois conceded that the claims would remain as they were at the moment; that is, acknowledged but unpaid, and most likely not to be.

Meantime Monroe had found voice to oppose Napoleon's demands of entry and navigation, as calculated to embarrass the revenue system of the United States, to offend foreign powers, and actually to defeat the policy of France by inclining the United States toward Britain. Marbois was going to pass by the arguments, but Livingston too observed that such commercial demands had not been made in previous conversations. Then Marbois quickly accepted the view. He said, however, that such French rights should have been discussed; it was an omission on his part; his Government had always contemplated them, for the honor of his Government required that it furnish a "publick motive for the cession distinct from money."

Monroe suggested the way out of this difficulty. They would concede the rights to France, not in perpetuity, but for twelve years, two more than stated in Madison's original instructions. Marbois as quickly agreed. Whether he did so with a straight face was not recorded in Monroe's account of the affair.[43]

Two days later on April 29, Livingston and Monroe came with an offer of their own. France could have fifty millions for Louisiana and twenty on account of the American claims. Marbois read so far and refused to proceed. It would have to be just as he had stated, eighty millions in all. So they gave in. France would get sixty millions for Louisiana and release also from the American claims. Marbois asked now if they might not advance something imme-

42. Monroe (Hamilton ed.), IV, 12, Monroe's journal, April 27, 1803.

43. Monroe (Hamilton ed.), IV, 499, Monroe's journal: addenda. See Miller, *Treaties*, II, 502–503.

diately, for he knew that Monroe had been authorized to spend two million dollars. They protested that they were already doing so; they were taking over the debt of France to their fellow citizens. That did not interest Marbois. He wanted cash in his own hands. They had eventually to accept a plan for paying in bonds which could be resold at once to foreign investors in the national debt of the United States.[44]

The arrangement was made with the English banking interests of Baring and Hope. Although Britain was again at war with France before the first of June, Alexander Baring was allowed to go to Paris in July and then to the United States for the new bonds. Without question the British Government knew that Napoleon would use the proceeds for war.[45]

This has been considered "striking proof" of British friendship for the United States. But it was more a demonstration of the price which the British were willing to pay in order to make sure that the United States, under the administration of the traditional "friend of France," took no part in the war even as a "benevolent neutral" on the side of France. Besides, the United States Treasury had begun making payments to the British Treasury under the Convention of 1802 on the account of those old American debts to English creditors incurred prior to the Revolution. Livingston and Monroe reported to Madison on May 13, 1803, that Baring and Hope were willing to take the new bonds on commission at the current price in England because they wished to keep up the credit of "our stock," as they were much interested in it. Gallatin remarked that they stood to gain three millions from the transaction.[46]

The negotiations were really at an end when Livingston and Monroe came up to Marbois' price. They still had to listen to him insist that the inhabitants of the ceded territory should be incorporated in the American Union. His purpose may have been to make sure that they obtained full liberties, privileges, and immunities as citizens in the United States. This was in accordance with ideas then so much in vogue, made famous by Thomas Jefferson himself in the Declaration of Independence as the "Laws of Nature and Nature's God"—that government derives its "just powers" from "the consent of the governed." But Marbois quite as likely was making doubly certain that the United States should not trade the land beyond the Mississippi and its inhabitants to Britain for other con-

44. Monroe (Hamilton ed.), IV, 14.
45. ASP FR, II, 559, Livingston and Monroe to Madison, May 13, 1803; 564, June 7.
46. Lyon, 248. Miller, *Treaties,* II, 488–491. King (King ed.), IV, 44–52. ASP FR, II, 559. Gallatin, *Writings,* I, 145–152, August 31, 1803.

siderations perhaps more immediately desired, and thus increase Britain's power.[47]

Years later in his *Histoire de la Louisiane*, Marbois quoted Napoleon as having said in May, 1803: "This accession of territory strengthens for ever the power of the United States; and I have just given to England a maritime rival, that will sooner or later humble her pride." But then, this too may only have been Marbois' way of calling attention in 1829 to those brilliant victories of American frigates over British in the War of 1812, without referring to the fact that the British fleet had driven the American fleet from the high seas, or mentioning what had happened to Napoleon after Waterloo.[48]

Final Agreements

LIVINGSTON and Monroe returned home that day, April 29, 1803, assured that Marbois would submit their project to Napoleon and that soon now Monroe would have his audience and dinner with the First Consul. This great event in the life of James Monroe came on the following Sunday, May 1. Their conversation, as he recorded it, adds nothing to the story of the negotiations, save one offhand remark and a prophecy more revealing of wishes than of prescience: "I am glad to see you. . . . You have been here fifteen days? . . . You speak French? . . . You had a good voyage? . . . You came in a frigate? . . . How many inhabitants has the federal city? . . . Well, Mr. Jefferson, how old is he? . . . Is he married or single? . . . Then he is a *garçon*? . . . Has he children? . . . Does he reside always at the federal city? . . ."

Between Monroe's replies there had fallen the casual remark that Livingston and he should have their affairs settled. Then came the prophecy: "You Americans did brilliant things in your war with England. You will do the same again. . . . You may probably be in war with them again."[49] How soon, where, in what associations, under what circumstances, the Little Corsican did not venture. Great prophets are not specific, do not ignore Delphic precedents. Those who wish strongly, however, often do think aloud.

You could wish, and yet it was really too much to expect that Britain's statesmen would risk voluntarily another war with both France and the United States. Addington in fact had already assured Rufus King in April that if Britain took New Orleans in making war upon France, she would do so only to turn New Or-

47. Jefferson (Ford ed.), II, 43. Monroe (Hamilton ed.), IV, 14.
48. Marbois (Am. ed.), 312.
49. Monroe (Hamilton ed.), IV, 15–16.

leans over to the United States. Had Napoleon heard King's corresponding remark that the United States must "at no distant day" annex the Louisiana country, he might have been amused. But he would not have been deceived into thinking that it meant American coöperation with France in this war upon Britain to do so, nor on the other hand, even Jefferson's brave union with Britain against France.[50]

The best for which either of these European powers could hope now was that the United States would remain neutral toward both on the seas, and endure the hardships of being a neutral commerce carrier provided they were allowed to take advantage of both in the vast interior of the North American continent. This would not be worth as much to France immediately as to Britain. But after all, Napoleon had sixty millions for his war chest, and it was coming, too, in good British money.

Monroe and Livingston met Marbois by appointment after their dinner with the First Consul, and settled their "affairs." It was the Frenchman who now took exception, but only to relatively minor details. The department of foreign affairs, said Marbois, did not like the opening article of the American project; it sounded too much like a "private transaction before a notary publick." That Talleyrand should be sensitive when everyone knew that it was so like an ordinary sale of property, is humorous. But from habit, it may be, one saves one's face with fine words about removing misunderstanding and strengthening friendship in diplomatic negotiations, even though one knows that everyone else knows the words mean nothing.[51]

Marbois objected also to any guarantee against France or Spain. It was useless, he said, to give it as against French interference because the cession itself was as strong a guarantee as France could make. It would be ungracious for France to guarantee against Spain, and besides, there was nothing to fear from Spain.

The latter was the better reason. No one, henceforth, ever would have to guarantee the safety of the United States against Spanish encroachment. But Spain many times thereafter may have wished that somebody had obligations to protect Spanish America from the United States.

Marbois had no objection to inserting the article from the Treaty of San Ildefonso describing the extent of the territory which France had taken back from Spain in 1800, and was now handing over to the United States. The clause reads: "The Colony or Province of

50. See above, pp. 434 f., 445.
51. Monroe (Hamilton ed.), IV, 16.

Louisiana with the Same extent that it now has in the hands of Spain, & that it had when France possessed it; and Such as it Should be after the Treaties subsequently entered into between Spain and other States." Marbois asserted personally that France would use her good offices with Spain to aid the United States in negotiating for the Floridas.[52]

When the treaty was signed, however, it made no reference to this matter. And when Monroe raised the question whether he should go on to Madrid, the French authorities attempted to discourage him. Cambacérès, Second Consul, in fact remarked that for the present he must not go. One interpretation of this is that Napoleon wished to keep the Floridas from the United States, in case he might at some later date wish to reëstablish the French interest in the politics of North America. A better explanation is to be found, however, in a subsequent letter from Livingston to Madison. Livingston felt that Napoleon and Talleyrand hoped to get more money out of the United States Treasury. Madison, too, thought that France was trying to "get her hand into our pocket."[53]

Robert Livingston did not value highly the good offices which Marbois promised. As he read those vague stipulations in the Treaty of San Ildefonso and reëxamined the course of events from 1763, he much preferred to believe that France had obtained West Florida, at least to the Perdido beyond Mobile, whether or not Spain had intended to cede it. Marbois had said he was sure that Mobile was within the cession by Spain. So Livingston went to Talleyrand to ask what France had meant to take from Spain. Talleyrand replied in his easiest manner: "I do not know. Then [persisted Livingston] you mean that we shall construe it our own way? I can give you no direction [was the reply]; you have made a noble bargain for yourselves, and I suppose you will make the most of it."

Livingston wasted no time in doing so. He wrote to Madison that very day: "Now, sir, the sum of this business is, to recommend to you, in the strongest terms, after having obtained the possession, that the French Commissary will give you, to insist upon this as part of your right; and to take possession, at all events to the river Perdido." He was positive that the American right was good; the time was favorable "without the smallest risk at home"; they should anticipate Britain's designs upon the country; once they had West Florida, East Florida would be theirs whenever they pleased.

52. Miller, *Treaties*, II, 499. Monroe (Hamilton ed.), IV, 16, Monroe's journal.

53. *Ibid.*, IV, 18. Lyon, 225–226. Cox, 102, 109–110. Monroe (Hamilton ed.), IV, 305 n., excerpt from Livingston's letter of September 21, 1804, to Madison. Madison (Hunt ed.), VII, 187 n., Madison to Livingston, July 5, 1805. See below, p. 536.

This was May 20, 1803, two days before France ratified the treaty of cession to the United States.[54]

All of these statements and counterstatements regarding the Floridas, whether Mobile was or was not in French Louisiana, what Spain did or did not retrocede to France and France pass on to the United States, seem to have been so much juggling in order to make the best case at every stage for one's own interest. When Livingston had been afraid that France would hold New Orleans and Louisiana, he had argued that the Floridas were not in the retrocession and had tried hard to keep Spain from yielding them to France. Marbois gave his personal opinion that Mobile was in the retrocession, but officially was extremely vague about it. Talleyrand said he did not know, when papers regarding the negotiations with Spain had passed through his office showing very clearly what France meant to take from Spain. The memory of the ex-Bishop of Autun was never that bad, except when it was advantageous to be so. As Napoleon had said during the negotiations about the boundaries, according to Marbois, "if obscurity did not exist, perhaps it would be good policy to put it there."[55]

Marbois had lingered upon the commercial privileges which France and Spain were to have in Louisiana for twelve years. But he readily admitted under argument that they could not expect more than preferential rights over other foreign countries, and those only for a period of time. The grand scheme of duPont de Nemours, Lebrun, and Napoleon—to allow France entry, navigation, and special agents along the course of the great inland waterway of the continent—had collapsed during the preliminary stages of the negotiation, if it ever had been taken seriously by any other than duPont de Nemours.[56]

Marbois had questioned also some features of the plan for settling the American claims. He had been afraid on May 8 that they might prevent the sale of Louisiana. Once sure that the American bonds from which the proceeds would come to the French Treasury were to be properly issued, transferred to Baring and Hope, and made redeemable so as to support their market value, the minister of the public treasury stopped worrying about the claims. The Americans could work out the details among themselves. Their Government was going to pay the bill.[57]

After he had seen the First Consul again on Monday, May 2, Mar-

54. ASP FR, II, 560–561, Livingston to Madison, May 20, 1803.
55. Marbois (Fr. ed.), 312.
56. Monroe (Hamilton ed.), IV, 14. See above, pp. 442–443, 488–489.
57. AAE CP EU, LV, ff. 420–421, Marbois to Talleyrand, May 8, 1803. Lyon, 228.

bois met with Livingston and Monroe to sign the treaty of cession. But the convention regarding the claims was not signed until the eighth or ninth. A third agreement was separately drawn to fix the amount at 60,000,000 francs, or $11,250,000, and to prescribe the manner in which payment should be made. All three papers were dated as if they had been signed on April 30, 1803.[58]

The bargain was complete. The United States had New Orleans, the whole of Louisiana, and a pretension at least to West Florida. Napoleon had more than his price for Louisiana, and release from his promise to pay the American claims. Ratifications only remained to be approved and exchanged.

Rufus King Released to Politics

As these agreements were completed in Paris, Rufus King, Federalist finished his work in London for the Republican administration of Thomas Jefferson. He had two things left to do. One was to keep Britain from landing troops in New Orleans as war broke out. The other was closely related. It was to sign the convention, which both Jefferson and Livingston had favored in the early stages of the negotiations with France, for settling the remaining disputes with Britain over the Canadian boundary, particularly the line from the Lake of the Woods to the Mississippi River.[59]

King had written to Livingston and Monroe on May 7 that he should know at once if New Orleans were ceded to the United States, and should have permission to announce the fact to the British authorities, for they were certainly going to send an expedition to take it, he said, unless it had been transferred to the United States. Livingston and Monroe, with the consent of the French Government (naturally, for the sixty million francs were already within sight), promptly replied that they had obtained New Orleans and the whole of Louisiana as it had been possessed by Spain. And, they added for good measure, he might also tell the British Government that they had taken care "so to frame the treaty as not to infringe upon any rights which Britain might claim to the navigation of the Mississippi."[60]

This statement was true enough, although they did not explain that they had given preference to French and Spanish shipping over British in American ports. This did not infringe upon the British right of free navigation of the river. King was tempted later to make a little Federalist capital of it when corresponding with

---

58. Monroe (Hamilton ed.), IV, 17. Miller, *Treaties,* II, 498–528.
59. See above, pp. 449–450.
60. ASP FR, II, 557, Livingston and Monroe to King.

Christopher Gore whom he had left in charge at London, but his candor overcame his politics. He admitted to Gore that the British would see the thing "in its true light."[61]

Rufus King had not waited for the reply from Livingston and Monroe, however, before going to the British prime minister on May 12 to declare that the cession was "probable." Addington responded that he hoped it had been done. He apparently had heard from Paris before King. The expedition, he said, would not proceed to New Orleans, for England would be satisfied if the United States obtained Louisiana. By the fifteenth, King had the letter from Livingston and Monroe, and announced the cession to Lord Hawkesbury. The secretary for foreign affairs was happy to reply from Downing Street on the nineteenth, formally declaring His Majesty's "pleasure" and especial satisfaction also with "the care which has been taken so to frame this Treaty as not to infringe any right of Gr. Britain in the Navigation of the Mississippi."[62]

The British ministers must have been gratified for the moment, as King had just agreed with Hawkesbury on the twelfth to the convention for settling the boundary disputes. It provided that the shortest line should be drawn from the northwest point of the Lake of the Woods to the nearest source of the Mississippi. Britain's domain in North America, therefore, was still to border upon the great continental waterway, notwithstanding the fact that the United States were now to possess both banks from its source to its mouth. If this convention held, the British claim to free navigation of the Mississippi would rest upon geography as well as treaty right. What Thomas Jefferson was to think, and his Senators to do, about the matter, however, proved quite different.[63]

Rufus King left England on May 21, 1803, to return to American politics. Another presidential campaign was approaching. Charles Cotesworth Pinckney had prior claims to the presidential nomination of the Federalist party, but there was the second place on the ticket open for a man of career and ambition. He had gone to England in 1796 for Washington to succeed Thomas Pinckney. His chief task had been to keep the United States on good terms with the British Government after the Jay Treaty had prevented war. He had done this well.[64]

61. King (King ed.), IV, 293–295, King to Gore from New York, August 20, 1803.

62. Ibid., IV, 255, 262, 263.

63. ASP FR, II, 584–591. King (King ed.), IV, 270. For Jefferson and the Senate, see below, pp. 526–527.

64. King (King ed.), IV, 264. For the political prospects to which King was returning see Vans Murray's letter to him from Baltimore, November 12, 1802, ibid., IV, 181–182.

In addition, if he could, he had been expected to iron out the difficulties which remained. He had done nothing about the claims for the slaves who had been taken with the British army at the close of the Revolution, but Jay himself had already allowed those claims to fall. He had been unable to establish the American position in regard to impressment of sailors into the British service, but he had tried persistently up to the moment of his departure. The British admiralty had declined to yield its advantage on that point, although using fair words about the inviolability of a crew on the "high seas." Lord St. Vincent had insisted that the "narrow seas" as well as Britain's territorial waters were within the jurisdiction of British municipal law. King, after weighing the disadvantage to his country in yielding to such an interpretation of *"mare clausum,"* had dropped the negotiation. The United States would still have to defend individual cases, to submit to exacting regulations about birth certificates and citizenship established prior to the Treaty of 1783, and to await the slow decisions of the British courts. The practical result would be that Americans would continue serving in the British navy or remain in British jails against their wishes and their rights.[65]

King furthermore had not been able to break down the British position regarding neutral American ships and their cargoes on the high seas and in West Indian waters. The British would make no concession to the principle *free ships free goods*. Nor had he succeeded in getting the commercial privileges which American merchants and shipowners desired in British ports. But he had obtained promises of change in the procedure of the British prize courts. He had solved the problems of American debts to English creditors incurred prior to the Revolution, other British claims, and the counterclaims of the United States for spoliations of American commerce by Britain during the previous war with France. He had accomplished by diplomacy with the British ministers what the mixed commissions under the Jay Treaty had failed to do after years of attempt at adjudication. Even though the very failure of those commissions had contributed greatly no doubt to the outcome, Rufus King deserved much credit. And he was likely to get it among Republicans as well as Federalists.[66]

Encouraged by a good personal reception in London and some

65. King (King ed.), IV, 256, conference with St. Vincent, May 13, 1803; 258, King to St. Vincent, May 15; 259–260, to Madison from New York, July, 1803. Zimmerman, 62–90. For previous negotiations on impressment, see above, pp. 131, 169, 303 f.

66. King (King ed.), IV, 261–262. For the Jay Treaty and the mixed commissions, see above, pp. 186–189.

progress up to the change of administration at home in 1801, stirred also perhaps by his own enthusiasm for Miranda's schemes in Latin America and the prospect of Anglo-American coöperation on a grand scale for the benefit of both Britain and the United States, Rufus King had urged the Republican administration to let him stay at his post in London. Or it may have been simply that he sensed from Jefferson's public statements, if he had not privately heard from the Administration, that the Republicans meant to keep him there as a Federalist friend of Britain to counteract misgivings of their course as traditional friends of France. In any case, he had written a private letter to Madison on October 8, 1801, justifying his wish to remain. The return of peace between Britain and France, he said, gave a better opportunity for the "revision of our treaty with this country" which he had hoped to secure. If Jefferson would confide the negotiation to him, he should willingly cross the Atlantic for a fortnight in Washington and return; or he should confer with Robert Livingston in London or in Paris as the President desired.[67]

Thomas Jefferson had not called Rufus King home for a conference, but he had soon put King in touch with the Republican plans entrusted to Robert Livingston. King had shifted his course at London to support of them. He had seen the importance of subordinating the revision of the Jay Treaty to expansion of solely American interests in the Mississippi Valley, and he had told the British foreign minister that in practically so many words. When he had gone to Paris in the fall of 1802, he had given Talleyrand no comfort at all as a Federalist expected to help undermine the Republican minister. Livingston shortly thereafter had broached his scheme to Napoleon through Joseph Bonaparte for the sale of Upper Louisiana. King, back again in London, had declared to the British prime minister in the following spring that the United States must soon "annex" Louisiana.[68]

Now this was an accomplished fact. The Federalist could return home knowing that he had served to the great advantage of his country the major purposes for which the Republican administration had kept him at his post in London. The United States were still at peace with Britain. And he had ably assisted in forestalling British action on the Mississippi while Livingston worked at removing the interest of France. He would be free now to play at politics as soon as he had made his report to his Government; his record would commend him for high office.

67. King (King ed.), IV, 266–267.
68. See above, p. 445.

Deferring to King's wish that he should not have to report in Washington, Jefferson and Madison made other arrangements. Albert Gallatin, third ranking Republican, called in New York upon the Federalist candidate for public attention. Gallatin could not get King's report at their first meeting on August 11, for another person was present. But a week later they were alone, and out it poured. He believed, said Rufus King, that he could have renewed the commercial treaty with Britain on terms satisfactory to America. He had got the West Indian admiralty courts improved. But he could do nothing with the "practical prejudices" of Lord St. Vincent upon impressment. Although the ministry in Britain was "most favorable" toward the United States, it probably would not last long. It was made of "little men." Livingston would do well in England as minister, except for his deafness. There was objection to Monroe. He would be received, but his situation would be "less comfortable and his services less useful than those of another person."

Both Gallatin and King concluded that Livingston's "precipitancy had been prejudicial to the United States," in that they might have got Louisiana for less money. But more interesting to us is what Gallatin reported to Jefferson about King's views in regard to Louisiana and the Floridas: "On the subject of Louisiana generally, Mr. King's opinions both as relating to New Orleans and the upper Country west of the Mississippi, seem to coincide with yours. . . . And he observed that Florida must necessarily fall into our hands, and that he hoped too much impatience would not be evinced on that subject."[69]

Thus released from the duties of the statesman, Rufus King turned to politics. He encouraged the protests of his Federalist friends in New England that Louisiana should not be incorporated into the Union, even though it had been acquired from France with that understanding. He ridiculed Jefferson's tentative idea of holding the American population out of the territory for a time. "Nothing but a cordon of troops," he said, could do it. He favored exchanging Louisiana for the Floridas. He later made fun of Monroe's mission to Madrid and dubbed him the "Knight of the Sorrowful Countenance." He was amused at the talk in Connecticut and upper New York "of *moving* to Louisiana, the country which will produce sugar & cotton & corn, &c. &c. ! ! !" So far, he wished perhaps to be ironic, but the truth forced him to go on: "and there can be no doubt," he said, "that the project of reserving the Lands west of the

69. Gallatin, *Writings*, I, 134–136, 140–144, to Jefferson, August 11, 18, 1803. King (King ed.), IV, 553–556.

Mississippi for posterity will be defeated by the Emigrants of the Eastern and Western States."[70]

It was the inevitable. Rufus King understood it as well and wished for it in his heart as much as Thomas Jefferson. The Federalist of New York, no more than the Republican of Virginia, was to be found among the provincials of the Atlantic Seaboard when the choice lay between the fears of party and the advantage of their country. Weeks before he knew that Jefferson would be reëlected, and a Republican Vice-President too, Rufus King had expressed his displeasure with the "croakings" of his friends in Washington, or as Livingston would have called them, the "Boston floppers." When they talked secession from the Union rather than face the fact that its future was imperial, Rufus King, however much he dreaded the spread of democracy, stood against them for empire.[71]

70. King (King ed.), IV, 302–303, to Gore, September 6, 1803; 339–341, to Gore, January 4, 1804; 586–599, 594, "Review of the Foreign Relations" of the United States; 325–326, to Gore, November 20, 1803.

71. Ibid., IV, 339–341, to Gore, January 4, 1804; 315–318, to Gore, October 24, 1803; 311–312, Livingston to King from Paris, October 14, 1803.

ACHIEVEMENT OF EMPIRE

Jefferson's Imagination

RUFUS KING had brought home the news of Louisiana and war in Europe; Thomas Jefferson's mind accordingly was at work upon the next phases of his problem, before the treaty itself arrived by special courier on July 14, 1803. How much territory had France ceded to the United States? How was it to be organized and administered? The President was not much concerned how they would pay for it, nor whether the Federalists would oppose. What if they did? He was practically certain now of a two-thirds vote in the Senate.[1]

After correspondence with Gallatin in the preceding January, Jefferson had agreed that there was no Constitutional barrier to acquiring new territory. He had said that it would be a "question of expediency," when they got to it, whether such territory could be organized as States in the Union under the Constitution as it then stood, but he thought that it would be safer to extend the Union of States into such territory only after they had amended the Constitution. He had committed himself in the election of 1800 to the doctrine of states rights and strict interpretation of the Constitution. He was sensitive to the fears in the older States that newer members of the Union would take control of the Federal Government from them. He knew that those misgivings might not stay within the Federalist party. So he began now to formulate an amendment to the Constitution which would maintain his political position at the moment but make it possible to admit new States from the Louisiana territory eventually.[2]

His plan was to make into a State as soon as possible the inhabited portion which lay below the latitude of the mouth of the Arkansas River, or perhaps only the thirty-first degree farther to the south. He would hold the remainder to the north and west as Indian territory into which the tribes now living east of the Mississippi could be removed. This would supplement the purpose of the Lewis and

1. AAE CP EU, LVI, ff. 3–11, Pichon to Talleyrand, July 7, 1803. Jefferson (Ford ed.), VIII, 249–251, Jefferson to Horatio Gates, July 11, 1803.
2. *Ibid.*, VIII, 241 n., to Gallatin, January, 1803.

Clark expedition up the Missouri River. It would also speed the settlement of the country to the east of the Mississippi, in which Jefferson's thoughts also included the Floridas. The American people
would then cross the Mississippi in time, advancing "compactly" as
they multiplied and laying off "range after range" of States beyond.
Until then, as he wrote to duPont de Nemours in the following
November, the Indians west of the Mississippi would be a constabulary force to hold the white population in check. Thomas Jefferson knew that there was more behind the Federalist outcry
against the purchase of Louisiana than the feeling that it was "rob-
bery of the public treasury." He appreciated Gallatin's counsel that
the settlement of the lands beyond the Mississippi would be "another delicate and difficult subject to introduce." Their "object
should at present be to restrain the population and settlements on
this side of the Mississippi."[3]

   This did not stop Jefferson's imagination from roaming the territory which had been acquired. By August 12 he not only had
found ample room for his plans beyond the Mississippi; but he had
also a sure way into the Floridas. He wrote from Monticello to his
friend Breckenridge, Senator from Kentucky, that the boundaries
of Louisiana which did not admit of question were the highlands
enclosing all the western tributaries of the Mississippi, including the
Missouri "of course" and the line drawn from the Lake of the Woods
to the source of the Mississippi. (It was a happy thought for his expedition into the Missouri country to establish competition with the
British traders.) Besides, the United States, he said, had some claim
to the seacoast reaching westward to the Rio Grande, and an even
better claim eastward to the Perdido between Mobile and Pensacola
for that had been "the antient boundary of Louisiana." He did not
then know that more recently General Victor's instructions had
been so drafted as to show that France considered the eastern boundary of her Louisiana would be the Mississippi, the Iberville, and Lake
Ponchartrain close to the island of New Orleans. It may be unfair
to say that if he had, he would not have cared. But Jefferson remarked to Breckenridge: "These claims will be a subject of negociation with Spain, and if, as soon as she is at war, we push them
strongly with one hand, holding out a price in the other, we shall
certainly obtain the Floridas, and all in good time."[4]

   3. *Ibid.*, VIII, 242 n.–244 n., to Breckenridge, August 12, 1803. *Gazette of the United
States,* Philadelphia, July 22, 1803, quoting *Trenton Federalist,* Gallatin, *Writings,* I,
156; remarks on the President's message, received October 4, 1803.
   4. Jefferson (Ford ed.), VIII, 243 n. For Victor's instructions, dated November 26,
1802, see Robertson, I, 361–374.

In the meantime the United States would exercise their natural right of free navigation on the Mississippi to the ocean "without waiting for permission." Easterners were objecting to the "vast extent of our boundaries" and proposing an exchange of Louisiana or part of it for the Floridas? Not so Thomas Jefferson: "We shall get the Floridas without," said he, "and I would not give one inch of the waters of the Mississippi to any nation. . . ."[5]

By the eighteenth of August, however, Jefferson had heard from Livingston that the French were not so pleased with their bargain; that Marbois and Talleyrand were now talking as though they would not sell, had they the thing to do over again. Was it a warning that Napoleon might repudiate the transaction before ratifications could be exchanged?[6]

Thomas Jefferson stopped working upon his Constitutional amendment. He wrote successive letters to the correspondents in whom he had confided, asking them to keep quiet about his plans for the Louisiana country. Congress should proceed, he said, to do what was necessary *"sub-silentio."* He confessed he still thought it "important" in this case to set an example against "broad construction" of the Constitution. He would prefer to appeal to the people for "new power." But if "our friends shall think differently, certainly I shall acquiesce with satisfaction."

After all, two thirds of the Senate were among those "friends." If they saw fit to act in the practical interest of the country, he should "acquiesce with satisfaction" indeed, confident "that the good sense of our country will correct the evil of construction when it shall produce ill effects." There are times when scrupulous persons take the advice of their "friends."[7]

Napoleon Regretful?

IT may seem that Jefferson was quite right in fearing a Napoleonic change of mind. Both Livingston and Monroe appear to have been convinced that the French were discontented with their bargain. Marbois gave them formal notice that the convention for paying the 60,000,000 francs had set "in a precise manner" three months after the exchange of ratifications as the longest period for "the consummation of this affair." "Every extraordinary delay beyond the

5. Jefferson (Ford ed.), VIII, 243 n.
6. ASP FR, II, 563, Livingston to Madison, June 3, 1803; 563–565, Livingston and Monroe to Madison, June 7, enclosing a note from Marbois and their reply.
7. Jefferson (Ford ed.), VIII, 244 n.–248 n., to Breckenridge, August 18, 1803, Thomas Paine, August 18, Madison, August 18, Levi Lincoln, August 30, and W. C. Nicholas, September 7.

terms fixed," said he, "places the contracting parties in the same situation as if they had never treated." As Talleyrand discussed with Monroe the order which should go to Pichon for transferring Louisiana, Talleyrand remarked that the First Consul had the right to annex a condition to the ratification "at any time before the exchange." Did this mean that Napoleon might double back and keep Louisiana?[8]

It did not, regardless of the fears of Livingston, Monroe, and Jefferson. Leclerc had failed in San Domingo. Victor's troops were needed at home, even if they could have eluded the British squadrons off the coast of Europe. Bernadotte did not try to leave for the United States, but returned to Paris. The time for such stalling had gone by. It was too late to get a force into New Orleans which could hold off the British fleet and maintain French authority against the Americans up the river until Napoleon had accomplished his purposes in Europe and restored communications with Louisiana.[9]

This move through Marbois and Talleyrand was no mere gesture. It served its purpose. It hastened Livingston to beg Madison "to get the ratification as soon as possible and to do all that on our part remains to be done." It roused Monroe to say to Talleyrand: "on our part and on our own responsibility if it is desired we would prevail on the house of Baring and Hope to advance the first payment, that is six million livres, before we heard from our government, in confidence that our conduct would be approved." It expedited the journey of Alexander Baring from Paris to Washington for the bonds of the United States with which the funds were to be provided for the French Treasury. And it hurried the treaty through the American Senate to the exchange of ratifications on October 21, 1803.[10]

Laussat, French prefect in New Orleans, longed for something to interfere with the transfer to the United States at the last moment, and when it was over lamented—"What a magnificent New France have we lost." But Napoleon, First Consul of France, wanted only to close the bargain quickly and get his money. A later time, perhaps, might bring another opportunity for France in the Americas, but that would be another time. The reality now was war with Britain in Europe. To be paid $11,250,000 by British bankers and

8. ASP FR, II, 565.

9. AAE CP EU, LV, f. 485, Talleyrand to Bernadotte, June 11, 1803. ASP FR, II, 563. For Gallatin's opinion that Napoleon intended to raise no serious objections to the sale, see his *Writings*, I, 145–152, August 31, 1803.

10. ASP FR, II, 563. Monroe (Hamilton ed.), IV, 35, to Madison, June 8, 1803.

assured neutrality by the United States were good compensations for a colonial domain that you were certain to lose anyway. It was amusing, too, if one had a sense of humor.[11]

The Floridas—and Texas

THE fear which reduced Jefferson's Constitutional scruples to silence in August had no effect, however, upon his expansive conception of "the vast extent of our boundaries." He wrote on September 21 to his scientific friend, William Dunbar of Natchez, that Louisiana included West Florida eastward to the Perdido beyond Mobile. He did not include the Texas country on the west when describing Louisiana to Congress in November; but, as he explained to Dunbar in the following March, he had not done so because he preferred to have "explanations" with Spain before publicly asserting the claim. Dunbar was soon to explore for him the region of the Red and Washita Rivers beyond the Mississippi.[12]

By January 31, 1804, Jefferson was certain that he had more than a good claim to Texas. He was positive, without those "explanations," that the whole region from the Perdido to the Rio Grande had been purchased from France. James Monroe still should go to Madrid and talk about it. One would be deferential still to the Spanish claim to West Florida, for the sake of appearances, and also to prevent possible reactions in Europe, particularly in France. In the meantime, one would not hesitate long over appropriating the use of West Florida which one's countrymen most desired. Without deference to Spanish protests, there should be entry and departure from the territory of the United States above West Florida on the navigable waters which flowed through it from the United States into the Gulf of Mexico.[13]

The President, his four Secretaries, and the Attorney General reached important conclusions on February 18. The waterway

11. Martin, *Louisiana,* II, 245. See also Laussat's reports to Decrès in Robertson, II, 29–59.

12. Jefferson (Ford ed.), VIII, 256 n., to Dunbar, September 21, 1803. ASP Miscellaneous, I, 344–384, Jefferson to Congress, November 14, 1803, submitting a "digest of information" on Louisiana. Jefferson (Washington ed.), IV, 537–541, to Dunbar, March 13, 1804. For Jefferson's "Limits and Bounds of Louisiana," dated September 7, 1803, and Dunbar's "Exploration of the Red, the Black, and the Washita Rivers," see the American Philosophical Society's *Documents Relating to the Purchase and Exploration of Louisiana.* In this collection is Jefferson's letter to du Ponceau of the Society, December 30, 1817, saying: "When we first made the purchase, we knew little of its extent, having never before been interested to enquire into it." This afterthought is hardly consistent with his instructions to Lewis and Clark and Gallatin's letter about the Missouri country. See above, pp. 461–466.

13. Madison (Hunt ed.), VII, 114–118, Madison to Livingston, January 31, 1804.

through the Iberville River and Lake Ponchartrain ought to be considered as within American jurisdiction, and Baton Rouge made a port of delivery. Governor Claiborne in New Orleans, therefore, should notify the Spanish official that he was not welcome in this district and that the remaining troops should withdraw. Fort Stoddert on the Tombigbee River above Mobile Bay should also become a port of entry. Monroe should be instructed "to negotiate as to our lines with Spain, & the extention of territory." He was to try for three different concessions: the Perdido River, the Appalachicola, or all of East Florida. In proportion to the success of his efforts, he was to yield these "equivalents": relinquishment of the American right to the Texas country eastward from the Rio Grande to the Sabine; stipulation that a breadth of territory, to remain unsettled for a period of years, should be fixed between Spanish and American settlements beyond the Mississippi; and payment to Spain of $1,-000,000.[14]

Six days later, Congress passed the "Mobile Act," for which John Randolph had introduced the original bill in November, extending the laws of the United States to the territory recently acquired from France. It stipulated that Natchez and vicinity were to remain a separate district, for entry from the Mississippi into the American territory east of the river. But it incorporated into a "District of Mississippi," with New Orleans as the sole port of entry, not only the new territory acquired from France but also "all navigable waters, rivers, creeks, bays, inlets, lying within the United States which empty into the Gulf of Mexico east of the Mississippi river." It authorized the President, whenever he thought it expedient, to make "the shores, waters and inlets of the bay and river of Mobile, and west thereof to the Pascagoula" into a separate district and to designate suitable ports of entry and delivery.[15]

Henry Adams and others following him have criticized this wording as ambiguous. They have pointed to it with contemporary opponents as revealing Jefferson's belief that the United States had acquired West Florida from France. There is no doubt that the act does manifest his claim to West Florida. But the phrase "navigable waters . . . lying within the United States . . ." is not as ambiguous as it might seem. Jefferson was ready to appropriate international waterways through foreign territory to the use of the American people, and to dissolve the conflict of jurisdictions in those waters for the advantage of the United States over Spain, as he had been

14. Jefferson (Ford ed.), I, 304–305, entry in Jefferson's "Anas."
15. Statutes at Large, II, 251–254.

long since with regard to navigation of the Mississippi. He was not yet ready to seize the lands of West Florida.[16]

The act was precisely written to meet the exact situation. The United States had title to the territory down to the thirty-first degree of latitude, by reason of the Treaty of 1783 with Britain confirmed by Spain in the Pinckney Treaty of 1795. The heads of navigation of most, if not all, of the important rivers flowing through West Florida into the Gulf were within territory indisputably American. Congress was, therefore, entirely within its legislative jurisdiction when it provided for customs districts and ports of entry. There is no ground for the charge that it was enacting seizure of Spanish territory. It was no more than presumptuous when it authorized the President to make the shores and waters of Mobile into a separate district whenever he thought it expedient to do so. The act was careful to avoid designating "shores" which were not "within the United States."[17]

Thomas Jefferson thought it expedient very soon to make the shores and waters of Mobile Bay into a separate customs district, but not until he had drawn again upon the wisdom of Albert Gallatin. The Secretary of the Treasury wrote on March 28, 1804, that they should designate Fort Stoddert as the port of entry, for this would prove to Spain that they had no intention of exercising jurisdiction within the territory in her possession. Jefferson proclaimed the new district on May 20 and named Fort Stoddert as the port of entry.[18]

John Randolph took exception to the proclamation and thereafter opposed Jefferson's efforts to ease the departure of the Spaniards from the Floridas. Apparently Randolph had expected the President to turn the presumption of the "Mobile Act" at once into fact. Following Randolph's line of thought, one authority on the history of West Florida has called Jefferson "shifty" and has declared that his proclamation "virtually annulled" the act. But it would not seem so. Jefferson was slow rather than uncertain.[19]

Irujo, Spain's minister in Washington, hotly protested the Act of Congress, sought the British minister's support, continued to berate Madison, and charge the Administration with double-dealing, even though he was reassured that American troops had not been sent to take possession and appeared to be mollified somewhat by Jeffer-

16. Adams, *United States*, II, 252. Cox, 97.
17. See above, pp. 92, 217, for the treaties of 1783 and 1795.
18. Gallatin, *Writings*, I, 183. *Annals*, 8 Cong. 2 Sess., 1234.
19. Cox, 100, 99.

son's proclamation. Irujo came much nearer than Randolph to understanding the policy of Jefferson, Gallatin, and Madison, but even he did not correctly interpret the purposes of the act and the President's supplementary proclamation.[20]

Those purposes were to defer for the time being to the Spanish claim of title to the lands of West Florida without compromising the counterclaim of the United States, and to secure immediately the right to use the navigable waterways which passed through those lands to the Gulf of Mexico. Jefferson would not satisfy Randolph by making the pretension to the lands into seizure. Obviously he did not intend to gratify Irujo by weakening in the slightest degree that pretension based upon the purchase of Louisiana from France. Jefferson intended that the United States should be poised at their undisputed boundary, prepared to take possession of the additional territory at the propitious moment either by means of Monroe's diplomacy in Madrid or exigencies created by the war in Europe. There was caution in this policy, and determination, but not deceit.

Secretary Madison had drafted the instructions to Monroe on April 15. He was to ascertain the views of the French Government on the way to Madrid, for much would depend upon its interposition. There were American claims for spoliations to settle in Madrid, but he was to be more concerned with territories. Spain should acknowledge that the United States had bought West Florida. If the Spaniards would not admit it, he was to hold his negotiations to the claims for damages to American commerce and make no arrangement in regard to the lands westward from the Mississippi to the Rio Grande. If they did acknowledge the title of the United States to West Florida, and settled the claims comprehensively, he might agree to an unoccupied area for a period of time between the Sabine River on the east, the watershed of the Missouri and its tributaries on the north, and on the far side the Colorado or some other river emptying into the Bay of St. Bernard.

In no case was Monroe to cede finally to Spain any part of the Texas country east of the Rio Grande, except in the event that Spain gave East Florida to the United States as well as acknowledged that West Florida belonged to them, "and in that event in case of absolute necessity only." He might do so then, provided he did not deprive the United States "of any of the waters running into the Missouri or Mississippi, or of the other waters emptying into the Gulph of Mexico between the Mississippi and the river Colorado

20. AAE CP EU, LVI, ff. 429–434, Pichon to Talleyrand, March 18, 1804. Cox, 98–99. Madison (Hunt ed.), VII, 123–140, 125, Madison to Livingston, March 31, 1804.

emptying into the Bay of St. Bernard." And he was to offer no guarantee of Spain's possessions.[21]

In other words, Jefferson was no longer willing to relinquish claim to the Texas country from the Sabine to the Rio Grande for the Floridas. He would concede only the region from the Rio Grande eastward to the Colorado in return for the whole of East Florida, and that only in case of "absolute necessity." He would give no guarantee to Spain against the consequences of the war in Europe or future conditions in the Americas. Such instructions seem to indicate that he was counting far more upon events than upon the success of Monroe in Madrid.[22]

British Rights on the Mississippi

WHAT was the President of the United States thinking about the northern limits of the Louisiana Purchase and Britain's rights west of the Lake of the Woods? By January 15, 1804, Jefferson's conception of American territory had swept forward easily to the forty-ninth degree of latitude, the line of agreement between France and Britain concerning trade at the time of the Treaty of Utrecht of 1713. The northern boundary, therefore, should run from the northwestern point of the Lake of the Woods "westwardly" to intersect the forty-ninth parallel and then proceed along that line until it reached the limits of the Spanish province "next adjacent." If the forty-ninth degree by any chance should cross the Missouri River, Jefferson was prepared. Then, the "dividing line shall pass around all those waters to the North" and drop back to the forty-ninth degree of latitude, and proceed to Spanish territory. What if Spain had no right that far to the north?—then, the forty-ninth degree should go on marking the boundary to the Pacific between the territory of the United States and British dominions in North America.[23]

This conception is startling, in the light of subsequent British and American rivalry there. At that time, however, it was of small import. Jefferson's fellow Americans in the West were not then anxious over the valley of the Red River of the North, nor the intermountain region farther into the Northwest. They were fascinated by the rich lands immediately across the Mississippi and along the Missouri and lured by the trade down the Mississippi, the lands, and the outlets to the sea through the Floridas.

21. Madison (Hunt ed.), VII, 141–153, Madison to Monroe, April 15, 1804.

22. Jefferson (Ford ed.), VIII, 309–312 and n. 1, Jefferson to Madison, July 5 and 6, 1804, commenting upon a discussion in the Cabinet where Gallatin had not been quite so expansive.

23. Am. Phil. Soc., *Documents relating to Louisiana*, 43–44.

Nor was Britain much concerned at that time over the great Northwest. She had her hands more than full with Napoleon's aspirations on the European continent, in the Mediterranean, and the Orient. She would have to leave the United States alone to do what they would in America, until later. It was too bad, but it was so.

Thomas Jefferson, however, was practical as well as prophetic. The treaty which Marbois had made with Livingston and Monroe had affected the international character of the Mississippi River and changed the question of navigation. It was now, reasoned Jefferson, a matter simply of American "municipal law." Should he be troubled by the fact that Rufus King had made almost simultaneously an agreement with Britain formalizing the promise of Livingston and Monroe? Should nothing in their treaty affect the British right of navigation? Thomas Jefferson did not think so. He set down as his opinion that the article in King's convention providing for the shortest line between the Lake of the Woods and the nearest source of the Mississippi was "nugatory." It should be expunged. His reasoning was that the Louisiana Treaty with France, as of April 30, 1803, was unknown to both Britain and the United States at the moment when their representatives signed the Convention of May 12, 1803, in London.[24]

We may not be impressed by that reasoning even though Rufus King now supported it. The fact was that King had reassured the British Government with respect to the navigation of the Mississippi after he had heard from Livingston and Monroe in Paris. But gone from Jefferson's thinking was the consideration which he had once seriously entertained, when it might have helped Livingston persuade France to cede New Orleans. Going swiftly in its wake was also the thought that the United States must live up to their commitments of 1783 and 1795 which gave Britain free navigation of the river.[25]

This, too, was a matter which the British had to let fall until they were done with Napoleon. When Rufus King's convention of May 12, 1803, came from the American Senate ratified on February 9, 1804, its provision for the line from the Lake of the Woods to the Mississippi was missing. But the influence of President Jefferson was apparent. "All the democrats except those from Vermont," remarked the Federalist Plumer, had "voted to expunge the fifth

24. *Ibid.*
25. King (King ed.), IV, 330–332, Madison to King, December 4, 1803, and King to Madison, December 9 in reply. For King's assurance to the British Government upon the basis of the statement of Livingston and Monroe to him, see above, p. 511.

Article." Timothy Pickering, commiserating King on the loss of his *"entirely satisfactory"* convention, wrote of these Jeffersonians: "Some of his *magnanimous* partisans in the Senate have openly avowed the propriety of pushing G. Britain *now* on any points we desire to gain; because her present critical situation will dispose her to yield (as they imagine) what in a time of peace she might refuse!"[26]

So it really was. Hammond in the foreign office·"hoped to God" that his Government would not accept the convention if altered by the Senate, and his Government did not. But neither did it demand satisfaction because the United States had broken the promise of Livingston and Monroe. Its European problems were too engrossing. And when Britain finally was in position at the close of the Napoleonic wars to do something about the line from the Lake of the Woods to the Mississippi, it was too late. The American people were entrenched on both banks of the river from source to mouth; free navigation was a question of purely domestic concern to them. Britain accepted, in the Convention of 1818 following the Peace of Ghent, the line from the Lake of the Woods down to the forty-ninth degree of latitude, and thence westward to the Rocky Mountains. This ran above the headwaters of the Mississippi, abandoning all claim to the navigation of the river. Thomas Jefferson and his *"magnanimous* partisans" had been very practical.[27]

Awaiting "Favorable Conjunctures"

THE Senate had met in special executive session on October 17, 1803, to consider the French treaties. The "friends" of Jefferson were not bothered with scruples about the Constitution, misgivings concerning the state of the Treasury, even fears of disloyalty in New England. Had not Jefferson rationalized the problem of the Constitution for them into terms of expediency and common sense? Gallatin could do the worrying about funds to meet the payments on the new bonds. Prospects were good for increasing revenues. Meanwhile Baring and Hope would advance the cash.

As for sedition in New England, were there no Jeffersonians in New England? There were, represented even in the Cabinet. Were there not Federalists, too, who desired New Orleans and the whole Louisiana country with the most eager of Jeffersonians? Indeed there were. The "friends" of Jefferson rushed the treaties through within

26. Plumer, 141. King (King ed.), IV, 360–364, *363,* Pickering to King, March 3, 1804. ASP FR, II, 584–591, text and papers sent to the Senate by Jefferson. J. Q. Adams, *Memoirs,* I, 269 ff., comments by Adams as a member of the Senate's special committee.
27. King (King ed.), IV, 341–343, Gore to King, February 8, 1804.

four days, ratifying them as they had not done the Convention of 1800, with no reservation whatsoever. The ratifications were exchanged the next day, October 21, 1803, in Washington. Two months later, December 20, Governor Claiborne of the Mississippi territory and General Wilkinson with a body of troops at New Orleans took over Louisiana from the French prefect, Laussat.[28]

Confidently awaiting that news, President Jefferson settled himself on January 8, 1804, to write at length a comfortable, gossipy, revealing letter to his protégé and political handy man, James Monroe, now minister at London, where he was to talk about matters of impressment and neutral rights before he journeyed to Madrid and proved, amicably if possible but proved none the less, that the Spaniards were losing not only New Orleans and Louisiana but also the Floridas, at least to the Perdido beyond Mobile: "We scarcely expect any liberal or just settlement with Spain," wrote Jefferson, "and are perfectly determined to obtain or to take our just limits." It was probable that the inhabitants of Louisiana on the eastern bank and "eastwardly to a considerable extent" would very soon ask to be received under the jurisdiction of the United States. Thus they would get possession of most of West Florida peaceably. For Mobile and the territory farther east, they would "await favorable conjunctures."[29]

This was a happy moment for Thomas Jefferson. Alexander Baring, apparently to his entire satisfaction, had completed his arrangements with the Treasury and was about to return with the bonds for the payments to Napoleon. Baring's departure offered "a confidential opportunity" to write Monroe "with less reserve than common conveyances admit." Jefferson could chatter at ease about his literary friends, political acquaintances in England and France, political subordinates and seekers after patronage in the United States. He could gloat a bit over the "federal leaders" who "have had the imprudence" to oppose the acquisition of Louisiana "pertinaciously," and who had caused "a great proportion of their quondam honest adherents to abandon them and join the republican standard." Four states only were hanging back. New Hampshire would join within the year, said he; even Connecticut was advancing "with a slow but steady step." Only Massachusetts and Delaware were uncertain. Republicanism in Massachusetts was "so flaccid in texture" and Delaware "so much affected by every little

28. Plumer, 14. Senate Ex. Journ. I, 450. Miller, *Treaties,* II, 528. Robertson, II, 225–231, Claiborne to Madison, December 20, 27, 1803.

29. Jefferson (Ford ed.), VIII, 289, to Monroe, January 8, 1804.

topical information" that he would "wait for them with patience & good Humour."[30]

Jefferson also trusted to the conveyance of Alexander Baring a plan for rewarding James Monroe which Monroe himself had already suggested. Congress was considering the bill for the government of Louisiana. It could be written, said Jefferson, so as to delay the appointment of the Governor for six months. If Monroe wanted the place, he could have it. The salary would be only $5,000, whereas he was now getting $9,000; and the expenses of entertaining as Governor of Louisiana would be greater. On the other hand, he would have there "the facility of getting the richest land in the world, the extraordinary profitablness of their culture." If he took his slaves with him, he might get himself immediately "under way" out of the debts which made his present salary and traveling expenses so attractive to him. It was his to decide, although naturally with "limited delay" as there were others in the Jeffersonian organization to be considered.[31]

There were things on Jefferson's mind at the moment, however, which he did not choose to entrust to Baring or spread before Monroe. Most assuredly neither time nor place nor person was right as yet for releasing those conclusions which he added on the following day to his memoir upon the limits of Louisiana—that the northern boundary ran above the headwaters of the Missouri and that the British right of navigation on the Mississippi rested now upon the discretion of the United States in administering their own municipal law. He told Monroe of this memoir and said that Secretary Madison would send him a copy, but that was all.[32]

Instead, Jefferson informed Monroe that the British chargé, Thornton, was wrong in thinking the United States were not now as friendly toward Britain as before the acquisition of Louisiana. Not so. They were "cordial and sincere." They were "anxious to see England maintain her standing, only wishing she would use her power on the ocean with justice."

Instead, he filled the remainder of the letter with an account—half-amused, half-vexed—concerning the performances of Mrs. Merry, wife of the new British minister. She resented the President's practice of escorting his guests to dinner "pele-mele." He did so, he said, because there was no hostess at the White House as he was a widower and he would avoid offense by giving precedence

30. *Ibid.*, VIII, 288.
31. Monroe (Hamilton ed.), IV, 156, 477. Jefferson (Ford ed.), VIII, 290.
32. See above, p. 525.

to anyone. Mrs. Merry resented so strongly, and made her feelings so obvious, that she created a diplomatic episode. She was a "virago," said Jefferson. Her husband was "reasonable" and a "good" man. But "if his wife perseveres, she must eat her soup at home, and we shall endeavor to draw him into society as if she did not exist."

Was there no time left to talk about boundaries with Britain and rights of navigation, or to expound the rights of neutrals on the high seas and to protest the illegality of impressing American sailors? Baring did not leave until days later. There was time to write a postscript on January 16, but it contained only this exuberance—"Louisiana was delivered to our commissioners on the 20th Dec."[33]

What a Loyal Virginian Should Do

JAMES MONROE had thought better of his hint about the governorship of Louisiana by the time this letter from Jefferson reached him in March, 1804. The high road to big things in politics did not run in that direction for him. The diplomatic career, not the administrative post though vice-regal, was the way to the top. There was no telling what political credit would come of a governorship even over so imperial a domain as Louisiana, but there was already in sight fame from his extraordinary mission in France, his assignment to London, and his forthcoming expedition to Madrid, if he played the part correctly.[34]

Monroe had already moved, in fact almost as soon as he had arrived at Paris in April, 1803, to undermine any conviction that Robert Livingston might cherish and advertise to the effect that it was he who deserved the honors for acquiring Louisiana. Then on May 25, 1803, just three days after Napoleon had ratified the conventions, Monroe had carefully advised the Virginian Senators and Breckenridge of Kentucky—by way of Secretary Madison—that the Administration at home was responsible for the outcome. Candor had made him reject any particular credit for himself, but he had made that disclaimer include Livingston too. The approach of war again in Europe had done much, he said, but it was the masterly statesmanship of Jefferson that had turned the trick and influenced Napoleon to sell.[35]

33. Jefferson (Ford ed.), VIII, 291–292. AAE CP EU, LVI, ff. 342–351, Pichon to Talleyrand, February 5, 1804.
34. Monroe (Hamilton ed.), IV, 153–163, to Jefferson, March 15, 1804.
35. Ibid., IV, 31–34, May 25, 1803. See above, p. 501.

On further reflection, Monroe had written again about the matter to Madison from London. By this time, July 26, he had concluded that his arrival in France had made up the Napoleonic mind. This view still left room for Jefferson and Madison, and for conditions in Europe, but there was more of Monroe in it. From what Marbois observed, and Livingston also, we should be more inclined to believe that it was the arrival of Ross's belligerent Federalist resolutions, before Monroe himself, that had put the final touch to a decision which had been taking shape for some time. But James Monroe did not express, if he considered, so deflating an idea. It does tend to adorn the record of Livingston rather than of Monroe.[36]

Then, as he found himself carried along by the eagerness of the French to have done with negotiations and to sell at their own price, Monroe had been put to it to find something to do with the $2,000,000 which Congress had authorized him to spend. Robert Livingston had wished to apply this sum to the American claims against France. His plan was not unreasonable, in view of the fact that the French insisted the American Government should assume those claims. Besides, they seemed to be making excellent progress on their own with Baring and Hope in arranging to cash the American bonds. Why should the American ministers have pressed other financial inducements upon them?[37]

Nevertheless it was true that Livingston was closely in touch with James Swan and other American claimants in Paris. It might have been that Livingston or some of his numerous relatives were personally interested in those claims. There was that undertone in the correspondence of the time. Dark insinuations were passing among Federalists that Livingston stood to gain from valuable grants of lands by the French Government before the transfer was made to the United States. It was easy for anyone who knew of John Marshall's past experiences with Talleyrand to suspect that, in whatever the French foreign minister interested himself, there was a scheme for personal profit at public expense. And Robert

36. Monroe (Hamilton ed.), IV, 56, to Madison, July 26, 1803.

37. *Ibid.*, IV, 35, 64–65, 72–73. For the Act of Congress, February 26, 1803, see Stats. at Large, II, 202. The debate is not recorded in the Annals as the matter was in executive session. But see *Annals,* 7 Cong. 2 Sess., 370–371, for a resolution concerning the purchase of New Orleans and the Floridas and a committee report in the House. See also Gallatin's report, October, 1803, in Rpts. of Secs. of Treas., I, 262–264, regarding allocation of the fund to the account of American claims. For subsequent references to them, see *ibid.,* I, 288, 299, 332, 358, 374, 392, 399.

Livingston, as he had told Madison, was on far better terms with
Talleyrand than James Monroe could ever be.[38]

These reflections seem to have been running through Monroe's
mind during the winter of 1803-4, although he had neither the
information nor the courage to present them in open accusation
against his colleague before the public at home. Rather, Monroe
harped upon the idea that Livingston and he should use the appro-
priation by Congress to guarantee the first payment due the French
Government from Hope and Baring, even though Alexander Baring had already gone to the United States for the new bonds. Then,
in spite of the fact that he no longer had any official connection with
the affairs of the United States in Paris, as Livingston was still minister to France and he was now minister to England, James Monroe
took the side of the American claims commissioners in Paris against
Livingston.

Talleyrand had forced Monroe to offer the guarantee, it would
seem, in order to scare the American Government into quickly ratifying the treaties. But Talleyrand had not pressed for actual payment in advance, once Monroe and Livingston had been so aroused
that they wrote home to cut Jeffersonian procrastination short. In
fact he had told Monroe that Napoleon had no desire for it, and
so Livingston had seen no good reason for making it. Still, Monroe
persisted. He was going to make sure that the money was not used
as Livingston wished, on account of the American claims.[39]

Monroe persisted so much in fact that the French authorities
finally agreed to accept the payment. Livingston gave in and signed
the guarantee with Monroe, although it was now far into December, 1803, and Baring was soon to leave Washington for London
with the bonds from the American Treasury.[40]

As for the quarrel between Livingston and the claims commissioners, Monroe vouched for them to Madison as his own friends.
In view of his opinion of Livingston by this time, and of himself,
this could mean nothing less than that they were right. They were

38. Monroe (Hamilton ed.), IV, 116, Monroe to Madison, December 17, 1803. King
(King ed.), IV, 335, Gore to King, December 20, 1803, concerning Swan and Livingston's candidacy for Vice-President; 315, Gore to King, October 21, 1803, concerning
alleged grants of land to Livingston and his family. See above, pp. 283–292.

39. Monroe (Hamilton ed.), IV, 34–36, to Madison, from Paris, June 8, 1803; 63–
69, to Livingston, from London, August 20; 71–74, to Madison, August 31; 78–92, to
Livingston, October 9; 99–100, to Madison, November 25; 149, to Madison, March 3,
1804.

40. Monroe (Hamilton ed.), IV, 124–130, Monroe to Madison, January 9, 1804; 131–
134, to Livingston, January 13. See also Gallatin, *Writings,* I, 158, Gallatin to Jefferson,
October, 1803.

honest. They were not personally interested, he said, in the claims. (The fact is that at least one, Fulwar Skipwith, was interested.) And Livingston? One would not like just yet to say in so many words that he was dishonest, but one would say:

> With respect to this old friend I have only to observe, that I have had but one opinion and wish since my association with him, it has been to put it out of his power and those about him to give an improper character to a particular transaction, to the injury of others & true principles, and that being done that he sho^d. be treated with the utmost kindness possible. . . .

He should be shown "a kind of general indulgence" and kept at his post in Paris until the spring of 1805, until after the business of the next vice-presidency had been settled without him. Then Monroe would wish him to return home "sensible of his errors, repentant of them, & grateful to the gov.^{t} for its kindness towards him." In other words, a young and faithful Virginian, with political aspirations of his own, should not allow an old New Yorker to proceed with his political shuffling without letting the elder Virginians at home know the trend of his game.[41]

James Monroe also made a point of relating in this letter to Madison how Lord Hawkesbury had complained about Livingston's memorial to the French Government on the question whether France should take Louisiana. James Swan had sent this paper to America as the cession to the United States was completed. It had appeared in the newspapers of July, 1803, and Federalist critics had pounced upon Livingston's remarks that the common sentiments and interests of France and the United States should form the "maritime code," help France to naval superiority, and "deliver the universe from the tyranny" of Britain. The *Gazette of the United States* in Philadelphia had declared that Jefferson ought to disavow "this impertinent charge of his minister."[42]

It was enough of an event for Hawkesbury to take notice and to have the British minister in the United States turn it to diplomatic advantage. But the British effort did not go beyond complaint. Livingston's memorial had been submitted in the summer

---

41. Monroe (Hamilton ed.), IV, 114–122, Monroe to Madison, December 17, 1803; 102–103, to Madison regarding Livingston, November 25. For treatment of these debts and claims, from a legal point of view, see Moore, V, 4433–4446. Pertinent documents are in ASP FR, VI, 154 ff. See also Miller, *Treaties*, II, 524–528. For Skipwith's claims, see Malloy, *Treaties*, I, 517–520.

42. Monroe (Hamilton ed.), IV, 101–102. Madison (Hunt ed.), VII, 60 n., Madison to Monroe, July 30, 1803. *Gazette of the United States*, Philadelphia, July 15, 19, 22, 1803. King (King ed.), IV, 293–294, King to Gore, August 20, 1803.

of 1802. The foreign office had received ample information from Whitworth since that time to show what were the real purposes of the American minister to France.[43]

Robert Livingston's explanation to Madison was adequate. He had not submitted the memorial to the French Government in his public character as minister. Besides, there was nothing in it which had not already been told officially to Britain. James Monroe's candor did not extend so far. It did not persuade him to write that Livingston had used this and other memorials to build up friendship with France for the advantage of the United States, just as Livingston then had cultivated Lord Whitworth to keep Spain from transferring West Florida to France—for the same purpose. James Monroe seems also to have quite forgotten how belligerent he himself had been in opposition to the Jay Treaty, and how he had even tried to get the United States into war with Britain not ten years past when he had been minister to France. Bygones should be bygones. Kindliness and indulgence should rule—so long as Robert Livingston did not get into American politics. But James Monroe was soon having other emotions.[44]

"He Will Poison What He Touches"

BY the time President Jefferson's letter arrived in March, 1804, the young diplomatist from Virginia was safely beyond the temptation of the governorship in Louisiana and he was looking forward to his negotiations in Madrid. He explained to Jefferson, as best he could, that he would like to keep the post at London and also go to Madrid when his instructions should arrive. Then Robert Livingston appeared in London, May 19, ostensibly "on a trip of amusement."[45]

Monroe again was irritated and suspicious. He told Madison that Livingston would not be welcome to the British Government because of that old "memorial" to France. He himself, he said, was placed "in rather an unpleasant dilemma" on account of it. Addington had given way to Pitt, and Harrowby was now at the foreign office instead of Hawkesbury. He did not know how he would stand with this new ministry. Mrs. Monroe had been experiencing much the same treatment at dinner as Mrs. Merry in the White House. His feelings increased as he learned from Harrowby that Living-

43. Madison (Hunt ed.), VII, 138, to Livingston, March 31, 1804. See above, p. 441 f.

44. ASP FR, II, 573–574, Livingston to Madison, November 15, 1803. See above, pp. 453, 235 f.

45. Monroe (Hamilton ed.), IV, 153–163, to Jefferson, March 15, 1804. See above, p. 528.

ston had come after conversing with Talleyrand and Marbois upon
the possibility of peace between Britain and France. The proposition was that, if Britain would take the lead as the party which had
broken the Peace of Amiens, and would relinquish Malta, "everything else would be made easy." Livingston had talked about it
with members of the opposition, and Fox was likely to ask an interview with Pitt. Livingston had then told him, admitted Monroe,
and asked his opinion; but in such a way, he concluded, as simply
to give him the information without really seeking his judgment on
the matter.[46]

Upon this vexation, Lord Harrowby piled complaint that the
Senate had ratified King's convention without the article on the
line to the Mississippi. Harrowby's conduct through the whole conference, said Monroe, "was calculated to wound & to irritate." He
had observed with "severity" that the article was expunged because
it ceded territory which the American Government did not wish
to yield. (It was the truth, but this did not lessen Monroe's distress.) Then, after Monroe had his orders for Madrid, and was
giving Harrowby a general idea of their nature and endeavoring
to obtain promises that all would go well while he was away, the
British foreign minister abruptly questioned whether the United
States had obtained West Florida in the cession of Louisiana as they
thought![47]

With these matters left unsettled in London to plague him,
James Monroe arrived at last in Paris in November, 1804, en route
to Madrid. He expected to enjoy the mediation of France as it had
once been promised; and he assumed that he would have the coöperation of Robert Livingston and General Armstrong who was to
succeed Livingston as minister to France. Instead, he found Talleyrand, though personally cordial, officially evasive. It was an unmistakable hint that Napoleon, now Emperor, would do nothing further for the United States without special compensations. Armstrong could not act, for he had not yet been officially received.
And Livingston, though quite willing to make the initial approaches to the French Government for Monroe, was not willing
to participate in the negotiations, and was frankly skeptical of the
procedure which Monroe wished to adopt.[48]

Robert Livingston was quite within his rights. They no longer

46. Monroe (Hamilton ed.), IV, 188–191, 207 n.–208 n., 205–217, to Madison, May
22, June 10, June 28, 1804.

47. *Ibid.,* IV, 194–197, 241–249, to Madison, June 3, September 8, 1804.

48. *Ibid.,* IV, 266–274, Monroe to Talleyrand, November 8, 1804, in Paris; 274–277,
to Livingston, November 13; 277–297, to Madison, from Bordeaux, December 16.

had a joint commission. This was James Monroe's sole responsibility. But Livingston did have a plan of action, and he offered it to Monroe. It was that the United States should make a loan to Spain if she would acknowledge that they had acquired West Florida. If President Jefferson would not follow their advice and seize the disputed region, Livingston would secure it by advancing money, in bonds of the United States, which Spain should pay back in seven annual installments. Monroe protested that they would pay twice for the area, as they would never get their money back; and furthermore, Livingston had not included East Florida in his plan. Livingston argued that they would get it "without paying a farthing"; for Spain, said he, would reimburse them with drafts on Mexico; they could include East Florida in the transaction; and in the interim, they would settle all disputes over the boundaries amicably.[49]

Monroe conceded that Livingston and he did have the same object in view, differing only in mode. But he would not adopt the plan. For, after he had talked with Marbois and with Hauterive in Talleyrand's office, he knew that the French were expecting the United States to pay for any adjustment of their difficulty with Spain; and he believed that whatever Spain got from the United States would then be paid to France on account of sums due her from Spain[50]

Livingston thought so too. He had written to Madison on September 21, 1804:

> While Spain wishes to limit us as much as possible, France wishes to make our controversy favorable to her finances. Yesterday Marbois again spoke to me on the subject of purchasing the Floridas and giving sixty millions for them, and even pressed the matter very strongly upon me. You see by this which way the wind sets. The distresses of Spain make them fear that she will not be able to comply with her engagements, and the threatening war and internal expenses render the state of the Treasury here very precarious.

This, from the man who had just gone over to England to talk of peace for France, is very revealing. But it does not disclose the matter about which James Monroe was giving himself so much worry.[51]

Monroe was coming to think that Livingston not only opposed him personally but was betraying the interests of their country. He

49. *Ibid.*, IV, 278–279. ASP FR, II, 574, Livingston to Madison, November 15, 1803.
50. Monroe (Hamilton ed.), IV, 282, 295.
51. *Ibid.*, IV, 305 n., excerpt from a letter of Livingston to Madison, September 21, 1804.

was piqued that Livingston when presenting him to Talleyrand and to Napoleon had not mentioned the fact that he was on his way to Madrid—although Livingston had already announced that fact and hardly needed to do so again. He expressed surprise when he discovered that Livingston would not coöperate with him in Paris, and declared that he had supposed they were acting together —even though Livingston had already told him that they were not. When he arrived in Bordeaux, on December 15, he poured out the whole controversy to Madison. So far as it concerned Livingston, he asserted, it was at an end. There had been "some warm discussion" but "no rupture." Monroe was deceiving only himself, if he meant it; for he took this occasion to give his version of an episode which had occurred in May, 1803, immediately after they had signed the treaty of cession; and he presented it in such a way that it discredited Livingston.[52]

The episode was this. Livingston had suggested to Azara, Spanish ambassador in Paris—when they were together in the French foreign office and Monroe was not present—that Azara should write to his Government proposing that it treat with the United States for the cession of Florida. At the same time Livingston was urging Monroe himself to go to Madrid, although Cambacérès, Lebrun, and even Napoleon were virtually warning him not to do so. Azara told Monroe of Livingston's suggestion, and Monroe then asked Livingston about it. As Monroe had recorded their conversation in his own journal in May, 1803, Livingston replied that he had made the suggestion to Azara, but also said "not to obtain the authority to treat here for it." When Monroe described the event to Madison on December 16, 1804, he did not include this fact. He did not report that Livingston had denied in May that he wished to have the negotiations in Paris. Let us leave it there—with Monroe's statement to Madison that he had come upon the episode in the first place "by accident" and to his "utter astonishment." Whether this were true or not, it did little credit to his recollection or his reporting of facts.[53]

When Monroe wrote again to Madison from Paris, July 6, 1805, on his disappointed way back from Madrid to London and further disappointment, he declared that Talleyrand had refused to aid his negotiation at Madrid because "a project of a very different character countenanced by our agents meaning Mr. L. was before our gov^t." It may be true that Livingston's plan for a loan to Spain was not sagacious. But it is going very far to state that the

52. *Ibid.*, IV, 288, 297.
53. *Ibid.*, IV, 19, 288.

French Government declined to aid Monroe in Madrid because Livingston had another plan before Madison and Jefferson. Monroe, however, went farther:

> Thus is appears by the clearest demonstration that the failure of that negotiation is entirely owing to the misconduct of that individual. Many facts go to prove that the many acts of his misconduct while here, are not attributable to folly alone. I have heretofore thought him entitled to that apology: but I am far from thinking so at present: indeed there is much reason to suspect him of the grossest iniquity. I give you this hint to put you on your guard. Be assured that he will poison what he touches.

Livingston's object, declared Monroe, was to get the appointment as minister to England. Could he say more? Yes, this:

> I sho.^{d} not be surprised if this gov.^{t} on seeing the stand made here & at Madrid, agnst the project submitted by him, to our gov.^{t}, apprehending its failure, in that extent, had charged him, with some other more reasonable, in the hope of better success. If he is admitted, in the least degree, into confidence, or if cause is given him, to infer that sacrifices wo.^{d} be made for peace, or that our councils balance, and are not decided, he will communicate the same here. In short he is the man of all others whom you sho.^{d} avoid, as most deserving the execrations of his country.

Whether this burst from conviction reached after examining evidence, or from a hope that somehow it would obscure his own failure and save his reputation with the Administration at home for the great things he still expected to do in London, is for those to decide who read at length through the papers of James Monroe. They will have also to search the papers of Robert Livingston and the French Archives for corroborative evidence before they finally decide. Until they do, we may be content with what is before us.[55]

Possibly Madison and Jefferson were influenced by this pseudo candor. They seem to have liked Monroe notwithstanding. How they could have continued to respect his intellect is another question. They had already received a different interpretation of this latest phase in the American policy of Talleyrand. Livingston himself had reported in September, 1804, that the French wished to use the American controversy with Spain for the benefit of their own finances. This, coupled with his equally explicit advice in the previous June—"I should not hesitate to take possession of West Florida and act as if no doubt could be entertained of our title"—

54. *Ibid.*, IV, 302–303.
55. Cox, 102–138, chapter on the "Failure of Monroe's Special Mission."

would appear sufficient to have guided Madison through the vaporings of Monroe. Livingston was not the dupe of Talleyrand, as Gerry had been at the time of the X Y Z affair. Nor was Livingston involved, as Monroe himself once had been with the Committee of Public Safety and the Directory.[56]

Robert Livingston deserved, not execrations, but thanks from his superiors. He saw clearly indeed "which way the wind sets." The United States needed West Florida for the outlets to the Gulf which its rivers would give to the produce of their settlements from Georgia to the Mississippi. They did not need to pay France for it now, nor Spain either for that matter.[57]

Let us accept as true the assertion of Livingston's secretary, Thomas Sumpter, to Monroe on October 1, 1803, that Livingston and others were planning to speculate in the lands of Florida. This does not prove that Livingston was intriguing with Frenchmen to pour American money into the French Treasury and to injure his own country. It proves that Robert Livingston sensed how the values of real estate would rise with the transfer of Florida and Louisiana to the United States. They did rise. The American officer who took over Upper Louisiana in March, 1804, and published his account in September, 1812, stated that "the cession raised the general mass of property in Louisiana more than four hundred per centum."[58]

Give full credence, nevertheless, to Sumpter's testimony without searching his motives. Concede, if we must, that there was substance in the gossip of Federalists that Livingston and his family had received large grants of land before the cession of Louisiana. Christopher Gore, who got this information from Hammond in the British foreign office and passed it on to Rufus King, said that he did not believe it. Concede it, even so. We cannot observe Robert Livingston close a notable career without appreciating his service to the American people. This began in the days of the Continental Congress when, as secretary in charge of foreign affairs, he took part in framing and strengthening the policy of separation from European affairs yet maintenance of every advantage in playing close to France. This he helped to do without blocking any overtures from Britain that were beneficial. He was a useful critic in the time of Washington and Adams of the too British policy of

56. Madison (Hunt ed.), VII, 124 n., Livingston to Madison, June 20, 1804. See also ASP FR, II, 561, for Livingston's report on May 20, 1803. See above, pp. 509–510.

57. Monroe (Hamilton ed.), IV, 305 n., Livingston to Madison, September 21, 1804.

58. Cox, 73 n., citing Monroe Papers, X, 1219, in the Library of Congress. Stoddard, 266.

Alexander Hamilton. Then, as minister to France, he applied determination and foresight as he watched Britain become "sour" over the Peace of Amiens and saw Napoleon's colonial ambitions fail in San Domingo. His career was closing now as the effort of the United States to gain more control east of the Mississippi triumphed suddenly in acquiring the whole of that imperial expanse from the great river to the Rocky Mountains.[59]

Old Federalists, like the young Republican Monroe, took pleasure in suspecting and criticizing this old Republican. It made for good politics at home. It also compensated somewhat for personal disappointments. But we must recognize this fact: Robert Livingston had won the right to be placed with Franklin, Washington, Jay, Hamilton, and Jefferson, statesmen who had the vision of empire on the North American continent, and made it reality. If he speculated in land as did contemporaries including James Monroe, Robert Livingston was neither the first nor the last American, prominent or obscure, to keep his own advantage well in mind as he served his country.

It seems clear that Thomas Jefferson really did not expect great things of James Monroe at Madrid, nor care very much if he did not accomplish them. Jefferson had instructed him through Madison in October, 1803, that he was not to go on to Madrid until he was told to do so. Then Jefferson had written personally in January, 1804, that they did not look for a settlement with Spain, that they were determined to obtain or to take what they themselves considered "just limits." Monroe was to govern his stay at Madrid, said Jefferson, by "the procrastinations of artifice or indolence" which he encountered in the Spanish authorities, and by his own determination to accept the appointment in Louisiana. That, said Jefferson, would "admit but of a limited delay." Later, to be sure, Madison did send specific orders to Monroe for his guidance in Spain. But they were so peremptory about West Florida and so exacting with regard to Texas and East Florida that Jefferson could hardly have expected them to prevail, certainly not if the anger of the Spanish minister, Irujo, reflected the feelings of his superiors in Madrid. It was James Monroe rather than Thomas Jefferson who hankered after the mission to Madrid. Jefferson preferred to wait for events to come.[60]

59. King (King ed.), IV, 315. See above, pp. 74 f., 228 n. 3, 232, 244.
60. Madison (Hunt ed.), VII, 71, Madison to Charles Pinckney, October 12, 1803. Monroe (Hamilton ed.), IV, 133, Monroe to Livingston, January 13, 1804. Jefferson (Ford ed.), VIII, 289. Madison (Hunt ed.), VII, 141–153, to Monroe, April 15, 1804. See above, pp. 524–525.

Nor did Thomas Jefferson expect great things of James Monroe at London. When he wanted the serious negotiating about neutral rights to begin, Jefferson sent William Pinkney back to collaborate with James Monroe. Pinkney had been one of the commissioners under the Jay Treaty for adjudicating the claims against Britain on account of spoliations of American commerce during the war with Revolutionary France, and he had achieved prestige and influence among Englishmen for his abilities.[61]

Why Thomas Jefferson used James Monroe at all, after his blundering abroad from 1794 to 1797 and his insubordination to George Washington, is a problem for the special students of Jefferson's character and the history of his party. We may venture, however, that Monroe had practical value as a lieutenant in Virginian politics. Was it also because he had been popular with the "men of the Western waters" ever since he had opposed John Jay in the Congress of 1786 about the closure of the Mississippi? Was he considered a political asset—so long as he shared his duties with others and did not get loose on his own? In any case, he was a devoted personal friend, a loyal follower, a faithful youngster. Jefferson at this time was sixty-one, Monroe forty-six. Some are wise in their twenties. Others emerge from adolescence late, if ever. Some lose political fortune irretrievably with the first mistake. Fame comes to others regardless.[62]

Old Federalists looked on while the young Republican began his diplomacy with the British Government in 1803. They found in the Monroe of those days none of that statesmanship in the legend which has grown about the famous doctrine of 1823. They noted the behavior which made him inconsequential to the ministry of Addington and then of Pitt. They judged him incapable of accomplishing anything in London, if he had the determination; and they doubted this, for Hammond told Christopher Gore that the British foreign office never saw nor heard of Monroe. So far as it was concerned, said Hammond, "he might as well be in Virginia."[63]

Little did these Federalists anticipate events in the train of Louisiana. They were, however, following war with Britain, to make this happy child of fortune President of the United States in 1817 after an easy victory over one of themselves, Rufus King, and with the approval of many of their own kind. Fate had in store for James

61. Updyke, 28–32. Madison (Hunt ed.), VII, 375–395, instructions to Monroe and Pinkney, May 17, 1806. King (King ed.), IV, 537, Gore to King, August 24, 1806.
62. See above, 104 f., 228 f.
63. King (King ed.), IV, 322, Gore to King, November 21, 1803.

Monroe preference then by a narrow margin over William H. Crawford, candidate of a still younger generation of Republicans also founding their aspirations upon the West. But fate had in mind too that James Monroe should become inconsequential again, before his term of office had expired, as these Westerners fought among themselves to decide who should take his place in 1825.[64]

"Our Rope of Sand"

MOST Federalists did not try like Thomas Jefferson in 1804 to peer into the future. Few save John Jay, Rufus King, and Alexander Hamilton had so bold imagination. They thought of the United States as a tight little confederacy on the Atlantic Seaboard, which they were appointed to rule for their aristocratic selves, with perhaps something, if there was any to spare, for those youthful democratic communities so like colonial dependencies beyond the Appalachians. These were called States, indeed, but they should not expect ever to be truly equal with the original thirteen, no matter what the Northwest Ordinance of 1787 had said about the future. If Westerners thought that they could join with Southerners in compelling New Englanders to accept a national policy which led to war again with Britain, Federalist New Englanders knew what they would do. They would break the vicious grip of democracy; they would abandon the Union; they would form their own confederacy under the protection of Great Britain.[65]

Thomas Jefferson, however, had dreamed of a galaxy of American States in the West before there had been a Northwest Ordinance. Now in 1804 he loosed his imagination again as hundreds of his countrymen rushed to Louisiana while others railed at democracy and plotted secession. Amidst a placid commentary upon the ancient philosophers, the doctrines of Jesus, the new work of Malthus on population, he remarked to Dr. Joseph Priestley on January 29, 1804: "I very early saw that Louisiana was indeed a speck in our horizon which was to burst in a tornado." Only their "frank & friendly development of causes & effects," he said, and Napoleon's "good sense" to perceive that the sequence was unavoidable "and would change the face of the world," had averted "that storm." They had not expected Napoleon to see the inevitable before he got into war again; but happily for them, he had done so; and now they were looking out upon an area doubled in size and open

64. Turner, *Rise of the New West*, 245–264.

65. King (King ed.), IV, 318–320, Gore to King from London, November 1, 1803, reflecting opinions from their "friends" in New England.

for the extension of their "free and economical" government, "a great achievement to the mass of happiness which is to ensue."

As for the other storm which he had long observed rising in American affairs, the man who had made "life, liberty, and the pursuit of happiness" classic in the Declaration of Independence had this to say to the English philosopher in 1804:

> Whether we remain one confederacy, or form into Atlantic and Mississippi confederacies, I believe not very important to the happiness of either part. Those of the western confederacy will be as much our children & descendants as those of the eastern, and I feel myself as much identified with that country, in future time, as with this; and did I now foresee a separation at some future day, yet I should feel the duty & desire to promote the western interests as zealously as the eastern, doing all the good for both portions of our future family which should fall within my power.[66]

Thomas Jefferson was preparing himself to face with equanimity Eastern fears of Western political and economic power, and to accept the consequence in dissolution of the Union, if it had to come. He was so serene about it in 1804 because he did not believe that it had to come. It was not until he heard of the Missouri Compromise of 1820, in his old age, not until after he had passed through another struggle with Britain for rights on the sea and mastery of this continent, not until he had lived to see his ideas of confederacy and democracy fused into ideals of nationality, that Thomas Jefferson cried out:

> . . . this momentous question, like a fire bell in the night, awakened and filled me with terror. I considered it at once as the knell of the Union. It is hushed, indeed, for the moment. But this is a reprieve only, not a final sentence. A geographical line, coinciding with a marked principle, moral and political, once conceived and held up to the angry passions of men, will never be obliterated; and every new irritation will mark it deeper and deeper.[67]

By that time the possible line of cleavage was no longer between East and West, between Atlantic and Mississippi confederacies separated by mountain barriers which gave some appearance of reality to division, but between North and South, sections economically diverse and politically at odds even though they were yoked together by national ties of more than blood, revolutionary tradition, and mutual dependence for safety from foreign encroachment. Jefferson could not live to witness the civil war which he

66. Jefferson (Ford ed.), VIII, 293–296.
67. *Ibid.*, X, 157, April 22, 1820, to John Holmes.

feared in 1820, nor those confederacies reunited into one republic afterwards upon democratic principles which he had done so much to promote.

But Thomas Jefferson was not wholly sanguine in 1804 that the expansion of the American people would occur without loss of friendship and coöperation between the Eastern and Western confederacies, if they had to be. Before a month had passed after his letter to Priestley, he wrote to Caesar A. Rodney, to regret that Rodney felt obliged at this time to retire from public life:

> I had looked to you as one of those calculated to give cohesion to our rope of sand. You now see the composition of our public bodies, and how essential system and plan are for conducting our affairs wisely with so bitter a party in opposition to us, who look not at all to what is best for the public, but how they may thwart whatever we may propose, tho' they should thereby sink their country.

To his Postmaster General, Gideon Granger of Connecticut, Jefferson wrote on April 16, 1804, another letter wise in the ways of politics and yet fearful that things might not come out as they should in accord with that wisdom.[68]

Granger had told him of a "federal scheme afloat"—the plan to form a coalition of Federalists and a minority of Republicans in New York, New Jersey, and New England. Jefferson knew that the Federalists could never return to power under their own name. He was equally convinced that they could hope to win over a minority only of the Republicans in those states. Still, they might do that; and if they did, they would surely dominate the coalition. "Thus," he said, "a bastard system of federo-republicanism will rise on the ruins of the true principles of our revolution." "The idea of forming 7 Eastern states," he declared, "is moreover clearly to form the basis of a separation of the Union. Is it possible that real republicans can be gulled by such a bait?" Jefferson sensed that they could not. He prayed, in seeming resignation to the ultimate triumph of good, that "crooked schemes" would end by overwhelming the schemers. And, after all misgivings had passed in review, he was confident that his prayers would be answered, for the time being at least.[69]

So ran the ways of practical politics. There were just too many "real republicans" living throughout New England and New York like Gideon Granger of Connecticut, interested in the patronage of the Federal Government. Besides, there were Federalists such as

68. *Ibid.*, VIII, 296–297, 298–300.
69. *Ibid.*, VIII, 298–300.

Alexander Hamilton and Rufus King, who would neither risk losing control of their party to a coalition nor forsake their own aspirations to empire, whatever their contempt for the rule of Jefferson and his democrats.

Senator Pickering of Massachusetts also was hoping and praying, but that "the people of the East" would realize they could not "reconcile their habits, views, and interests with those of the South and West" who were "beginning to rule with a rod of iron" and would make the Constitution "assume any shape as an instrument to crush the Federalists." "The independence of the judges is now directly assailed," said he, "and the majority are either so blind or so well trained that it will most undoubtedly be destroyed." Should the Federalists sit still until their principles were overwhelmed even in the Eastern States? They should not. The principles of their own revolt from George III pointed to the remedy—"separation." Jefferson's friends were planning to make him President for life![70]

Timothy Pickering's correspondent, George Cabot, Federalist sage of Massachusetts, saw the matter in much the same light as Thomas Jefferson. Cabot mourned the helplessness of New England's aristocrats, but he knew that its common people would never rise and strike in 1804 at the call of Timothy Pickering. He replied: "Even in New England, where there is among the body of the people more wisdom and virtue than in any other part of the United States, we are full of errors, which no reasoning could eradicate, if there were a Lycurgus in every village. *We are democratic* altogether, and I hold democracy in its natural operation to be *the government of the worst.*" His conclusion was wise. The people of New England would not rebel unless some cause intervened "which should be very generally felt and distinctly understood as chargeable to the misconduct of our Southern masters, such, for example, as a war with Great Britain, manifestly provoked by our rulers."[71]

Timothy Pickering was no Lycurgus, Spartan law giver to Helots of Massachusetts, that is certain. If he had been, he could not have been in every village, much as his spirit commanded him. The elections of 1804 in Massachusetts and the District of Maine confirmed George Cabot's opinion. James Sullivan, Republican, received 23,979 votes to 30,007 for the Federalist, Governor Strong,

70. Lodge, *Cabot,* 337–341, Pickering to Cabot, January 29, 1804. Pickering Papers, XIV, 93.

71. Lodge, *Cabot,* 341–344, Cabot to Pickering, February 14, 1804. Pickering Papers, XXVII, 53.

standing for reëlection. The Republican party gained seats in the
Legislature. And Alexander Hamilton and Rufus King still had
influence among Federalist New Englanders.[72]

Disregarding personal danger, Hamilton threw himself against
the conspiracy which followed the ratification of the Louisiana
treaty by the Senate. The plan was to elect Aaron Burr Governor
of New York with Federalist votes; Burr was then to swing New
York and New Jersey into line with New England and help to form
the Northern Confederacy. That he could, or would, have led New
York and New Jersey out of the Union if he had been chosen Governor is beside the point. The course ran straight to the dueling
ground of Weehawken, as Hamilton prevented the election of Burr.

One of Hamilton's last acts was to write to his old henchman,
Theodore Sedgwick of Massachusetts. Whether or not he willed
it so, Hamilton struck hard in behalf of Thomas Jefferson. He told
Sedgwick that he had wished to write a long letter explaining his
view of the events and his own intentions for the future. There
was time left now however, he said, to express "but one sentiment."
It was:

> . . . dismemberment of our empire will be a clear sacrifice of great
> positive advantages without any counterbalancing good, administering
> no relief to our real disease, which is *democracy,* the poison of which,
> by a subdivision, will only be the more concentrated in each part, and
> consequently the more virulent. King is on his way for Boston, where
> you may chance to see him, and hear from himself his sentiments. God
> bless you.

Then Alexander Hamilton faced the morrow and Aaron Burr.[73]

Federalist Lamentations

NOTES taken by John Quincy Adams at the time and his subsequent recollections would prove that Rufus King, signer of the
Constitution, fought disunion in 1804, if we did not have Hamilton's word that King was returning to his native Massachusetts
to declare his "sentiments." Adams had stopped at New York,
April 8, on his way home from Washington. He had called upon
Aaron Burr and heard him say that he would not be a candidate
for the governorship of New York except for "the absolute necessity of interposing to save the country from ruin by these family
combinations, &c., &c., &c." Then Adams "spent the evening"
with King, and "found Mr. Pickering there." He dined on the tenth

72. Robinson, 42.
73. Hamilton (Lodge ed.), X, 457–458, July 10, 1804.

with King and passed another evening, this time "in particular conversation." He enlarged upon these notes later, when writing as President of the United States in 1829 to defend himself against the charges of Federalists in Massachusetts. He recalled how King had told him, after Pickering had withdrawn, that Pickering had been going over with both Hamilton and himself that day the scheme for separating the States. King had asked if Adams had heard of it in Washington. Yes, he had—"much, but not from Colonel Pickering." Then King had said that he entirely disapproved of the project, and was happy to tell Adams that so did General Hamilton. Adams had "rejoiced" to hear it. He himself was "utterly averse to the project," he wrote, and "much concerned at the countenance" which he had heard it was receiving in Connecticut and in Boston.[74]

John Quincy Adams had just become the junior Senator from Massachusetts and so had not been present in October when the Louisiana treaty had been ratified or he might have voted with Pickering against it, as he did later against the act enabling the President to take possession of the territory. He distinguished then between the power to acquire lands and the power to incorporate them in the Union as the treaty with France stipulated, without first having an amendment to the Constitution. He held that the treaty-making power alone could not make new Territories and States in the Union. But this was far from agreeing with Timothy Pickering that the Federalists ought to destroy the Union because they had not been able to stop the purchase of Louisiana. Adams stood with Hamilton, Jefferson, and King for empire.[75]

Still, being otherwise good Federalists in 1804, John Quincy Adams and Rufus King "lamented" together that evening: "one inevitable consequence of the annexation of Louisiana to the Union would be to diminish the relative weight and influence of the Northern section." This would aggravate the evil of representation based upon slavery according to the three-fifths rule in the Constitution, and it would weaken the "line of defence against foreign invasion."

They conceded, however, that Jefferson's "alternative" had been "Louisiana and the mouths of the Mississippi in the possession of France, under Napoleon Bonaparte." This would have been insufferable. They felt therefore, as the situation was now, that a "fearful

74. J. Q. Adams, *Memoirs*, I, 313, April 10, 1804. H. Adams, *Docs. relating to N. E. Federalism*, 147–148, J. Q. Adams, *To The Citizens of the United States* replying to "Appeal of the Massachusetts Federalists, January 28, 1829."

75. Senate Ex. Journ., III, 303, October 26, 1803. J. Q. Adams, *Memoirs*, I, 266, 268. For Adams' coolness toward Pickering see also *ibid.*, I, 287–289, January 11–15, 1804.

cause of war" had been removed; and henceforth, that France would be changed by her "altered and steadily operating interests" into a "natural ally" again.[76]

So Adams and King reasoned and found some comfort in 1804, according to Adams' memory in 1829. Neither seems to have taken thought that evening—with Jefferson, Gallatin, Livingston—of the British fleet. But it had checked even a Napoleon Bonaparte on his way to empire in the Americas. Could it not as easily have kept the United States from New Orleans and the lower Mississippi in 1804, while troops from Canada, and then settlers, followed the traders across the portages to the Missouri, the Red River of the North, and the upper Mississippi?

Having the advantage of retrospect, we conclude that Britain had all that she could do then to save herself and her interests in Europe from Napoleon, without undertaking at the same time to expand her colonial domain in America. We think, as evidently her statesmen did then, that she had little choice but to purchase American neutrality by financing Napoleon's sale of Louisiana for him. We feel confident that the hordes of American pioneers would have overwhelmed British authority in the trans-Mississippi country for their own Government as effectively as they influenced Napoleon to abandon Talleyrand's plan in Louisiana. But could they really have done so in 1804?

There can be no definitive answer. What might have been is blocked for us by immediate events from which our judgment cannot be shaken free. The historical facts are that the British fleet and landing force which had all but come in 1803 did appear before New Orleans in 1814 and also that, when they arrived, it was too late. When Britain finally had conquered her fears of French invasion and Napoleon's rule in Europe, the American pioneers had made the Mississippi Valley their own. Their increase along the tributaries of the great river, from Ohio to Missouri, from Illinois to Louisiana, had been tremendous between those significant years. And they were eager to take the offensive even against Britain. Indians would not have said that their "conquest of Louisiana" had been either "noiseless" or "bloodless," but Europeans had to admit that it was "unrelenting," and successful.[77]

Perhaps Rufus King was too inspired that evening in 1804 by his own triumphs in London to consider the menace of the British fleet. His ultimatum to Addington and the prime minister's as-

76. H. Adams, *Docs. relating to the N. E. Federalism,* 148.

77. Twelfth Census, 1900, Vol. I, part 1. Quotations from Pelzer in Iowa *Journ. Hist. and Pol.,* XI, 21–24.

surance in 1803 that Britain would be pleased to see the United States take Louisiana may have obscured for him the British antipathy to the westward expansion of the United States. Possibly his early visions with Miranda of empire for both Britain and the United States had been stirred again by his letters from Christopher Gore. It may have been impossible for him to conceive that Britons would not voluntarily share with Americans the fruits of victory over absolutism and tyranny. (There indeed would have been more than enough to go around.) But John Quincy Adams was not thinking in the atmosphere of 1804 when he published his account of their "conversation." He wrote in 1829, years after Andrew Jackson had defeated Wellington's veterans before New Orleans on January 8, 1815, and after the Monroe Doctrine of 1823 (to which Adams himself contributed greatly) had defied Britain as well as the Holy Alliance of European monarchs.[78]

There is irony in this. Jackson's success at New Orleans was one of the very few in that strange war which Americans could acclaim without question as an American victory. More significant are the facts which Adams must have observed as a peace commissioner in 1814—before the Battle of New Orleans. Britain's diplomats at Ghent recognized the power of the United States in America. They took the position of the weaker party on the defensive. They sought an Indian buffer state and terms of security for the British dominions against American encroachment. They abandoned pretension to the use of the Mississippi River, letting fall Rufus King's convention of 1803. They accepted final conditions of peace that were hardly commensurate with British achievements against American arms on both land and sea from 1812 to 1814.[79]

It is usual to say that the British were war-weary in 1814 and too involved still in European affairs, in spite of their triumph over Napoleon, to relish continuing a minor imbroglio with the American people. That no doubt is largely true. But it is as evident that Britons understood the meaning in the rapidly increasing strength of the United States. Arrangements were made in 1817 to limit naval forces on the Great Lakes; and in 1818, joint claims to the Oregon country beyond the Rockies were acknowledged. The boundary of western Canada was fixed at the forty-ninth degree of latitude, as Jefferson had presumed in 1804.[80]

78. See above, p. 316 f. King (King ed.), IV, 298–300, Gore to King, August 30, 1803; 308–309, September 22; 313–314, October 21; 321–322, November 21. For King's subsequent attitude toward Miranda, see *ibid.*, IV, 517–532, 1805–1806.

79. Updyke, 198–234, 217. Miller, *Treaties*, II, 574–584.

80. Miller, *Treaties*, II, 645–654, 658–662.

There is irony, too, in the Monroe Doctrine. It depended for its reality upon the British fleet, and Britain's desire to protect the Latin American Republics from Mexico to the Argentine for the benefit of her own commerce and industry. Canning boasted with much truth that he had called the New World into existence to redress the balance of the Old. But equally significant is the fact that he resented the American doctrine as a warning to Britain quite as much as to the continental powers. The United States had compelled Spain to yield East Florida in 1819 without hesitating over Britain's old claims to the territory, and without compensating her for the high-handed execution of her subjects in the process. And before President Monroe's famous message to Congress in 1823, John Quincy Adams as Secretary of State had announced that Cuba was a "natural appendage" to this continent which in fifty years would become virtually a part of the "North American Union." It was due notice given to the British fleet cruising in the West Indies.[81]

These things the British had seen and heard, had chosen to make nothing of them, and to concentrate their attention upon other interests around the Caribbean and in South America. Perhaps that is why John Quincy Adams recorded no personal observations upon the British menace to New Orleans and the newly acquired domain of the American people across the Mississippi River in 1804 when he published his account in 1829.

The Far View Again

THE President of 1804 had no such advantages of afterthought upon the relative weaknesses of the old enemy, Britain, and the comparative reformations in the character of the "natural ally," France. Thomas Jefferson could not even be sure in 1804 that the "crooked schemes" in New England would end once and for all in confounding the schemers. George Cabot's opinion was prophetic. Southern leaders did have to face Northern threats of secession as they got the United States into another war with Britain. Active sedition was to appear in the Northeast, and Hartford Conventionists were to have their say about amendments to the Constitution, before the Jeffersonian President, James Madison—luckily saved from British capture by his flight from Washington—could announce that the Treaty of Ghent marked the end of a war "signalized by the most brilliant successes." He was to be fearfully anxious before he could greet the angry resolutions of those New

81. Temperley, *Canning*, 154. Perkins, *Monroe Doctrine*, 248–250. Adams, *Writings*, VII, 369–372, to Hugh Nelson, April 28, 1823.

Englanders with the tolerant good humor of the victor abroad and at home.[82]

Thomas Jefferson and James Madison were to have grave experiences before this happy outcome. There was to be the dark conspiracy in the Southwest of Aaron Burr and James Wilkinson, commander of the American Army but paid agent of Spain. Notwithstanding Wayne's victory at Fallen Timbers, Jay's Treaty, and the Treaty of Greenville, British agents continued to intrigue with the Indians under Tecumseh in the Northwest. And Britain raided American neutral ships and impressed American sailors until the spirit of this country rose to the hysteria of war. France, too, despoiled American commerce. And Spain stubbornly refused to acknowledge the loss of West Florida even though American settlers there revolted and obtained annexation to the United States.

The "War Hawks" of the West forced Madison at last to declare war upon Britain. Even Jefferson himself, stirred by their ambition, pride, and fear, came to think in 1812 that "the seeds of genius" needed only "soil and season to germinate" and would "develop themselves among our military men." Said he then: "The acquisition of Canada this year, as far as the neighborhood of Quebec, will be a mere matter of marching, and will give us experience for the attack of Halifax the next, and the final expulsion of England from the American continent."[83]

All these experiences Thomas Jefferson could not anticipate in 1804 and forestall in the name of peaceful expansion. But he could look confidently to the future of the United States in the light of what had then come to pass. He was safely reëlected President of the United States. The Federalists had not broken the Union. Britain and France were no longer ancient enemy and natural ally, enabled by that relationship to confuse and divide counsels in the American Government on affairs of state. The American people were responsible only to themselves now, freed from all obligations of the French alliance, real or professed. Both Britain and France stood clearly in view as foreign states—both hostile to the westward advance of the American people, but thoroughly engrossed again in war upon each other. They might ravage American commerce on the seas, but they could hardly keep the Government of the American nation from extending its law into the continent with its people.

The long quest of America's statesmen from Franklin to Jefferson, of Jay, Washington, Hamilton, Livingston, even John Adams,

82. Richardson, I, 552, February 18, 1815.
83. Jefferson (Ford ed.), IX, 365–367, to William Duane, August 4, 1812.

had come to achievement. The United States had title to the whole Mississippi Valley, not merely the eastern portion caught between British forts on the Great Lakes and Spanish posts in the Indian country to the south; they had both banks of the great river and all of its tributaries far across the plains to the Rocky Mountains. Franklin's "street door" on the Mississippi was now to be an interior portal to a vast territory entirely American. Gone were France and all French pretensions worth the name. Talleyrand still planned, it may be, but the hope of empire which he had inherited from Moustier, Collot, Adet, Fauchet was futile—though Napoleon III had yet to learn. The American nation faced Britain alone. Spain lingered, but Spain was too impotent to be anything of an obstacle, so impotent in fact as to invite American aggression. As for the Indians, once so dangerous in the time of Pontiac, so determined before "Mad Anthony" Wayne, so obstinate still in the Southwest, Thomas Jefferson no longer had to fear.

The Delawares, he was happy to report to Congress, had ceded their lands to the Government from the Wabash down to the Ohio. Those beyond the Mississippi might serve as a constabulary force to hold white men in check until they had properly taken up the land on this side. But about those Indians too Jefferson was beginning to change his mind. Perhaps Rufus King was right. It would take a cordon of troops constantly on patrol to hold white men back from the Missouri, the Arkansas, the Red River valleys. Before Lewis and Clark had returned from their "literary pursuit" into the far Northwest, Thomas Jefferson had spoken to Congress once more upon the wisdom of peace with Europe, but about Indians with an overtone that was different:

> . . . the endeavors to enlighten them on the fate which awaits their present course of life, to induce them to exercise their reason, follow its dictates, and change their pursuits with the change of circumstances, have powerful obstacles to encounter . . . they, too, have their anti-philosophers, who find an interest in keeping things in their present state, who dread reformation, and exert all their faculties to maintain the ascendency of habit over the duty of improving our reason, and obeying its mandates.[84]

There were bounds to the attributes of peace. An Indian philosophy of live-as-you-have-and-as-you-please, if it endeavored to stand in the way of the American people and their rising empire, was entitled to respect henceforth no more than the rival aspirations of Frenchmen, Britons, or Spaniards. This was hard. It was ruthless. But it was true to the character of this people.

84. Jefferson (Ford ed.), VIII, 345, March 4, 1805, Second Inaugural.

APPENDIX

ACKNOWLEDGMENTS

THE materials for this book have been gathered in the course of teaching the history of the United States over a period of years in Yale University and Phillips Academy, and the volume has been written with the students of those classes constantly in mind. It could not have been done without the aid of the particular studies of such experts in their respective fields as Clarence W. Alvord, Edward S. Corwin, Samuel Flagg Bemis, Henri Doniol, William K. Woolery, William R. Manning, William S. Robertson, Frederick Jackson Turner, Arthur Preston Whitaker, E. Wilson Lyon, Frederick L. Nussbaum, Charles A. Beard, James A. James, and Isaac J. Cox. I have tried to show my indebtedness to their scholarship. If I have anywhere failed to do so, it has been inadvertently; or else the conclusions of these specialists have become so much a part of the fabric of American historiography that it is difficult to give proper credit to the original authority. In any case my obligation to them is gratefully acknowledged. The pertinent works of Henry Adams, the Edward Everett Hales, Bernard Faÿ, Andrew C. McLaughlin, Paul C. Phillips, Thomas M. Marshall, Frank Monaghan, Mary Treudley, Beverley W. Bond, Villiers du Terrage, Edmond G. P. F. Fitzmaurice, Mildred S. Fletcher, Alfred T. Mahan, Samuel E. Morison, James B. Perkins, William R. Riddell, William A. Robinson, and others have also been kept at hand during the construction of the manuscript. Documentary sources are cited in the footnotes and the accompanying bibliographical list. They have been studied independently whenever possible. The *Guide to the Diplomatic History of the United States* published by Samuel Flagg Bemis and Grace Gardner Griffin in 1935 has been invaluable both in uncovering material and indicating its importance. Special thanks for great courtesy and assistance are due to Grace Gardner Griffin and Thomas P. Martin in the Manuscripts Division of the Library of Congress, officials in the Department of State, Walter B. Briggs and his associates in the Harvard College Library, to the Sterling Memorial Library of Yale, the Massachusetts Historical Society, the Oliver Wendell Holmes Library of Andover, and the Connecticut Historical Society in Hartford. Arthur Preston Whitaker has read the whole of the manuscript with particular helpfulness through the tangle of Spanish affairs upon which he is an authority. Archibald Freeman, Howard Rice, and Phelps Putnam have most generously given both historical and literary criticism. Allen Johnson's precision and the curiosity of Frederick Jackson Turner, under both of whom it was a privilege to study, have been constant influences.

ARTHUR BURR DARLING

ABBREVIATIONS

AAE CP EU—Archives Étrangères, Correspondance Politique, États-Unis. Also Mémoires et Documents and Suppléments.
AHR—The American Historical Review.
AHA Rpt.—The American Historical Association Reports.
ASP FR—American State Papers, Foreign Relations.
ASP IA—American State Papers, Indian Affairs.
MHS—The Massachusetts Historical Society.
MVHR—The Mississippi Valley Historical Review.

BIBLIOGRAPHY

Papers and Transcripts

CONNECTICUT HISTORICAL SOCIETY. Papers of Oliver Wolcott jr.

DEPARTMENT OF STATE, ARCHIVES. Consular letters, Cape Haitien, September, 1797—October, 1799.

—— Dispatches from Rufus King, "England," vol. IX.

—— Dispatches from Robert Livingston and James Monroe, "France," vols. VIII, VIIIa.

—— Instructions to ministers, February, 1797—September, 1800, vols. IV, V. Madison's letter of instructions to Livingston, September 28, 1801, is in Instructions to consuls, vol. I.

HARVARD COLLEGE LIBRARY, Treasure Room. Fenno's *Gazette of the United States*, Philadelphia, 1791–95.

—— Oswald's correspondence and reports, May, 1782—January, 1783; selections from Fitzherbert's papers. Transcripts in the Sparks collection, vol. XL.

—— B. F. Stevens' facsimiles of manuscripts in European archives relating to America, 1773–83.

LIBRARY OF CONGRESS, Manuscripts Division. Henry Adams' transcripts from French and British state papers.

—— Archives affaires étrangères, correspondance politique, États-Unis; mémoires et documents; suppléments. Photocopies of the originals in France.

—— Alexander Hamilton's papers.

—— Thomas Jefferson's papers.

—— Robert Liston's papers. Correspondence with Grenville and relevant papers from the archives of Canada and Nova Scotia. Typescripts.

MASSACHUSETTS HISTORICAL SOCIETY. John Marshall's journal while in Paris, September 27, 1797—April 11, 1798. Manuscript copy with names included. In the Pickering papers, LI, 539–657.

—— Timothy Pickering's papers. For a "historical index" to them, see MHS Collections, 6th series, vol. VIII.

Published Materials
Correspondence Diaries Writings Documents
(Arranged for person of interest rather than editor)

ADAMS, ABIGAIL. Letters of Mrs. Adams, the wife of John Adams. 1848. (C. F. Adams ed.)

ADAMS, JOHN. The life and works of John Adams. 1856. (C. F. Adams ed.)

———, ——— Warren-Adams letters, MHS Collections, vols. LXXII, LXXIII. 1917, 1925. (W. C. Ford ed.) Chiefly correspondence among John Adams, Samuel Adams, and James Warren.

ADAMS, JOHN QUINCY. Memoirs. . . . 1874. (C. F. Adams ed.)

———, ——— ——— Writings. . . . 1913. (W. C. Ford ed.)

ADAMS, SAMUEL. Writings. . . . 1908. (H. A. Cushing ed.)

AMERICAN STATE PAPERS. Documents, legislative and executive. 1832-61.

AMES, FISHER. Works. . . . 1854. (Seth Ames ed.)

ANNALS OF CONGRESS. 1849. (Gales and Seaton publishers.)

ANNUAL REGISTER, THE. 1806.

ATTORNEYS GENERAL, THE. Official opinions. . . . 1852.

BAYARD, JAMES A. "Papers . . . 1796-1815," AHA Rpt. 1913, vol. II. (E. Donnan ed.)

BLOUNT, WILLIAM. "Documents on the Blount conspiracy, 1795-1797," AHR X, 574-606 (1904-1905). (F. J. Turner ed.)

BONAPARTE, NAPOLEON. Correspondance de Napoléon Ier. 1861.

BRISSOT DE WARVILLE. The commerce of America with Europe . . . shewing importance of the American revolution to France. 1794. Clavière co-author.

BURKE, EDMUND. Writings and speeches. 1901.

CABOT, GEORGE. Life and letters. . . . 1878. (H. C. Lodge)

CANADA. Report of the Public Archives. . . . 1872– (Brymner ed.)

CHALMERS, G., ed. A collection of treaties between Great Britain and other powers. 1790.

CIRCOURT, A. DE, ed. Histoire de l'action commune de la France et de l'Amérique pour l'indépendance des États-Unis par George Bancroft. 1876. Documents in 3d. vol.

CLARK, GEORGE ROGERS. "Correspondence of Clark and Genet," AHA Rpt. 1896, I, 930–1107. (F. J. Turner ed.)

COLLOT, VICTOR. A journey in North America. 1826.

CONTINENTAL CONGRESS. Journals. . . . 1774-86. 1904-34. (W. C. Ford and J. C. Fitzpatrick eds.)

——— ——— Letters of members. . . . 1921-34. (E. C. Burnett ed.)

CUMBERLAND, RICHARD. Memoirs. . . . 1807.

DONIOL, H., ed. "Conférences de M. de Rayneval avec les ministres Anglais," Revue d'Histoire Diplomatique, VI, 62–89 (1892).

———Histoire de la participation de la France à l'éstablissement des États-Unis d'Amérique, correspondance diplomatique et documents. 1884-99.

DOYSIÉ, A., ed. "Journal of a French traveller in the American colonies, 1765," AHR XXVI, 726-747; XXVII, 70-89 (1920-1922).

DROPMORE PAPERS. The manuscripts of J. B. Fortescue Esq. preserved at Dropmore. 1892-1927. (Historical Manuscripts Commission.) They contain reports from Gouverneur Morris to Grenville in 1796. Gouverneur has been confused with Robert Morris in the index (vol. III).

DuPont, Victor. "DuPont, Talleyrand, and the French spoliations," MHS Proceedings, 49, 63–79 (1915–16). (S. E. Morison ed.)
Durand, J., ed. New materials for the history of the American revolution. 1889. Translations from documents in the French archives.

Ellicott, Andrew. The journal of. . . . (2d ed.) 1814.
England. "English policy toward America in 1790–1791," AHR VII, 706–735; VIII, 78–86 (1901–03).

Folwell, R., printer. The laws of the United States of America. 1796. "Published by Authority."
Fox, Charles James. Memorials and correspondence. . . . 1853–57. (Lord John Russell ed.)
France. Archives parlementaires de 1787 à 1860. . . . 1867–1914.
—— "Correspondence of the French ministers to the United States, 1791–1797," AHA Rpt. 1903, vol. II. (F. J. Turner ed.)
—— "Documents on the relations of France to Louisiana, 1792–1795," AHR III, 490–516 (1897–98). (F. J. Turner ed.)
Franklin, Benjamin. Writings. . . . 1905–1907. (A. H. Smyth ed.)
Fries, John. The two trials of John Fries. . . . 1800. (T. Carpenter reporter.)

Gallatin, Albert. Report on finances, October, 1803. Printed in the Reports of the Secretaries of the Treasury, I, 263 ff.
——, —— Writings. . . . 1879. (H. Adams ed.)
George the Third. Correspondence. . . . 1760–1783. 1927. (Sir John W. Fortescue ed.)
Godoy, Manuel de. Memoirs. . . . 1836.

Hamilton, Alexander. Works. . . . 1850. (J. C. Hamilton ed.)
——, —— Works. . . . 1903. (H. C. Lodge ed.)
Henry, Patrick. Life, correspondence, and speeches. 1891. (W. W. Henry ed.)
Higginson, Stephen. "Letters . . . 1783–1804," AHA Rpt. 1896, I, 704–841. (J. F. Jameson ed.)

Iredell, James. Life and correspondence. . . . 1857–1858. (G. J. McRee ed.)

Jay, John. Correspondence and public papers. . . . 1890. (H. P. Johnston ed.)
Jefferson, Thomas. The correspondence of Jefferson and Du Pont de Nemours. 1931. (G. Chinard ed.)
——, —— Correspondence between Thomas Jefferson and Pierre Samuel Du Pont de Nemours, 1798–1817. 1930. (D. Malone ed.)
——, —— Documents relating to the purchase and exploration of Louisiana. 1904. It contains Jefferson's paper on "The limits and bounds

of Louisiana," dated September 7, 1803, and Dunbar's account of "The exploration of the Red, the Black, and the Washita rivers," under the date, October 16, 1804. (From the collections of the American Philosophical Society.)

——, ——Writings. . . . 1892–1899. (P. L. Ford ed.)

KING, RUFUS. Life and correspondence. . . . 1894–1900. (C. R. King ed.)

McHENRY, JAMES. Life and correspondence. . . . 1907. (B. C. Steiner.)

MADISON, JAMES. Writings. . . . 1900–1910. (G. Hunt ed.)

MALLOY, W. M., ed. Treaties, conventions. . . . 1776–1909. 1910.

MALMESBURY. Diaries and correspondence of James Harris, first earl of Malmesbury. 1845.

MANGOURIT, MICHEL A. "The Mangourit correspondence in respect to Genet's projected attack upon the Floridas, 1793–1794," AHA Rpt. 1897, 569–679. (F. J. Turner ed.)

MARTENS, G. F. VON, ed. Receuil des traités . . . depuis 1761. . . . 1817–.

MICHIGAN PIONEER AND HISTORICAL SOCIETY. Collections. . . . 1877–.

MILLER, HUNTER, ed. Treaties and other international acts of the United States of America. 1931–.

MONROE, JAMES. A view of the conduct of the executive in the foreign affairs of the United States connected with the mission to the French Republic. . . . 1797.

——, —— Writings. . . . 1898–1903. (S. M. Hamilton ed.)

MOORE, J. B. History and digest of international arbitrations to which the United States has been a party. . . . 1898.

MORRIS, GOUVERNEUR. Diary and letters. . . . 1888. (A. C. Morris ed.) To avoid the granddaughter's sense of delicacy, see "A diary of the French revolution." 1939. (B. C. Davenport ed.)

MOUSTIER. "Correspondence of the Comte de Moustier with the Comte de Montmorin, 1787–1789," AHR VIII, 709–733; IX, 86–96 (1902–04). (H. E. Bourne ed.)

MURRAY, W. VANS. "Letters of William Vans Murray to John Quincy Adams, 1797–1803," AHA Rpt. 1912, 343–715. (W. C. Ford ed.)

NEW ENGLAND. Documents relating to New England Federalism. (1877) 1905. (H. Adams ed.)

PAINE, THOMAS. Writings. . . . 1894–1896. (M. D. Conway ed.)

PINCKNEY, CHARLES. "Charles Pinckney's reply to Jay, August 16, 1786, regarding a treaty with Spain," AHR X, 817–827 (1904–05). (W. C. Ford ed.)

PITKIN, T. A statistical view of the commerce of the United States of America. . . . 1835.

PLUMER, WILLIAM. Memorandum of proceedings in the United States Senate, 1803–1807. 1923. (E. S. Brown ed.)

RANDOLPH, EDMUND. Accounts. . . . Executive Documents of the Senate, 50th Cong. 2d sess., No. 58 and Journal of the Senate, 50th Cong. 2d sess., pp. 101, 128. 1888–89.
——, —— Political truth. . . . 1796. Published anonymously.
——, —— A vindication of Mr. Randolph's resignation. 1795.
RICHARDSON, J. D., ed. Messages and papers of the Presidents. 1900.
ROBERTSON, J. A., ed. Louisiana under the rule of Spain, France, and the United States, 1785–1807. 1911.
RUSSELL, PETER. The correspondence of the Honourable Peter Russell, with allied documents relating to his administration. . . . 1932–1936. He was the governor of Upper Canada during the absence of Simcoe on leave. (E. A. Cruikshank ed.)

ST. CLAIR, ARTHUR. The St. Clair papers, life and public services. . . . 1882. (W. H. Smith ed.)
SCHMIDT, C., ed. Receuil des principaux textes législatifs et administratifs concernant le commerce de 1788 a l'an XI. In the Bulletin d'Histoire Économique de la Revolution. . . . 1912.
SCOTT, J. B., ed. Armed neutralities of 1780 and 1800. 1918.
—— The controversy over neutral rights between the United States and France, 1797–1800. 1917. Cited as Scott.
SIMCOE, JOHN GRAVES. Correspondence. . . . 1923–26. (E. A. Cruikshank ed.)
STRACHEY, HENRY. Papers. . . . In: The Sixth Report of the British Historical Manuscripts Commission. 1877–78.
SURREY, N. M. MILLER. Calendar of manuscripts in Paris for the history of the Mississippi Valley. 1908

TALLEYRAND. Correspondance diplomatique . . . : le ministère de Talleyrand sous le Directoire. 1891. (G. Pallain ed.) Cited as Pallain.
—— Correspondance diplomatique . . . : la mission de Talleyrand à Londres en 1792. 1889. (G. Pallain ed.)
—— Memoirs. . . . 1891–1892. (Broglie ed.) Introduction by Whitelaw Reid.
—— "Mémoire lu à l'Institut," April 4, 1797, printed in The Pamphleteer, IV, 463 ff. (1813–28). It was followed by an essay on the advantages to be obtained from New Orleans.
TOUSSAINT LOUVERTURE. "Letters of Toussaint Louverture and of Edward Stevens, 1798–1800," AHR XVI, 64–101 (1910–1911). (J. F. Jameson ed.)
TRUMBULL, JOHN. Autobiography, reminiscences and letters, from 1756 to 1841. 1841.

UNITED STATES. Diplomatic correspondence . . . 1783–1789. 1837.
—— Journal of the executive proceedings of the Senate. Volume III, October, 1803.
—— Public statutes at large.

—— State papers and public documents. . . . 1819. (T. B. Wait publisher.)

—— State trials . . . during the administrations of Washington and Adams. 1849. (F. Wharton ed.)

—— The United States and Spain in 1790; An episode in diplomacy described from hitherto unpublished sources. 1890. (W. C. Ford ed.)

UNITED STATES CENSUS. A century of population growth, 1790–1900.

VAUGHAN, BENJAMIN. "Letters . . . ," MHS Proceedings, 1903, 2d series, XVII, 406–438. (C. C. Smith ed.)

WASHINGTON, GEORGE. Diaries. . . . 1748–1799. 1925. (J. C. Fitzpatrick ed.)

——, —— Farewell Address. 1935. (V. H. Paltsits ed.)

——, —— Writings. . . . 1889–1893. (W. C. Ford ed.)

——, —— Writings. . . . 1834–1837. (J. Sparks ed.)

WHARTON, F., ed. The revolutionary diplomatic correspondence of the United States. 1889. Cited as Wharton.

WHITWORTH, LORD. England and Napoleon in 1803; Being the despatches of Lord Whitworth and others. 1887. (O. Browning ed.) Cited as Browning.

WITT, C. H. DE. Thomas Jefferson; Etude historique sur la démocratie Americaine. 1861. Documents in the appendix.

WOLCOTT, OLIVER. Memoirs of the administrations of Washington and John Adams. 1846. (G. Gibbs ed.)

——, —— "Secretary Wolcott's report, December 14, 1795," ASP Finance, I, 360, 371. On the American debt to France.

WOODBURY, LEVI. Report on cotton as Secretary of the Treasury. . . . 1836. Executive Documents, 24th Cong. 1st sess., No. 146.

Books and Articles

ADAMS, E. D. *The influence of Grenville on Pitt's foreign policy, 1787–1798.* 1904.

ADAMS, H. *History of the United States of America* (1801–17). 1891.

—— *The life of Albert Gallatin.* 1879.

ALDEN, G. H. *New governments west of the Alleghenies before 1780.* 1897.

ALLEN, G. W. *Our naval war with France.* 1909.

ALVORD, C. W. *The Mississippi Valley in British politics; A study of the trade, land speculation, and experiments in imperialism culminating in the American revolution.* 1917.

ANDERSON, F. M. "The enforcement of the alien and sedition laws," AHA Rpt. 1912, 115–126.

AUSTIN, J. T. *The life of Elbridge Gerry.* With contemporary letters. 1828–29.

BANCROFT, G. *History of the formation of the Constitution of the United States of America.* 1882. The appendix contains letters and papers (indexed) "from his own collections of authentic copies."

—— *History of the United States, from the discovery of the American continent.* 1859. This edition has footnotes with citations.

BARBÉ-MARBOIS, F. *Histoire de la Louisiane et de la cession de cette colonie par la France aux États-Unis.* . . . 1829.

—— The history of Louisiana, particularly of the cession of that colony to the United States of America. . . . (American translation.) 1830.

BASSETT, J. S. *The Federalist system, 1789–1801.* 1906.

BASTIDE, L. *Vie religieuse et politique de Talleyrand-Périgord.* . . . 1838.

BEARD, C. A. *Economic origins of Jeffersonian democracy.* 1915.

BEMIS, S. F. *The diplomacy of the American revolution.* 1935.

—— *The Hussey-Cumberland mission and American independence.* . . . 1931.

—— *Jay's treaty; A study in commerce and diplomacy.* 1923.

—— "The London mission of Thomas Pinckney, 1792–1796," AHR XXVIII 228–247 (1922–23).

—— *Pinckney's treaty; A study of America's advantage from European distress, 1783–1800.* 1926.

—— "Relations between the Vermont separatists and Great Britain, 1789–1791." With documents, AHR XXI, 547–560 (1915–16).

—— "Washington's farewell address: a foreign policy of independence," AHR XXXIX, 250–268 (1933–34).

BEMIS, S. F. (ed.) *The American secretaries of state and their diplomacy.* 1927–29.

BEVERIDGE, A. J. *The life of John Marshall.* 1916–19.

BOND, B. W. *The Monroe mission to France, 1794–1796.* 1907.

BROWN, W. G. *The life of Oliver Ellsworth.* 1905.

CARTER, C. E. *Great Britain and the Illinois country, 1763–1774.* 1910.

CHANNING, E. *A History of the United States.* 1905–25.

CLARK, G. L. *Silas Deane, a Connecticut leader in the American revolution.* 1913.

CONWAY, M. D. *Omitted chapters of history disclosed in the life and papers of Edmund Randolph.* 1888.

CORWIN, E. S. *French policy and the American alliance of 1778.* 1916.

COX, I. J. *The West Florida controversy, 1798–1813; A study in American diplomacy.* 1918.

CRUZAT, H. H. "General Collot's reconnoitering trip down the Mississippi and his arrest in New Orleans," *Louisiana Historical Quarterly,* I, 303–320 (1908).

DAVIS, W. W. H. *The Fries rebellion, 1798–1799.* . . . 1899.
Dictionary of National Biography.

ELLERY, E. *Brissot de Warville; A study in the history of the French revolution.* 1915.

FARRAND, M. "The Indian boundary line," AHR X, 782–791 (1904–05).

FAUCHILLE, P. *La diplomatie française et la ligue des neutres de 1780, 1776–1783.* 1893.

FAŸ, B. *Franklin, the apostle of modern times.* 1929.

—— *The revolutionary spirit in France and America; A study of moral and intellectual relations between France and the United States at the end of the eighteenth century.* 1927. Tr. by R. Guthrie.

FENWICK, C. G. *The neutrality laws of the United States.* 1913.

FITZMAURICE, E. G. P-F. *Life of William, earl of Shelburne, afterwards first marquess of Lansdowne.* (2d ed.) 1912. With extracts from his papers and correspondence.

FLANDERS, H. *The lives and times of the chief justices of the Supreme court of the United States.* 1855–58.

FLETCHER, M. S. "Louisiana as a factor in French diplomacy from 1763 to 1800," MVHR XVII, 367–376 (1930–1931).

FUGIER, A. *Napoléon et l'Espagne, 1799–1808.* 1930.

GAYARRÉ, C. *History of Louisiana.* (3d ed.) 1885.

GILMAN, D. C. *James Monroe in his relations to the public service during half a century, 1776–1826.* 1893.

GUINNESS, R. B. "The purpose of the Lewis and Clark expedition," MVHR XX, 90–100 (1933–34).

GUTTRIDGE, G. H. *David Hartley, an advocate of conciliation, 1774–1783.* 1926.

GUYOT, R. *Le Directoire et la paix de l'Europe des traités de Bâle à la deuxième coalition (1795–99).* 1911.

HALE, E. E., AND E. E. jr. *Franklin in France.* 1887.

HAMMOND, M. B. *The cotton industry; An essay in American economic history.* Am. Econ. Assn. Publications, new ser., No. 1, December, 1897.

HILL, C. E. *Leading American treaties.* 1922.

HOWARD, G. E. *Preliminaries of the revolution, 1763–1775.* 1905.

HYNEMAN, C. S. *The first American neutrality . . .* (1792–1815). Illinois Studies in the Social Sciences, XX, Nos. 1, 2. 1934.

JAMES, J. A. "French opinion as a factor in preventing war between France and the United States, 1795–1800," AHR XXX, 44–55 (1924–25).

—— *The life of George Rogers Clark.* 1929.

—— "Louisiana as a factor in American diplomacy, 1795–1800," MVHR I, 44–56 (1914–15).

JAY, WM. *The life of John Jay, with selections from his correspondence and miscellaneous papers.* 1833. Cited as Jay.

JUNG, TH. *Lucien Bonaparte et ses mémoires, 1775–1840. . . .* 1882–1883.

KAPP, F. *The life of John Kalb, major-general in the revolutionary army.* 1870.

LOKKE, C. L. "Jefferson and the Leclerc expedition," AHR XXXIII, 322–328 (1927–28).

LOMÉNIE, L. DE. *Beaumarchais et son temps*. . . . (2d ed.) 1858.

LYMAN, TH. *The diplomacy of the United States*. (2d ed. with additions.) 1828.

LYON, E. W. "The Directory and the United States," AHR XLIII, 514–532 (1937–38).

—— *Louisiana in French diplomacy, 1759–1804*. 1934.

McLAUGHLIN, A. C. "The western posts and the British debts," AHA Rpt. 1894, 413–444.

MacLAY, E. S. *A history of the United States Navy from 1775*. . . . 1894.

MAHAN, A. T. *The influence of sea power upon the French revolution and empire, 1793–1812*. 1892.

MANNING, W. R. "The Nootka Sound controversy," AHA Rpt. 1904, 279–478.

MARSHALL, J. *The life of George Washington*. 1805–07.

MARSHALL, T. M. *A history of the western boundary of the Louisiana purchase, 1819–1841*. 1914.

MARTIN, F. X. *The history of Louisiana, from the earliest period*. 1829.

MILLER, J. C. *Sam Adams, pioneer in propaganda*. 1936.

MONAGHAN, F. *John Jay, defender of liberty*. . . . 1935.

MORISON, S. E. *The life and letters of Harrison Gray Otis, Federalist, 1765–1848*. 1913.

NEWCOMB, J. T. "New light on Jay's treaty," *Am. Journ. Int. Law* (October, 1934) XXVIII, 685 ff.

NUSSBAUM, F. L. *Commercial policy in the French revolution; A study of the career of G. J. A. Ducher*. 1923.

OGG, F. A. "Jay's treaty and the slavery interests of the United States," AHA Rpt. 1901, I, 273–298.

PELLEW, G. *John Jay*. 1890–92.

PELZER, L. "The Spanish land grants of Upper Louisiana," *Iowa Journ. . . . History and Politics* (January, 1913) XI, 3–37.

PERKINS, D. *The Monroe doctrine, 1823–1826*. 1927.

PERKINS, J. B. *France in the American revolution*. 1911.

PHILLIPS, P. C. *The West in the diplomacy of the American revolution*. 1913.

PICKETT, A. J. *History of Alabama, and incidentally of Georgia and Mississippi, from the earliest period*. 1851.

RENAUT, F. P. *La question de la Louisiane, 1796–1806*. 1918.

RICE, H. C. *Barthélemi Tardiveau; A French trader in the West*. 1938. With letters from Tardiveau to Crèvecœur, 1788–1789.

—— "James Swan: agent of the French Republic, 1794–1796," *New England Quarterly* (September, 1937) X, 464–486.

RIDDELL, W. R. *The life of John Graves Simcoe, first lieutenant-governor . . . of Upper Canada, 1792–1796.* 1926.

RIDINGS, S. P. *The Chisholm trail; A history of the world's greatest cattle trail. . . .* 1936.

ROBERTSON, W. S. "Francisco de Miranda and the revolutionizing of Spanish America," AHA Rpt. 1907, I, 189–528. With documentary appendix.

—— *The life of Miranda.* 1929.

ROBINSON, W. A. *Jeffersonian democracy in New England.* 1916.

ROLOFF, G. *Die kolonialpolitik Napoleons I.* 1899.

ROSE, J. H. *William Pitt and the great war.* 1911.

SLOANE, W. M. "The world aspects of the Louisiana purchase," AHR IX, 507–521 (1903–4).

SOREL, A. *L'Europe et la révolution française.* 1885–1904.

SPARKS, J. *The life of Gouverneur Morris.* 1832.

STODDARD, A. *Sketches, historical and descriptive, of Louisiana.* 1812. By the American officer who took over Upper Louisiana in 1804.

STODDARD, L. *The French revolution in San Domingo.* 1914.

TANSILL, C. C. *The United States and Santo Domingo, 1798–1873.* 1938.

TEMPERLEY, H. *The foreign policy of Canning, 1822–1827.* 1925.

THOMAS, C. M. *American neutrality in 1793; A study in cabinet government.* 1931.

THOMPSON, I. "The Blount conspiracy," East Tenn. Hist. Soc. Publications, No. 2. (1929).

TRESCOT, W. H. *The diplomatic history of the administrations of Washington and Adams, 1789–1801.* 1857.

TREUDLEY, M. "The United States and Santo Domingo, 1789–1866," *Journ. . . . Race Development* VII, 83–145, 220–274 (1916–17).

TUDOR, WM. *The life of James Otis, of Massachusetts. . . .* 1823.

TURNER, F. J. "The origin of Genet's projected attack on Louisiana and the Floridas," AHR III, 650–671 (1897–98).

—— "The policy of France toward the Mississippi Valley in the period of Washington and Adams," AHR X, 249–279 (1904–5).

—— *Rise of the new West, 1819–1829.* 1906.

UPDYKE, F. A. *The diplomacy of the war of 1812.* 1915.

UPHAM, C. W. *The life of Timothy Pickering.* 1867. Begun by Octavius Pickering.

VAN SANTVOORD, G. *Sketches of the lives and judicial services of the chief justices of the Supreme court of the United States.* 1856.

VAN TYNE, C. H. *The war of independence; American phase. . . .* 1929.

VATTEL, E. *The law of nations; or, Principles of the law of nations. . . .*

1796. The first American edition corrected and revised from the latest London edition translated from the French.

VILLIERS DU TERRAGE, M. *Les dernières années de la Louisiane française.* . . . c 1904.

WARREN, C. *The Supreme court in United States history.* 1922.

WHITAKER, A. P. "Alexander McGillivray," *North Carolina Hist. Rev.,* V. 181–204, 289–310 (1928).

—— "France and the American deposit at New Orleans," *Hisp. Am. Hist. Rev.* (November, 1931) XI, 485–502.

—— "Louisiana in the treaty of Basel," *Journ. of Modern History* (March, 1936) VIII, 1 ff.

—— *The Mississippi Question, 1795–1803; A study in trade, politics, and diplomacy.* 1934.

—— "New light on the treaty of San Lorenzo: An essay in historical criticism," MVHR XV, 435–454. (1928–29.)

—— "The retrocession of Louisiana in Spanish policy," AHR XXXIX, 454–476 (1933–34).

—— *The Spanish-American frontier: 1783–1795.* Cited as Whitaker.

WHITE, K. "John D. Chisholm," East Tenn. Hist. Soc. Publications, No. 1. (1929).

WINSOR, J. *The westward movement* . . . *1763–1798.* 1897. Cited for maps.

WOOLERY, W. K. *The relation of Thomas Jefferson to American foreign policy, 1783–1793.* 1927.

YELA UTRILLA, J. F. *España ante la independencia de los Estados Unidos.* . . . 1925. Documents in 2d vol.

ZIMMERMAN, J. F. *Impressment of American seamen.* 1925.

INDEX

A BOUKIR Bay, effect of Nelson's victory at, 325, 331, 339, 412

Adams, Abigail, on Franklin, Mme Helvetius, 90–91; Adams to, on his problems, 249–250, 302; illness, 324, 350; Federalist appreciation of, 344; and Adams' opponents, 366 f.

—— Charles F., on Franklin, 90

—— Henry, his story of the Bonapartes and Louisiana examined, 493–494; his criticism of Mobile Act considered, 522–524

—— John, plan of 1775, 9; "plan of treaties," 10; instructions from Congress (1779–80), 28; and Vergennes, 43, 87–88; Vaughan, Laurens and, 46; and Franklin, 46–49, 89–91; his contribution to the Peace of 1782–83, 87–88; in London, 103, 110–112; his treaty with the Netherlands, 127; advices to Washington (1790), 141; deciding vote against the non-importation bill (1794), 178, 231; his inheritance from Washington, 243–244; and Election of 1796, 247–248, 272; and French "assaults," Collot's journey, 249 f.; reports from J. Q. Adams to, 254; and the West, 258 f.; and Wilkinson, W. S. Smith, 259; and British "secret plots," 266 f.; his exposure of Blount, and Liston, 273 f.; pro-American, 275; the mission of Pinckney, Marshall, and Gerry (1797), 276 f.; caustic on the Directory, 279; his policy of neutrality, 279–280; admonitions to Gerry, 281; and preparations for war with France, 293–295; his French policy determined by danger from Britain, 302 f., 333; and impressment, 303–305; and naval coöperation with Britain, 303 f., 457; and Captain Jones of the *Chesterfield*, 304; his policy toward Britain (1798), 307 f.; and Hamilton, 310, 320; instructions to King, April 2, 1798, 310; his Dominican policy, and Liston, 311 f., 354, 364; and Toussaint Louverture, 315–316; his policy on war (1798), 325–326; and Miranda, 316–328; and the state of the Union, 329–333; and du-

Pont de Nemours, 332; orders to Pickering, Oct. 20, 1798, 335–336; requests of Gerry, 336–337; and Federalist opposition to renewed negotiations with France, his threat to resign, 337–347, 350–351, 364–375; and Fries 351–354; mission of Ellsworth, Davie, and Murray (1799), 375–386; his retirement, 386–389; Jefferson in agreement with, 391; his European policy compared with Jefferson's, 398, 412–413; in Pickering's thinking, 470

—— John Quincy, on "new yoke of the English," 205; his comment on Monroe (1797), 244; on France and Election of 1796, 248; on Washington, 248; his reports from The Hague (1796), 254; minister in Berlin, instructions to, 281; reports on European conditions (1798), 302; letters from Murray to, 302; on Far West, 310; letters to his mother, 333; Liston on his letters home, 344; his plan regarding *free ships free goods*, 379 f.; letters from Murray to, on Pickering, 388; on Jefferson in 1796, 397; and the "federal scheme" of 1804, reflections with King, 546–550

—— Samuel, growth of his feeling for independence, 4–5; La Luzerne on, 30

Addington, Henry (Sidmouth), to King on supplies for American fleet, 404; negotiations with Otto (Oct., 1801), 405–406; and King's pronouncement on Louisiana (Apr., 1803), 445, 480, 493, 507–508, 548–549; resignation, 534

Adet, Pierre A., and the Jay Treaty, 196–197, 393; and Election of 1796, 243, 247–248; and Collot, views on the West, and Elijah Clarke, 250 f.; Victor duPont and Fulton, 259; report to Talleyrand, 260; Irujo working for, 262 f.; and Liston, 268; arrival in Paris, 283; Otto on, 296; appraisal of Jefferson (1796), 299, 397; and expedition to New Orleans (1802), 433

Admiralty Courts, British, in West Indies, 312 f., 515

Africa, pirate states of, 391, 403; British interest in, 399